LACTOR 19

TIBERIUS TO NERO

EDITED BY M.G.L. COOLEY

MAJOR CONTRIBUTIONS BY
A.E. COOLEY
M.T. GRIFFIN
A. HARKER
B.M. LEVICK
S. MOORHEAD
E.C. OTHEN
B.W.J.G. WILSON
T.P. WISEMAN

TIBERIUS TO NERO

ISBN: 0-903625-34-2
ISBN: 978-0-903625-34-2

TABLE OF CONTENTS

List of illustrations and credits

The four photographs in Section J are reproduced courtesy of the British Museum non-commercial image service. The four photographs from Aphrodisias are courtesy of R.R.R. Smith and New York University Excavations at Aphrodisias.

Bibliography and Abbreviations

AE	*L'Année épigraphique*
Barrett	A.A. Barrett, *Caligula: the Corruption of Power* (London 1989)
BGU	*Aegyptische Urkunden aus den Königlichen/ Staatlichen Museen zu Berlin, Griechische Urkunden*
Birley	*A.R. Birley, The Roman Government of Britain (Oxford 2005)*
BMC	H. Mattingly, *Coins of the Roman Empire in the British Museum,* volume I: *Augustus to Vitellius,* (London 1923)
Brill-Pauly	Brill's New Pauly: *Encyclopedia of the Ancient World* (Leiden, 2002–2009)
CIL	T. Mommsen et al. edd., *Corpus Inscriptionum Latinarum* (Berlin 1866–)
Claridge, *Rome*	A. Claridge, *Rome, an Oxford Archaeological Guide,* 2nd ed. (Oxford 2010)
Cooley, *RG*	A.E. Cooley, *Res Gestae Divi Augusti* (Cambridge 2009)
EJ	V. Ehrenberg & A.H.M. Jones, *Documents Illustrating the Reigns of Augustus and Tiberius* (2nd edn 1976)
Fasti Ostienses	Bargagli and Grosso, *I Fasti Ostienses* (Rome 1997)
Gow & Page	A.S.F. Gow and D.L. Page, *The Greek Anthology, the Garland of Philip* (1968)
Griffin	M.T. Griffin, *Nero: the End of a Dynasty* (1984)
IAph2007	J. Reynolds, C. Roueché, G. Bodard, *Inscriptions of Aphrodisias* (2007), available http://insaph.kcl.ac.uk/iaph2007
IGRRP	*Inscriptiones Graecae ad Res Romanas Pertinentes*
ILN	*Inscriptions Latines de Narbonnaise*
ILS	*Inscriptiones Latinae Selectae* (ed. Dessau) [online e-book at Internet Archive: http://www.archive.org/details/inscriptionesla01dessgoog]
InscrIt XIII/2	*Inscriptiones Italiae* XIII – *Fasti et Elogia*, fasc. 2, *Fasti Anni Numani et Iuliani*, ed A. Degrassi (1963)
IRT2009	*Inscriptions of Roman Tripolitania*, by J. M. Reynolds and J. B. Ward-Perkins, enhanced electronic reissue by Gabriel Bodard and Charlotte Roueché (2009) http://irt.kcl.ac.uk/irt2009/
LACTOR 15	J. Edmondson, *Dio: the Julio-Claudians* (1992)
LACTOR 17	M.G.L. Cooley & B.W.J.G. Wilson, *The Age of Augustus* (2003)
Levick, *Tib*	B.M. Levick, *Tiberius the Politician* (1976)
Levick, *Claud*	B.M. Levick, *Claudius* (1990)
MAMA	*Monumenta Asiae Minoris Antiqua*
Millar, ERW	F.G.B. Millar, *The Emperor in the Roman World, 31* BC – AD *337* (2nd edition London 1992)

NSc	*Notizie degli scavi di antichità*
OCD	S. Hornblower and A. Spawforth, edd., *The Oxford Classical Dictionary* (3rd edition, Oxford 1996)
OGIS	*Orientis Graeci Inscriptiones Selectae*, ed. W. Dittenberger (1905)
Page	D.L. Page, *Further Greek Epigrams* (1981)
PIR	*Prosopographia Imperii Romani* (ed. E. Klebs *et al.* Berlin 1897–8; 2nd edition 1933 and ongoing)
P.Oxy	*Oxyrhynchus Papyri*
RIC	C.H.V. Sutherland, *The Roman Imperial Coinage,* volume I revised ed. (London 1984)
RPC	A. Burnett, M. Amandry and P.P. Ripollès, *Roman Provincial Coinage I: From the Death of Caesar to the Death of Vitellius* (London and Paris, 1992)
SEG	*Supplementum Epigraphicum Graecum*
Sherk	R.K. Sherk, *The Roman Empire: Augustus to Hadrian* (1988)
SIG	*Sylloge Inscriptionum Graecarum*
Smallwood	E.M. Smallwood, *Documents Illustrating the Principates of Gaius, Claudius & Nero* (1984)
Syme, *AA*	R. Syme, *The Augustan Aristocracy* (Oxford 1986)
Syme, *RP*	R. Syme, *Roman Papers,* ed. A.R. Birley (Oxford)
Syme, *Tacitus*	R. Syme, *Tacitus* (Oxford 1958)
Wiseman, *New Men*	T. P. Wiseman, *New Men in the Roman Senate, 139 BC–AD 14* (Oxford 1971)

Preface

This volume aims to provide source material for students of the Roman Empire under Tiberius, Caligula, Claudius, and Nero. It does not include material from Tacitus' *Annals* or Suetonius' *Lives of the Caesars*, since these are readily available in a variety of formats. Nor does it include material from Dio's *Roman History*, since this is easily accessible as LACTOR 15. Instead it concentrates on a much greater range of material, in most cases more contemporary than Tacitus, Suetonius and Dio. I hope that the volume will be of use to students and teachers of the A2 level Roman History option in the UK, and some knowledge of Augustus is assumed (as on this module), but I hope it will also be of use to students at English-speaking universities.

The material has been structured in a similar way to LACTOR 17, The Age of Augustus. Part I consists of long texts of various genres mostly written by contemporaries. Part II is arranged by themes most relevant to the fairly traditional approach of a political history concentrating on the emperors (as currently required by A level). This sourcebook is not intended as a textbook for social history.

This book will certainly contain inconsistencies, sometimes due to the ancient evidence, sometimes due to the number of contributors to the book and the oversight of the editor. For these and for other mistakes of fact, interpretation, or proof-reading, I most sincerely beg the reader's pardon.

It is a great pleasure to thank the many people who have spent a great deal of their free time on this book and shared freely their expertise. Most of the literary texts were translated by Brian Wilson, with the exception of Seneca's *Apocolocyntosis* and Philo's *Embassy to Gaius*, by Emma Othen. I am very grateful for the notes provided by various experts on the some of the ancient authors: Barbara Levick on Velleius, Miriam Griffin on Seneca the Younger, Andrew Harker on Josephus, and Peter Wiseman on *Octavia*. Sam Moorhead provided a great deal of help on the coins, and I am grateful to the British Museum for the photographs of the coins from their superb collection, many of which were taken specially for this book by Victoria Wolfe (George Washington University), and also to Bert Smith and the New York University Excavations at Aphrodisias for allowing their photographs of the Sebasteion to be reproduced here. Some material here has been reworked from the JACT 'Teachers' Notes' produced by Zahra Newby, Penny Goodman, and myself. Thanks are also due to Andrew Harvey for his work in setting and printing a long and difficult script.

Far my greatest debt, however, is due to my wife Alison, for her continued support throughout this project, in translating and commenting on the large number of inscriptions, and in all other ways. This book is dedicated with love to her and to our children, Emma and Paul.

August 2011

M.G.L. Cooley
Head of Scholars, Warwick School

Notes on Literary Sources

Minor authors are given brief introductions where passages from their works are given.

Calpurnius Siculus: nothing is known about him, except for the 7 pastoral poems ascribed to him. The literary style is similar to other hexameter verses produced around the time of Nero, and the references to a comet, a young emperor who gave games and is thought of as a literary patron fit Nero and almost no other possible emperor. His name suggests a possible link to the Calpurnius Piso family.

Dio (probably L. Claudius Cassius Dio Cocceianus) was born *c.* AD 163/5 into one of the most prominent Greek families in Bithynia (NW Turkey). He had a distinguished career, over about 40 years, as Roman senator and governor, retiring after his second consulship in ad 229. Dio's *Roman History* is written in Greek and covered the entire period from Rome's foundation to his own day. However significant parts of his original accounts of the Julio-Claudian emperors are lost, though these survive in the form of summaries made by Xiphilinus (ad 1070s) and Zonaras (AD 1118). Where Tacitus' *Annals* are lost, Dio can provide the only surviving chronological account. For a selection of the most valuable parts of Dio's history, see Jonathan Edmondson, LACTOR 15.

Frontinus. Sextus Julius Frontinus lived from about AD 30 to AD 104, and was given important positions by the emperors Vespasian, Domitian, Nerva and Trajan, including three consulships. His *Strategems*, written after AD 84, give examples of military tactics from Greek and Roman history. In AD 97, Nerva appointed him Aqueducts Commissioner, and while in this post, he wrote a book about the history, administration and maintenance of the aqueducts he was responsible for (*de aquis urbis Romae* – The Aqueducts of Rome). This book includes a wealth of technical information, facts and figures about the system in his day as well as exact quotations of earlier statutes.

Aulus Gellius, born between AD 125 and 128 seems to have published his 'Attic Nights' around AD 180. He explains the title as emanating from his decision to write up notes he made from his reading on a great variety of subjects, during the long winter nights in Attica, but says he only completed the project 30 years later as an instructive entertainment for his children. His value lies in his repeating material which he read, but which is not now preserved elsewhere.

Josephus (Flavius Iosephus), AD 37/8 – *c.* 100. Jewish historian, see **E1** for his own description of himself and his writings and Introduction to Section E.

Juvenal (Decimus Iunius Iuvenalis), Roman satirist, active *c.* AD 120. His 16 poems satirise and exaggerate aspects of contemporary Roman life. Juvenal often uses historical examples to back up his point. These are often explained in ancient commentaries which sometimes completely misidentify figures, and occasionally provide important historical information.

Lucan (M. Annaeus Lucanus), AD 39-65, poet, grandson of Seneca the Elder, nephew of Seneca the Younger. For his life, see **P11b** and **R36**, for his epic poem on the Civil Wars, see **T16**.

Martial (Marcus Valerius Martialis), AD 38/41 to 101/4, was born and died at Bilbilis in Spain. He moved to Rome *c.* AD 64, as a protégé of Seneca the Younger. He published 15 books of epigrams on a huge variety of themes, beginning in AD 80 with a *Book on the Shows* for the inauguration of the Flavian Amphitheatre.

Philo, an old man at the time of his embassy to Gaius, was a leading Hellenised Jew of Alexandria, who wrote extensively in Greek on Jewish themes. See Introduction to Section D.

Pliny the Elder (Gaius Plinius Secundus) AD 23/4 to 79. Prominent equestrian, commander of the fleet at Misenum at the eruption of Vesuvius. See **R14–R15**.

Pliny the Younger (Gaius Plinius Secundus), *c.* AD 61 to *c.* 112). Nephew and heir of Pliny the Elder. Originally from Comum in N. Italy, he works his way up to the suffect consulship in AD 100: his career is also known from an inscription (*ILS* 2927). He published 9 books of letters to friends on a variety of literary, social, political and historical matters. Pliny refers to selecting and arranging 'letters which were written with some degree of care' (*Letters* 1.1), so the letters are intended to portray him in a good light to other members of the upper classes. A tenth book contains letters to Trajan and his replies on questions concerning his governorship of Bithynia-Pontus where he died in office.

Plutarch, *c.* AD 45–120 is best known for his biographies of Greek and Roman leaders, *Parallel Lives* linking the lives of Greeks and Romans, and often drawing moral conclusions. His *Moralia* includes moral and philosophical essays, literary criticism. It also includes a section on famous sayings of kings and emperors.

Quintilian (Marcus Fabius Quintilianus) born *c.* AD 35 in Spain became the best known teacher of rhetoric in Rome. *The Orator's Education* (*Institutio Oratoria*) gives lengthy and detailed advice on writing speeches, including many famous remarks of historical figures and judgements on Roman authors.

Seneca the Elder (Lucius Annaeus Seneca) *c.* 50 BC – *c.* AD 40) was born in Corduba in Spain, a landowner and gentleman of leisure who first visited Rome in the 30s BC to study rhetoric and then to supervise the education of his three sons. He was ambitious for them, and two became consuls. In old age the Elder Seneca dedicated to his sons a work on declamation, using his astounding memory for recalling what he had heard in the schools of rhetoric (perhaps supplemented by written sources). Of this work, five books of *controversiae* and one of *suasoriae* survive, containing excerpts from the best performances he had heard. His history from the start of the civil wars almost to his death is lost.

Seneca the Younger (Lucius Annaeus Seneca, shortly before 1 BC – AD 65), orator, dramatist and Stoic philosopher, was born in Corduba, S. Spain. His family was of Italian origin and equestrian status, which meant substantial wealth and high social standing. A hugely important literary and political figure in this period.

Seneca began his political career late in the reign of Tiberius, an emperor Seneca was to depict unflatteringly, remarking on his meanness throughout his reign and on his paranoia in his last years (e.g. *Ben.* 2.7.–8; 3.26.1; 5.25.2). Under Caligula, Seneca and his brother, Novatus, achieved the next senatorial office, despite Caligula's envy of Seneca's success as an orator (Dio 59.19 and Suet. *Gaius* 53). In 41 his friendship with Caligula's sisters led to his being tried before the senate, on a charge of adultery with Julia Livilla, and relegated to the island of Corsica. There he remained, writing consolations to his mother Helvia and to Claudius' freedman Polybius until 49 when, through the influence of Claudius' new wife Agrippina, he was recalled to Rome and given a praetorship. Agrippina thought his recall would counter the unpopularity of her marriage, as Seneca was already a well-known author: by then his long treatise *On Anger* was planned and probably partly written. She also wanted him to tutor her son Lucius Domitius Ahenobarbus in rhetoric, not in philosophy. Novatus, bearing the adoptive name L. Junius Gallio Annaeanus by 52, benefited too: he became proconsul of Achaia (Greece). It may be now too that the third brother Mela became a procurator of imperial estates (Tac. *Ann.* 16.17).

When Nero became *princeps* in October 54, Seneca was not merely his teacher, but one of the principal *amici principis*, the imperial speech-writer and key publicity agent. Working closely and harmoniously with the praetorian prefect, Sextus Afranius Burrus, also a provincial (from Gaul) and also a protégé of Agrippina, Seneca managed to control and guide the adolescent *princeps*, 'using now the reins and now the spur' (*On Anger* 2.21.3, cf. Tac. *Ann.* 13.2.1), as reflected in the mixture of flattery and admonition in *On Clemency*, dedicated to Nero in late 55 or 56 (Section G). Seneca and Burrus managed to retain their authority with by providing a less austere alternative to Agrippina's censorious nagging, but after Nero disposed of his mother in 59 and Burrus died in 62, Seneca saw that his influence was over. In that year Nero divorced Claudius' daughter Octavia, who had failed to produce a child, and married the beautiful Poppaea Sabina (**J27**), who was pregnant with his daughter. Faenius Rufus and Ofonius Tigellinus succeeded Burrus as praetorian prefect. Seneca asked to retire from court to concentrate on his philosophical writing (Tac. *Ann.* 14.53-4), though by that time he had probably already written most of the tragedies and the philosophical works that survive, except possibly for the later books of the *Natural Questions* and the *Letters to Lucilius* (*De Providentia*, also addressed to Lucilius is undateable). Nero refused his request, and Seneca remained, to outward appearances, a favoured *amicus*. After the great fire of July 64, Seneca was again refused permission to retire and withdrew to his room, handing over most of his wealth to the Emperor (Tac. *Ann.* 15.45). In April of 65 he was ordered to commit suicide, officially for participation in the Pisonian conspiracy, though Tacitus was probably right to believe that he was innocent but possibly cognisant of the plot (*Ann.* 15.60, 61). Sadly, the last words he recorded are only mentioned, not preserved, by Tacitus (*Ann.* 15.63), though the act of dictation was immortalised by Reubens in his painting of Seneca's death.

Statius (Publius Papinius Statius), Roman poet, born around ad 50 in Naples. He wrote an epic poem, *Thebaid* on the struggle for Thebes between Oedipus' sons and a collection of poems, *Silvae*, published in the 90s, which celebrate various occasions in the lives of a circle of upper-class friends.

Strabo was born in Amasia in Pontus, probably around 64 BC, into a family that enjoyed close involvement with the local ruling dynasty. His great literary achievement was a 47-book historical work, which is almost entirely lost. However, we do have his 17-book *Geography,* which was compiled during the reigns of Augustus and Tiberius, and provides an account of the entire world known to the Romans. Strabo's material came largely from older literary sources, but his mixture of Greek education, Pontic background, and Roman connections, provides us with one of the most important and extensive contemporary sources on the Roman world at the accession of Tiberius.

Suetonius (Gaius Suetonius Tranquillus), born *c.* AD 69, died after AD 130, author of *Lives of the Caesars*. He was an equestrian who worked as imperial secretary for

Trajan and Hadrian in the AD 110s, involving him in administrative tasks such as helping to handle the emperor's correspondence. Thus Suetonius had direct access to the imperial archives, including documents such as personal letters from the time of Julius Caesar and Augustus. He drew on this material as he began working on his *Lives of the Caesars*, sometimes quoting it directly in his biographies. However after being dismissed from the imperial staff in AD 122, he lost his privileged access to the archives, so that from *Nero* onwards it is clear that he was restricted to using publicly-available source material such as senatorial decrees, narrative histories already written by earlier authors and oral reports.

Suetonius is writing biography, not history. So while the structure of the *Lives* is very broadly chronological, the bulk of each biography is usually thematic. Suetonius also places greater emphasis on the private lives and personalities of the emperors – often from a very 'gossipy' perspective.

Tacitus (Publius Cornelius Tacitus) was born *c.* AD 56 probably in Gaul. He came to Rome by AD 75 and had a senatorial career under the Flavian emperors. He was praetor in 88, consul in 97 and proconsul of Asia in 112–13. While his most prestigious posts were held under Nerva and Trajan, his career started and was developed under the Flavians (as he admits in *Histories* 1.1). Tacitus began his literary career around AD 98, with various minor works, including a biography of his father-in-law, Agricola. His *Histories* covered the period AD 69–96: only the first five books survive, covering the wars of succession which followed Nero's death. He then went back to cover the period AD 14–68 in *Annals* written in 18 books. Of these, books 1–6 (covering AD 14-37, but with most of book 5 lost) and books 11–16 (covering AD 47–66) survive.

Like Suetonius and Pliny the Younger, Tacitus sees the reigns of earlier emperors through the lens of his experiences under Domitian. Thus themes such as the origins of treason trials under Tiberius or the autocracy of Gaius and Nero are given prominence. A major theme in Tacitus' writings is the loss of liberty. For his attitude to the writing of history, see **R3**.

Valerius Maximus compiled his book of 'Memorable deeds and sayings from the City of Rome and foreign nations' in the reign of Tiberius (AD 14–37). He makes no claim to originality merely to make a convenient selection from famous authors.

Velleius Paterculus: historian, 20/19 BC to after AD 30. See introduction to **C**.

Editorial Conventions for Texts of Inscriptions

[ ]	square brackets enclose words or letters which are missing in the original test and have been restored by the editor or translator.
[…]	dots in square brackets indicate words or letters missing in the original text.
( )	round brackets are used to expand words abbreviated in the original text.
…	dots outside brackets mark where the translator has omitted part of the text.
[5]	numbers in square brackets indicate line numbers of an inscription
~~Nero~~	text struck through indicates a deliberate deletion or erasure of a text in antiquity.

The Coinage Reform of AD 64

Pliny tells us in his *Natural History* (33.47 = **T21**) that Nero reduced the weight of the gold *aureus* (Pliny calls it the gold *denarius*) from 40 to 45 to the pound. It is likely that he knew this from dealing with the coins themselves, rather than from having any direct access to information about theoretical weights. The gold *aureus* did indeed fall in weight in AD 64. It had been 7.85 grams under Augustus and ranged between 7.7 and 7.6g in Nero's reign until AD 64. It then fell to between 7.4 and 7.2g after 64. However, the fineness of the coins remained at about 99% gold. Pliny does not mention the silver *denarius* but it was also reduced in weight from 96 to 84 to the pound, *c.* 3.89 to 3.41g. Furthermore, the fineness of the coins was reduced from around 98-96% to around 94% silver. There was a simple way for the populace to distinguish pre- and post-reform coins: the pre-reform coins had a bare-headed portrait of Nero; the post-reform coins showed him wearing a laurel wreath.

We cannot be certain about the reason for such changes in the coinages, but if the state paid its debts at the same price levels after the reform, it would obviously benefit from such debasement. However, in the long-term, over the next couple of centuries, continued debasement led to high inflation, culminating in the third century ad. It is also argued that changes were required in the weight of coins to maintain a ratio of 25 silver *denarii* to one gold *aureus*.

Nero began to strike large numbers of base metal coins from AD 62 at Rome – brass *sestertii*, brass *dupondii*, copper *asses*, brass *semisses* and copper *quadrantes*. However, from AD 64 the output increased enormously, partly due to the opening of the mint at Lugdunum (Lyons). There is no doubt that an increasing proportion of the coinage was now made of base metal and one can assume that the state paid more of its debts in these low value coins.

Roman Coin	HS equivalent	material	diameter	weight*	notes
aureus	100 HS	gold	18mm	8g	Augustan
denarius	4 HS	silver	18mm	4g	3rd century bc
sestertius	1 HS	brass	35mm	28g	Augustan
dupondius	½ HS	brass	28mm	14g	
as	¼ HS	copper	28mm	10g	traditional unit
semis	1/8 HS	brass	17mm	3g	
quadrans	1/16 HS	copper	17mm	3g	

* notional weights up to AD 64, though in practice coins staying in circulation become slightly worn and less heavy.

In the East, Greek (Attic) coinage was commonly used, base on the drachma, a silver coin, weighing, at 4.36g, slightly more than a *denarius* but notionally equivalent to it. The Alexandrian drachma used in Egypt was notionally equivalent to 1 HS.

A guide to monetary values	Sesterces
The budget surplus on Gaius' accession was around	2,700,000,000
Gaius' wife, Lollia Paulina apparently wore jewellery worth	40,000,000
The property qualification for a Roman senator, established by Augustus was	1,000,000
The property qualification for a Roman equestrian, established by Augustus was	400,000
The annual pay of a Roman legionary was	900
Discharge payment for Roman legionary veterans was	12,000
The town council at Pompeii occasionally allocated, for funerals of local dignitaries	2,000
The annual corn dole of 60 *modii* (measures) was worth around	300-360
Gaius gave two cash gifts to Roman citizens in June and August of ad 37 (**J19e**), of	75
A tunic (of unknown quality) at Pompeii cost	15
A cup of Falernian (high quality) wine at a bar in Pompeii cost	4
A cup of cheap wine from the same bar cost	1

Glossary

aedile: the most junior magistrate with full senatorial status.
***as* (pl. *asses*)**: the base-unit of Roman currency, a small value coin.
augur: a priest, especially responsible for predictions based on flights of birds.
Augustalis: a priest involved in emperor-worship.
Augustus: as well as the name adopted by Octavian, it comes to be part of the name or title of Gaius, Claudius and Nero and thus can effectively mean 'emperor'. '**Augusta**' becomes applied to Livia and various other imperial women. '**Augusti**' can refer to the imperial family.
aureus: the highest value coin, made of gold, worth 100 sesterces.
censor: traditionally one of two senior senators, elected for eighteen months every five years, responsible for revising the roll of the senate, according to financial and moral standards.
civic crown: (*corona civica*) traditionally an honour awarded for saving the life of a citizen in battle, but usurped by Augustus for ending civil wars, and reduced to little more than an element of imperial decoration.
client: a citizen who voluntarily paid his respects to a richer, more powerful patron, in return for his protection.
cognomen: the last of a Roman's names, sometimes a type of 'nickname', but often distinguishing not just an individual, but a branch of a large family.
colony: a settlement of Roman citizens (often army veterans) with its own local constitution.
consul: the highest political office in the republic. Two consuls were elected each year to serve for one year.
cursus honorum: the 'career path' of a member of the senatorial classes.
denarius: small silver coin worth 4 sesterces.
dictator: magistrate appointed in time of emergency in the Roman republic.
Divus/Diva: 'God(dess)', especially of those officially deified.
equestrian: (1) a member of this class in Rome, almost equal in status to the senatorial class. (2) equestrian statue: statue of a man on horseback (compare *pedestrian*)
fasces: symbols of the authority of a magistrate carried by his attendants
fasti: publicly inscribed lists of various sorts: dates, consuls, etc.
freedman: a slave, formally set free by his master, automatically becoming a Roman citizen (and the client of his former master).
genius: the spirit of a person (or place).
imperator: originally a title given by Roman troops to their general after a major victory, such as would merit a triumph, adopted by Augustus as part of his name and used as part of the emperor's official title, though also to mark military victories.
imperium: the power invested in a magistrate (*e.g.* consul, praetor or governor).
imperium maius: (greater power), i.e. power outranking that of a consul or governor, granted to certain members of imperial family, *e.g.* Germanicus in the East.
laurel crown: originally worn by a general in his triumph, but adopted as a symbol of the emperor.

legate: 1) anyone to whom authority is delegated, *e.g.* a military officer. 2) ***legatus Augusti propraetore*** (legate of August with the power of a praetor) – the official term for someone appointed to govern a (major) imperial province.

libation: liquid (usually wine) poured as an offering to gods or spirits of the dead

ludi saeculares: (Centennial Games) games held once every 100 or 110 years, to celebrate a new age.

macellum: meat and fish market-building.

magistrate: an official elected for a year both at Rome and in local government.

manumission: the formal freeing of a slave, resulting in his attaining citizenship.

military tribune: one of 6 officers in a Roman legion subordinate to the legionary commander. Usually one was of senatorial class, the other five equestrians, the post was effectively a step on the *cursus honorum*. Occasionally centurions were promoted to this post.

municipium: a city within the Roman empire whose citizens were also Roman citizens and which was allowed to govern itself on a Roman model.

novus homo: (new man) – term applied to the first member of a family to become a senator, or the first to become consul, or occasionally to do both (as abnormally, Sejanus).

pater patriae: Father of the Fatherland. Title granted to Augustus in 2 bc and adopted by Gaius, Claudius and Nero. Though honorific it suggested absolute authority over the empire similar to that of a father over his family.

patron: a more wealthy and important citizen who looked after the interests of poorer clients in return for their support and public deference.

pedestrian: pedestrian statue: statue of a man standing up (compare *equestrian*)

plebs: the proper term for the ordinary citizen body of Rome.

pontifex maximus: chief priest, a post taken on accession by all emperors after Augustus.

portico: a colonnade around a central (open-air) area.

praetor: annually 'elected' magistrate ranking between consul and quaestor. Ex-praetors governed the less important public provinces.

Praetorian guard: elite bodyguard of the emperor. The only troop stationed in Italy.

Praetorian prefect: commander of the guard, an increasingly powerful position.

prefect: someone 'put in charge of' something: often an appointee of the *princeps.*

princeps: the word, meaning 'leader' of 'chief' was the one chosen by Augustus to designate his position.

princeps iuventutis: (leader of the younger generation) – title invented by Augustus for his grandsons to show that they would become *princeps.*

proconsul: a former consul, retaining his former official power, usually as governor of a major public province.

procurator: someone taking care of something for the *princeps*, from an estate to a minor imperial province.

propraetor: someone granted the power of a praetor, usually as governor of a minor public province.

quaestor: a junior magistrate and member of the sentate, sometimes employed effectively as the *princeps'* secretary (*e.g.* **P3q**).

quindecimvir: a member of a college of fifteen priests in charge of sacrifices, chosen by the *princeps* as a permanent honour.

republican: modern usage to refer to the period when Rome was governed by elected magistrates (rather than emperors), roughly 510–50 BC.

Salii: an archaic college of priests who sang a hymn on public occasions.

septemvir: a member of a college of seven priests responsible for feasts put on in honour of Jupiter at Games. A signal honour, chosen by the *princeps*.

sesterces: the unit of currency in Rome.

suffect: replacement magistrate, especially consul, appointed in republic after death of incumbent, but under principate, pairs of suffect consuls are usually appointed as a way of sharing the honour of a consulship more widely.

tribe: all citizens were formally a member of one of 35 tribes, by this period of no discernible significance.

tribunician power: the power of one of ten republican magistrates elected to protect the interests of the plebs. Augustus adopts the power as symbolic and useful, and also to ease the succession to Tiberius. For later emperors it mostly marks their regnal years.

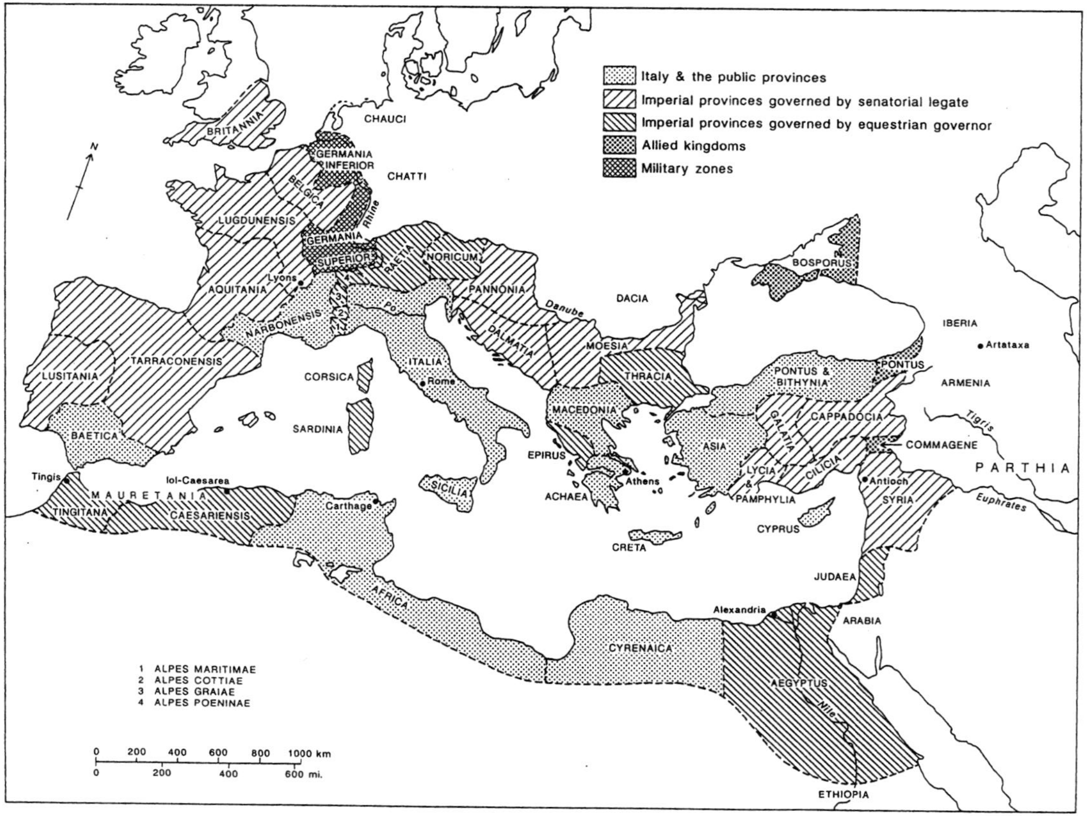

The Roman Empire in AD 46

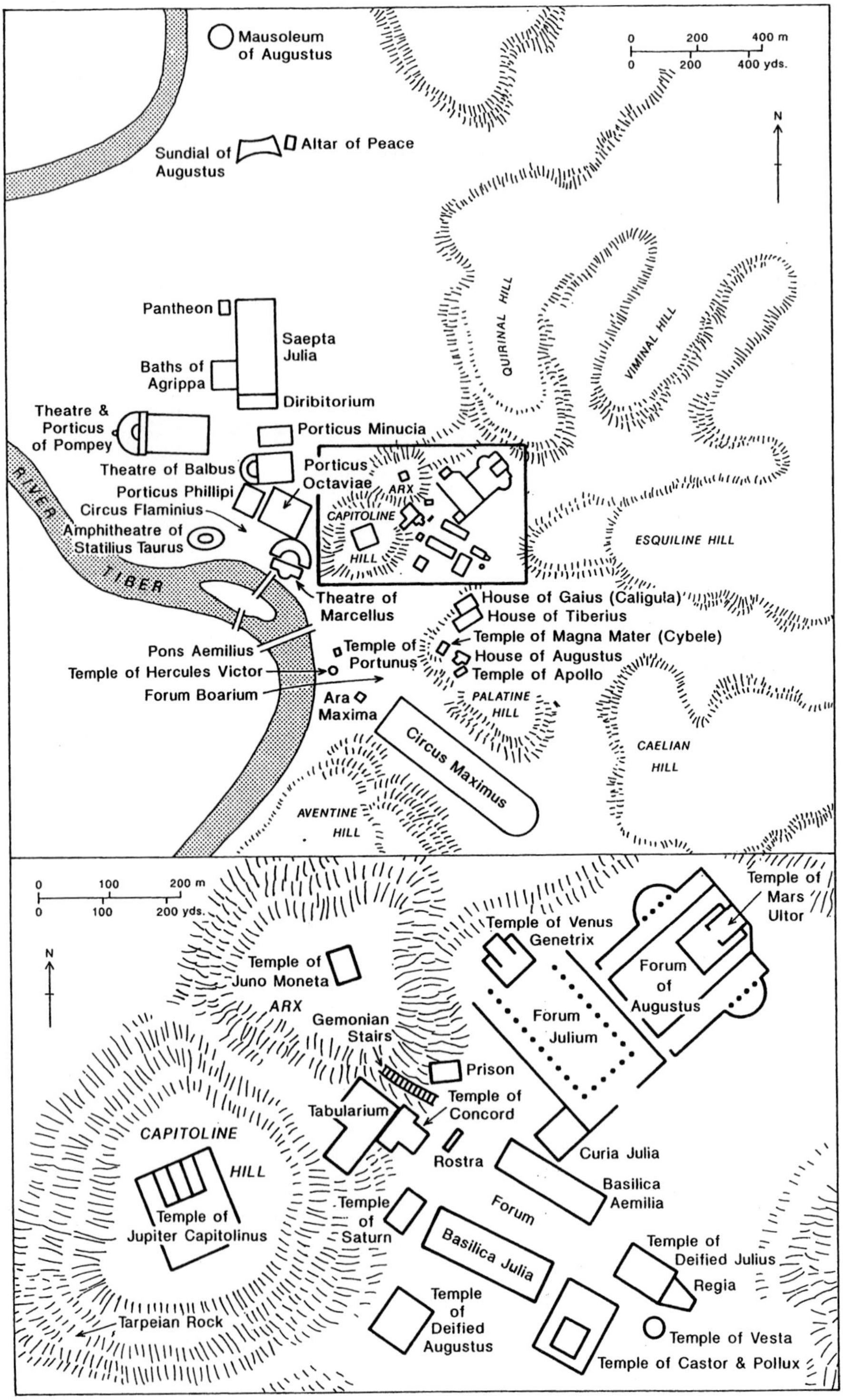

The City of Rome under Claudius

SECTION A

THE ACTS OF THE ARVAL BROTHERS
(ACTA FRATRUM ARVALIUM)

Introduction: The Arval Brothers were an archaic priesthood revived by Augustus. They worshipped the obscure Dea Dia in a sacred grove just outside Rome, at modern Magliana. Increasingly, their activities focused on honouring the emperor and his family, celebrating imperial anniversaries. The 12 members of the college were important senators at Rome, including members of the imperial family, and held position for life, being replaced by co-option on death. Their acts of worship were recorded on stone inscriptions. Some of these have survived almost intact, others in a more or less fragmentary state, thus providing, for certain periods, a version of official court history. Bibliography: J. Scheid, *Commentarii fratrum arvalium qui supersunt* (Rome 1998) no.2. J. Rupke, Fasti Sacerdotum (Oxford 2008) for definitive lists of Brothers and biographies.

After two passages on the Arval Brothers, the numbering used here divides the records according to year and entry, so A38d is the fourth preserved record for AD 38. Square brackets indicate a gap in the text. As the rites tend to follow obvious patterns and wordings, involve a limited number of people, and may well be repeated from year to year, these can usually be filled in with a degree of certainty.

A1 The origin of the Arval Brothers

But Masurius Sabinus, in the first book of *Memorable Deeds*, following some historians writes that Acca Larentia was the nurse of Romulus. "This woman lost one of her twelve sons to death. In his place Romulus offered himself as her son and called himself and her other sons the "Arval Brothers". Since then, the college of the Arval Brothers has been maintained, twelve in number, with the special symbols of priesthood being a crown of ears of corn a white headband."

[Aulus Gellius, *Nights in Attica*, 7.7.8 = Masurius Sabinus, fr. 14]

Masurius Sabinus was a leading Julio-Claudian lawyer and teacher of law. He wrote on sacred, private and public law and his learning was admired by Tiberius who gave his legal opinions imperial authority. Gellius has also given the more common view that Acca, whose name was often mentioned in the early records of Rome, was a prostitute who made a lot of money which she bequeathed to Romulus or the Roman people.

A2 Arval Brothers priests for life

Amongst his first acts, Romulus created the institution of the priests of the fields (*arvorum sacerdotes*) and nominated himself the twelfth brother among the others who were the sons of Acca Larentia who brought him up. This priesthood was given as its most sacred emblem, a crown of ears of corn bound by a white headband, the first crown for the Romans. This honour is only ended by death and stays even with those exiled or imprisoned.

[Pliny, *Natural History* 18.6]

A15a – 1 June, AD 15: Paullus Fabius Persicus co-opted

On 1 June on the Palatine in the Temple of Apollo, [Tiberius Caesar] Augustus, *pontifex maximus*, master of the [Arval] Brothers co-opted Paullus Fabius [Persicus] in place of Paullus Fabius Maximus and [called] him to the sacred rites.
[The following were present: Drusus Ca]esar, M. Ca[ecil]i[us Cor]nutus, L. Domitius Ah[enobarbus, T. Q]uinctius Cr[ispinus Valerianus, … *(name lost)*], Paullus Fa[bius Persicus, …*(name lost)*].

[*AFA* 3, lines 4–11]

The Fabii were one of Rome's most aristocratic families. Paullus Fabius Maximus, consul 11 BC, was a friend of Augustus, who committed suicide shortly before Augustus' death (LACTOR 17, F5.1–2, P1, P18). Persicus was his son: as he was not consul until AD 34, he must have been around 20 when co-opted.

A20a – unknown occasion late in AD 20

(A list of names, T. Quinctius Crispinus Valerianus, L. Calpurnius Piso the pontifex, M. Caecilius Cornutus, Paullus Fabius Persicus, Cn. Pompeius the augur, alone survives just before the entry below, recording the consuls and first event of AD 21.)

[*AFA* 4a, lines 2–6]

A21a – 11 January AD 21: prayers and rites

When Tiberius Caesar, for the fourth time, and Drusus Caesar, [for the second time, were consuls].

11 January, [*(location lost?)*] T. Quictius Crispinus Valerianus, president, with clean hands and covered [head], under the open sky, [facing east announced] a sacrifice to the Dea Dia.

"That all may be good, propitious, favourable, and prosperous [for the people of Rome, the Quirites], and for the Arval Brothers, for Tiberius Caesar Augustus, for Julia Augusta, their children and grandchildren [and their whole house!] There shall be a sacrifice [this year to the Dea Dia …*(date lost)*]."

[*AFA* 4a, lines 7–19]

A21b – 20 May AD 21: illness of Sulla Felix

[Since T. Quictius Crispinus Valerianus, president] of the Arval [Brothers informed them] that [Sulla] Felix, [priest …] who was [hindered by] illness [and was unable] to be present at the [sacrifices] to the Dea Dia [on *(dates lost)*]. [M. Valerius Messall…] was appointed as his replacement. The following were present: [T. Quinctius Crispinus] Valerianus, president, [Drusus] Caesar, [son of Tiberius, … *(name lost)*…, M. Valerius] Messall […*(name lost)*…, M. Caecilius] Cornutus, [Paullus Fabius Persi]cus, Sex. [Appuleius].

[*AFA* 4b, lines 1–15]

M. Valerius Messalla Messallinus is either the son (cos 3 BC) or grandson (cos AD 20) of M. Valerius Messalla Corvinus (Augustan aristocrat (see on consuls of AD 20 = **B20**)).

A21c – 30 May AD 21: C. Pomponius Graecinus co-opted

When Mamercus Aem[ilius Scaurus] and Cn. Trem[ellius were consuls], on 30 May. Since T. Qui[nctius Crispinus] Valerianus, [president] of the Arval [Brothers] informed [them that another] had [to be summoned] by the Arval [Brothers] to the rites [of the Dea Dia] in [place of] the deceased [Sulla Felix], they [co-opted C. Pomponius] Graecin[us as Arval Brother] in the traditional [way]. The following were present: [T. Quinctius Crispinus] Valer[ianus, president, …*(and other names lost)*]

[*AFA* 4b, lines 16–28]

C. Pomponius Graecinus was consul in AD 16, see **B16**.

A27a – 4 Jan, AD 27: vows for Tiberius and Julia Augusta/Livia

[When L. Calpurnius Piso and M. Licinius] Cra[ssus were consuls, on 4 January, on the Capitol, L. Calpurnius Pis]o the Pontifex, [president, on behalf of the college of Arval] Brothers [undertook vows for the safety of Tiberius] Caesar Au[gustus, *pontifex maximus*, in his 28th year of tribunician power, consul four times, and for

Ju]lia Augusta. [After making sacrifices on the Capitol he fulfilled the vows which] the previous year's president had made, and undertook the vows for the coming year, dictated by T. Quin[ctius Crispinus Valerianus], in the exact terms [written below]:

[Jupiter, Greatest and Best], if Tiberius Caesar [Augustus, son of Divus Augustus, *pontifex maximus*, in his 28th year of tribunician] power, [consul four times, and Julia Augusta, whom I consciously] mention, shall be [alive and well for the state and Roman People, the Quirites,] on 4 [January in the next year for the Roman People, the Quirites;] and if you preserve [those people, whom I consciously mention, from dangers which happen or are to happen before that day; and if you grant them as prosperous] a situation [as I consciously name; and if] you see to it that [you preserve them] in the same condition as [at present or better], then I vow, [on behalf of the college of Arval Brothers,] a golden [ox to you. Jupiter, Greatest and Best, on the terms according to which] I have vowed that you will have [a golden ox which I have vowed this day, if you do this accordingly], I vow, [on behalf of the Arval Brothers that ... pounds of gold and ... pounds of silver will be offered] as a gift to you [*(in a place? lost)*, from their resources].

[Queen Juno, on the terms according to which I have vowed that] Jupiter, Greatest and Best [will have a golden] ox [which I have vowed this day], if you do this accordingly, I vow to a golden cow [to you, on behalf of the Arval Brothers].

[Minerva, on the terms according to which I have vowed that] Jupiter, Greatest and Best will have a golden ox [which I have vowed this day], if you do this accordingly, I vow to a golden cow to you, [on behalf of the Arval Brothers].

[Dea Dia, on the terms according to which I have vowed that] Jupiter, Greatest and Best will have a golden ox, [which I have vowed this day], if you do this accordingly, [I vow to a] golden [cow to you], in the grove, [on behalf of the Arval Brothers].

[The following were present: L. Pis]o the Pontifex, Pa[ullus Fabius Persicus, L. Caninius Gallus, Cn. Domiti]us Ahen[obarbus, *(and others – names lost)*].

[*AFA* 5a–e, lines 1–32]

Much of this very fragmentary entry can be restored from very similar vows made at the start of other years, compare **A38a**, **A54a**.

A27b – 30 Jan AD 27: birthday of Julia Augusta/Livia

[On 30 January, *(name lost)*, on behalf of the college of Arval Brothers sacrificed a male ox] on the Capitol [to Jupiter Greatest and Best], in honour of the birthday of Julia Augusta.

[The following were present: T. Quinctius Crispinus V]alerianus, L. Caninius Gallus, [Cn. Domitius Ahenobarbus?].

[*AFA* 5f, lines 1–6]

A27c – shortly after 30 Jan AD 27: statue in honour of Tiberius and Julia Augusta/Livia

[On *(date lost)*, L. Piso the Pontifex, president], had a [statue] placed [in the grove of the Dea Dia], together with a plaque, a base, and the following inscription:

For the year's well-being of [Tiberius Caesar Augustus, son of Divus Augustus], *pontifex maximus*, holder of tribunician [power, consul, father of the fatherland, and of Julia August]a, his mother, in the fourth presidency [of L. Piso the Pontifex].

[*AFA* 5f, lines 7–14]

A27d – 19 May AD 27: various rites in the grove

(Fragments for 19 May show L. Piso conducting vows and sacrifices to Dea Dia.)

[*AFA* 5g, lines 4–7]

A28a – 4 January, AD 28: vows for Tiberius and Julia Augusta/Livia

*(Fragments recording exactly the same vows as **A27a** above.)*

[*AFA* 6, lines 1–6]

A35a – 23 September, AD 35: birthday of Augustus

[On 23 September, Paullus Fabius Persicus, vice-president, on behalf of the Arval Brothers, sacrificed a male ox on the Capitol] to Jupiter Greatest and Best, [in honour of the birthday] of Divus Augustus.

The following were present: Paullus Fa[bius Persicus, L. Caninius] Gallus, Taurus Statilius [Corvinus, … *(another name lost)*].

[*AFA* 7, column II, lines 1–3]

A35b – 16 November, AD 35: birthday of Tiberius

On 16 November, the same vice-president sacrificed [a male ox on the Capitol to Jupiter Greatest and Best], by decree [of the senate, in honour of the birthday] of Tiberius Caesar Augustus, son of Divus Augustus, [*pontifex maximus*], in his 2[7th year] of tribunician power, [five times consul].

The following were present: Paullus Fa[bius Persicus, L. Caninius Gal]lus, Taurus Statili[us Corvinus, … *(another name lost)*].

[*AFA* 7, column II, lines 4–10]

A36a – 3/4 January, AD 36: vows for Tiberius

*(Significant fragments show vows being undertaken in the same terms as **A27a** above, by the president, L. Caninius Gallus, though for Tiberius alone (Livia died in AD 29)).*

[*AFA* 7, column II, lines 11–23]

A37a – 13 January, AD 37: vows for Tiberius, by order of the consuls

On 13 January on the Capitol, [Taurus Sta]tilius Corvinus, president of the [Arval] Brothers, by order of the consuls summoned his colleagues [to fulfil and] undertake [vows] for the well-being of Tiberius Caesar.

[The following were present]: Taurus Statilius Corvinus, L. Caninius [Gallus] [Paullus Fab]ius Persicus, Cn. Domitius.

[*AFA* 8a, lines 1–6]

A37b – 23 January, AD 37: sacrifice for Tiberius, by order of the consuls

On 23 January on the Capitol, [Taurus Stat]ilius Corvinus, president of the Arval Brothers, by order of the consul, and by consent of the senate, summoned his colleagues and sacrificed two male oxen to Jupiter Greatest and Best for the safety and well-being of [Tiberius Caesar] Augustus.

[The following were present]: Taurus Statilius Corvinus, Fabius [Persicus, … *(name lost)*], L. Caninius Gallus, Cn. Domitius.

[*AFA* 8a, lines 7–14]

A37c – 17 May, AD 37: sacrifices and co-option of M. Furius

["C. Caesar August]us Germanicus [greets] his [colleagues the Arval Brothers]. [In place of M. Furi]us Camillus, [I co-opt, by my own judgement], M. Fu[rius …] as our colleague and Arval [Brother].

[*AFA* 11b, lines 7–14]

Though the names are fragmentary, we seem to have another case of a son replacing his father. Furius Camillus was consul in AD 8; for another son, Arruntius Camillus, see **B32**.

A38a – 3 January, AD 38 (vows for Gaius)

(Probably starts with prayers for the imperial house, similar to those of ***A27a****)*

Jupiter, Greatest and Best, on the terms according to which [I have vowed that you will have a golden ox which] I have vowed this day, if you do this accordingly, I vow, on behalf of the Arval Brothers that 25 pounds of gold and 55 pounds of silver will be offered [as a gift to you], from their resources.

Queen Juno, on the terms according to which I have vowed that Jupiter, Greatest and Best will have a golden ox which I have vowed this day, if you do this accordingly, I vow to a golden cow to you, on behalf of the Arval Brothers.

Minerva, on the terms according to which I have vowed that Jupiter, Greatest and Best will have a golden ox, if you do this accordingly, I vow to a golden cow to you, on behalf of the Arval Brothers.

In the same terms he made vows to the Dea Dia, to Well-Being, to Divus Augustus.

The following were present: Paullus Fabius Persicus, Cn. Domitius Ahenobarbus, M. Furius Camillus.

[*AFA* 12a, lines 3–15]

A38b – 7 January, AD 38: fulfilment of vows for Gaius

On 7 January, Taurus Statilius Corvinus, vice-president, on behalf of the college of Arval Brothers, fulfilled the vows which he had made on 3 January for the safety of Gaius Caesar Augustus Germanicus, and sacrificed a cow in the grove of the Dea Dia.

[*AFA* 12a, lines 16–19]

A38c – 11 January, AD 38: vows for Gaius

On 11 January, [Taurus Statilius Cor]vinus, vice-president, on behalf of the college of Arval Brothers, [… with clean hands and covered] head, [under the open sky, facing east, *(place lost)*, announced the sacrifice to the Dea Dia:]

"That it may be [good], propitious, [favourable, and prosperous for Gaius Caesar Augustus] Ger[manicus, president, and for his] sisters, [for the people of Rome, the Quirites, and for the Arval Brothers, and] for me! [There shall be] a sacrifice [in the grove and in the house] of Gaius Caesar Augustus German[icus, president]:

on 27 May [at his house],
on 29 May [in the grove and at his house],
on 30 May [at his house].

[*AFA* 12a, lines 20–23 and *AFA* 12b, lines 1–7]

A38d – 30 January, AD 38: birthday of Julia Augusta/Livia

On 30 January, Taurus Statilius Corvinus, vice-president, on behalf [of the college of Arval Brothers], on the Field [of Mars], at the Altar of Peace, [sacrificed …]

The following were present: Paullus Fabius Persicus, [… *and others (names lost)*.

Taurus Statilius Corvinus, vice-president, [on behalf of the college] of Arval Brothers sacrificed a male ox on the Capitol to Jupiter Greatest and Best, in honour of the birthday of Julia Augusta. The following were present: Paullus Fabius Persicus, Cn. Domitius Ahenobarbus, M. Furius Camillus.

[*AFA* 12b, lines 8–11 and *AFA* 12c, lines 1–4]

A38e – 31 January, AD 38: birthday of Antonia

On 31 January, Taurus Statilius Corvinus, vice-president, [on behalf] of the college of Arval Brothers sacrificed a male ox on the Capitol to Jupiter Greatest and Best, in honour of the birthday of Antonia Augusta.

[*AFA* 12c, lines 5–7]

A38f – 18 March, AD 38: Gaius hailed as *Imperator*

On 18 March, Taurus Statilius Corvinus, vice-president, [on behalf] of the college of Arval Brothers sacrificed on the Capitol three adult animals to Jupiter, Juno and Minerva, and, [in front of the] new temple, one to Divus Augustus, because on this day Gaius Caesar Augustus Germanicus [was hailed] *Imperator* by the senate.

The following were present: Paullus Fabius Persicus, Cn. Domitius Ahenobarbus, M. Furius Camillus, Appius Iunius Silanus.

[*AFA* 12c, lines 8–14]

This commemorates Gaius being hailed as *Imperator* by the senate on 18 March, 37, two days after the death of Tiberius, marking their official recognition of his succession. See Barrett, *Caligula,* 53.

A38g – 28 March, AD 38: Gaius entered Rome

On 28 March,Taurus Statilius Corvinus, vice-president, [on behalf] of the college of Arval Brothers sacrificed [on the Capitol] three adult animals to Jupiter, Juno and Minerva, and, in front of the new temple, one to Divus Augustus, because on this day, Gaius Caesar Augustus Germanicus entered Rome.

The following were present: Paullus Fabius Persicus, M. Furius Camillus, Appius I[unius Sila]nus.

[*AFA* 12c, lines 15–20]

This commemorates Gaius' arrival in Rome on 28 March, 37, accompanying Tiberius' body from Misenum: see **J2g** and Levick, *Tiberius* 219–20, Barrett, *Caligula,* 55–6.

A38h – 18 April, AD 38: sacrifice to Dea Dia

On 18 April, Taurus Statilius Corvinus, vice-president, [on behalf] of the college of Arval Brothers made sacrifice in expiation for a branch which had fallen through old age in the Grove of the Dea Dia and ordered the branch [to be burnt].

[*AFA* 12c, lines 21–23]

A38i – 23 April, AD 38: sacrifice to Augustus

On 23 April, [Taurus Statilius C]orvinus, vice-president, [on behalf] of the college of Arval Brothers [sacrificed a male] ox at the Theatre of Marcellus, in front of the statue of Divus Augustus. [The following were present: Paullus F]abius Persicus, Cn. Domitius Ahenobarbus, M. Fu[rius Camillus, Appius Iunius Si]lanus.

[*AFA* 12c, lines 24–28]

The calendar at Praeneste records the dedication of this statue to Augustus in AD 22 by Livia and Tiberius (**K3**). The date is not recorded as having had any previous significance to Augustus in any Augustan calendar or in Ovid's *Fasti* (4.863–900). It disappears from the *AFA* after this year.

A38j – 24 May, AD 38: birthday of Germanicus, father of Gaius

On 24 May, [Taurus Statiliu]s [Corvi]nus, vice-president, [on behalf] of the college of Arval Brothers sacrificed a male ox on the [Capit]ol to Jupiter Greatest and Best, in honour of the birthday of Germanicus Caesar.

On the same day in the Temple of Jupiter Stator:

Letters were read out from Gaius Caesar Augustus Germanicus co-opting as Arval Brothers, L. Annius [Vin]icianus in place of C. [Pomponius Graecin]us; [C. Caecina Larg]us in place of Tiberius Caesar [son of] Drus[us]; C. Calpurnius Piso in place of M. Silanus. The following were present: M. Furius Camillus, Appius Iunius Silanus, Paullus F[abius Persicus].

[*AFA* 12c, lines 29–37]

L. Annius Vinicianus: part of the assassination of Gaius in 41 (Jos. *JA* 19.18–20) and conspired against Claudius in 42; C. Caecina Largus: see **B42**; C. Calpurnius Piso (cos 57 – **B57**) must have been in his twenties when appointed.

A38k – 27 May, AD 38: sacrifice to Dea Dia

On 27 May, C. Caesar Augustus Germanicus, president of the college of [Arval] Brothers, in his own house, which had previously belonged to his grandfather Tiberius Caesar, carried out, in the open air, a sacrifice on the altar of the Dea Dia.

The following were present: M. F[urius C]ami[llus], Appius Iunius Silanus, Cn. D[omitius] Ahenobarbus, [Paul]lus Fabiu[s Persi]cus, C. Caecina Largus, Tauru[s Statilius] Corvinus, L. Anni[us] Vinicianus, [C. C]alpurnius Piso.

[*AFA* 12c, lines 38–44]

A38m – 29 May, AD 38: sacrifice to Dea Dia and entertainment

On 29 May, Taurus Statilius Corvinus, vice-president, on behalf of the college of [Arval] Brothers sacrificed a cow in the Grove of the Dea.

On the same day, and in the same place, C. Caesar Augustus Germanicus, [president] of the college of Arval Brothers, together with Appius Silanus, priest of the Dea Dia, sacrificed a special lamb and gave a signal to chariots and stunt-riders.

The following were present: Paullus Fabius Persicus, Cn. Domitius Ahenobarbus, M. Fur[ius] Camillus, C. Caecina Largus, L. Annius Vinicianus, C. Calpurnius Piso.

[*AFA* 12c, lines 45–53]

Compare **A53a, A58b, A59h**.

A38n – 26 June, AD 38: sacrifice at Altar of Augustan Providence

On 26 June, Taurus Statilius Corvinus, vice–president, on behalf of the college of Arval Brothers sacrificed a cow in the Field of Agrippa at the Altar of Augustan Providence.

The following were present: Paullus Fabius Persicus, M. Furius Camillus, Appius Iunius Silanus.

[*AFA* 12c, lines 54–58]

The Altar of Augustan Providence is mentioned on the *SCPP* (**P3f**) and was perhaps created to celebrate Augustus' adoption of Tiberius. It comes to represent the divine personification of the emperor's care for the Roman empire, and is quite frequently represented on coins from Tiberius to Vitellius, e.g. *RIC* Tiberius 81; *BMC* Tiberius 146. No trace of it remains.

A38o – 26 June, AD 38: sacrifice in honour of Jupiter

In the consulship of Ser. Asinius Celer and Sex. Nonius Quinctilianus

On 1 July,Taurus Statilius Corvinus, vice-president, on behalf of the college of Arval Brothers sacrificed a male ox on the Capitol, in front of the statues of ex-consuls, in honour of Jupiter Greatest and Best.

The following were present: Paullus Fabius Persicus, M. Furius Camillus, Appius Iunius Silanus.

[*AFA* 12c, lines 59–65]

A38p – 4 July, AD 38: sacrifice at the Altar of Peace

On 4 July, Taurus Statilius Corvinus, vice-president, on behalf of the college of Arval Brothers sacrificed a cow at the Altar of Peace in the Field of Mars. The following were present: Paullus Fabius Persicus, M. Furius Camillus, Appius Iunius Silanus.

[*AFA* 12c, lines 66–70]

This celebrated the beginning of the Altar of Augustan Peace in 13 BC. See LACTOR 17, C20 for the date of this public holiday on calendars and K13 for the monument itself.

A38q – 1 August, AD 38: sacrifice in honour of Augustus' conquest of Egypt

On 1 August, Taurus Statilius Corvinus, vice-president, on behalf of the college of Arval Brothers sacrificed a male ox in front of the new Temple to Divus Augustus.

The following were present: Paullus Fabius Persicus, M. Furius Camillus, Appius Iunius Silanus.

[*AFA* 12c, lines 71–76]

This celebrated the capture of Alexandria in 30 BC by Octavian/Augustus after his defeat of Antony and Cleopatra. See LACTOR 17, C21 for the date of this public holiday on calendars.

A38r – 31 August, AD 38: birthday of Gaius

On 31 August, Taurus Statilius Corvinus, vice-president, on behalf of the college of Arval Brothers sacrificed a male ox on the Capitol to Jupiter Greatest and Best, in honour of the birthday of C. Caesar Augustus Germanicus.

The following were present: Paullus Fabius Persicus, M. Furius Camillus, Appius Iunius Silanus.

[*AFA* 12c, lines 77–82]

A38s – 21 September, AD 38: Gaius made *pater patriae*

On 21 September, Taurus Statilius Corvinus, vice-president, on behalf of the college of Arval Brothers sacrificed on the Capitol three adult animals to Jupiter, Juno and Minerva, and, [in front of his new tem]ple, one to Divus Augustus, because on this day, Gaius Caesar Augustus Germanicus accepted the title Father of the Fatherland offered him by unanimous decision of the senate.

The following were present: Paullus Fabius Persicus, M. Furius Camillus, Appius Iunius [Silanus, P. Me]mmius [Reg]ulus, C. Caecina, L. Annius Vinicianus, [C. Calpurniu]s Piso.

[*AFA* 12c, lines 83–91]

Dio (59.3.2 = LACTOR 15, B3) tells us that Gaius accepted all Augustus' titles shortly after his accession, with the except of *pater patriae*, father of the fatherland, which he took soon afterwards. This record shows the date as 21 September, AD 37. For the honour, see LACTOR 17, H38 and Barrett, *Caligula* 70–71.

A38t – 23 September, AD 38: Augustus' birthday; Drusilla's deification

On 23 September, [Taurus Statilius Cor]vinus, vice-president, [on behalf] of the college of Arval Brothers [sacrific]ed [a male ox] in the new temple of Divus Augustus, in honour of the birthday of Divus Augustus.

[The following were present: Paullus Fabius P]ersicus, Cn. Domitius Ahenobarbus, [M. Furius Camillus, P. Mem]mius Regulus, C. Caecina Largus, [...], [C. Calpurniu]s Piso.

[On the same day, for the consecration of Drusill]a, in the new Temple of Divus Augustus, the college of [Arval] Brothers [... D]rusilla [...] Diva Drusilla [...]

[*AFA* 12c, lines 92–103]

For Drusilla, see **J22** and Barrett, *Caligula* 86–9.

A38u – 24 September and 16 November, AD 38: various rituals

(Meagre fragments show sacrifices of a male ox on 24 September and on 16 November, with ritual expiation of a fallen branch at some date in between.)

[*AFA* 12c, lines 103–109 and *AFA* 12d, lines 1–10]

A39a – 1 January, AD 39: Gaius' consulship

When C. Caesar Augustus Germanicus, for a second time, and L. Apronius Caesianus were consuls (AD 39), and Appius Iunius Silanus was president of the Arval Brothers.

On 1 January, [L. Salvius Otho, priest] and vice-president on behalf of the college of Arval Brothers [sacrificed] on the Capitol a male ox to Jupiter, a [cow] to Juno [and a cow to Minerva], and, [in fr]ont of the statues of ex-consuls, another male ox to Divus Augustus at his [new] temple, [in honour of the con]sulship of [C. Caesar Augustus Germanicus ...]

[*AFA* 13abcd, lines 1–10]

A39b – January to March, AD 39: various sacrifices

*(Sufficent fragments to restore as the next three entries sacrifices to mark the birthdays of Livia (30 January), Antonia (31 January) and the acclamation of Gaius as Imperator by the senate (18 March) on exactly the same formulae as for AD 38 (**A38d–f**). Those present included Paullus Fabius Persicus, Taurus Statilius Corvinus, C. Caecina Largus, and P. Memmius Regulus.)*

[*AFA* 13e, lines 1–17]

A39c – Unknown date, AD 39: sequence of sacrifices

[...] sacrificed [...] to Minerva a cow, [to Well-Being a cow,] to Divus Augustus a male ox; [also] in the Temple of Concord [a cow; also on] the Palatine to Divus Augustus a [male] ox, and at the Altar of Providence, a cow.

The following were present: Cn. Domitius, Ca[ecina Largus, Taurus] Statilius Corvinus.

[*AFA* 13fgh, lines 1–8]

Record of sacrifices to Jupiter and Juno must have preceded that to Minerva. Sacrifice to Concord suggests a political context in which unison has *not* been apparent. While that to Providence shows a wish to thank the gods for taking care of the status quo. The likely context is failure of Gaetulicus' conspiracy (see **A39e** below).

A39d – 24/26 October, AD 39: birthday of Agrippina the Elder

On 2[.] October, [L. Salvius Otho], priest and vice-president on behalf of the [college of] Arval Brothers sacrificed a male ox on the [Capitol] in honour of the birthday of Agrippina, wife of Germanicus [Caes]ar, mother of Caesar [Ger]manicus …].

The following were present: Cn. Domitius, Paullus Fabius Persicus, C. Caecina Largus.

[*AFA* 13fgh, lines 9–16]

A39e – 27 October, AD 39: Gaetulicus' conspiracy detected

On 27 October, on account of the uncovering of wicked [plots against Gaius Germanicus] by Cn. Lentulus Gaetulicus … [L. Salvius] Otho, priest [and vice-president on behalf of the college of Arval] Brothers [sacrificed …]

[*AFA* 13fgh, lines 17–22]

For Cornelius Lentulus Gaetulicus and his conspiracy, see **A39c** above; **B26**; **P5**; Barrett, *Caligula* 101–6.

A40a – 24 May, AD 40: birthday of Germanicus

On 24 May, […the vice]-president in the presidency of [P. Memmius Regulus, on behalf of the college] of Arval Brothers sacrificed a male [ox to Jupiter], a cow to Juno [and a cow to Minerva in honour of] the birthday of Germanicus [Caesar].

[The following were present: …] M. Silanus, C. Caecina [Largus, Taurus Sta]tilius Corvinus.

[*AFA* 14 column I, lines 1–9]

A40b – 1 June, AD 40: sacrifice to Dea Dia

On 1 June, […the vice]-president in the presidency of P. Memmius Reg]ulus, on behalf of the college of Arval Brothers [sacrificed] a cow to the Dea Dia.

The following were present: [Imperator C. C]aesar Augustus Germanicus, [C. Caecina L]argus, Taurus Statilius [Corvinus, L. A]nnius Vinicianus, C. [Calpurnius] Piso, M. Silanus.

[*AFA* 14 column I, lines 10–18]

A40c – 2/5 June, AD 40: sacrifice to Drusilla

On 2/5 June, […the vice]-president in the presidency of [P. Memmius Reg]ulus, on behalf of the college of [Arval] Brothers sacrificed a ma[le ox to Jupiter], a cow to [Juno] and a cow to Minerva in honour of the birthday of [Diva Drusilla] Augusta.

[The following were present: C. Ca]ecina L]argus, M. Silanus, [L. Annius Vini]cianus, C. Calpurnius Piso.

[*AFA* 14 column I, lines 19–26]

A44a – 12 January, AD 44: Claudius *pater patriae* (father of the fatherland)

On [12] January, sacrifice to Jupiter because Tiberius Claudius Caesar Augustus Germanicus was called father of the fatherland. [On] the Capitol a male ox to Jupiter, a cow to Juno, a cow to Minerva, a cow to Prosperity, a male ox to Divus Augustus, a cow to Diva Augusta.

The following were present: C. Caecina Largus, L. Vitellius, Paullus Fabius Persicus, Taurus Statilius Corvinus, C. Piso, M. Silanus, L. Silanus, Magnus Pompeius.

[*AFA* 17, lines 3–14]

Claudius initially refused the title *pater patriae* (Dio 60.3.2 = LACTOR 15 C3), but took it in January 42 (*RIC Claudius* 90–91 = *BMC Claudius* 181–4, showing Claudius PP and COS II).

A44b – 17 January, AD 44: anniversary of deification of Julia Augusta/Livia

On 17 January, [In honour of] the consecration of Diva Augusta, in the [new] temple, a male ox to Divus Augustus, a cow to [Diva] Augusta.

The following were present: C. Caecina Largus, L. Vitellius, Paullus Fabius Persicus, Taurus Statilius Corvinus, C. Piso, M. Silanus, L. Silanus, Magnus Pompeius.

[*AFA* 17, lines 15–23]

For Augusta's deification, see **L22**.

A45a – Unknown Date in AD 43 or 45.

[Paullus Fabius] Persicus [sacrificed] a male ox to Jupiter. Marcus Silanus was present.

[*AFA* 18, lines 1–2]

A45b – 23 and 24 September, in AD 43 or 45: celebrations of Augustus' birthday

On 23 September, for the birthday of Divus Augustus, L. Vitellius, president, on behalf of the college of Arval Brothers, sacrificed a male ox to Jupiter on the Capitol and a cow at the altar of the Julian clan.

The following were present: C. Caecina La[rgus, M]. Silanus, Statilius [Corvinus]. On 24 September, L. Vi[tellius, president], on behalf of the college of Arval [Brothers], sacrificed a male ox [to Divus Augustus] on the Palatine and a cow [to Diva Augusta ... (*names of those present lost)*].

[*AFA* 18, lines 3–17]

A53a – 29 May, AD 53: sacrifice to Dea Dia and entertainment

[... in the presidency?] of T. Sextius Africanus, [... (name lost)] on behalf of the college of Arval Brothers, sacrificed a cow at the altar to the Dea Dia. Next, inside the temple, at the hearth, he sacrificed and made offering to the Dea Dia of a special lamb. When the sacrifice had been completed, wearing a veil and a crown, he gave a signal to chariots and stunt-riders to leave the starting-gates.

There were present in the college: M. Silanus, P. Memmius Regulus, L. Salvius Otho, Messalla Corvinus.

[*AFA* 20, lines 1–14]

Presumably 29 May, see **A38m, A58b, A59h.**

A53b – 12 October, AD 53: Augustalia

When Q. Caecina Primus and P. Trebonius were consuls,

On 12 October, the *Augustalia*, in the new temple, in the presidency of T. Sextius Africanus, A. Vitellius, vice-president, on behalf of the Arval Brothers, sacrificed a male ox to Divus Augustus, and a cow to Diva Augusta.

The following were present: Nero Caesar, leader of the younger generation, P. Memmius Regulus, L. Salvius Otho, M. Silanus, C. Piso, Messalla Corvinus.

[*AFA* 20, lines 15–30]

A54a – 28 June, AD 54: vows for young Nero, *princeps iuventutis*

On 28 June, on the Capitol, [(name lost), president], on behalf of the Arval Brothers [undertook vows for the health] of Nero Claudius Drusus Germa[nicus Caesar ... at the dictation of (name lost) ...] in exactly these following words:

Jupiter, Greatest and Best, we pray [and beseech you that you] preserve [safe] and unharmed Nero Claudius, leader of the younger generation, offspring [of Agrippina Augusta, son of Tiberius Claudius Caesar Augustus Germanicus], divine *princeps* and [public] parent; and that at the [first] opportunity you make him exempt for the future [from any serious sickness. If this is, and shall be the case, and if you] bring this about, then [we vow that you will have] a golden ox. Jupiter, Greatest and Best, on the [terms] according to which [we have vowed that you will have a golden ox] which we have vowed this day, if you [do] this accordingly, [then] we vow [the 25 pounds of gold and 55 pounds of silver] which the College of Arval Brothers [has decreed as a gift to you].

Queen Juno, on [exactly the same] terms according to which we have vowed that Jupiter, [Greatest and Best will have a golden ox] which we have vowed this day, [if you do this accordingly, we vow to a golden cow to you], on behalf of the College of Arval Brothers. Minerva, on [exactly the same] terms according to which [we have vowed that Queen] Juno, [will have a golden cow], if you do this accordingly, [we vow to a golden] cow [to you], on behalf of [the College] of Arval Brothers. Public Well-Being of the Roman People, the Quirites, [we pray] and beseech you that you preserve safe and unharmed Nero Clau[dius, leader of the younger generation, offspring of Agrippina Augusta, son of Tiberius Claudius Caesar Augustus G] ermanicus, divine *princeps* [and public parent]; and that at the first [opportunity you make him exempt for the future from any serious] sickness. [If this is, and] shall be the case, and if you bring this about, then [we vow that you will have a golden ox].

The following were present: [... (name lost) ...,] M. Junius Silanus.

[*AFA* 22, lines 1–29]

Scheid explains the unusual description of Claudius as 'divine *princeps'* (lines 8 and 24) as showing that Claudius was *princeps* at the time of the ceremony, but dead and deified by the time the inscription was made, probably at the end of the year. The inscription is interesting for showing how very clearly Nero was officially marked as Claudius' successor, with these elaborate vows being made for his health, and with his position as *princeps iuventutis* – 'leader of the younger generation' (see **A53b** and **J30a**). Nero was 16½, Claudius nearly 63, Britannicus (not mentioned) was 13½ .

A55a – 11 December, AD 55: in honour of Nero's father

When Gnaeus Lentulus Gaetulicus and T. Curtilius M[ancia were consuls].
On 11 December, P. Memmius Regulus, vice-president, [on behalf of the Arval] Brothers, [on the instruction? of] Nero Claudius Caesar Augustus Germanicus, *princeps* [and parent of his people sacrificed a male ox] on the Sacred Way, in front on the house of the Domitiii, in honour of the memory of Domitius [his father].

[*AFA* 24, lines 1–5]

A55b – 15 December, AD 55: Nero's birthday

On 15 December, P.Memmius Regulus, vice-president, [in honour of the birthday] of Nero Claudius Caesar Augustus Germanicus, [*princeps* and parent of his people], on behalf of the college of Arval Brothers sacrificed a male ox on the Capitol to Jupiter Greatest and Best, [a cow to Juno, a cow to Minerva] a male ox to Public Well-Being, a [bull] to his own divine spirit.

The following were present in the college: P. Memmius Regulus, [*name(s) lost*], Faustus Cornelius [Sulla, *name(s) lost*].

[*AFA* 24, lines 6–13]

A57a – 1 January, AD 57: Nero's second consulship

[M.] Salvius Otho, [vice-president, on behalf of the college] of Arval Brothers, in honour of the second consulship [of Nero Claudius Caesar Augustus Germanicus] sacrificed a male ox to Jupiter Greatest and Best], a cow to Juno], a cow [to Minerva] on the Capitol, and a male [ox to Divus Augustus and a cow] to Diva Augusta [and a male ox to Divus Claudius] in front of [the new temple].

[*AFA* 25a, lines 1–7]

A57b – unknown date in AD 57: all members of college present

C. Vipstanus Apronianus, president, M. Valerius Messalla Corvinus, consul designate, Sulpicius Camerinus, Faustus Cornelius Sulla Felix, T. Sextius Africanus, C. Piso, A. Vitellius, L. Salvius Otho Titianus, P. Memmius Regulus, L. Piso, M. Salvius Otho, M. Aponius Saturninus.

[*AFA* 25b, lines 1–5]

This entry is unusual in naming all twelve members of the college as present at a ritual not preserved.

A57c – 6 November, AD 57: Agrippina's Birthday

Under the same consuls, on 6 November, the birthday of Agrippina Augusta.

C. Vipstanus Apronianus, president, on behalf of the college of Arval Brothers sacrificed on the Capitol a male ox to Jupiter, a cow to Juno, a cow to Minerva, a cow to Public Well-Being, a cow to Concord.

The following were present in the college: C. Vipstanus Apronianus, president, M. Valerius Messalla Corvinus, consul designate, Sulpicius Camerinus, Faustus Cornelius Sulla Felix, T. Sextius Africanus.

[*AFA* 25b, lines 6–13]

A57d – 4 December, AD 57: Nero's tribunician power

Under the same consuls, on 4 December, in honour of the tribunician power of Nero Claudius Caesar Augustus Germanicus, C. Vipstanus Apronianus, president, on behalf of the college of Arval Brothers sacrificed on the Capitol a male ox to Jupiter, a cow to Juno, a cow to Minerva.

The following were present: C. Vipstanus Apronianus, president, M. Valerius Messalla Corvinus, consul designate, ~~A. Vitellius~~, Faustus Cornelius Sulla Felix, Sulpicius Camerinus, C. Piso, P. Memmius Regulus, M. Aponius Saturninus, T. Sextius Africanus.

[*AFA* 25b, lines 14–21]

The date of Nero's tribunician power is unclear: Gaius and Claudius took the power on their accession date. In Nero's case, this would be 13 October, 54 (see **A58d**). The date celebrated above may have been that on which a popular assembly formally ratified the senate's decree. The name of Vitellius (emperor in AD 69) was deleted, but is still legible.

A57e – 11 December, AD 57: Birthday of Nero's father

Under the same consuls, on 11 December, in honour of the birthday of Cn. Domitius Ahenobarbus, C. Vipstanus Apronianus, president, on behalf of the college of Arval Brothers sacrificed on the Sacred Way a male ox to the memory of Cn. Domitius.

The following were present: C. Vipstanus Apronianus, president, M. Valerius Messalla Corvinus, [consul designate, P.] Memmius Regulus, T. Sextius Africanus, C. Piso, M. Aponius Saturninus, Sulpicius Camerinus, A. Vitellius.

[*AFA* 25b, lines 22–27]

Nero's father was consul in 32 (see **B32**), and Arval from 27–39 (e.g. **A27a**, **A39c–d**). **A55b, A58g**, the record for the following year's sacrifice, shows that the Sacred Way (*via sacra*) was the (prestigious) location of the Domitius family house.

A57f – 15 December, AD 57: Nero's birthday

Under the same consuls, on 15 December, in honour of the birthday of Nero Claudius Caesar Augustus Germanicus, C. Vipstanus Apronianus, president, on behalf of the college of Arval Brothers sacrificed on the Capitol [a male ox] to Jupiter [...]

[*AFA* 25b, lines 28–31]

For Nero's birth in AD 37, see **R26** and Suet, *Nero* 6.1.

A58a – early AD 58: vows and sacrifices

(Meagre fragments for the first two months of AD 58 shows vows and sacrifices undertaken for the health of Nero and his wife, Octavia.)

[*AFA* 26a–lr, lines 1–32]

A58b – 29 May, AD 58: sacrifices to Dea Dia and entertainments

[On 29 May ... sacrificed] a special lamb to the Dea Dia; when the sacrifice had been completed, wearing a veil and a crown, he gave a signal to chariots and stunt-riders to leave the starting-gates.

The following were present: L. Salvius Otho Titianus, president, M. Valerius Messalla Corvinus, consul, C. Piso, Sulpicius Camerinus, L. Piso.

[*AFA* 27, lines 1–3]

A58c – 12 October, AD 58: Augustalia

When A. Paconius Sabinus and A. Petronius Lurco were consuls, on 12 October, L. Salvius Otho Titianus, president, on behalf of the college of Arval Brothers, sacrificed a male ox to Divus Augustus, a cow to Diva Augusta, a male ox to Divus Claudius.

The following were present: L. Salvius Otho Titianus, president, C. Vipstanus Apronianus, Sulpicius Camerinus, C. Piso, A. Vitellius, P. Memmius Regulus.

[*AFA* 27, lines 4–8]

A58d – 13 October, AD 58: in honour of Nero's imperium

Under the same consuls, on 13 October, in honour of the rule (*imperium*) of Nero Claudius Caesar Augustus Germanicus, L. Salvius Otho Titianus, president, on behalf of the college of Arval Brothers sacrificed on the Capitol a male ox to Jupiter, a cow to Juno, a cow to Minerva, a cow to Public Prosperity, a ox to his own divine spirit, a male ox to Divus Augustus, a cow to Diva Augusta, a male ox to Divus Claudius.

The following were present: L. Salvius Otho Titianus, president, C. Piso, C. Vipstanus Apronianus, M. Valerius Messalla Corvinus, A. Vitellius, Sulpicius Camerinus, P. Memmius Regulus, T. Sextius Africanus.

[*AFA* 27, lines 9–14]

Nero was proclaimed emperor immediately after Claudius' death (Suet., *Claud* 45 and Tac. *Ann.* 12.69)

A58e – 6 November, AD 58: Agrippina's Birthday

Under the same consuls, on 6 November, in honour of the birthday of Agrippina, mother of Augustus Germanicus, L. Salvius Otho Titianus, president, on behalf of the college of Arval Brothers sacrificed on the Capitol a male ox to Jupiter, a cow to Juno, a cow to Minerva, a cow to Public Well-Being, a cow to Public Concord.

The following were present: L. Salvius Otho Titianus, president, C. Vipstanus Apronianus, consul designate, L. Piso, P. Memmius Regulus.

[*AFA* 27, lines 15–18]

The offering to Public Concord was no doubt intended to suggest a good relationship between Nero and Agrippina (a sacrifice added since the previous year (**A57c**)). Tacitus, however, begins his account of AD 59 (*Annals* 14.1.1) with reference to Nero's 'long premeditated crime' (matricide).

A58f – 4 December, AD 58: Nero's tribunician power

Under the same consuls, on 4 December, in honour of the tribunician power of Nero Claudius Caesar Augustus Germanicus, L. Salvius Otho Titianus, president, on behalf of the college of Arval Brothers sacrificed on the Capitol a male ox to Jupiter, a cow to Juno, a cow to Minerva.

The following were present: L. Salvius Otho Titianus, president, M. Aponius Saturninus, Sulpicius Camerinus, C. Vipstanus Apronianus, consul designate, M. Valerius Messalla Corvinus, P. Memmius Regulus.

[*AFA* 27, lines 19–23]

See comments on **A57d** above.

A58g – 11 December, AD 58 (Birthday of Nero's father)

Under the same consuls, on 11 December, in honour of the birthday of Cn. Domitius Ahenobarbus, L. Salvius Otho Titianus, president, on behalf of the college of Arval Brothers sacrificed on the Sacred Road, in front of the house of the Domitii, a male ox to the memory of Cn. Domitius.

The following were present: L. Salvius Otho Titianus, president, M. Valerius Messalla Corvinus, C. Vipstanus Apronianus, consul designate, T. Sextius Africanus, Sulpicius Camerinus, P. Memmius Regulus, M. Aponius Saturninus.

[*AFA* 27, lines 24–8]

A58h – 15 December, AD 58: Nero's birthday

Under the same consuls, on 15 December, in honour of the birthday of Nero Claudius Caesar Augustus Germanicus, L. Salvius Otho Titianus, president, on behalf of the college of Arval Brothers sacrificed on the Capitol a male ox to Jupiter, a cow to Juno, a cow to Minerva, a cow to Public Well-Being, a cow to Concord in honour of Agrippina Augusta, an ox to his own divine spirit.

The following were present: L. Salvius Otho Titianus, president, C. Vipstanus Apronianus, consul designate, M. Valerius Messalla Corvinus, C. Piso, Sulpicius Camerinus, M. Aponius Saturninus, T. Sextius Africanus, P. Memmius Regulus.

[*AFA* 27, lines 29–34]

A59a – 3 January, AD 59: Vows for Nero's safety

When C. Vipstanus Apronianus and C. Fonteius Capito were consuls,

On 3 January, L. Piso, president, on behalf of the college of Arval Brothers undertook vows for the safety of Nero Claudius Caesar Augustus Germanicus, son of Divus Claudius, grandson of Germanicus Caesar, *pontifex maximus*, in his 5th year of tribunician power, hailed victorious commander 6 times, consul three times, and designated for a fourth time, and for Octavia, his wife. After making sacrifices on the Capitol he fulfilled the vows which the previous year's president had made, and undertook the vows, dictated by C. Vipstanus Apronius the consul, in the exact terms written below: two male oxen to Jupiter, two cows to Juno, two cows to Minerva, two cows to Public Well-Being, at the new temple, two male oxen to Divus Augustus, two cows to Diva Augusta, two male oxen to Divus Claudius.

The following were present: T. Sextius Africanus, M. Aponius Saturninus, P. Memmius Regulus, C. Piso, Sulpicius Camerinus, L. Salvius Otho Titianus.

[*AFA* 27, lines 35–48]

A59b – 12 January, AD 59: a meeting in the Pantheon

Under the same consuls, on 12 January, in the Pantheon in the presence of L. Calpurnius Piso, president.

C. Vipstanus Apronianus, consul, L. Salvius Otho Titianus, M. Aponius Saturninus, M. Valerius Messalla Corvinus, Sulpicius Camerinus, T. Sextius Africanus, Arval Brothers, L. Calpurnius Piso, president, proclaimed a sacrifice to the Dea Dia, as dictated by L. Salvius Otho Titianus, on 27 May in the house,

on 29 May in the grove and in the house,

on 30 May in the house.

Those mentioned above were present.

[*AFA* 27, lines 49–56]

A59c – 25 February, AD 59: adoption of Nero

Under the same consuls, on 25 February in honour of the adoption of Nero Claudius Caesar Augustus Germanicus, L. Piso, president, on behalf of the college of Arval Brothers sacrificed on the Capitol a male ox to Jupiter, a cow to Juno, a cow to Minerva, a cow to Public Well-Being.

The following were present: P. Memmius Regulus, T. Sextius Africanus, M. Valerius Messalla Corvinus, Sulpicius Camerinus, L. Salvius Otho Titianus, M. Aponius Saturninus.

[*AFA* 27, lines 57–63]

For Nero's adoption in AD 50, when aged 12, see Tac. *Ann.* 12.25–6. Suetonius, *Nero* 7.1 wrongly gives Nero's age as 10.

A59d – 4 March, AD 59: Nero's *comitia consularia*

Under the same consuls, 4 March in honour of the *comitia consularia* of Nero Claudius Caesar Augustus Germanicus, L. Calpurnius Piso, president, on behalf of the college of Arval Brothers sacrificed on the Capitol a male ox to Jupiter, a cow to Juno, a cow to Minerva, an ox to his own divine spirit.

The following were present: M. Valerius Messalla Corvinus, L. Salvius Otho Titianus, C. Vipstanus Apronianus, consul, T. Sextius Africanus, P. Memmius Regulus, C. Piso, M. Aponius Saturninus.

[*AFA* 27, lines 64–70]

The *comitia consularia* (voting assembly for the consulship) presumably refers to Nero being elected as consul for AD 60 (**B60**).

A59e – 5 March, AD 59: Nero *pontifex maximus*

Under the same consuls, on 5 March [in honour of] the pontificate of Nero Claudius Caesar Augustus Germanicus, L. Calpurnius Piso, president, on behalf of the college of Arval Brothers sacrificed [on the Capitol, a male ox] to Jupiter, a cow to Juno, a cow to Minerva, an ox to his own divine spirit.

The following were present: T. Sextius Africanus, Sulpicius Camerinus, P. Memmius Regulus, L. Salvius Otho Titianus, M. Valerius Messalla Corvinus, M. Aponius Saturninus.

[*AFA* 27, lines 71–2 and *AFA* 28a–c, lines 1–5]

Nero was made chief priest (*pontifex maximus*) on 5 March 55.

A59f – 28 March, AD 59: extraordinary meeting of the brothers

Under the same consuls, on 28 March, the following were present on the Capitol: C. Vipstanus Apronianus, consul, [L. Piso, P.] Memmius Regulus, Sulpicius Camerinus, T. Sextius Africanus, consul designate, [M. Valerius] Messalla Corvinus, M. Aponius Saturninus, L. Salvius Otho Titianus, C. Piso. [On this day no] sacrifice was made.

[*AFA* 28a–c, lines 6–9]

This unprecedented meeting without any vows or sacrifices being made must relate, like the next entry, to the murder of Agrippina. They may have met to agree and make the formal announcement of the days of thanksgivings a week later. The murder is reported in detail by Tacitus, *Annals* 14.1–12, who says it took place at the *Quinquatrus* festival (19–23 March: Ovid, *Fasti* 3.809–10). The official version was a naval accident, followed by Agerinus' failed assassination of Nero and her suicide. Tacitus attests various celebrations (14.10.1 and 14.12.1, as does Dio 62.15.1).

A59g – 5 April, AD 59: thanksgiving for Nero's safety

Under the same consuls, on 5 April, in honour of the days of thanksgiving proclaimed for the safety of Nero Claudius Caesar [Augustus Germanicus, L. Calpurnius] Piso, president, on behalf of the college of Arval Brothers, and by decree of the senate, sacrificed [on the Capitol] a male ox to Jupiter, a cow to Juno, a cow to Minerva, a cow to Public Well-Being, a cow to Providence, an ox to his own divine spirit, a male ox to Divus Augustus.

The following were present: C. Vipstanus Apronianus, consul, P. Memmius Regulus, L. Salvius Otho Titianus, Sulpicius Camerinus.

[*AFA* 28a–c, lines 10–16]

A59h – 29 May, AD 59: sacrifice to Dea Dia

Under the [same] consuls, on 29 May, [L. Piso, president], on behalf of the college of Arval Brothers, sacrificed at the altar to the Dea [Dia two sows in] expiation, then a cow. Next, inside the temple, at the hearth, [he sacrificed] and made offering to the [Dea Dia] of a special lamb. When the sacrifice had been completed, [wearing a veil and a crown], he gave a signal to chariots and stunt-riders to leave the starting-gates.

There were present in the college: C. Vipstanus Apronianus, consul, L. Salvius Otho Titianus, P. Memmius Regulus, Sulpicius Camerinus.

[*AFA* 28a–c, lines 17–23]

A59i – 23 June, AD 59: vows for Nero's safe return

Under the same consuls, on 23 June, [for the safe] return of Nero Claudius Caesar Augustus Germanicus, [L. Calpurnius Piso], president, on behalf of the college of Arval Brothers, sacrificed [on the Capitol a male ox to Jupiter], a cow [to Juno], a cow to Minerva, a cow to Public Well-Being, [a cow] to Prosperity, a cow to [...]; furthermore in the new temple, a male ox to Divus Augustus, a cow to Diva [Augusta], a male ox [to Divus Claudius]; furthermore in the Forum of Augustus, an ox to Mars the Avenger, an ox to [his own] divine spirit.

The following were present: M. Valerius Messalla Corvinus, P. Memmius Regulus, Sulpicius Camerinus, L. Salvius Otho Titianus.

[*AFA* 28a–c, lines 24–33]

Tacitus describes Nero's welcome on his return from the Bay of Naples (*Ann.* 14.13.2: compare Dio 62.16).

A59j – 11 September, AD 59: Nero's safe return

When T. Sextius Africanus and M. Ostorius Scapula were consuls.

On 11 September, for the [safe] return of Nero Claudius Caesar Augustus Germanicus, [L. Piso], president, on behalf of the college of Arval Brothers, sacrificed on the Capitol a male ox to Jupiter,[a cow] to Juno, a cow to Minerva; furthermore in the Forum of Augustus, an ox to his own divine spirit, a cow to Public Well-Being; furthermore [in front of] the house of the Domitii, a cow to the Household Gods.

The following were present: P. Memmius Regulus, L. Salvius Otho Titianus, C. Vipstanus Apronianus, M. Aponius Saturninus, T. Sextius Africanus.

[*AFA* 28a–c, lines 34–9]

A59k – 12 and 13 October, AD 59: Augustalia and Nero's *imperium*

*(fragmentary entries for 12 October and 13 October AD 59 can be restored as for the same dates in AD 58: **A58c, A58d**).*

[*AFA* 28a–c, lines 40–50]

A59m – 11 December, AD 59: birthday of Nero's father

[Under the same consuls], 11 December, [L. Piso, president, on behalf of the college] of Arval Brothers sacrificed on the Sacred Road, [in front of the house of the Domitii,] a male ox to the memory of Cn. Domitius.

[The following were present: M. Aponius] Saturninus, A. Vitellius, C. Vipstanus Apronianus, [*one lost name*], Sulpicius Camerinus, T. Sextius Africanus, L. Salvius Otho Titianus.

[*AFA* 28de, lines 3–8]

A59n – 15 December, AD 59: Nero's birthday

[Under the same consuls, on 15] December, in honour of the birthday of Nero Claudius Cae]sar Augustus Germanicus, [L. Piso, president, on behalf of the college] of Arval Brothers sacrificed on the Capitol a male ox to Jupiter, a cow to Juno, a cow to Minerva, a cow to Public Well-Being, a cow to Prosperity, an ox to his own divine spirit.

The following were present: A. Vitellius, M. Aponius Saturninus, L. Salvius Otho Titianus, Sulpicius Camerinus, C. Vipstanus Apronianus, P. Memmius Regulus, C. Piso.

[*AFA* 28de, lines 9–14]

The previous year **A58h** had seen a sacrifice to 'Concord in honour of Agrippina Augusta'.

A60a – 1 January, AD 60: Nero's fourth consulship

In the fourth consulship of Nero Claudius Caesar Augustus Germanicus, son of Divus Claudius, grandson of Germanicus Caesar, great-grandson of Tiberius Caesar Augustus, great-great-grandson of Divus Augustus, *pontifex maximus*, in his 7th year of tribunician power, hailed victorious commander 7 times, and of Cossus Lentulus, son of Cossus.

On 1 January, in honour of the consulship of Nero Claudius Caesar Augustus Germanicus, Sulpicius Camerinus, president, on behalf of the college of Arval Brothers, sacrificed on the Capitol a male ox to Jupiter, a cow to Juno, a cow to Minerva, an ox to his own divine spirit.

The following were present: Sulpicius Camerinus, president, L. Piso, T. Sextius Africanus, M. Aponius Saturninus, L. Salvius Otho Titianus, P. Memmius Regulus, C. Piso.

[*AFA* 28de, lines 15–23]

A60b – 3 January, AD 60: vows for Nero's safety

Under the same consuls, on 3 January, Sulpicius Camerinus, president, on behalf of the college of Arval Brothers undertook vows for the safety of Nero Claudius Caesar Augustus Germanicus, son of the Divus Claudius, grandson of Germanicus Caesar, great-grandson of Tiberius Caesar Augustus, great-great-grandson of Divus Augustus, *pontifex maximus*, in his 7th year of tribunician power, hailed victorious commander 7 times, consul four times, and for Octavia, his wife. After making sacrifices on the Capitol he fulfilled the vows which the previous year's president had made, and undertook the vows, dictated by M. Aponius Saturninus: two male oxen to Jupiter, two cows to Juno, two cows to Minerva, two cows to Public Well-Being, at the new temple, two male oxen to Divus Augustus, two cows to Diva Augusta, two male oxen to Divus Claudius.

The following were present: Sulpicius Camerinus, president, A. Vitellius, L. Piso, M. Aponius Saturninus, P. Memmius Regulus, L. Salvius Otho Titianus.

[*AFA* 28de, lines 24–32]

(After the start of a record for 11 January, other entries for AD 60 are lost, up until…)

A60c – 15 December, AD 60: Nero's birthday

[Under the same consuls, on 15 December,] in honour of the birthday of Nero [Claudius] Caesar Augustus Germanicus, [Sulpicius Camerinus, president, on behalf] of the college of Arval Brothers [sacrificed] on the Capitol a male ox to Jupiter, a cow to Juno, a cow to Minerva, a cow to Public Prosperity, a cow to Concord, an ox to his own divine spirit.

The following were present: Sulpicius Camerinus, president, M. Aponius Saturninus, C. Vipstanus Apronianus, L. Salvius Otho Titianus, T. Sextius Africanus.

[*AFA* 28f, lines 1–10]

A63a – ? January, AD 63: list of names

[The following were present in the college: Q. Tillius Sassius, president, Sulp]icius Camerinus, L. Salvius [Otho Titianus, L.] Piso, son of Lucius, Q. Volusius Saturninus, [C. Vipstanus Ap]ronianus, C. Piso.

[*AFA* 29, column I, lines 1–4]

A63b – 12 January, AD 63: sacrifices vowed to Dea Dia

Under the same consuls, on 12 January, [in front of the temple? of] Concord, Q. Tillius Sassius, president, on behalf of the college of Arval Brothers, assisted by Q. Volusius Saturninus, T. Sextius Africanus, L. Salvius Otho Titianus, announced a sacrifice to [the Dea Dia]

On 27 May, in the house.

On 29 May, in the grove and in the house
On 30 May, in the house
The following were present in the college: Q. Tillius Sassius, president, Q. Volusius Saturninus, T. Sextius Africanus, L. Salvius Otho Titianus.

[*AFA* 29, column I, lines 5–16]

A63c – 21 January, AD 63: Poppaea gives birth

Under the same consuls, on 21 January, on the Capitol, the fulfilment of vows undertaken for Poppaea Augusta giving birth safely, [Q. Tillius Sassius, president, on behalf of the college of Arval] Brothers, [sacrificed a ox to Jupiter,] a cow [to Juno]

[*AFA* 29, column I, lines 17–23]

Tacitus hints at Poppaea being pregnant at the time of her marriage in 62 (*Ann.* 14.61.4). For the birth, Tacitus, *Annals* 15.23.1, including vows undertaken by the senate, and *Octavia* 590–2 = **H9**.

A63d – before May, AD 63: sacrifices for Poppaea and her child, Claudia

Under the same [consuls], on [date lost], in the presidency of Q. Tillius Sassius, A. Vitellius, on behalf of the [college of] Arval [Brothers], sacrificed on the [Capit]ol in honour of the arrival [of Nero Claudius] Caesar Augustus G[ermanicus and Poppaea] Augusta and Claud[ia Augusta, an ox to Jupiter,] a cow to Juno, [a cow to] Minerva, a cow to Public [Well-Being, a cow to Prosperity], a cow to Hope, [an ox to his own] divine spirit, [a cow to the divine spirit] of Poppaea Aug[usta], a cow [to the divine spirit of Claudia] Augusta.

The following were present: [A. Vitellius, Sulpicius] Camerinus, [*(name lost)*..., L. Vitel]lius, C. Piso.

[*AFA* 29, column II, lines 1–15]

Claudia Augusta, the daughter of Nero and Poppaea survived 4 months (Tac. *Ann.* 15.23.3; **J27, L34–L35**).

A66a – Unknown date in AD 66: anniversary of the Pisonian conspiracy?

... det]ection
... to Mars?
... to Provid]ence
... on the same most hallowed day
... a cow to Honour, a cow to Eternal [...]
[The following] were [present]: M. Aponius Sa[turninus],
... [Q. Tilli]us Sassius, L. Salvius Otho [Titianus]

[*AFA* 30, column I, cd, lines 2–8]

A probable reconstruction (compare A66g, A66h below)

Under the same consuls, on *(date lost)* in the second presidency of Emperor Nero Claudius Caesar Augustus, father of the fatherland, M. Aponius Saturninus, vice-president, at the dictation of L. Salvius Otho Titianus, undertook vows on the Capitol for the detection of evil conspiracies: a male ox to Jupiter, a cow to Juno, a cow to Minerva, an ox to Mars, a cow to Providence (*and one other sacrifice)*. On the same most hallowed day *(other sacrifices),* a cow to Honour, a cow to Eternal Rule, *(other sacrifice(s))*.

For this conspiracy, see **P11**, and for this entry, Griffin, *Nero,* page 285, note 75.

A66b – Unknown date in AD 66: sacrifices relating to Tiridates?

[Under the same consuls *(date lost)*] in the presidency of Emperor
... instruct]ed L. Salvius Otho Titianus
... on the Capitol, in honour of the laurel (wreath)

... a cow to Juno, a cow to Minerva, a male ox to Jupiter ...
... a cow to ... a cow to Peace, in front of the arch ...
... The following were present *(around four names lost),* C. Vipstanus Apronianus
[*AFA* 30, column I, cd, lines 9–14]

A probable reconstruction (compare A66h–i below)
Under the same consuls *(date lost)* in the second presidency of Emperor Nero Claudius Caesar Augustus, father of the fatherland, the college of Arval Brothers instructed L. Salvius Otho Titianus that in place of the vice-president, M. Aponius Saturninus, on behalf of the Arval Brothers, on the Capitol, in honour of the laurel wreath of Emperor Nero Claudius Caesar Augustus Germanicus, he should sacrifice a male ox to Jupiter, a cow to Juno, a cow to Minerva, a male ox to Jupiter the Victor, a cow to *(lost),* a cow to Peace, in front of the arch of Double Janus.

A66c – Unknown date in AD 66: further sacrifices relating to Tiridates?

[Under the same consuls *(date lost)* in the presi]dency of Emperor
... instructe]d L. Salvius Otho Titianus
... on the Capitol, in honour of the thanksgivings
... a cow to Minerva, a cow to Prosperity, a cow to Clemency
... the following were present: L. Salvius [Otho Titianus]
(two names lost), T. Sextius Africanus, Q. [Tillius Sassius]
[*AFA* 30, column I, cd, lines 15–21]

A probable reconstruction (compare A66h–i below)
Under the same consuls *(date lost)* in the second presidency of Emperor Nero Claudius Caesar Augustus, father of the fatherland, the college of Arval Brothers instructed L. Salvius Otho Titianus that in place of the vice-president, M. Aponius Saturninus, on behalf of the Arval Brothers, on the Capitol, in honour of the thanksgivings decreed by the senate, he should sacrifice a male ox to Jupiter, a cow to Juno, a cow to Minerva, a cow to Prosperity, a cow to Clemency...

A66d – Unknown date in AD 66: sacrifices, including to Nero's deified daughter

[...] M. Aponius Saturninus, [vice-president, on behalf of the Arval Brothers *(for unknown occasion)*...] made a sacrifice on the Capitol [and in the new temple of Divus Augustus, a male ox to Jupiter,] a cow [to Juno, a cow] to Minerva, [a male ox to Divus Augustus, a cow to Diva Augusta, a male ox to Divus Claudius, a cow to Diva Clau]dia the maiden, [a cow to Diva Poppaea Augusta,] a bull to [the divine spirit of Nero Claudius Caesar Augustus Germani]cus, [...].
[*AFA* 30, column I, cd, lines 23–28]

A66e – Unknown date in AD 66: sacrifices to Diva Poppaea and Statilia Messalina

In the presidency of Emper[or Nero Claudius Caesar Augustus, father of the fatherland, M. Aponius Saturni]nus, [vice-president, on behalf of the College] of Arval Brothers, in honour of the] laurel (wreath) of Emperor [Nero Claudius Caesar Augustus Germanicus, sacrificed in the new temple [of Divus Augustus] a male ox to Divus Augustus, [a cow to Diva Augusta, a male ox to Divus Claudius, a cow to Diva Claudia the maiden], a cow to Diva Poppaea Augusta, [a bull to the divine spirit of Nero Claudius Caesar Augustus Germanicus], a cow to [the divine spirit] of Messallina.
[*AFA* 30, column II, cef, lines 3–8]

The reference to a laurel wreath suggests continued celebrations of Nero's triumph over Tiridates.

A66f – 17, 19 June, AD 66 (worship of Dea Dia)

(Fragments record a banquet on 17 June in honour of the Dea Dia and expiatory sacrifices on 19 June in honour of the Dea Dia.)

[*AFA* 30, column II, cef, lines 8–19]

A66g – Unknown date in AD 66: detection of conspiracy of Annius Vinicianus?

When M. Arruntius [...
Having carried out the sacrifice ...
[con]spiracies, in the presidenc[y of ...
[Satur]ninus [on behalf of] the college of [Arval] Bro[thers ...
[a cow] to Juno, a cow to Minerva ... a cow to [Pro]vidence, [an ox to] M[ars]
The following were prese[nt:

[*AFA* 30, column II, cef, lines 20–26]

A probable reconstruction (compare also A66a above)

When M. Arruntius and M. Vettius Bolanus were consuls, on *(date lost),* having carried out the sacrifices which the Arval Brothers had vowed to do in honour of the detection of evil conspiracies, in the second presidency of Emperor Nero Claudius Caesar Augustus, father of the fatherland, Saturninus, on behalf of the college of Arval Brothers, in fulfilment of the vows, sacrificed a male ox to Jupiter, a cow to Juno, a cow to Minerva, *(one other sacrifice),* a cow to Providence, an ox to Mars.

For this mysterious conspiracy, see **P11**, Suet. *Nero* 36 and Griffin, *Nero* 178–9.

A66h – 25 September, AD 66: vows for safe return of Nero & Messalina

Under the same consuls, on 25 September, [in the second presidency of Emperor Nero Claudius Caesar Augustus, father of the fatherland,] the vice-president, M. [Aponius Saturninus, at the dictation of L. Salvius Otho Titianus, vowed sacrifices for the safe] return of Emper[or Nero Claudius Caesar Augustus and of Messallina, his wife.

[The following were present:] M. Aponius Satuninus [... *(a few other names lost)*]

[*AFA* 30, column II, cef, lines 27–30]

This entry refers to Nero setting off for his tour of Greece.

A66i – 12 October, AD 66: Augustalia

[Under the same consuls, on 12 October, and] in the [second] presidency of Emp[eror Nero Claudius Caesar Augustus, father of the fatherland, in honour of the Au]gustalia, [the vice-president, M. Aponius] Saturninus [on behalf of] the col[lege of Arval Brothers in the new temple sacrificed a male ox] to Divus Au[gustus, a cow to Diva Augusta, a male ox to Divus Claudius,] a cow to [Diva Claudia] the maiden, [a cow to] Diva Poppaea Augusta.

The following were present: M. Aponius Saturninus], vice-president, C. V[ipstanus Apronianus *and probably one other*].

[*AFA* 30, column II, cef, lines 30–34]

(fragmentary entries for 13 October AD 66 can be restored as for ***A58d****).*

SECTION B

THE *FASTI CONSULARES* (LIST OF CONSULS)

B1: Running like a Caesar's candidate

Lucius Galba said to a man making little effort to run for a ball, "You are running like a Caesar's candidate!"

[Quintilian, *The Orator's Education,* 6.3.62]

The consulship. Augustus started by monopolising one of the consulships, but gave it up in 23 BC, thereafter holding it only for the years in which his grandsons came of age, 5 and 2 BC. In these years, he and his colleague resign the consulship in favour of suffect consuls (originally appointed only after a death). From then a pattern emerges of six-month consulships under Augustus and Tiberius, while under Claudius, two-month consulships become quite common. Thus far more senators could reach the top of the political ladder than under the republic. At the same time the honour can be differentiated: a consul taking office at the start of the year (*consul ordinarius*) has far greater prestige than one appointed later in the year (*consul suffectus*). Consuls may also be honoured by being given a longer consulship than others; by being given a second or even third consulship; the first named consul of a pair also has precedence. The greatest honour is sharing the consulship with a reigning emperor.

The Fasti Consulares. Reference to the consuls remains the standard official way of dating documents within the Roman empire. So, for example, Tacitus in his *Annals* marks each new year by naming the new consuls (see Ginsburg, *Tradition and Theme in the* Annals *of Tacitus* (1981)). But although Tacitus (suffect consul in 97) resolutely ignores suffect consuls in his *Annals*, ordinary documents from Pompeii and Herculaneum show great care being taken to give the correct (suffect) consuls for a given date. That this information must have been available in towns around Italy is confirmed by the *Fasti Ostienses* (Lists from Ostia), though these were unusual in being carved on stone and including historical events and local magistrates. The official list will have been inscribed in Rome, but does not survive for this period. The list that follows is therefore reconstructed from various sources, and certainly has some omissions, for example of those known to have been consuls but whose consulships cannot be dated.

The consular election. One of the powers formally granted to Vespasian in AD 69/70 is that all candidates for any magistracy whom he recommends should be elected. (Law on the Power of Vespasian, 10–13 = LACTOR 17, H52) Unlike with many other of Vespasian's powers, no precedent is offered, but it almost certainly formalised what had already happened at Tiberius' accession when 'elections were transferred from the citizens' assemblies to the senate ... Tiberius guaranteed that he would not recommend more than four candidates, who would have to be appointed without rejection or canvass.' (Tacitus, *Annals* 1.15.1 = LACTOR 17, F15.1). This leads to there being 'Caesar's candidates' who would know they would be elected without the need to run for election (see Quintilian at start of the this section). Tacitus describes Tiberius' method of conferring honours thus, 'He would confer posts of honour by considering the nobility of a candidate's ancestry; the distinction of his military service; his record in civic life, so that it was sufficiently clear that there were no better candidates.' Tacitus, *Annals* 4.6.2.

Bibliography: The Fasti are published in Degrassi, *Inscriptiones Italiae* 13.1 (1947 onwards, with commentary in Latin). EJ and Smallwood give lists of names for their respective periods. Documents, especially from Pompeii and Herculaneum, have added many names to these lists. An up-to-date list appears in A.E. Cooley, *Cambridge Handbook to Latin Epigraphy*, Appendix 1. Bargagli and Grosso, *I Fasti Ostienses* (1997, Latin text, Italian commentary) contains all the material from Ostia. *Prosopographia Imperii Romani* (ed. E. Klebs et al. Berlin 1897–8; 2nd edition 1933 and ongoing: text in Latin) gives biographical details and sources for all the consuls, but parts of alphabet are very out of date. Most consuls have an entry in Brill's New Pauly: *Encyclopedia of the Ancient World* (Leiden, 2002–2009).

[In the list below, the names of *consules ordinarii* appear in bold, with suffect consuls appearing below the consuls they replaced.]

14 Sex. Pompeius — Sex. Appuleius

Sextus Pompeius: somehow related to Augustus, according to Dio 56.29.5. Also distantly related to Pompey the Great.

Sextus Appuleius: son of the consul of 29 BC and therefore Augustus' (step) great-nephew.

15 Drusus Caesar — C. Norbanus Flaccus

M. Junius Silanus

Drusus Caesar: Tiberius' son, made consul aged 26, fifteen years before the official minimum, the same age as his adoptive brother Germanicus (cos AD 12).

C. Norbanus Flaccus: his father had been consul with Augustus in 24 BC.

M. Junius Silanus: from a very prominent Julio-Claudian family, see **J33**. Victim of Caligula in 38 (Philo, *Leg.* 62–5 = **D6**, *Leg.*71–3; Dio 59.8) and replaced as Arval in **A38j.**

16 Sisenna Statilius Taurus — L. Scribonius Libo

C. Vibius Rufus — C. Pomponius Graecinus

Sisenna Statilius Taurus: younger son of one of Augustus' most trusted generals. His brother had been consul in AD 11.

L. Scribonius Libo: great-nephew of Scribonia, Augustus' first wife, and also great-grandson of Pompey the Great (Syme *AA* Table XIV). His brother, Marcus, is first victim of *maiestas* trials – Tac. *Ann.* 2.27–32.

C. Vibius Rufus: an aspiring orator, married to Cicero's widow, Publilia (Dio 57.15.6).

C. Pomponius Graecinus: *novus homo*; friend of the poet Ovid who addresses poems to him from exile (*ex Ponto* 1.6, 2.6, 4.9), the last anticipating his consulship and his brother's. Probably also a former *legatus* of Tiberius. Coopted Arval in 21, replaced in May 38 (**A38j**).

17 L. Pomponius Flaccus — C. Caelius Rufus

C. Vibius Marsus — L. Voluseius Proculus

Pomponius Flaccus: *novus homo*; brother of Pomponius Graecinus, suffect in the previous year. Brief description in Velleius, 129.1. An officer and drinking partner of Tiberius (Suet. *Tib.* 42.1) and a literary man. Governor of Moesia in 18, defeated King Rhescuporis of Thrace by subterfuge (Tac. *Ann.* 2.66–7). Appointed governor of Syria in 32 (Tac. *Ann.* 6.27.2).

C. Caelius Rufus: son of the suffect of 4 BC, but known for nothing except his consulship.

C. Vibius Marsus: a man of distinguished ancestry, renowned for his learning (Tac. *Ann.* 6.47.2). Survives malicious accusation through death of Tiberius in 37. Governor of Syria in 47 (Tac. *Ann.* 11.10.1).

L. Voluseius Proculus: *novus homo* (Wiseman, *New Men,* no.511), otherwise little known.

18 Tiberius Caesar Augustus III — Germanicus Caesar II

L. Seius Tubero

Livineius Regulus

C. Rubellius Blandus — M. Vipstanus Gallus

Tiberius Caesar Augustus: Tiberius had been consul in 13 BC and with Gnaeus Calpurnius Piso in 7 BC.

Germanicus Caesar: Germanicus had been consul in AD 12. He was absent from Rome for his whole consulship (Tac. *Ann.* 2.53.1).

L. Seius Tubero: probably an adopted brother of Sejanus (Syme, *AA* 305), Tacitus describes him (*Ann.* 4.29.1 – AD 24) as an intimate friend of Tiberius.

Livineius Regulus: unknown, except as a courageous defender of Piso (Tac. *Ann.* 3.11.2).

C. Rubellius Blandus: Tacitus *Annals* 6.27 bemoans the marriage in AD 34 of Livia Julia to this man whose grandfather was (only) an equestrian (in fact a well-known teacher – Sen. *Controv.* 2 pr. 5). Syme (*AA* 225) suggests some personal connection with Tiberius must explain his remarkable rise from *novus homo.*

M. Vipstanus Gallus: *novus homo* (Wiseman, *New Men,* no.499) probably father of consul of 48.

19 M. Junius Silanus Torquatus — L. Norbanus Balbus
P. Petronius

M. Junius Silanus Torquatus: had married Aemilia Lepida, great-granddaughter of Augustus. First of their five children born shortly before Augustus' death. See **J33**.

L. Norbanus Balbus: an amateur trumpeter, whose playing early on his first day as consul was mistaken for a war-signal, alarming a crowd of well-wishers! (Dio 57.18.3) Possibly the man slain by Gaius' German bodyguard after his assassination (Jos. *JA* 19.123 = Section E with note).

P. Petronius: governor of Asia 29–35, long-standing friend of Claudius and 'expert in Claudius-speak' – Sen. *Apocol.* 14.2. Father-in-law or grandfather-in-law of emperor Vitellius (Suet. *Vit.* 6).

20 M. Valerius Messalla Messalinus — M. Aurelius Cotta Maximus Messalinus

M. Valerius Messalla Messalinus and **M. Aurelius Cotta**: this pair of consuls, nephew and uncle, each held office for the whole year, 'a distinction unique in the reign of Tiberius' (Syme *AA* 230). The distinction derives from M. Valerius Messalla Corvinus, consul with Octavian/Augustus in 31 BC, aristocrat, scholar, patron. He was father of Aurelius (who, by adoption, took his *nomen* from his mother's family) and grandfather (by a different marriage) of Valerius Messalla Messalinus. See Syme *AA*, Table IX.

21 Tiberius Caesar Augustus IV — Drusus Caesar II
Mamercus Aemilius Scaurus — Cn. Tremellius

Tiberius Caesar Augustus IV: consul as colleague for his son, see Tacitus, *Annals* 3.31.1.

Drusus Caesar II: given a second consulship, aged 32, 6 years after his first, exactly like his late adopted brother, Germanicus.

Mamercus Aemilius Scaurus: Tacitus (*Ann.* 6.29.3) describes him as 'of distinguished ancestry, powerful eloquence, scandalous lifestyle'; Seneca the Elder, who will actually have known him, as 'a man of enormous eloquence and also charm, who never allowed anyone's folly to pass without criticism.' (*Controv.* 1.2.22; see also 10 pref. 2–3). Seneca the Younger mentions his sexual perversions at *Benefits* 4.31.3–4. He had offended Tiberius 'whose anger against him was implacable' in the accession debate – Tac. *Ann.* 1.13.4. Eventually he was forced to suicide in 34, through enmity of Macro (Tac. *Ann.* 6.29.3) and the 'evil nature and unfortunate talents of his accuser, Tuscus' (Sen. *Suas.* 2.22).

Cn. Tremellius: unknown except as giving a consular date (*PIR*^{2} T337).

22 D. Haterius Agrippa — C. Sulpicius Galba

D. Haterius Agrippa: a relative of Germanicus (Tac. *Ann.* 2.51.1): most probably his mother was a daughter of Agrippa and Marcella, Augustus' niece (Syme *AA* 145). His father had been suffect in 5 BC. For Tacitus (*Annals* 6.4.4), 'He was all the more loathsome because lethargic through sleep or staying awake to indulge his lusts, his idleness gave him no reason to fear the emperor's cruelty, but he plotted the destruction of men of note in bars and brothels.'

C. Sulpicius Galba: from a patrician family, son of the suffect of 5 BC, elder brother of the emperor Galba. He fell seriously from favour with Tiberius refusing to let him draw lots for a province to govern in 36, whereupon he committed suicide (Tac. *Ann.* 6.40.2; Suet. *Galba* 3.4).
Two or more suffect consuls are likely to have been elected for this year, but are unknown.

23 C. Asinius Pollio — C. Antistius Vetus
C. Stertinius Maximus

C. Asinius Pollio: eldest son of C. Asinius Gallus and Vipsania, Tiberius' first wife. His grandfathers were thus the homonymous literary patron of Augustus' time and M. Agrippa.

C. Antistius Vetus: from a family who had served Augustus well: grandfather, suffect 30 BC, helped pacify Spain; father, consul 6 BC and governor of Asia. His younger brother is suffect in 26, and his son gains an iterated consulship under Claudius.

C. Stertinius Maximus: *novus homo* (Wiseman, *Nem Men,* no.415).

24 **Ser. Cornelius Cethegus** — **L. Visellius Varro**

C. Calpurnius Aviola — P. Cornelius Lentulus Scipio

Ser. Cornelius Cethegus: known only from a variety of sources as giving his name to the year, but probably from the Cornelius Lentulus clan (see on the suffect of this year, below).

L. Visellius Varro: son of the suffect of AD 12.

C. Calpurnius Aviola: a revolt in Gaul in AD 21 had been put down by Acilius Aviola, imperial governor of Gallia Lugdunensis (NW & Central France). Syme, *AA* 378 assumes that he was then adopted into the Calpurnian *gens.* Later a member of Claudius' consilium in AD 41.

P. Cornelius Lentulus Scipio: no fewer than seven member of this aristocratic and numerous clan held consulships under Augustus: this man, the son of the suffect of AD 2, had commanded a legion in Africa two years before his consulship (Tac. *Ann.* 3.74.2; see also Syme *AA* 297–8 and Table 21).

25 **Cossus Cornelius Lentulus** — **M. Asinius Agrippa**

C. Petronius

Cossus Cornelius Lentulus: see comments on the Cornelii Lentuli immediately above. His father had been consul in 1 BC and was still influential throughout the reign of Tiberius, including as City Prefect, 33–36 (See **U1**). Syme describes this consul as 'only a date' (*AA* 298 and Table 21).

M. Asinius Agrippa: younger brother of C. Asinius Pollio, consul in 23, see above. He died a year later – a man whose 'life had been worthy of his distinguished, though not ancient family' (Tac. *Ann.* 4.61).

C. Petronius: probably younger brother of Publius Petronius (cos suff 19) and grandson of P. Petronius, prefect of Egypt under Augustus.

26 **Cn. Cornelius Lentulus Gaetulicus** — **C. Calvisius Sabinus**

Q. Iunius Blaesus — L. Antistius Vetus

Cn. Cornelius Lentulus Gaetulicus: see comments on the Cornelii Lentuli in AD 24. His father had been consul in 1 BC before defeating the Gaetulians and acquiring the *cognomen* for his second son (see LACTOR 17, E116.2, M4, N10). He went on to command the army in Upper Germany from AD 29 to 39; survived betrothing his daughter to a son of Sejanus (Tac. *Ann.* 6.30), perhaps through the continued influence with Tiberius of his father, City Prefect 33–36; but was executed for conspiring against Caligula (**A39e**); Dio 59.22.5 = LACTOR 15.79). Also a poet (Pliny, *Letters* 5.3.5; D.L. Page, *Further Greek Epigrams*, 51–60). See also Syme *AA* Index and Table 21.

C. Calvisius Sabinus: bore the same name as his grandfather and father, consuls in 39 BC and 4 BC. He survived a *maiestas* charge in AD 32 (Tac. *Ann.* 6.9.3) and went to govern Pannonia late in 36, but was ensnared in the same plot in 39 as his fellow consul (and perhaps brother-in-law) Gaetulicus (Dio 59.18.4 = LACTOR 15.76).

Q. Iunius Blaesus: cousin of Sejanus. Son of the suffect of AD 10 who as governor in Africa received, in 22, what was to be the last ever acclamation as *imperator* (victorious commander) outside the imperial family (Tac. *Ann.* 3.74.4). The father did not survive the fall of his nephew, Sejanus. The son did, but was forced to suicide in 36 when Tiberius treated his priesthood as vacant. (Tac. *Ann.*6.40.2).

L. Antistius Vetus: younger brother of the consul of 23 – see above.

27 **L. Calpurnius Piso** — **M. Licinius Crassus Frugi**

P. Cornelius Lentulus — C. Sallustius Passienus Crispus

L. Calpurnius Piso: the son of the Piso condemned by the senate over the death of Germanicus (see **P3**). His grandfather, father and uncle had all held consulships under Augustus (23 BC, 7 BC, 1 BC). He went on to be City Prefect at the death of Tiberius (See **U1**) and outlived his son, the consul of 57 (Pliny, *Letters* 3.7.12).

M. Licinius Crassus Frugi: his father, consul 14 BC, came from the distinguished Piso Frugi family and was adopted into the even more distinguished family of Licinius Crassus. He married Scribonia, great-great-granddaughter of Pompey the Great. In 41 their son, Pompeius Magnus, married Antonia, daughter of

Claudius (Dio 60.5.70, Suet. *Claud.* 27.2), which made son and parents a threat to Messalina and they were eliminated in AD 47 (Suet. *Claud.* 29.1–2).

P. Cornelius Lentulus: undistinguished member of a prominent clan (see on consuls of AD 24, 25, 26).

C. Sallustius Passienus Crispus: see extract from Suetonius' biography on him, **U5**. Son of L. Passienus Rufus, cos 4 BC, adopted by Sallustius Crispus, 'successor' of Maecenas as minister of Augustus (Tac. *Ann.* 3.30.2 = LACTOR 17, R27), he has a second consulship in 44.

28	**C. Appius Junius Silanus**	**P. Silius Nerva**
	L. Junius Silanus	C. Vellaeus Tutor

C. Appius Junius Silanus: from a family very prominent under the Julio-Claudians, see J33. His father had been consul in 10, his uncle suffect in 15. Arval (**A38f – A39a**).

P. Silius Nerva: his family had become prominent with his homonymous grandfather, companion of Augustus (Suet. *Aug.* 71.2), consul 20 BC. His three sons (two adopted into nobler families) had all reached the consulship under Augustus, in AD 3, 7, 13.

L. Junius Silanus: suffect for his distant cousin (see above).

C. Vellaeus Tutor: not prominent (*PIR*[1] V233).

29	**L. Rubellius Geminus**	**C. Fufius Geminus**
	A. Plautius	L. Nonius Asprenas

L. Rubellius Geminus: presumed to be a close relative of Rubellius Blandus, suffect in 18 (*PIR*[2] R113).

C. Fufius Geminus: son of the suffect of 2 BC, but apparently owed his consulship to Livia's favour (Tac. *Ann.* 5.2.2. After Livia's death in 29, he and his wife fell (Dio 58.4.5), his mother apparently executed for mourning her son (Tac. *Ann.* 6.10.1).

A. Plautius: led the invasion of Britain and was its first governor: for his career, see **N33.**

L. Nonius Asprenas: his father had been suffect in AD 6, his uncle consul in AD 8. Both governed provinces in the early years of Tiberius' reign (Tac. *Ann.* 1.53.6; *AE* 1933, 265).

30	**M. Vinicius**	**L. Cassius Longinus**
	L. Naevius Surdinus	C. Cassius Longinus

L. Cassius Longinus and M. Vinicius: see Tacitus, *Annals* 6.15.1 – AD 33, 'Caesar, after long consideration of who should be husbands for his granddaughters, when they reached marriageable age, chose L. Cassius and M. Vinicius. Vinicius' family came from outside Rome: he was born at Cales. His father and grandfather had been consuls, the rest of his family was of equestrian class. He was of gentle disposition and mannered in speech. Cassius' family was Roman, plebeian, but ancient and distinguished. Brought up very strictly by his father, he was notable more for his affability than for hard work. He married Drusilla, daughter of Germanicus, Vinicius married Iulia, her sister.' Cassius was to lose Drusilla to incest with Gaius (Suet. *Cal.* 24.1). Vinicius was the patron of Velleius (96.2, 104.2 = LACTOR 17, section E). Vinicius fell victim to Messalina in 46 (Dio 60.27.4).

L. Naevius Surdinus: his father (*PIR*[2] N16) was a senator under Augustus, *praetor c.* 10 BC, but nothing else is known about his consular son (*PIR*[2] N17).

C. Cassius Longinus: distinguished jurist; younger brother of L. Cassius Longinus (above). He married (date unknown) Junia Lepida, a granddaughter of Julia the Younger (Augustus' granddaughter). In 65 they both fell victim to Nero (Tac. *Ann.* 16.7–9), Cassius 'for his ancestral wealth and upright character'. He was allowed to die in exile.

31	**Tiberius Caesar Augustus V**	**L. Aelius Seianus**
	Faustus Cornelius Sulla	Sex. Tedius Valerius Catullus
	L. Fulcinius Trio	P. Memmius Regulus

Tiberius Caesar Augustus V and L. Aelius Seianus: Tiberius holding the consulship for the first time in 10 years in partnership with Sejanus was no doubt intended as a signal honour, since his previous two consulships as emperor were held with Germanicus and Drusus. Other honours were promised or expected: consulships with Tiberius every five years (Dio 58.4.4); tribunician power (Dio 58.6.2); betrothal to Livilla, Tiberius' widowed daughter-in-law (Tac. *Ann.* 5.6.2, 6.27.1) or perhaps to Livia Julia, daughter of Drusus (Dio 58.3.9). In fact Sejanus follows Tiberius' four consular colleagues in dying a violent and miserable death, as noted by Dio 57.20.1–2.

Faustus Cornelius Sulla: great-great-grandson of two of the most prominent generals/politicians of the late republic, Sulla and Pompey the Great. His father had been Arval under Tiberius (**A21b–c**). See Syme, *AA* table XVI. His brother is consul in 33.

Sex. Tedius Valerius Catullus: obscure (see Syme *AA* 241).

L. Fulcinius Trio: consul from 1 July. Lawyer, 'whose talents were well-recognised amongst prosecutors and who was eager for notoriety' (Tac. *Ann.* 2.28.3). Prominent in *maiestas* trials under Tiberius (Tac. *Ann.* 2.28–30; 3.10–13) he succumbs to one in 35 (*Ann.* 5.11.1, 6.38.2).

P. Memmius Regulus: consul from 1 Oct and crucial in helping Tiberius to remove Sejanus (Dio 58.9.3, 10.6–8). For further details, see **U4**.

32	**Cn. Domitius Ahenobarbus**	**L. Arruntius Camillus Scribonianus**
		A. Vitellius

Cn. Domitius Ahenobarbus: grandson of Mark Antony and Octavia (Augustus' sister); father of Nero. See **J13**.

L. Arruntius Camillus Scribonianus: son of Furius Camillus, cos AD 8, descendant of Pompey the Great and Sulla; adopted son of L. Arruntius, one of the most influential senators of the time. His aristocratic pedigree leads to him being the figurehead of the revolt against Claudius in AD 42 – see **P7**

A. Vitellius: eldest son of a Roman equestrian who had served as procurator of Augustus. Uncle of the emperor Vitellius. He died in office (Suet. *Vit.* 2.2).

33	**Servius Sulpicius Galba**	**L. Cornelius Sulla Felix**
	L. Salvius Otho	C. Octavius Laenas

Servius Sulpicius Galba: the future emperor Galba, consul for six months. He had been a favourite of Livia (Suet, *Galba* 5.2 and *Galba* 1–9 for details of his ancestry and career).

L. Cornelius Sulla Felix: younger brother of Faustus Cornelius Sulla, the consul of 31 (see above).

L. Salvius Otho: his father had been brought up in Livia's household, and it was through her that he became a senator and married a noblewoman. Salvius was a close friend of Tiberius, whom he ressembled, giving rise to rumours that he was an illegitimate son of the emperor (Suet. *Otho* 1.1–2). Arval 39–53, see **A39e** and **A53b**. His son was the emperor Otho.

C. Octavius Laenas: in charge of Rome's aqueducts AD 34–38 (**K32**). A *novus homo* (Wiseman, *New Men* no. 289). Family from Marruvium (on the Fucine Lake, Central Italy).

34	**Paullus Fabius Persicus**	**L. Vitellius**
	Q. Marcius Barea Soranus	T. Rustius Nummius Gallus

Paullus Fabius Persicus: son of Paullus Fabius Maximus, cos 11 BC and intimate friend of Augustus: Persicus had succeeded his father as Arval in AD 15 (**A15a**), and was still alive under Claudius (**A44b**).

L. Vitellius: father of the emperor Vitellius and 'the most successful politician of his age' (*OCD*). A friend of Antonia (Tac. *Ann.* 11.3.1), he gained further consulships in 43 and 47 under Claudius who left him in charge of Rome during the invasion of Britain. Tacitus praised his governorship of Syria (35–37), but roundly condemned his sycophancy (*Ann.* 6.32.4). Suetonius gives more details of character and career (*Vitellius* 2.4–3.1).

Q. Marcius Barea Soranus: the Marcii were a famous Roman clan, though Barea Soranus' place in the clan is not clear. He governed Africa (**M30**). His son was consul in 52, his granddaughter, Marcia Furnilla 'of illustrious pedigree' – Suet. *Tit.* 4.2, was the first wife of the young Titus, later to become emperor.

T. Rustius Nummius Gallus: not prominent (PIR^2 R234).

35 **C. Cestius Gallus** — **M. Servilius Nonianus**

D. Valerius Asiaticus — P. Gabinius Secundus

C. Cestius Gallus: senator by 21 (Tac. *Ann.* 3.36.2), in 32, prosecuted two friends of Sejanus (Tac. *Ann.* 6.7.2).

M. Servilius Nonianus: son of the consul of AD 3. Also a major literary figure, see **R9**.

D. Valerius Asiaticus: the first consul from Gallia Narbonensis, nonetheless a man of very great wealth and influence, a friend of Antonia (Tac. *Ann.* 11.3). Prominent in 41 in the assassination of Gaius and its aftermath (**E21**), and a possible senatorial candidate for emperor (**E28**). Second consulship in 46; falls victim to Messalina a year later (Tac. *Ann.* 11.1–3, reviewing his whole career).

P. Gabinius Secundus Successful command of the army in the Lower Rhine, around AD 41 gets him the honorific *cognomen* Chaucicus (Suet. *Claud.* 24.3; Dio 60.8.7)

36 **Sex. Papinius Allenius** — **Q. Plautius**

C. Vettius Rufus — M. Porcius Cato

Sex. Papinius Allenius: Dio 59.25.5b confusedly describes him as the son of Anicius Cerialis (see **B65**), implicated in a plot against Caligula in AD 40. Seneca's version (**P5b**) is more likely.

Q. Plautius: younger brother of A. Plautius, suffect in 29.

C. Vettius Rufus: only known from fasti. Not even in PIR^1 (1898).

M. Porcius Cato: of famous family (see **M12** and note), Tac. describes him in 28 as an ex-praetor eager for the consulship by acting as an informer (4.68–70). He was made Aqueducts Commissioner in 38 (**K32**), but fell later that year (predicted at *Annals* 4.71.1 described, presumably in lost book 7).

37 **Cn. Acerronius Proculus** — **C. Petronius Pontius Nigrinus**

C. Caesar Augustus — Ti. Claudius Nero Germanicus

A. Caecina Paetus — C. Caninius Rebilus

Cn. Acerronius Proculus: Not known except for being consul and for his daughter, Acerronia being the intimate friend of Agrippina killed in the shipwreck (Tac. *Ann.* 14.5.6, Dio 61.13.3).

C. Petronius Pontius Nigrinus: probably son of L. Pontius Nigrinus attested as praetor in 20, adopted by the consul of 25 (*PIR*^{2} P812), but not otherwise known.

C. Caesar Augustus: the emperor Gaius. This, his first consulship, lasted two months from 1 July (Suet, *Cal.* 17.1). He allowed the *ordinarii* to serve their six-month term, refusing the senate's offer to make him consul immediately on becoming *princeps* (Dio 58.27.1, 59.6.5).

Ti. Claudius Nero Germanicus: the future emperor Claudius, Gaius' uncle and nearest adult male relative.

A. Caecina Paetus: see Pliny 3.16.4 for his suicide after involvement in the revolt of Gaetulicus in AD 42 (see **P7a**), but the consul of that year, Caecina Largus seems to be no relation.

C. Caninius Rebilus: son of suffect of AD 12. A man of bad reputation according to Seneca *On Benefits* 2.21.5, describing the virtuous Graecinus rejecting a donation from him.

38 **M. Aquila Iulianus** — **P. Nonius Asprenas**

Sex. Asinius Celer — Sex. Nonius Quintilianus

M. Aquila Iulianus: unknown except as a name on consular dates (*PIR*^{2} A982).

P. Nonius Asprenas: he may have been involved in Gaius' assassination and was killed by the German bodyguard in the aftermath (Jos. *JA* = **E15**, **E17**, **E19**, **E25**).

Sex. Asinius Celer: son of C. Asinius Gallus and Vipsania, Tiberius' first wife. His two elder brothers had been consuls in 23 and 25 (see above). Pliny, *NH* 9.67 records his reckless expenditure in Gaius' reign. Seneca, *Apocol.* 13.5 (= **F13**) lists him among friends of Claudius put to death by him.

Sex. Nonius Quintilianus: son of consul of AD 8 and grandson of C. Sosius, cos 32 BC. He had been tribune of the plebs in 32 (Tac. *Ann.* 6.12.1).

39	**C. Caesar Augustus II**	**L. Apronius Caesianus**
	Q. Sanquinius Maximus II	Cn. Domitius Corbulo
	A. Didius Gallus	Cn. Domitius Afer

C. Caesar Augustus II: Gaius was consul for 30 days (Suet, *Cal.* 17.1).

L. Apronius Caesianus: his father was suffect in AD 8, and an important commander under Tiberius. As a teenager, Caesianus helped his father to a victory (Tac. *Ann* 3.21.4) which he commemorated in a now fragmentary poem (*ILS* 939 = CIL 10.7257 = Anth Lat 2.2.1525). Despite close alliance to Sejanus, Apronius was able to get away with making a public joke about Tiberius' baldness, which Tiberius took well (Dio 58.19.1–2). Apronius was consul for 6 months (Dio 59.13.2).

Q. Sanquinius Maximus II: prefect of the city (Dio 59.13.2). Suffect consul before 32 (Tac. *Ann.* 6.4.3). It is not clear why he was honoured as the first man outside the imperial family to hold a second consulship since 26 BC (Barrett, *Caligula* 92). He died in 47 as governor of Lower Germany (Tac. *Ann.* 11.18.1).

Cn. Domitius Corbulo: Nero's general – see **N45–N50**. Corbulo was half-brother to Caesonia, Gaius' mistress and fourth wife: see **J15a**.

A. Didius Gallus: governor of Britain, 52–57 – see **N35**.

Cn. Domitius Afer: from Nemausus (Nîmes) in Gallia Narbonensis (Jerome, *Chronicle* p.179H). Made his reputation as an outstanding orator (Quintilian, 10.1.118; Tac. *Dialogus* 15.5; less positively *Ann.* 4.52, 4.66.1, 14.19). According to Dio 59.19–20, flattery and acting ability turned Gaius' hatred into the gift of the consulship. Aqueducts Commissioner AD 49–59 (**K32** and Tac. *Ann.* 14.19).

40	**C. Caesar Augustus III**	
	C. Laecanius Bassus	Q. Terentius Culleo
	M. Cluvius Rufus	M. Furrius Augurinus

C. Caesar Augustus III: Gaius was consul for just 13 days, entering this consulship in Lugdunum, Gaul, as sole consul because the consul designate died the day before entering office (Suet, *Cal.* 17.1).

C. Laecanius Bassus: not from a prominent family, ran large-scale pottery production from Istrian peninsular (PIR^2 L30). Urban praetor AD 32 (fasti Arvales). His son becomes consul in 64.

Q. Terentius Culleo: probably son or grandson of Terentius Culleo, proconsul of Sicily under Augustus. (*PIR*^{2} T69 and T70).

M. [Cluvius Rufus]?: See **R11** for this prominent historian and senator whose consulship is not certain for this year, but who is described as an ex-consul at Gaius' assassination (**E14**).

M. Furrius Augurinus: an Augurinus is mentioned in Sen. *Apocol.* (3.4) as dying in the same year as Claudius.

41	**C. Caesar Augustus IV**	**Cn. Sentius Saturninus**
	Q. Pomponius Secundus	
	Q. Futius Lusius Saturninus	M. Seius Varanus
	P. Suillius Rufus	Q. Ostorius Scapula

C. Caesar Augustus IV: Gaius was consul for just 7 days (Suet, *Cal.* 17.1).

Cn. Sentius Saturninus: his grandfather and father had been consuls (19 BC and AD 4). See **E22** for Sentius' speech to the senate urging action to restore the republic in the aftermath of Gaius' assassination. He was a victim of Nero's last years (Tac. *Hist.* 4.7).

Q. Pomponius Secundus: half-brother of Caesonia the wife of Gaius (**J15a**). Saved by Claudius after Gaius' assassination (Jos. *JA* 19.264), he joined the rebellion of Scribonianus a year later (Tac. *Ann.* 13.43).

Q. Futius Lusius Saturninus: July to October: killed by Claudius in 43: **F13**; Tac. *Ann.* 13.43.2.

M. Seius Varanus: July to October: known only as date on a writing tablet from Pompeii.

P. Suillius Rufus: a former quaestor of Germanicus, banished by Tiberius (Tac. *Ann.* 4.31.3). Half-brother or step-father of Caesonia, wife of Caligula (**J15a**). 'A venal and dreaded figure in Claudius' reign' according to Tacitus, *Annals* 13.42–3, describing his condemnation in 58 engineered by friends of former victims (e.g. Valerius Asiaticus, Tac. *Ann.* 11.1–6).

Q. Ostorius Scapula: probably grandson of Q. Ostorius Scapula, prefect of the praetorian guard (2 BC), nephew or great-nephew of P. Ostorius Scapula, prefect of Egypt in the last decade of Augustus, cousin of the second governor of Britannia (see **N34**).

42 Ti. Claudius Caesar Augustus II — C. Caecina Largus

C. Cestius Gallus
Cornelius Lupus

Ti. Claudius Caesar Augustus II: Claudius' first consulship was under his nephew Gaius. He held this consulship for two months (Suet. *Claud.* 14).

C. Caecina Largus: unusually consul for the whole year (Dio 60.10.1). Arval from 38 (See **A38m, A45b**); close companion of Claudius (Tac. *Ann.* 11.33–34).

C. Cestius Gallus: son of consul of 35. Went on to be governor of Syria (Tac. *Ann.* 15.25.3).

Cornelius Lupus: attested on coins as proconsul of Crete under Tiberius. A close friend of Claudius, but done to death by Suillius Rufus under Claudius (Seneca, *Apocol.*13.5, Tac. *Ann.* 13.43.2 – death must have been in lost books of Tacitus, so before AD 47).

43 Ti. Claudius Caesar Augustus III — L. Vitellius II

Sex. Palpellius Hister	L. Pedanius Secundus
A. Gabinius Secundus	
Q. Curtius Rufus	Sp. Oppius

Ti. Claudius Caesar Augustus III: another two-month consulship (Suet. *Claud.* 14, confirmed by Pliny, *NH* 10.35 and epigraphically (*AE* 1969–70, no.98, p.29)); Dio 60.21.2 wrongly says six months.

L. Vitellius II: see on his first consulship in 34.

Sex. Palpellius Hister: A *novus homo* (Wiseman, *New Men* no. 304), whose home territory of Istr(i)a only became part of Italy under Augustus. His full career is given by an inscription from Pola (= Pula in Croatia), *ILS* 946. This explains his rise, describing him as companion of Tiberius, appointed by Augustus. Praetor in 27, Claudius appoints him governor of Pannonia in 50 (Tac. *Ann.* 12.29).

L. Pedanius Secundus: only the second known consul from Spain (after Cornelius Balbus in 40 BC), and the first from Hispania Tarraconensis, Pedanius came from Barcino (Barcelona). His consulship marks the rise of his own family (see cos suff 61), and others from the provinces: see Syme, *Tacitus* App. 80, 82, 87. City Prefect, probably from 56, he was murdered by his own slave in 61 (Tac. *Ann.* 14.42–43).

A. Gabinius Secundus: presumably brother (PIR^2) or son (Brill-Pauly) of the consul of 35, see above.

Q. Curtius Rufus: see **U11** and Tacitus' scathing verdict (*Annals* 11.21). This is probably also the writer of a suriving history of Alexander the Great.

Sp. Oppius : Not prominent, but father or uncle of cos ord 84 (C. Oppius Sabinus).

44 C. Sallustius Passienus Crispus II — T. Statilius Taurus

Sabinus P. Pomponius Secundus	
T. Axius	T. Mussidius Pollianus

C. Sallustius Passienus Crispus II: suffect consul in 27. See **U5**.

T. Statilius Taurus: son of the consul of AD 11, grandson of M. Valerius Messalla Corvinus (see on AD 20) and of T. Statilius Taurus, one of Augustus' leading generals. See Syme *AA*, Table IX. Governor of Africa. Father of Statilia Messalina, Nero's third wife, he falls victim to Agrippina in 53 (Tac. *Ann.* 12.59).

Sabinus P. Pomponius Secundus: eminent through personal connections and talents; half-brother of Caesonia, wife of Gaius (**J15a**, Syme, *Tacitus* 289 n.3). Convicted for supporting Sejanus (Tac. *Ann.* 5.8) and possibly imprisoned (Dio 59.6.2 – confused). Greatly admired by Quintilian (10.1.98), 'far the greatest of poets I have seen myself', by Pliny the Elder who wrote his biography (**R14**), and by Tacitus who also records his honorary triumph for a victory in Germany in 50 (*Ann.* 12.27–8).

T. Axius: unknown prior to discovery of his name as consul on a document from Herculaneum.

T. Mussidius Pollianus: career inscription, *ILS* 913 shows that he was governor of Gallia Narbonensis.

45	**M. Vinicius II**	**T. Statilius Taurus Corvinus**
	Ti. Plautius Silvanus Aelianus	
	M. Pompeius Silvanus	A. Antonius Rufus
	P. Fabius Firmanus	L. Tampius Flavianus

M. Vinicius II : cos 30 – see above.

T. Statilius Taurus Corvinus: second son of the consul of AD 11, grandson of M. Valerius Messalla Corvinus (see on AD 20) and of T. Statilius Taurus, one of Augustus' leading generals. See Syme *AA*, Table IX. Conspired against Claudius (Suet. *Claud.* 13.2). He was Arval AD 35–44/5 (**A35b–A44b**).

Ti. Plautius Silvanus Aelianus: see **U3** for this man, son of a leading figure under Augustus and Tiberius.

M. Pompeius Silvanus: later governor of Africa (**M69**), tried and acquitted of corruption there as an old man in 58 (Tac. *Ann.* 13.52). Aqueducts Commissioner AD 71–3 (**K32**), second consulship, probably in 75.

A. Antonius Rufus: not prominent.

P. Fabius Firmanus: unknown prior to discovery of his name as consul on a document from Herculaneum.

L. Tampius Flavianus: parallel career to Pompeius Silvanus (above): also governor of Africa, where he played with a dolphin (Pliny *NH* 9.26); succeeded Pompeius as Aqueducts Commissioner, AD 73–4 (**K32**), before sharing a second consulship with him.

46	**D. Valerius Asiaticus II**	**M. Junius Silanus**
	C. Antistius Vetus	
	Q. Sulpicius Camerinus	
	D. Laelius Balbus	
	C. Terentius Tullius Geminus	

D. Valerius Asiaticus II: see above on his suffect consulship of 35.

M. Junius Silanus: the great-great-grandson of Augustus and dubbed 'the golden sheep' by Caligula. See **J33** for this very prominent family. Arval 40 to 54 (**A40a–A54a**).

C. Antistius Vetus: the fourth generation C. Antistius Vetus to hold the consulship (father cos. 23).

Q. Sulpicius Camerinus: from patrician family, son of consul AD 9; father of a Flavian consul. Juvenal 7.90–1 mentions Camerini as synonymous with wealthy aristocrats. He was later tried and acquitted of corruption as governor of Africa in 58 (Tac. *Ann.* 13.52). Arval 57–63 (**A57d–A63d**).

D. Laelius Balbus: this man or his father (PIR^2 uncertain L48/9) is mentioned as a leading orator by Quintilian 10.1.24; and prosecuted for *maiestas* (Tac. *Ann.* 6.47.1 and 6.48.4). The consul of 6 BC was probably a direct ancestor.

C. Terentius Tullius Geminus: Tacitus records a Tullius Geminus making a prosecution for libel in AD 62 (*Annals* 14.50.1); Legate of Moesia sometime between 50 and 53 (Brill-Pauly, Tullius II.3).

47	**Ti. Claudius Caesar Augustus IV**	**L. Vitellius III**
	C. Calpetanus Rantius Sedatus	M. Hordeonius Flaccus
	Cn. Hosidius Geta	T. Flavius Sabinus
		L. Vagellius
		C. Volasenna Severus

Ti. Claudius Caesar Augustus IV: Claudius was consul to preside over the Centennial Games.

L. Vitellius III: see on his first consulship in 34.

C. Calpetanus Rantius Sedatus: in post in March: inscriptions show that he was curator of public records at Rome in 45; Legate in Dalmatia after 47

M. Hordeonius Flaccus: ineffective governor in Germany in 69–70 (Tac. *Hist.* 1.56) eventually killed by his own mutinous troops (*Hist.* 4.36).

Cn. Hosidius Geta: military commander in Mauretania (Dio 60.9.1). Either he or a brother, Gaius, also commanded a legion in the invasion of Britannia (Dio 60.20.4). In post for last 6 months of the year.

T. Flavius Sabinus: elder brother of the emperor Vespasian. Like him, commanded a legion in the invasion of Britannia (Dio 60.20.3). Killed in December AD 69 after 35 years of public service, 12 as city prefect (Tac. *Hist.* 3.75).

L. Vagellius: known from the Neronian law from Herculaneum, see **K33**.

C. Volasenna Severus: known only as a consular date. P. Volasenna, probably a brother, and consul around 53 is known from a coin to have been governor of Asia around 61.

48 A. Vitellius — L. Vipstanus Poplicola Messalla

L. Vitellius

A. and L. Vitellius: sons of L. Vitellius, Claudius' greatest supporter and his fellow consul the previous year (Suet. *Vit.* 3.1). Aulus Vitellius, only 34 years old when consul was briefly emperor in AD 69, see Suetonius *Vitellius*. Aulus was Arval from 57 (**A57d**). Lucius was Arval 63–9 (**A63d**).

L. Vipstanus Poplicola Messalla: his father had been suffect in 18, his mother a member of the patrician Valerius Messalla family (Syme, *Tacitus* 615 and *AA*, Table IX).

49 Q. Veranius — C. Pompeius Longinus Gallus

L. Mammius Pollio — Q. Allius Maximus

Q. Veranius: for his career including governorship of Britannia, see **N36**.

C. Pompeius Longinus Gallus: unknown (Syme, *Tacitus* 560n).

L. Mammius Pollio: known only for proposing, as consul designate, marriage of Octavia and Nero (Tac. *Ann.* 12.9).

Q. Allius Maximus: propraetorian legate in Africa, AD 42 (**M30**).

50 C. Antistius Vetus II — M. Suillius Nerullinus

Q. Futius — P. Calvisius

C. Antistius Vetus II: see AD 46 on his first (suffect) consulship.

M. Suillius Nerullinus: son of the notorious accuser, Suillius Rufus, one of Claudius' first consuls (**B41**). Nero intervenes to prevent his sharing his father's fate (Tac. *Ann.* 13.43).

Q. Futius: known only as a consular date.

P. Calvisius: own achievements unknown, but presumably brother of P. Calvisius Ruso (cos suff. 53).

51 Ti. Claudius Caesar Augustus V — Ser. Cornelius Salvidienus Orfitus

L. Calventius Vetus Carminius

T. Flavius Vespasianus

Ti. Claudius Caesar Augustus V: Claudius was consul for the whole of his 10th anniversary as emperor; the year of his 60th birthday, and of Nero's coming of age (attested as consul at the end of the year in an inscription (*AE* 1973, no.139, p.40) despite Suetonius giving it as six months (*Claud.* 14)).

Ser. Cornelius (Scipio) Salvidienus Orfitus: by adoption, a member of the famously aristocratic Cornelius Scipio clan (see on consuls of AD 24). Despite a sycophantic proposal in AD 66 (Tac. *Ann.* 16.12) Nero had him killed for apparently trivial reasons (Suet. *Nero* 37.1) through the prosecution of Aquilius Regulus (Tac. *Hist.* 4.42). Nonetheless 4 successive generations of Orfitus' descendants are known as consuls.

L. Calventius Vetus Carminius: governor of Lusitania, leading to his son, suffect in 81, acquiring the name L. Carminius Lusitanicus; otherwise unknown.

T. Flavius Vespasianus: the future emperor Vespasian. Like his elder brother, the consulship was a reward for commanding a legion in the invasion of Britannia (Suet. *Vesp* 4.2).

52	**Faustus Cornelius Sulla Felix**	**L. Salvius Otho Titianus**
		Q. Marcius Barea Soranus
		L. Salvidienus Rufus Salvianus

Faustus Cornelius Sulla Felix: son of consul of 31; had married Claudius' daughter Antonia soon after 47. This and his aristocratic pedigree incur suspicion and eventual murder (Tac, *Ann.* 13.23.1, 13.47.1, 14.57). Arval 55–58 (**A57b – d**).

L. Salvius Otho Titianus: elder son of M. Salvius Otho, cos 33, who was a favourite of Claudius (see Suet. *Otho* 1.2–3) who made him patrician. Arval 57–69, see **A57b**, **A66h**. Titianus' younger brother, Otho was briefly emperor in 69.

Q. Marcius Barea Soranus: son of the suffect of AD 34. Tacitus makes much of Nero's persecution of him and his fellow Stoic, Thrasea Paetus (*Annals* 16.21–33 (the manuscripts fail before Soranus' death)).

L. Salvidienus Rufus Salvianus: little known (PIR^2 S120).

53	**D. Junius Silanus Torquatus**	**Q. Haterius Antoninus**
	Q. Caecina Primus	P. Trebonius
	P. Calvisius Ruso	

D. Junius Silanus Torquatus: a great-great-grandson of Augustus. Forced to suicide in 64 (Tac. *Ann.* 15.35). See **J33** for his family.

Q. Haterius Antoninus: his grandfather (suffect AD 5) and father (AD 22) had been consuls. He is one of the noblemen to receive an annual subsidy from 58 'even though he had squandered his inheritance on a luxurious lifestyle.' (Tac. *Ann.* 13.34).

Q. Caecina Primus and **P. Trebonius:** known only as consular names.

P. Calvisius Ruso: his own achievements are not known, but was father of two Flavian consuls, one, P. Calvisius Ruso Iulius Frontinus, who was the great-grandfather of the emperor Marcus Aurelius.

54	**M'. Acilius Aviola**	**M. Asinius Marcellus**
	M. Junius Silanus	A. Pompeius Paulinus
		Vell(a)eus Tutor

M'. Acilius Aviola: probably son of suffect cos of 24. Aqueducts Commissioner AD 74 to 97 (**K32**).

M. Asinius Marcellus: great-grandson of Asinius Pollio (cos 40 BC) who had brought the family to prominence under Augustus. Marcellus' grandfather, father and two uncles had all been consuls (8 BC, AD 23, 25, 38). He was disgraced in 61 after conspiring to forge a will (Tac. *Ann.* 14.40).

M. Junius Silanus: from the less prominent branch of the family (**J33**); son of consul of 28.

A. Pompeius Paulinus: wealthy son of equestrian from Arles (S. France) – Pliny *NH* 33.143. Brother-in-law of Seneca (*On Shortness of Life* 1.1). Prefect of the corn-supply, 49–55; *c.* 54–56 commander of army of Lower Germany (Tac. *Ann.* 13.53.1 and inscriptions from stone camps at Bonn and Neuss). In 62 Nero appointed him to reform public revenues (Tac. *Ann.* 15.18.3 and *Customs Law of Asia*, **M58a**).

Vell(a)eus Tutor: not prominent.

55	**Nero Claudius Caesar Augustus I**	**L. Antistius Vetus**
	N. Cestius	
	P. Cornelius Dolabella	L. Annaeus Seneca;
	M. Trebellius Maximus	
	P. Palfurius	
	Cn. Cornelius Lentulus Gaetulicus	T. Curtilius Mancia

Nero Claudius Caesar Augustus I: Nero's first consulship was for two months (Suet. *Nero* 14).

L. Antistius Vetus: member of a very prominent J-C family: his father (AD 26), grandfather (6 BC), great-grandfather (30 BC), uncle (AD 23) and first cousin (AD 46 and 50) had all been consuls. His daughter marries Rubellius Plautus, son of Tiberius' granddaughter Julia. Vetus fails to persuade his son-in-law to resist Nero's order to suicide (AD 62, Tac. *Ann.* 14.57–9) and himself commits suicide in 65 (Tac. *Ann.* 16.10–12). See also *OCD* page 113.

N. Cestius: only known as a consular date (PIR^2 C689).

P. Cornelius Dolabella: there had been consuls of this name in 44 BC, and AD 10, presumably father and grandfather of this aristocrat.

L. Annaeus Seneca: from Corduba in Spain; the philosopher, writer and tutor of Nero. Consul from May to October. See source introductions.

M. Trebellius Maximus: governor of Britain, 63–9, see **N39**.

P. Palfurius: not prominent (PIR^2 P67) but his name suggests origin in Tarraconensis in Spain (Syme *Roman Papers* 4.88), fitting in with many consuls from Spain/S. Gaul in this period.

Cn. Cornelius Lentulus Gaetulicus: son of the consul of 26; his selection perhaps advertised imperial clemency (his father was linked with Sejanus and 'conspired' against Caligula).

T. Curtilius Mancia: commander of the upper army in Germany in 58 (Tac. *Ann.* 13.56). Seems from legal sources (*FIRA* i 100) to have owned great estates in the province of Africa, which he failed to bequeathe away from his son-in-law (Pliny *Letters* 8.18.4).

56	**Q. Volusius Saturninus**	**P. Cornelius Scipio**
	L. Iunius Gallio Annaeanus	T. Cutius Ciltus
	P. Sulpicius Scribonius Rufus	P. Sulpicius Scribonius Proculus
	L. Duvius Avitus	P. Clodius Thrasea Paetus

Q. Volusius Saturninus: his grandfather had been suffect in 12 BC. His father, suffect AD 3, lived to 93 to see this son of his old age as consul (Tac. *Ann.* 13.30.2, **U12**). Arval in 63 (**A63a**).

P. Cornelius Scipio: elder son of the suffect of AD 24 (See Syme, *AA* Table XXI); with his half-brother, suffect in 68, the last descendant of one of the most prominent families of the Roman Republic.

L. Iunius Gallio Annaeanus: Seneca's brother, adopted by the orator Junius Gallio. Pliny, *NH* 31.62 mentions his recent consulship.

T. Cutius Ciltus: not prominent – not in PIR^2; Brill-Pauly Cutius 1.

P. Sulpicius Scribonius Rufus and **Proculus**: Dio 63.17.3 describes these brothers as doing everything together – consuls, governors of Upper and Lower Germany, summoned to Greece by Nero in 67 and committing suicide. Also Tacitus *Annals* 13.48 and *Histories* 4.41 (destroyed for their wealth).

L. Duvius Avitus: from Vasio (Gallia Narbonensis), like the powerful Burrus. Duvius governed Aquitania (Pliny, *NH* 34.37) and Lower Germany (AD 58, Tac. *Ann.* 13.54 and 13.56). A fragmentary inscription of his career has been found at Vaison (*ILS* 979).

P. Clodius Thrasea Paetus: famous Stoic and champion of senatorial freedom. See Tacitus, *Annals* 13.49, 14.12, 14.49–50, 15.20–1, 16.21–35; Pliny, *Letters* 3.16.10, 6.20, 8.22, Griffin, *Nero* 165–6.

57	**Nero Claudius Caesar Augustus II**	**L. Calpurnius Piso**
		L. Caesius Martialis

Nero Claudius Caesar Augustus II: Nero is attested as consul for the whole year, despite Suetonius' suggestion that he was consul for six only months (Suet. *Nero,* 14).

L. Calpurnius Piso: son of the consul of AD 27 who outlived him. Not the conspirator against Nero, but probably the subject of the *Laus Pisonis* (see **R37**). Arval in AD 57 and president in AD 59 (**A57b, A59a–n**). Aqueducts Commissioner (**K32**). Killed as governor of Africa in aftermath of civil war, 69/70 (Tac. *Hist.* 4.48–50).

L. Caesius Martialis: only known as a consular date (PIR^2 C200).

58 **Nero Claudius Caesar Augustus III** — **M. Valerius Messalla Corvinus**

C. Fonteius Agrippa

A. Paconius Sabinus — A. Petronius Lurco

Nero Claudius Caesar Augustus III: Nero was consul for four months (Suet. *Nero,* 14).

M. Valerius Messalla Corvinus: Great-grandson of the famous Augustan aristocrat of the same name (see on AD 20). Tacitus, *Annals* 13.34 mentions his ancestry and poverty. He was the fourth and last successive generation of this family to be consul ordinarius. Arval 57–59 (**A57b–A59i**). See Syme *AA*, Table IX.

C. Fonteius Agrippa: his father had gained money and a praetorship from prosecuting Scribonius Libo (Tac. *Ann.* 2.30, 32) in AD 16. This man was Aqueducts Commissioner AD 66–8 (**K32**), Governor of Asia, 68/9 then appointed Governor of Moesia by Vespasian (Tac. *Hist.* 3.46).

A. Paconius Sabinus: other members of his family had served Tiberius and Claudius in more minor roles. His father, legate of Gaius Silanus in Asia, had accused Silanus (Tac. *Ann.* 3.67.1) but himself succumbed to *maiestas* charges (Suet. *Tib.* 61.6). His brother, Q. Paconius Agrippinus, had been quaestor of Crete and Cyrene under Claudius.

A. Petronius Lurco: not prominent, other than as consul (PIR^2 P284)

59 **C. Vipstanus Apronianus** — **C. Fonteius Capito**

T. Sextius Africanus — M. Ostorius Scapula

C. Vipstanus Apronianus: linked (it is not certain how) to the Apronii and Vipstani families (with consuls in AD 8, 39, 18, 48). Arval from 58 to death in 86 (*e.g.* **A58c**).

C. Fonteius Capito: presumably great-grandson of consul of 33 BC and grandson of consul of AD 12.

T. Sextius Africanus: nobleman. Agrippina the Younger believed that his marriage to Junia Silana (sister-in-law of Caligula) might be dangerous (Tac. *Ann.* 13.19). Arval 57–66 (**A57b–A66c**).

M. Ostorius Scapula: his father, Publius, had governed Britain AD 47–52 (see **N34**). Marcus had served under his father, winning the civic crown (Tac. *Ann.* 12.31.4). Nero, fearing his reputation as a soldier, ordered his execution in 66 (Tac. *Ann.* 16.14–5).

60 **Nero Claudius Caesar Augustus IV** — **Cossus Cornelius Lentulus**

C. Velleius Paterculus — M. Manilius Vopiscus

Nero Claudius Caesar Augustus IV: Suetonius, *Nero* 14 tells us that Nero was consul for six months, adopting the practice of six-month consulships (*Nero* 15) which certainly seems to hold for 59–68.

Cossus Cornelius Lentulus: son of the consul of 25; see also comments on the Cornelii Lentuli on AD 24.

C. Velleius Paterculus: probably the son of Velleius the historian (**Section C**).

M. Manilius Vopiscus: the name suggests he came from Spain (Syme, *Tacitus* 602 note). Statius praises the villa at Tivoli of him or his son (*Silvae* 1.3). His grandson is consul in 114.

61 **P. Petronius Turpilianus** — **L. Caesennius Paetus**

Cn. Pedanius Salinator — L. Velleius Paterculus

P. Petronius Turpilianus: governor of Britain, see **N38**.

L. Caesennius Paetus: Caesennii are not prominent in previous generations. His disastrous command in Armenia is recorded by Tacitus, *Annals* 15.6–17. Nonetheless appointed governor of Syria under Vespasian, 70–2 (Jos. *Jewish War,* 7.59, 7.219ff), and marries a woman called Flavia Sabina (*ILS* 995) who must be a member of the Flavian dynasty.

C. Velleius Paterculus: probably another son of Velleius the historian (**Section C**).

Cn. Pedanius Salinator: the Pedanii come from Barcino (Barcelona) in Spain (Syme, *Tacitus,* 785). His brother, cos suff 43. This man's son is Cn. Pedanius Fuscus Salinator is consul around 84; his grandson of the same name, consul 118, married Hadrian's niece (Syme, *Tacitus,* App.87, nos 15–16).

62 **P. Marius (Celsus?)** — **L. Afinius Gallus**
Q. Iunius Marullus — T. Clodius Eprius Marcellus

P. Marius (Celsus?) :– cognomen is uncertain. Aqueducts Commissioner, AD 64–6, (**K32**) but otherwise unknown (he is not the Marius Celsus, consul designate for 69 (Tac. *Hist.* 1.14.1).

L. Afinius Gallus: little known (PIR^2 A437).

Q. Iunius Marullus: only known as pandering to Nero's cruelty (Tac. *Ann.* 14.48.2).

T. Clodius Eprius Marcellus: of very humble birth, he made his mark through oratory (Tac. *Dial* 5.7 and 8.1–3). Great honours shown on an inscription (*ILS* 992) from near Capua, his home town: priesthoods, governor of Cyprus and Asia (70–73); consul II (AD 74). Trial in AD 79 (Dio 65.16.3f) and suicide.

63 **C. Memmius Regulus** — **L. Verginius Rufus**
T. Petronius Niger — Q. Manlius Tarquitius Saturninus

C. Memmius Regulus: the son of the consul of 31.

L. Verginius Rufus: a remarkable man who twice refused the chance to become emperor, see **P13c, h, i**.

T. Petronius Niger: Tacitus provides a lengthy character sketch of Nero's notorious courtier at *Annals* 16.18, in context of his forced suicide in 66 (*Ann.* 16.17–20). He is quite likely to be the famous author of *Satyrica*, which includes 'Trimalchio's Dinner Party'.

Q. Manlius Tarquitius Saturninus: governor of Africa 71/2.

64 **C. Laecanius Bassus** — **M. Licinius Crassus Frugi**
C. Licinius Mucianus — Q. Fabius Barbarus Antonius Macer

C. Laecanius Bassus: son of cos suff 40. Best known for dying of anthrax in AD 79 (Pliny, *NH* 26.5 and 36.205).

M. Licinius Crassus Frugi: very aristocratic. Father cos 27, grandfather (adopted by the famous Licinii Crassi) cos 14 BC. His mother, Scribonia, was great-granddaughter of the brother of Scribonia (Augustus' first wife) and great-great-granddaughter of Pompey the Great (see Syme *AA* Table XIV). Victim of Nero (Tac. *Hist.* 1.48.1).

C. Licinius Mucianus: character sketch Tacitus, *Histories,* 1.10. Legionary legate under Corbulo in the East (Pliny, *NH* 5.83) and governor of Lycia/Pamphylia shortly after 57. Nero appointed him governor of Syria. His support for Vespasian's bid for power was crucial and he remained Vespasian's chief adviser (cos II 70, cos III 72) until his death some time before AD 77.

Q. Fabius Barbarus Antonius Macer: little known; possibly of provincial origin (Syme, *Tacitus* 787)

65 **A. Licinius Nerva Silianus** — **M. Julius Vestinus Atticus**
C. Pomponius Pius — C. Anicius Cerealis

A. Licinius Nerva Silianus Publius Pasidienus Firmus: probably maternal grandson of the consul of AD 7, keeping his father's very uncommon name (Pasidienus) alongside that of his more aristocratic mother's clan, Licinius, and one derived from his great-grandfather, Silius Nerva, cos. 20 BC, close friend of Augustus. He was praetorian governor of Bithynia under Claudius, 48–50, as shown by coins.

M. Julius Vestinus Atticus: son of L. Vestinus from Vienne in Gaul, very close friend of Claudius (Claudius' speech to senate, *ILS* 212 = **M11**). Husband of Statilia Messalina (**J28**), soon to marry Nero. Highly intelligent (Tac. *Ann.* 15.52.3) with biting wit, close companion of Nero who came to hate him and had him falsely accused and killed (Tac. *Ann.* 15.68.2–3).

C. Pomponius Pius: member of a family very prominent under the Julio-Claudians, with great-uncles, uncle and father all consuls (AD 16, 17, 44 and 41 respectively).

C. Anicius Cerealis: according to Tacitus, *Annals* 16.17, Anicius had revealed a plot to kill Gaius (possibly involving his step-son – see **P5b** and note). Opposed to Nero, despite proposing his worship (Tacitus, *Annals* 16.17, 15.74.3). Forced to suicide in AD 66.

66	**C. Luccius Telesinus**	**C. Suetonius Paullinus II**
	M. Arruntius …	M. Vettius Bolanus

C. Luccius Telesinus: family background unknown: friend and follower of Apollonius of Tyre who voluntarily shared the exile of the philosophers under Domitian (Philostr. *Life of Ap* 7.11)

C. Suetonius Paullinus II: for this governor of Britain, see **N37**)

M. Arruntius …: the rest of his name is lost in Acts of the Arval Brothers – see **A66g**.

M. Vettius Bolanus: commanded a legion under Corbulo in Armenia (Tac. *Ann.* 15.3.1 and Statius, *Silvae* 5.2.31–50 written in praise of his son. A *novus homo* who went on to govern Britain 69–7 and later Asia, and was made patrician by Vespasian (Statius 5.2.28).

67	**L. Iulius Rufus**	**.. [Fonteius?] Capito**
		L. Aurelius Priscus
	M. Annius Afrinus	C. Paccius Africanus

L. Iulius Rufus: died of anthrax in AD 79 (Pliny, *NH* 26.5 and 36.205).

.. (Fonteius?) Capito: only the name Capito is preserved on the *Fasti* at Antium, but this is almost certainly the commander of the army in Lower Germany, killed on suspicion of plotting against Galba (Tac. *Hist* 1.7 and elsewhere; also Suet, *Galba* 11; Plut. *Galba* 15; Dio 64.2.3).

L. Aurelius Priscus: only known from dating (PIR^2 A1580).

M. Annius Afrinus: governor of Pannonia between AD 71 and 73 (*CIL* 3.4109).

C. Paccius Africanus: apparently responsible for prompting Nero to destroy the Proculi Scribonii brothers the previous year (see **B56** and Tac. *Hist.* 4.41). Governor of Africa 77–78 (*AE* 1949, 84).

68	**Ti Catius Asconius Silius Italicus**	**P. Galerius Trachalus**
	Nero Claudius Caesar Augustus V	
	C. Bellicius Natalis	P. Cornelius Scipio Asiaticus

Ti Catius Asconius Silius Italicus: a *novus homo*, he owed his very early and *ordinarius* consulship, aged 42, to literary and cultural interests and/or zeal as a prosecutor. **See R38.**

P. Galerius Trachalus: 'The most pleasing voice I have ever heard, delivery good enough for the stage, and a handsome appearance,' according to Quintilian, 10.1.119.

Nero Claudius Caesar Augustus V: Nero deposed one consul (Pliny, *Panegyric* 57.2) or even both (Suet. *Nero* 43.2) to try to deal with the Vindex/Galba uprising.

C. Bellicius Natalis: from Vienne in Gaul which helped Vindex's rebellion so perhaps a symbolic choice installed to replace Nero.

P. Cornelius Scipio Asiaticus: son of the consul of 24 by his second marriage to Poppaea Sabina, mother of Nero's wife. (See Syme, *AA* Table XXI).

SECTION C

VELLEIUS PATERCULUS, *HISTORY OF ROME* (2, 124.1 – END)

Introduction: Velleius' forbears came from south of Rome, winning citizenship in the Social War (90–88 BC). His grandfather served with Pompey, Brutus, and the father of Emperor Tiberius. He was born in 20 or 19 BC, went with Gaius Caesar to the East, then served under Tiberius in Germany, and the Balkans. He entered the senate in AD 7, and reached the praetorship of AD 15. His Greek and Roman History, in two books, is summary, becoming fuller with the Augustan and especially the Tiberian periods. It was written c.AD 30 and dedicated to M. Vinicius, consul that year. Velleius as a contemporary and eye-witness was ideally placed to write Augustan political and military history, but his conventional patriotism and bias towards the official point of view, particularly his fawning on Tiberius (typical of the senate of his day, as its decree on Cn. Piso the Elder shows (**P3d**, **P3g**, **P3i**) though excusable in a subordinate, loyal to his commander, vitiate his work for some scholars. But he is a valuable foil to the hostile Tacitus, Dio, and Suetonius: he is offering the same material with a different slant (see notes). The last chapters of his work are devoted to the rise of L. Aelius Sejanus, Prefect of the Praetorian Guard since 14 and an increasingly close adviser to Tiberius. He reached the consulship, held jointly with his patron in 31 and so thought to be leading to a grant of imperium and tribunician power, the prerogatives of an emperor and his heir. Readers differ sharply in their views of Velleius' attitude towards Sejanus; that is because, while his devotion to Tiberius is unshakeable, he knew that the political situation in 30 was on a knife edge, and that Sejanus' opponents, the family of Germanicus, were not finished: it was probably Gaius Caesar (Caligula) who brought about Sejanus' downfall late in 31. There is no reason to believe that Velleius was involved in it, but we hear no more of him after 30.[1] His sons, however, both reach the consulship under Nero (60 and 61 – see Section B).

C1 Tiberius' accession

[124.1] I have not the time, for I must hasten on. But even if time were available, no man would have the capacity to describe the general anxiety of those times following the death of Augustus, the senate's alarm, the popular turmoil, the universal fear, and the boundary upon which we stood between safety and destruction.[2] Suffice to say only what was said by all: "We feared the ruin of the world; we found it not even stirred. So great was the majesty of one man that there was no need of arms to defend the good or to resist the bad." [124.2] But there was one battle, metaphorically speaking:[3] the state's battle with Caesar, as the senate and people of Rome sought to persuade him to succeed to his father's post, and his battle with them as he strove for the right to be the equal of others as a citizen rather than as emperor to stand above them.[4] At last reason not ambition won the day, once he realised that whatever he

---

1 For more on Velleius' career and fate, see B.M. Levick, 'Velleius Paterculus the Senator' in E. Chambers' (ed.) forthcoming conference papers on Velleius.

2 *Universal fear*: There were real dangers, from foreign enemies (Germans, Parthia); discontented armies (Germany and Pannonia); and rival claimants, real (Postumus) or suspected (Germanicus). For the precautions that Tiberius took at Augustus' funeral, see Tac. *Ann.* 1.8.6f. Postumus was immediately killed: Tac. *Ann.* 1 6.1; Suet. *Tib.* 22; Dio 57.3.5; LACTOR 17, J48; Vell. 93.2 and 112.7.

3 *There was one battle*: Velleius' presentation of what scholars have misleadingly called the 'hesitation' of Tiberius to take over the principate; compare Tac. *Ann.* 1.11f., which looks more like an inconclusive debate between Tiberius and the senate on the form that his principate was to take, and Dio 57.3.3.

4 *Succeed to his father's post*: The military metaphor that Velleius uses here of the principate ('post') is repeated in the official decree on Cn. Piso the Elder (**P3j** – line 129), as well as informally by Augustus himself in his letter to Gaius about the succession (in Gellius, *Attic Nights* 15.7.3 = LACTOR 17, J57) and by Ovid ironically of Augustus leaving his post to read Ovid's verses (*Tristia* 2.229 = LACTOR 17, G56). Metaphor was necessary because there was no single position to take over.

refused to guard must necessarily perish. He is the only man whose lot it has been to refuse the principate for longer, almost, than others fought to usurp it.[5]

[124.3] Once his father had been given his due place in heaven,[6] his body adorned with human honours, his name with the title of divinity, the first duty of the new princeps was to organise the voting assemblies along the lines recorded by Divus Augustus in his own hand.[7] [124.4] On this occasion my brother and I were lucky enough, as Caesar's candidates,[8] to be nominated for the praetorship immediately after the noblest of candidates and those who had held priesthoods,[9] thus acquiring the unique privilege of being the last of the candidates recommended by Divus Augustus and the first of those supported by Tiberius Caesar. [10]

C2 Mutinies in the legions, AD 14

[125.1] The nation's prayers and wisdom were rapidly rewarded. For it very soon became clear to us what we might have suffered had we failed to persuade Tiberius to accept, and how greatly we profited from our success in persuading him. The army, which was campaigning in Germany under the direct and personal command of Germanicus, and the legions which garrisoned Illyricum,[11] were simultaneously overtaken by a mad and overwhelming desire to cause chaos by demanding a new commander, a new constitution, and a new republic. Indeed they even had the nerve to threaten to impose their demands on the senate and the emperor himself.[12] [125.2.] They wanted to fix their own level of pay and the terms of their engagement, and it

---

5 *The only man ... to refuse the principate for longer ... than others fought for it*: rhetoric. Velleius, like most senators, and Augustus, but not Tiberius, regarded the position necessarily as one of dominance, with the emperor taking the initiative; for Tiberius' view, see Suet. *Tib*. 27–9.

6 Death and deification: 17 Sept; Tac. *Ann*. 1.10.8; Dio 56.46. The ascent was witnessed: Dio 56.42.3.

7 *Voting assemblies*: this is the transfer of elections to the senate recommended by Augustus in his political testament: see Tac. *Ann*. 1.11.3 and 15.1, with Dio 56.33.

8 *Caesar's candidates*: Politicians canvassed for candidates they supported; the emperor did likewise, and those candidates he supported were called 'Caesar's candidates'. See Suet. *Aug*. 56.1 and **B1**.

9 *Immediately after the noblest of candidates and those who held priesthoods*: There were twelve places available, and since Tiberius undertook not to support more than four candidates (see Tac. *Ann*. 1.15.2), who would have been sure of election, there should have been two nobles in front of Velleius and his brother (another useful military man: see 115.1). Nobility is a rank, hereditary in the male line, won under the Republic by all who attained the consulship. See also note 47 below.

10 *Last of the candidates recommended by Divus Augustus*: The consular elections were over when Augustus died; the praetorian and others followed the 'accession' of Tiberius, but besides drawing up his political testament, Augustus had decided which candidates he wished to support, and Tiberius kept the same list.

11 *The army, which was campaigning in Germany*: The Romans had been campaigning beyond the Rhine since 12 BC, with the intention of creating further provincial territory there, provisionally up to the Elbe. The commanders had been members of the imperial family, when available: Nero Drusus (Germanicus' father) 12–9 BC; Tiberius 9–7, AD 4–6, and 9–12; and since 12, Germanicus. His first task, however, had been to expel Germans from Gaul and pacify the Gauls after the defeat of Varus. His command was confirmed on Augustus' death and he was holding a census when the mutiny broke out in the Lower Rhine army (*legiones* I, V, XX, XXI); at the same time *legiones* VIII, IX, and XV mutinied in Pannonia. See Tac. *Ann*. 1.16–51 and Dio 57.4.1–6.1.

12 *A new commander...republic*: Tacitus tells of troops offering to replace Tiberius with Germanicus (*Ann*. 1.35.3), and there was talk of rushing the pretender Agrippa Postumus to the Rhine armies (Suet. *Aug*, 19.2), but there is little evidence that most of the men wanted anything more than improved pay and conditions: the new emperor would be amenable when threatened with mutiny.

even looked as if they were prepared to make a fight of it.[13] Swords were drawn, and so convinced were the soldiers of their own inviolability that it almost became a full scale mutiny. There was no shortage of followers; all they lacked was someone to lead them into battle against their own country.[14] [125.3] But Tiberius' long experience as an army commander soon calmed their fury and put an end to this general breakdown of military discipline.[15] Many were punished severely;[16] some were bought off by promises, where it was possible to do so without undermining respect for their general's standing.[17] This combination of severe sanctions against the ringleaders and limited measures against the rest settled the matter.

[125.4] Germanicus' handling of this crisis had been generally fairly vigorous; but Drusus had recourse to a more traditional and old-fashioned severity.[18] His father had despatched him into the very heart of an army mutiny whose fires were already well and truly ablaze.[19] He chose what was for himself the high risk option, rather than taking a more restrained approach which might have set a disastrous precedent for the future. He chose to suppress the mutineers with the same brute force as they had themselves used to threaten him. [125.5] In all this he was admirably supported by Junius Blaesus, a man whose military skills were more than matched by his political know-how. A few years later as proconsul in Africa he was awarded the richly deserved decorations of a military triumph and the title of *imperator* (victorious general).[20] But in the two Spanish provinces and their armies, by contrast, absolute peace and quiet reigned. Marcus Lepidus held the supreme command there, and I have already written about his remarkable personal qualities and his outstanding military

[13] *They wanted to fix their own level of pay*: Legionaries were required to serve for 16 years, with four more years as reservists with the colours; the legal term was regularly exceeded (30–40 years was alleged), and they demanded that the 16-year limit should be strictly observed, with no supplementary service (Tac. *Ann.*1.17.5). Praetorian guardsmen, by contrast, served sixteen years all told and received 8 sesterces a day, compared with 2½ for legionaries. Discharge bounties were proportionate, but many did not live to receive their due (Suet. *Tib.* 48.2). It was another complaint that they were instead being sent to settle on useless land (Tac. *Ann.* 1.17.3).

[14] *They lacked ... someone to lead*: Probably this alludes to Germanicus' refusal of their offers.

[15] *Tiberius' long experience*: first major campaign in the Alps, almost 30 years before (15 BC: Vell 95.1; Dio 54.22; LACTOR 17, G42, G44, N14, N15. But Tacitus' account shows how difficult he found it to bring the mutiny to an end.

[16] *Many were punished severely*: Germanicus allowed the troops to 'try' the ringleaders and loosed loyal soldiers against the mutineers: Tac. *Ann.*1.44.2f.; 48.

[17] *Bought off by promises*: Germanicus began by offering improvements, producing a forged letter from Tiberius (Tac. *Ann.* 1.36.3). His conduct did in fact undermine respect for his standing, both among the troops and at home, and promises were retracted the following year, or not carried out (1.52.3).

[18] *Drusus had recourse to a more traditional ... severity*: Velleius prefers the methods of Drusus Julius Caesar ('old-fashioned', *prisca*, is a word of approval for him) perhaps as an ex-officer, certainly because Drusus was the son of Tiberius by blood.

[19] *His father had dispatched him*: Drusus was a civilian at Rome and of no attested military experience, when Tiberius sent him to Pannonia, probably immediately after he knew of the mutiny, with a new Prefect of the Praetorian Guard, Sejanus, to advise him and command his escort (Tac. *Ann.* 1.24). The mutiny was brought to an abrupt end on the night of 26 Sept., as a result of an eclipse of the moon, and ringleaders slaughtered (1.28f.).

[20] *Junius Blaesus*: This man, Q. Junius Blaesus, suffect consul AD 10, was governor of Pannonia and in charge of the rebellious legions. He was Sejanus' mother's brother, so Velleius' comments on him, made before Sejanus' downfall, are not unexpected. How he came, irregularly, by his African command in 21 is told by Tacitus, Ann. 3.32–35; 3.58.1; 3.72.4. Blaesus conducted a successful but not finally decisive campaign. He evidently perished in 31 along with his nephew (Tac. *Ann.* 5.7.2).

service in Illyricum.[21] He had a principled understanding of what was the right course of action and the natural authority to ensure that his views prevailed. Dolabella, a man of uncomplicated nobility of character, showed a similar commitment and devotion to duty in his command of the Illyricum coastline.

C3 Panegyric on the last sixteen years of Tiberius' rule

[126.1] Could anyone enumerate in detail all that has been achieved over the last sixteen years,[22] since it is perfectly apparent to the hearts and minds of us all? Caesar deified his father not so much by imperial decree as by his own display of religious devotion.[23] He did not call him a god; he made him one. [126.2] Respect has been restored to public life;[24] political conspiracy eliminated from it.[25] Scheming for high office has been banished from elections, factional strife from the senate;[26] justice,[27] fairness, and commitment to hard work, qualities long buried and forgotten, have been brought back to the body politic. The magistrates have recovered their authority, the senate its former majesty and the law courts their solemnity;[28] riots in the theatre are a thing of the past.[29] Everyone now is driven by a desire to do what it right and

---

[21] *The two Spanish provinces: Marcus Lepidus*: He is not known from elsewhere to have governed a Spanish province; his service under Tiberius in Illyricum is described by Velleius 2.114f. His political integrity won him general respect, and he was considered a man capable of running the Empire, if the opportunity offered (see Tac. *Ann.* 1.13.2; 4.20.2f.; 6.27.4, his obituary, AD 33). His children, however, became fatally embroiled with members of the imperial family: see **J20**.

[22] *All that has been achieved over the last sixteen years: i.e.*, August 14 to August 30. The summary of Tiberius' achievements is rhetorical, the substance hard to pin down, and there is a curious resemblance to the encomium on Augustus' own principate in 2.89, suggesting that the last years of Augustus left something to be desired.

[23] *Religious devotion*: Technically it was a senatorial decree, not an imperial order, that deified Augustus (Tac. *Ann* 1.11.1). Too much had been done beforehand towards the deification for anyone to resist, but it was advantageous to Tiberius, as that of Caesar had been for Octavian.

[24] *Respect has been restored*: The word *fides* has financial connotations, and suggests the chronic difficulties (shortage of cash) that were to lead to the crisis of AD 33 (Tac. *Ann.* 6.17), which Tiberius took action to resolve.

[25] *Political conspiracy ... scheming for high office*: Augustus and Tiberius' effective transfer of elections to the senate meant that hustings, violence, and bribery of non-senatorial voters ceased (Tac. *Ann.* 1.15.1; compare 1.81).

[26] *Factional strife*: With the deadly weapon of a charge of diminishing the majesty (*maiestas*) of state or emperor available to opponents, politicians needed caution in conducting rivalries – which did not diminish.

[27] *Justice*: votive altars found in Rome and near Capena (30km north of Rome) refer to Tiberius as 'best and most just *princeps*' **J2f** and *ILS* 3783.

[28] *The magistrates ... the senate ... the law courts*: For Tiberius insisting on the proper functioning of officials and the senate's role, see Tac. *Ann.* 4.6.2f.; Suet. *Tib.* 30; Dio 57.7–9; for judicial matters Tac. *Ann.* 1.75.1. All these, parts of the *res publica*, were institutions that the Republican-minded Tiberius hoped to see working independently. That was paradoxical when there was an all-powerful man at the helm (compare Suet. *Tib.* 29); he adopted a bullying tone before the end (e.g.,Tac. *Ann.* 6.12 of AD 32). The senate's 'majesty' (*maiestas*) was a novelty of the principate: majesty properly belonged to the Roman People, but they became less significant under Augustus and the senate's authority was emphasised as its real power diminished.

[29] *Riots in the theatre*: Velleius is deceiving himself: Tac. *Ann.* 1.54.2, 1.77; Suet. *Tib.* 37.2; Dio 57.14.10; Tiberius absented himself from Rome in 21–22 and from 26 onwards, escaping encounters with the public.

fitting; if not, they are compelled to do so by force.[30] [126.3] Good deeds are admired; evil deeds punished. The lower orders respect, but do not fear, the higher; the higher orders claim precedence over, but do not despise, the lower.[31] When was the price of corn ever more stable?[32] When were the blessings of peace more delightful to us all? The Augustan Peace has spread to the lands of the east and west, to the very limits of the north and south,[33] and keeps every corner of the whole wide world safe and free from the fear of pirates and brigands.[34] [126.4] Blind chance has brought losses to citizens and cities alike; the emperor's generosity has made their losses his own. The cities of Asia have been restored;[35] the provinces set free from the exploitation of their governors.[36] For those who deserve it, honour is there for the taking; for criminals, punishment is slow but sure.[37] Influence gives way to fairness; ambition to merit. Our best of emperors is teaching his citizens by example to do what is right; his power makes him supreme; his example greater still.[38]

C4 Praise of Sejanus as Tiberius' assistant

[127.1] It is common enough for eminent men to employ distinguished assistants in the management of their affairs.[39] The two Scipios recruited the Laelii, and elevated

---

[30] *A desire to do what is right and fitting*: Wishful thinking, and part of the official view of Tiberius' principate, as shown by the *SC de Pisone patre* of AD 20 (**P3**), where the effect of the moral teaching and example of members of the imperial family is stressed. What gave rise to this idea was indeed Augustus' and Tiberius' (probably galling) didactic attitude (e.g. Tac. *Ann.* 1.13.1; Suet. *Tib.* 29) and illustrated by many of speeches and letters in the *Annals* (e.g. 3.53f.). Tiberius is specifically referred to as teaching his peers in 126.4 below.

[31] *The higher orders claim precedence*: Tiberius expected the lower orders at Rome to know their place, but for conscientiousness towards material duties see next notes.

[32] *The price of corn*: For problems over grain, see **K10–K19** and Tac. *Ann.* 4.6.4 praising Tiberius' efforts.

[33] The Augustan Peace: To have brought peace to the world was one of Augustus' boasts in his *Res Gestae*, and Tiberius worked to maintain it: *tranquillitas* at home and abroad was a leading principle: Rome could no longer afford expensive wars of aggression (see Tac. *Ann.* 6.32.1; 2.65.1).

[34] *Pirates and brigands*: Tiberius represented the revolt of Tacfarinas in Africa (AD 17–24, see **N6**) as mere brigandage: Tac. *Ann.* 3.73.2 ; for an episode in Italy (AD 24), see *Ann.* 4.27.

[35] *Blind chance*: Disasters included fires at Rome in 22 and 27, along with the collapse of the amphitheatre at Fidenae (Tac. *Ann.* 3.72.2; 4.62f.), and earthquake in Asia in 17 (Tac. *Ann.* 2.47f.; **M3–M5**; compare Dio 57.17.7 and the unfavourable Suet. *Tib.* 48.2). Tacitus gives Tiberius credit for help after these disasters and for generosity overall: *Ann.* 4.64.1f.; 6.45.1; compare Dio 57.10.3.

[36] *The provinces set free*: Tac. *Ann.*1.2.2 says that that the provinces welcomed the coming of the principate because of the greater control of provincial governors; for Tiberius' care see Tac. *Ann.* 4.6.4) but the list of offenders is not short: Cn. Piso in AD 20 (but for an earlier an offence: Tac. *Ann.* 3.13.1); C. Silanus in 22 (Tac. *Ann.* 3.66.1) and Tiberius significantly is shown referring to provincials as sheep to be sheared (Suet. *Tib.* 32.2).

[37] *Punishment is ... sure*: The case of Piso (previous n.) is a case of delayed punishment, but Velleius is referring to Tiberius in terms appropriate to divine vengeance.

[38] *Our best of Emperors*: The title 'Optimus princeps' was conferred formally on Trajan in 114, but was used informally before that, (e.g. *ILS* 159 – see note 26) and of Tiberius in a governor's pronouncement: S. Mitchell, *JRS* 66 (1977) 107, l.7. Velleius' contemporary, Valerius Maximus, also uses the term (2 Pref.).

[39] *Employ distinguished assistants*: Velleius eases the awkward introduction of Sejanus by referring in Roman style to precedent (he is ceremonious: *Sejanus Aelius* reverses the normal order of family name and *cognomen*).

them to positions of equality with themselves;[40] Divus Augustus brought in Marcus Agrippa,[41] and immediately after him Statilius Taurus.[42] The fact that they lacked an aristocratic pedigree did not prevent them from winning promotion to repeated consulships and triumphs, as well as a number of priesthoods. Matters of high policy require administrators of outstanding ability, [127.2] and practical necessity requires that those who serve the national interest should be reinforced by high status, and their effectiveness assured by the authority of their position. [127.3] With such precedents to guide him, Tiberius Caesar brought in just such an outstanding administrator in Sejanus Aelius, to assist him in all the burdens of the principate – and he retains that position to this day.[43] His father was a leading figure in the equestrian order; his mother claimed descent from some of the most ancient and distinguished families in Rome, holders of innumerable public offices. His brothers, cousins, and uncle were all of consular rank;[44] his own loyalty to the emperor and capacity for hard work has been matched by a physical strength that more than equals his intellectual vigour. [127.4] He is a man of good natured seriousness of character and a somewhat old fashioned sense of humour.[45] His energy is masked by a deceptively relaxed manner; he has sought no personal advantage and for that reason has been granted every kind of distinction;[46] his personal modesty is in sharp contrast to the high regard which others have for him; his life, like his general demeanour, shows no signs of stress; yet his is a sharp and always restless intelligence.

[128.1] There is nothing to choose between the long standing regard felt for this man in the court of public opinion and the emperor's own judgement of him. In this there is nothing new; it has always been the habit of the senate and people of Rome

---

40 P. Cornelius Scipio Africanus, Hannibal's conqueror, consul 205 BC, and his friend C. Laelius, a *novus homo*, consul 195, is paradigmatic, and the impression it made was reinforced by Scipio's grandson P. Cornelius Scipio Africanus Aemilianus, consul 147 BC, who destroyed Carthage, and his friend C. Laelius, consul 140. Cicero asked Pompey in 62 BC to let him play Laelius, *i.e.*, political adviser, to Pompey's Scipio (Cic. *Fam.* 5.7.3).

41 Velleius continues with Augustus and his low-born but able contemporary M. Vipsanius Agrippa (63 – 12 BC), who was responsible for the victories of Naulochus in 36 BC (over Sex. Pompeius) and Actium in 31 (over Antony and Cleopatra). He married Augustus' daughter Julia in 21 and became the father of the two heirs Gaius and Lucius Caesars; in 18 he was awarded the tribunician power and by 12 he was sharing *imperium* with Augustus as a near-equal partner in power.

42 T. Statilius Taurus, consul in 37 and 26 BC, was another new man, second to Agrippa and Prefect of the City in 16 BC; importantly, members of his family survived into the following reigns: his sons were consuls in 44 and 45 (**B44–B45**); his daughter, Statilia Messalina (**J28**) was Nero's third wife.

43 *To assist him with all the burden of the Principate*: 'Companion/assistant in his labours', is the standard description of Sejanus' position, used by Tiberius himself, perhaps as early as AD 20, and in formal speeches: Tac. *Ann.* 4.2.3; Dio 57.19.7; 58.4.3.

44 *A leading figure in the equestrian order*: L. Seius Strabo was Prefect of the Praetorian Guard and after AD 14 Prefect of Egypt. Sejanus' maternal relations are not securely established: the best representation is that of R. Syme, The *Augustan Aristocracy* (Oxford, 1986) Table XXIII. For his uncle, Junius Blaesus, see note 20 above; the other consuls were jurists.

45 *Good-natured seriousness, etc.*: This sketch has been much discussed and is close to that of Tac. *Ann.* 4.2.3. On the surface it is entirely laudatory, but it has features in common with Sallust's portrait of the villainous L. Sergius Catilina in his *Bell. Cat.* 5.1–5. Velleius has reservations about Tiberius' controversial aide. *Old-fashioned: 'prisca'* again (see note 18).

46 *He sought no personal advantage*: in 25 he asked Tiberius for the hand of Drusus Caesar's widow, and was refused (Tac. *Ann.* 4.39f.).

to equate what is most noble with that which is the best.[47] Three hundred years ago, before the Punic War,[48] they raised a new man, Tiberius Coruncanius to the highest pinnacle of public office, the consulship, as well as conferring upon him all sorts of other honours, and even the office of *pontifex maximus*.[49] [128.2] Then there was Spurius Carvilius,[50] an equestrian by birth, and soon afterwards Marcus Cato,[51] a new man and an immigrant to Rome from Tusculum, and Mummius,[52] the conqueror of Achaia – they were all advanced to the offices of consul and censor, and awarded triumphs. [128.3] Nothing was known of Gaius Marius' origins. But until his sixth consulship he was universally regarded as Rome's first citizen (*princeps*).[53] Marcus Tullius Cicero was so highly regarded that his recommendation could win high office for almost anyone he wished.[54] As for Asinius Pollio, they denied him nothing which could be earned by honest toil and sweat, even by the noblest in the land.[55] They clearly realised that the highest rewards should be bestowed on those whose character revealed the noblest qualities. [128.4] It was that natural impulse to follow their example which led Caesar to put the qualities of Sejanus to the test, encouraged him to share the burdens of imperial office, and persuaded the senate and people of Rome to recruit to the defence of their own security the very man whom experience had showed them to be best suited to the task.[56]

---

47 In theory Romans awarded office to merit, especially military merit (*virtus*); in practice, birth was supremely important, and *nobiles* regarded themselves as morally superior too. *Nobiles* had held the consulship, or who had an ancestor in the direct male line who had held it; under the principate the criteria became less rigorous. Like Sejanus, the men Velleius goes on to name are all *novi homines*, 'new men', variously defined as men who did not qualify as *nobiles*, or who had not held any office entitling them to sit in the curule chair of office (curule aedileship, praetorship) or who were the first in their family to enter the senate.

48 *Before the Punic War*: The first war lasted from 264 to 241 BC, the second 218–202 BC.

49 *Tiberius Coruncanius*: Consul 280, Dictator 246, and the first plebeian *pontifex maximus* (chief priest) *c*. 254 BC. C. Julius Caesar was *pontifex maximus* from 63 BC until his death; he was followed by the triumvir M. Lepidus and after his death in 12 BC by Augustus and all succeeding emperors.

50 Spurius Carvilius: Consul 293 and 272 BC, censor ?289, he is an obscure figure, but built a shrine to Fors Fortuna (Livy 10.46.14), a deity favoured by the Plebs and cultivated by Sejanus: Dio 58.7.2f.); a temple was dedicated to her in 16 (Tac. *Ann*. 2.41.1).

51 *Marcus Cato*: M. Porcius Cato, consul 195, was the celebrated censor and moralist, began his career as a protégé of a patrician, L. Flaccus. Tusculum was 24km south-east of Rome.

52 *Mummius*: conquered Achaia (mainland Greece) as consul in 146 BC. His reputation was tarnished by his destruction of Corinth and the introduction of un-Roman wealth to the city.

53 *Marius*: He began as a *protégé* of the leading family of the Caecilii Metelli, but broke away; his career suffered and he did not reach the consulship until 107. After military success in Africa, Gaul, and Italy, his sixth consulship of 100, saw him forced to abandon the radical allies who had supported him, and his position was so weakened that he had to go abroad. His last attempt at pre-eminence brought him through violence to the consulship of 87, but he died early in the year.

54 *M. Tullius Cicero*: the orator and statesman (106–43 BC) was a kinsman of Marius. He won his way as a defence counsel, and reached the consulship of 63 BC. As a senior consular he possessed influence in the senate and at the hustings; he used it for the last time, and fatally, in 44–3 by recommending the advancement of Octavian. With such extra-constitutional power Velleius moves to another aspect of Sejanus' position (compare his uncle Blaesus's appointment to Africa, note 20).

55 *Asinius Pollio*: C. Asinius Pollio, consul 40 BC, was a supporter of Julius Caesar and kept out of the disputes between Antony and Octavian. He became an influential historian of the period 60–42.

56 *Persuade the senate and people to recruit ...*: For Sejanus' consulship and fall in AD 31, see **P4**. *Defence of security*: This reveals the tensions that rivalry for the succession had generated: Nero and Drusus Caesars, the eldest sons of Germanicus were in disgrace and imprisoned (Tac. *Ann*. 5.3.3; 6.23f.; Suet. *Tib*. 54.2, along with their mother the elder Agrippina; Gaius (Caligula) was untouched, living with his grandmother Antonia, soon to be summoned to Capri by his grandfather Tiberius (Suet. *Cal*.10.1).

C5 Highlights of Tiberius' reign

[129.1] I have set out, so to speak, the broad characteristics of Tiberius Caesar's principate; let me now examine some of the details.[57] What a shrewd move it was to summon Rhascupolis to Rome, after he murdered his nephew, Cotys, the co-ruler of his Thracian kingdom. In a matter of such importance he had the outstanding services of Pomponius Flaccus, a man of consular rank, a skilful operator when it came to any form of delicate operation, but also a man of simple integrity, who always deserved but never demanded the highest accolades for his achievements.[58] [129.2] Then there was the trial of Drusus Libo.[59] How impressive was the serious attention which Tiberius gave to the case, not in his position as emperor, but in his role as a member of a senatorial jury; how impressive the speed with which he disposed of that ungrateful revolutionary! How well he had trained his own Germanicus[60] and imbued him with such understanding of military principles that, when his service was done,[61] he welcomed him home as conqueror of Germany and loaded that young man with the highest honours,[62] giving him a triumph whose scale matched his achievements in magnificence. [129.3] How often and how generously he gave largesse to the people,[63]and willingly enhanced the census rating of individual senators, when he could do it with the senate's blessing – his aim being to prevent honourable poverty depriving senators of their status without encouraging a general extravagance.[64] What honours he heaped upon Germanicus before sending him to the provinces overseas! What guile he showed when, with the help of Drusus his son and lieutenant,[65] he used salutary enticements (if I may so describe them without disrespect to the emperor) to force Maroboduus to emerge like a serpent from his secret den, when he was stubbornly clinging to the very borders of the territories he had seized.[66] He treated him honourably; but kept him on a very tight rein. When Sacrovir, the Gallic chieftain, and Florus Julius launched a ferocious revolt, how remarkable was the speed, the courage, with which he suppressed it, with the result that the people of Rome learned

---

57 *Some of the details*: *Rhascupolis*: For the attempt of this dependent monarch to seize the whole of Thrace, and Tiberius' strategy for avoiding warfare (AD 19), see Tac. *Ann.* 2.64–7.

58 *Pomponius Flaccus*: consul AD 17, see **B17**. Velleius was close to members of this family and obtained information from them. They survived Sejanus' fall by astute political footwork (Tac. *Ann.* 5.8.2).

59 *The trial of Drusus Libo*: See **P1**.

60 *Trained his own Germanicus*: Velleius insists on Tiberius' affection for his adopted son, in contrast with the opinion of Tacitus; the training had been during Germanicus' service in the Balkans and Germany, AD 7–12.

61 *When his service was done*: For Germanicus' campaigns, see note on **N3–4**. He did not wish to be recalled, but Tiberius insisted (Tac. *Ann.* 2.26.5), not necessarily out of fear or envy, but because of the costliness of such campaigns. In 17 Germanicus celebrated a triumph decreed in 15 (Tac. *Ann.* 1.55.1).

62 *Highest honours*: these also included a second consulship (**B18**) and extraordinary powers for his mission in the East (*SCPP* lines 33–6 = **P3e**).

63 *Largesse to the people*: See e.g. Tac. *Ann.* 2.42.1; 3.29.3; Suet. *Tib.* 54.1.

64 *Enhanced the census rating*: This was a prerogative of the immensely wealthy *princeps* from Augustus onwards when many senators were comparatively impoverished and could not maintain the required rating of 1 million sesterces: it was probably resented. For examples of help and (just) rebukes, see **U15–U16**; Tac. *Ann.* 1.75.3; 2.37. By referring applicants to the senate the already unpopular emperor was avoiding an invidious task.

65 *Drusus his son and lieutenant*: Drusus held an overriding command in the Balkans from AD 17 to 20, winning an ovation for his successes (Tac. *Ann.* 3.19.3).

66 *Maroboduus*: A formidable opponent of Rome who built up a kingdom in the territory of the present Czech Republic. Tiberius was about to attack him in AD 6 when the Pannonian revolt broke out. Here he is compared with a wild animal (as provincials are compared with sheep: see note 36).

of his victory before they knew that they were at war, and got news of his success before they were even aware of the danger.[67] [129.4] As for the war in Africa, which caused a general panic and seemed to be growing more dangerous by the day – under his auspices and thanks to his strategic genius it was soon suppressed.[68]

C6 Tiberius' buildings in Rome

[130.1] What wonderful public buildings he erected in his own name or that of his relatives![69] And now he is building a temple to his father with a lavish expenditure which, to an unbelievable degree, reflects his family devotion.[70] His restoration of the fire-damaged buildings of Gnaeus Pompey is a splendid tribute to his generosity of spirit.[71] For he believes that any building erected as a memorial to famous men should be preserved, as if it were a tribute to his own family. Note also his remarkable generosity on many other occasions, but especially after the recent fire on the Caelian hill, [130.2] when from his own resources he made good the losses of citizens of every order.[72] Consider his recruitment for the army, something which has always been a source of special anxiety – it was carried through without fuss and without any of the usual panic associated with a military levy.[73]

C7 Tiberius' misfortunes

[130.3] It may seem unnatural and impertinent for a humble mortal like myself to dare to utter this complaint to heaven – but I shall: what has Tiberius done to deserve the abominable conspiracy of Drusus Libo against him,[74] and then to earn the bitter enmity of Silius and Piso, men whose high status he either established or enhanced?[75] For him these strokes of fortune indeed seemed cruel enough; but now I shall turn to others that were far worse. What did he do to merit the loss of his sons in their youth,

---

67 *Florus and Sacrovir*: The revolt led by these two Gallic nobles, prompted by debt and misgovernment, took place in 21 and was immediately repressed by C. Silius (Tac. *Ann.* 3.40–6). Tacitus deplores Tiberius' failure to keep the senate informed on progress (3.47.1).

68 *War in Africa*: The rebellion led by Tacfarinas lasted from AD 17 until 24, see **N6–7**. Although Africa was a public province the commander was still said to be fighting under the auspices of the Emperor (LACTOR 17, M3–M4), who was free with advice for generals.

69 *Wonderful public buildings*: Possibly the temple to Augustus (**K6–7**) and the restored theatre of Pompey (see next notes), but also the Temple of Castor and Pollux and the Temple of Concord, completed before Tiberius came to sole power, and perhaps a minor dedication of AD 16 (Tac. *Ann.* 2.41.1). Tiberius was accounted niggardly in this regard: Tac. *Ann.* 6.45.1; Suet. *Tib.* 47.

70 *The temple to his father*: see **K6–7**.

71 *Fire-damaged buildings*: The theatre of Pompey was damaged in 22: Tac. *Ann.* 3.72.2f.; **P4c**.

72 *The Caelian Hill*: This fire took place in 27: Tac. *Ann.* 4.64; Suet. *Tib.* 48.1.

73 *Recruitment for the army*: Tiberius' difficulties in finding Italian recruits, and his complaints on the subject, are recorded in Tac. *Ann.* 4.4.2.

74 *Abominable conspiracy of Libo Drusus*: see **P1**.

75 *Silius*: C. Silius Caecina Largus, consul AD 13, was governor of Lugdunensian Gaul and had put down the revolt of AD 21 (Tac. 14. 18f. and see note 67). Accused of extortion on his return in 24, he also had a charge of disloyalty levelled against him, and committed suicide. According to Tacitus, it was his loyalty to Germanicus' family that was the reason for the attack (he had won the triumphal decorations in 15 as a legate of Germanicus (Tac. *Ann.* 1.72.1). Piso: see Tac. *Ann.* 2.55–3.20 and **P3**. There is no reason to believe that he was in any sense an enemy of Tiberius: his failing lay in tactless and aggressive loyalty.

and of Drusus his grandson?[76] But those were personal tragedies. [130.4] Now we must turn to more shameful matters.[77] Let me tell you, Marcus Vinicius,[78] that these last three years have brought him heart-rending distress.[79] It was a fire devouring his very heart, and all the more destructive for the fact that he kept it secret for so long. It was the sorrow, the fury, the shame he was compelled to endure because of his daughter-in-law, Agrippina, and his grandson, Nero.[80] The death of his mother, which occurred at the same time, could only aggravate his distress.[81] [130.5] She was a peerless lady, in everything more like a goddess than a mortal being,[82] who exercised her power only to help those in adversity or to enhance their rank and high position.

C8 Velleius' prayer

[131.1] Let me finish with a prayer.[83]
Jupiter, Lord of the Capitol,
Mars Gradivus,[84] author and defender of Rome's great name,
Vesta, guardian of Rome's eternal flame,
Gods and goddesses all,
Who have taken our vast empire[85] to the summit of all earthly greatness,
In the name of Rome's people I call upon you,
To you I offer up this prayer:
Guard, preserve, and defend our present condition, our peace, our emperor,
[131.2] Grant him the longest life of mortal men,

---

76 *Loss of his sons*: Germanicus died in Syria in 19 (Tac. *Ann.* 2.72.2; **J7g–i; J8**), Drusus at Rome in 23 (Tac. *Ann.* 4.8.1f.; **J10d**; poison was alleged only when Sejanus fell), and the twin grandson Ti. Drusus Julius Caesar Nero in 23 (2. 84.1 and 4.15.1).

77 *More shameful matters*: The alleged disloyalty of family members.

78 *Marcus Vinicius*: consul AD 30, to whom the work is dedicated.

79 *These last three years*: That would be from 27 to 29.

80 *Agrippina ...and ...Nero*: compare Tac. *Ann.* 5.3–5.5. Agrippina (**J9**), grand-daughter of Vipsanius Agrippa and of Augustus, had given Germanicus nine children, had played a conspicuous part during the campaigns in Germany and opposed Cn. Piso and his wife in Syria. After Germanicus' death her hopes rested on her eldest surviving sons Nero (**J17**) and Drusus (**J18**) Caesars. Ill feeling and misunderstanding developed when Tiberius refused them premature advancement; angry words and popular feeling on their behalf, and allegations of homosexual acts on the part of Nero were reported to the absentee princeps and led to their incarceration and ultimately death, Agrippina's in 33 (Tac. *Ann.* 6.25.1), Nero's in 31 (Suet. *Cal* 7; Dio 58.8.4). His younger brother Drusus starved in 33 (Tac. *Ann.* 6.23; Suet. *Tib.* 54.2; 61.1; Dio 58.22.4; 58.25.4).

81 *The death of his mother*: Livia (Julia Augusta since 14) died in 29, and Velleius differs from Tacitus (compare *Ann.* 5.1f.) in regarding this as a cause of distress to Tiberius. There is also disagreement, no doubt going back to gossip of the time, about her attitude towards Agrippina, hostile in Tacitus (but compare *Ann.* 5.3.1), and about her effect on the Tiberian principate: Velleius delivers the same 'official' line as the *SCPP* lines 114–18 = **P3h**: she rightly had great influence, and properly used it sparingly, only to advance the deserving and mitigate distress; for the factual basis of this view, see Seneca. *Clem.* 1.9; Tac. *Ann.* 2.34.2–4; Suet. *Otho* 1.1; Dio 55.14–21.

82 *More like a goddess*: Except on some informal monuments using the word 'dea' (*ILS* 119), Livia was not deified until her grandson Claudius became emperor in 43 (**L22**); he needed all the divine ancestors he could muster.

83 *Let me finish with a prayer*: The extreme tension of the last years of Tiberius, developing during Sejanus' ascendancy inform this unexceptionably worded *votum* (bargain made with the gods, in this case implicitly, for the safety for the state/emperor).

84 *Mars Gradivus*: Mars, father of Romulus, was the originator of the Roman People.

85 *Vast empire: moles*, 'mass' was the word that Tiberius used in his opening address to the senate (Tac. *Ann.* 1.11.1) when he appealed for their help in running it.

And when his task is done,[86]
Grant him successors to the end of time,
Men with shoulders strong as we have found his own to be,
To bear as bravely the burden of Rome's universal empire.
Prosper the aspirations of all our citizens, where they are virtuous;
Where they are wicked, cast them down to dust.

[86] *Task is done:* Velleius again uses the military '*statio*' (see note 4) for the *princeps*' position.

SECTION D

PHILO, *EMBASSY TO GAIUS* (SELECTIONS)

D1 Josephus on Philo's embassy

[257] Meanwhile, as a result of civil unrest in Alexandria between Jewish and Greek inhabitants, three representatives of each faction were chosen to appear before Gaius. … [259] Philo, the leader of the Jewish delegation, was a man held in the greatest esteem, brother of Alexander the alabarch, and a very experienced philosopher.

[Josephus, *Jewish Antiquities,* 18.257, 259]

Introduction: Philo's *Legatio ad Gaium – Embassy to Gaius* is an account of the delegation sent by the Jews of Alexandria, and led by Philo in AD 39/40. Philo was the leading Hellenised Jew in Alexandrian society, a philosopher, writer, and political leader. His literary output, all written in Greek, was enormous, with his main works being on the first five books of the Old Testament. Philo, already an old man at the time of his embassy, must have written up his account shortly after Gaius' death. The embassy went to complain about maltreatment of the Jews of Alexandria by the Greeks, though was in part 'overtaken by events' in news of Gaius wishing to be worshipped at the Temple in Jerusalem.

D2 High hopes on Gaius' accession

Following Tiberius' death on 16 March AD 37, Philo relates how Gaius' accession was eagerly greeted. Other sources confirm this euphoria: on his first entry into Rome as emperor, well-wishers lined the streets calling him affectionately 'star' or 'chick' (Suet. *Cal.* 13). There were said to be 160,000 sacrifices and offerings over the first three months of his reign (Suet. *Cal.* 14.1). Inscriptions from Assos (*ILS* 8792), a league of Greek cities (**J19f**), and Cyzicus (**M46**) show that Gaius was received in a similar way in the provinces. There was reason for optimism: Gaius published a 'balance sheet' (*ratio*) on accession (Suet. *Cal.*16.1; Dio 59.9.4 = LACTOR 15 B7), which showed a considerable surplus of 2,700 million sesterces (Suet. *Cal.* 37.3; Dio 59.2.6 = LACTOR 15 B2 gives figures of 2,300 or 3,300 million).

[8] Looking at Gaius after the death of Tiberius Caesar, who was not amazed and awe-struck by his prosperity, which was marvellous and beyond all description? For he had succeeded to an empire of the whole earth and sea, an empire safe from civil war, under the rule of law, and fully integrated with all its parts in unison, east, west, south and north, the Greek with the barbarian, and the barbarian with the Greek, the soldier with the civilian, and the civilian with the soldier, all in harmonious agreement for the shared enjoyment and advantage of peace.

[9] He found an inheritance of vast accumulated goods ready to hand, very numerous stores of money, silver and gold, some in bullion, some in coin, and some as valuables in the form of drinking cups and other things which are devised for show; also huge forces, infantry, cavalry, navy, revenues supplied with an ever-flowing rush as if from a fountain; [10] a dominion not only of the most vital and greatest parts of the inhabited world, (or what someone would rightly call the inhabited world, namely what is marked out by two rivers, the Euphrates and the Rhine, the latter dividing us from the Germans and all the wilder races, the former from the Parthians, the Sarmatians and the Scythians, races which are no less brutal than the Germans) but rather, as I said already, a dominion extending from sunrise to sunset, both within the ocean and beyond it. The people of Rome rejoiced in all these benefits, as did all of Italy and the races of both Europe and Asia.

[11] They had never exulted so completely and universally under any of the previous emperors. It was as though they were not just hoping that they would obtain and enjoy advantages both as individuals and communally, but as if they believed that they already had the full complement of good fortune, with prosperity waiting at hand. [12] At any rate there was nothing to see throughout the cities other than altars, offerings, sacrifices, men splendidly clad in white robes and garlands, beaming goodwill from cheerful faces, feasts, assemblies, musical contests, horse races, merrymaking, all-night festivals with flutes and lyres, jollity, licence, holidays, pleasures of every kind for every sensation. [13] At that time the rich did not take precedence over the poor, nor the famous over the obscure, nor money-lenders over debtors, nor were masters superior to slaves. Instead, the times granted equality before the law, with the result that the Golden Age, as depicted by the poets, no longer was thought a fiction of the myth, on account of the abundance and well-being, the freedom from grief and fear, and the universal good cheer found night and day among people and households alike, which continued uninterrupted throughout the first seven months of his reign.

[Philo, *on the Embassy to Gaius* 8–13]

D3 Gaius' illness and recovery

In the autumn of AD 37 Gaius fell ill (Suet. *Cal.* 14.2; Dio 59.8.1–2). The nature of his ailment is unknown: for a summary of modern speculation, see Barrett, *Caligula* 73. A second wave of euphoria greeted his recovery; the Alexandrian Jews, for example, celebrated with sacrifices (*Leg.* 356).

[14] But in the eighth month a serious illness struck him down: for he had exchanged the lifestyle he followed just a little before, while Tiberius was alive, which was comparatively simple, and therefore more wholesome, for one of sumptuous extravagance. His health was attacked by the combination of a lot of strong drink, eating of delicacies, appetites that were not sated even when the stomach was full, ill-timed hot baths and vomiting, and more drunkenness immediately again and binge-eating, lusts for boys and for women and everything else that destroys the soul and body and the bonds that join the two together. The rewards of self-restraint are health and strength, whereas the wages of self-indulgence are weakness and sickness bordering on death.

[15] It was the start of autumn, the final sailing time for seafarers returning from their trading posts everywhere to their own home ports and harbours, especially those who have the intention of avoiding wintering abroad. So, with it still being the sailing season, the report that he was ill spread everywhere, and people abandoned their pampered lifestyle and became subdued. Every house and city was filled with anxiety and sorrow, with their recent joy balanced by an equally matched grief. [16] For all parts of the inhabited world shared his illness, and the sickness they experienced was more severe than the one which afflicted Gaius. For his was an illness of the body only, whereas theirs was a sickness of everyone everywhere, a threat to their mental well-being, their peace of mind, their hopes, and the sharing and enjoyment of the good times. [17] For they continually thought of the great and numerous troubles which arise from anarchy: famine, war, the laying waste and ravaging of the country, confiscation of property, abductions, fears of enslavement and death, untreatable fears for which there is no healer and only one cure – the recovery of Gaius.

[18] At any rate, when his sickness began to abate, even those who live as far as the ends of the world found out quickly (for nothing is faster than rumour) and every city was in suspense, continually thirsting for a better report, until his complete recovery was reported by visitors. On account of his recovery all continents, all islands, considering it their own personal salvation, turned back afresh to the same happiness as before. [19] For no one remembers so much joy being felt by any one country or race over the appointment and deliverance of its leader as was felt by the whole world over Gaius, both when he started his reign and when he recovered from his indisposition. [20] For they rejoiced as if they were beginning now for the first time to move from a roaming and brutish life to a life of community and shared interests; from a wilderness of pens on the mountainside to be settled in walled cities; and from an unprotected existence to be given a place under a guardian, a shepherd, as it were, and head of a civilised flock. But they rejoiced in ignorance of the truth, [21] because the human mind is blind to perceiving what is to its advantage, and it can only use conjecture and guesswork, rather than knowledge.

[Philo, *on the Embassy to Gaius* 14–21]

D4 Death of Tiberius Gemellus

After his recovery Gaius compelled three members of his innermost circle to commit suicide; Tiberius Gemellus, Marcus Silanus and Naevius Macro. Tiberius had made Gaius and Tiberius Gemellus his joint heirs. This will was annulled in order for Gaius to accede to the throne with the help of Macro and Gaius subsequently adopted Gemellus (Dio 59.8.1). Philo groups together the enforced suicides, suggesting that the three were connected. Macro and Silanus may have transferred their allegiance to Gemellus during Gaius' illness, which Gaius considered an act of betrayal when he recovered. Other sources hint at a plot centred around Gemellus involving Silanus (Dio 59.8.1–3; Suet. *Cal.* 23.3, 29.1) as well as agreeing with Philo's portrayal of Gaius' growing resentment towards Silanus' advice and interference (Dio 59.8.4–6). Agricola's father-in-law prosecuted a man named Marcus Silanus at this time, who could well be this character (Tac. *Agr.* 4.1). The three seem to have died towards the end of AD 37 or the beginning of AD 38.

[22] Anyway, the man who had recently been considered to be a saviour and benefactor, the one who would rain down new streams of blessings on both Asia and Europe, to the indestructible happiness of all, both as individuals and all together, immediately 'began from the sacred line', as the saying goes. He changed to savagery, or rather revealed the ferocity which he had veiled with a mask of hypocrisy. [23] He killed his cousin, who had been left as his equal partner in the empire and the more rightful successor (for Gaius was Tiberius' grandson by adoption, but his cousin was Tiberius' grandson by birth), alleging treachery, though his age would not allow such a charge: for the poor boy was just moving from childhood to adolescence. [24] Indeed, some men say that if Tiberius had lived a little longer, Gaius would have been put out of the way, having come under suspicions that could not be dispelled, and the true grandson would have been appointed the sole ruler and inheritor of his grandfather's power. [25] But Tiberius was snatched away by his destiny first, before he had brought his plans to their conclusion: and Gaius thought that by clever planning he would evade the criticism which would arise if he transgressed in his duty towards his partner.

[26] This was the stratagem he used: having collected together the men in authority, he said, "I wish to follow the decree of the deceased Tiberius, and to make him who is my cousin by birth, but my brother by affection, my partner in the imperial power: you observe, yourselves, that he is still a mere child in need of guardians, teachers,

and tutors. [27] For what greater blessing could there be than for the massive weight of rule not to weigh down on a single soul or one body, but to have someone able to lighten and relieve it? And I will exceed tutors, teachers, and guardians. I now appoint myself his father, and him my son."

[28] Having deceived those present and the lad himself with these words – for the adoption was a trap, not to give him the ruler's power he expected but to deprive him of the power he had already – Gaius plotted against his rightful co-heir and equal partner with considerable safety and paying no heed to anybody. For according to the Roman laws, absolute authority over the son lies with the father, even aside from the fact that his power as emperor meant he was not accountable to anyone, since no one had the boldness or the power to call any of his actions into question. [29] Just as in the wrestling ring, a champion takes on and throws down the challenger, so Gaius, showing no pity for their shared upbringing, their kinship or his youth, dispatched this unfortunate, short-lived lad, his fellow ruler and fellow heir, who had once been expected to be sole emperor. He was, after all, the one most closely related to Tiberius, and grandsons – when their fathers are dead – are counted like sons in their grandparents' eyes.

[30] It is said that he was even ordered to kill himself by his own hand, with a centurion and a military tribune as supervisors, who had been told not to take part in the sacrilege on the grounds that it was not permitted for the descendants of emperors to be destroyed at the hands of others. For in the midst of his lawless and impious deeds Gaius remembered law and piety, whilst making a parody of their true nature. But the lad was unskilled, for he had not seen anyone else killed nor had he yet trained in the armed exercises which, on account of ever-impending wars, are usually the preparatory training for boys being reared for leadership. First he stretched out his neck to those who had come and told them to kill him. [31] Then, when they did not do it, he took the sword himself and on account of his lack of experience and knowledge he asked the most likely spot, so that he might break off his wretched existence by a well-aimed strike. They, like teachers of misfortune, both told him and showed him the part where it was necessary to apply the sword. He, having been given his first and last lesson, became under compulsion his own murderer, unfortunate child.

[Philo, *on the Embassy to Gaius* 22–31]

D5 Death of Macro

Naevius Macro had been the Praetorian Prefect instrumental in securing Gaius' accession after Tiberius' death on 16 March AD 37, perhaps even to the extent of speeding up Tiberius' demise (Tac. *Ann.* 6.50.5; Dio 58.28.3–4). Macro liaised with the senate and ensured that Tiberius' will, in which he had left Gaius and his grandson Tiberius Gemellus as joint heirs, was annulled (Philo *Leg.* 23; *Flacc.* 10; Dio 59.1.1; Suet. *Cal.* 14.1). Macro was forced to commit suicide shortly after Tiberius Gemellus and his father-in-law Marcus Silanus were compelled to do the same in AD 37. It may well be the case that during Gaius' serious illness in the autumn of AD 37 Macro and Silanus, expecting Gaius to die, had transferred their allegiance to Gemellus, an act of conspiracy in the eyes of Gaius when he recovered (Dio 59.8.1–3; Suet. *Cal.* 23.3).

Macro's death is reported at very great length in Philo's *Leg.* 32–61. This shorter version comes from Philo's attack on A. Avitius Flaccus, who as prefect of Egypt (AD 32–38) had been pro-Greek and thus anti-Jewish. Flaccus had been condemned to death, perhaps somehow implicated in the 'conspiracy' against Gaius mentioned above.

[11] He had a friendship with Macro, who exerted complete influence over Gaius in the early days and who, according to report, had played a major role in his gaining power and, even more importantly, in his survival. [12] Tiberius had often been inclined to remove Gaius on the grounds that he was malicious and not naturally suited to rule, and also because of his fear for his grandson – he was afraid that Gemellus would become an extra burden to Gaius once he himself was dead. But each time Macro would remove his suspicions and praise Gaius as sincere, worthy and sociable, and especially inclined to defer to his cousin: as a result Gaius would surely be willing to yield the principate to him alone, or at least to give him the leading position.

[13] Taken in by these reports, Tiberius unwittingly left behind an implacable enemy to himself, his grandson, his family, to Macro who advocated his cause, and to all humanity. [14] For when Macro saw Gaius changing his habits and giving free rein to his impulses, wheresoever and whensoever they took him, he would chastise and advise him, believing that he was the same Gaius who had been so moderate and cooperative while Tiberius was still alive. But the ill-starred Macro paid the ultimate penalty for his too optimistic benevolence, when he was destroyed with his whole house, wife and children, as being superfluous, tiresome and annoying. [15] For whenever Gaius spotted him approaching in the distance, he would say this sort of thing to his companions: "Let us not smile, let us look serious. Here is our plain-speaking adviser, who has now begun to play tutor to a grown man and ruler just when he has dismissed and parted company with those who tutored him from early childhood."

[Philo, *against Flaccus* 11–15]

D6 Death of Silanus

Marcus Junius Silanus, suffect consul in AD 15 (**B15**) came from a family which had married into Augustus' own. At Augustus' death, his only male descendant (besides Agrippa Postumus) was the baby son of Silanus' cousin, Silanus Torquatus, and Aemilia Lepida, Augustus' great-granddaughter. Four more of their children survived into adulthood (see **J33**, Family Trees). Silanus was a close friend of Tiberius (Dio 58.9.5) and in AD 33, the emperor gave Silanus' daughter in marriage to Caligula (Tac. *Ann.* 6.20.1).

[62] When Macro too had been slaughtered, household and all, Gaius prepared himself for a third treacherous attack, an even more serious one. Marcus Silanus had been his father-in-law, a man full of spirit and distinguished in his descent. After his daughter died young, Silanus continued to pay attention to Gaius, showing a fondness more typical of a true father than of a father-in-law. He thought that in all fairness he would receive a like affection in return if he made his son-in-law like a son to him. But he was unaware how mistaken and badly deceived he was. [63] For he always offered the advice of a guardian, holding back nothing which could benefit and improve Gaius' character, lifestyle and leadership, especially since he had strong grounds for speaking freely in both his exceptionally noble lineage and his kinship with him by marriage. In fact his daughter had died not long before, with the result that the rights of her relatives had become obscured – had all but expired – though some last remnants of the breath of life existed within their body. [64] But Gaius took Silanus' advice as insolence, since he thought himself the wisest and most moderate of all men and also the most courageous and just, and hated his instructors more than his sworn enemies.

[65] So he got it into his head that Silanus was also a nuisance, who would block him having things entirely his own way. Then, dismissing any thought of his dead wife's spirits taking revenge on him for disposing of her father, who had become his own father-in-law, he treacherously killed him.

[Philo, *on the Embassy to Gaius* 62–65]

D7 Gaius likens himself to demigods and gods

Philo here begins a bitter tirade against Gaius, noting that he began to liken himself to and dress like demigods such as Heracles, Dionysus and the twins Castor and Pollux, and wearing their attributes in public. Philo's allegations that Gaius then moved on to imitate gods are repeated in other sources (Dio 59.26.5–7; Suet. *Cal.* 52). While this behaviour may appear strange to us, and appals the Jewish Philo, Gaius was considered a god by his subjects, particularly those in the east of the empire who were used to giving cult worship to their leaders.

[86] All these, Gaius, were and are even now esteemed on account of the good deeds they undertook and were considered worthy of worship and the highest honours. So tell me; have you done anything similar to make you puffed up with pride? [87] Did you imitate Castor and Pollux in their brotherly love? Where shall I begin? Your brother and co-heir you slaughtered in the first bloom of his manhood, you unfeeling and merciless monster, and your sisters you later exiled. Did they too really cause you to fear losing power? [88] Did you imitate Dionysus? Have you become an inventor of new delights, like he was? Did you fill the inhabited world with merriment? Can Asia and Europe not contain the gifts that have come from you?

[89] So as the instigator of general destruction and murder you discovered skills and sciences by which you changed pleasures and delights into cheerless sorrow and a life that all people everywhere found not worth living. Because of your unquenchable and insatiable greed you appropriated for yourself all good and fine things from east and west, and from the other regions of the whole world, whether to the south or the north. And in return you gave and sent them the products of your own bitterness and such harmful and noxious things as venomous and cursed souls habitually generate. Is it because of these things that you have been revealed to us as the new Dionysus? [90] Or was it Hercules you also rivalled, in your unwearied labours and untiring deeds of heroism, when you filled both continents and islands with good order and just dealing, with fertility and prosperity and an abundance of the other benefits which a secure peace brings about? Did you, you degenerate, you utter coward, you who emptied the cities of all that brings about health and happiness, and displayed them full of the causes of disorder and uproar and the height of misery?

[91] Tell me, Gaius, is it because of the great harvests you have produced – harvests of destruction – that you are seeking to gain a share of immortality, so that you may bring about disasters that are not short-term and ephemeral, but everlasting? I think the opposite – that even if you did seem to have become a god, you would at any rate change back to a mortal existence on account of your villainous practices. For if virtues confer immortality, vices are completely destructive. [92] So you are hardly to be counted with the Dioscuri, the most loving of brothers, since you became the death and ruin of your brothers. Nor are you to share the honour of Heracles or Dionysus who benefited the life of men, since you are an evil-doer and have corrupted what they achieved.

[93] So great a madness came over him, a frenzy which bedevilled and befuddled his mind, that passing by the demigods he went on to assail the honours paid to Hermes and Apollo and Ares, gods considered to be greater and divine on both sides. [94] To deal with Hermes first, he dressed up with staffs, sandals and mantles, displaying order in disorder, consistency in confusion, and method in his madness. [95] Then, whenever he pleased, he would take the one lot off, and change his appearance and trappings into Apollo's, putting crowns of the sun-rays on his head, taking a bow and arrows in his left hand, and holding out the Graces in his right, to show that it was proper for him to offer good things readily, and for these good things to be arranged in the better position on the right, whereas punishments should be less prominent and be allotted the inferior place on the left.

[96] Well-trained choirs immediately stood by, singing paeans to him, who just a little while before had been calling him Bacchus and Evius and Lyaeus and honouring him with hymns, when he took on the garb of Dionysus. [97] Often he would also put on a breastplate and advance with sword in hand, wearing helmet and shield, being addressed as Ares, and on each side the servants of the new Ares advanced with him, a company of cut-throats and public executioners, ready to offer their evil services to a master of murderous impulses and a great thirst for human blood.

[Philo, *on the Embassy to Gaius* 86–97]

Summary of 98–180: *After pointing out that Gaius was not like Hermes, Apollo or Ares (98–113), Philo presents the Alexandrian Greeks as using Gaius' dislike of Jewish religion to attack the Jews in Alexandria (114–139), making clear that the Jews had previously been content with Roman rule (140–161). The Jews only get an initial hearing despite the efforts of the freedman Helicon.*

D8 Philo's attempts to gain an audience with Gaius

As F. Millar has shown, the Roman empire worked on a 'petition and response' model. Provincials with a grievance could take their case directly to the *princeps.* But ambassadors also have to follow the *princeps* around and await their turn, and/or bribe imperial freedmen to gain an audience. Though Philo is outraged by the treatment of their embassy, here and in **D10**, 'it is merely an extreme instance of the fact that the work of an emperor was fitted into the framework of the leisured existence of an upper-class Roman.' (Millar, *Emperor in the Roman World*[2]*,* page 23).

[181] Initially Gaius welcomed us in the plain by the Tiber when he was leaving the Gardens of Agrippina. He returned our greeting and waved his right hand, suggesting a favourable response, and sent Homilus, the official in charge of receiving embassies with the message, "I will personally hear your case when I am free." As a result everyone in our group, and all those deluded by immediate appearances, rejoiced as if we had already succeeded. …

[185] We had come to the Bay of Naples from Rome, following Gaius to Puteoli as he switched between his many country estates. He had gone down to the seaside and was spending time in his luxurious villas.

[Philo, *on the Embassy to Gaius* 181 and 185]

D9 Gaius' proposed desecration of the Temple in Jerusalem

Rioting between the Greeks and Jews in Alexandria led Philo's embassy to Gaius. But while waiting to see Gaius, Philo's delegation meets others from Judaea concerned with the even more serious matter of Gaius' attempt to raise a statue of himself in the Jewish Temple.

[186] We were concentrating on our case, in the expectation of being summoned at any moment, when someone approached us, glancing around in panic with bloodshot eyes, and gasping for breath. He drew us a little way apart from some other people who were there, and said, "Have you heard the news?" ... [188] Sobbing and struggling for breath, he just about managed to say, "Our temple is no more: Gaius has ordered that a colossal statue of himself as Zeus be set up in the inner sanctuary."

[Philo, *on the Embassy to Gaius* 186 and 188]

***Summary of 189–348**: Philo explains what had prompted Gaius' proposals and the response to them. In Jamnia in Syria, the Greek residents of the city had set up an altar to the imperial cult, which the Jews tore down; Gaius retaliated by decreeing that the temple in Jerusalem be converted into an imperial shrine by having a statue erected in it of himself in the guise of Jupiter. The governor Petronius, realising that the measure would provoke a riot, urged the sculptors to take their time with the statue. In the meantime, he wrote to Gaius urging him to reconsider. Gaius insisted that Petronius continue. The end of the affair is unclear. One tradition reports that King Agrippa, a friend of Gaius, intervened and persuaded Gaius to give up the plan late in AD 40; another states that Gaius' death in January AD 41 ended the attempt. The whole affair is recorded at great length in* Leg. *184–348; Josephus,* JA *18.257–301.*

D10 Philo's embassy to Gaius

Philo here records the eventual meeting with Gaius opposite a Greek embassy. It occurred after Gaius' German expedition (*Leg.* 356), i.e. between September AD 40 and Gaius' assassination in January AD 41. Gaius' opening question to the delegation could suggest that the meeting occurred after the conclusion of the Temple affair. The substance of Philo's delegation was as follows. In AD 38 there had been a period of rioting between the Greeks and Jews of Alexandria. The cause of the riot was the peculiar status held by the Alexandrian Jews. They were not Alexandrian citizens, yet enjoyed many of the privileges enjoyed by Alexandrian citizens, and some which were not; their community was ruled by a council (*Flacc.* 74), whereas the Alexandrian Greeks were forbidden to convene one of their own. When the Alexandrian Jews paraded the Jewish King Agrippa I through the city in AD 38, the Greeks responded with violence to which the prefect Flaccus had allegedly turned a blind eye. He had also issued an edict declaring the Jews 'foreigners and aliens' and herded them into a section of the city. Thirty-eight members of the Jewish council were marched to the theatre, flogged, tortured, hanged and even crucified. Philo provides a full account in *Flacc.* 29–96 and *Leg.* 120–37.

Gaius replaced and executed Flaccus in AD 38–9 and may have considered the matter closed. Philo presents Gaius as a madman here, who was a hostile judge and mocking towards the Jews. He does admit, however, that Gaius did listen to the arguments presented by the Jews. The Jews wanted to discuss their 'sufferings and claims' i.e. what they had suffered in AD 38 and their status and position in Alexandria, which Flaccus had destroyed. The issue of the imperial cult was clearly discussed, and Josephus' version of the meeting also focuses on this (*JA* 257–60). Gaius' view that the Jews were not criminals, alongside Philo's preceding phrases ('God took pity on us and turned Gaius' heart to mercy' and Gaius 'became gentler') suggests that the Jewish exemption from the imperial cult was confirmed at least verbally. There is no evidence that Gaius dealt with the other issues concerned or sent his judgement to Alexandria in the form of a letter; perhaps his assassination prevented this. Claudius issued his own judgement on the matter in his letter sent to Alexandria in October AD 41 (see **M6**).

[349] It is right to record both what we saw and what we heard when we were summoned to contend in the debate about our citizenship. For as soon as we entered, we realised from his expression and his movement that we had not come before a judge but before an accuser, more hostile than those ranged against us. [350] For this is how a judge would act: first he would sit with councillors chosen on merit, for the subject under scrutiny was of great significance, having not been heard for four hundred years, but being brought up now for the first time to the detriment of hundreds of thousands of Alexandrian Jews. The opposing parties would stand on either side, with their advocates. The judge would hear in turn the prosecution and the

defence, each for the period of time measured by the water-clock. Then he would rise and consult with the council as to what verdict ought to be publicly given according to strict justice. But what he actually did, revealed the overbearing arrogance of a cruel tyrant. [351] Far from doing anything that I have just suggested, he sent for the stewards of the Gardens of Maecenas and the Gardens of Lamia, which were near to each other and to the city. He was spending three or four days there, and that was where the dramatic performance aimed at our whole nation was to be staged, to the grief of us who were present. And he gave orders that all the accommodation was to be opened up for him, for he wished to carry out a careful scrutiny of each property.

[352] When we were brought in to him, as soon as we saw him, we greeted him by bowing to the ground with complete respect and reverence, addressing him as Imperator Augustus. So moderately and benevolently did he respond that we abandoned hope not only for our case but for our lives! [353] For at once showing his teeth and snarling at us, he said "Are you the god-haters, the ones who don't believe I am a god, a god universally acknowledged among other nations but not to be named by you?" And stretching out his hands to heaven he uttered the start of a prayer, which it was a sin to listen to, let alone repeat verbatim.

[354] How great a joy immediately filled the ambassadors on the other side, who thought from Gaius' first words that their mission had already succeeded! They gesticulted, danced about and uttered blessings on him under the names of all the gods. [355] When he saw that Gaius was delighted to be addressed as being of superhuman nature, the hateful sycophant Isidorus said, " O Lord, you will hate these men here present and those who share their nationality even more if you understand their malice and disrespect to you. For when all men were bringing sacrifices of thanksgiving for your deliverance, these men alone could not bear to make sacrifice. And when I say 'these men' I include the other Jews also." [356] We cried out with one accord "Lord Gaius, we are being slandered: for we too sacrificed – sacrificed whole hecatombs at that, and we did not just pour out the blood on the altar and carry the flesh home for a feast and merrymaking, as is the custom for some to do, but gave the victims to the sacred fire to be burnt whole. And this we have already done three times, not once: first when you inherited the empire, second when you escaped that severe sickness which the whole inhabited world shared with you, and the third time in the hope of victory in Germany." [357] He said, "Granted this is true, you have sacrificed, but to another, even if it was on my behalf. So what good is it? For you have not sacrificed to me." Immediately a deep trembling fear gripped us when we heard this remark on top of his opening one, and this fear spread even to the point of being seen in our expressions.

[358] While he was saying this he was going through the rooms, himself surveying the men's quarters, the women's rooms, the chambers on the ground floor, those above, all of them, finding fault with some as defective in construction, but forming designs for others and giving further instructions on making them even more luxurious. [359] Then we were driven along, following him up and down, with our enemies mocking and jeering at us as in mimes at the theatre. For the whole situation was a sort of mime: the judge had adopted the role of the accuser, and the accusers the role of a poor judge, who has regard for his own hostility but not for the reality of the truth. [360] But when

it is the judge who accuses the man on trial – and so powerful a judge at that – it is necessary to be silent: for silence too can be a form of defence, and it was particularly so for us, since we were unable to respond to any of the points he was asking and pressing, because of our customs and laws checking our tongues and shutting and sewing up our mouths.

[361] When he had given some of his instructions about the buildings, he asked a very important and solemn question: "Why do you abstain from pork?" In response to the question again there was a great burst of laughter from the opposition, some out of sheer delight, others as a deliberate flattery, to make it seem that his remark had been delivered with style and wit. As a result some of the servants following the emperor were annoyed at the disrespect shown to the emperor, with whom even a measured smile is unsafe, except for those who are very close friends. [362] We replied, "Different things are lawful for different people, and the use of some is forbidden to our opponents, just as others are to us." And someone else said, "Just like many do not eat lamb, although it is very easily available." Gaius laughed and said "A good choice, at any rate, for it is not tasty."

[363] Belittled and jeered in such as way, we were helpless. Then eventually he said mockingly, "We want to learn what rights you claim concerning your citizenship." [364] We began to speak and tell him, but when he had had a taste of our plea in justification and realised that our case was not easily dismissed, he cut off our earlier arguments before we could bring in the stronger ones, and dashed off at full speed into a large chamber. He walked around it and gave orders for the windows around it to be restored with transparent stones resembling white glass, which do not block the light but check the wind and the blazing heat from the sun. [365] Then coming forward in a relaxed manner, he asked in a more measured tone, "What are you saying?" But when we began to continue with the points that came next, again he ran into another room, where he ordered original pictures to be put up.

[366] With our case so mangled and interrupted (indeed virtually knocked to pieces and crushed to death), we gave up hope. With no strength left, and all the time expecting nothing other than death, we no longer kept our souls in these bodies, but in our anguish they had gone forth out of us, to entreat the true God to restrain the anger of the one who falsely claimed that name. [367] And God, taking compassion on us, turned Gaius' spirit to pity: he relaxed into a more gentle mood and pronounced thus: "They seem to me to be unlucky people rather than wicked, and foolish in not believing that I have been allotted the nature of a god." Then he went off, ordering us to be gone too.

[Philo, *on the Embassy to Gaius* 349–367]

SECTION E

JOSEPHUS, *JEWISH ANTIQUITIES* 19.1–275

E1 Josephus and his writing in his own words

[20.259] This now concludes my account of *Jewish Antiquities* and I shall turn my attention to the *Jewish War*. My first volume has covered the whole period from the origins of man until the twelfth year of Nero's reign, and gives a full record of all that happened to the Jewish nation in Egypt, Syria, and Palestine, [260] their sufferings at the hands of the Assyrians and the Babylonians, and the brutalities meted out to them by the Persians, the Macedonians, and after them by the Romans. I believe that I have given an accurate and comprehensive full account of all these events.

[263] My Jewish contemporaries all agree that my knowledge of Jewish history and custom is far superior to their own. I have also made it my business to develop a wide knowledge of Greek learning and literature, having made a detailed study of the language. But my own regular use of the Jewish tongue has prevented me from achieving total accuracy in spoken Greek.

[267] At this point I now conclude my *Jewish Antiquities*. It consists of sixty thousand lines in twenty volumes. If heaven so wills it, I shall in due course compose a chronological account of the war and subsequent events up to the present day – namely the thirteenth year of the reign of Domitian Caesar and the fifty-sixth year of my own life.

[Josephus, *Jewish Antiquities* 20.259–60, 263, 267]

Joseph, a priest from Jerusalem, first came to prominence as an ambassador to Nero. He was a commander for the Jews in the Jewish revolt of AD 66–73. When his company was trapped by the Romans, they decided on a collective suicide pact. The Jews drew lots and killed each other. Josephus, almost certainly through manipulating the process, was the sole survivor and later surrendered to the Roman forces led by Vespasian and Titus. He acted as a negotiator for the Romans during the siege of Jerusalem in AD 70 and this earned him the favour of the Flavian dynasty. He was given Roman citizenship, as Flavius Iosephus, and a generous pension, which allowed him to complete his historical and apologetic treatises. The *Jewish War*, the account of the revolt of AD 66–73, was written around AD 75; *Jewish Antiquities* was written around AD 94. His latest work was an autobiography written around AD 99.

Introduction to *Jewish Antiquities* 19.1–275

Josephus presents here the story of the final conspiracy against Gaius. His reign had been marred by plots and attempted coups starting as early as AD 37 when he saw fit to execute his adopted son, Tiberius Gemellus, his father-in-law, Marcus Junius Silanus, and his Praetorian Prefect, Macro. A more serious attempt followed in AD 39, involving his brother-in-law, Marcus Lepidus and the governor of Upper Germany, Gaetulicus. The more frequent executions of senators and equestrians during AD 40 could perhaps be due to Gaius' growing paranoia or an increase in the number of plots; Josephus' accounts suggests several conspirators were working independently during AD 40–41.

Josephus' account focuses on the role of Cassius Chaerea, a tribune in the Praetorian Guard. His motives are presented as an honourable desire to end the reign of a tyrant and restore liberty to the Romans and personal dislike for Gaius. It is Chaerea who inspires his wavering fellow conspirators to act and who plays a role in the actual killing. After relating the story of Claudius' accession, Josephus presents the execution of the brave Chaerea, who insisted he be killed with the same sword which he had used to kill Gaius (Jos. *AJ* 18.267–271).

However many scholars do not accept the portrayal of the heroic Chaerea as historically plausible. A return to the 'liberty' of the Republican era was perhaps an aspiration of some senators; but Rome had now been under the rule of one man for seventy years and any senator who knew his history would not want to return to the civil wars which had marred the late Republic. In all likelihood Chaerea was part of a coup to replace Gaius. Many leading senators of the day could have been the real driving force behind the assassination of Gaius: Annius Vinicianus, Valerius Asiaticus, Paulus Arruntius, or even Gaius' uncle Claudius (on whom see the footnotes below). Perhaps chosen as a scapegoat because his name evoked the assassin of Julius Caesar (Gaius Cassius Longinus), Chaerea was then discarded by his sponsor in the aftermath of the assassination.

Whatever faults, inconsistencies and errors are contained within Josephus' account it is the earliest surviving testament to these events, written before Suetonius' biography, Tacitus' missing historical account and Cassius Dio's third century history. Its importance is elevated by the clear use of a contemporary source; parts of the work, such as the events described in the theatre, clearly come from an eyewitness account. Josephus' source is likely to be a senator present at the assassination of Gaius named Marcus Cluvius Rufus. Rufus was a member of Nero's court and was governor of Spain during the civil war of AD 69. He composed his Histories, which survive only fragments cited by later writers, under Vespasian. Josephus describes a 'Clavition' (emended to Cluvius) as present in the theatre on the day of Gaius' death and this is generally believed to be the historian Rufus. Tacitus used Rufus' histories as a source for some events in Nero's reign (Tac. *Ann.* 13.20.3; 14.2.4). If Rufus' work did cover the reign of Gaius too, then it is likely to have been a hostile account (see **R11**).

E2 Josephus' introduction: Gaius' madness

[1] Gaius' madness was now an offence to god and man. He showed it not only in his sacrilegious conduct towards the Jews in Jerusalem and all the surrounding territory, but also exported it to infect every land and sea which was subject to the rule of Rome, inflicting on all of them innumerable misfortunes to a degree unprecedented in recorded history.[1] [2] Rome herself above all became only too aware of the sheer horror of his actions, since he afforded her no special treatment compared with other cities. He plundered and laid waste her citizens, but in particular the senate and those of its members who were patricians or highly respected for their distinguished ancestry. [3] He also devised innumerable attacks upon the so-called *equites*, men whose status and financial power gave them a prestige equivalent to that of the senate in the eyes of ordinary citizens, since it was from them that senators were recruited. He would take away their privileges, order them into exile, put them to death and confiscate their property – indeed, the motive for such executions was usually in order to seize their possessions.[2]

E3 Gaius usurps divine honours

[4] His own deification was going to be his next step, since he was now claiming from his subjects honours no longer appropriate for mortal men. When he visited the temple of Jupiter, known as the Capitol and the most sacred of all Rome's temples,

[1] Gaius' 'madness' is a reference to his despatching the governor Petronius to Syria in the autumn of AD 39 with the brief to erect Gaius' statue in the Temple in Jerusalem, thereby desecrating it for the Jews whose beliefs prevented them from worshipping the emperor. (Jos. *JA* 18.257–309; Philo *Leg.*186–337).

[2] Other sources support Josephus' depiction of a reign of terror, attributing to Gaius many acts of torture, exile, compelled suicides and executions: at least a dozen senatorial victims are known by name: see **T3–T12, D4–D6, P5**. For the position of senators and equestrians, see introduction to section **U**.

he brazenly addressed the God as his brother.[3] [5] His other actions were no less symptomatic of his madness. He decided that it was simply unacceptable to take a trireme to make the crossing from Puteoli, a coastal city in Campania, to Misenum. [6] Since he was lord of the ocean, he felt entitled to demand the same sort of service from the sea as he did from the land. So he built a bridge nearly four miles long to link the two promontories and enclose the whole bay, and then he drove across it in his chariot. Since he was a god, he observed, that was the right and proper way for him to travel. [4]

[7] There was not a temple in Greece that he left un-plundered. All their paintings, sculptures, and other statuary and dedicatory offerings he ordered to be collected and brought to him, insisting that it was wrong for beautiful objects to be anywhere except in the most beautiful place in the world – and that just happened to be Rome.[5] [8] With all this material looted from Greece he adorned his palace and gardens and all his other properties throughout the land of Italy. He even dared to give orders for the statue of Zeus by Pheidias, the Athenian, which was worshipped by the Greeks at Olympia and therefore known as the 'Olympian Zeus', to be brought to Rome.[6] [9] In this he failed. The architects told Memmius Regulus, who had been tasked with moving the statue, that any attempt to do so would destroy it. Reports say that this was why Memmius postponed the removal, but that he was also influenced by a series of portents too powerful to be ignored. [10] He explained all this in a letter of apology to Gaius for his failure to carry out his instructions. It would probably have cost him his life, but he was saved by the fact that Gaius died first.[7]

[11] His madness was so far advanced that when his daughter was born he carried her up to the temple of Capitoline Jupiter and placed her upon the knees of the statue, declaring that she was the child of both himself and Jupiter and that he had decided that she had two fathers, but he refused to say which of them was the greater. [12] That was the sort of activity that everyone had to put up with.[8]

E4 Informers

He even allowed domestic slaves to make accusations against their masters on whatever grounds they wished. Whatever the accusations, they were all equally deadly, since most of them were designed to please the emperor and had been instigated by him. [13] Polydeuces, for example, a slave of Claudius', had the nerve

---

[3] Gaius took a particular interest in Jupiter, which Aurelius Victor (*Caes*. 3.10) claims was the origin of Gaius' incestuous interest in his sisters. Gaius allegedly liked to be addressed as Jupiter Latiaris, a version of Jupiter worshipped from Rome's early days (Dio 59.28.5; Suet. *Cal*. 22.2). Gaius also seems to have started to build a house for himself in front of this temple of Jupiter and began a bridge from the Capitol to the Palatine, where he resided (**L14**, Suet. *Cal*. 22.4; Dio 59.28.2). Gaius may have erected a statue of himself in the temple as an offering to Jupiter.

[4] Suet. *Cal*.19.1, Dio 59.17.1 and Sen. *Brev. Vit*. 18.5 = **T10** also report this.

[5] Pausanias 9.27.3 reveals that a bronze statue by Lysippus, the Eros, was taken from Thespiae. Philo *Leg*. 365 = **D10** shows Gaius arranging for pictures to be hung in one of his villas.

[6] Dio 59.28.3 and Suet. *Cal*. 22.2 suggest that Gaius intended to replace the head of Zeus with his own image and make this, one of the seven wonders of the world, into the cult statue in a temple for himself.

[7] For Regulus' career, see **U4**. The history following a 'reign of terror' is often full of such stories of narrow escapes from death. Gaius' death is alleged to have also saved Petronius the governor of Syria (Jos. *JA* 18.304–309).

[8] Gaius' daughter Julia Drusilla by his last wife Milonia Caesonia (**J15**) was born in AD 39 shortly after their marriage (Dio 59.23.7; Suet. Cal. 25.3–4).

to lay charges against him. Gaius found it perfectly acceptable to attend the hearing against his own uncle on what amounted to a capital charge, because of course he was hoping for an opportunity to get rid of him, though it did not work out like that for him.[9] [14] He had by now filled the whole world of which he was the emperor with informers and wicked men, creating an extensive slave-tyranny over their owners. As a result, conspiracies were becoming commonplace. Some were motivated by bitterness and a desire for vengeance for sufferings endured; others because they intended to eliminate the man before some random circumstance brought death to themselves.

E5 God's providence

[15] His end came at a critical moment for the general rule of law and the happiness of all mankind. Our own nation was teetering on the very brink of disaster and would have been totally destroyed had it not been for his sudden demise. [16] But in addition to that, his downfall offers excellent proof of the power of God and gives comfort to all those who are who are afflicted by any form of adversity. As for those who think that the good times will never end, it offers a sharp reminder that good fortune unaccompanied by virtue always turns out badly in the end. So for all those reasons I intend to give a detailed and accurate account of all that happened.

E6 Conspiracies against Gaius

[17] There were three different plans for the assassination of the emperor, each of them under the leadership of a good man. One group was led by Aemilius Regulus, a native of Spanish Corduba, who was eager to get rid of Gaius personally, or with the help of his team. [18] A second group, led by the military tribune Cassius Chaerea, was being put together to support them. A significant addition to those plotting against the tyranny was Annius Vinicianus.[10]

[19] The reasons for their hatred varied. For Regulus it was a general sense of outrage and a hatred of the injustice of Gaius' actions. Temperamentally hot-tempered and a man of independent spirit, he was therefore reluctant even to conceal their plans and, as a result, communicated their intentions to many of his friends as well as any others who seemed to him to be men of action.[11] [20] Vinicianus joined the conspiracy because he wanted revenge for the Lepidus affair.[12] Lepidus had been one of his closest friends and one of the best of Romans, but Gaius had put him to death. He also feared for his own safety, since once Gaius developed one of his regular vendettas, it

---

[9] Other members of the imperial family and Gaius' entourage fared poorly during his reign. His cousin and adopted son Gemellus and his father-in-law Marcus Junius Silanius were compelled to commit suicide (**D4**, **D5**; Suet. *Cal.* 23.3; Dio 59.8.1–4); Marcus Lepidus (**J20**) was executed (Sen. *Ep.* 4.7; Dio 59.22.6–7); his sisters Agrippina (**J21**) and Livilla (**J23**) were exiled (Suet. *Cal.* 29.1; Dio 59.22.8), as was Gaius' friend Tigellinus Ophonius (Dio 59.23.9); Sextus Pompeius was starved to death (Sen. *Tranq.* 11.10). Suet. *Claud.* 9.1 refers to Claudius being hounded by prosecutions. Presumably Gaius did not consider Claudius important enough to warrant removal.

[10] Josephus implies here that the three groups were working together although his account later contradicts this. Dio names Chaerea and a tribune named Cornelius Sabinus as the main forces behind this conspiracy (Dio 59.29.1).

[11] Regulus is otherwise unknown and not mentioned later in Josephus' narrative.

[12] Marcus Aemilius Lepidus was Gaius' brother-in-law (see **J20**).

meant death for all alike.[13] [21] Chaerea felt deeply offended by the insults regularly cast upon his manhood by the emperor. As he had also been a close personal assistant to Gaius and therefore daily at risk, he regarded it as the duty of a free man to bring about his demise.[14] [22] But the three also agreed that their plans should be discussed by all those who had witnessed the sacrilegious madness of the emperor and were eager to eliminate him, so as to avoid the dire emergency which threatened others. If all went well, it would be a noble achievement to have launched such a great enterprise for the safety of the city and the empire, even if it brought about their own deaths. [23] Chaerea was the one most eager to press ahead with their plans. He was eager to remedy the slur to his reputation, but as tribune he also had unrestricted access to Gaius, and therefore would have the best opportunity to kill him.

[24] This was the time when the chariot races were being held – a spectacle which is immensely popular with the Roman people. They flock enthusiastically to the Circus Maximus and large groups of them petition the emperors for whatever they want. Those emperors who decide that their demands are irresistible are naturally very popular.[15] [25] On this occasion they were making desperate requests to him to reduce taxes and grant some relief from the serious burden they entailed. But he would have none of it, and as the shouts grew louder and louder he sent his officials into different parts of the crowd with orders to arrest those who were shouting, drag them forward, and execute them immediately.[16] [26] He issued the order; those so instructed carried it out. The victims of this barbarity were very numerous. As for the people, when they saw what happened they controlled themselves and stopped shouting, since they could see with their own eyes that any such petitions for financial help could only lead to their own deaths. [27] This served only to fire even further Chaerea's determination to launch his attempt and to put an end to Gaius' brutal savagery towards his fellow men. There were many occasions at banquets when he had been on the point of action, but on balance had judged it better to hold back. He no longer had any doubts about the decision to kill the emperor, but was still waiting for the ideal opportunity. He had no desire to take the plunge and then fail; he wanted complete success for his plans.

E7 Cassius Chaerea

[28] By now Chaerea had a long record of military service, though his close association with the emperor gave him no pleasure at all. But then Gaius put him in charge of collecting taxes and all the other revenues that were owing to the imperial treasury, but were now overdue because their rates had been doubled. So he contrived his own method of delaying the collection rather than following the emperor's

---

13 Vinicianus' name suggests a family link with Gaius' brother-in-law, Marcus Vinicius, the husband of Livilla. He was accused of treason in AD 32 together with his father Annius Pollio (Tac. *Ann.* 6.9.3–4) and later joined Camillus Scribonianus' conspiracy against Claudius (Dio 60.15.1). Given this, he is likely to have been a more important figure than Josephus suggests and perhaps replacing Gaius was his motivation.

14 Chaerea had distinguished himself as a centurion during the mutiny on the Rhine which followed Augustus' death in AD 14 (Tac. *Ann.* 1.32.5). He had now been promoted to a tribunate of the Praetorian guard (Suet. *Cal.* 56.2) in command of one of the nine cohorts of the guard.

15 These are possibly the *ludi Romani*, held annually between the 4–19 September, the last five days of which were given to chariot racing.

16 Gaius is reported to have increased taxes but not to have doubled them (Suet. *Cal.* 40–1; Dio 59 28.8–11).

instructions to the letter. [29] Because of his sensitive approach and sympathy for those who were the victims of these exactions he enraged Gaius, who denounced his dilatory approach to tax collection as pathetic. He heaped insults upon him and whenever as duty officer he asked for the password of the day, Gaius would give him words with female associations, many of them obscene. [30] This was a case of the pot calling the kettle black, since Gaius himself had dubious connections with certain cult rituals, which he had himself instituted. He would put on women's clothes and devise wigs and other female disguises to make himself look like a woman. But that did not stop him having the gall to embarrass Chaerea for the same "offences."[17] [31] Every time he was given the password, Chaerea was enraged by this, the more so when he passed it on and was laughed at by his fellow officers who received it from him. In fact they devised a game in which they would call out some appropriately offensive word, whenever he was about to go and collect it.[18] [32] All this inspired Chaerea to collect allies for his plans, since he had every reason to feel outrage.

E8 The actress Quintilia

There was a man of senatorial rank called Pompedius, who had held almost every official position, but followed the Epicurean philosophy and lived a life of calculated non-involvement in public affairs.[19] [33] He had an enemy, one Timidius, who denounced him for speaking of the emperor in insulting terms.[20] He summoned as a witness Quintilia, one of the acting fraternity, but one whose remarkable beauty was widely admired, not least by Pompedius. [34] But she thought that to give evidence against her lover would be a terrible thing, since the charge was false and would certainly lead to his death. When she refused to testify, Timidius called for torture with the enthusiastic support of Gaius, who ordered Chaerea to get on with it immediately and put her to the test. He used to employ Chaerea for murder cases and any others that required evidence under torture, on the calculation that he would carry out his duties with particular severity, so as to avoid the accusation of effeminacy.

[35] On her way to the torture Quintilia pressed the foot of one of the conspirators to encourage him to keep his nerve and not to be afraid that she would break under the pain. She would endure it with the courage of a man. The torture, inflicted by Chaerea unwillingly but under compulsion from his superior, was excruciating. But she gave nothing away and when they brought her back to Gaius, the very sight of her appalled all those who saw her. [36] Even Gaius felt a modicum of pity for her, when he saw how terribly disfigured she had been by her sufferings. He dismissed the charge against both her and Pompedius, and honoured her with a gift of money,

---

17 Gaius introduced various mystery religions into Rome. His dressing as goddesses (e.g. Dio 59.26.5–10 and 26.7 as a Maenad, a follower of Bacchus) and other gods (**D7**) probably belong in the context of the initiation ceremonies of these cults.

18 As well as criticising Chaerea's ability to collect taxes efficiently, Gaius allegedly mocked his voluptuousness and effeminacy, see **P6b**, also Suet. *Cal.* 56.2; Dio 59.29.2; Pausanias 9.27.3.

19 Named as Pomponius in Dio 59.26.4, unnamed in Suet. *Cal.*16.4; perhaps the Pompeius Pennus of **T9**.

20 Perhaps 'Timinius', a better attested Roman name.

as compensation for the ruin of her mutilated beauty and the unbearable suffering she had endured.[21]

E9 Chaerea tries to enlist Clemens the praetorian prefect

[37] All this caused Chaerea the utmost distress, since he felt personally responsible for the sufferings of those whom even Gaius felt deserved sympathy. He spoke to Clemens, the praetorian prefect, and Papinius a military tribune like himself.[22] [38] "Well, Clemens," he said, "at least in our capacity as the emperor's guards we have done everything possible to keep him safe. Of those who have formed conspiracies against his rule, thanks to our forethought and hard work we have slain some, and tortured others so brutally that even he felt pity for them. In fact, we are perfect examples of military virtue."

[39] Clemens said nothing. But he blushed and showed by his look that he was thoroughly ashamed of the orders he had carried out, though concern for his own safety made him reluctant to risk referring directly to the madness of the emperor. [40] It was enough, however, to encourage Chaerea to speak openly and without regard for the risks as he catalogued the dire state of affairs in Rome and the empire. [41] He pointed out that though Gaius might be nominally responsible for such abuses, if they were honest enough to face the truth, it was clear where responsibility really lay.[23] "I tell you, Clemens," Chaerea continued, "it is I and Papinius here, and you more than either of us, who are responsible for torturing the people of Rome and indeed the whole of mankind. We cannot claim that we are simply following Gaius' orders; [42] it is by our own choice, if we act as his agents in committing such atrocities upon our fellow citizens and subject peoples, when it is perfectly possible for us to put a stop to it. We are not real soldiers; we are simply his bodyguards and public executioners. We are not bearing arms in defence of the freedom and empire of the Roman people; we are guarding the life of a tyrant, who has reduced the lives and minds of his people to slavery. And in so doing we have become an offence to heaven for the daily slaughter and torture of our people.

But the time will surely come, when another of the emperor's minions will inflict the self same fate upon ourselves. [43] For in his attitude towards us, Gaius will not make decisions out of gratitude for what we have done. His suspicions will be what count, and these will increase in proportion to the number of murders he has perpetrated. There will never be an end to the mad frenzy of his killings, since he is not motivated by a desire for justice, but pleasure. We shall end up as human shields, there for target practice, when our duty demands that we should be making plans for public safety and

---

[21] This tale, which Dio and Suetonius present as a plot against Gaius is presented by Josephus as separate from Chaerea's own. According to Suetonius, an unnamed freedwoman, probably Quintilia, received 800,000 sesterces as compensation for her torture, and if the identification with Pompeius Pennus is correct, 'Pompedius' kissed Gaius' golden sandal in gratitude (**T9**). On Gaius' penchant for torture see Suet. *Cal.* 27–28, 30.1 and **T5–T6**.

[22] Marcus Arrecinus Clemens was commander of the guard at this time (Tac. *Hist.* 68.2; Suet. *Tit.* 4.2). This Papinius may be a relative of the Papinius executed by Gaius (**P5b** and note).

[23] Josephus presents this episode to highlight Chaerea's bravery. However Suet. *Cal.* 56.1 states that the praetorian prefects knew about the plot, Dio 59.29.1 names Clemens as a conspirator, and Claudius later saw fit to replace him as praetorian prefect.

the defence of freedom, while at the same time taking decisions for our own security from danger."[24]

[44] Clemens clearly approved of what Chaerea had in mind, but he urged him to be discreet in case the news leaked out. It would be best if such confidential matters were prevented from reaching a wider audience before its success was complete. If the conspiracy became generally known, they would suffer the consequences; he would prefer to leave everything till time brought some real hope of success. Sooner or later they were bound to get a lucky break. [45] "But," he explained, "old age prevents me personally from taking part in such a risky venture. As for the plans, which you have devised and described to me, it might be possible for me to suggest something less risky, but how could anyone come up with anything more admirable?"

E10 Clemens approaches Sabinus, a military tribune

[46] So Clemens went off, thinking about what he had heard and reviewing his own response to it. Chaerea, on the other hand, was deeply alarmed and hurried off to Cornelius Sabinus, one of his fellow tribunes, whom he knew very well to be an admirable man, a champion of liberty, and for that reason thoroughly dissatisfied with the present state of affairs.[25] [47] He was eager to get on with the plans he had already decided upon, but thought it a good idea to include Sabinus. He was also afraid that Clemens might let the news leak out, especially since he regarded delays and procrastination as a sign of lack of real commitment. [48] Sabinus was delighted by the whole idea. He had already reached the same conclusion, but had not known whom he could safely confide in and had therefore kept quiet about his support for their ideas. But now that he had chanced upon someone who had shown that he would not only conceal what he had been told, but had also made clear his own intentions, he was all the more enthusiastic and begged Chaerea to avoid any further delay.

E11 Clemens enlists Vinicianus

[49] They turned next to Vinicianus, very much a kindred spirit in the quality of his principles and the high ideals by which he lived. But as far as Gaius was concerned he was suspect, because of the death of Lepidus, since they had been close friends, and this made Vinicianus fear the worst at his hands. [50] Gaius was, of course, a source of terror to all those in high positions, since he was never likely to hold back from some mad attack upon any or all of them. [51] They were all very well aware of each others' dislike of the present situation, but through fear of the danger they hesitated to share with one another directly their true feelings and their loathing for Gaius. But indirectly they understood how much they all hated him, and so in matters of mutual interest they continued to feel the utmost goodwill towards one another.

[52] After an exchange of pleasantries when they met, Vinicianus was allowed as usual to chair the meeting by virtue of his distinguished position, since he was an aristocrat of the highest nobility, and because he was universally admired, especially in discussions of policy. [53] He opened the proceedings by asking Chaerea

---

[24] Upon his execution for conspiracy, Betelienus Capito had named Gaius' companions and prefects as his fellow conspirators (Dio 59 25.7–8; compare Suet. *Cal.* 56.1).

[25] Dio 59.29.1 and Suet. *Cal.* 58.2 give Sabinus and Chaerea equal importance in the formation of the plot.

what password he had received for the day, since the insults he had endured on the password issue were notorious throughout the city.

[54] Chaerea laughed, and did not hesitate to reciprocate the trust Vinicianus had shown in agreeing to meet with them like this. "For me," he said, "the password *you* have given us is 'Freedom,' and I am grateful to you for your inspiration to even greater efforts than I can inspire in myself.[26] [55] With your support I need no further words to urge me on; we are of one mind before the meeting has even started. I am only armed with a single sword, but that will be enough for both of us. [56] So let us act; let us get on with the job. Take the lead; order me anywhere you like, and I will go there. I have total faith in your help and support. For men who have committed themselves to action, there is no such thing as shortage of cold steel; for when action calls, it is courage that steels men's hearts. [57] I have launched myself into this endeavour with no thought for what may happen to myself. Time is too short to scrutinise the dangers to myself. All my thoughts are focused on the pain I feel at the enslavement of my country, which was once a bastion of freedom, at the ruination of our most precious tradition of the rule of law, and, thanks to Gaius, at the destruction of all mankind. [58] You have clearly judged me and found me worthy of your trust, since our minds are as one and you have not abandoned me. May I prove worthy of your trust."

[59] Vinicianus recognised the sheer intensity of his words, embraced him warmly, and offered every encouragement to his audacity. Having praised and embraced him again, he sent him off with prayers and entreaties to the gods. [60] Some people insist that their prayers were heard. For, as Chaerea was going into the senate house, a voice was heard from the crowd shouting encouragement and urging him on to action and bidding him finish his task and make heaven as his ally. [61] They say that Chaerea at first thought that one of the conspirators had betrayed him and that he was about to be arrested. But in the end he realised that the cry was to encourage him, though he never knew whether one of the conspirators was sending him a warning or the voice of God, who watches over the affairs of men, was seeking to bolster his courage. [62] The news of the conspiracy was now widely known, and everybody present at the senate house was armed, senators, equestrians, and those of the military who were in on the plot. There was no one present who would have not have regarded the death of Gaius as the greatest blessing.[27]

E12 Callistus

[63] For that reason and to the best of their ability, each man was eager not to let the show down through lack of the necessary courage. All were committed to the execution of the tyrant with all the determination and strength, whether of word or deed, of which they were capable. [64] This included even Callistus, one of Gaius' freedmen, whose power had reached the pinnacle of any single man's capacity

---

[26] Julius Caesar's assassin Brutus had used this as a password at the battle of Philippi (Dio 47.43.1).

[27] Yet, from the remaining narrative, the plot cannot have been as widely known as is suggested here.

and matched that of the tyrant himself.[28] [65] He had reached this position of unprecedented authority by terrorising all and sundry and by the acquisition of enormous wealth through bribery and an arrogant contempt for any individual. Above all, he fully understood the psychology of Gaius, his ruthlessness, and his implacable refusal to listen to any plea in mitigation, once he had found someone guilty. Nor had he any illusions about the danger he was in personally for many reasons, but in particular because of his great wealth.

[66] This was why he even began to pay court to Claudius, secretly shifting his allegiance to him, in the hope that the empire would pass to Claudius if Gaius were eliminated. He wanted to lay the foundations for his own future position and the equivalent of his present power by building up a credit account of favours done and kind words exchanged. [67] He even risked spreading the news that he had been ordered to get rid of Claudius by poison, but had found numerous ways of getting round his instructions. [68] It was a story which, I suspect, was invented by Callistus as part of his campaign to win over Claudius, since if Gaius had once decided to do away with him he would have refused to tolerate Callistus' excuses. As for Callistus himself, if he had been ordered to do the deed, he would have regarded it as perfectly acceptable; and if he had failed to carry out his master's orders to the last detail, he would have reaped the inevitable reward on the spot. [69] For myself, I see the hand of God in Claudius' escape from the crazed attentions of Gaius, and I believe that Callistus was pretending to have done Claudius a favour, when in fact he had done nothing of the sort.[29]

E13 Procrastination

[70] Chaerea's fellow conspirators kept putting off the action from day to day, because many of them lacked the nerve to strike. Chaerea himself would never willingly have tolerated any postponement, since he regarded all opportunities as good enough for action.[30] [71] And there were many such opportunities, for example, when Gaius went up to the Capitol to make sacrifices for his daughter. While he was standing on the palace roof throwing gold and silver coins down to the crowds, a simple push would have sent him headlong, since the roof overlooking the forum is very high; or again during the celebration of the cult rituals, which Gaius himself had set up. [72] On those occasions his mind was completely focused on the proper conduct of the ritual, and he was blindly confident that there would not be any attempt on his life. As long as no divine power protected the emperor from meeting the fatal blow, [73] Chaerea was certain that, whether he himself were armed or not, he would have the strength to dispose of Gaius. But he was exasperated by the hesitations of his fellow conspirators, fearing that they were letting their opportunities slip away.

---

[28] The freedman Gaius Julius Callistus was to become one of Claudius' most influential advisers (**S25–S27**; Tac. *Ann.* 11.38, 12.1–2). Tac. *Ann.* 11.29 suggests that Callistus had played a major role in this final conspiracy against Gaius in Tacitus' missing account. Dio 59.29.1 and Suet. *Cal.* 56.1 attest his importance at this time.

[29] Gaius cannot have considered Claudius a serious threat or he would have removed him, as Josephus states. Callistus was possibly involved in a plot to make Claudius emperor but may simply have cultivated potential future alliances in order to preserve his influential position.

[30] Josephus describes the delays of several months here.

[74] They understood that his only ambition was the restoration of the rule of law, and that his sense of urgency was entirely for their own good. Nevertheless, they urged on him at least some small further delay, for fear that something might go wrong with the plan and the whole city be turned upside down in the search for all those who had been privy to the plot, while any future attempts however brave, would find no opening, since Gaius would have taken even more elaborate precautions against them. [75] The best thing, they suggested, would be to make the attempt during the celebration of the Palatine Games. They are held in honour of Augustus, the first Caesar to transfer power from the people to himself. A covered scaffolding structure is set up a little in front of the palace and the Roman nobility, their wives and children, and Caesar himself watch the ceremonies from there.[31] [76] With tens of thousands of other spectators crammed together in such a small area, they said, it would be easy for them to launch their attack on him as he entered and there would be no way in which his bodyguards could help him, even if any of them wanted to do so.[32]

[77] Chaerea accepted this reluctantly and it was agreed to make the attempt on the first day of the forthcoming festival. But Chance proved stronger than their intentions and imposed a number of delays, with the result that they missed the normal three appointed days of the festival and were hard put to it achieve their objective on the final day of its extended programme.[33] [78] In the end, Chaerea called the conspirators together and delivered a short speech. "The time," he said, "which we have already wasted by putting off our heroic venture is a disgrace to us all. But it will be even more terrible if the news leaks out and the whole plan collapses. Gaius' brutality will become even worse. [79] Don't we realise that every extra day we allow to his tyranny is another day stolen from the freedom of our people? It is our duty in future to be fearless, and by winning for others the gift of everlasting freedom, to make ourselves the object of wonder and honour for future generations."

[80] They could not deny that he was absolutely right, but were unable to bring themselves to act immediately; they simply stood there in miserable silence. Chaerea spoke again. "My noble friends, why are we still hesitating? Can't you see that this is the last day of the festival and Gaius is about to set sail?" [81] (He was in fact getting ready to sail for Alexandria to make a tour of Egypt). "He is a reproach to the glorious name of Rome. It cannot be right to let him slip through our fingers, to go strutting arrogantly over land and sea.[34] [82] We would be rightly condemned if it was some Egyptian that found his arrogance too much for free men to endure and carried out his execution in our place.[35] [83] Well I for my part can't stand any more of your prevarication; I shall go to face the danger this very day and accept the outcome, whatever it may be, with a high heart. Even if I could, I would not put it off any longer.

31 This temporary stage was set up in front of the complex of houses which formed the imperial property.

32 The *ludi Palatini* (Suet. *Cal.* 56.2) were instituted by Livia in honour of the deified Augustus. The three-day festival began on January 17 (the wedding anniversary of Augustus and Livia) on the Palatine hill.

33 Dio 59.29.6 reports that Gaius extended the festival by three days in order to allow himself to perform in a tragedy. This would bring the date to 22 January. However Suet. *Cal.* 58.1 records the date of his assassination as 24 January, making this the eighth day. Assuming Dio is correct about the additional three days, perhaps the festival had already been extended to five days before AD 41.

34 Suet. *Cal.* 49.2, Philo *Leg.* 172, 250–3, 338 report this proposed visit. January would have been an odd time to sail but Philo states that he intended to follow a coastal route, spending each night on land.

35 Egyptians were stereotyped by Greek and Roman writers as uncultured and uncivilised.

Nothing could be more shameful for any man's sense of honour than that another man should kill the emperor, while he himself remained alive, robbed for ever of the honour for such a glorious deed."

E14 The start of the last day of the Palatine Games

[84] So saying, he himself got ready for action, and at the same time gave fresh impetus to the others, so that they were all now keyed up for the attempt and unwilling to put it off any longer. [85] At dawn Chaerea himself hurried off to the Palatine, wearing his equestrian's sword, which convention required as part of a tribune's uniform, when on his day as duty officer he asked the emperor for the password, as required. [86] A crowd was already gathering on the Palatine with much pushing and shouting, as they tried to grab a good vantage point from which to watch the spectacle. Gaius always derived pleasure from the popular enthusiasm for these proceedings, and for that reason no special seating had been reserved for the senate or the *equites*. As a result they all sat together with men and women, slaves and freemen mixed up together. [87] When his procession entered, Gaius made a sacrifice to Caesar Augustus, in whose honour these games were being held. As one of the victims fell, it happened by chance that the toga of a senator named Asprenas was spattered with its blood. At this Gaius laughed loudly; but for Asprenas it proved to be a very clear omen, since he was slaughtered immediately after Gaius.[36] [88] Witnesses record that Gaius was in unusually good form that day, surprising all those whom he chanced to meet with his genial greetings. [89] Once the sacrifice was over, he took his seat for the show surrounded by all his most influential friends.[37]

[90] Let me explain the way the theatre was built, since it was a wooden structure, put together in the same way every year. It had two doors, one leading out to the open air, the other into a portico, with its own exits and entrances, so as to spare those separately gathered there from being disturbed by the general comings and goings. There was another doorway from the stage itself to an area separated by interior partitions to give the actors and other performers a space to which they could retire and rest.

[91] By now the crowd was seated, and Chaerea had taken his place, together with his fellow tribunes, not far from Gaius, who occupied the right wing of the theatre. Taking great care that he was not overheard as he spoke, a senator called Bathybius, a former praetor, asked Cluvius, an ex-consul sitting beside him, if any news had reached him of a forthcoming *coup d'etat*. [92] "Not a whisper," he replied. "Well, Cluvius," said Bathybius, "the play for today is called The Tyrant's Assassination." "Be quiet, my friend," said Cluvius, "Let not the Commons hear this testament …"[38] [93] Massive quantities of harvest fruits were scattered among the spectators, together with many rare birds whose scarcity made them highly valued by their owners, and

---

[36] Publius Nonius Asprenas the consul of AD 38 may also have been involved in the plot. Suetonius gives other portents and omens of the forthcoming assassination (Suet. *Cal.* 57.1–3).

[37] Josephus later reveals the identities of some of these friends – Vinicianus (96), Asprenas (98), Claudius, Marcus Vinicius, Decimus Valerius Asiaticus, Paullus Arruntius (102).

[38] A slight adaptation of Shakespeare, *Julius Caesar* 3.2.130 here renders Jospehus' slight adaptation of Odysseus' words to Agamemnon in Homer's *Iliad* 14.90–91.

Gaius watched with delight as fights for their possession and tugs-of-war developed among the spectators.[39]

[94] It was at this point that two portents occurred. First of all a mime was enacted, in which a tribal chieftain was captured and crucified. And then the dancer performed *Cinyras*, in which Cinyras himself and his daughter, Myrrha, are murdered, with masses of artificial gore scattered around the crucified chieftain and Cinyras.[40] [95] It is also generally agreed that this was the same day of the year as the one on which Philip King of Macedon, Amyntas' son, was murdered by Pausanias, one of his Companions, as he entered the theatre.[41]

E15 The tension builds

[96] Gaius was in two minds, whether to stay in the theatre until the end of the show, because it was the final day of the festival, or to bathe, have a meal, and then return as he had normally done. Vinicianus, who was seated behind him, was afraid that they might waste their moment of opportunity. He got up to go, and when he noticed that Chaerea had already left ahead of him, he hurried forward to catch up with him and offer him some encouragement. [97] But Gaius good-humouredly gave a tug at his toga and asked, "Where are you off to, my dear chap?" Vinicianus, out of apparent respect to the emperor, sat down again, though his real motive was sheer terror. But after a brief delay he got up to leave again. [98] On this occasion Gaius did not delay him as he went out, assuming that he was going out to answer a call of nature. Meanwhile Asprenas, who was eager to bring their plans to a successful conclusion, was also urging Gaius to follow his previous practice and to go out, have a bath and lunch, and then come back again.[42] [99] Chaerea's associates had assigned key locations for each other appropriate to the demands of the situation, and their task was to remain at their posts without fail, however exhausted they felt. But they were finding the delay and the constant postponement of the action very hard to take, since it was already around three o'clock in the afternoon.[43]

E16 The assassination

[100] With Gaius constantly putting off his departure, Chaerea indeed was all for going back into the theatre and attacking him where he sat. He realised that this would involve the widespread slaughter of senators and such *equites* as were present, but despite this anxiety he was keen to act, since he believed that the casualties involved counted for little when set against the safety and freedom of the whole people. [101] The conspirators had even turned back towards the theatre entrance when the volume of noise increased, alerting them to the fact that Gaius had got up to leave. They rushed back to their positions and began to hold back the crowd, pretending that they did not want the emperor to be annoyed, but in fact because they felt it would make

---

39 The un-Roman name of Bathybius is otherwise unknown – it could be a garbled form of Vatinus. Cluvius is probably the historian Cluvius Rufus, see **R11**, an ex-consul by AD 65 (Suet. *Nero* 21.2).

40 The dancer Mnester was a close friend of Gaius (Suet. *Cal.* 36.1, 55.1, 57.4). In Ovid's version (*Met.* 10.298–552), Cinyras actually committed suicide while Myrrha metamorphosed into a tree. Suet. *Cal.* 57.4 reveals the mime as Catullus' *Laureolus*.

41 Philip, the father of Alexander the Great, was actually murdered in the autumn of 336 BC.

42 The plan required Gaius to be attacked in a narrow passage between the theatre and the palace; his habit of leaving the theatre during lunch provided an excellent opportunity for the attack.

43 Suet. *Cal.* 58.1 says the 'seventh hour' (one o'clock).

things safer for their attack, if they could contrive to keep him in an open space well clear of anyone who might come to his aid. [102] Gaius' uncle, Claudius, Marcus Vinicius, his brother-in-law, and Valerius Asiaticus led the way out, and respect for their high standing meant that no one could have blocked their way, even if they had wanted to. The emperor followed, accompanied by Paulus Arruntius.[44] [103] But once he was inside the confines of the palace, he left the direct route taken by Claudius and his party, which was lined with his own personal slave attendants, [104] and turned down a deserted passageway which was a short cut to the baths, where he intended at the same time to pay a visit to the troop of boys from Asia, who had been sent to sing at the mysteries which he was presiding over and, in some cases, to join in the Pyrrhic dances in the theatres.[45]

[105] There Chaerea met him and requested the password for the day. Gaius gave him one of his usual repertoire of humorous words, and Chaerea reacted immediately and without hesitation. He denounced Gaius violently, drew his sword, and struck him a ferocious blow. But it was not fatal.[46] [106] Some people maintain that Chaerea deliberately planned to avoid slaying the emperor with a single stroke, so as to make his vengeance all the sweeter with a succession of blows.[47] [107] I myself am not convinced by this. On these sorts of occasion fear ensures that there is no time for careful calculation. If Chaerea had any such plan he would, in my opinion, have been guilty of inordinate stupidity in gratifying his lust for revenge rather than ensuring for himself and his fellow conspirators a speedy escape from danger. There were a number of means by which help could have reached Gaius, if he had not been despatched on the spot, and in that case Chaerea would have had to give up all thought of his own vengeance, and instead reckon on the vengeance of Gaius' for himself and his friends. [108] This was the sort of occasion when, even if the operation went well, it was better to operate silently and avoid the anger of those who might come to the emperor's assistance; and while it was still uncertain whether they would succeed or not, it was madness to lose his life and his opportunity. But still, in this case, judgement is a matter of each to his own choice.

---

44 Marcus Vinicius the husband of Gaius' sister Livilla had been consul in AD 30. Valerius Asiaticus was suffect consul in AD 35 and consul in 46. Seneca alleges that Gaius' criticism of Lollia Saturnina's sexual performance drove Asiaticus to conspire against Gaius (Lollia was Asiaticus' wife: **T3**). Tacitus has Messalina's agent Sosibus name Asiaticus as the 'principal author' of the conspiracy (Tac. *Ann.* 11.1). The name of 'Paulus Arruntius' is garbled in the manuscripts of Josephus but he may be a relative of a leading politician Lucius Arruntius, whom Tacitus considered worthy of ruling (Tac. *Ann.* 1.13.2) and therefore related to Lucius Arruntius Camillus Scribonianus who rebelled against Claudius in AD 42 (**P7**).

45 Dio 59.29.6 tells us that these were noble Greek boys summoned to sing a hymn to Gaius. Pyrrhic dances were a type of ballet. The palace complex consisted of separate buildings and Gaius is outside here not in a narrow passageway as the conspirators had intended. Suet. *Cal.* 58.1 has Gaius meeting the boys in an underground passageway or cellar (crypta), stopping there longer than he needed to as the choir leader complained of a cold.

46 In Suet. *Cal.* 58.2 Sabinus asked for the password. Suetonius provides two versions of the curse: '*hoc age*!' the phrase used when a sacrificial animal was killed or '*accipe ratum*' ('take this as the fulfilment of my vow'). Suetonius agrees that the first blow was not fatal. On the other hand Sen. *Const.* 18.3 = **P6b** has Chaerea cutting through Gaius' neck with one blow.

47 Perhaps a case of dramatic irony here – Gaius allegedly had enjoyed watching lingering deaths himself (*e.g.* Suet. *Cal.* 30.1).

[109] Gaius had been severely dazed by the pain of the blow, which had struck him between the shoulder and the neck before being blocked by his collar-bone from penetrating any further. He neither shouted out in terror nor did he call to his friends, whether because he did not trust them or because he was too confused to think clearly. Groaning in agony, he tried to make his escape by running forward.[48] [110] Cornelius Sabinus was there waiting for him, having anticipated how he was likely to react. He knocked Gaius to the ground and as he struggled to his knees the conspirators surrounded him and at a single word of command from Cornelius they hacked at him with their swords, shouting encouragement to each other and acting as if they were in competition. In the end it was Aquila who delivered the *coup de grace,* striking the blow that finally finished him off. All our sources are agreed on that point.[49] [111] But the honours really go to Chaerea. He may have had the help of many others in carrying out the deed, but he was the first to think of the idea, and much the first to come up with a method of execution. [112] He was the first to risk speaking to the others and that took some courage. Then, when they individually accepted the murder plot, he brought the scattered elements together and welded all the details into a coherent plan. Where intelligent leadership was needed, he proved the outstanding personality, with a gift for inspirational oratory to spur them on when their courage faltered. [113] And then, when the critical moment for action arrived, it is clear that he made the first move and bravely seized the chance to strike, leaving Gaius nearly dead and a sitting duck for the others. In short, justice requires that, whatever the others may have done, the credit should be given to the intelligence, courage, and hard work put into the operation by Chaerea.

[114] So died the emperor Gaius, lying where he fell, robbed of life by his many wounds.[50]

E17 The assassins flee, the German bodyguard reacts to news of Gaius' death

[115] Once they had settled their scores with Gaius, Chaerea and his friends realised that there was no hope of escaping to safety if they went back by the way they had come. They were alarmed by the implications of what they had done, since the dangers of assassinating the tyrant were far from trivial. Fools that they were, the general populace admired and adored their emperor, while the soldiery would be out for blood, once they began to look for him. [116] The alleyways where they had done the deed were narrow and blocked by a massive crowd, both the slave attendants and that day's duty detachment of the imperial bodyguard. [117] So they fled down other streets until they reached the house of Germanicus, the father of their recent victim, Gaius. The house was physically joined to the palace, which was itself a single building with extensions put up by members of the imperial family and honoured with the names of those responsible for the building, or even just laying the foundations, of each individual section.[51] [118] Having thus avoided the attentions of the mob they

---

48 Suet. *Cal.* 58.3 has Gaius calling for help and his litter bearers coming to his aid.

49 Suet. *Cal.* 58.3 has thirty assassins, some of who aimed at his genitals in revenge for Gaius' sexually deviant behaviour. Dio 59.29.7 claims some even tasted Gaius' flesh. Aquila is otherwise unknown.

50 Recalling Dio's quip that Gaius finally learnt that he was not a god (Dio 59.30).

51 The location of this is unknown. Gaius had extended the buildings which made up the Palatine complex as far as the forum and the assassins may have ventured this way (Suet. *Cal.* 22.2)

were safe for the time being, since no-one was as yet aware of the disaster which had overtaken the emperor.

[119] The first to learn of the death of Gaius were his German bodyguards, soldiers named after the tribe from which they had been recruited and known as the Celtic contingent.[52] [120] Like all their nation, they are a fiery tempered tribe to an extent rare among other barbarians. They act without thought of the consequences, and being physically immensely strong they tend to achieve considerable success in battle by their initial assault on any they have identified as their enemies. [121] When they learned of the murder of Gaius, they went berserk, being naturally inclined to make their judgements on the basis of their own advantage rather than the rights and wrongs of the whole issue. And Gaius was, of course, immensely popular with them, because he had kept their goodwill by generous donatives. [122] With swords drawn they combed the palace complex searching for Caesar's murderers. They were led by Sabinus, a military tribune, who owed his promotion to such a command not to the merits and nobility of his ancestry, but to his own physical strength, since he was a gladiator.[53]

[123] Because Asprenas was the first man they came across, they butchered him. He was the one whose toga was spattered with the blood of the sacrifices, as I mentioned above, and it certainly proved to be an evil omen for his future. The next to encounter them was Norbanus, one of Rome's noblest citizens with many army commanders in his ancestry.[54] [124] They showed no respect for his status, but he was remarkably strong and grappled with the first of his attackers. He grabbed his sword and made it clear that he would sell his life dearly, but in the end he was overwhelmed by the sheer numbers of those surrounding him and fell beneath innumerable wounds. [125] Anteius was their third victim, one of the senate's most distinguished members. Unlike the previous two, it was no accident that brought him into contact with the Germans. He was only too glad to be a spectator, delighted to be present, to see with his own eyes Gaius lying there, and to feast his hatred on the sight. His father, Anteius senior, had been driven into exile by Gaius, but this was not enough for the emperor, and so he sent soldiers after him to kill him. [126] That was why Anteius was there, gazing with relish upon the spectacle of Gaius' corpse. But when the uproar began in the palace, he realised that he needed to hide. Even so, he could not escape the Germans' intensive search parties, and their murderous intentions towards the innocent and guilty alike. Such was the end of these three men.[55]

---

52 Augustus had instituted this unit of Batavians in 30 BC (Suet. *Aug*. 49.1; Dio 55.24.7).

53 Not the same man as the conspirator Cornelius Sabinus. This Sabinus later became a lover of the empress Messalina (Dio 60.28.2).

54 Suet. *Cal*. 58.3 describes the senators killed by the Germans as 'innocent' although they may have been involved in the conspiracy. Norbanus Balbus (Josephus gives his name as 'Barbaros') may be the consul of AD 19 or his son.

55 Anteius is otherwise unknown. He may have been a relative of Publius Anteius Rufus, a friend of Agripinna (Tac. *Ann*. 16.14) and/or Anteia, wife of Helvidius Priscus (the younger) (Pliny *Ep*. 9.13.4).

E18 Reaction in the theatre to the news

[127] When the news of Gaius' death reached the theatre, there was shock and disbelief. Some there were who welcomed the news of his elimination with absolute delight and would have long ago regarded such an event as a blessing for themselves. But their own terror made them refuse to believe it. [128] There were others whose hopes were diametrically the opposite, because they had no wish for any such thing to happen to Gaius. They too refused to believe it, because they could not imagine that any man would have the courage for such a deed.[56] [129] These included stupid women, children, the whole slave population, and some of the soldiery – these last because they took his pay and were in effect accomplices in his tyranny, since their support for his brutality inflicted terror on the leading citizens and brought status and profit to themselves. [130] As you would expect from that sort of rabble, his harem of female fans, together with the younger generation, were captivated by the shows and gladiatorial battles which he staged, and by the pleasures of the meat-handouts from his sacrifices, officially issued to keep the common people fed, but in fact designed to satisfy the emperor's own crazed and savage appetites. [131] As for the slaves, they were now free to argue with their owners and felt no respect for them as a result, since the emperor's own protection enabled them to escape punishment and it was only too easy for them to give false evidence against their masters and be believed. By laying information about their masters' wealth they could even win their own freedom, as well as grow rich on the proceeds of their testimony, since the standard reward was one eighth of the property of those accused.

[132] As for the senators, if any of them thought the news was true, either because they had previous knowledge of the plot or because it seemed to be an answer to their prayers, they remained silent, not only concealing their delight at the news but also to avoid giving any appearance of even having heard it at all. [133] Some of them feared that their hopes would be disappointed and that they would then be punished for having prematurely revealed their true feelings. But those that were privy to the conspiracy, because they were participants, were even more careful to conceal their feelings. They did not know who else was involved, and were afraid that if they spoke openly to anyone who would profit by the survival of the tyranny, they might be denounced and punished if the emperor lived. [134] This was because another rumour was doing the rounds to the effect that Gaius had been wounded, but not fatally, and was alive and in the care of his doctors.

[135] In fact no one trusted anybody enough to have the courage to reveal what he really thought. If his information came from a friend of Gaius, he was suspect as being sympathetic to tyranny; if from someone who hated him, the very fact that he had nothing good to say about him rendered his information totally unreliable. [136] Some even reported – and this above all was a source of despair and demoralisation to the senators – that oblivious to the dangers and indifferent to the need for treatment to his wounds, Gaius had escaped to the forum and just as he was in his bloodstained condition he was even now addressing the crowd. [137] Such were the irrational suggestions spread by determined rumour-mongers. What was believed depended on

56 According to Suet. *Cal.* 60 the people thought that Gaius had made up the rumour of his demise to gauge their reaction.

the particular prejudices of the hearers. But none of them dared to leave their seats in the theatre for fear of being denounced if they were the first to go out. Judgement would be passed on them, not for their real intentions in departing, but according to the particular interpretation which the prosecutors and jury chose to place upon their decision to leave.

E19 A massacre averted

[138] But when a mass of Germans with drawn swords surrounded the theatre, all the spectators feared the worst, reacting with terror whenever anyone entered the place, being convinced that they were about to be hacked to pieces by them on the spot. They had no idea whether to pluck up their courage and depart, nor any confidence that it would be safe to remain there for the time being. [139] When the troops broke in, the theatre echoed with the shouts of the people, which turned to cries to the soldiers for mercy. They pleaded that they had no knowledge of what was going on, no information about the intentions of the rebels (if there really had been a rebellion), and no idea of what had actually happened. [140] They begged to be spared, and not to be punished for something for which they were not to blame, in revenge for the outrageous audacity of others, urging the soldiers to leave them alone and to set up a search for the perpetrators of the deed, whatever it was. [141] All this and more they cried out, weeping and beating their faces, as they called upon the gods and uttered whatever kinds of prayers and invocations the imminent danger suggested to them. Each spoke with all the eloquence of one whose very life depended on his words.[57]

[142] The soldiers' rage melted away in the face of such entreaties, and they changed their minds about attacking the spectators. It would have been an act of savagery, and now seemed so even to them, despite their anger, once they had contented themselves with fixing the heads of Asprenas and their other two victims on the altar.[58] [143] This simply increased the distress of the spectators, as they contemplated the distinction of these men and felt pity for their deaths. The dangers of suffering a similar fate themselves seemed just as close and no less terrifying, since it was still far from certain that in the end they would be able to avoid it. [144] So even those with reason to be Gaius' most bitter enemies were deprived of any opportunity for delight at his death, since their own chance of sharing his fate still rested in the balance and they had as yet no certainty or cast-iron guarantee for their survival.

[145] There was a man called Evarestus Arruntius, a professional auctioneer. Thanks to his loud voice, an essential for that profession, he was rolling in money and had as much wealth as the richest of the Romans, and as a result both then and later was able to do pretty much what he liked around the city. [146] He dressed himself up as if he was in the deepest possible mourning, even though he hated Gaius as much as anyone. But fear is a more powerful instructor, and survival strategy a more potent source of profit, than any immediate sense of pleasure. [147] So he came into the theatre dressed in all the paraphernalia of one attending the funeral of a most highly respected citizen,

[57] The level of detail here again suggests that Josephus used an eye-witness account in this section, most likely Cluvius Rufus (see introduction to this narrative and **R11**).

[58] See section 87 on Asprenas.

and announced that Gaius was dead. This immediately put an end to any rumours born of ignorance about what had happened.[59]

[148] By now Arruntius Stella had arrived and backed by their tribunes was calling the Germans to order, instructing them to sheathe their weapons, and making clear to them that Gaius was now dead.[60] [149] It is perfectly clear that this was what saved all those in the theatre and anyone else who happened to meet the Germans elsewhere. Had they had any hope that Gaius was still alive, they would undoubtedly have perpetrated every atrocity imaginable. [150] Their loyalty to him was excessive, and they would have willingly sacrificed their own lives to protect him from plots or from falling victim to such a disaster as occurred. [151] But once the full facts of Gaius' death were clear to them, they abandoned their frenzied search for revenge, since any display of inordinate loyalty towards the man who would repay them was futile, when he was already dead. They also feared that if they persisted with their wildly undisciplined behaviour, the senate might turn upon them, if they came to power, and likewise the next emperor, if anyone established himself in that position. [152] It was touch and go, but that was the moment when the Germans gave up the crazed lust for revenge, which had overtaken them at the death of Gaius.

E20 Vinicianus arrested but released by Clemens

[153] Chaerea, meanwhile, was profoundly anxious for the fate of Vinicianus. He was afraid that he might have encountered the Germans and been murdered. So he went round the soldiers, begging them to do everything possible for his safety, and by means of intensive interrogation making sure that had not lost his life. [154] In fact Vinicianus had been brought to Clemens, who had ordered his release, along with many other members of the senatorial order, declaring that their deed was just, its conception admirable, and its execution free from any taint of cowardice.[61] [155] "Tyranny," he declared, "motivated by the enjoyment of unbridled violence never lasts. After all, a tyrant has no means by which to make his life end happily, since he is hated by all good men and true. [156] The sort of calamity which Gaius suffered happened because he had become his own worst enemy, long before the conspirators laid their plots against him. He taught even his closest friends to declare war upon him, by his treatment of all those who found his atrocities unbearable and his indifference to all principles of justice intolerable. As a result, though he was destroyed by those who will be called his assassins, in effect he died by his own hand."[62]

---

59 Arruntius Evarestus is likely, given his Greek cognomen, to have been a freedman, perhaps of the Arruntius Stella of the subsequent section or of the Paulus Arruntius from 102.

60 Tacitus mentions a L. Arruntius Stella who organised Nero's games in AD 55 (*Ann.* 13.22). As he seems to have had authority over the Germans, he may well have been Clemens' colleague as Praetorian Prefect.

61 Clemens was presumably holding the inquiry into Gaius' murder, referred to in 158, although this is unlikely to have taken place in the theatre.

62 Clemens' favourable portrayal here may well reflect that his son and daughter were prominent in the Flavian period when Josephus was writing this work; his son M. Arrecinus Clemens, was a suffect consul in AD 73 and his daughter, Arrecina Tertulla, was the first wife of the emperor Titus (Suet. *Tit.* 4.2).

[157] The guards had at first been ferociously strict, but they were now beginning to relax, and there was a general move to get up and leave the theatre. The one who contrived their escape without any objections from the guards was Alcyon, the physician. He had been forcibly carried off to attend to some of the wounded, and he now despatched some of the people with him ostensibly to get the medical supplies required for treating the injured, but in fact to remove safely out of harm's way.[63]

E21 The senate meets while the soldiers turn to Claudius

[158] In the meanwhile, a meeting of the senate had been convened, while the popular assembly gathered in their usual meeting place in the Forum.[64] Both gatherings were holding investigations into the murder of emperor, the people with serious intention, the senate merely going through the motions. [159] The official presiding over the popular assembly was an ex-consul by the name of Valerius Asiaticus, The people were still in a riotous mood, furious that the murderers of the emperor had still not been detected. When they all began to shout vociferously, demanding to know who had done the deed, he replied: "I wish I had done it myself."[65]

[160] The consuls then published a decree containing denunciations of Gaius.[66] They instructed the people, meanwhile, to go home and the soldiers to return to barracks, promising the people every hope of relief from their grievances, and the soldiers rewards, if they retained their traditional discipline and refrained from riotous destruction. There was every reason to fear that, if they ran wild and turned to looting and pillaging the temples, the city would suffer an orgy of destruction. [161] By now the whole body of the senate had assembled in response to the urgency of the situation, with those who had plotted the assassination of Gaius very much to the fore. Their confidence was fully restored and they were full of a sense of their own importance, since they thought that they would now be in control of government business.[67]

---

63 This is presumably the surgeon mentioned by the elder Pliny, who allegedly charged exorbitant fees (*NH* 29.22).

64 Suetonius (*Cal.* 60), Dio 60.1.1 and Josephus himself in his *Jewish War* (*JW* 2.5) report that this meeting took place in the Capitol, since the 'Julian' senate house bore the name of Gaius' family. The people seem to have gathered informally rather than as an official popular assembly, which met to ratify laws or the election of magistrates; although the appearance of a presiding magistrate could suggest otherwise. The repetitions and inconsistencies in this meeting in sections 158–160 and the subsequent meeting in sections 160–168 suggest that Josephus may have combined two contradictory sources here; there may only have been one meeting.

65 Compare the allegation in Tac. *Ann.* 11.1 that Asiaticus was the 'principal author' of the conspiracy during his trial for treason under Claudius. Dio 59.30.2 has Asiaticus speaking in a similar way to the Praetorian Guard instead.

66 The consuls were Cn. Sentius Saturninus and Q. Pomponius Secundus. Both men were removed by later emperors, perhaps indicating an involvement in this conspiracy; Pomponius under Claudius (Tac. *Ann.* 13.43), Saturninus under Nero (Tac. *Hist.* 4.7). Other sources give further detail about the edict and actions taken by the senate. The consuls ordered the urban cohorts to secure the forum and Capitol (Suet. *Claud.* 10.3; Jos. *JW* 2.205); transferred the public treasury from the Temple of Saturn to the Capitol (Dio 59.30.3); decided to wipe out the family of the Caesars, including women and children and destroy the temples set up to them (Orosius 7.6.3; Vict. *Caes.* 3.16; Suet. *Cal.* 60); and wrote a letter to Claudius.

67 Dio 59.30.3 reveals 'These men (the consuls) together with the prefects and the followers of Sabinus and Chaerea, were deliberating what should be done.'

[162] That was the general situation when Claudius was unexpectedly kidnapped from his home.[68] The soldiers had held a meeting to discuss what needed to be done. They realised that a republican government was incapable of controlling such a vast empire, and if it was established, it would certainly not govern in the interests of the army. [163] But if one man seized power, it would be a significant disadvantage to themselves in every way if they had not helped him to achieve it.[69]

[164] While matters were still in a state of flux, therefore, it seemed best to them to choose Claudius as emperor. He was the dead Gaius' uncle, and of those who had gathered for the meeting of the senate, there was none who was his superior either in the distinction of his ancestry or in his commitment to his own learned studies.[70] [165] If they made him emperor, he would be likely to feel a debt towards them and repay them with gifts. No sooner said than done. Claudius was kidnapped by the soldiers.

E22 Sentius Saturninus makes a speech proclaiming freedom

[166] Despite a show of reluctance, Gnaeus Sentius Saturninus wanted the throne and had already staked his claim to it. He had heard of the kidnap of Claudius, but he now he rose to address the senate without giving any hint of anxiety, gave an encouraging address that matched his character as a free man of the noblest birth. This is what he said.[71]

[167] "Men of Rome, we are free at last. We have waited long years for its arrival; we never believed we would possess it; but now, unbelievable as it may seem, we truly possess the glorious dignity of freedom. How long it will last, we cannot tell; that rests upon the will of the gods, whose gift to us it is. But it is enough that for the moment it is a blessing to delight in, and if we are robbed of it once again, enough that while it lasted it was a source of such blessing. [168] It is sufficient for those that love our traditional values to live for a single hour, thinking like free men, in a country whose laws are freely made and under laws by which our city once grew great. [169] I cannot tell you of that earlier period of freedom; I was born, alas, too late. But as I feast myself to bursting point upon our present situation, I count those blessed who were born and brought up in those glorious days; and I honour no less than the very gods themselves those men who, though all too late, have in our own time granted us to taste, at least, the self-same gift of freedom.

[170] And though I pray that for the rest of time to come our present liberty will never pass away, yet this single day would be sufficient for the younger ones among us, while for those that have grown old it will be worth a lifetime: for those that are old, if only they may pass away having lived to experience its blessings; for those that are young, that they have received a lesson in the traditional values, and how they

68 Claudius was last seen in sections 102–3 leaving the theatre and seems to have returned to the imperial complex rather than his own house.

69 In a Republic there would be no reason for a Praetorian Guard (compare Tac. *Hist.* 1.5, 25; Dio 53.11.5).

70 Claudius was the brother of Gaius' father, Germanicus, but unlike Germanicus had not been adopted into the Julian family. He was a member of the Claudian family which had first held the consulship in 495 BC.

71 The effect of the speech on the excesses of tyranny may lose some of its force considering Josephus' allegation that Saturninus, who delivered the oration, was manoeuvring for power himself.

were once established, [171] values which were their highest aspiration for those from whom we are sprung. As for ourselves, because we live to enjoy this hour, there is nothing of greater consequence than that we decide to live by those same traditional values; for they alone are the source of freedom for all mankind. [172] I myself have learned what happened in the past, from hearsay; but I know, and have seen from bitter personal experience, what are the evils with which tyranny can fill the state. Tyranny destroys our values; tyranny steals freedom from those of noble ambition; tyranny teaches men the arts of flattery and fear. For it leaves the ordering of men's affairs, not to the wisdom of the law, but to the passions of the powerful.

[173] Ever since Julius Caesar devised the destruction of democratic government, subverting the state by turning upside down the rule of law, and making himself more powerful than justice by becoming a slave to his own personal desires, our city has been forced to suffer every evil known to man.[72] [174] Those who succeeded him as our rulers have all competed with each other to destroy the constitution of our ancestors, and as best they could to create for our citizens a wilderness of all that is most honourable. They thought that it would add to their own security, if they could live among men unworthy of the name, not just by dissipating the natural pride of those admired for their outstanding virtues, but by decreeing the total annihilation of all such men for ever. [175] There have been many such tyrants in the past, and they have all been conspicuous for the intolerable savagery that each wrought in his reign. But Gaius, who today lies dead, above all others was unique, not only in the savagery he showed towards his fellow citizens, but also in giving free rein to a frenzy of rage that was truly bestial towards his relatives and friends. In his wild fury against men and gods alike he inflicted on everyone sufferings worse than the injustices of the most vindictive of those who lust for vengeance. [176] For tyranny, pleasure for its own sake is simply not enough, not even when enjoyed to arrogant excess, or by doing violence to property or marriage. It finds its total satisfaction only in hounding to destruction the families and households of its enemies.

[177] For tyrants, every form of freedom is an enemy; they will have no truck with friendship or goodwill, even to those who are willing to discount their own sufferings. For every tyrant knows full well what evils he has perpetrated, and even if his victims generously overlook their own misfortunes, no tyrant can ever forget what wickedness he has wrought. As a result, they can never feel free from suspicious fears, and trust only those whom they have been able to destroy utterly.

[178] Those are the evils, which you have now shaken off; you have made yourselves subjects only to one another. This is the only form of constitution, which guarantees goodwill for the present, safety from conspiracy for the future, and the glory that belongs to a well-conducted city. It is now your duty to take thought and to provide all that is conducive to the general good, and where proposals do not meet with your approval, to make your disagreement clear. [179] In this there is now no danger whatsoever, since we are no longer subject to the rule of a tyrant, who is unaccountable for the damage he does to the city, and has the power to remove

---

72 Even before Caesar's perpetual dictatorship of 44 BC, he had been a pre-eminent figure for fifteen years, holding several consulships and dictatorships in the period 60–45 BC.

arbitrarily anyone who dares to speak out in opposition. [180] For our tyranny was born of nothing other than indifference and our failure to argue against the tyrant's wishes. [181] We have succumbed to the temptations of a peaceful coexistence with our tyrants and so have learned to live like slaves. Some of us have ourselves endured unbearable misfortunes; others have watched disasters strike down our neighbours. All of us have feared to face death bravely; and so all of us have learned to endure death most shamefully.

[182] But now our first duty is to confer upon those who removed a tyrant from our midst the very highest honours we can bestow – upon Cassius Chaerea above all others. For with the help of heaven, by his intelligent planning and decisive action, this one man has shown himself to be the source of all our freedoms. [183] It is altogether right and fitting than we should now remember him, both for his skilful planning and his willingness to be the first to venture all for freedom in a time of tyranny, by deciding in our time of liberty to confer these honours freely, as the first and public decision of a free people. [184] It is the noblest action possible, and one that is altogether worthy of free men, that we should seek to repay those who have served us well – as this man has served each and every one of us. He is not to be compared with Brutus and Cassius, who slew the tyrant Gaius Julius Caesar. For they but fanned the flames of furious insurrection and fierce civil strife for Rome; but this man has both slain a tyrant and also cleansed our city from the horrors he inflicted on us."[73]

[185] So much for the speech of Sentius. It was rapturously received by the senators and those equestrians who were present. One of them, Trebellius Maximus, leapt up and snatched the ring from Sentius' finger, which had a stone set in it, engraved with a portrait of Gaius. He must have realised that Sentius had forgotten about it, being too wrapped up in his own oratory and plans for the future. So he smashed it.[74]

[186] It was by now well into the night, and then Chaerea asked the consuls for the password. "Freedom", they replied. There was a stunned silence and an almost total disbelief at what had happened. [187] It was a hundred years from the original destruction of the republic to this moment, when the giving of the password reverted to the consuls, the very men who had been the commanders of Rome's armies in the days before the city was ruled by tyrants.[75] [188] Chaerea accepted the password and passed it to those of the soldiers who were loyal the senate. They amounted to four cohorts, units that regarded the lack of an emperor as more honourable than tyranny.[76] [189] They now went off with their tribunes, while the general populace also began to

---

73 Veneration of Caesar's assassins Marcus Junius Brutus and Gaius Cassius Longinus was often used as a thinly veiled attack on the emperors during the first century AD; Cremutius Cordus was tried in AD 25 for praising the pair in a political pamphlet (Tac. *Ann.* 4.34–35, **P4c**) and Cassius Longinus was punished for having a bust of his ancestor Cassius in his house inscribed with the slogan 'to the leader of the cause' (Tac. *Ann.* 16.7; Dio 62.27.1–2).

74 Marcus Trebellius Maximus became governor of Britain between AD 63–9 (**N39**).

75 This hundred years presumably counts from Julius Caesar's support from Pompey and Crassus in the consular elections of 60 BC or from his consulship of 59 when his fellow consul resorted to forbidding all senate meetings on a religious technicality, and Caesar ignored him (Dio 38.6).

76 Four cohorts may be a slip for three, as at Jos. *JW* 2.205. The three would be the three urban cohorts (Tac. *Ann.* 4.5.3; Suet. *Claud.* 10.3). No praetorian cohorts are likely to have supported the Republic.

withdraw, rejoicing and full of optimism, and proud to have become masters of their own destiny and no longer subject to an overlord. For them Chaerea was the hero of the hour.

E23 The murder of Gaius' wife and baby daughter

[190] But Chaerea himself was worried that Gaius' wife and daughter had survived. He wanted the destruction of the complete family, since if any of them survived they would threaten to bring ruin upon the city and its laws. As well as that, he personally wanted the whole business thoroughly completed as a way of satisfying his own loathing for Gaius. So he sent the tribune Julius Lupus to kill Gaius' wife and daughter.[77] [191] Lupus was related to Clemens, and that was why they chose him for the task, so that as a participant in the murder of the tyrant, even at second hand like this, Clemens might enjoy some reflected glory in the eyes of the citizenry, and be thought by them to have had a share in the original planning of the whole conspiracy. [192] Some of the conspirators thought that it was excessively savage to treat Gaius' wife with such brutality. They argued that Gaius himself was naturally vicious and his actions in exhausting the city by his cruelty and wiping out the flower of its people were not in any way the result of her encouragement. [193] But others denounced her as the evil genius behind all these misfortunes. They said that she was responsible for all Gaius' crimes, having driven him mad by dosing him with a drug designed to enslave his mind and excite his sexual passion for her. In fact, they argued, she was totally responsible for the shipwreck of the city's fortunes and those of the worldwide empire Rome controlled.[78]

[194] In the end it was decided that she must die, since those who vigorously opposed the idea were unable to do any more to help her. Lupus was duly sent on his mission. He wanted to avoid any delay in carrying out his duties, seeking to ensure the prompt completion of his task for those who had sent him, so as to avoid any blame for failing in his duty to the people of Rome. [195] When he reached the palace, he found Gaius' wife, Caesonia, lying on the ground by the body of her husband, lacking any of the conventional marks of respect which are traditionally paid to the dead. She was stained with blood from his wounds, utterly distraught with misery, and with her daughter sprawled beside her. The only sounds that could be heard were her reproaches to her husband for not believing her repeated warnings to him.

[196] There were two opinions at the time about what she said; there still are, since those that hear them give them whatever degree of significance matches their own prejudices. One point of view was that her words showed she had been urging him to give up his mad savagery towards the citizenry, and to rule with moderation and respect for traditional values, so as to avoid bringing upon himself a destruction that matched his own brutality to others. [197] Others argued that news had reached her of the conspiracy, and that she had been urging Gaius to avoid delay and to eliminate them all immediately, even if they were innocent, so as to ensure his own safety. This,

[77] The murder of Gaius' wife and daughter was brutal (Dio 58.11.5). The debate over her life must have been intense as Caesonia belonged to an influential and well-connected family **J15a**. Her niece, Domitia Longina, became Domitian's empress in Josephus' lifetime.

[78] For this story see Suet. *Cal.* 50.2 and Juvenal 6.614–26 – **J15b**.

they said, was the true meaning of her complaint: she had warned him, but he had lacked the guts to take the necessary action.

[198] So much for Caesonia's words and the general verdict of posterity on what she meant. When she saw Lupus approaching, she pointed to Gaius' body, inviting him with tears and sobs to come nearer. [199] When she realised from his demeanour that he had a fixed purpose, and that he was approaching her without showing any evidence of distaste for his task, she understood why he had come. She bared her throat very readily, but whimpered in the way one would expect of those who know well that their last hours have come. She urged him not to delay in bringing down the curtain on the final act of the drama that had been composed for her family. [200] And so she died, bravely, at the hands of Lupus, who then killed her little daughter, and then hurried back to Chaerea and his friends, so as to make sure he was the first to bring them the news.[79]

E24 Obituary of the Emperor Gaius

[201] Gaius died in the fourth year of his reign as Emperor of the Romans, four months before its completion. As a man, even before he came to the throne, he was a flawed character, who had turned viciousness into a fine art. Pleasure he found irresistible; slander a delight. Danger terrified him; for that reason he was savagely violent towards those whom he did not fear. Glutted with power, he used it for one purpose only: to do violence to others. He showed ludicrous generosity to those who least deserved it, and as the source of that generosity he used murder and judicial mayhem. [202] He aspired to be, and to be seen to be, superior to the laws of god and man; yet he was a slave to the plaudits of the multitude. All that the law adjudges criminal and base, and seeks to punish, this he regarded as a source of virtue. [203] Indifferent to friendship, however loyal and long standing, he would inflict punishment for the least offence on those who incurred his anger. He hated everything to do with traditional values, and once he had set his heart on something, he found any opposition to his commands intolerable – hence his incest with his own sister.[80] [204] This was the source of the deep hatred for him among the ordinary citizens, a hatred that grew ever more intense as time went by. As a crime it was unheard of for centuries, and induced in everyone incredulity, and loathing for the perpetrator.

[205] He constructed neither great public buildings, which could be said to be for the benefit of contemporaries or future generations, nor even a palace. The one exception was the harbour planned for the area of Rhegium and Sicily, intended to provide facilities for the grain ships from Egypt. [206] This was certainly a major undertaking and an invaluable anchorage for sailors. But he never saw it through, and it was abandoned, half finished, thanks to his own half-hearted interest in it.[81] [207] The reason was clear: he was fascinated by the futile, and poured millions into pleasures, which served no useful purpose beyond his own gratification. All this robbed him of any ambition for more demonstrably substantial achievements.

---

79 Suet. *Cal.* 59 states that Caesonia was stabbed with a sword, her daughter smashed against a wall.

80 Josephus refers here to Drusilla; Suet. *Cal.* 24 and Dio 59.3.6 allege incest with the other two also.

81 Gaius in fact undertook much building during his reign; in addition to this harbour he also constructed aqueducts (**K24**, **K26**; Suet. *Cal.* 21, but they were completed and dedicated by Claudius, **K27**).

[208] By contrast, he was an outstanding public speaker, with a profound understanding of Greek, as well as his native Latin. He could speak off the cuff, and would reply to speeches laboriously composed by others after much cogitation, in such a way as to appear immediately more convincing than anyone else, even on the most weighty subject. All this he owed to his own natural talent, which he complemented with practice and hard work.[82] [209] He was great-nephew to Tiberius, whom he also succeeded as emperor, and this gave him great incentive to take his education seriously, since Tiberius himself had manifestly achieved the highest distinction in such matters. Gaius had a love of the fine arts, and in following the example of one who was both kinsman and guide, he achieved great distinction among his contemporaries.

[210] Nevertheless, the benefits which he had gained from his education could not protect him from the ruinous effects of his acquisition of power. For the virtue of moderation is hard to acquire for those who have the power to act as they please and without restraint. [211] At first, thanks to his education and desire for a high reputation in lofty pursuits, he was eager to cultivate the friendship of men who were in everyway admirably suitable; but ultimately his sadistic extremes put them off from the friendship they had originally shown him, and once this had developed into absolute hatred, they plotted against him, and finally killed him.

E25 Claudius discovered and carried off by the soldiers

[212] As I explained above, Claudius had broken away from the route taken by Gaius. Finding the palace in a state of panic and disorder at the death of Caesar, he had no idea how to get to safety. Finding himself enclosed by a narrow alleyway, he remained there in hiding.[83] He had no reason to expect any danger beyond the fact that he was of noble birth, [213] since he had lived discreetly in his private life, content with his circumstances and devoted to his studies, particularly Greek. In every way he steered clear of any sort of action that might lead to trouble.[84]

[214] By this stage blind panic had infected the mob and the whole palace was full of rampaging soldiers, while the emperor's bodyguard was displaying cowardice and indiscipline more appropriate to civilians. Then there was the Praetorian Guard, the cream of the Roman army, who were holding a council of war to discuss their next move. Those involved could not have cared less about avenging the death of Gaius, since he had got what he deserved. [215] Their concern was with their own future and how best to take advantage of the situation, since even the Germans were wreaking vengeance on the assassins simply to gratify their own savagery, and not out of any concern for the general good. [216] Claudius was much troubled by all this and feared for his own safety, especially since he had seen the heads of Asprenas and the other victims being carried past him. So he stood where he was, in the darkness, cowering into a doorway reached by a few steps.

---

[82] Suet. *Cal.* 53 and Dio 59.19.3–6 attest his skill as an orator. See also Section R, introduction and **R16–35.**

[83] According to Suet. *Claud.* 10.1 Claudius was separated from the emperor by the crowd of assassins and then made his way into a room called the Hermaeum in the imperial complex, where he learnt of the murder and then hid himself on the balcony behind curtains. Dio 60.1.2 has him hiding in a dark corner.

[84] Claudius' scholarly nature is emphasised in other sources, e.g. Suet. *Claud.* 3.1, 41–42, **R22–R25**.

[217] Gratus, one of the palace guards, spotted him but failed to identify him because of the darkness, though he could see enough to realise that it was a man lurking there, as if in ambush. He went closer and when Claudius asked permission to leave, he rushed at him, caught hold of him, and then recognised him. "Here's Germanicus," he shouted to his mates, who were with him. "Let's take him off and make him emperor." [218] Claudius realised that they were fully prepared to kidnap him, and was terrified that they might kill him in return for the death of Gaius. He begged for mercy, reminding them that they had never suffered anything untoward at his hands, and that he had had nothing to do with planning what had just happened. [219] Gratus grinned and took him by the arm. "Stop fussing about little details like saving your life. Keep an eye on the big picture – the empire. The gods care for the whole of mankind and have taken it from Gaius and given it to you, as a reward for your virtuous life. So, go for it! The throne of your ancestors is yours for the taking." [220] Then he hoisted him onto his shoulders and carried him off, since, overwhelmed with a combination of joy and terror at what he had heard, he was incapable of walking on his own two feet.[85]

[221] By now more bodyguards were collecting around Gratus. When they saw Claudius being carried along and, as they thought, being dragged off for punishment, there were angry looks. They objected to the idea of punishing a man whose whole life had been spent well away from the public gaze, and had himself faced considerable dangers during the reign of Gaius. Some even shouted that he should be handed over to the consuls to decide his case. [222] As more and more soldiers began to gather, the mob of civilians fled, but for Claudius there was no way forward, since he was too weak to walk, and his litter-bearers had given up all hope of safety for their master and had made a dash for their own, when he was first seized by Gratus.

[223] By now they had come to the open area of the Palatine where, according to tradition, Rome's first settlements were established. They had almost reached the building, where a far larger gathering of soldiers had congregated. They greeted the appearance of Claudius with delight, since they were determined to make him emperor out of admiration for his brother Germanicus, whose fame lived on among all those who had known him.[86] [224] But there was also a degree of calculation in their actions. They remembered how greedy the leading figures in the senate had been when they were last in power, and how many mistakes they had made. [225] There were other considerations too: a return to senatorial government was totally unrealistic; but if all power reverted to the control of one man, they themselves would face dangers from the fact it had been seized by a single individual. But there was now an opportunity for Claudius to take power with their help and support, and he was bound to remember their favours and repay the debt in a manner appropriate to such a gift.

[226] They went through all these factors in discussions with each other and in their own minds, as well as explaining them to new arrivals as they joined them. Once this had all been explained to them, they welcomed the proposals enthusiastically, massed

[85] According to Suetonius (Claud. 10.2) a soldier spotted his feet under the curtain and dragged him out; as Claudius begged for his life, he was proclaimed emperor. According to Dio (60.1.1–3), Claudius was recognised by soldiers who were plundering the palace and proclaimed emperor by them.

[86] For Germanicus see **J7** and **J8**.

ranks in close formation around Claudius, and headed for their camp, carrying his litter on their shoulders so that nothing should obstruct their progress.[87]

E26 The reaction of senate and people

[227] There was a sharp division of opinion between the people and the senate. The senators longed for a return to their former status, being desperate to shake off the disgrace of slavery imposed on them by the arrogance of tyrants, now that they had a chance to do so after so long. [228] The people on the other hand had no love for the senate, and realised that the emperors acted as a curb for its rapacity and were a source of protection for themselves. They were delighted by the kidnap of Claudius, imagining that if he became emperor he would protect them from the civil wars, which had prevailed in the days of Pompey.

[229] Once the senate learned that Claudius had been brought to the Praetorians' barracks by the soldiers, they sent a delegation of their most distinguished members to him to point out to him forcibly that it was his duty to make no attempt to seize the throne by force. [230] He should rather defer to the senate, recognising his subordinate position as but one individual among many, and should allow the law to take responsibility for managing the state in the general interest. They begged him to remember what terrible damage previous tyrants had done to their city, and what great dangers he himself, like them, had faced under the rule of Gaius. Since he hated the cruel insolence of any tyranny, when exercised by the others, let him not in a moment of impetuosity do deliberate violence to his fatherland.[88] [231] If he listened to their arguments and showed that, as in the past, he was firmly committed to avoiding any involvement in public life, then there would be many honours for him, voted by a free people. It was, they argued, by yielding due obedience to the law that ruler and ruled alike could earn the praise they deserved for virtuous conduct. [232] But if he refused to see sense and to learn wisdom from the death of Gaius, they themselves would certainly not tolerate it, since they had the support of a large part of the army, ample supplies of weaponry, and a large body of slaves well able to use them. [233] Hope and Chance counted for much on these occasions, and the gods themselves fought only for those with goodness and virtue on their side – in other words, those who were fighting for their country.[89]

[234] Veranius and Brocchus, members of the senatorial delegation, were both tribunes of the people, and that was the message they delivered. They then fell at his knees, beseeching him like suppliants not to inflict upon their city a disastrous war, for they now realised that Claudius was protected by a large force, and that compared to him the consuls carried very little clout.[90] [235] They suggested that if he was determined to claim the throne, he should receive it as a gift of the senate, since he

---

87 Suet. *Claud.* 10.2 has a terrified Claudius being pitied by the people who thought he was being led off to execution.

88 This argument may have been strengthened by the reports that Claudius' father and brother had favoured a return to the Republican government (Tac. *Ann.* 1.33.2, Suet. *Tib.* 50.1, *Claud.* 1.4; Tac. *Ann.* 2.82.2).

89 Suet. *Claud.* 10.3 has Claudius summoned by the senate; Dio 60.1.3–4 reports how the delegation forbade Claudius to become emperor but yielded once their own soldiers had accepted Claudius.

90 For Q. Veranius, see **N36**; Brocchus may be the Sertorius Brocchus who acted as the governor of an eastern province under Claudius.

would then exercise power under better omens and divine approval, as a result of receiving it without violence and with the goodwill of those that handed it to him.

[236] Claudius fully realised that the senate's delegation was an audacious bluff, but for the moment his own inclination veered towards avoiding confrontation. By now he had recovered his nerve and was no longer afraid of them, thanks to the soldiers' own confidence and the advice of King Agrippa, who urged him not to allow the unsolicited opportunity of gaining such a glorious kingdom to slip through his fingers.[91]

E27 King Agrippa intervenes

[237] Having been much honoured by Gaius, Agrippa had attended to his corpse and done all that loyal obligation required of him. He had placed it upon a bier, and dressed it in whatever clothing he could lay hands on, and then made his way back to his bodyguards and told them that Gaius was alive but very badly wounded, and that doctors would be coming to attend to him. [238] When he heard of the kidnap of Claudius by the soldiers, he forced his way through to him and found him in a confused state, and ready to give way to the senate's demands. He urged him to take a grip on himself and make a bid for the empire. [239] After giving this advice to Claudius, he went home, only to receive a summons from the senate. He smeared his head with scent, to make it appear as if he had come from a party which just broken up, and asked the senate what Claudius had been up to. [240] They told him how the land lay and asked him in return what he thought about the whole situation. He said that though he was willing to die for the honour of the senate, his advice was to look only to their practical advantage and ignore all personal considerations. [241] If they wanted to make win control of the empire, they would need weapons and soldiers for their own security; otherwise, if they launched an attempt without proper preparation, they would probably fail. [242] They replied that they had ample weapons and would supply the finance, and that they had a significant body of troops on their side, which they could weld into a fighting force by liberating slaves.

"Well, Gentlemen of the senate," replied Agrippa, "I only hope that you gain your hearts' desire. But I will tell you this straight, since the key issue is your own safety. [243] You must be well aware that the army which will be fighting for Claudius has had long years of military training; our troops will be the flotsam and jetsam of humanity, combined with slaves who have found themselves unexpectedly released from slavery and will therefore be hard to discipline. We shall be fighting professionals, while leading an army of men who don't even know how to draw a sword. [244] My advice is to send a delegation to Claudius to persuade him to renounce his office. I myself am very willing to join that delegation." [245] After this speech, amid general agreement, he was sent off with the rest of the embassy. Having secured a private meeting with Claudius, he described the general confusion of the

[91] Agrippa (10 BC – AD 44(?)), the grandson of Herod the Great of Judaea, had been sent to Rome as a boy, as were many relatives of friendly kings. He grew up in the imperial household, forging strong relations with Tiberius, Gaius and Claudius (**J5c**). Dio 60.8.2 acknowledges Agrippa's role but provides no details. Josephus' other account, *JW* 2.206–10 gives Agrippa a much more passive role in Claudius' accession, realising that the intervention of the soldiers had immediately put Claudius into a pre-eminent position.

senate and recommended to him that he should reply in lofty tones, as if he already exercised an emperor's authority.[92]

[246] Claudius replied that he was not at all surprised that the senate objected to the idea of being ruled by anyone, since they had been brutally treated by the savagery of previous holders of the imperial throne. But under his own gentle sway they would taste for themselves an era of moderation in what would be an empire nominally, but in fact a commonwealth shared by all. His own life's journey had passed through many different experiences, which they themselves had witnessed, and it would be greatly to their advantage to trust him. [247] The delegates were won over by this speech and were sent on their way. Meanwhile Claudius called the army together and made a speech, in which he made them swear to remain truly loyal to him, issued a donative of 5,000 denarii to each member of the praetorian guard and proportionately larger sums to their officers, promising similar sums to the armies generally, wherever they were stationed.[93]

E28 Response of the senate

[248] The consuls then summoned the senate to the temple of Victorious Jupiter while it was still night.[94] Some of them, who were still hiding in the city, were in two minds when they heard the call. Others had already departed for their private estates in the country, having given up all hope of liberty, since they saw all too clearly how the situation would develop. They had decided that it was better to spend a life of leisured idleness, free from the dangers of slavery, than to put their own safety at risk striving to emulate the glorious achievements of their ancestors. [249] Nevertheless about a hundred of them at a maximum turned up for the meeting, and began to debate the current situation. Suddenly there was a shout from the soldiers who had supported them, demanding that they should choose an emperor and commander in chief, rather than ruin the empire with a plethora of leaders. [250] They made it clear that as far as they were concerned the empire should be entrusted to a single ruler rather than to the general population, but that they left it to the senate to decide who deserved such a lofty position. This left the senate with the worst of both worlds: they had failed to win the much-vaunted liberty of which they had spoken earlier, yet they were terrified of Claudius.[95]

[251] Nevertheless, there were some whose aristocratic families and marriage alliances made them eager for the throne. For example, Marcus Vinicius, could claim distinction both by reason of his own noble birth and because of his marriage to Julia, Gaius' sister. He was eager to make a pitch for the crown, but the consuls discouraged him by raising one argument after another against it. [252] Valerius Asiaticus had similar ambitions, but was held back by Vinicianus, one of the emperor's murderers.

92 This is the embassy referred to at 229 above.

93 In Suet. *Claud.* 10.4, a formal parade of the Praetorians took place on the following day. Suetonius states that he offered 15,000 sesterces per man (less than Josephus' figure of 5,000 *denarii* = 20,000 sesterces, but still 17 years' pay for an ordinary legionary) and adds that Claudius was the first of the Caesars to buy the loyalty of the troops. A donative followed every future accession.

94 Probably the temple of Jupiter Optimus Maximus on the Capitol, where triumphal processions ended, and where the senate had already met (see note 64).

95 Suet. 10.4 has the crowd favouring Claudius; Jos. *JW* 2.211 has a single soldier speaking out for him.

If those who were ambitious for the empire had been given free rein to challenge Claudius, the result would have been a slaughter of unparalleled proportions.[96] [253] The reason was that there were gladiators in significant numbers, soldiers of the city's night watch, and the rowers from the fleet – and all of them were pouring into the Praetorians' barracks. And so of the several candidates for the post, some withdrew in order to spare the city further bloodshed, others out of fear for their own safety.

E29 The final chance to restore senatorial government is lost

[254] At daybreak that morning Chaerea and his accomplices came forward to try and talk to the soldiers.[97] But when they saw them raising their hands for silence and looking as if they were about to speak, most of the soldiers raised shouts of protest, demanding that they should not be allowed to say anything, since they had made up their minds and everyone there was determined to be ruled by one man. They demanded an immediate decision on their emperor-to-be. [255] The senate was reduced to impotence; they could not control the crowd, nor could they reach a decision on the choice of emperor, since on the one hand the troops refused to listen to them, yet on the other hand Gaius' assassins refused to allow them to give way to the soldiers' demands.

[256] At this point Chaerea lost his temper. If they wanted an emperor, he declared, he would give them one, if someone could bring him the password from Eutychus. [257] Eutychus was a charioteer of the green faction, much admired by Gaius, and the soldiers were fed up with the unpaid labour of building stables for his horses.[98] [258] This and much more was the sort of vulgar abuse that Chaerea threw at them, before finally demanding that they bring him the head of Claudius. "You've been ruled by a madman," he shouted; "are you going to give the empire to a lunatic?" [259] But the soldiers refused to take any notice of his words. They drew their swords, raised their standards, and marched off to join those who had sworn allegiance to Claudius.[99]

So they were left there, the senate without military support, and the consuls reduced to the level of any ordinary citizen. [260] Shock and demoralisation prevailed, since they had absolutely no idea what to do next, since they had clearly infuriated Claudius. Their attitude changed to one of regret for their actions and mutual abuse for their mistakes. [261] At this point Sabinus, one of the assassins, stepped into the middle and threatened to kill himself rather than help to make Claudius emperor and see slaves take over the government once again. He denounced Chaerea for cowardice if, after the leadership he had shown in his contempt for Gaius, he now thought that life was worth living when their actions had failed to restore freedom to their country. [262] At this Chaerea declared that he was perfectly prepared to die, but that he wanted first to test thoroughly the quality of Claudius' currency.

---

[96] Claudius honoured Vinicius and Asiaticus with consulships in AD 45 and 46 respectively; however both died shortly after this – Vinicius allegedly poisoned by Claudius' empress Messalina for refusing her advances (Dio 60.27.4) and Asiaticus was compelled to commit suicide following suspicions of a plot against Claudius (Tac. *Ann.* 11.1–3). On Vinicianus see section 18–20 and **P7**.

[97] Daybreak on January 23.

[98] The greens were chariot racing team favoured by Gaius who gave Eutychus 20,000 gold pieces, according to Suetonius, *Cal.* 55.2.

[99] Dio 60.3.4 and Suet. *Claud.* 11.1 confirm this, as Chaerea was executed for plotting to kill not only Gaius but also Claudius.

E30 Claudius firmly in command

[263] So much for the activities of the senatorial party. But from all sides there was a mass movement towards the praetorian camp, as people hurried to pay their respects to Claudius. One of the two consuls, Quintus Pomponius, was particularly unpopular with the troops, because he had summoned a meeting of the senate in the spurious name of liberty. They went for him with drawn swords and would have done for him, if Claudius had not stopped them.[100] [264] Having snatched the consul from certain death, he seated him next to himself, but failed to accord anything like the same respect to the rest of the senators who had accompanied him. Some of them were prevented from speaking to Claudius by the soldiers and even beaten up by them, while Aponius sustained serious injuries and left the scene. All of them were in very real danger.[101]

[265] But then King Agrippa went up to Claudius and suggested that he might adopt a more conciliatory approach to the senators, pointing out that if anything disastrous happened to them, he would not have anyone else to rule over. [266] Claudius took his advice and called a meeting of the senate on the Palatine. He was carried through the city by the Praetorians, who acted as his escort and treated the crowds with considerable brutality.[102] [267] Of Gaius' assassins, Chaerea and Sabinus now came forward openly, but were prevented from approaching Claudius on the instructions of Pollio, whom Claudius had recently appointed praetorian prefect.[103]

E31 The fates of those involved

[268] When Claudius reached the Palatine, he called his friends together and asked for a vote on the fate of Chaerea. Their verdict was that the action had been a glorious one, but the man himself they denounced for disloyalty, and stated that justice required that he be punished as a deterrent to others in the future.[104] [269] So he was led away to execution, together with Lupus and a number of other Romans. It is said that Chaerea accepted his fate in a noble manner and that his face betrayed nothing of his true feelings, except that he chided Lupus for bursting into tears. [270] And when Lupus took off his toga and complained of the cold, Chaerea even joked to the effect that the cold never did any harm to a wolf.[105] Crowds followed to watch the spectacle. Then, when they reached the place of execution, Chaerea asked the soldier if he had any experience of butchery, or was this the first time he had wielded the executioner's sword. He then told him to go and get the sword with which he himself had put an end to Gaius. And so he died, lucky enough to be killed with a single blow. [271] But

---

[100] In Jos. *JW*. 2.213 Agrippa intervenes to warn Claudius of the danger and that if he did not restrain the praetorians, then he would risk losing the men who could support his rule.

[101] This could well be the Aponius Saturninus who fell asleep at one of Gaius' auctions and woke up to find that his nodding of his head during his sleep had bought him thirteen gladiators (Suet. *Cal.* 38.4).

[102] Clearly security was very tight (Suet. *Claud.* 35; Dio 60.3.2). It was perhaps at this point that the senate voted Claudius 'all the powers of the principate' (Dio 60.1.4).

[103] Rufrius Pollio (Dio 60.23.2) and his colleague Catonius Justus (60.18.4) were presumably appointed at the same time; Gaius' prefects' failure to protect him cannot have endeared them to Claudius.

[104] Perhaps Chaerea's jibes against Claudius (section 258) ensured his fate. The emphasis on Lupus in the ensuing sections suggests that the murder of Gaius' wife and daughter was also partly to blame for their executions.

[105] A Latin pun also made by J.K. Rowling (Remus Lupin).

Lupus lost his nerve and died rather less tidily. He failed to expose his neck properly and it took a number of blows to finish him off.[106]

[272] A few days later, when the ritual sacrifices to the dead were offered, the Roman people made offerings for their own relatives, but also honoured Chaerea by casting a share of the sacrifice into the fire for him, together with prayers that he should look kindly upon them and not be angry with them for their ingratitude. So ended the life of Chaerea.[107]

[273] As for Sabinus, not only was he acquitted by Claudius of all responsibility for the murder, but he was even allowed to retain the post of tribune, which he held. But he could not face the idea that he had failed to keep faith with his fellow conspirators, so he committed suicide, falling upon his sword until it had pierced him right up to the hilt.[108]

[274] Claudius moved decisively to purge the army of all the elements whose loyalty was suspect, and then issued a proclamation to the effect that Agrippa's rule (as tetrarch of Galilee), conferred on him by Gaius, was confirmed, accompanied by a official encomium of the king for his loyalty. He extended his kingdom by adding to it Judea and Samaria, the lands ruled by Herod, his grandfather, [275] in recognition of the debt owed to him by virtue of his kinship to Herod. To these he added Abila, once ruled by Lysanias, and from his own territory all the mountain regions of Lebanon. Finally he ratified by oath a treaty of alliance with Agrippa, in a ceremony held in the centre of the Forum in Rome.[109]

---

[106] How many 'other Romans' is unclear. Dio 60.3.4 refers to 'certain others'; Suet. *Cal.* 59 and *Claud.* 11.1 refers to a few tribunes and centurions, under the impression that Caesonia was killed by a centurion.

[107] This festival (*placandis Manibus*) started on February 13 and lasted until February 22.

[108] Fulfilling the promise he had made earlier (section 261).

[109] Josephus' story here returns to the career of Agrippa. Dio 65.15–16 and Pliny relate that two men prominent in Josephus' tale, Vinicianus and Pomponius, were executed for joining the rebellion to oust Claudius initiated by Arruntius Scribonianus several years later (**P7**).

SECTION F

SENECA, *THE* APOCOLOCYNTOSIS *OF DIVUS CLAUDIUS*

'Seneca composed a work which he entitled Apocolocyntosis (Gourdification), as though it were some kind of deification'.

Introduction: The work is entitled by the best and oldest manuscript 'Divi Claudii ΑΠΟΘΗΟCIC (sic – Greek short and long 'e' and 'o' are confused) Annaei Seneca per satiram' (The Apoth<eo>sis of Claudius the god in satirical mode). The title that we use is derived from the passage of Cassius Dio quoted above (60.35.2). He was writing a century and a half after Seneca's death and is discussing the death of Claudius whom he believes to have been poisoned by Agrippina and Nero. There is no reason to deny that what Dio describes is the work we have. The Greek title *Apocolocyntosis* clearly plays on the Greek word *apotheōsis*. A *colocuntē* is a gourd, and there is some evidence that *cucurbita* (the Latin equivalent) could be used to describe a numskull, whose skull is as empty as a dried gourd. But Seneca's farce does not show Claudius becoming a pumpkin or any other kind of gourd. It was probably designed to entertain Nero's intimate circle at around the time of Claudius's politically-motivated consecration as a god, an event that could have taken place a month or so after his death on 13 October 54. A suitable occasion for its reading might have been the Saturnalia festival in mid-December (compare 8.2; 12.2), the new emperor's first 'Christmas party'.

Seneca took over a Hellenistic literary form called Menippean satire: it combined prose and verse, the serious and the comic. The serious aspect of the work shows in the similarities it exhibits to Nero's first speech to the senate (Tac. *Ann.* 13.4, compare Suet. *Nero* 10), written for him by Seneca. Claudius is criticised for the power of his freedmen (6.2; 15.2), the venality of the court (9.4; 12.2; 12.3, v. 28), his monopolisation of jurisdiction and his exercise of it without regard for proper procedure (7.5; 12.3, vv. 19–28; 10.4; 14.2). Augustus is held up as the good example (10–11), who vetoes the deification of Claudius, the bad example (11.4–5), and Nero is praised for the emergence of proper legal forms (4.1, vv. 23–4; 12.2). But the farcical element predominates. Claudius is laughed at for trivial faults: his voice (5.3), his walk (5.2), his undignified conduct (4.3); philosophers are ridiculed (2.2), and even Augustus' obsession with his achievements, as in the *Res Gestae*, and with his family, raises a laugh (10.2–3). Only Nero is sacred: flattery of his voice and beauty, and celebration of the Golden Age he inaugurates (4.1, vv. 8–32) appear elsewhere in Neronian writers. Here they are used to encourage Nero to stay on the right path.

[The edition of P.T. Eden, *Seneca* Apocolocyntosis (Cambridge, 1984) has a useful introduction, translation and commentary, which is, however, geared to the Latin text.]

F1 Introduction and 'historiography'

[1.1] I want to record for posterity[1] the debate which took place in heaven on 13 October in the new year which was the start of an age of prosperity. There will be no concession to any grudge or partiality. This report is absolutely true. If anyone wants to know where I obtained my information, first, I shall not reply, if I do not want to. Who is going to force me? I know that I have been given freedom of action, since he met his fate, that man who had truly exemplified the saying that one ought to be born either a king or a fool. [1.2] If it suits me to give an answer, I will say whatever comes into my mouth. Who ever required sworn testimonies from an historian? Yet if it is necessary to produce my source, inquiry should be made of the man who saw Drusilla going to heaven: he will say he saw Claudius making the same journey '*with unequal*

[1] In this first chapter Seneca ridicules the claims of Greek and Roman historians to impartiality and the use of reliable sources, particularly eye-witnesses.

paces'.[2] Whether he likes it or not, he is bound to see everything that is transacted in heaven: he is in charge of the Appian Way, the road on which, you know, both Divus Augustus and Tiberius Caesar went to the gods.[3] [1.3] If you ask this man, he will tell you, if you are alone: he will never say a word in the presence of more than one. For ever since he swore in the senate that he had seen Drusilla ascending to heaven and, in return for such good news, found nobody believes what he saw, he has bound himself on oath not to give evidence, even if he had seen a man murdered in the middle of the forum. What I heard from him then I report plainly and clearly, as surely as I wish him hale and hearty.

F2 Date of Claudius' death

[2.1] *Now Phoebus had reduced the curvèd path of light*
With shorter route. Now waxed the hours of dusky Sleep.
Victorious Cynthia now increased her realm,
And loathsome Winter gnawed the pleasing charms
Of wealthy Autumn. Now, with Bacchus forced to age,
The late grape-gatherer plucked the few remaining grapes.

[2.2] I think it is easier to understand if I say: the month was October, the day was the thirteenth. I cannot tell you the hour for certain (philosophers agree with each other more readily than clocks)[4], but it was between the sixth and seventh hour. [2.3] "This is too boorish! All poets enjoy these conventions so much that, not content just to describe sunrises and sunsets, they even disturb the midday siesta. Is this all you have to say about such a splendid time of day?"

Now Phoebus had completed half his chariot-ride.
More close to Night, he shook his tired reins,
By angled path sent down his redirected light:

then Claudius began to gasp his last and could not find the way out.

F3 The Fates discuss Claudius' allotted span of life

[3.1] Then Mercury, since he had always been delighted by Claudius' qualities, took one of the three Fates aside[5] and said, "Why are you allowing the poor man to be tortured, you cruel woman? Will he never have rest, though he has been tormented so

[2] Julia Drusilla, sister of Caligula, was deified on her death in 38 (**J22**; **A38t**); a senator Livius Geminius, was apparently bribed, to attested on oath that he had seen her ascending to heaven (Dio 59.11.4). Seneca mocks Claudius's erratic gait (compare 5.2) by invoking Virgil's description of Ascanius trying to keep up with his father Aeneas (*Aen.* 2.723).

[3] Augustus died at Nola (Tac. *Ann.* 1.5.3), Tiberius at Misenum (Tac. *Ann.* 6.50; **J2g**). In both cases their bodies were brought back to Rome on the Appian Way.

[4] Seneca's words appear in Latin below a sundial designed in 1986 in Benson Court, Magdalene College, Cambridge.

[5] Mercury was the god who escorted the souls of the dead to the underworld; the three fates were Clotho, Lachesis and Atropos.

long? It is sixty-four years since he started his struggle against life.[6] Why do you hold a grudge against him and the state? [3.2] Allow what the astrologers say to become true at some point: they have been carrying him off every year, every month since he became the emperor. And yet it is not surprising if they are wrong and no one knows his appointed hour: for nobody ever thought that he had been born. Do what must be done: '*Give him over to death, let his superior reign in his vacated court.*' [3.3] But Clotho said, "By Hercules, I was keen to give him a little bit more time, until he gave the citizenship to these very few who remain without it," (for Claudius had decided to see all Greeks, Gauls, Spaniards and Britons wearing the toga)[7] "but since it pleases you that some foreigners are left over to spread their seed, and since you order it to be so, let it be so." [3.4] Then she opened a little box and brought out three spindles: one belonged to Augurinus,[8] the next to Baba, the third to Claudius. "These three I shall order to die in one year, separated by tiny intervals of time, and I shall not dismiss Claudius unaccompanied. For it is not right for a man who just now used to see so many thousands of men following him, going before him, and surrounding him, to be left suddenly on his own. He will be satisfied with these familiar friends in the meantime."

F4 The Fates spin a golden thread of life for Nero

[4.1] *She spoke these words, then turning thread around*
Her ugly spool, she broke the royal season of
The dullard's life. But Lachesis, her locks tied back,
Her hair adorned, with laurel wreathed her tresses
And her brow. She took white threads of snow-white fleece
To shape with lucky touch; and this, teased out, assumed
A wondrous hue. The sisters wondered at their work:
Cheap wool transformed to precious ore, a Golden Age
Descended on a lovely thread. And yet there was
No limit set: the fleeces they teased out were blessed –
Glad they were to fill their hands: their work delightful.
Their task went quickly of its own accord,
Soft threads descending freely on the twisted spool.
The years of Nestor and Tithonus too were passed.[9]

---

6 Claudius was born on 1 August 10 BC (Suet. *Claud.* 2.1). He was disabled, being notably unable to control his physical movements. His mother, Antonia, is (shockingly) said to have referred to him as an unfinished monster (Suet. *Claud.* 3.2). But even now an MP with cerebral palsy can apparently be mocked in the House of Commons by 'honourable' members (widely reported in UK media, 5 February 2011).

7 Wearing the toga was the mark of a Roman citizen. There is no evidence that Claudius was unduly generous with citizenship, but Seneca may be alluding to his famous speech advocating the admission to the senate of some Gallic chieftains, in which he apparently praised the progressive admission to citizenship of worthy provincials (*ILS* 212 = **M11d**; Tac. *Ann.* 11.24 = **M12**).

8 M. Furrius Augurinus was suffect consul in 40 (**B40**).

9 Nestor in Homer's *Iliad* 1.250–2 had seen two generations pass away and was now ruling over the third. Tithonus was a Trojan prince abducted by Dawn to be her lover. She asked Zeus to grant him immortality, but forgot to ask also for eternal youth, so he withered away.

Phoebus attended,[10] *singing his own song of joy*
At what's to come. In joy he plucked the strings,
Then passed the wool. His music charmed their ears,
Beguiled away their toil. And while they greatly praised
Their brother's song and lyre, their hands had spun
More than they should: and their impressive work
Transcended human destiny. "Do not reduce it, Fates,"
Said Phoebus, "Let him go beyond the span
Of human life, as one like me in countenance
And beauty; not inferior in song or voice.
For he shall bring an age of plenty for the weary,
And will break the silence of the laws.
He's like the Morning Star, who as he rises
Scatters fleeing stars. Or like the Evening Star
Who rises when the stars return. Or like the Sun,
Who shines as soon as rosy Dawn dissolves the dark
And brings the day; the Sun looks down upon the world,
Begins to drive his chariot from the starting box.
Now such a Caesar is at hand, such a Nero Rome
Shall look upon. His lovely neck with flowing hair,
His shining face with gentle radiance gleams."

[4.2] This is what Apollo said. But Lachesis, since she herself also felt a fancy for such a very good-looking man, responded generously and gave Nero many years from her own supply. However, in the case of Claudius, they ordered everyone '*to send him out of the house rejoicing and saying fair words*'. And Claudius did indeed splutter out his life, and from that time ceased even to appear to live. But he expired while he was listening to some comic actors, so you know that I have good reason to fear them.[11] [4.3] These were the final words of his that were heard among men, after he had let out a greater sound from that part from which he used to talk more readily: "Oh dear, I think I've shitted myself." Whether he did so, I don't know; he certainly did shit up everything else.

F5 Claudius' arrival in heaven

[5.1] It is quite unnecessary to report what went on afterwards on earth, as you know this very well and there is no danger of the events which made such a joyful impression on the public being forgotten: no one forgets his own good luck. Listen to what happened in heaven: my source will be responsible for the reliability of this report. [5.2] A message was brought to Jupiter that there was a new arrival, someone of good height, very white-haired; that he was making some sort of threat, for he kept wagging his head; and that he was dragging his right foot. The messenger said he had asked what nationality he was, but that he had made some reply with a confused noise

10 Phoebus, another name for Apollo, is the leader of the Fates and also the god whom Augustus had identified with and whom Nero emulated as a poet and charioteer. The inauguration of a new Golden Age, comparable to the Augustan Age celebrated in Virgil's Fourth Eclogue, is to be found in pastoral poetry of the early Neronian period, see **T15**.

11 Seneca follows the official version of Claudius' death. According to Suet. *Claud.* 45, the announcement was delayed, comic actors being brought in, as if at his request, after he was dead.

and an incoherent sound. The messenger hadn't understood his language: he was neither Greek nor Roman nor of any known race. [5.3] Then Jupiter ordered Hercules, who had wandered all over the world and seemed to be acquainted with all nations, to go and find out what race of men he belonged to. Then, at his first glimpse, Hercules was indeed shocked, in that he had thought he had already seen and feared every sort of monster. When he saw his shape, as of a new species, his unusual manner of movement, his voice, which was not that of a land animal but similar to the normal call of sea beasts, rough and confused, he thought that his thirteenth labour had come to him. [5.4] But when he looked more closely it seemed to be some sort of person. So he approached and said, as was very easy for a Greekling, '*Who are you, and whence do you come? Of what sort are your city and parents?*' Claudius was glad that there were men of learning there: he hoped that there would be some place for his histories.[12] And so he spoke up himself, indicating that he was Caesar by means of a verse of Homer: '*The wind carrying me from Ilium brought me to the Cicones.*' (The next verse, however, was truer, and likewise from Homer: '*There I sacked the city and destroyed the people.*')

F6 The goddess Fever mocks Claudius as a Gaul

[6.1] And he would certainly have deceived Hercules, who was pretty dim, if the goddess Fever had not been there. Abandoning her own shrine, she alone had come with him, leaving all the rest of the gods in Rome. "That fellow," she said, "is telling you downright lies. I can assure you – I have lived with him for so many years – that he was born at Lyons. You are looking at a fellow citizen of Munatius. I tell you, he was born at the sixteenth milestone from Vienne, a true Gaul. And so he did what a Gaul ought to do – he captured Rome. I guarantee to you that he was born at Lyons where Licinus ruled for many years.[13] But, with a wider stamping-ground than any long-distance mule-driver, you ought to know that many miles intervene between the Xanthus and the Rhône. [6.2] At this point Claudius grew incandescent with rage and showed it by mumbling as loudly as he could. What he was saying, though, no one could begin to understand. Actually, he kept ordering Fever to be taken away. Using that familiar gesture of his uncontrollable hand (it was steady enough for this one purpose) with which he usually had people beheaded, he had commanded her neck to be severed. You would think they were all his own freedmen: so little attention did anyone pay him.[14]

---

[12] Claudius recognises the quotation from Homer (*Ody.* 1.170), from whom he himself liked quoting (Suet. *Claud.* 42.1). He replies with *Od.* 9.39, indicating his descent from Aeneas, claimed by previous emperors as Julii and so by Claudius, and his arrival among barbarians (the Romans). He wrote several historical works, in Latin and in Greek (Suet. *Claud.* 41–2; **R25**).

[13] Claudius was born at Lugdunum. His mother Antonia was accompanying his father Drusus who was campaigning against the Germans. Munatius Plancus founded the colony when governor of Transalpine Gaul 44–43 BC (*ILS* 886). Licinus, born in Gaul and freed from slavery by Julius Caesar, made himself notorious for extortion as Augustus' procurator of Gallia Lugdunensis (Dio 54.21. 2). The other details, the distance between Lugdunum and the colony of Vienna in Gallia Narbonensis to the south ('a true Gaul' emphasises the less civilised character of Tres Galliae) and the sack of Rome by the Gauls in the fifth century BC were in Claudius' speech (see n.7), which is perhaps being ridiculed again.

[14] Seneca alludes to Claudius' tendency to anger (Suet. *Claud.* 38.1) and his subservience to his freedmen secretaries (Suet. *Claud.* 25.5; Dio 60.2.4; **S23–S29**).

F7 Hercules questions Claudius

[7.1] Then Hercules said, "You there, listen to me, and stop playing the fool. You have come to a land where mice gnaw iron. Quickly tell me the truth, or I'll shake the nonsense out of you." And so as to be the more daunting, he adopted a tragic style and said:

[7.2] *Hasten to tell me the place which you claim for your birth,*
Or struck by my cudgel you'll fall to the earth:
Fierce are the kings that this club has so frequently slain.
What sound do you utter with voice so unclear?
Tell me what country, what people your shaking head reared!
For when I was seeking the far-off domains
Owned by the three-bodied king whose great cattle I drove
Inland to the town of Inachus, I saw
Loom o'er two rivers a ridge, which at morning the Sun,
Apollo looks straight in the face at his rise;
There flows the Rhône in its greatness with current so swift,
The Saône, with its shallows, meanders along
Quietly washing its banks and unsure where to roam
Can that be the nurse of your life and your home?

[7.3] These words he said with spirit and courage enough, but nonetheless he was not master of his own mind and he feared the slings and arrows of a fool. When Claudius marked the mighty man, he forgot to quibble, and realised that whilst no one had been his equal at Rome, there he did not have the same degree of influence: a cock struts supreme on his own dunghill. [7.4] And so, as far as he could be understood, he appeared to be saying this: "I did hope, Hercules, that you, the bravest of the gods, would stand by me in front of the others, and if anyone asked me for a sponsor, I was going to name you, who have got to know me best. For if you delve in your memory, I was the one who used to dispense justice in front of your temple for whole days in the months of July and August.[15] [7.5] You know how great a list of plaints I deliberated there, when I was listening to the advocates day and night. If you'd stumbled into that, as brave as you may seem to yourself, you would have preferred to clean out the sewers of Augeas: I drained off much more bullshit. But since I wish …"

(there is a short gap in the text at this point)

F8 Discussions of what sort of god Claudius would be

[8.1] "It isn't surprising that you have made a forced entry to the senate-house: nothing is closed to you. Just tell us what sort of god you wish that fellow to become. He cannot be an '*Epicurean god, having no trouble himself nor causing any to others*.' A Stoic? How can he be, as Varro says, '*spherical, with no head, with no foreskin*?'[16]

---

[15] Seneca emphasises Claudius' passion for trying cases by mentioning the two summer months when the courts were usually not very busy and most residents of Rome fled the city (compare Suet. *Claud.* 23.1).

[16] The Epicureans believed in the existence of gods in human shape but thought that they took no interest in human affairs and enjoyed themselves, like perfect Epicureans. For the Stoics, god was identical with the cosmos, which they imagined as round, or with the rational principal that infused the universe and appeared in humans as reason.

But now I see, there *is* something of the Stoic god about him: he has no head and no heart. [8.2] By Hercules, if he had sought this favour from Saturn, whose month he celebrated the whole year as Carnival emperor,[17] he would not have got it. Is he to be introduced as a god by Jupiter, whom he convicted of incest, as far as was in his power! For he executed his son-in-law Silanus. "On what grounds, pray?" Because of his sister, the most charming of all girls, whom everyone else called Venus: but Silanus preferred to call her Juno. [8.3] "Why his own sister, I ask you?" he says. You fool, look it up! You're allowed half of it in Athens, the whole thing at Alexandria.[18] '*At Rome the mice lick the millstones*' you say, but is he the man to straighten our immorality? He will not know what he is doing in his own bedroom: already he is '*scanning the zones of heaven*'. He wants to become a god? Is it not enough that he has a temple in Britain,[19] that the barbarians now worship him and pray, '*to find the fool well-disposed*' as if he were a god?

F9 The senate of the gods meets in debate

[9.1] At last it occurred to Jupiter that senators were not allowed to state an opinion or to debate while ordinary persons were loitering in the senate.[20] "I had permitted you to ask questions, gentlemen of the senate," he said, "but you have made a complete dog's dinner. I desire you to keep to the correct procedure of the senate-house. What must this man think of us, whatever kind of fellow he is?" [9.2] When Claudius had been sent out, Father Janus was the first called on for his opinion. He had been designated as consul for the afternoon of 1 July, a fellow who is always looking '*forwards and backwards simultaneously*', as far as his own street leads. He spoke at length and eloquently, because he lived in the Forum, but the shorthand writer could not keep up and so I do not report him in case I should misquote what he said.[21] [9.3] He spoke a lot about the greatness of the gods: this honour ought not to be given indiscriminately. "Once it was a great thing to be made a god," he said. "now you have made it a Bean farce. And so that I don't appear to be making a judgement on an individual rather than an issue, I propose that after today no one should be made a god from these who '*eat the fruit of the earth*' or from these whom the '*grain-giving*

---

[17] Claudius extended the Saturnalia festival from one day to five (Dio 60.25.8), but Seneca means that Claudius indulged in eating, drinking and dicing more than was appropriate for a *princeps* (compare Suet. *Claud.* 33.1, 39.1).

[18] L. Junius Silanus Torquatus, great-great-grandson of Augustus through his mother Aemilia Lepida, daughter of the younger Julia, had been betrothed to Claudius' daughter Octavia in AD 41 (**J33a**). Agrippina, wanting to increase Nero's chances of becoming Emperor by marrying him to Octavia, had Silanus accused of incest with his sister Junia Calvina and had him struck off the senate rolls. He committed suicide in 49 on the day that Agrippina married Claudius (Tac. *Ann.* 12.3–4, 12.8). Jupiter was married to his sister Juno. At Athens Cimon had been married to his half-sister Elpinece by the same father; in Egypt the Ptolemies regularly married their full sisters or brothers.

[19] The temple to Divus Claudius was in the Roman colony of Camulodunum (Colchester) and was a focus of discontent in the big rebellion of 60–1 (Tac. *Ann.* 14.32.1; **L21**).

[20] Seneca imagines the meeting of the gods following the protocol of the Roman senate, where non-members had to leave unless specially invited and the presiding officer, here Jupiter, would make a proposal and then call on senators in order of rank to give their opinion, starting with the consuls designate. These opinions could take the form of a senatorial decree and the presiding officer, at the end of the debate, would use them to formulate the issue in asking senators to vote with their feet.

[21] Cicero's secretary Tiro invented a system of shorthand, and this was doubtless employed in producing the *senatus acta diurna* (Roman equivalent of 'Hansard') instituted by Julius Caesar in 59 BC (Suet. *Jul.* 20.1).

earth' nourishes. Anyone who is made, named or depicted as a god in contravention of this resolution of the senate, is to be given to the spirits and flogged with canes among the new recruits in the next gladiatorial games." [9.4] Next to be asked for his opinion was Diespiter, the son of Vica Pota, himself also a consul-designate and a money-changer. He used to make ends meet by selling citizenship rights. Hercules sidled up to him and gave him a nudge. So Diespiter made a proposal in these words: [9.5] "Since the divine Claudius is a blood-relation of both Divus Augustus and, no less, Diva Augusta, his grandmother,[22] whom he himself commanded to be a goddess, and since he far excels all mortal men in wisdom and since it is in the public interest for there to be someone who can '*gobble boiled turnips*' with Romulus, I propose that from this day Divus Claudius should be every bit as much a god as anyone before him who became a god with excellent justification, and that this event be added to Ovid's *Metamorphoses*."[23] [9.6] A range of opinions was expressed and Claudius seemed to be winning the vote. For Hercules, who saw that his iron was in the fire, kept dashing this way and that and saying "Don't go against me, my own position is on the line; then if you want something, I'll pay you back. One good turn deserves another."

F10 Augustus speaks against Claudius

[10.1] Then, at his turn to express his opinion, Divus Augustus got up and spoke with the utmost eloquence. "I call you to witness, conscript fathers," he said, "that from the time when I became a god, I have not uttered a word: I always mind my own business. And yet I can no longer conceal or repress the feelings of grief exacerbated by shame. Was it for this that I secured peace on land and sea? Was it for this that I suppressed the civil wars? Was it for this that I founded the city on a basis of law, adorned it with monuments, so that . . . ? What am I to say, conscript fathers? I can find no words! They all fall short of my outrage. So I must take refuge in that well-known saying of a very eloquent man, Messalla Corvinus – '*The power of my position shames me.*'[24] [10.3] This man, gentlemen of the senate, whom you think couldn't disturb a fly, used to kill people as readily as a dog squats on its haunches. But why should I myself speak on the subject of the men he killed, many and distinguished though they were. I have no leisure to lament public disasters when faced with the troubles of my family. And so I will ignore the former and concentrate on the latter. For I know that '*the knee is closer than the shin*', even if my ankle does not. [10.4] That fellow whom you see, who has been hiding for so many years under my name,[25] returned the favour to me by

[22] Claudius was descended indirectly from Augustus through his mother Antonia Minor, who was the daughter of Antony and Augustus' sister Octavia. He was descended from Augustus' second wife Livia through his father Drusus, who was her younger son by her first husband Ti. Claudius Nero. She had been adopted into the Julian gens and renamed Julia Augusta on Augustus death, but neither Tiberius on her death or Caligula later had her granted divine honours. It was Claudius who did (**L22**; Suet. *Claud.* 11.2; Dio 60.5.2).

[23] This poem ended with the deification of Julius Caesar being decreed in a senate of the gods and that of Augustus being predicted (Ovid, *Met.* 15.745–870).

[24] M. Valerius Messala Corvinus, a distinguished senator, was the first to hold the new post of Prefect of the City. Appointed *c.* 25 BC, he resigned after a few days, saying he did not know how to act (Tac. *Ann.* 6.11.3), being concerned that the *imperium* he had been given had not been properly delimited. Here Augustus is ashamed of the powerful position of *princeps* that he held, since Claudius' tenure shows it was open to arbitrary abuse.

[25] Claudius was the first *princeps* not entitled by descent to the name Caesar, which up to now had been a family name, a cognomen of the Julian gens, but now became a name assumed by all *principes* and later also by expected successors, natural and adopted, of *principes*.

killing two Julias, my great-granddaughters, one by the sword, the other by starvation, and one great-great-grandson, L. Silanus: you, Jupiter, will see whether Silanus was in the wrong – certainly you have done the same, if you are going to be just.[26] Tell me, Divus Claudius, why you condemned any one of these men and women whom you put to death before you got to know their cases, or even heard them. Where is this kind of thing customary? It is not so in heaven.

F11 Augustus lists Claudius' victims

[11.1] Look at Jupiter, who has been reigning for so many years. One person's leg he has broken – that of Vulcan whom '*he hurled from the threshold of heaven, having taken him by the foot*'.[27] He also became angry with his wife and hung her up: did he ever kill? Yet you killed Messalina, whose great-great uncle I was as much as I was yours. "I don't know," do you say? May the gods curse you: your ignorance is much more shameful than the fact that you killed her![28] [11.2] Gaius Caesar's death did not stop Claudius targeting him. Gaius had killed his own father-in-law: Claudius killed his son-in-law as well. Gaius forbade the son of Crassus being called "the Great": Claudius restored his name but removed his head. In one household he killed Crassus, Magnus and Scribonia: [29] admittedly not exactly as royal as the family of Assaracus, but nobles nonetheless. Indeed Crassus was so stupid that he was even qualified to reign. [11.3] Is this the man you now want to make a god? See his body, born when the gods were in foul mood. In short, let him spit out three words without hesitation and he can have me as his slave. [11.4] Who will worship this man as a god? Who will believe in him? As long as you make such gods, no one will believe that you are gods. This is the heart of the matter, conscript fathers: if I have conducted myself honourably among you, if I have not answered anybody too bluntly, avenge the wrongs done to me. I am putting forward this proposal as my considered opinion" (and this is what he read out from his tablet): [11.5] "Since Divus Claudius has put to death his father-in-law Appius Silanus, his two sons-in-law Magnus Pompeius and L. Silanus, his daughter's father-in-law Crassus Frugi, a man as like himself as one egg is to another, Scribonia his daughter's mother-in-law, his own wife Messalina, and others too numerous to mention, I propose that a severe example be made of

---

26 The two Julias were victims of Messallina, Claudius' first wife. Julia (**J16**), the daughter of Tiberius' son Drusus and Livia Julia (Claudius' sister, **J11**), was accused by Suillius Rufus, the noted Claudian prosecutor, and condemned to death (Dio 60.18.4; Tac. *Ann.*13.43.3) and Julia Livilla (**J23**), the daughter of Germanicus, who was Claudius' brother and Tiberius' adopted son, was banished on a charged of adultery with Seneca (Dio 60.8.5). As Tiberius was Augustus' adopted son, they counted as his granddaughters. On Silanus see 8.2 and note 18.

27 Homer, *Iliad* 1.591.

28 On Jupiter's punishments, see the *Iliad* 1.586ff. and 15.18 ff. Augustus was the great-great uncle of Valeria Messallina (**J25**), who, according to Tac. *Ann.* 11.30–8, had married the consul designate Gaius Silius and was ordered to commit suicide by Claudius' freedman Narcissus. Claudius only found out when at dinner.

29 Caligula had his father-in-law Marcus Junius Silanus, (suff. cos. AD 15), whose daughter Junia Claudia was his first wife, commit suicide in 38; Claudius killed his father-in-law (really his stepfather-in-law) C. Appius Junius Silanus (cos. 28) without trial after he had arranged his marriage to Messallina's mother Domitia. The son-in-law Claudius killed is probably Cn. Pompeius Magnus, the son of M. Licinius Crassus Frugi (cos. 27) and Scribonia. In 41 he married Antonia, Claudius' daughter by Aelia Paetina. The name reflected maternal descent from Pompey the Great. He was deprived of his *cognomen* 'Magnus' = 'Great' by Caligula (Suet. *Cal.* 35.1) and killed by orders of Claudius (Suet. *Claud.* 29.1). The three killed in one household are thus this man and his parents.

him, that no exemption from prosecution be granted to him, and that he should be deported as soon as possible, and leave heaven within thirty days and Olympus within three." [11.6] Members rose to their feet to support this proposal. There was no delay, Mercury dragged him out, twisting his neck, down to the underworld from heaven '*whence they say no-one returns*.'

F12 Claudius' funeral

[12.1] While they were going down the Sacred Way,[30] Mercury inquired what such a crowd of people could mean, whether it was Claudius' funeral. And indeed it was a most elegant affair with no effort spared, so that you would immediately realise that it was a god's funeral cortège. There was so great a crowd, such a great collection of trumpeters, horn-players, and players of every kind of brass instrument, that even Claudius could hear it. Everybody was joyful and in high spirits. [12.2] The Roman people were walking about like free citizens. Agatho and a few advocates were wailing, but their grief was plainly heartfelt. The legal experts were coming out of their hiding-places, pale and slight, scarcely drawing breath, like people who were only just coming to life again. One of them, when he saw the advocates putting their heads together and lamenting their change in fortune, came up and said, "I kept on telling you the Saturnalia wouldn't last forever."[31] [12.3] Claudius, when he saw his own funeral, understood that he was dead.[32] For in a mighty *grand finale* they were chanting a dirge:

Pour forth your tears and beat at your breasts,
Cries full of woe should ring in the square.
Dead is the fellow brilliant of mind
None in the whole world braver than he.
  He could do all:[33]
Ride at full speed overtaking the swift;
Rout rebel Parthians; harass the Mede
Though lightly armed; unshaking his hand
Stretches his bow to shoot at the Mede
Turning their backs in headlong retreat.
Rich were their clothes now peppered with wounds.[34]
Under his rule the Britons beyond

---

[30] The Sacred Way was the main route to the forum from the southeast and was the scene of many processions, here Claudius' funeral.

[31] By encouraging litigation and arrogating jurisdiction to himself, Claudius had encouraged advocates like Suillius Rufus (**B41** and note) who made fortunes by bribery and collusion. Meanwhile the legal experts were unemployed, as Claudius interpreted the laws in his own idiosyncratic way (Suet. *Claud.* 14).

[32] Claudius' absent-mindedness is much remarked: he was, for example, unaware of Messallina's marriage to someone else and of her death (11.1 and note 28): see Suet. *Claud.* 4.5; 39.

[33] The emphasis on Claudius' personal military achievement is ironic. Having no military record when he became *princeps*, he was eager to make up for it by taking 27 imperial salutations, more than Augustus' 21.

[34] In fact, by the time of Claudius' death, Rome had once more lost control of Armenia to Tiridates, brother of the Parthian king. Nero's first foreign policy venture was to send the general Domitius Corbulo to regain Armenia and stabilise the Parthian frontier. Seneca refers to the Parthians by the names of Persians and Medes who occupied the territory in the great days of the Greek struggle against Persia.

Shores of the seas unknown until then;
Tribal Brigantes with indigo shields,
Bowed to his word,
Bent down their necks now subject to Rome.
Great Oceanus shakes at the powers
Legally wielded in Rome's new domain.[35]
Weep for the man who mastered his briefs
Quickest of all – one side of the case
More than enough for him to have heard.
Who now will listen as judge at the courts
All the year round?
Minos who judges a silent great throng
Lord of a hundred cities of Crete
Leaving his bench resigns it to you.[36]
Strike at your breasts with hands full of grief
Advocates, venal tribe that you are.
Mourn, modern poets, and you, more than all,
Gamblers at dice who raked in the cash.

F13 Claudius' victims welcome him to the underworld

[13.1] Claudius was delighted with this eulogy, and wanted to watch for longer. But the Talthybius[37] of the gods laid a hand on him and pulled him away, with his head covered so that he could not be recognised, across the Field of Mars, and went down to the underworld between the Tiber and the Covered Way. [13.2] The freedman Narcissus had already taken a short cut to be ready to receive his patron, and he ran up to meet him, fresh and gleaming, as he was straight from the bath,[38] and said: "For what purpose have gods come to men?" "Be quick!" said Mercury, "and announce that we are coming." [13.3] Quick as a flash, Narcissus flew off. It was downhill all the way, the descent was easy. And so, in spite of his gout, Narcissus came in a short space of time to the door of Dis, where Cerberus was lying, or, as Horace says, "the hundred-headed beast". Narcissus (who used to keep a whitish bitch as a pet) was a tiny bit shocked when he saw that hairy black hound, certainly not the sort of thing you would like to encounter in the dark, and in a loud voice he announced "Claudius will be coming." [13.4] The crowd came forward with clapping and singing "*We*

35 The conquest of the southern part of Britain by Aulus Plautius and the creation of a Roman province there constituted Claudius' most significant military achievement (**N13–N30**). He spent sixteen days there in AD 43 and was hailed by the troops as *imperator* (victorious commander). He celebrated a triumph for it at Rome in 44. On that occasion Claudius acquired a naval crown to signify his victory over Ocean, of which he boasts also in the speech on the admission of Gallic senators (*ILS* 212 = **M11d**). The Brigantes were not conquered until the reign of Vespasian, though Ostorius Scapula (**N34**) put down a revolt against their queen Cartimandua, who was friendly to Rome.

36 Minos, the legendary king of Crete, was one of the judges in the underworld: it is Aeacus, however, who condemns Claudius (14–15).

37 Talthybius was Agamemnon's herald in the *Iliad*: the 'Talthybius of the gods' is Mercury.

38 Narcissus, Claudius' freedman *ab epistulis* (in charge of his letters), was one of his closest political associates and a defender of the interests of Britannicus against Agrippina, whose marriage to Claudius he had opposed. Seneca alludes here to his enforced stay at the baths of Sinuessa in Campania for his gout (Dio 60.34.4); as soon as Claudius was dead Narcissus was driven to suicide by Agrippina (Tac. *Ann.* 13.1). Seneca therefore has him reach the underworld before Claudius who had made a detour to Olympus. For Narcissus, see **S25**.

have found him, let us rejoice".[39] Here was Gaius Silius, a consul designate, Juncus, a former praetor, Sextus Traulus, Marcus Helvius, Trogus, Cotta, Vettius Valens, Fabius, Roman equestrians whom Narcissus had ordered off to execution. In the middle of this crowd of singers was Mnester the pantomime artist, whom Claudius had made shorter to suit Messalina, for appearance's sake.[40] [13.5] The rumour that Claudius had arrived spread quickly. First of all, the freedmen Polybius, Myron, Arpocras, Ampheus, and Pheronaotus[41] flew up, all of whom Claudius had sent ahead so that he might have attendants everywhere. Then the two prefects Justus Catonius and Rufrius Pollio.[42] Then his trusted friends, Saturninus Lusius and Pedo Pompeius and Lupus and Celer Asinius, of consular rank.[43] Finally his brother's daughter, his sister's daughter, his sons-in-law, his fathers-in-law, his mothers-in-law, clearly all his relatives.[44] They formed a line to meet Claudius. [13.6] When Claudius saw them, he cried out "*All full of friends*! How did you come here?" Then Pedo Pompeius said "What are you saying, you cruellest of men? You ask how? Who else but you sent us here, you murderer of all your friends? Let us go into the court. In this place *I'm* going to show *you* the magistrates' benches."

F14 Judgement passed on Claudius in the underworld

[14.1] He led him to the court of Aeacus, who presided over cases under Sulla's legislation on murder.[45] Pedo requested the court to record Claudius' name; he charged him with having killed thirty-five senators; three hundred and twenty-one Roman equestrians; other persons, '*as many as grains of sand and flecks of dust*'.

---

39 This is the ritual cry of the followers of Isis when a new Apis bull, regarded as an incarnation of Osiris, is discovered. Like Osiris, Claudius is a god (in the view of humans) and has died.

40 To deal with the crisis of Messallina's marriage to Silius (see note 28), Narcissus had himself put in charge of the praetorian guard for a day and presided over the trials of those present at the wedding. Of the other seven people named here, all but Helvius, Cotta and Fabius are mentioned by Tacitus (*Ann.* 11.35–36). The pantomime actor Mnester was apparently beheaded.

41 Claudius was notorious for giving too much influence to his freedmen. Two of those named here are otherwise known. Polybius was his *a studiis* (Suet. *Claud.* 28) and *a libellis*, in which capacity Seneca had addressed to him from exile a consolation on the death of his brother in hopes of being recalled (see **S24**, **T13–T14**): he was accused by Messallina and put to death (Dio. 60.31.2). Arpocras is presumably the Harpocras of Suet. *Claud.* 28 who was given the privilege of overseeing entertainments.

42 The first is mentioned as a victim of Messallina in 48 by Dio 60.18.3; the second was praetorian prefect from 41 until 48 (Jos. *AJ* 19.14.5, compare Dio 6–23.2).

43 The *amici principis* were usually high-ranking senators and equites whom the emperor would call in to advise him on political matters or to try cases with him (**U6**). Seneca's brother Junius Gallio is described by Claudius on an inscription as 'my friend'. Pedo Pompeius (also mentioned in 14.2) is otherwise unknown. Lusius Saturninus, consul under Tiberius, and Cornelius Lupus, consul in 42, were victims of Suillius Rufus who was acting to please Messallina (Tac. *Ann.* 13.43). Asinius Celer had been consul in 38.

44 They are Julia Livilla (note 26; **J23**), daughter of Germanicus; Julia (note 26; **J16**), daughter of Livia Julia; L. Junius Silanus (note 18; **J33a**), Gn. Pompeius Magnus (see note 29), C. Appius Junius Silanus (note 29), M. Licinius Crassus Frugi (note 29), the father of his son-in-law; Domitia Lepida (**J14**), Messallina's mother, sentenced to death by Claudius in 53 (Tac. *Ann.* 12.64–65), and Scribonia, mother of his son-in-law (note 18).

45 The *Lex Cornelia de secariis et veneficiis*, passed by the dictator Sulla in 81 BC, was still the statute that governed the standing court under the empire (though murder by men of rank could also be tried then before the senate or the emperor). Cases of judicial malpractice resulting in condemnations in the criminal courts could be tried under this law.

Claudius could not find an advocate.[46] [14.2] At last Publius Petronius came forward, an old crony of his,[47] a fellow with Claudius' own eloquence, and requested an adjournment. It was not granted.[48] Pedo Pompeius put the case for the prosecution accompanied by loud shouts. The counsel for the defence began to try to reply. Aeacus, a man of the greatest justice, forbade it and having heard only one side of the case, condemned Claudius, with the words, "*If you were to suffer that which you wrought, immediate justice would be done.*" [14.3] There was an immense silence. Everyone was struck dumb, astonished by the novelty of this procedure. They began to say that this had never happened before. To Claudius it seemed more unjust than unprecedented.[49] There was a long discussion over the nature of the penalty, as to what should be done to him.[50] Some said that Sisyphus had done his carrying for a long time, that Tantalus would die of thirst unless someone helped him, that poor Ixion's wheel ought to have the brake on at some point. [14.4] But it was decided that no relief should be given to any of the old-timers, so that Claudius himself should never expect similar mercy. It was resolved that a new punishment should be fixed, that they should devise a pointless task for him, one with the prospect of gratifying some desire but without any chance of success. Then Aeacus ordered him to play dice with a dice-box that had a hole in it. And already Claudius had begun to seek the ever-vanishing dice and to make no headway.[51]

F15 Conclusion: Claudius punished

[15.1] *For every time he cast the dice, they kept*
Escaping through the hole that formed the base.
So, gath'ring them inside the rattling box,
Resolved to throw again, he always failed.
For like a man at once about to play and search,
Each die recoiled and slipped, a traitor, through
His very grasp, just like the useless weight
Which rolls off Sisyphus' neck just as
He scales the mountain's topmost peaks.

[15.2] Suddenly Gaius Caesar appeared and began to claim Claudius as his slave. He produced witnesses who had seen Claudius being beaten by him with whips, canes and fists.[52] The judgement was made. Aeacus awarded Claudius to Gaius Caesar. Gaius handed him over to his freedman Menander, to be his secretary for law-suits.[53]

---

[46] Seneca imagines the underground tribunal following the procedure of the Roman standing courts. First the accuser asks the presiding magistrate for permission to charge Claudius; that granted, he produces a written indictment. The quotation is from Homer *Iliad* 9.385.

[47] Publius Petronius had been suffect consul in 19, so he could have known Claudius long before his accession.

[48] As Augustus had suggested (11.5).

[49] For this Claudian habit, compare 12.3, v. 21; Suet. *Claud.* 15.2; Dio 60.28.5.

[50] In the standing court the penalty prescribed by statute would be imposed, but Seneca borrows from the freer procedure used before the emperor, as in the judge not hearing both sides of the case.

[51] Claudius was addicted to dicing (12.3, v. 30; Suet. *Claud.* 33.2) where it is said that he had written a book on it. His punishment is an activity as futile as that of Sisyphus, and Tantalus.

[52] Witnesses confirm that Caligula when emperor had treated Claudius as a slave: see Suet. *Claud.* 8–9.

[53] The final punishment also fits Claudius' faults when emperor. He was under the influence of his freedmen, so here he is assigned as a slave assistant to one with the specific job of looking after the emperor's legal cases.

SECTION G

SENECA, *ON CLEMENCY*

Introduction: This incomplete essay, in two books, is the only work of Seneca to be dedicated to the Emperor Nero. It is more securely dated than most of his writings, for Seneca gives the age of his addressee as nineteen, which indicates the period from 15 December of 55 to 14 December of 56 (*Clem.* 1.9.1). Nero had been *princeps* for a year and two months.

As in the *Apocolocyntosis*, Augustus is held up as a model (1.9.2–10; 1.15–16), but in this work Seneca stresses Nero's superiority: whereas Augustus' clemency was 'exhausted cruelty' after an early career marked by the proscriptions and civil war, Nero's clemency is unstained by violence or cruelty (1.9.1; 1.11.1–2, compare 1.1.6). Herein lies a problem. In February of 55 Nero, who is now said not to have spilled a drop of human blood, had murdered Claudius' natural son Britannicus: none of the ancient sources doubts that Nero had Britannicus poisoned at a dinner in the palace. However, the murder was carried out so discreetly that the official version, that Britannicus had had an epileptic fit, was credible, and Seneca and Burrus chose to believe it, probably being among those who received lavish presents from the Emperor (Tac. *Ann.* 13.15–18). Even if they did not sign up to the clichés being circulated about fraternal discord being traditional and kingship being indivisible, they would have felt that the important thing was to convince Nero and the reading public that the renunciation of Claudian cruelty and injustice at the start of the reign would be maintained.

Seneca's composition is a mixture of several literary forms: it is a panegyric of Nero (and ancient panegyric always carried an element of admonition), a Romanised version of the Hellenistic treatises *On Kingship*, and a philosophical treatise on one virtue, rolled into one. The technical analysis of clemency is delayed by Seneca until Book II, of which we only have seven chapters. There would also have been a discussion of how to acquire the virtue and make its practice habitual (1.3.1), possibly in a third book. In *On Clemency* the view taken of the Emperor's role is different from the constitutional notion of power emananting from, and shared with, the senate that Nero had proclaimed in his first speech to that body (Tac. *Ann.* 13.4). Here the role of the *princeps* is repeatedly likened to that of a king (1.3.3; 1.8.1); Nero is said to behave as if he were obliged to obey the laws (1.1.4), and to have unrestricted power (1.11.2; 1.8.5); the safeguard of liberty is the self-restraint of the ruler (1.5.2). In fact, Seneca is expressing a more realistic view of the *princeps'* position, in which constitutional form is unimportant: '*principes* and kings and whatever other name the guardians of the public order bear' protect society from chaos, and at Rome, in particular, 'Caesar has long identified himself so thoroughly with the state that neither one could be withdrawn without the ruin of both: Caesar needs strength and the state needs a head' (1.4.3.).

The notes in this section are hugely endebted to S. Braund's superb commentary, *Seneca,* De Clementia, Oxford 2009.

G1 Introduction (1.1)

[1.1] I have started this essay on Clemency,[1] Nero Caesar, in order to act for you as a sort of mirror. I wish to reveal you to yourself, so as to show you how you will achieve the highest pleasure known to man. For although the true reward for virtuous action lies in the action itself, and virtue is its own and only due reward,[2] there is nonetheless a certain pleasure to be derived from a conscious examination of one's own virtuous actions. There is pleasure, too, in contemplating the vast multitude of your people,

---

1 Clemency (*clementia*) was a virtue of Julius Caesar much praised by his contemporaries, especially Cicero (*e.g. Letters to Atticus* 9.16 which includes Julius Caesar's response). A temple to Caesar's Clemency was voted by the senate (Appian, *Civil Wars* 2.106; Dio 44.6.4). It was one of the four key virtues on Augustus' 'Shield of Virtues' set up by the senate in 28/7 BC (*RG* 34.2, EJ22 = LACTOR 17, H24). Tiberius claimed to exercise it in his treatment of Piso (*SCPP* line 91 = **P3g**) and the senate voted an altar to Clemency with statues to Tiberius and Sejanus (Tac. *Ann.* 4.74.2). Tacitus (*Ann.* 13.11) comments on Nero's early professions of clemency in speeches written by Seneca, who had also attributed it to Claudius (**T14**). A sacrifice was made to Clemency by the Arval Brothers (**A66c**). Titus' clemency was the subject of Mozart's last opera, *La Clemenza di Tito* (K621).

2 It was the essential tenet of Stoicism that virtue was its own reward.

so prone to discord and sedition, so ungovernable, almost revelling in activities destructive of others or themselves if conventional restraints are broken, and then being able to hold an inner discourse with oneself along the following lines.

G2 How Nero should be able to reflect on himself (1.2 – 1.4)

[2] "Of all mankind can I really be the one whom it has pleased the gods to choose to act as their representative on earth? I am the arbiter of life and death for the nations; in my hands I hold the destiny and condition of all mankind; what Fortune intends to be the lot of each and every mortal man she declares through my lips; by my decrees cities and nations find reason to rejoice; no corner of the world may prosper without my consent and encouragement; my peace keeps restrained and sheathed a million swords – and at my nod they will all be drawn. Which nations will be utterly destroyed, which ones depopulated, which will receive their freedom and which will lose it, which kings will become my slaves and whose heads will be adorned with royal diadems, which cities will crumble to the dust and which will rise again – all this depends on my decrees alone.[3]

[3] "And yet, for all these vast powers, nothing has moved me to inflict unjust punishment, neither anger nor the impetuosity of youth, neither man's rash folly or intransigence, which can so often try the patience of the most tranquil spirit, not even that fearful lust for glory itself, which flaunts its power by the use of terror and is the all too frequent implement of overweening empire. My sword I keep hidden, or rather sheathed. When blood is shed, I am parsimonious of even the meanest citizen's blood; though he lacks all other possessions, no one who bears the name of man will fail to find me generous.[4]

[4] "Severity I keep concealed; clemency always at the ready. I keep a guard upon myself, like one destined to render his account to the very laws, which I have summoned from the darkness of disuse back to the light of day.[5] My heart bleeds for the tender youth of one, for the ripe old age of another; one I have pardoned for his distinguished status, another for his low estate; and when I can find no good cause for pardon, then by sparing myself the pain of inflicting pain, I show pity to myself. This very day, if the immortal gods demand that I must render my accounts, I am ready to submit the records of all humanity."

---

3 Seneca does not overstate Nero's powers as *princeps*. He was the highest 'court of appeal' (see Millar, *ERW* 507–27; LACTOR 17, H44–51 for the position as judge established by Augustus). For ecstatic responses to the emperor's decrees, see e.g. Tac. *Ann.* 13.8; LACTOR 17, H34, or **M46**. For peace see contemporary poetry – Calpurnius Siculus, 1.42–62 = **T15a–b**; *Apocolocyntosis* 10.2 = **F10**; and Nero's closing of the Gates of Janus in 64 – **N52**. In 67, Nero decreed 'freedom' to Achaia – see **M14–M15**: Vespasian removed it a few years later (**M16**). Tacitus states that the relatives of King Prasutagus of the Iceni were treated as slaves (*Annals* 14.31.1). Nero would crown Tiridates as King of Armenia with great spectacle in Rome in AD 66: **N54**, **Q16**, Dio 63.4–5, Suet. *Nero* 13.1.

4 Seneca may be proclaiming Nero's superiority to the young Octavian/Augustus who 'aged nineteen, raised an army on my own initiative' (*RG* 1.1), and was just 20 at the time of the proscriptions. Calpurnius Siculus talks of Clemency turning swords into tools of peace, *Ecl.* 1.59 = **T15b**.

5 Seneca makes a contrast with Claudius (no doubt thinking of his own exile). This theme is found elsewhere at the start of Nero's reign – *Apocol.* 4.1.23–4, 10.4 = **F4**, **F10**; Calp. Sic. 1.71–2 = **T15b**; Tac. *Ann.* 13.4. Suetonius reports on Claudius as judge in *Claudius* 14–15 and 29.

G3 The blessings Nero has brought (1.5 – 1.9)

[5] This then, Caesar, is the declaration you may boldly make, that you have kept safe all that was committed to you as trustee and guardian; nothing has diminished the state, whether by violence or covert fraud. For this is that most laudable of all accomplishments, unprecedented amongst previous emperors, that your avarice has been for innocence. Your labours have not been in vain: your goodness has won gratitude and plaudits at the bar of history. You are the object of thanksgivings; no single man has ever been so dear to anyone as you to all the Roman people; for them you are a mighty and long-enduring blessing.

[6] But in this you have laid a mighty burden on yourself.[6] No one now talks of Divus Augustus or the early years of Tiberius Caesar, since the only example they would have you follow is your own – a taste of your principate has so narrowed the field of competition.[7] This would have been a formidable task had your own virtues been a temporary expedient, rather than inherent in your own nature. For none can wear an actor's mask for long; that which is spurious soon reverts to type. But that which is based on underlying reality, born as it were from its own inherent nature, grows with the passing of the years and develops into something greater and better.

[7] For as long as it was uncertain how those great natural talents of yours would develop, the Roman people resembled a gambler playing for high stakes. But now the nation's prayers have been safely granted, and there is no danger that you will suddenly forget your own principles. Too much success makes men greedy, and none can ever so curb desires that they evaporate with their fulfilment. The ladder of ambition leads to ever-escalating aspirations, and the unexpected fulfilment of their hopes only serves to drive men on to hopes beyond the dreams of avarice. But all your citizens must perforce acknowledge that they are truly blessed, and that no further blessing can be added to this their present felicity save the promise that it will last for ever.[8] [8] The sources of such a declaration – one which humankind is universally reluctant to acknowledge – are many: a sense of security, which is profound, abundant riches, the rule of law, which reigns over all wrongdoing; the fact that with their own eyes men can see the realisation of the ideal state, where nothing can obstruct the ultimate fulfilment of their liberty except the fact that they enjoy the freedom to destroy it.[9] [9] But above all else, the admiration for your clemency is universal, extending from the highest to the least of all your citizens. For men perceive or expect other blessings in proportion to their lot in life; but when it comes to clemency, all men hope to receive it in equal measure. For there is no one on this earth so convinced of his own total innocence that he does not feel reassured to think that Clemency stands nearby, ready to bring relief for human errors.[10]

---

6 For the 'burden of empire' Ovid, *Fasti* 1.616; Tacitus on Tiberius' 'accession speech' *Annals* 1.11.1; compare Suet. *Tib.* 24.2; Sen. *Consolation to Marcia* 2.3.

7 Seneca makes explicit a flattering comparison with Augustus (compare note 4), and with Tiberius' early years (compare Suet. *Tib.* 26–40 with 41–3).

8 Compare Calpurnius Siculus, **T15**; Sen. *Apocol.* **F4**,: for initial euphoria at Gaius' accession, Philo, *Leg.* **D2**; doubts about how Titus would be, Suet. *Tit.* 7.1; and about Nero, Tac. *Ann.* 13.6.

9 Augustus claimed to have championed liberty (*RG* 1.1). Sen. *Apocol.* 1.1 and 12.2 = **F1**, **F12** claims that Claudius' death brought about liberty for the Roman people.

10 Seneca is probably thinking of statues of the goddess (see note 1).

G4 In praise of clemency (2.1 – 2.2)

[2.1] I am very well aware that there are some who think that clemency simply gives encouragement to the wicked.[11] After all, it never comes into play until there has been a crime, and it is the only virtue which serves no useful purpose among innocent men. But first of all, in this it resembles medicine, which likewise serves no useful purpose except for the sick, but is highly respected by those who are well, just as clemency is admired even by the innocent, even though it is invoked only by those who deserve to be punished. There is a second consideration too: clemency can have an application even for those who are innocent, since sometimes bad luck takes the place of wrongdoing; and clemency not only comes to the aid of innocence, but often of virtue also, since the contemporary situation may bring it about that deeds which are admired may nonetheless be punished. In addition to that, there are many people who may well return to innocent ways, if only they receive a remission of their sentence.

[2] Nevertheless, forgiveness should not be too widely distributed, since if you remove the distinction between virtue and vice, confusion develops, accompanied by an upsurge of bad behaviour. Good judgement in all things is the right approach, based on a clear understanding of which characters are capable of reform, and which are beyond redemption. We need an exercise of clemency which is neither extravagantly general nor yet totally excluded, since it is just as cruel to pardon everyone as to pardon no one. We need to steer a middle course, but because such a policy of moderation is difficult to sustain, if there is to be any degree of imbalance, it should veer in the direction of humanity.

3.1 – 3.3 Seneca introduces his approach to the theme (omitted here)

G5 The emperor in battle as the embodiment of the state (3.4 – 4.3)

[3.4] There is nothing irrational about the way in which peoples and cities are all alike in their love for their kings and their determination to protect them, even to the extent of sacrificing themselves and all they possess, wherever the safety of their ruler requires it. It is not that they regard their own lives as valueless, nor is it an act of madness, when for the sake of a single man so many thousands are willing to face the sword, or by the deaths of many to save the life of one, who sometimes may be old and feeble.[12] [5] Look at it like this. The whole body is the servant of the mind. It may be so much larger and more conspicuous, and the mind an insubstantial thing, remaining permanently concealed, its location a matter of uncertainty. But despite this, hands, feet and eyes all do its bidding; the skin is its defence, and at its command we rest or rush busily about. If it is a greedy master and it so orders us, we scour the seas for profit; if it is ambitious, men have often before thrust their right hands into

---

11 A similar argument in an historical context is given to Cato by Sallust in his account of the Catiline War (52 BC) arguing that those involved must be punished rather than spared, as a warning to others.

12 Seneca perhaps invites a favourable comparison of the young Nero with Claudius.

the fire, or of their own free will plunged into the abyss.[13] The state is similar. Its vast multitude of citizens are centred upon the life of a single man, are ruled by his spirit, and guided by his mind. Were they not sustained by his wisdom, they would all crush and destroy themselves by the sheer brute force of their own numbers.

[4.1] And so we see that it is in fact their own safety that men are in love with, when for the sake of a single ruler they lead ten legions at once out to battle,[14] when they rush to fight in the front line, or suffer wounds from battling their enemies face to face, all lest their leader's standards be put to flight. For he is the chain that binds them all in one and holds the state together, his the breath of life for all these thousands, who in themselves are nothing but a burden and a prey to others, if once their emperor's guiding mind is taken from them.

While yet their king is safe, united is the hive;
But should he once be lost, their bond of unity cannot survive.[15]

[2] A disaster such as that would mean the end of Rome's peace;[16] it would bring ruination to the fortunes of a mighty people. Our people will steer clear of such a dire calamity only so long as they understand how to accept the guiding reins of government; if once they break loose and by some mischance get the bit between their teeth and refuse to let it be replaced, then the very unity of the state, the total structure of our mighty empire will break down and fall apart, and the end of our nation's rule will coincide with the end of its capacity to be ruled.[17] [3] For that very reason it is hardly surprising that emperors and kings and all those responsible for a nation's welfare, by whatever name they are called, are loved more dearly even than those who are related to us by bonds of kinship. For if sensible men place the public interest above their own private advantages, it must surely follow that the ruler who is the very centre and pivot of a people's fortunes must be more precious to them all. Many years ago Caesar dressed himself in the garments of our state in such a way that the one could not be separated from the other without the destruction of them both.[18] For though he needed power, the state needed its head.

---

13 Seneca refers to two examples from early Roman history, as told by Livy: in 507 BC Gaius Mucius showed Roman fortitude by holding his own right hand in a flame after being captured on a mission to assassinate the Etruscan king, thus earning the name 'Scaevola' ('Leftie') Livy 2.12–13. Marcus Curtius was a young equestrian who, in obedience to an oracle saved his country by jumping on horseback into a chasm which had suddenly opened in the forum (Livy 7.6: this was one of three possible ancient explanations of the *Lacus Curtius* monument in the Roman Forum, still partially preserved). Livy's famous books on Rome's early history may also be Seneca's source for the body = state analogy, which though already used by Aristotle (4th century BC) is employed by Livy (2.32).

14 Seneca exaggerates: no example is known from Roman history of a single army made up of ten legions. Eight legions were stationed on the Rhine in two separate armies.

15 The quotation is from Virgil, *Georgics* 4. 212–3. Virgil wrongly speaks of a king bee rather than a queen (as do Roman authors generally).

16 The phrase used by Seneca, *Romana pax,* seems particularly to have referred to end of civil war.

17 Seneca digresses from his message about clemency to stress the necessity of monarchy to Rome's continued prosperity. The ordinary people can hardly have been expected to read Seneca's treatise, but the senatorial élite can be expected to take warning about the dangers of removing Nero.

18 Seneca uses the name Caesar here, as usually, to refer to Augustus. His language here would more naturally mean 'Caesar dressed the state in himself.' In either case, the equivalence of state and ruler is clear (*'L'État c'est moi,'* as Louis XIV of France may have said).

G6 The need for clemency in a ruler (5.1 – 5.7)

[5.1] It may perhaps appear that I have digressed somewhat from the original subject of this essay, but I can assure you that it is in fact deeply relevant. For if, as I have so far tried to demonstrate, you are the heart and soul of the state and the state is your body, it should be clear to you, I think, how essential the quality of clemency is. For though you may appear to be showing clemency to another, in fact you are showing it to yourself. It follows, therefore, that you should be clement even to the most reprehensible citizens in the same way as you would be tolerant of your own limbs, if they fail you; and if there is ever need to let blood, like a surgeon you must keep a steady hand to avoid cutting more deeply than is absolutely necessary. [2] So, as I have been suggesting, the quality of clemency is a natural attribute of all humanity, but is a particularly attractive quality in rulers, since they have both greater opportunities to preserve life, and more abundant material on which to demonstrate that quality. Cruelty in a private individual does little harm; savagery in a ruler is tantamount to war. [3] All virtues are equivalent to each other; none is more admirable or noble than any other.[19] But some virtues are particularly suited to particular personalities. Greatness of heart well becomes each mortal man, even the humblest of humankind. For what can be more admirable or more courageous than to beat back the blows of misfortune. But when the luck is running with you, greatness of heart has ampler opportunity to reveal itself – it is far more conspicuous in a magistrate than in a commoner.

[4] Wherever Clemency makes her dwelling place, she is for that household a source of joy and tranquillity; but in a palace she is all the more wonderful because she is more rare. There lives a man whose anger none can resist, whose sentence, however severe, even those subject to his condemnation will acknowledge, whom none will challenge, from whom none will even beg for mercy, least of all when the fire of his wrath is kindled. But can anything be more remarkable than that such a man should hold himself in check and exercise his own power more generously and with more restraint, thinking to himself 'every man has the power to take a life illegally, but only I have the power to preserve it.'?

[5] Nobility of mind brings honour to those of high position; failure to match nobility of mind to such position, or even to surpass it, simply degrades that high position. The true sign of such nobility of mind is calmness and tranquillity, the ability to rise above both injustice and misfortune. Women rage with anger; wild animals, though not the nobler kind, are the ones that bite and maul their prostrate victims. When elephants and lions have felled their victims, they move on; it is the lower orders of animal that never relent.[20] [6] A savage and inexorable anger ill befits a king; such conduct barely raises him above that of the one to whose level his rage reduces him. But if he grants life or high position to those who have risked all and deserve to lose them, he does what is possible only for someone who exercises power. Life is a possession we may take even from a superior; but it is a gift we may grant only to an inferior. [7] To save a life is the peculiar privilege of the loftiest position; never does it more deserve our

[19] That all virtues are equal was a principle of Stoicism, repeated by Seneca, *Epistles* 113.16.

[20] The noble lion is contrasted with wolves and bears by Ovid, begging an end to his exile, *Tristia* 3.5.31–6.

admiration than when it exercises a power, which is the prerogative of the gods, by whose good gift it comes that all of us, evil and good alike, are born into the light of day. An emperor should claim as his own prerogative the gods' own attitude of mind: he should rejoice to behold a proportion of his citizens, because they are good and useful; others he should regard as making up the numbers. That some of them exist should bring him pleasure; he should simply tolerate the rest.

6.1 – 7.3 Seneca reflects on how few people are without guilt (omitted here)

G7 The people are sovereign; the burdens of office (7.4 – 8.7)

[7.4] Men of humble rank are relatively free to use violence, to quarrel, to turn to brawling at the drop of a hat, and generally indulge their propensity to lose their tempers. When small men fight, the blows fall lightly. But for a ruler to raise his voice or use intemperate language is unbecoming to his majesty. [8.1] You will regard it as a serious matter to deprive kings of the right to say what they think, when such is the privilege of their most humble subject, arguing that such constraints amount to slavery, not sovereignty. You are absolutely right. But have you not realised that that sovereignty is a noble slavery for you? Those who are simply one of a crowd, blending with them and attracting no notice, enjoy a very different situation from your self. Their virtues have a long struggle to gain recognition; their vices remain invisible. But all your deeds and words are the subject of gossip and rumour. For that reason anyone who enjoys a lofty reputation, irrespective of his merits, must take the greatest care of all to preserve its character intact. [2] There are so many things, which you must not do but I can, thanks to your benevolence. I can walk through any part of the city I choose all alone, unescorted by any companion, without a weapon in my home or at my belt. But you, in the midst of the peace which you have created, must live forever armed. You cannot escape your destiny; it hedges you about, and if ever you come down to the level of ordinary men, the attributes of royalty can never be left behind. [3] This is indeed the slavery of greatness – that it can never be reduced to the level of the ordinary. This is the inescapable condition which you share with the gods. For heaven keeps them prisoners on high, so that they have no more power to come down from their lofty heights than it is safe for you to do so. You are nailed to your palace pinnacle. [4] Our activities, by contrast, are observed by few; we can go out, return, and change our clothes without public knowledge. But you can no more hide yourself than can the sun. You live in the bright glare of public observation; all eyes are fixed upon you. Are you thinking of "popping out for a moment"? No chance – you will "emerge".[21] [5] You cannot hold a conversation without your every word being transmitted to all the nations upon earth. Your anger makes the whole world tremble, because wherever your blows fall, they shake the surrounding landscape. Lightning strikes the few; it terrifies the many. Inevitably, the punishment meted out by mighty potentates terrifies far more than it afflicts, for when the potentate is all-powerful, men will not ask what he has done, but rather how much more he might be going to do.

[21] The identification of ruler as the sun was common in Hellenistic ruler-cult. Antony named his son by Cleopatra 'Helios' (= Sun in Greek), Plutarch, *Antony* 36.3. Louis XIV of France would be known as the 'Sun-King'. The metaphor was common too: Pompey allegedly said he was a rising sun, Sulla a setting sun (Plutarch, *Pompey* 14.4) while Tiberius said the same of Macro's desertion of him for the rising sun of Gaius (Tac. *Ann.* 6.46.4; compare Dio 58.28.4).

[6] So now, bear this is mind also: when private citizens patiently put up with injuries, it makes them all the more liable to further injury. But kings, by contrast, by gentleness will gain far greater security. Their frequent punishments may suppress the hatred of a few; they certainly stir the anger of the whole community. [7] The inclination to savagery should always be less compelling than the reasons for it. Otherwise, just as coppiced trees sprout a far greater number of branches, and many kinds of plant are pruned to make them grow the more profusely, so the cruelty of kings simply increases the number of their enemies by the very act of eliminating some of them. For the parents and children of those who have been killed, together with the relatives and friends all take the place of individual victims.

9.1 – 10.3 The example of Augustus (omitted here)[22]

G8 True Clemency (10.4 – 11.3)

[10.4] Not merely to offer safety to your enemy, but to guarantee it personally, even when you know that there will be many willing to express their anger on your behalf and seek to ingratiate themselves with you by shedding another's blood – that is true forgiveness. [11.1] Augustus was like that in his old age – or rather as he approached it. As a young man he had a quick temper, which flared up easily, leading him to take many actions on which he looked back with regret. Even if they make allowances for your youth contrasted with the maturity of his advanced old age, none will think to draw comparisons between your gentleness of temper and that of Divus Augustus. Restraint and clemency were certainly the keynotes of his reign – but only in later years, after the seas of Actium were stained with Roman blood, only after his own fleet as well as that of his enemy Sextus Pompeius were shipwrecked off Sicily, only after the sacrifice of Roman victims on the altars of Perusia and the subsequent proscriptions.[23]

[2] I do not give the name of clemency to what is merely an exhausted savagery. No, Caesar, it is the clemency you display which constitutes true clemency, a clemency which is not born of remorse for brutality, which has no stain upon its record, and which has never shed the blood of fellow-citizens. For in an omnipotent ruler this is moderation in its truest sense and the mark of a comprehensive love for all humanity as for oneself: to remain unaffected by greed, unmoved by natural impetuosity, uncorrupted by the base example of predecessors in testing the limits of one's power over others, and to choose instead to blunt the cutting edges of imperial might. [3] You have given to us, Caesar, a state unstained with blood. But the achievement which rightly constitutes your proudest boast is the fact that nowhere in the whole wide world have you shed one drop of human blood.[24] What makes it all the greater and

---

22 This section, detailing examples of Augustus' clemency, can be found in LACTOR 17, P11; H29; P15).

23 Seneca rounds off his section on Augustus by giving examples of Augustus' (Octavian's) considerable ruthlessness in his rise to the principate. For further details see LACTOR 17, H8 (this passage), H7, P11.

24 Nero had in fact murdered Britannicus early in AD 55. But the official version was that Britannicus died of an epileptic fit (Tac. *Ann.* 13.16, Jos. *JA* 20.153) and even Tacitus could admit that removing an obvious rival for power was a crime that many could forgive (*Ann.* 13.17).

the more remarkable is the fact that no one so young has ever had the sword of empire committed to his charge.[25]

G9 The difference between king and tyrant (11.4 – 12.3)

[11.4] Clemency, therefore, not only makes rulers more honoured, but also more secure. Clemency is the adornment of empires, but also their best guarantee of safety. How else does it happen that kings grow old and can hand on their kingdoms to their children and grandchildren, while the power of tyrants is dishonoured and short lived? How does a tyrant differ from a king?[26] In the visible characteristics of prosperity and unbridled power they are both alike. But tyrants use cruelty as a source of pleasure; kings only out of just cause and sheer necessity.

[12.1] 'What do you mean? Don't kings also make a habit of killing? They do; but only when it is in the public interest. Tyrants do it for pleasure. The difference between a tyrant and a king is to be measured by his deeds, not his title. Dionysius the Elder has every right to be admired more than many kings;[27] but nothing can deny Lucius Sulla the name of tyrant, since he never stopped killing until he ran out of enemies.[28] [2] It is no defence to argue that he gave up his dictatorship and returned to civilian life, since no tyrant ever drank so eagerly of human blood.[29] He once ordered the mass execution of seven thousand Roman citizens all together, and as he reclined at the nearby temple of Bellona, the goddess of war, and listen to the mingled shrieks and groans of so many thousands as they were put to the sword, he remarked to a panic stricken senate, "To business, gentlemen of the senate. It is just a few traitors being executed on my orders." He wasn't lying – as he saw it, they were just "a few".[30]

[3] I shall return to Sulla in due course, when we examine the nature of the anger we should show towards our enemies,[31] especially when men from the very same citizen

---

25 Nero, born 15 December AD 37 (Suet. *Nero* 6.1, **A57f**) was not yet 17 at Claudius' death on 13 October, AD 54 (Suet. *Claud.* 45). Octavian (Augustus) had raised an army at the age of 19 (*RG* 1.1). Gaius was 24 on his accession in March 37.

26 Seneca breaks away from the traditional Roman use of *rex* (king) as a term of abuse deriving from the last king of Rome, Tarquin the Proud. He had earlier (1.3.3) mentioned *rex* or *princeps* as if equivalent. Here he uses *rex* to mean 'good king' and *tyrannus* to mean 'bad king' or 'tyrant'.

27 Dionysius I was sole ruler of Syracuse between 405 and 367 BC. Nepos, the Roman biographer, writing under Augustus, gave a character summary (*On Kings* 2.2–3) in which he praised his many personal qualities, but mentions his ruthlessness in maintaining his power.

28 Sulla (Lucius Cornelius Sulla Felix) 138–78 BC. Twice led his armies against Rome; plundered cities of the Greek East; dealt severely with towns and areas of Italy opposed to Rome. He made himself dictator in 82/1 BC, and instituted proscriptions (legalised murder of personal and political opponents, and confiscation of their property: lists of the names of the proscribed were published in Rome and their killers were rewarded.) Confiscated land was given to his veterans. As dictator Sulla also carried out much-needed reforms of the senate. Having done this he resigned the dictatorship and soon retired to private life, dying soon afterwards.

29 Tacitus makes Tiberius predict of Gaius that 'he would have all of Sulla's vices and none of his virtues.' (*Ann.* 6.46.4)

30 7,000 Roman citizens: this represents the army which had fought against Sulla in the civil war. Seneca elsewhere (*Benefits* 5.16.3) describes it as 'two legions'. The standard account will have been Livy, book 88 which now survives only in a summary, giving the figure as 8,000. For other Julio-Claudian writers, Sulla is an example of cruelty and tyranny: Strabo, 5.4.11; Velleius 2.28.2–4; Elder Seneca, *Controv.* 9.2.19; Lucan 2.139–232.

31 Presumably in the lost book 2 or 3.

body acquire the name of enemy by breaking away and going over to the enemy. But in the meantime, as I was saying, it is the quality of clemency that really emphasises the distinction between a tyrant and a king. Both may be equally defended by their bodyguards. But the one uses his weaponry to keep the peace; the other to suppress great hatred by the use of terror. Yet all the time he cannot view without suspicion the very hands of those to whom he has entrusted his own safety.

G10 The fears of a tyrant (12.4 – 13.3)

[4] The tyrant is always at sixes and sevens with himself. He is hated because he is feared; but because he is hated he needs to be feared. And as that hatred gets out of control, he never knows what madness will ensue. As a result he adopts a policy encapsulated in that dreadful motto, which has driven many to their downfall, *"Let them hate me, so long as they fear me."*[32] Fear in moderation keeps hearts and minds in check; but fear as a permanent condition, when it is intense and drives men to extremes, will excite the moderate to desperate measures and extreme reactions.[33] [5] In the same way, a line of feathers on a rope may suffice to keep wild animals contained. But if a rider goads them from behind with the point of a javelin, they will try to escape through the very obstacles they had hitherto avoided, and will run roughshod over their previous fears. There is no courage so extreme as that induced by dire necessity. Fear works best when it leaves room for confidence, offering greater grounds for optimism than fear of danger. Otherwise, if someone usually uninvolved in public life feels just as threatened as those who are, he will be all too willing to take risks and throw away a life that is already in the power of another.

[13.1] A calm and gentle king will have a loyal bodyguard, dedicated to the security of the community. The soldiers will realise that that they are serving the safety of the state and will be proud to do so, gladly putting up with every hardship, as if each were protecting his own father. But inevitably, a savage and bloodthirsty ruler will be surrounded by a resentful body of men.[34] [2] No one can have good and loyal servants, if he uses them as agents of torture, bringing death to others by rack and steel, and throwing victims to them as he would to wild beasts in the arena. Such a man must be more troubled and apprehensive than any prisoner on trial would be. For he now lives in fear of men and gods alike, since all are the witnesses and avengers of his crimes. Yet he has now reached a state in which it is impossible to amend his ways. Of all the other miseries his cruelty brings in its train, this must surely be for him the most extreme: he has no choice but to persevere; he cannot turn back to better ways. His crimes can only be defended by yet further crimes. Can any condition be more pitiable than to be one for whom there is now no choice but to be wicked? [3] How wretched he must seem, to himself at least. But for others to feel pity for him would be criminal – after all he exercised his power through robbery and slaughter; at

[32] From *Atreus* by the Roman tragedian Accius, whose works are completely lost. This was very famous line, quoted by several other authors, *e.g.* Cicero, *Philippics* 1.34, and parodied by Tiberius, according to Suetonius (*Tib.* 59.2).

[33] Machiavelli, *The Prince,* 17 'From this arises the question whether it is better to be loved more than feared, or feared more than loved. The reply is, that one ought to be both feared and loved, but as it is difficult for the two to go together, it is much safer to be feared than loved, if one of the two has to be wanting.

[34] Seneca is presumably thinking of Caligula, assassinated by members of his own guard (**E16**). So too was Domitian in AD 96.

home and abroad alike he created a universal sense of paranoia; for fear of violence he had recourse to violence; he placed no trust in the loyalty of friends or the love of his own children. When he has contemplated his own deeds, both past and future, and has bared the secrets of his soul, so filled with the record of his crimes and tortures, such a man must often be afraid of death, but yet more often must desire it, since he must hate himself far more than all his underlings do.

G11 The rewards of good rule (13.4 – 13.5)

[4] Contrast this with one whose loving care extends to all, who in matters great and small alike stands as the universal guardian; who nourishes each portion of the state as if it were a part of his own being; who inclines to leniency, even though his own advantage indicates severity, and thus reveals a deep reluctance to turn his hand to cruel punishments; who banishes from his mind all hostility and ferocity; who, in his desire that his governance should win the approbation of his citizens, exercises power with a calm concern for the good of all; who counts himself abundantly blessed, if he can share his blessings with his people; whose conversation is congenial, and ease of access and manner welcoming; whose appearance is pleasant (which is what the public particularly likes); who is generous to worthy petitions, yet not harsh to those which are not; such a ruler is loved, guarded, and revered by all his citizens. [5] What people say of him in secret is just what they say in public. They become eager to bring up sons and we hear no more of the state-induced sterility of evil times, since all can now be sure that their children will be for ever grateful that they have lived to see an age like this.[35] Such an emperor is guarded by his own good deeds; he has no need of bodyguards; the weapons he wears are mere accessories of fashion.

G12 The ruler as a father figure (14.1 – 14.3)

[14.1] What then are his duties? Simply those of any good parent, who sometimes will rebuke his children gently, sometimes with threats, and sometimes even with blows. But no father in his right mind will disinherit a son for his first offence. Only when those offences are so serious and so numerous as to exhaust his patience, and when he fears offences even more dreadful than those he has already castigated, only then will he reach for his stylus and rewrite his will. Before he does so he will make many attempts to rescue one whose character has reached a fairly bad situation, but not without hope of change; only when he has despaired of success will he resort to the ultimate sanction. No one resorts to punishment until he has tried every other remedy. [2] A parent is bound to act in this way. So too is an emperor, whom in no spirit of futile flattery we have called the Father of the Fatherland,[36] Various other honorific titles have been accorded to our rulers. Some have been called Great or Fortunate, some August, in our efforts to heap whatever titles we could upon those whose

[35] A wish to have children once peace was established (by Augustus) is also expressed in the *Laudatio Turiae* 8/2 BC (LACTOR 17, T37f), and, according to Velleius, 2.103.5, on Tiberius' adoption by Augustus.

[36] The title *pater patriae* – Father of the Fatherland – was adopted by Augustus in 2 BC and is given as his culminating honour in the *Res Gestae* (35.1: see LACTOR 17, C13, H38, K28, M20 and Suet. *Aug.* 58.2, Dio 55.10). Tiberius refused the title (Tac. *Ann.* 1.72.1) but Gaius and Claudius both accepted it (*e.g. RIC* Gaius 46, Claudius 50). Nero initially refused it (Suet. *Nero* 8.1) but probably accepted it in late 55– late 56 (Griffin, *Nero* 252 n.73; *RIC* Nero 8).

majesty was matched by their desire for glory.[37] But when we call a ruler the Father of the Fatherland, we are telling him that we have given him over his country the *patria potestas*, the father's rights over his family, which carries with it a duty of the most generous care for his children's welfare and indifference to his own concerns.[38] [3] For any father to disinherit a son would be like cutting off one his own limbs. He would be reluctant to do it, and having done so, he would yearn to bring it back. He would have hesitated long and often; and in the execution of the deed his groans would be profound. You could almost claim that any man who is quick to condemn, is happy to condemn; any man who punishes too much, punishes unjustly.

15.1 – 16.1 Examples of punishments inflicted by fathers (omitted here)[39]
16.2 – 17.3 Analogies from teaching, farming and medicine (omitted here)

G13 Treatment of slaves and free men (18. 1 – 18.3)

[18.1] To exercise control over slaves with restraint is praiseworthy.[40] A slave may be simply a possession, but you should always remind yourself that it is not a question of how much suffering your slave can endure without retaliation, but rather how much latitude the principles of natural justice and equity will allow you, since they demand that even captives and purchased slaves are entitled to merciful treatment. These same principles require, with an even greater degree of justification, that free men, those native to our country, and all men of good repute should not be treated like slaves but rather as men who, by virtue of their lower rank, have been entrusted to your care as their guardian, rather than their slave-master. [2] Even slaves are entitled to seek sanctuary at your statue.[41] Whatever licence is allowed in the treatment of slaves, there are some things which, in the treatment of any human being, the common rights of all living creatures render absolutely illegitimate. For example, public opinion loathed Vedius Pollio even more intensely than his slaves did, because he used to fatten up his moray eels on human blood, and if any of his slaves annoyed him in any way at all, he would order him to be thrown into his fishpond, which was nothing less than a snake pit. What a vile creature! He deserved to die a thousand deaths, whether he threw his slaves as food to the very eels which he intended to eat himself in due course, or simply kept eels for the fun of feeding them on such delicacies.[42]

[3] Just as cruel masters face are pointed at with loathing and hatred all over the city, so too with kings. The injuries they inflict are more widespread, while their evil deeds and the hatred they inspire become the raw material for history books. Would it not

---

37 Great (Magnus) was a cognomen adopted by Pompey; Fortunate (Felix) by Sulla; for the name Augustus, see LACTOR 17, H22, H23.

38 *Patria potestas* – was a father's legal jurisdiction over his family, including the power of life and death.

39 Included in LACTOR 17, H48.

40 Seneca's humane attitude to his own slaves is shown in his *Epistle* 47.

41 The right of slaves to seek refuge 'at shrines of gods or statues of emperors' became established in law (Gaius, *Institutes* 1.53). Tacitus laments the spread of this practice under Tiberius (3.36.1) and examples are given by Suetonius (*Aug.* 17.5; *Tib.* 53.2) and later by Pliny, *Letters* 10.74.

42 Vedius Pollio, a freedman who became and equestrian under Augustus was notorious for his luxury and cruelty. Seneca gives a fuller version at *On Anger* 3.40.1–4 = LACTOR 17, H40.

be better never to have been born, rather than to add your name to the record of those whose birth has proved disastrous for their country?[43]

19.1 – 19.6 Seneca draws analogies from bees having kings[44] (omitted here)

G14 The good ruler offers hope of a golden age (19.7 – 19.9)

[19.7] What could be more delightful than to live amidst a people united in their hopes for your long life and whose prayers for their ruler are uttered without the need for official supervision?[45] To find that the slightest indication of your ill health excites men's fears and not their hopes? To know that there is nothing so precious to any citizen that he would not gladly sacrifice it for the health of his supreme protector? [8] Surely any man so blessed must feel it also as his duty to himself to stay alive? And in so doing, he has shown by constant proofs of his benevolence that the state in no sense belongs to him, but rather that he belongs to the state. Against such a man, no one would dare to raise his hand; every man would wish to protect him from ill fortune, if he could. For under him justice, peace, chastity, security, and honour flourish and abound;[46] under him the state grows rich and overflows with an abundance of all good things. Men look to such a ruler with the same intensity of feeling as that with which we would gaze with awe and veneration on the gods, if the immortals did but grant us such facility.[47] [9] So now, tell me this. Is it not true that a ruler who conducts his life in the manner of a god, who is kindly and generous, and uses his power for the good of all, is his position not already second only to that of the gods themselves? It will bring you credit if you make this your ambition, the standard you aspire to: that the extent of your Great Goodness shall be the true measure of your Great Power.[48]

G15 Justice: clemency in offences against oneself (20.1 – 20.3)

[20.1] A ruler usually inflicts punishment for one of two reasons: as retribution for offences either against himself or against another. Let me first discuss this generalisation as it applies to the ruler himself, since it is more difficult to exercise restraint when the motivation is a personal grievance than when it is used for its deterrent effect. [2] There is no need for gratuitous advice at this point on the need to be cautious in believing allegations, to dig out the truth, to be prejudiced in favour of innocence, and to realise that the establishing of innocence is as much the duty of the judge as the interest of the accused party.[49] This is not a matter of clemency, but of justice. I would strongly urge any ruler that, even when he is clearly the injured

---

[43] The phrase is strikingly similar to a phrase of Nero's father at his son's birth, as reported by Suetonius, *Nero* 6.1.

[44] See note 15 above.

[45] Public prayers were offered for the well–being of the emperor at the start of the year, preserved in the Acts of the Arval Brotherhood (Section A, *e.g.* **A59a**), mentioned by Tac. *Ann.* 16.22; Suet. *Nero* 46.2. A 'guard' was checked that public prayers made by chief magistrates followed the exact wording (Pliny, *NH* 28.11).

[46] For similar blessings, suggestive of a golden age, see Calpurnius Siculus **T15**, Sen. *Apocol.* 4.1.23–5 = **F4**.

[47] Compare Philo on the great expectations at the start of Caligula's reign = **D2**.

[48] Seneca uses the terms *optimus* and *maximus*, most usually found in conjunction in the cult title *Iuppiter Optimus Maximus* – Jupiter, Greatest and Best, Rome's chief god.

[49] Compare Machiavelli, *The Prince* 17 'And when he is obliged to take the life of any one, let him do so when there is proper justification and manifest reason for it;'.

party, he should nevertheless keep his feelings under control, impose no penalty if he can safely avoid it, and a mild one if he must, and to prove far more open to pleas for clemency where his own interests are concerned than those of others. [3] It is no mark of a generous spirit to be open-handed with what belongs to another; clemency rather is the quality to be found in one who concedes to another what he denies to himself. It is to be found in one who, though goaded by a sense of his own grievances, does not rush to vengeance, but realises instead that to put up with offences against himself, though his powers are absolute, represents true generosity of spirit, and that the noblest thing on earth is a ruler whose wrongs remain unpunished.

[21.1] Revenge usually brings about two results: it provides compensation to the aggrieved party, or future security. The position of an emperor is too great for him to need compensation, and his strength too obvious for him to seek confirmation of it by injuring another. I say this of cases when he has been attacked and abused by his inferiors; for if he sees people he once regarded as his peers now beneath him, he has enough revenge.[50] Slave or snake or arrow may kill a king. But he who saves a life can only be greater than the one he saves.

G16 Preserving friendly kings (21.2 – 21.3)

[21.2] The ruler who has the power of life and death over others has a duty to use this heavenly prerogative with magnanimity. This is particularly the case with those who, he knows, once enjoyed a pinnacle of power like his own.[51] If he has now acquired such arbitrary power over them, he has already more than satisfied any need for vengeance and met all the requirements of genuine punishment. Any man that owes his life to another has lost his own; any king who has been toppled from his high position to kneel before his enemy's feet has had to await the verdict of another on his right to his life and his kingdom. If he lives, he lives to the glory of the man that spared him, and by his very survival he confers more glory on his conqueror than ever he would have done, if he had been removed from the eyes of the world. For he remains a permanent reminder of the virtues of another; displayed in a general's triumph he would have rapidly disappeared from sight.[52]

[3] But if it has proved possible to leave his kingdom safely in his hands and to restore him to the heights from which he fell, the admiration for the man who was content to take nothing from that conquered king except his glory is massively enhanced. This is like celebrating a triumph over his own victory, by declaring that he has found no spoils worthy of his victory amongst his conquered foes.

---

[50] Seneca is aware that Nero had not been brought up within the imperial family (Suet. *Nero* 6.3), unlike Tiberius, Gaius and even Claudius. There were others of equal descent from Augustus too (see family tree). All were dead by the end of Nero's reign.

[51] Seneca is thinking of friendly kings (see **M39–M51**). Nero was to restore Tiridates as King of Armenia in AD 66: **N54, Q16**; Dio 63.5.2–3, 'I am making you king of Armenia, to ensure that both you and they realise that I have the power not only to take away kingdoms but to bestow them.' Sacrifices recorded by the Acts of the Arval Brotherhood (**A66c**), connected with Tiridates include one to Clemency. The reality was different for Armenia, but Nero did annexe Pontus from King Polemon (see **M48** and Suet. *Nero* 18).

[52] Cicero, writing of a Roman triumph (*Verrines* 2.5.77) says 'the same day marks the end of the victor's command and of the vanquished's life.'

22.1 – 22.2 Seneca discusses crime and punishment in general terms (omitted here)

G17 Parricide under Claudius (23.1 – 23.2)

[23.1] You will find, also, that the commonest crimes are those which are most commonly punished. Your father Claudius had more parricides sewn up in the sack in just five years than our records show us were similarly punished throughout the whole of human history. Far fewer sons dared to commit this ultimate offence against heaven during the period when the crime lay outside the constraints of the law. In this our leading statesmen showed a singular wisdom and a profound understanding of man's natural instincts. They decided that it was better to close their eyes to such a crime, by treating it as impossible and beyond the audacity of any man, rather than making it obvious that it could happen by imposing punishments for it. As a result, the development of parricide coincided with the institution of the law against it; the penalty itself showed to those sons the possibility of committing such a crime. Family loyalty reached its all time low once we began to see more sacks than crucifixions.[53]

[2] In states where men are rarely punished, a sort of consensus in favour of lawful conduct develops, and it is generally encouraged as conducive to the public well-being. If once a state believes that it is law-abiding, it will be. There will be far greater anger felt against those who ignore the consensus in favour of restrained behaviour, when people see that the offenders are few. Believe me, the real danger lies in showing our citizens how many more villains there are.

G18 Tolerance is better (24.1 – 24.2)

[24.1] A proposal was once laid before the senate that slaves should be distinguished from free men by their dress. But it soon became clear that there would be significant risks, if our slaves became aware of the comparatively low numbers of our free citizens. You must realise that there will be exactly the same problem if we adopt a policy of pardoning no one. It will rapidly become apparent how greatly the worse elements in society outnumber the better. High numbers of punishments reflect as badly on an emperor as do high numbers of deaths on a doctor. The kinder the ruler, the more readily he is obeyed. [2] Human temperament is by nature contradictory; it battles readily against opposition and difficulties, and is more willing to follow by choice than to be led by compulsion. Just as spirited horses with high pedigrees respond more willingly to a light touch upon their reins, so too a willingness to be law-abiding is an automatic consequence of a policy of leniency. And the state regards such a policy as desirable, because it serves its interests. In this way, therefore, leniency proves more effective than severity.

25.1 – 26.3 Seneca discusses cruelty (omitted here)

G19 The civic crown (*corona civica*) (26.4 – 26.5)

[26.4] Tyrants do not constrain their mad fury even against their relatives; they rage against family and stranger alike. They start with the murder of individuals and soon slide into total genocide; soon they think it a mark of power to burn homes to the ground and to put antique cities to the plough. To order the execution of one or two is

[53] The ancient punishment for parricide was to be sewn up in a sack with a snake, monkey and dog, and thrown into water (Digest 48.9.9 and Cic. *pro Roscio* 71).

not seen as sufficiently commanding. Without the simultaneous massacre of a whole host of wretched human beings, the tyrant feels that his cruelty has been forcibly curtailed.[54]

[5]* * *[55] True happiness lies in granting to the many the gift of safety, in recalling men to life from death itself, and in earning the civic crown by deeds of clemency. No insignia of honour is a greater adornment of the lofty eminence of a ruler's position, no decoration more beautiful than the civic crown, awarded for saving the lives of citizens.[56] Nothing can match it – neither weapons captured from your foes, nor chariots spattered with barbarian blood, nor even the spoils of war itself. This is the power of a veritable god – to save life by the hundred all across the state. But to take life by the hundred and utterly at random, that is the power of conflagration and destruction.

BOOK II

G20 Nero wishes he had never learned to write (2.1.1 – 2.1.4)

[2.1.1] One remark of yours above all others, Nero Caesar, encouraged me to write on clemency. When you made it, I well remember, I was deeply impressed by what I heard, and later I repeated it to many others. It was a noble sentiment, generous-hearted, and full of compassion, a sudden exclamation, unrehearsed and not intended for others to hear, a clear manifestation of your own kindly nature battling against your lofty destiny as emperor. Burrus,[57] your prefect, an outstanding personality, born to serve you as emperor, was about to execute a couple of robbers, and was pressing you to sign the official declaration, stating their names and the reasons for your decision that they should die. This had been frequently postponed and he was urging that it should finally be done. You were both equally reluctant, but when he produced the document and handed it to you, you exclaimed, "I wish I had never learned to write." [3] What a wonderful comment![58] Every nation upon earth should have heard it, whether they dwell within the boundaries of our empire, or lie adjacent to our borders and lack the certainty of liberty, or those who have the courage and strength to rise against us. It was an inspired comment, which should have been addressed to a gathering of all the nations of mankind, and used as an oath to which all emperors and kings would swear allegiance. The words might have come from the long lost golden age of human innocence, and should serve to bring it back to us again.

[4] Now, surely, the time has come for all to unite in a general campaign for justice and upright living, an end to envy of what belongs to others, which is the source of all malice and ill-feeling, a return of love of family, integrity, honesty and moderation, and a time when vice, which has for so long abused its reign among us, is to be exiled and at long last yield place to an era of purity and happiness.

54 Seneca, *On Anger* 2.5.5 (= LACTOR M76) records Volesus, proconsul of Asia under Augustus, executing 300 and boasting 'Now that's the act of a real king'.

55 Part of the text seems to have been lost at the start of this section.

56 The civic crown was traditionally awarded for the act of saving the life of a fellow citizen in war (Pliny, *NH* 22.13 = LACTOR 17, H14). Augustus appropriates this award in 28/7 BC as one of his honours, for saving citizens in general by putting an end to civil war, see LACTOR 17, H20 with many further references. For a very recent 'real' example of the award, see Tac. *Ann.* 12.31.

57 Sextus Afranius Burrus, see **U25**.

58 Suetonius also reports this remark (*Nero* 10.2) which clearly became known through Seneca.

G21 Seneca claims to be no flatterer (2.1 – 2.2)

[2.1] It is our privilege to hope and trust that in large measure this is the future you hold out for us, Caesar. Your gentleness of nature will gradually diffuse its influence throughout the body of our empire, and all mankind will be transformed into a likeness of yourself. It is the head that brings health to the body; from the head derive all its qualities of liveliness and vigour or depressive feebleness, depending on whether the mind is active or demoralised. But there will be citizens and allies who deserve this blessing, and as a result moral integrity will return throughout the world. Everywhere your own hands will be spared the need for retribution.

[2] Bear with me while I develop this point a little further. My purpose is not to curry favour with you, for that is not my habit, since I would rather give offence by speaking the truth than please by flattery.[59] No, my purpose is simply this: I want to remind you constantly, to make you totally familiar with all your own admirable deeds and words, so that what now comes naturally to you and as if on impulse may in time become a matter of deliberate policy. I cannot help remembering that there are many famous but deplorable remarks, which have become part and parcel of human intercourse and acquired a certain proverbial quality. For example, "Let them hate me, so long as they fear me." There is a similar Greek saying, in which the writer bids the whole earth be consumed by fire – once he is dead; and others of this kind.[60] [3] Somehow or other, clever minds, when dealing with horrible and offensive material, have a knack of giving a neat turn of phrase to violent and aggressive sentiments. But I have never heard any memorable remark from the lips of one who is good and kind.

My point is simply this. I fully appreciate that you are reluctant and hesitate to do it, but sometimes it is essential that you write the sort of document that made you hate the very idea of writing. But, as on this occasion, you must always do it with the utmost hesitation and only after much delay.

3.1 – 7.5 Seneca offers further definitions of clemency, pity and pardon (omitted here), before the manuscripts break off in mid-sentence and the rest of the treatise is lost.

---

[59] Machiavelli devotes a whole chapter of his work (23) to 'How flatterers must be shunned'!

[60] The first (Latin) quotation has been used earlier (12.3). The Greek saying is from a lost tragedy. Dio has it quoted by Tiberius the express his indifference to Gaius succeeding him (Dio 58.23.4) and it was apparently quoted during the Great Fire of AD 64, receiving the rejoinder from Nero – 'in fact while I am alive' (Suet. *Nero* 38.1).

SECTION H

OCTAVIA (SELECTIONS)

Octavia is the only surviving example of a *fabula praetexta*, a Roman play on a historical theme. Such plays often dealt with events in the distant past, but contemporary subjects were also presented, as in Naevius' *Clastidium*, on M. Marcellus' victory in 222 BC, or Ennius' *Ambracia*, on M. Fulvius Nobilior's victory in 189 BC, or L. Balbus' play about his own role in the civil war (Pollio in Cic. *Fam.* 10.32.3). There is no need to suppose that *praetextae* ceased to be written under the principate; no doubt they were usually loyal flattery of the emperor (compare *Phaedrus* 5.7.23–8, Suet. *Aug.* 89.3, Pliny, *Paneg.* 54.1–2), but attacks on unpopular figures, like Nero and Poppaea in *Octavia*, would be possible once they were safely dead. How and why the text of this play was preserved is not known, but its survival to the present is due to its incorporation (probably about 1200) into the 'A-group' of manuscripts of Seneca's tragedies. That it is not by Seneca is clear from references to events after Seneca's death in AD 65 (e.g. in **H11**).

When was it written? Recent editors suggest a date under Vespasian (A.J. Boyle) or Domitian (R. Ferri), but the total absence of pro-Flavian material counts against that. The playwright makes Nero dwell on the cruel famine that will follow his burning of Rome (line 833), but Tacitus regarded the food shortage in 64 as a minor item, quickly remedied (*Ann.* 15.39.2); that may suggest that the play's perspective is from close to the events, perhaps the autumn of 68, as suggested independently by Patrick Kragelund and T.D. Barnes in 1968. For more details, see T.P. Wiseman, *The Principal Thing* (Classical Association Presidential Address, 2001).

There is no consensus about act division in *Octavia*. The scene divisions and summaries in *italics* below simply attempt to give the reader some sort of context for the extracts within the play as a whole.

Scene 1 (lines 1–272): *In the opening scene Octavia and her Nurse lament her plight and the series of crimes that brought it about. While Octavia confesses her loathing of Nero, the Nurse for safety's sake urges prudent acceptance of her lot.*

H1 Claudius' marriage to Agrippina; Silanus' suicide (137–149)

NURSE: Poor girl, in vain you call upon the shade of your
Dead father; for down there among the dead he feels
No love or care for you, his own child. He even could prefer
Another's offspring to his own son, Britannicus,
And to himself betrothed his brother's daughter, binding her
As partner to an unholy bed and lamentable marriage.[1]
Hence sprang a catalogue of crimes: murder and treachery,
Lust for a kingdom and a thirst for sacrilegious blood.
A son-in-law, Silanus, was slaughtered, sacrificial victim to
The marriage of his father-in-law, – a crime abominable
And all lest he come to power by marriage to yourself.
He was surrendered, gifted to a woman's wiles, and falsely charged
He stained with his own blood the house-gods of his ancestors.[2]

---

1 For Claudius' marriage to his niece Agrippina and adoption of her son L. Domitius Ahenobarbus as Claudius Nero, see Tac. *Ann.* 12.1–3 (AD 48), 12.25 (AD 50). The law legalising the marriage is **J12d**.

2 Octavia's fiancé L. Junius Silanus (**J33a**), like Nero a great-great-grandson of Augustus (Sen. *Apocol.* 10.4 = **F10**), was prosecuted by L. Vitellius in 48, and committed suicide on the day of Claudius' marriage to Agrippina (Tac. *Ann.* 12.3–4 and 12.8.1, Suet. *Claud.* 29.1–2).

H2 Agrippina murders Claudius (160–166)

NURSE: Then Piety, the holy bond of family, fled away
On trembling footsteps, and with murderous tread
A savage Fury entered the empty palace, and defiled
With Hell's own firebrand the sacred gods of Home,
In madness shattering the laws of Nature and of Right.
A wife for her husband concocted foul poisons,[3] but then
Herself fell victim to her own son's crime.

H3 Britannicus' death and funeral (166–173)

NURSE: You, too, lie dead, Britannicus,
Unhappy lad, to be bewailed by us for evermore, who lately
Were the world's bright constellation, the strong pillar
Of Augustus' house. But now alas, no more you are than ashes,
Light as the air, a mournful shadow, over whom
Even that savage stepmother wept tears, when to the pyre
She gave your sweet corpse for burning, while the raging fire
Robbed us of that sweet countenance and limbs that bore
Cupid's own likeness.[4]

H4 Acte and Poppaea (193–200)

NURSE: She that first dared to violate your marriage-bed, that slave
Who long ago had seized possession of her master's heart,
Now humble and afraid, she fears assuredly the one preferred
Above herself, and puts up monuments by which she shows
Herself deceived, and offers proof of terrors in her heart.[5]
Winged Cupid, the treacherous and deceitful god, will soon
Abandon her as well. Lovely though she may be,
Proud of her wealth, her joy will be short-lived.

H5 Messalina's bigamy (257–269)

OCTAVIA: Long since has our house been crushed beneath the anger
Of the gods. Hard-hearted Venus first afflicted it
With my poor mother's madness, making her forget
Her duty to her rightful husband, spurning the law,
So that though already married she in her madness mad

[3] Agrippina allegedly employed the poison expert Locusta to kill Claudius (Tac. *Ann.* 12.66–67, Dio 60.34.2–3, compare Suet. *Claud.* 44.2–3).

[4] For the death of the 14-year-old Britannicus in 55, allegedly by poison, see Tac. *Ann.* 13.15–17, Suet. *Nero* 33.2–3, Dio 61.7.4.

[5] For Nero's mistress the freedwoman Claudia Acte, see Tac. *Ann.* 13.12–13 (AD 55), 14.2.1 (AD 59), Suet. *Nero* 28.1, 50, Dio 61.7.1. She was a woman of wealth: inscriptions reveal that she had property at Velitrae, Puteoli and in Sardinia, and about twenty of her own slaves and freedmen are attested at Rome and elsewhere.

A second, unholy marriage.[6] *But the avenging Fury came,*
With torched hair running wild and girded with snakes,
To that cursed wedding-bed, and from their chamber stole
The marriage-torches, and in blood extinguished them.
The emperor's heart she fired with savage rage
And drove him to commit unholy murder.[7] *So by the sword*
My poor unhappy mother, Messalina died, and for ever after
She left me overwhelmed in grief perpetual. Husband and son
She dragged to the shades below, and thus betrayed to ruin
Our fallen house.

Scene 2 (lines 273–376): *In a lyric ode the Chorus of Roman citizens sing of the foundation of the Roman tradition of liberty in the expulsion of the Tarquins, on whom their own forefathers had taken vengeance, and liken the early tyrants' crimes to the recent murder of Agrippina by Nero. They lament the impiety and degeneracy of the present century.*

H6 **Nero murders Agrippina** (310–376)

CHORUS: Our century too has seen
A son's crime, sacrilegious,
Abomination supreme.
An emperor made captive
His mother and sent her
To sea in ship he designed
As a floating coffin,
He sent her far out
On the savage Tyrrhenian sea,[8]

Obeying orders, the sailors
Leave the calm harbour waters
In haste, and the shattered sea
Sings to the slap of their oars.
Into the deep she sails on the wind.
Then with a crash the hull
Splinters, her ribbing dissolves,
Labouring now she swallows the sea.
A tumult of noise batters the stars;
Women's screams add to the tumult;
Before their eyes stalking the decks
Comes grisly Death, from whom each
For himself seeks refuge. Some, stark naked,

---

6 Messalina bigamously married C. Silius in 48 (Tac. *Ann.* 11.26–31, Suet. *Claud.* 26.2, 29.3, Dio 60.31.3–4). The idea that she was driven to it by Venus may derive from her destruction of Julia Livilla (**J23**) in 41 and Julia (**J16**) the daughter of Drusus in 43 (Dio 60.8.5 and 18.4, Tac. *Ann.* 13.32.3 and 13.43.2); since both women were great-granddaughters of Augustus (Sen. *Apocol.* 10.4), the goddess could be thought of as avenging her own descendants.

7 For Claudius' execution of Messallina without a hearing, see Tac. *Ann.* 11.34–38, Dio 60.31.4–5, **P8c**.

8 In fact, a bay at the north end of the Bay of Naples, between Puteoli and Bauli (Tac. *Ann.* 14.4.2).

Cling to the shattered ship's timbers,
Breasting the waves; some swim for the shore;
Fate dooms many to death in the deep.

The Augusta, Agrippina,
Rips up her robes, tears out her hair,
And drenches her cheeks with her tears
Of despair. But all hope of safety is lost.
Fired up in her rage, and doomed to defeat
By disaster, she shouts, "Is this my reward,
For all the great things I have done
For you, Nero my son? I confess,
I deserved such a ship as my death-trap,
Since I brought you to birth, gave you light,
And – fool that I was – gave you empire and
Title of Caesar. Ah! Claudius, husband,
From Acheron's depths, now look up,
Feast your eyes on the pain of my punishment.
Poor soul, it was I who was author and cause
Of your death, the demise of your son.
I deserve all I get, as unburied I go,
Carried off to confront you in Hades,
Overwhelmed by the wild sea's waves."

While she speaks the billowing sea
Stops her mouth, as she plunges into
Its waves; submerged she sinks down,
Yet rises again and, driven by terror,
She thrashes the waters till, exhausted,
She gives up the struggle. But loyalty
Still lingered, hidden in silent hearts; so now
Scorning their fear of dread death, to the last
Of their broken strength many dared to bring
Help to their queen.[9] They urge her with shouts
As she drags leaden limbs to the shore;
In their arms they lift her to safety.

But what profit was there for you, in this
Pointless escape from savage sea waves?
You are doomed to a death by the sword
Of your son, in a crime that posterity
Scarcely will credit, and subsequent centuries
Barely believe. Nero rages: his mother's escape
From the sea, her very survival, is to him

9 According to Tacitus (*Ann.* 14.5.3), Agrippina's life was saved by her companion Acerronia calling out that she was the empress and attracting the attention of the murderers, while Agrippina remained sensibly silent.

A deep disappointment. His unholy mind
Dreams up a huge second offence against
Heaven itself. In his dash for the death
Of his unhappy mother he brooks no delay.
A servant, sent to do his bidding, carves open
The breast of his queen with his sword.[10]
As she dies the poor woman begs
That agent of death to bury his terrible sword
Deep in her womb. "Here! This is the place;
Here bury your sword, as deep as you can.
It brought forth a monster." [11]
Those were her final words. Then with one
Last groan, through those fearsome wounds
She set her grim spirit free.

Scene 3 (Lines 377–592)

Seneca appears and in a long speech expresses regret for his recall from exile (to be Nero's tutor) and laments the decline of human morality. Wickedness he says has reached its peak, at which moment Nero appears and orders the execution of Plautus and Sulla. He remains deaf to Seneca's suggestion that mercy is a safer and surer approach for a ruler (compare the De Clementia*), a lesson perhaps aimed at the new Emperor Galba, who if the early dating of the play is correct, may have been sitting watching the play among the ranks of Roman senators.*

H7 Plautus and Sulla killed (462–471)

NERO: I can endure no longer these attempts to shed my blood,
Aimed at my sudden overthrow, despised and un-avenged.
Their distant exile has not cracked their spirits; rather
With crazed obstinacy Plautus and Sulla still persist
In arming their confederates in crime to murder me.
They may be far away, but still their popularity here
In Rome remains intense; it nourishes their hopes in exile.[12]
These suspect enemies of mine must be exterminated
By the sword, my hated wife must perish, following
In the footsteps of the brother whom she loved.
The loftiest trees must be cut down.

H8 Messalina's adultery; Octavia's illegitimacy? (533–537)

SENECA: Octavia will fill your halls with offspring all divine,
Daughter of a deity and glory to the clan of Claudius.
Like Juno she has gained the right to share a brother's bed.

---

[10] Anicetus, commander of the Misenum fleet, was a freedman (Tac. *Ann.* 14.3.3 and 14.7.3, Dio 61.13.2).

[11] The last words in Tacitus (*Annals* 14.8.4) are more laconic: 'Strike my womb!'

[12] Faustus Cornelius Sulla and Rubellius Plautus (**J29**) had been banished in 58 and 60 respectively (Tac. *Ann.* 13.47, 14.22), Sulla for his patrician birth and his marriage to Claudius' other daughter Antonia (Tac. *Ann.* 13.23.1), Plautus for his descent from Augustus and the old-fashioned dignity of his behaviour (Tac. *Ann.* 13.19.3, 14.22.1). If their popularity was real, and not just – as Tacitus suggests – Nero's paranoia, it may have been based on the clients and freedmen that aristocratic families could still rely on (Tac. *Hist.* 1.4.3).

NERO: Her mother's adultery cancels her line's legitimacy. And though
She was my wife, her heart was never joined in love to mine.

H9 **Poppaea's child** (589–592)

NERO: Let me approve what Seneca disapproves. For too long now
I have delayed an answer to the prayers of all my people.
Poppaea carries in her womb a part and token of myself.
So now, let us designate tomorrow as our wedding day.[13]

Scene 4 (Lines 593–645)

The ghost of Agrippina appears as a Fury seeking vengeance both for her husband's murder and for her own matricide. On this, Nero's wedding day, she puts a curse on the marriage and prophesies his downfall.

H10 **Agrippina's *damnatio memoriae*** (608–613)

GHOST OF AGRIPPINA: Even my blood could not eliminate my own son's hatred;
This savage tyrant rages still against his mother's name;
He wants all record of my deeds of love for him destroyed,
My statues cast down, and throughout the world
Memorial inscriptions to me everywhere erased
On pain of death.[14] Yet this was the self same world
My own ill-fated love once gave him for a kingdom
While yet a boy. That gift is now my own dire punishment.

H11 **Nero's fate; *domus aurea*; Tiridates** (614–631)

GHOST OF AGRIPPINA: My dead husband, Claudius, fiercely haunts my spirit
And in my guilty face thrusting his firebrands
He presses his attack, and threatens me, and blames
Me for the death and tombstone of his son
Britannicus, and demands his murderer's death.

Spare me a moment longer; his death shall come. I ask
But a brief delay, and then this avenging Fury plans a death
Such as that sacrilegious tyrant well deserves: lashes,
A coward's flight, and other penalties so great he will surpass
The thirst of Tantalus, Sisyphus' grim toils, Tityos' vulture,
Pecking his liver, and the torture wheel that breaks Ixion's limbs.[15]
Let him, in all his arrogance, erect a marble palace decked

---

13 Nero and Poppaea were married in 62 (Tac. *Ann.* 14.59–60); Poppaea's child, (named Claudia!) was born just before 21 January, when the Arval Brothers record sacrifices (**A63c**). Tac. *Ann.* 15.23 records the baby's birth, death and deification. By 66 the Arvals sacrifice to Diva Poppaea and Diva Claudia (**A66d–e**).

14 In fact, there is not much evidence for the erasure of Agrippina's inscriptions: see Harriet I. Flower, *The Art of Forgetting: Disgrace and Oblivion in Roman Political Culture* (Chapel Hill 2006) 189–94. But Agrippina was denied a proper memorial by Nero (Tac. *Ann.* 14.9.1).

15 The senate sentenced Nero to be flogged to death (Suet. *Nero* 49.2); he fled in secret from the imperial property to a freedman's house (*Nero* 48.1–2); and all he had to drink was a little water from a pool (*Nero* 48.3–4).

In gold, let his armed cohorts guard their general's gates,
Let the exhausted world, reduced to penury, bequeath to him
All its resources, suppliant Parthians bow to kiss
His bloodstained hands,[16] and all the kingdoms of earth
Bring him their riches, yet that day, that time will come,
When he shall surrender up his guilty soul for all his crimes,
And to his enemies lay bare his throat, and die,
Deserted, destroyed, in utter destitution.

Scene 5 (Lines 646–690)
In a lyric passage Octavia, divorced and exiled, prepares to leave the palace, but foresees her own death. As she departs the Chorus protest at Poppaea's elevation and lament the lost courage of the Roman people to resist the tyrant.

Scene 6 (Lines 690–780)
Poppaea's tells her Nurse of an ominous dream, in which the earth gapes open and she sees Agrippina as a menacing fury, and then her former husband Crispinus being murdered by Nero. At the end of the scene the secondary Chorus of her supporters sing a hymn to her beauty.

H12 Death of Crispinus (728–733)

POPPAEA: In my dream I saw Crispinus, my former husband, coming near
Together with my son;[17] with him a company
Of Nero's victims. He hurried to embrace me and to share
Our kisses, long forgotten. But at that moment into my house
There burst a trembling Nero, who in my husband's throat
Buried his savage sword. And then at last almighty terror
Jolted me from my slumbers and I woke. My face shook,
A horrid tremor ran throughout my limbs, while my heart
Beat wildly, and my fear stifled my screams. But now, dear Nurse,
Your kindly love and faithful loyalty have calmed my fears.

Scene 7 (Lines 780–819)
Against a background of noisy revelry from wedding guests within the palace, the Messenger describes the popular protests, in which Poppaea's statues are overthrown and plans are being made to attack the palace. The Secondary Chorus declare that no one can overcome the power of Love and remind us that it was Love that destroyed the kingdom of Priam. The audience will remember too that, according to rumour, only four years previously Nero sang of the Fall of Troy while he watched Rome burn.

---

[16] Nero staged a great spectacle for the formal submission and crowning of Tiridates in 66 (Suet. *Nero* 13; Dio 63.1–6; Pliny, *NH* 33.54 = **Q16**). The marble palace in line 624 is the Domus Aurea, created from the ruins of the fire in 64 (Tac. *Ann.* 15.42.1; **K41–K44**).

[17] Rufrius Crispinus, one of the praetorian prefects dismissed by Agrippina in 51 (Tac. *Ann.* 12.42.1); by 58 he had been succeeded as Poppaea's husband by M. Salvius Otho (ibid. 13.45–6, Suet. *Otho* 3). He was banished to Sardinia in 65 and committed suicide the following year (Tac. *Ann.* 15.71.4, 16.17.1–2). His son by Poppaea was drowned by his own slaves while still a boy, supposedly on Nero's orders (Suet. *Nero* 35.5).

H13 **Popular uprising** (780–805)

MESSENGER: All soldiers in the palace now on guard must
Leap to its defence – the people have gone wild with rage
They're up in arms attacking it. Look how scared
The prefects are – they're calling in the army to defend
The city. This is madness, but it started mindlessly; it won't
Give way to fear of force – indeed it's gaining strength.
CHORUS: Whence comes this mad frenzy that afflicts their minds?
MESSENGER: Their ranks are all siding with Octavia. They're raging
And in their wild frenzy are hell bent on atrocity.
CHORUS: What risks are they prepared to take? Tell us their plans!
MESSENGER: To give back to Octavia, the house-gods of Divus Claudius,
And to restore her marriage to her brother, with her due share of empire.
CHORUS: All these are now Poppaea's, by marriage contracts mutually agreed.
MESSENGER:That's why they're all fired up to back Octavia – it's stubborn lunacy,
It's disproportionate, but it's driving them to mindless violence.
Wherever a statue, whose bright marble and refulgent bronze
Stands with a likeness to Poppaea's looks, now it lies fallen,
Toppled with bare hands by the crowd, or torn down
With savage iron hooks, while one by one they tear apart
The limbs with their nooses, trampling them down, till finally
In filthy mud they all lie buried.[18] Their mingled shouts and cries
Are well-matched with their deeds. I dare not tell you more.
They're getting ready now to put a ring of fire round the palace,
If he will not sacrifice his new wife to the anger of the people,
Meet their demands, and give back to Octavia her household gods.
He has to be told of these civic disturbances
From my own lips. I must hurry now. Those are the prefect's orders.

Scene 8 (Lines 820–876)

An enraged Nero bursts onto the scene, threatening revenge, and complaining that his Prefect should have burned the city and broken the people's spirit by brutal suppression. He orders the exile and execution of Octavia, for fomenting the uprising. The Chorus, diminished and demoralised, respond with an ode on the dangers of popular favour.

H14 **Great Fire of Rome** (825–833)

NERO: But now, for their crimes, death is too slight a punishment;
For their impiety the mob deserves a retribution far more dire.
Octavia, too, my suspect wife and sister, she to whom
The fury of the people would subject me, she
To assuage my pain must render up her life
And with her blood alleviate my anger.

---

[18] Tacitus calls the disturbances an armed uprising (*seditio*), and makes Poppaea complain that Octavia's supporters 'dare in peace what scarcely happens in war' (Tac. *Ann.* 14.61.1 and 3); Suetonius, however, mentions nothing more than shouting (Suet. *Nero* 35.2). Dio's narrative does not survive, but his account of the fall of Sejanus in 31 (58.11–12) shows vividly what the angry populace was capable of, and what Poppaea was afraid might happen to her.

Now, let this city's buildings crumble beneath my flames,
And let my guilty populace succumb to fiery ruin and
Vile poverty, famine and savage starvation, with all its woes.[19]

Scene 9 (lines 900 – end)

In a final series of lyric exchanges, Octavia resigns herself to death ("There is no god of righteousness now"), while the Chorus seek to comfort her with reminders of the many imperial women who have suffered similar fates before her.

H15 Fates of imperial women (929–957)

CHORUS: Let past examples give you strength; many
Already the woes your household has endured.
Was Fate to them unkinder than to you?

Yours, Agrippina, is the tale
Which I must first unfold.
Mother of many children,
Agrippa's daughter and
Augustus' too, by marriage,
A Caesar's wife, your name
Shone bright in glory
All across the world.[20]
So many times your heavy womb
Brought children forth as
Promises of future peace.
But your reward was exile, beatings
And cruel chains,
Their deaths, your grief, and death
At the last, after protracted torture.[21]

Then Livia Julia, blessed in her husband,
Drusus, blessed in her children, she
Who rushed to criminality and paid
The due penalty for a filthy crime.[22]
Her daughter, Julia, shared
Her mother's fate, dying by the sword
After long years, with no charge laid against her.[23]

---

19 The food shortage after the fire of July AD 64 is mentioned briefly at Tac. *Ann.* 15.39.2.

20 "The term *nurus* [daughter-in-law] includes not only a son's wife but also a grandson's." (Paulus in *Digest* 23.2.14.4). The elder Agrippina (**J9**) was the wife of Germanicus Caesar, who was the son (by adoption) of Tiberius and thus grandson (by adoption) of Augustus.

21 She was banished in 29, beaten in captivity, and starved to death in 33 (Suet. *Tib.* 53.2, Tac. *Ann.* 6.25.1). Her sons Nero Caesar (**J17**) and Drusus Caesar (**J18**) were also beaten in captivity and starved to death, in 31 and 33 respectively (Suet. *Tib.* 54, Tac. *Ann.* 6.23–4).

22 Germanicus' sister, sometimes called Livilla (**J11**), wife of Tiberius' son Drusus and mother of twin sons (Tac. *Ann.* 2.84.1); mistress of Sejanus (ibid. 4.8.3–4), starved to death in 31 (Dio 58.11.6–7).

23 Julia, grand-daughter of Tiberius, executed at Messallina's instigation in 43 (Tac. *Ann.* 13.32.3, Suet. *Claud.* 29.1, Dio 60.18.4)

Then there was Messalina, your own mother,
What could she not achieve in earlier days
When she was ruler of the emperor's court
By virtue of his love for her, and as
His children's mother. She too became
The slave of a slave, and died
By a soldier's savage sword.[24]

And what of Agrippina, she who once
Could rightly hope for royal rule and then
Divinity, as Nero's all-powerful mother?
Was she not first assaulted by the hands
Of murdering sailors, and then slashed
To lingering death by swords,
To lie, a sacrificial victim
To her cruel son?

H16 Octavia's exile and death (958–972)

OCTAVIA: That savage animal, that tyrant, plans to send
Me also to the sad land of shadows and the dead.
Why should I vainly plead for pity or delay?
Soldiers! Drag me away to death, since now
The Fates have left me at your mercy.

Ye gods in heaven, be my witnesses –
Forget it, you foolish woman; prayers
Serve no purpose, when you are hated
By all the gods of heaven. Therefore, I call
On Tartarus to be my witness, goddesses too
Of Erebus, avengers of men's crimes,
And you, my father Claudius, that he deserves
A death and punishment resembling mine.[25]
I can no longer find
Due cause to hate the death he plans for me.

Come sailors, prepare your craft,
Spread out your sails upon the waves,
And let the ship's helmsman catch
The wind, and seek the shores
Of Pandateria.[26]

---

[24] The 'slave' is the freedman Narcissus, in charge of the Praetorians for the execution of Messallina (**P8c**, Tac. *Ann.* 11.33–34, 11.37).

[25] Nero died on the anniversary of Octavia's death (Suet. *Nero* 57.1), and was afraid that he would be decapitated like her (Suet. *Nero* 49.4).

[26] The small island of Ventotene, 25 miles off the coast of Italy. Also imprisoned there were Augustus' daughter Julia from 2 BC to AD 14 (Tac. *Ann.* 1.53.1, Dio 55.10.14), his granddaughter Agrippina from 29 to 33 (Suet. *Tib.* 53.2, *Gaius* 15.1), and Domitian's niece Flavia Domitilla from 95 (Dio 67.14.2).

SECTION J
IMPERIAL FAMILY

If only I had lived unmarried, or died childless! – Augustus

This section arranges personal and family information on members of the imperial family, including emperors, in roughly chronological order, with a brief introduction to each. Family trees, given at intervals throughout the period (AD 14, 31, 37, 41, 54, 68), appear at the end of the book. Adoptions, multiple marriages, and inter-marriages make the trees complicated. So does the repeated use of family names: hence the use of numbers and letters, so that Drusus son of Tiberius = **J10** (also in cross-references and on family trees, with sources on him lettered a to h). Augustus (above) was quoting Homer (*Iliad* 3.40), according to Suetonius, *Augustus* 65.4).

J1 Livia (Julia Augusta, later Diva Augusta) 58 BC – AD 29

Livia was born on 30 January 58 BC (**A38d**). A member, by birth, of the Claudius clan, Livia married another member of this famously aristocratic family, Tiberius Claudius Nero. She bore him two children, Tiberius and Drusus, but even while pregnant with Drusus married Octavian (Augustus) (Tac. *Ann.* 1.10.5). Her 51-year marriage to Augustus produced a miscarriage, but no children (Pliny, *NH* 7.57; Suet. *Aug.* 63.1). Her huge influence over Augustus and Tiberius is unquestionable (Vell. 130.4–5; SCPP 114–8; Sen. *Clem* 1.9; Tac. *Ann* 2.34.2–4; Suet *Otho* 1.1; Dio 55.14–21), though sources differ about its use. Tacitus' *Annals* is very hostile to Livia, though his 'obituary' is more balanced (*Ann.* 5.1 = LACTOR 17, J26). For the senate and Livia, see Tac. *Ann.* 1.14. Suetonius preserves some of Augustus' letters to Livia (Suet. *Claud.* 4). Livia also brought up Caligula (Suet. *Cal* 10.1; and 23.2 for his view). She was deified by her grandson, Claudius (Sen. *Apocol.* = **F9.5**; Suet. *Claud.* 11.2; **A44b, A53b**).

Modern treatment: Barrett, *Livia, First Lady of Imperial Rome* (New Haven, 2002) includes 70 page appendix of all sources for Livia. Images: portrait bust from the Fayum, Egypt in Copenhagen, Ny Carlsberg Glypotek (Kleiner, 54); BM Livia bust; Sard sealstone BM Gem 1975

J1a Honestus, epigram to Livia Augusta

Augusta, twin Caesars, sceptred gods, her proudest boast,
    Twin torches for Peace she lit for every nation;
The Muses' choruses her wisdom suited most;
    Her genius was the whole wide world's salvation.

[Honestus, 21]

Honestus (of Corinth?) wrote 10 epigrams included in the 'Greek Anthology'. A further 12 epigrams with his name were found inscribed on statue bases at Thespiae in Greece, home to a festival in honour of the Muses. Nine of these honour the Muses; one honours Thamyris, the lyre-player blinded for challenging the Muses (Homer, *Iliad* 2.594–600); one is very fragmentary; the last (above) is to an Augusta, who, closely linked to two Caesars, can only be Livia, wife of Augustus and mother of Tiberius.

J1b Honoured in the Agora at Athens

Julia Augusta the Counsellor, mother of Tiberius Augustus, the council of the Areopagus.

[Greek: EJ 89]

This statue-base of Hymettian marble was found reused near the *bouleuterion* (council chamber) at Athens, and this has influenced the choice of an unusual epithet, 'Boulaia' = 'Counsellor' for Julia Augusta.

J1c Honoured at Anticaria (Baetica, Spain), AD 14/29

To Julia Augusta, [daughter] of Drusus, (wife) of Divus [Augustus], mother of Tiberius Caesar Augustus, *princeps* and saviour, and of Drusus Germanicus; mother of the world. Marcus Cornelius Proculus, pontiff of the Caesars.

[*CIL* 2. 2038 = EJ 123]

J1d Tiberius and Julia Augusta, *sestertius* of AD 23 (mint of Rome)

Obv: *Carpentum* drawn right by two mules. The front is decorated with two Victories, the side with two standing figures

S P Q R IVLIAE AVGVST (the Senate and People of Rome for Julia Augusta [Livia])

Rev: Large S C (by decree of the senate) in centre of coin

TI CAESAR DIVI AVG F AVGVST P M TR POT XXIIII (Tiberius Caesar Augustus, son of Divus Augustus, *pontifex maximus*, in his 24th year of tribunician power)

[*BMC* Tiberius 76; *RIC* Tiberius 51]

The coin was struck to celebrate the recovery of Livia (also known as Julia Augusta) from illness in AD 23. The *carpentum* was a covered two wheeled carriage, sometimes used to transport religious object not to be seen by the public. In Republican Rome, where wheeled traffic was restricted, it could only be used by married woman, but this privilege too was withdrawn. It is possible that Livia was allowed to use the *carpentum*, or it was used to move religious items used in the ceremony of thanksgiving after her recovery.

J2 TIBERIUS 42 BC – AD 37

Tiberius was born on 16 November (**A35b,** Suet. Tib. 5). He was just over three when his mother Livia married Octavian/Augustus. His career under Augustus in covered by Suetonius, *Tiberius* 6–21, with other sources in LACTOR 17, J33–42. Velleius, who served under Tiberius in Germany and the Balkans provides an adulatory account of Tiberius as general and emperor (LACTOR 17, Section E; this volume, Section **C**). Tiberius' reign was fully covered by Tacitus' *Annals*, but the two-year period AD 29–31 is completely lost from the manuscripts. So too is, presumably, an account of his funeral from *Annals* book 7 (see **J2g** below). His own unwillingness to rule is summed up in a letter to the senate quoted by Tacitus, *Annals* 6.6.1 and Suet. Tib. 67.

Modern treatment: Levick, *Tiberius the Politician* (London 1976).

J2a Tiberius on *Aureus* of AD 13–14

Obv: Augustus, laureate, right
CAESAR AVGVSTVS DIVI F PATER PATRIAE (Caesar Augustus, son of Divus, father of the fatherland)

Rev: Tiberius, head bare, right
TI CAESAR AVG F TR POT XV (Tiberius Caesar, Son of Augustus, in his 15th year of tribunician power)

[*BMC* Augustus 506; *RIC* Augustus 225]

This *aureus* showing Tiberius' portrait coupled with that of Augustus can be dated to the last year of Augustus' life. Tribunician power marked the principal successor and gave him all the powers he needed to rule. Tiberius had first been granted this power in 6 BC for a five-year period, and for further ten-year periods on his adoption in AD 4 and in AD 13.

J2b Oath of allegiance to Tiberius, Cyprus, AD 14

[By] our Aphrodite Acraea and our Maiden Persephone and our [Apollo] Hylates and our Apollo Kerynetes and our saviours the Dioscuri and Hestia of the council who is shared by the island, and the gods and goddesses who are the ancestral deities shared by the island, and the descendant of Aphrodite, god Augustus Caesar, and everlasting Rome, and all the other gods and goddesses; we ourselves and our descendants swear to obey and be obedient, to show goodwill by land and sea, to reverence [*blank*] Tiberius Caesar Augustus, son of Augustus, with all his house, and to have the same man as friend and enemy that they have, and along with the other gods to propose and vote for [?religious rites] only for Rome and Tiberius Caesar Augustus, son of Augustus [*blank*] and for the sons of his blood and for nobody else at all…

[Greek: Mitford, *JRS* (1960) = Levick 126 = EJ 105*]

Similar oaths from the Augustan period have been discovered (LACTOR 17, H37). This particular example from near the ancient site of Palaipaphos shows the uncertainity surrounding Tiberius' accession. The inscription on a white marble slab includes spaces equivalent to about twelve letters left deliberately blank, where the imperial title *autokrator* (the Greek equivalent of *imperator*) could be added at a later date. This seems to reflect knowledge that Tiberius had rejected this title (Suet. *Tib.* 26.2), but doubt as to whether this rejection would persist. In the event, these blank spaces remained uncompleted. The phrasing of the oath also implies that it was not centrally imposed, but was composed in Cyprus. By alluding to 'sons of his blood', the oath inadvertently excludes Tiberius' principal heir, Germanicus, who was his adopted son. T.B. Mitford, 'A Cypriot Oath of Allegiance to Tiberius' *JRS* 50 (1960) 75–79.

J2c Decree on the accession of Tiberius, Messene (Achaia), AD 14

To god Augustus [Caesar] and to Tiberius Caesar Augustus, the Secretary of the Council and priest [of god Augustus] Caesar…

[only small fragments survive of the next thirteen lines]

… whenever the seer prays … and … Augustus Caesar, let [someone] bring in the magistrates, and swear … in the entrance-ways each man … [of god] Augustus Caesar and of Tiberius Caesar [Augustus] and their descendants. Let there be a great feast with lambs in [the imperial shrine…] let the [priest] of Augustus in that year carry the torch … approaching the shrine and first from those on the right hand side… alone … to give light to us and to all men … Augustus, and … of Tiberius Caesar and those who begot him and those who bore him, himself… and goddess Livia, his mother, and the wife [of god Augustus Caesar], and Antonia and Livilla, sacrifices … every year in succession, just as also … priest [of Augustus] and let them carry the torch… [fragmentary couple of lines]… and all those living in the city are led out, … a holiday over three days in a row, and to celebrate competitions – athletics for boys and young men, and horse-racing of the youth on the birthday – and weapons of the victors to be dedicated each year after the sacrifice, and to send an embassy to Rome to the imperator Tiberius Caesar, to express our distress that the god is no longer manifest among us, but to salute Tiberius as imperator, and to congratulate him as he deserves, and according to our prayer that he become leader of the whole world, and to lament bitterly about those who have wickedly taken over the city and to entreat that we may receive some pity.

[Greek: *SEG* 41 (1991) 328]

Fragments from the bottom of a pedimental stele were found in excavations of the Sebasteion (imperial shrine) at Messene. These partially preserve a decree showing the city's response to the death of Augustus and accession of Tiberius: the Messenians established games in honour of Tiberius and sent an embassy to Rome to lament Augustus' death, congratulate Tiberius, and to seek help with some local problems (probably a dispute with Sparta – compare Tacitus *Annals* 4.43 for the dispute between Sparta and Messene over control of the temple of Diana Limnatis, settled in favour of the Messenians by the senate in AD 25).

J2d Tiberius the heavy drinker

Forty years ago, under Tiberius Caesar, drinking on an empty stomach, with a drink of wine before food, became the fashionable thing to do as a result of foreign methods, and the opinions of doctors who always seek to recommend themselves by some novelty. The Parthians have a reputation for this; Alcibiades won a reputation for it among the Greeks; and among us, Novellius Torquatus of Milan, who held every office between praetor and proconsul, acquired his *cognomen* 'Eighteen-Pints' from the amount he drank in one go, as a sort of stunt, while Tiberius watched. This was in the emperor's old age when he had become strict and even cruel: in fact when a younger man himself he had been quite a hard drinker, and it is thought that what had recommended Lucius Piso as Tiberius' choice for city prefect was two days and nights of drinking without a break at his house when he had just become *princeps*.

[Pliny, *Natural History* 14.143–6]

Suetonius, *Tiberius* 42, gives further details of Tiberius' drinking habits, including his nickname Biberius Caldius Mero – roughly 'Drinker of strong mulled wine' or, vaguely keeping the puns 'Bibulous Poured Us Beero'. He also mentions an obscure candidate being made quaestor after meeting a drinking challenge set by Tiberius. No doubt this was Novellius Torquatus whose career is known from an inscription *CIL* 14.3602. Lucius Calpurnius Piso was famous for his drinking (Suet. *Tib.* 42; Seneca, *Letters* 84.14), but this did not affect his health (died aged 80 – Tac. *Ann.* 6.10.3) or his efficiency (Velleius 2.98; remarkable tribute from Tacitus, *Ann.* 6.10–11). For L. Piso as city prefect, see **U1**. Brother-in-law of Julius Caesar, consul and winner of triumphal ornaments under Augustus, he did not owe his appointment to his own or Tiberius' drinking habits.

J2e Imperial family honoured at Lepcis Magna, AD 14/19

[... constructed and consecrated this temple with the statues of god Augu]stus and of Rome and of Tiberius Augustus and of Julia Augusta and of Germanicus and of Drusus Caesar and of Agrippin[a wife] of Germanicus and [of Livia wife of Dru]sus and of Antonia mo[ther of Ger]manicus and of Agripp[ina mother] of Drusus. And the entirety of the statue of the god Augustus and the throne of the statue of god Augustus. [.... of the statue to god] Augustus and the covering of the statue of Germanicus and of Drusus Caesa[r and ...] for Tiberius Augustus and the quadriga for [Germani]cus and for Drusus C[aesar] and the bronze door and the soffit of the portico and the courtyard of the temple and the porticoes were offered at the expense ...., when the *sufetes* were BLYTN son of Anno G. Saturninus and Bodmelqart son of Bodmelqart Tapapi... RYQL

[*IPT* 22]

This is the dedicatory inscription in Punic of the Temple of Rome and Augustus, AD 14/19, paid for by the local magistrates (*sufetes*). This is one of a series of building-inscriptions in which the local élite wished to associate themselves with Rome. They are careful to honour Tiberius' adopted and real sons equally, listing their wives and mothers. Agrippina, mother of Drusus is Vipsania Agrippina, daughter of Marcus Agrippa, and Tiberius' first wife. Fragments of colossal statues of members of the imperial family were found nearby. [Levi della Vida and Amadasi Guzzo, *Iscrizioni puniche della Tripolitania (1927–1967)* (1987)]

J2f Dedication to Tiberius, Flaminian Way, Italy AD 32/3

To Tiberius Caesar Augustus, son of Divus Augustus, *pontifex maximus*, consul five times, in his 34th year of tribunician power, best *princeps*, and most righteous preserver of the fatherland. For his safety and well-being, Aulus Fabius Fortunatus, road-builder, consul and praetor, first Augustalis, in fulfilment of a public vow.

[EJ 85 = *ILS* 159: Via Flaminia, near Capena]

J2g Tiberius' death and funeral

16 March: Tiberius Caesar passed away at Misenum.
29 March: His body was carried into Rome by soldiers.
3 April: He was given a public funeral.

[Fasti at Ostia, fragment Ch = EJ p 43]

The death and burial of Tiberius was commemorated in the public calendar inscribed at Ostia. See Tac. *Ann.* 6.50.1; Suet. *Cal.* 13 and 15 and Sen. *Apocol.* = **F1.2**. The distance from Rome to Misenum is around 130 miles, mostly along the Appian Way.

J2h Tiberius' funerary urn from Augustus' mausoleum

The bones of Tiberius Caesar, son of Divus Augustus, *pontifex maximus*, in his 38th year of tribunician power, hailed victorious commander 8 times, consul 5 times.

[Rome, *ILS* 164]

This is the inscription on a large marble cinerary urn, now lost but recorded during the Renaissance, from Augustus' Mausoleum in Rome.

J2i Marble head of Tiberius in British Museum

[Marble head of Tiberius: British Museum (GR 1812.6-15.2 (Sculpture 1880))]

This marble head of Tiberius is slightly larger than life-size (48cm high). It is very similar to others created for Tiberius' adoption as his heir in AD 4 and presents Tiberius, then in his mid-forties, in the style that had become typical for Augustus' blood relations, which Tiberius was not. See further, S. Walker, *Greek and Roman Portraits*, London (British Museum Press) 1995.

J3 Drusus 38 BC – 9 BC

Nero Claudius Drusus, the younger brother of Tiberius, was the second son of Livia by her first husband, Tiberius Claudius Nero. However she divorced him to marry Octavian while pregnant, and Drusus was therefore born into Octavian's household (Suet. *Claud.* 1.1). He married Antonia, younger daughter of Octavia and Mark Antony. His military success, death on campaign, and stated wish to restore the republic (Suet. *Tib.* 50.1, *Claud.* 1.4) assured his lasting popularity, which was harnessed by his son, Claudius (**J3b** below). See also LACTOR 17, J28, J43–7.

J3a Drusus' sexual fidelity

Drusus Germanicus was the outstanding glory of the Claudian family, an egregious ornament of his fatherland, and above all, someone who by the greatness of his own achievements at an early age, remarkably matched both his imperial step-father and brother, those twin divine eyes of the state. It is well established that he kept his sexual activity confined to love for his wife.

[Valerius Maximus, *Memorable Doings and Sayings*, 4.3.3]

Valerius Maximus was writing about AD 30. For his praise of Antonia's chastity, see **J5b** below.

J3b Claudian *aureus* showing his father's German victories, *c.* AD 41–5 (Rome)

Obv: Head of Nero Claudius Drusus wearing laurel wreath
NERO CLAVDIVS DRVSVS GERMANICVS IMP (Nero Claudius Drusus, Germanicus, Commander)

Rev: Two shields crossed, with two pairs of crossed spears and trumpets, in front of standard (*vexillum*)
DE GERMANIS (over Germany)

[*BMC* Claudius 104; *RIC* Claudius 73]

All coins in Drusus' name were struck under his son, Claudius. This coin celebrates Nero Claudius Drusus' victories over the Germans between 12 and 9 BC, but there were also victories over the Chatti and Maurusii in Claudius' reign (Tac. *Ann.* 11.16–19). Another coin, showing a trimphal arch, was also struck under Claudius to celebrate Drusus' German victories (*RIC* 71; *BMC* 100)

J4 Antonia the Elder 39 BC – AD 33

Elder daughter of Mark Antony and Octavia. Married the aristocratic L. Domitius Ahenobarbus, and had three surviving children, Gnaeus Domitius Ahenobarbus, the father of Nero, and two daughters, both known as Domitia Lepida (**J14**). She died after her son's consulship in AD 32, as shown by an anecdote reported in Sen. *Controv.* 9.4.18.

J5 Antonia the Younger 36 BC – AD 37

Younger daughter of Mark Antony and Octavia. Born on 31 January (**A38e**). Married to Drusus (**J3**), son of Livia, and mother to Germanicus, Claudius and Livilla (**J11**). The five Julio-Claudian emperors were her uncle, her brother-in-law, her grandson, her son, her sister's great-grandson. She was hugely influential, see **J5c** below. Her advice may have been crucial on persuading Tiberius that Sejanus was a threat – Josephus = **P4e**. Tacitus' account of this episode and her death is lost (see **J5d** below). Gaius honoured her as Antonia Augusta (Suet. *Cal* 15.2; Dio 59.3.3–4; **A38e**). Her memory was maintained by her son Claudius (Dio 60.5.1; **J5e**; **N26**) despite her apparent view of him (Suet. *Claud.* 3.2).
Modern treatment: Kokkinos, *Antonia Augusta, Portrait of a Great Roman Lady,* (London 1992). Images: portrait bust of unknown provenance, see Kleiner fig. 114; Kokkinos fig 83); British Museum: Antonia portrait bust (BM Sculpture 1985).

J5a Honoured at Ilium, AD 14/19

Antonia, niece of god Augustus, wife of Drusus Claudius, brother of Imperator Tiberius Augustus, son of Augustus, and mother of Germanicus Caesar; and Tiberius Claudius Germanicus; and Livia goddess Aphrodite wife of Anchises. She has provided the most abundant and greatest beginnings of the most divine family. Philo, son of Apollonios, honoured his goddess and benefactress at his own expense.

[Greek: *IGRRP* IV 206 = EJ 93]

The Julian family had special links to Ilium, ancient Troy, via Aeneas, son of Aphrodite and Anchises. We are offered here a selective picture of Antonia's place within the imperial family, emphasising her kinship to Augustus, but omitting the fact that she was also Antony's daughter. The inscription perhaps dates from AD 18, when Germanicus visited Ilium (Tacitus, *Annals* 2.54.2). There are other alternative interpretations of the phrase translated here as 'She has provided the most abundant and greatest beginnings of the divine family' (focusing upon her role as mother). Kokkinos, for example, translates as 'fullest and greatest principles', and interprets it as referring to Antonia's moral leadership within the family. [N. Kokkinos, *Antonia Augusta. Portrait of a great Roman lady* (1992) 196 n.29 for discussion]

J5b Antonia refuses to remarry after the death of Drusus

Antonia too surpassed the masculine renown of her family in her feminine virtues, by matching her husband's love with her own outstanding loyalty. After his death, though in the prime of life and beauty, she lived with her mother-in-law in place of a husband. In the same bed the one lost her vigour of youth, while the other grew old in her widowhood.

[Valerius Maximus, *Memorable Deeds and Sayings* 4.3.3]

Valerius has just mentioned the great virtues of her husband Drusus, who died in 9 BC, when Antonia was only 27 – see **J3a**. Valerius also praises the chastity of Livia (Antonia's mother-in-law, who died in AD 29) in terms which suggest she was still alive at the time of writing (6.1.pref).

J5c Antonia's influence at court: Agrippa's Upbringing in Rome

[143] Shortly before the death of King Herod the Great [4 BC], Agrippa was still living in Rome. He had been brought up with Drusus, the son of the emperor Tiberius, and remained a very close friend of his. He also came to enjoy the friendship of Antonia, the wife of the Elder Drusus, Tiberius' younger brother, thanks to the fact that she greatly admired Agrippa's mother, Berenice, who had asked her to sponsor his advancement. … [166] Once Agrippa had been accepted into Antonia's friendship, he made it his business to cultivate her grandson Gaius (Caligula), who was widely admired thanks to his father's popularity.

[Josephus, *JA* 18.143 and 166]

Antonia's household included two future emperors: her grandson Gaius (Suet. *Cal.* 10.1, 24.1, 29.1) and son, Claudius. Also other descendants by other marriages of her father, Mark Antony, such as Ptolemy of Mauretania (Dio 51.15.6; Suet, Cal. 26.1; Sen, *de Tranq.* 11.12) and Cotys of Thrace (**M46**). Also several other future friendly kings, such as Agrippa I and Antiochus IV of Commagene (Dio 59.24.1). For other possible connections, see Kokkinos, *Antonia Augusta,* 1992, page 25 and notes. Her influence also helped senators (Tac. *Ann.* 11.3.1).

J5d Death recorded on Calendar at Ostia for AD 37

1 May: Antonia met her end.

[Fasti at Ostia, fragment Ch = EJ p 43]

The accounts of her death in Suetonius (*Cal.* 23.2) and Dio (59.3.6) unconvincingly blame Gaius.

J5e Antonia: *dupondius* of Claudius (AD 41 or later)

Obv: Draped bust of Antonia right with hair in long plait
ANTONIA AVGVSTA

Rev: Claudius, with toga covering his head, standing, holding *simpulum*
TI CLAVDIVS CAESAR AVG P M TR P IMP, S C (Tiberius Claudius Caesar Augustus, *pontifex maximus*, with tribunician power, hailed victorious commander, by decree of the senate)

[*BMC* Claudius 166; *RIC* Claudius 92]

Claudius honoured his mother posthumously (Dio 60.5.1; **N26**). In this issue of coins he is depicted as a priest conducting religious rites in honour of his mother.

J5f Base of Statue of Antonia from Herculaneum

Of Antonia Augusta, mother of Tiberius Claudius Caesar Augustus Germanicus, *pontifex maximus*. L. Mammius Maximus, at his own expense.

[*ILS* 150 = *CIL* 10.1417]

J6 Julia (the Younger) *c.* 19 BC – AD 28

Julia, daughter of Julia and Agrippa and thus granddaughter of Augustus was born around 19 BC, married to L. Aemilius Paullus *c.* 4 BC. Tacitus records her death in AD 28 after 20 years of exile (supported by Livia) on an Adriatic island off the coast of S. Italy (*Annals* 4.71.4). Modern treatment: Fantham, *Julia Augusti* (Oxford 2006), chapter 9.I

J7 Germanicus 15/16 BC – AD 19

Nero Claudius Drusus Germanicus was born on 24 May (**A38j**), the son of Drusus (**J3** – Tiberius' brother) and Antonia (**J5**). His father died when he was about six (Suet. *Claud.* 1.3). In AD 4, when Augustus adopted Tiberius, Tiberius in turn adopted his nephew (Tac. *Ann.* 4.57.3; Suet. *Tib.* 15.2; Dio 55.13.2), as Germanicus Julius Caesar. He is groomed for rule with consulships in AD 12 and 18 (**B18**) and command in Germany (Tac. *Ann.* 1.31.2) and then overall command in the East (Tac. *Ann.* 2.43.1; Velleius = **C125.4, 129.2–3**; *SCPP* lines 30–37 = **P3e**). Tacitus gives a very full account of Germanicus' career and death (*Ann.*1.31–2.83). His early death results in a series of public honours (**J8a–q**) and ensures his lasting popularity (**J7p**), and sympathy for his family (Tac. *Ann.* 2.83; Suet. *Cal.* 15.2; Tac. *Ann.* 14.7.3 (forty years later)). Suetonius gives a mini-biography of Germanicus in *Caligula* 1–7. Married to Agrippina the Elder who bore him nine children.

Modern treatment: Barrett, *Caligula* (London 1989), chapter 1.

J7a Birthday

May 24: [the birthday of Germanicus] Thanksgiving to Vesta.

[Fasti at Cumae, = EJ p.49]

The occasion is confirmed by **A38j**. Vesta was goddess of hearth and home.

J7b Germanicus' Naval Expedition, AD 16: extract from an epic poem

[1.15] Latin rhetoricians have tended to be somewhat half-hearted in their descriptions of the Ocean. They either skated over the subject or simply lacked interest in it. None of them could match Pedo's vigorous descriptions, when describing Germanicus' naval expedition.

And now with the sun and daylight far behind,
They find themselves in darkness, exiles indeed
From the very limits of their familiar world's own boundaries.
Boldly now they go where none has gone before,
Through the forbidden land of shadows, to creation's limit
And the world's last shores.
And now it seems that Ocean –
He who bears beneath his sluggish waves
Monsters abominable, savage sawfish, sharks, the sea's
Own hunting-dogs, Ocean, it seems, swells up
To engulf their ships, Ocean whose crashing waves
Enlarge their fears; and even now beneath his muddy ooze
Their vessels sink; their fleet, abandoned by the winds'
Wild breath and the indifferent fates, falls prey
To the fierce denizens of the deep, in savage death dismembered.
But one, the look-out high on the lofty prow, with straining eyes
Battles to break through the all-blinding fog. Nothing avails.
In vain he struggles, but his world is stolen, lost to view.
And now, into words, he pours his thwarted heart's lament.
"Where are we heading? Daylight has fled away.
The world is lost, and Nature's last eclipse engulfs it all
In everlasting night. Is it that we seek new tribes, who dwell
Far off in lands beyond the hinges of the world, beyond
The northern pole, a people untouched by blasts of cruel wars?
The Gods themselves recall us; they forbid the eyes of mortal men
To see and know the final end of things. How with our oars
Dare we to violate these un-traversed seas, and waters not our own?
How can we dare disturb the gods' own quiet homes?"

[Seneca the Elder, *Suasoriae* 1.15 = Albinovanus Pedo, fragment 1]

In the summer of AD 16 Germanicus moved the majority of his army down the River Ems (just on the German side of the Germany-Netherlands border) to the North Sea. The aims of the expedition are not clear as it was ended by a disastrous storm. Albinovanus Pedo was a well-known literary figure and friend of Ovid (e.g. Quintilian 6.3.61, 10.1.90; Seneca, *Contr.* 2.2.12; Ovid, *ex Ponto* 4.10.3, 4.16.6) and was probably also the prefect mentioned by Tacitus as serving under Germanicus in AD 15 (*Annals* 1.60.2). He was presumably therefore involved in the expedition described in the epic poem above, and probably by Tacitus, *Annals* 2.23–24. Of Albinovanus Pedo's poetry, only the passage above survives, in the quotation by the Elder Seneca. See Courtney, *Fragmentary Latin Poets,* 315–9; Goodyear, *Annals of Tacitus* II, 243–4 (sceptical of any connection); Syme, *History in Ovid,* 88–9.

J7c Germanicus Olympic victor, AD 17

Germanicus Caesar, son of Imperator Tiberius Caesar Augustus, victor at the Olympic games with his four-horse chariot. Marcus Antonius Pisanus, to his own patron. To Olympian Zeus.

[Greek: *SIG*[3] II 792 = Sherk 33]

This text is inscribed in Greek on a limestone block from a statue base found near the temple of Zeus at Olympia. Tiberius had won this event 16 or more years earlier (EJ 78 = LACTOR 17, J39).

Germanicus' visit to Alexandria, AD 18–19: J7d–e

In addition to the account of Germanicus' visit to Egypt in Tacitus' *Annals* (2.59–61), papyri offer further insight into Germanicus' activities there, recording edicts (**J7d**, **M59**) and a speech (**J7e**) he made at Alexandria, together with the crowd's response. These papyri (of early first century AD from Oxyrhynchus) were not official records, and it remains unclear who actually wrote them, but they offer a unique insight into Germanicus through his own words. It is unclear whether Germanicus deliberately overstepped the mark in making this visit without Tiberius' permission, but it should be remembered that, as the grandson of Mark Antony, his rapturous reception may not have been exactly welcome to the emperor, despite also being his heir apparent.

J7d Edict in response to acclamations, AD 19

Germanicus Caesar, son of Augustus, grandson of Divus Augustus, proconsul, says: "Your goodwill, which you always display whenever you see me, I welcome, but your acclamations, which are hateful to me and fitting for the gods, I altogether reject. For they befit only the one who is actually the saviour and the benefactor of the whole human race, my father and his mother, my grandmother. The things for which I receive credit are implications of their divinity, so that, if you disobey me, you will force me to appear before you seldom."

[Greek: *Select Papyri* II no.211 = LACTOR 8 no.7b = EJ 320(b)]

In this edict, Germanicus responds to his enthusiastic reception at Alexandria by asking the people to be more restrained in the honours they give to him. He requests that divine honours be reserved only for Tiberius and Livia. [A.S. Hunt & C.C. Edgar (1956) *Select Papyri* II (Loeb Classical Library: Heinemann & Harvard University Press); L.A. Post, 'A new reading of the Germanicus papyrus', *AJPhil* 64.1 (1944) 80–82]

J7e Germanicus addresses the people at Alexandria

The magistrate: "I have given both the decrees to the Imperator himself." The Imperator: "I, sent by my father, men of Alexandria..." The crowd shouted: "Hooray! Lord, good luck! You will get blessings!" The Imperator: "You set great store, men of Alexandria, on my talking with you; hold on until the time when I finish the answer to each of your questions, then make your feelings clear. Sent, as I said, by my father to settle the overseas provinces, I have an extremely hard commission. First there is the voyage and being dragged away from my father and grandmother, mother, brother and sister, my children and close friends. The command in front of me [...] the house [...] that there is a new sea, that I may first gaze on our city." The crowd shouted: "Good luck!" The Imperator: "Even before, I considered it was the most brilliant sight, first of all because of the hero and founder, to whom there is a kind of common debt on the part of those who have the same ideals, and then because of the benefits of my grandfather Augustus and of my father [...] is, I think, right for me, and so I say nothing more." The crowd shouted: "Hooray! Extra long life to you!" The Imperator said: "What each of you knows, I remembered and I found these things multiplied, treasured up in your prayers. For decrees have been written down to do us honour even when a few men have been gathered together [---]"

[Greek: LACTOR 18 no.167 = *P.Oxy.* XXV 2435 recto = Sherk 34a]

Although the imperator is nowhere named, the context shows that it must be Germanicus: in particular, his reference to his mission 'to settle the overseas provinces' closely echoes the official language used of the same mission in the *Tabula Siarensis* (**J8b**; *SCPP* lines 30–37 = **P3e**), and the list of family members fits his situation at the time. Germanicus appears a bit disingenuous here, given that his actual mission certainly did not include going to Alexandria. The two decrees mentioned at the start were probably issued by the Greek council of the city. Germanicus strikes an informal pose in talking of the hardships involved in being far from his family, even though his wife Agrippina was travelling with him. His references to the city's splendour, and its foundation by Alexander the Great were likely to win over the Alexandrian crowd, and the whole account gives a vivid impression of his enthusiastic reception, and the interaction between crowd and speaker.

J7f Germanicus honoured on Lesbos

Germanicus Cla[udius Caesar], son of *imperator* ~~Tiberius Caesar~~ Augustus, grandson of [*imperator*] Caesar Olympian Augustus, benefactor; [the high-priest] Dam[archos], son of [Leo]n.

[Greek: IG XII 2, 540 = EJ 94]

An inscription from a statue base honouring Germanicus at Eresus on the island of Lesbos. It is unclear why the names Tiberius Caesar have been deleted. For further honours for his family, see **J2c** above.

J7g Germanicus' death, AD 19

10 October: Sacrifices for the death of Germanicus.

[Fasti at Antium, = EJ p.53]

J7h Germanicus' interment, AD 19

8 December: no business on account of the death of Germanicus

[Fasti at Ostia, fragment Cd left 33–4 = EJ p.41]

Compare Tacitus. *Annals.* 2.72–73.

J7i Burial in the Mausoleum

Germ[anicus Caesar, son] of Tiberius Augustus.

[H. von Hesberg & S. Panciera, *Das Mausoleum des Augustus*, (1994) 128–29 no.XII]

This fragmentary marble plaque was found in the Mausoleum of Augustus at Rome, where Germanicus' ashes were interred.

J7j Bassus: On the Death of Germanicus

Ye Guardians of Death, close all Hell's roads with bars;
With iron bolts close fast each portal-gate;
I, Hades, declare, 'Germanicus is not mine; he's of the stars;
No vessel on Acheron could convey a soul so great.'

[Bassus 5 = Palatine Anthology 7. 391]

(Lollius?) Bassus wrote 13 Greek epigrams of no literary merit (according to Gow and Page, *The Greek Anthology*, who describe this one as 'pretentious in style and absurd in content' 2.194). It does, however, show something about Germanicus' reputation. Another poem on Germanicus' death received a cash reward from Tiberius (Tac. *Ann.* 3.49.1).

J7k Germanicus' enduring popularity helps Gaius' succession

[205] When he returned to Capri, Tiberius fell ill. At first the affliction was trivial, but as the symptoms grew more severe he feared for his life and instructed Evodus, the most important of his freedmen, to summon his children to his bedside, since he wanted to speak to them before he died. [206] He no longer had any legitimate children, since Drusus his only son was already dead. But Drusus' son, Gemellus, still remained, together with Tiberius' grand-nephew, Gaius, the son of Germanicus. The latter was now a young man, very well educated since he had been a diligent and conscientious student, and generally popular in Rome thanks to the admirable qualities of his father, Germanicus. [207] Germanicus had achieved the highest possible reputation amongst the common people, and owed his popularity to an easy-going manner and ready accessibility and his reputation to the fact that he deliberately avoided any claims to superiority. [208] Thanks to this he was greatly admired by the people and senate alike, but also by all of Rome's subject peoples. Those who knew him were won over by the easy charm of his conversation; those who did not by the reports they received from those had met him. [209] His death was greeted by a universal outpouring of grief. This was not the artificial expression of sorrow from those who sought to pay court to their rulers, but a genuine sense of grief amongst a people who felt he was one of their own. Each felt his death as a personal loss to himself, such was his ability to get on easily with anyone he met. [210] As a result of all this, his son derived a great advantage amongst all he met, but especially with the soldiery, for whom it became a matter of personal honour that he should inherit the empire, even if it cost them their own lives.

[211] After instructing Evodus to bring his children to him the next morning about dawn, Tiberius prayed to the gods of Rome to show him some sort of clear sign of who should succeed him as emperor. He was eager to hand over the empire to his grandson, but he trusted in the god to reveal their future to him rather more than he believed in his own opinion and judgement.

[Josephus, *JA* 18.205–211]

For Tiberius' possible heirs, see on Gemellus below (**J24**).

J7m Caligula made emperor because of Germanicus

[1] This is the moment, my dear Liberalis, when I should like to make excuses for the gods. There are occasions when we cannot help exclaiming, "What was providence doing when it placed Alexander's idiot half-brother Arrhidaeus on his throne?" [2] Do you imagine that this was intended as an honour for Arrhidaeus himself? Certainly not. It was an honour paid to his father and his brother. Why did providence make Gaius Caesar emperor of the whole world, when he was a man so greedy for human blood that he ordered it to be spilt in front of him as eagerly as if he wanted to drink it himself. Think! Do you imagine that this was an honour paid to Gaius himself? Of course not – it was paid to his father, Germanicus, and to his grandfather and great-grandfather, and all those other equally distinguished ancestors who preceded them, even though they lived out their lives as private citizens no more distinguished than the rest of their contemporaries.

[Seneca, *On Benefits*, 4.31.1–2]

Philip Arrhidaeus was the son of the dynast Philip of Macedon and half-brother of Alexander the Great. Though widely thought to be unfit to rule, he became king Philip III of Macedon in 323 BC. As Seneca seems to be thinking of blood relatives, the grandfather of Gaius Caesar will be Germanicus' father by birth, the Emperor Tiberius' brother (Nero Claudius) Drusus; the great-grandfather meant could be Ti. Claudius Nero (Livia's first husband) or, more probably, the Emperor Augustus, grandfather of Caligula's mother Agrippina.

J7n Caligula celebrating Germanicus, *denarius* of AD 37 (mint of Lugdunum)

Obv: Head of Gaius Caligula, right

C CAESAR AVG GERM P M TR POT (Gaius Caesar, Augustus, Germanicus, *pontifex maximus*, with tribunician power).

Rev: Head of Germanicus, right

GERMANICVS CAES P C CAES AVG GERM (Germanicus Caesar, father of Gaius Caesar Augustus Germanicus).

[*BMC* Gaius 13; *RIC* Gaius 12]

Gaius, who owed his popularity to his father (**J7k, J7m**), honoured him and his mother (**J9d**) on coins.

J7p Germanicus remembered in a third-century army calendar

24 May: public thanksgiving on account of the birthday of Germanicus Caesar to the memory of Germanicus Caesar.

[Fink, R.O., Hoey, A.S. and Snyder, W.F., *The* Feriale Duranum (1940) 136]

The *Feriale Duranum* of A.D. 225/7 is the calendar of an auxiliary unit stationed at Dura Europus (Syria), preserved on papyrus. It is thought that this copy reflects official religious festivals of the army throughout the empire.

J7q Basalt bust of Germanicus from Egypt

[Basalt bust of Germanicus: British Museum (GR 1872.6-5.1 (Sculpture 1883))]

This bust of Germanicus is slightly larger than life-size (44.5cm high). Basalt can be quarried in Egypt. The damage done to the nose looks deliberate and may have been part of the same Christian superstition regarding pagan statues which led to the cross being carved on his forehead. See further, S. Walker, *Roman Art*, London (British Museum Press) 1991.

J8 Senatorial decrees honouring the dead Germanicus

Tacitus (*Annals* 2.83) offers a brief synopsis of the honours decreed to the dead Germanicus by the senate. His account can be compared with the epigraphic record of the same decrees. In terms of his selection of material, Tacitus focuses upon the unprecedented honours, omitting honours already previously awarded to Gaius and Lucius Caesars, perhaps as a way of reflecting Germanicus' unique character and popularity. The text of the *Tabula Siarensis*, a fragmentary bronze tablet found at Siarum near modern Seville in Baetica, overlaps partially with, and is continued by the text of the *Tabula Hebana*, a fragmentary bronze tablet found at Heba in Etruria. This tablet contains the text of a bill (*rogatio*), to be presented by the consuls for ratification by the people in the Assembly (in response to which they could simply vote yes or no), but in this case, the text was engraved even before that ratification had taken place. Senatorial decrees had no formal legal force, but by issuing instructions for its document to be circulated and inscribed around Italy and the provinces, the senate did its utmost to give its proposals the force of law. The finding of the inscription at Siarum, which was not a colony, indicates that the text was distributed even further than had been prescribed by the senate. Together, the inscriptions offer insights into the senate's relationship with Tiberius and other members of the imperial family. They illustrate the deferential attitude of the senate towards Tiberius and the inclusion of women within the family council to be consulted about what honours were deemed appropriate. It also emphasises the universal mourning of the whole of Roman society at Germanicus' death. The honours voted imitated those given earlier to Augustus' heirs apparent Gaius and

Lucius (**J8k** with note; LACTOR 17, J61, J64), and acted in their turn as a template for honours when Tiberius' son Drusus subsequently died in AD 23.
Text: M.H. Crawford, ed., *Roman Statutes* I 37 = Sherk 36 = EJ 94a (Tab. Hebana only).

J8a Introduction

[... of Germanicus Caesar, who] ought never to have [died.]
[... about the honours] of Germanicus Caesar which he deserved [... and concerning] this affair through consultation of Tiberius Caesar Augustus, [our] leader, [...so that] an abundance of proposals might be made available to him and so that he with his accustomed [...] might choose [from all these] honours which the senate decreed were to be granted, those [which he himself and Julia] Augusta his mother, and Drusus Caesar, and the mother of Germanicus Caesar, [with his wife if possible] having been summoned by them for this discussion, considered could suitably be adopted, on this matter they decreed as follows:

[*Tabula Siarensis* Fragment a, lines 1–8]

Agrippina was absent from Rome, still travelling back from Syria with Germanicus' ashes.

J8b Triumphal arch in Rome

It was agreed that a marble arch should be erected in the Circus Flaminius at public [expense, placed] near the place in which statues had been [set up] to Divus Augustus and to the Augustan household by Gaius Norbanus Flaccus. The arch should include representations of conquered peoples, [and it should be inscribed] on the front of this arch that the senate and people of Rome [have dedicated] this monument [...] to the memory of Germanicus Caesar, since he, after the defeat of the Germans in war and [---] after they had been removed from Gaul, and the military standards recovered, and the perfidious [defeat] of an army of the Roman people avenged, having put in order the affairs of the Gallic provinces, was sent as proconsul to the overseas provinces and in setting them and the kingdoms of that region in order according to the instructions of Tiberius Caesar Augustus, [and also after he had given] a king to Armenia, unsparing in his effort, before by senatorial decree [he entered the city with an ovation] by decree of the senate, met his death in the service of the state. It was agreed that above this arch should be placed a statue of Germanicus [Caesar] in a triumphal chariot, and on either side of him statues of Drusus [Germanicus, his] natural [father] and brother of Tiberius Caesar Augustus, and of Antonia his mother, [and of Agrippina his wife, and] of Livia his sister, and of Tiberius Germanicus his brother, and his sons and daughters.

[*Tabula Siarensis* Fragment a, lines 9–21]

a marble arch: whereas during the Republic, honorific arches were set up on the intitiative of the honorand, here we see a significant shift towards the decision being taken by the senate and people of Rome.

Circus Flaminius: used for the celebration of games, and for the holding of assemblies and markets, this space on the southern Field of Mars was especially associated with triumphs, being where the triumphal army would assemble before entering Rome. Other monuments celebrating members of the imperial family were already clustered nearby, notably the portico of Octavia and theatre of Marcellus.

Norbanus Flaccus, consul in AD 15: this is the earliest known monument celebrating the Augustan household.

military standards recovered: Germanicus campaigned against the Germans between AD 12–16, regaining the standards lost by Varus in AD 9 when he and his three legions had been wiped out by Arminius in the Teutoburg Forest (Tacitus, *Annals* 2.41.1).

Armenia: the kingdom of Armenia served as a buffer between the empires of Rome and Parthia. For Artaxias see **M43**; Tac. *Ann.* 2.64.1).

Tiberius Germanicus his brother: i.e., Claudius.

J8c Triumphal arch in Syria

And it was agreed that another arch should be built on the ridge of Mount Amanus, which is in Syria [... or if any] other place [seemed] more suitable to Tiberius Caesar Augustus, our leader, [in those regions whose] care and guardianship [he had himself entrusted] to Germanicus Caesar by the authority [of the senate;] also that his statue should be set up and an inscription befitting [the achievements of Germanicus Caesar] should be inscribed.

[*Tabula Siarensis* Fragment a, lines 22–26]

J8d Triumphal arch near the burial mound of Germanicus' father, Drusus

It was agreed that a third arch either [be built onto or be placed near the burial mound] which [the army had at first begun to construct on its own initiative] for Drusus, the brother of Tiberius Caesar Augustus, and then [had completed] with the permission of Divus Augustus [...] should be set up [of Germanicus] Caesar, receiving back [the military standards from the Germans; and that] the Gauls and Germans who [live] this side of the Rhine, [whose communities were ordered by Divus] Augustus [to conduct] religious rites at the burial mound [of Drusus, should be instructed to undertake a ...] sacrifice, making offerings [each year on the day on which Germanicus Caesar had died;] and, since there was in this region [where the burial mound of Drusus is ... on the birthday] of Germanicus Caesar [... done according to this decree of the senate.]

[*Tabula Siarensis* Fragment a, lines 27–34]

This cenotaph (9 BC) has been identified at Mainz-Kastel, in the modern district of Wiesbaden. It was used as a focal point for expressions of loyalty by both the Roman army and the local peoples (Suetonius, *Claudius* 1.3).

J8e Other monuments to mark his place of death and cremation

It was [likewise] agreed that [a monument should be set up] in the forum [at Antioch where the body of Germanicus Caesar had been cremated...]; and likewise [that a tribunal should be set up at Daphne, where Germanicus Caesar had breathed his last [...]

[*Tabula Siarensis* Fragment a, lines 35–7]

J8f Public mourning on the anniversary of his death

[And it was agreed that each year on 10 October at this altar] which is [in front of the burial mound ... in his memory] offerings [should be discharged publicly] for [his] departed spirit [by the officials of the *sodales*] *Augustales* clothed in dark togas, those of them for whom [it will be legal and proper to wear] an undyed toga, with the same sacrificial rite with which [offerings are dispatched publicly] for the departed spirirts of Gaius and Lucius Caesars. And it was agreed that a bronze tablet [should be placed] near this [burial mound, and on it this senatorial] decree should be inscribed in a similar way as the decrees of the senate had been inscribed which had been [passed in honour of Gaius and Lucius Caesars.] And it was agreed that [it should be permitted to the magistrates of the Roman people and to those who shall be in charge of jurisdiction in] a municipality or colony of Roman or Latin citizens] to perform no important business publicly on this day, nor that there should on this [day henceforth be public banquets,] nor marriage or betrothal ceremonies of Roman citizens, and that no[-one] should take [a loan from another] or give one to another, and that games or [shows] should not take place [nor ...] be heard.

And it was agreed that the Augustan theatrical games, [which before this] were usually [held on 12 October,] should be held on 28 October, by which [...] the days of the theatrical games [...] the day on which Germanicus Caesar [had] died.

[*Tabula Siarensis* Fragment b, column I, lines 1–14]

10 October: the day on which Germanicus had died (**J7g**).

[altar ... burial mound]: the scene has now shifted to the Mausoleum of Augustus in Rome.

sodales Augustales: a priesthood created to maintain the cult of Augustus in AD 14 (Tac. *Ann.* 1.54.1).

Gaius and Lucius Caesars: heirs presumptive of Augustus who died in AD 4 and 2 respectively.

J8g Eulogies to Germanicus by Tiberius and Drusus to be inscribed in public

[...] leader [...] because also the day(s) [...] and through speeches [...] to approve his (its) enthusiasm [...that] the urban and [rural] tribes should attend [...] had promised; and so it was agreed [that ... statues] of Germanicus Caesar in triumphal [dress should be set up at the expense of the urban plebs] in the public forecourts in which Divus Augustus [and ...] had placed [statues of Drusus] Germanicus, with an inscription of the urban plebs [...; likewise that the scroll] which Tiberius Caesar Augustus [had read out] in the senate on 16 December [and] had published [beneath] his edict, should be inscribed on bronze and fixed in a public place, [wherever] it pleased; and it was agreed that the senate considered that it would be all the more appropriate, because the innermost [feelings of Tiberius] Caesar Augustus contained not so much a eulogy of Germanicus Caesar his son, as the course of his whole life and a true witness of his virtue, for it to be handed down in eternal remembrance, and because Tiberius himself had testified in this same pamphlet that he wished not to dissemble and judged it to be useful to the youth of the next generation and of generations to come.

Likewise, so that the loyalty of Drusus Caesar might be better attested, it was agreed that the pamphlet which he had read out at the most recent meeting of the senate should be inscribed on bronze and fixed in the place decided upon by his father and himself.

[*Tabula Siarensis* Fragment b, column II lines 1–19]

urban and [rural] tribes: the *plebs urbana* was divided into thirty-five voting-tribes.

Tiberius ... wished not to dissemble: this unexpected statement offers a contemporary echo of Tacitus' characterisation of Tiberius (e.g. *Annals* 1.11.2).

J8h Senatorial decree to be inscribed in public places around the empire

And likewise it was agreed that this senatorial decree should be inscribed on bronze, along with the senatorial decree which was passed on 16 December, and that this bronze should be fixed on the Palatine, in the portico which is near Apollo's temple, in the consecrated space in which the senate was held.

And likewise it was agreed that the senate wished and considered it right, so that the loyalty of all orders towards the Augustan household and the consensus of all citizens in honouring the memory of Germanicus Caesar might more readily be apparent, that the consuls should publish this senatorial decree beneath their edict, and that they should order the magistrates and ambassadors of the municipalities and colonies to send a written copy to the municipalities and colonies of Italy and to those colonies which were in the provinces; and that those who were in charge of the provinces would be acting properly and correctly if they took pains to see that this senatorial decree should be fixed in as crowded a place as possible.

And it was agreed that Marcus Messalla and Marcus Aurelius Cotta Maximus, the incoming consuls, when they will have entered office – on the first occasion as far as the auspices allow – without giving notice of two or three *nundinae*, should see that a statute concerning the honours for Germanicus Caesar is presented to the people. They agreed. In the senate were two hundred and eighty-five. This senatorial decree was made one by a second motion.

[*Tabula Siarensis* Fragment b, column II lines 20–31]

nundinae: the period between two market days (i.e. eight days)

In the senate were two hundred and eighty five: this does not look a very impressive quorum from a senate of six hundred members.

J8i Further honours

(A further section is very fragmentary but mentions equestrian statues of Germanicus being brought out and then returned to the temple of Concord, and also the hymn of the Salii.)

[*Tabula Siarensis* Fragment b, column III lines 1–12]

J8j Statues of Germanicus and Drusus his father

And it was agreed that on the Palatine, in the portico which is near Apollo's temple, in the consecrated space in which the senate usually meets, [among the likenesses] of men of distinguished talent, likenesses should be set up of Germanicus Caesar and of Drusus Germanicus, his natural father [and the brother] of Tiberius Caesar Augustus, inasmuch as he too was of fertile talent, above the capitals of the columns of [the roof] by which the statue of Apollo is covered.

[*Tabula Hebana*, lines 1–4]

J8k Germanicus' name inserted into the hymn of the Salii

And it was agreed that the Salian priests should insert into their hymns the name of Germanicus Caesar [to] honour his memory, an honour which has also been accorded to Gaius and Lucius Caesar, the brothers of Tiberius Caesar Augustus.

[*Tabula Hebana*, lines 4–5]

The Salian priests were established by Numa, the second king of Rome. By this time the archaic Latin verse of their hymn had become incomprehensible, but it invoked both the gods in general and individual gods by name. Augustus' name had been added to the hymn, perhaps in 29 BC (*RG* 10.1). This created a precedent for the inclusion of the names of other members of the imperial family, including Gaius and Lucius Caesar, Germanicus and, later, Drusus. Unlike Augustus, however, they were given this honour only after their death.

Gaius and Lucius Caesar, the brothers of Tiberius Caesar Augustus: a rather inventive interpretation of their relationship, given that Tiberius had only been adopted by Augustus after both Gaius and Lucius had died in AD 4, and so the tie of brotherhood was, at best, only retrospective.

J8m Germanicus to give his name to new voting panels

[And it was agreed that to the ten] centuries of the Caesars which usually cast their vote concerning the selection of consuls and praetors, five should be added; and that the first ten centuries [which] will be summoned to vote should be named for Gaius and Lucius Caesars, the five following for Germanicus Caesar; and in all those [centuries] the senators and equestrians of all the jury-panels which have been or will be established for the purpose of public trials should cast [their vote;] and whoever, for the purpose of selecting magistrates, shall summon into the enclosure the senators to cast their vote and those for whom it shall be permitted to pronounce an opinion in the senate and likewise the equestrians, according to the statute which the consuls Lucius Valerius Messalla Volesus and Gnaeus Cornelius Cinna [Magnus] passed, he [should see] that, insofar as it shall be possible, the senators, and likewise equestrians of all the jury-panels [which] have been or will be established for the purpose of public [trials], cast their vote [in the fifteen centuries;]

[*Tabula Hebana*, lines 6–12]

selection of the consuls and praetors: a pre-election process that guaranteed these individuals' election.

Lucius Valerius Messalla Volesus and Gnaeus Cornelius Cinna [Magnus]: consuls in AD 5

J8n Detailed arrangements for the new voting panels

[13] And as to the selection by lot which according to that statute is [laid down] or prescribed for the nine hundred, or those called 'guardians' , for the ten centuries of the Caesars, the person for whom it shall be appropriate according to that statute or according to this bill to undertake the selection by lot of the nine hundred or those called ['guardians',] should undertake it for the fifteen centuries, just as if it were appropriate according to that staute for the selection by lot [of the nine hundred] or 'guardians' to be undertaken or carried out for the fifteen centuries.

[16] And that on that day on which, according to that statute which the consuls Lucius Valerius Messalla Volesus and Gnaeus Cornelius Cinna Magnus passed or according to this bill, the senators and equestrians [will be obliged] to attend in order to cast their vote, [he,] under the supervision of the praetors and the tribunes of the plebs, should order fifteen large wicker baskets to be placed in front of his tribunal, into which the voting tablets may be put; and likewise he should order as many waxed voting tablets to be placed next to the baskets as shall seem [to him to be necessary;] likewise he should also see that whitened boards, on which the names of the candidates have been written, be placed in a place in which they may [most] easily [be read;]

[21] Then, in sight of all the magistrates and those who shall be [about to cast] their vote, seated on benches, as they used to sit when the vote was cast for the ten centuries of the Caesars, [he] should order that balls, as balanced in weight as possible, for the thirty-three tribes – Succusana and Esquilina being excluded – be thrown into a revolving urn and [the selection by lot] declared; the selection by lot is made of which senators and equestrians ought to cast their vote into which basket, provided that the selection by lot [for] the first [centuries] which are named for Gaius and Lucius Caesars should be made in such a way that two [tribes] each are allotted to the first, second, third and fourth baskets, three [to] the fifth basket, two each to the sixth, seventh, eighth and ninth baskets and three to the tenth; for those which are named for Germanicus Caesar [the selection by lot should be made in such a way] that two tribes each are allotted to the eleventh, twelfth, thirteenth and fourteenth baskets, and three tribes to the fifteenth; in such a way that when he shall have summoned one tribe, whose [lot] has been drawn, [he should call in order] the senators and those for

whom it shall be lawful to pronounce an opinion in the senate who shall be from that tribe and should order them to approach the first basket and cast their vote; then, when they have cast their vote in this way [and] have returned to the benches,] he should call the equestrians from the same tribe [and order them] to cast their vote [into] the same basket; then he should select by lot [another and] another tribe and [call] the senators of each [tribe,] and then the equestrians, [and so] they should cast their vote [into the basket into which] they will be obliged to cast their vote; [lines 32–8] [provided that, as] shall regard the vote of those individuals, [if there] shall be [any from the tribe Succusana] or Esquilina, likewise, if [in] any tribe there shall be no senator or if there shall be no equestrian and there shall [not] be [...] of senators, and as regards the sealing of the baskets after the votes have been cast and the handing over to the praetors who are or shall be in charge of the treasury [so that] they may be taken down do the voting-enclosure [with the votes] of the selection, and concerning the checking of the seals, and the distribution of the votes, [he should observe all these things which] have been written down [or included] for [this] purpose in that statute which the consuls Cinna and Volesus passed concerning the ten centuries of the Caesars, and in the case of the <fifteen> centuries he should perform and do and see to the performance and doing of all the same things as it would be appropriate for him to perform and do [in the case of the ten] centuries of the Caesars according to that statute which [the consuls Cinna and Volesus passed;] and whatever shall be performed in this way, that should be legal and binding;

[38] [Then after] the votes [of that selection] from the fifteen centuries of Gaius and Lucius Caesar and of Germanicus Caesar have been taken down and counted, [and the tablet of that century which shall have been chosen by the lot has been brought forward,] he who shall hold that selection [should read out] that tablet, just [as] would be appropriate for him to read out [the tablet of that century which] had been [chosen by lot] <from> the ten centuries [of Gaius and Lucius Caesar, according to that statute which] the consuls [Lucius Valerius Messalla] Volesus and Gnaeus Cornelius Cinna Magnus passed; provided that he see that any tablet of a century of Gaius [and Lucius Caesars which shall have been drawn by lot] is read out [under the name] of Gaius and Lucius Caesars, and such candidates as [may be] selected by that century are each of them [announced under their name;] and that he see that any tablet from those centuries which [are named] for Germanicus Caesar [according to this bill which shall have been drawn by lot] is read out under the name of Germanicus Caesar, and such candidates as [may be selected] by that century [are each of them] announced [under that name;] and that the group of centuries which by this bill is added to [the group of the centuries of Gaius and Lucius Caesars] should proceeed just as is [prescribed] or laid down for that group, which is of the ten centuries, to proceed according to the statute which [the consuls] Cinna and [Volesus passed,] that it should proceed; and that [the person,] who [shall hold] a selection for the election of consuls and praetors [according to this bill,] should see that an account be kept [of all the tribes] and the vote should be cast in this way; as for everything else, which [is not] explicitly written down in this bill, [it all] should be performed, done and observed [just as] in that statute which the consuls Cinna and Volesus passed.

[*Tabula Hebana*, lines 13–50]

J8o Germanicus' curule chair to be visible during games of the Augustales

And it was agreed that during the games of the Augustales, [when the seats of the *sodales*] shall be placed in the theatres, the curule chairs of Germanicus Caesar should be placed among them, [with crowns of oak leaves, in memory] of his priesthood; these chairs, once the temple of Divus Augustus shall be completed, [should be carried] out of that temple, [and in the meantime] should be replaced [in the temple] of Mars the Avenger and carried out from there; and that whoever [shall see to the holding of] the aforementioned games, [he] should see [that they] are [placed [in the theatres] and, when they shall need to be replaced, that they are replaced in that temple.

[*Tabula Hebana*, lines 50–54]

J8p Equestrians to perform religious rites in the Field of Mars

[And] it was agreed that, [since it has been prescribed that] the temples of the gods should remain closed [until the bones of Germanicus] Caesar were interred in the burial mound, also those who shall be of the [equestrian] order, [those of them who] shall have [the ?broad?] stripe, those who shall wish to perform their duty and [shall be able to do so] as far as health and household [religious rites] are concerned, [they] should come into the Field of Mars [without] the stripe, those who shall possess a public horse, they should come into the Field of Mars with the double narrow-striped toga.

[*Tabula Hebana*, lines 54–57]

J8q Temples to be closed on the anniversary of his death

And it was agreed that on [10 October, on which day Germanicus Caesar died,] the temples of the immortal gods which [are or shall be in the city of Rome or nearer to the city [of Rome than one mile] should be closed [each year,] and that those who hold or [shall hold] the contracts for maintaining these temples [should see] that this be done in this way; [and that on the same day the officials] of the *sodales Augustales* who shall be in office each year should see that offerings are performed [for the departed spirits of Germanicus] Caesar in front of the burial mound [of Divus Augustus;] or if one or more of the officials [shall not be able to attend] that sacrifice, [those who] shall be obliged to hold that office in the following year [should perform] in the place of those who [shall not be able to perform] that duty …

[*Tabula Hebana*, lines 57–62]

J9 Agrippina the Elder 14 BC – AD 33

Born on 24/6 October (**A39d**). For her family, see **J9a**, **J9c** and Suet. *Cal.* 7. Her marriage to Germanicus linked Augustus' own descendants with those of those of Livia (Tac. *Ann.* 5.1.2). She bore nine children of whom six survived, and fully supported her husband (Tac. *Ann.* 1.33, 1.69), travelling with him to Germany (Tac. *Ann.* 1.40–41) and the East (Tac. *Ann.* 2.54.1). Her relationship with her step-father, Tiberius, never likely to be happy, given his treatment of her mother (Julia (**J6**) – Tac. *Ann.* 1.53.1) is encapsulated in the stories told by Tacitus and Suetonius (*Ann.* 4.52–54 and *Tib.* 53). Nevertheless her own popularity was huge (Tac. *Ann.* 2.43) and heightened by the loss of her husband (Tac. *Ann.* 2.75.1, 3.1, 3.3.2, 3.4.2; *SCPP* 137–140 = **P3j**). Sejanus brings about her fall (Tac. *Ann.* 4.12, 4.17, 4.67). Tacitus' *Annals* breaks off just after reporting Tiberius' denunciation of Nero and his mother Agrippina the Elder in the senate in AD 29 (5.3–4; see Velleius = **C7** for the official version at the time). Sejanus' own fall does not result in her release and she dies in AD 33 (Tac. *Ann.* 6.25; Suet. *Tib.* 53.2; *Octavia* 932–40 = **H15**). Her death day was celebrated under Tiberius, but Gaius gave his mother posthumous honours on his accession (**J9b–d** below).

Modern treatment: Barrett, *Agrippina* (London 1996), chapter 3; Fantham, *Julia Augusti* (Oxford 2006), chapter 9.II

J9a Epitaphs to three sons of Germanicus and Agrippina

Gaius Caesar, son of Germanicus Caesar was cremated here.
Tiberius Caesar, son of Germanicus Caesar was cremated here.
[...] Caesar, son of Germanicus Caesar was cremated here.

[Rome, *ILS* 181, 181a, 181b = *CIL* 6.888–890]

These square marker-stones were found near Augustus' mausoleum and commemorate three sons of Agrippina and Germanicus who died in infancy or childhood, Suet. *Cal.* 7.1.

J9b Caligula celebrating Agrippina, *aureus* of AD 37 (mint of Lugdunum)

Obv. Head of Gaius Caligula, right
C CAESAR AVG GERM P M TR POT (Gaius Caesar Augustus Germanicus, *pontifex maximus*, with tribunician power).

Rev. Bust of Agrippina, right, with hair in pigtail
AGRIPPINA MAT C CAES AVG GERM (Agrippina, mother of Gaius Caesar Augustus Germanicus)

[*BMC* Gaius 7; *RIC* Gaius 7]

This coin forms part of a series, all with exactly the same obverse, showing popular ancestors of Gaius: his parents, Agrippina and Germanicus (**J7n**), and his great-grandfather, Augustus (*BMC* 8, *RIC* 8–9).

J9c Funerary urn of Agrippina the Elder

The bones of Agrippina, daughter of Marcus Agrippa, granddaughter of Divus Augustus, wife of Germancius Caesar, mother of the *princeps* Gaius Caesar Augustus Germanicus.

[Rome, probably from Augustus' mausoleum: *ILS* 180 = Smallwood 84a]

A large marble urn of Luna marble (reused in the medieval period as an official grain measure) presumably dating from AD 37 when Gaius Caligula became *princeps* and brought his mother's ashes to Rome from Pandateria where she had died in 33. Caligula's act of filial devotion in restoring her memory and ensuring her burial in the dynastic mausoleum gained him popular acclaim (Suet. *Cal.* 15.1; Dio Cassius 59.3.5), as did his similar actions for his brother Nero (**J17d**). Consequently, the description of Agrippina here emphasises Gaius' importance, and shows his early adoption of the title of 'Augustus'.

J9d Agrippina's ashes returned to Rome, brass *sestertius*, AD 37–41

Obv: Draped bust of Agrippina, right, her hair in a ponytail
AGRIPPINA M F MAT C CAESARIS AVGVSTI (Agrippina, daughter of Marcus [Agrippa], mother of Gaius Caesar Augustus)

Rev: *Carpentum* drawn left by two mules, the cover supported by figures at the corners, and with an ornamented side.
S P Q R MEMORIAE AGRIPPINAE (the Senate and People of Rome, to the memory of Agrippina)

[*BMC* Gaius 85; *RIC* Gaius 55]

The carpentum (see **J1d** and note) was presumably used to transport the ashes of Agrippina when they were returned to Rome (see **J9c** and note).

J9e Cameo of Agrippina the Elder

[Cameo of Agrippina: British Museum (GR 1899.7-22.2 (Arundel Collection, Gems 3593))]

This cameo, measuring 2.9cm × 4.5cm was created by intricate carving of sardonyx with its alternating layers of colour. Quite a few examples of this art form (perhaps commissioned as gifts from and to members of the imperial family) survive from the early part of the first century AD, including the *Gemma Augusta* and the *Grand Camée de France*. See further, S. Walker, *Greek and Roman Portraits*, London (British Museum Press) 1995.

J10 Drusus *c.* 13 BC – AD 23

Nero Claudius Drusus was the son of Tiberius and Vipsania, named Drusus after his uncle. He became Drusus Julius Caesar in AD 4 when Augustus adopted Tiberius, but was simultaneously supplanted as his father's heir, since Augustus required Tiberius in turn to adopt Germanicus. The intention was to pave the way for a direct descendant of Augustus to inherit his power, as Germanicus was married to Augustus' granddaughter Agrippina. Three years younger than Germanicus, his cousin and brother by adoption, Drusus too is given experience of empire with consulships in AD 15 and 21 (**B15**), and command in Germany (Velleius = **C2**, **C5**). Tacitus' *Annals* gives a full account of Drusus' career (books 1–4), Suetonius a much briefer one (*Claud.* 1). Drusus married his cousin, Livilla (**J11**); they had one surviving daughter, Julia. His death in AD 23 was thought natural: only after Sejanus' fall was he said to have been poisoned by Sejanus and Livilla (Tac. *Ann.* 4.7–11). Drusus was later honoured by his son, Claudius (Suet. *Claud.* 11.3)

A portrait in the British Museum, BM 1886,1113.1, is possibly Drusus.

J10a Drusus' birthday

October 7: Birthday of Drusus Caesar. Thanksgiving to Vesta.

[Fasti at Cumae, = EJ p.53]

J10b Drusus and Germanicus on bronze coin from Pergamum (Asia), AD 14–19

Obv: Bare head of Germanicus right
ΓΕΡΜΑΝΙΚΟΣ ΚΑΙΣΑΡ (Germanicus Caesar)

Rev: Bare head of Drusus right
ΔΡΟΥΣΟΣ ΚΑΙΣΑΡ (Drusus Caesar)

[*RPC* 2367/2]

The coin (diameter 18mm) perhaps dates from AD 18, when Germanicus visited Lesbos and other cities on the coast of NW Asia Minor (Tacitus, *Annals* 2.54.1).

J10c Drusus' triumph over Illyricum, AD 20

May 28: Drusus [Caesar] triumphed over Ill[yricum]

[Fasti at Ostia, fragment Ce = EJ p.41]

J10d Drusus honoured at Caudium (Italy), AD 23

To Drusus Caesar, son of Tiberius Augustus, grandson of Divus Augustus, great-grandson of Divus Julius, twice consul, in his 2nd year of tribunician power.

[*NSc* (1924) 514 = LACTOR 8 no.11 = EJ 90]

J10e Drusus' death, AD 23

September 14: Funerary rites for the death of Drusus Caesar.

[Fasti on Oppian Hill and at Antium, = EJ p.52 = Sherk 28E = *InscrIt* XIII/2 p.510]

J10f Tiberius' grief for his son

Tiberius Caesar lost both Drusus, his own son, and Germanicus, the son he had adopted. For his son, Drusus, he nevertheless delivered the eulogy from the Rostra, standing there with the corpse laid out before him for everyone to see, covered only by a shroud to ensure that as *pontifex maximus* his own eyes should not rest upon a corpse. And while all Rome wept, his facial expression never changed. Thus he gave to Sejanus, standing at his side, an example of how patiently he could bear the loss of those most dear to him.

[Seneca, *On Consolation, To Marcia* 15.3]

Germanicus had been cremated in Syria (**J8e**), and Tiberius made no public appearance either at the ceremonies that attended the arrival of his ashes in Rome or their interment in the Mausoleum of Augustus (Tac. *Ann.* 3.3–4). One reason Tacitus suggests is that his facial expression registering grief would be viewed as hypocritical, whereas in the *SCPP* the senate specifically notes the signs of Tiberius' great and enduring grief for Germanicus' death and urges him to end his grief and change his expression to one of rejoicing, devoting himself to his surviving son Drusus, who will hopefully assume Tiberius' position one day (lines 125–131 = **P3j**), while *Tabula Siarensis* (**J8g**) praised him for *not* dissembling. Just as Tiberius had urged the public to show restraint in their mourning and to resume their ordinary activities after Germanicus' death (Tac. *Ann.* 3.6), so he conducted business as normal between Drusus' death and funeral and forbade a long period of mourning (Tac. *Ann.* 4.8; Suet. *Tib.* 52.1–2; Dio 57.22.3). Tacitus mentions Tiberius' eulogy (Tac. *Ann.* 4.12.1), and shows his punctilious disapproval of priests' viewing corpses on an earlier occasion (1.62.2). The point about the warning to Aelius Sejanus, Tiberius' powerful Prefect of the Praetorian Guard gains force from the ambiguity of the Latin verb *perdere*, which means 'to lose' or 'to destroy'.

J10g Honours at Rome for Germanicus and Drusus, AD 23 or later

The urban plebs of the 35 tribes to Germanicus Caesar, son of Tiberius Augustus, grandson of Divus Augustus, augur, *flamen Augustalis*, consul twice, hailed victorious commander twice; money collected.

The urban plebs of the 35 tribes to Drusus Caesar, son of Tiberius Augustus, grandson of Divus Augustus, great-grandson of Divus Julius, pontiff, augur, *sodalis Augustalis*, consul twice, in his 2nd year of tribunician power; money collected.

[*ILS* 168 + 176 = *CIL* VI 909–10 = EJ 92(a)/(b)]

This pair of dedications was found together by the Tiber at the foot of the Aventine (the hill associated with the plebs of Rome). Drusus held tribunician power for the second time in AD 23 (Tac. *Ann.* 3.56.3), the year of his death. Given the close similarities of the two dedications in terms of both form and content, it seems likely that the plebs was honouring both men posthumously. In any case, they were certainly intended to be viewed as a pair, emphasising the way in which both Germanicus and then Drusus were regarded as in similar positions within the succession (see also **M66**).

J10h Arch of Drusus dedicated in AD 30

15 March: Arch of Drusus dedicated.

[Fasti at Ostia, fragment Cb, right = EJ p.42]

J11 Livi(ll)a 13 BC – AD 31

Livi(ll)a Julia (Livia in Tacitus and inscriptions, Livilla in Suetonius and Dio) was the daughter of Drusus (**J3**, the brother of Tiberius) and Antonia Minor (Tac. *Ann.* 4.3.3). She was born around 13 BC, and married to Gaius Caesar, Augustus' grandson (Tac. *Ann.* 4.40.4; Dio 55.10). Soon after his death in AD 4, she married her cousin Drusus (**J10**, son of Tiberius), bearing a daughter (**J16**) and twin boys (**J24**; Tac. *Ann.* 2.84.1). According to Tacitus, Sejanus was: her lover (*Ann.* 4.3.3); the instigator of plots against her mother and husband (4.12, 4.60); her would-be or even actual husband (4.39–40, [5].6.2, 6.8.3 (referring to Sejanus and Tiberius' son-in-law)); also possible father of her son, Gemellus (Suet. *Tib.* 62.3). Implicated in Sejanus' fall (*Ann.* 6.2.1) she was killed by her uncle, Tiberius, or starved by her mother, Antonia (Dio 58.11.7, *Octavia* 941–3 = **H15**).

J12 Claudius 10 BC – AD 54

Tiberius Claudius Nero Germanicus was born at Lyons on 1 August, 10 BC, the youngest child of Drusus and Antonia Minor. Ill health and handicaps perhaps caused by cerebral palsy led to him being kept out of a public 'career' under Augustus (Suet. *Claud.* 4.7; LACTOR 17 J68 – remote position in imperial family monument) and Tiberius (see **J8b**; *SCPP* line 148 = **P3j**; Tac. *Ann.* 3.18.4). Though consul under Gaius (**B37**, Suet. *Cal.* 15.2) he was remained a butt of humour (Jos. = **E4**, **E12**; Suet. *Cal.* 23.3). It is not clear whether he played any part in Gaius' assassination, but he rapidly becomes the army's choice (Jos. = **E25–30**; Suet. *Claud.* 10). Tacitus' *Annals,* lost for the start of his reign, gives a detailed account of the later part and of his death. The insults he was subjected to are vividly and unpleasantly displayed in Seneca's *Apocolocyntosis* (see Section **F**) and Suetonius' biography (e.g. *Claud.* 3, 5, 8). There is ample evidence of his scholarship, hard work and good administration (**R22–R25**, **K10–K30**), while problems are often attributed to his freedmen and wives. For his first two marriages to Plautia Urganilla and Aelia Paetina, and his children by them, see Suet. *Claud.* 26–27: for his other marriages and children, see **J12h**, Agrippina (**J21**), Messalina (**J25**), Antonia (**J26**), Octavia (**J31**), Britannicus (**J32**). Much of his personal character emerges from his speeches and edicts (e.g. **M6, M8, M9, M11**). For his death on 13 October AD 54, see **P9**. Nero had him officially deified but allowed worship and his temple to lapse, but he was 'rehabilitated' by Vespasian (Suet. *Claud* 45).

Modern treatment: Levick, *Claudius* (London 1990).

J12a Claudius' Birthday

August 1: Birthday of Tiberius Claudius Germanicus

[Fasti Vallenses = EJ p.50]

Compare Suet. *Claud.* 2.1.

J12b Claudius and the praetorians, *aureus* of AD 41–2 (Rome)

Obv: Head of Claudius with laurel wreath, looking right

TI CLAVD CAESAR AVG P M TR P (Tiberius Claudius Caesar Augustus, *pontifex maximus*, with tribunician power)

Rev. Claudius, wearing a toga, clasping the hand of a long-haired soldier with shield and legionary eagle (*aquila*)

PRAETOR RECEPT (*praetorianis receptis*; the praetorians received)

[*BMC* Claudius 8; *RIC* Claudius 11]

This coin, related to **K1**, shows Claudius accepting the loyalty of the praetorian guard, a concept often represented by the clasping of hands.

J12c Claudius and his family at Arneae (Lycia): before AD 48

[Valeria Mes]sali~~na, wife of [Imperator Tiberius Claudius Caes]ar Au[gustus~~]: the people and [council] of the Arneates.

Tiberius Claudius Caesar Britannicus, son of Imperator Tiberius Claudius Caesar Augustus: the people of the Arneates.

Tiberius Claudius Caesar Augustus Germanicus, god manifest, saviour of our people: the council and people of the Arneates honoured (him) with the foremost [honours].

[Greek: Smallwood 136]

These honours are for Claudius and his family before Messalina's downfall in AD 48.

J12d The law allowing Claudius to marry his niece

It is lawful to take as a wife the daughter of one's brother: this first came into practice when Divus Claudius took Agrippina, the daughter of his brother, as his wife. But it is unlawful to take as a wife the daughter of one's sister.

[Gaius, *Institutes* 1.62]

Tacitus gives details about the proposals in the senate (*Annals* 12.5–12.7; compare Suet. *Claud.* 26.3)

J12e Claudius and his family honoured at Ilium, *c.* AD 53/4

To [Tibe]rius Claudius Caesar A[ugustus] Germanicus and Julia A[ugu]sta Agrippina and their children and to the senate and Athena of Ilium and the People: Tiberius Claudius Philocles, son of [...], and his wife, Claudia Parmen[is], daughter of [Parmeni]o, dedicated the stoa at their own expense and provided all of the furnishings in it.

Octavia, daughter of Augustus

Antonia, daughter of Augustus

Tiberius Claudius Britannicus, son of Augustus

Nero, son of Caesar Augustus: the Council and People (honoured) the kinsman of the city.

[Greek: Smallwood 101 = *IGRRP* IV 208–09]

The second set of texts accompanied statues of each of the children of Claudius. Octavia and Britannicus were children of Messalina, whereas Antonia (**J26**) was daughter of Aelia Paetina. All were eventually killed by Nero. The statue group perhaps dates from 53/54. For the links between the Julio-Claudians and Ilium, explaining why Nero is a kinsman of the city, see **J5a**. Claudius further encouraged such association, granting tax exemption to the city, perhaps in response to a speech made by the young Nero (Suetonius, *Claudius* 25.3, Nero 7.2; Tacitus *Annals* 12.58.1).

J12f Dynastic monument at Rome

To Imperator Caesar Augustus, son of Divus, *pontifex maximus*, consul eleven times, in his 11th year of tribunician power: the trumpeters (set this up).

To Nero Claudius Caesar Augustus Germanicus, son of Divus Claudius, grandson of Germanicus Caesar, great-grandson of Tiberius Caesar Augustus, great-great-grandson of Divus Augustus, *pontifex maximus*, in his 2nd year of tribunician power, hailed victorious commander, consul: the trumpeters (set this up).

To Tiberius Claudius Caesar Augustus Germanicus, son of Drusus, *pontifex maximus*, with tribunician power, hailed victorious commander, consul twice: the trumpeters and buglers of Rome (set this up).

To Julia Augusta Agrippina, daughter of Germanicus Caesar, wife of Divus Claudius: … of Rome (set this up).

[*AE* (1996) 246a–d]

Fragments of dynastic monuments set up by the professional associations of musicians who performed on official occasions were found at Rome in the area where the Arch of Constantine was later built. The earliest dedications are to Augustus in 12 BC, followed by Tiberius some time between 8 BC and AD 4. At Claudius' accession, a larger monumental base was set up for two or three statues (possibly of Messalina and Germanicus alongside Claudius himself), and the inscription of Augustus from 12 BC was reinscribed upon it. In AD 55/56, Nero and Agrippina were added. In this way, the musicians kept abreast of the changing profile of the dynasty, with the dedication in honour of Agrippina being stuccoed over in 59. The monument itself disappeared in the aftermath of the Great Fire of 64.

J12g A Contemporary View of Claudius

[5] Crispus Passienus often used to remark that there were some men whose high opinion he would rather have than any gift; others from whom he would rather have the gift. By way of example he said that would prefer the high opinion of an Augustus, but a gift from Claudius. [6] My own opinion is that we should never seek a gift from anyone whose judgement is worthless. Consider the implications. Should a gift be refused, if it is offered by a Claudius? On the contrary! It should be accepted, but as a windfall, a gift of Fortune, who one fully realises may turn nasty at any moment. So why do we try to make a distinction between things that are thoroughly mixed together? A gift is not a gift if it lacks its better part – the fact that it is given with judgement.

[Seneca, On Benefits, 1.15.5–6]

For Crispus Passienus, see **U5**. The *princeps* was expected to show good judgement in dispensing favours, but Claudius was accused of making indiscriminate grants of citizenship to individuals and groups (Dio 60.17.4–7, compare *Apocol.*3.3), and Tac. *Ann.* 12.61.2 criticises him for giving the inhabitants of Cos immunity from Roman taxation, not in recognition of its many services to Rome but as a personal favour to his Coan doctor (**R42** and note). Yet **M9c** shows the Emperor justifying his own mass grant of Roman citizenship to some Alpine tribes, in terms of service to Rome. However, the charge of making grants to those who bribed his minions (Dio 60.17.5, compare Suet. *Claud.* 25.5) cannot be written off in the light of **M76**.

J12h Claudius' family

Claudius had already put his previous wife Messalina to death in a fit of jealousy, but he had two children by her, Britannicus and Octavia. [150] There was also Antonia, his eldest child, born to his first wife, Paetina. He now also betrothed Octavia to Nero – this was the name he later gave to Domitius, when he adopted him as his son.

[Josephus, *Jewish Antiquities* 20.149–50]

J12i Bronze head of Claudius found in Suffolk

[Bronze head of Claudius: British Museum (P&EE 1965.12-1.1)]

This bronze, life-size head (30cm high) was torn from a statue. It was found in the River Alde at Rendham, Suffolk in 1907. As bronze statues are rarely found, being easily and profitably melted down, it has been suggested that the statue could have been spontaneously destroyed, perhaps even in the sack of Camulodunum (Colchester) in AD 61. See T. Potter, *Roman Britain* (British Museum Press) 1997.

J13 Domitius Ahenobarbus *c.* 2? BC – AD 41

Gnaeus Domitius Ahenobarbus was born on 11 December (**A57e**), the son of Antonia Major and Lucius Domitius Ahenobarbus. His year of birth is unclear. 2 BC would fit a consulship held early for an aristocrat connected to the imperial family; if so the boy depicted on the *ara pacis* and usually thought to be him must be an elder brother who did not survive (Syme, *AA* 155–6). Suetonius gives a character sketch (*Nero* 5), but with the stated wish (*Nero* 1.1) to show how Nero inherited each ancestor's vices and degenerated further. He was betrothed to 'the younger Agrippina' in 28 (Tac. *Ann.* 4.75) He was consul in 32 (**B32**) and died when his son, Nero was three. He is later honoured by Nero (Tac. *Ann.* 13.10.1, **A58g, A59m**).

J13a Velleius on Domitius and his family

Seven Domitii preceded this most unassuming young man, Gnaeus Domitius: all were only sons, but all attained the consulate and priesthoods, and almost all attained the honour of a triumph.

[Velleius, 2.10.2]

Velleius had every reason to compliment this aristocrat who was married to Tiberius' granddaughter.

J14 Domitia Lepida *c.* AD 1 – 54

Domitia Lepida was the younger daughter of Antonia the Elder and L. Domitius (Nero's grandfather). Tacitus sets out her relationships in *Annals* 12.64 (but confuses elder and younger Antonia). She married

M. Valerius Messalla Barbatus (Suet. *Claud.* 26.2), bearing Messalina, third wife of Claudius (Tac. *Ann.* 11.37); then Faustus Cornelius Sulla (suffect 31), by whom she bore Faustus Sulla (cos 52: Zonaras 11.9); finally C. Appius Junius Silanus (Dio 60.14.3). She had brought up Nero (Suet. *Nero* 6.3) and doubtless hoped for influence on his accession, but instead was done to death by Agrippina (Tac. *Ann.* 12.65.1, Suet. *Nero* 7.1). Modern treatment: Syme, *The Augustan Aristocracy* (Oxford 1986), chapter 12.

J15 Caesonia *c.* AD 5–41

Milonia Caesonia was Caligula's fourth wife, whom he married, probably in the spring of AD 39, while she was pregnant with their child (Suet. *Cal.* 25.3–4). Caesonia and the baby are murdered over Caligula's body (Jos. *JA* = **E23**).

J15a Caesonia's half-brothers

(Pliny is talking about the length of pregnancies)

Vistilia, wife of Glitius, and later of Pomponius and Orfitus, men of the highest class had four children by them, all born in the seventh month. She also gave birth to Suillius Rufus in the eleventh, Corbulo in the seventh (both these became consuls) and later Caesonia, wife of the emperor Gaius, in the eighth month of pregnancy.

[Pliny, *Natural History* 7.39]

Vistilia's seven children by six husbands, led to her daughter Caesonia bringing a large range of marriage connections to her marriage to Gaius in AD 39. Vistilia herself was presumably daughter or sister of Sextus Vistilius whom Tiberius forced to suicide in AD 32, and who had been a close friend of Tiberius' brother, Drusus (Tac. *Ann.* 6.9.2).

Glitius: their son may have been the P. Glitius Gallus exiled for his part in the Pisonian conspiracy of AD 65 (Tac. *Ann.* 15.56.4, 15.71.3).

Pomponius Secundus: probably had two sons by Vistilia: Q. Pomponius Secundus, suffect consul AD 41 and P. Pomponius Secundus, poet, suffect consul in AD 44. The latter was a close friend of Pliny who wrote his biography (see **R14**) and the most likely source of information about his mother's pregnancies.

Orfitus: their son could have been the consul of AD 51, Ser. Cornelius Salvidienus Orfitus.

Suillius Rufus: the prosecutor, consul 41(**B41**) could have been Vistilia's husband or son.

Domitius: Cn. Domitius Corbulo (cos 39), the famous general (**N45–N50**).

Milonia Caesonia: mother of three daughters and 'not in her first youth' by her marriage to Gaius in AD 39.

See Syme, Roman Papers II 805–14 = *JRS* 60, 1970, 27–39; Beagon, *NH Book 7* pages 187–8.

J15b Juvenal on Caesonia

The drug trade is booming: this dealer's got magical formulas,
And that recreational compound from Thessaly, so strong
That a wife can befuddle the wits of her husband, till he fancies a session
Of spanking, and she warms his backside with the sole of her sandal.
No wonder you're out of your mind, your memory so totally gone
That you cannot remember what you've recently done. Even *that* you can bear
So long as you don't go completely berserk, like Nero's mad uncle Caligula,
For whom Caesonia, his wife, once concocted a cocktail called "Mad Horse,"
From compounds of foal's forehead membrane, new born, still unable to stand.
So what will a woman not do, if an emperor's wife will do that?
In those days the whole world was in flames, its structures collapsing, as if
Queen Juno herself had driven great Jupiter mad. Those mushrooms
Agrippina gave Claudius will turn out less harmful by far.
After all, they just killed off one doddering dotard and ordered him down
To some heaven in Hades, still shaking his old palsied head and his lips

Still slurping saliva. But Caligula's potions brought fire and brimstone to Rome,
The torturer's rack, for the senate its slaughter, as he blended its blood
With the blood of equestrian nobles. For that was the price of a mare's foal,
The penalty paid for one witch.

[Juvenal, *Satires* 6. 610–626]

On Juvenal, *Satire* 6, see below on Messalina, **J25b**.

J16 **Julia** (Tiberius' granddaughter) ***c.* AD 6–43**

Julia Livia was the daughter of Drusus (son of Tiberius) and Livi(ll)a. She must have been born around AD 6/7 and married her first cousin Nero Caesar (**J17**) in AD 20 (Tac. *Ann.* 3.29.4). Dio says she was engaged to Sejanus (Dio 58.3.9) but Sejanus' engagement may have been to her mother, Livi(ll)a (Tac. *Ann.* [5].6.2, 6.8.3). She did marry Rubellius Plautus (see **B18**, **J29**) in AD 33. She fell victim to Messalina's scheming (Tacitus' narrative lost, but references at *Ann.* 13.32.3 and 13.43; also Sen. *Apocol* **F10.4**; *Octavia* 944–6 = **H15**; Suet *Claud.* 29.1; Dio 60.18.4).

J16a **Statue at Aphrodisias**

Julia, daughter of Drusus Caesar

[*IAph2007* 9.31]

For the Sebasteion at Aphrodisias see **L36**. The inscription in Greek is from a statue base of different type from those in **J20a**, **L36** but presumably from the same period.

J17 **Nero Caesar AD 6–31**

Nero Julius Caesar was the first child of Germanicus and Agrippina, thus great-nephew and, by his adoption of Germanicus, grandson of Tiberius. His coming-of-age and marriage to his first cousin, Julia (daughter of Drusus and Livilla) is recorded by Tacitus in AD 20 (*Annals* 3.29.4; **J17b**, *SCPP* = **P3j**). The death three years later of his uncle and father-in-law, Drusus, made him obvious heir to Tiberius (Tac. *Ann.* 4.8.4–5. Tiberius was then aged 63). Sejanus then plots his fall in alliance with Nero's younger brother, Drusus (Tac. *Ann.* 4.59–60, 4.67). Tacitus' *Annals* breaks off just after reporting Tiberius' denunciation of Nero and his mother Agrippina the Elder in the senate in AD 29 (5.3–4; see Velleius = **C130.4** for the official version at the time). Tiberius claimed in his autobiography (lost) that Sejanus killing Nero was his reason for killing Sejanus, though Suetonius rejects this, blaming Tiberius for Nero's death (*Tib.* 61.1; *Cal.* 7), which occurred in AD 31 (Dio 58.8.4). Gaius gave his eldest brother posthumous honours on his accession (Suet. *Cal.* 15.1; *Claud.* 9.1).

Modern treatment: Levick, *Tiberius,* 157–8, 162–3, 168–170, 175–6. Nero Caesar is omitted from the index to Oxford World's Classics translation of *Annals.*

J17a **Nero Caesar honoured on Lesbos**

The people (honoured) Nero Julius Caesar, son of new god Germanicus Caesar and goddess Aeolis harvest-bringer Agrippina.

[Greek: *IG* XII 2, 212 = EJ 95]

This inscription is recorded as from Mytilene on the island of Lesbos, one of the places visited by Germanicus and his family in AD 18 (Tacitus, *Annals* 2.54.1).

J17b **Nero Caesar comes of age**

AD 20, June 7: Nero put on the *toga [virilis]*. A gift of money was distributed.

[Fasti at Ostia, fragment Ce = EJ p.41]

J17c **Titles of Nero Caesar, AD 27–9**

Nero Caesar, son of Germanicus Caesar, grandson of Tiberius Caesar Augustus, great-grandson of Divus Augustus, *flamen Augustalis*, *sodalis Augustalis*, *sodalis Titius,* Arval Brother, *fetialis* priest, *quaestor*. By decree of the senate.

[Rome, *ILS* 182 = CIL VI 913 = EJ 96]

Presumably a statue base, and datable between his quaestorship in 27 (Tac. *Ann.* 3.29.1) and condemnation by the senate in 29 (Tac. *Ann.* 5.3).

J17d Funerary urn of Nero Caesar

Bones of Nero Caesar, son of Germanicus Caesar, great-grandson of Divus Augustus, *flamen Augustalis*, quaestor.

[Rome, Augustus' mausoleum: *ILS* 183 = Smallwood 85a = *CIL* VI 887]

Inscribed upon a cinerary urn from the Mausoleum of Augustus at Rome, that once matched that of Agrippina the Elder but is now lost (**J9c**). Gaius Caligula retrieved his brother's ashes from the island of Pontia, where he had died in exile. The name of his grandfather Tiberius is pointedly omitted (contrast the previous inscription), as having been responsible for his death.

J17e Drusus and Nero Caesar on bronze coin from Tingis (Mauretania), AD 23–29

Obv: Head of Drusus Caesar, left
DRVSVS

Rev: Head of Nero Caesar, right
NERO IVL TIN (Nero; Julian [Colony at] Tingis)

[*RPC* 865]

Tingis, modern Tangier in Morocco, opposite Gibraltar had received Roman citizenship from Octavian in 38 BC (Dio 48.45), so was independent of the kingdom of Ptolemy (**M40–M41** and **N8–N9**) who was first cousin, once removed, to the new heirs apparent (see **M39**). Like many coins minted in the provinces, this one is very rare and poorly preserved.

J18 Drusus Caesar AD 7–33

Drusus Julius Caesar was the younger brother of Nero Julius Caesar (**J17**). He came of age at the start of AD 23 (Tac. *Ann.* 4.4.1) He married Lepida, a descendant of Scribonia (Augustus' first wife – Tac. *Ann.* 6.40.3). Having joined Sejanus in plotting against his elder brother (Tac. *Ann.* 4.59–60, 4.67), he falls victim to Sejanus (account lost in Tacitus, *Annals* 5, and only preserved vaguely in excerpts of Dio (58.3.8–9)) and is imprisoned under the palace in Rome (Suet. *Tib.* 54.2; Tac. *Ann.* 6.23.2). Sejanus' own fall does not result in Drusus' release and his miserable death by starvation and posthumous vilification in AD 33 are recorded by Tacitus and others (*Ann.* 6.23.2; Suet. *Tib.* 54.2; 61.1; Suet. *Cal.* 7; Dio 58.22.4; 58.25.4). Gaius gave his elder brother posthumous honours on his accession (Suet. *Claud.* 9.1).

Modern treatment: Levick, *Tiberius* (London 1976), pages 166–74 and 206–7.

J18a Drusus Caesar honoured in the Troad

To Drusus Caesar, son of Germanicus Caesar, grandson of Tiberius Augustus, great-grandson of Divus Augustus, pontiff. By decree of the town councillors.

[*ILS* 185]

This inscription, found in the area around ancient Troy could date from Germanicus' visit to Troy in AD 18 (Tacitus, *Annals* 2.54.2; compare J5a).

J19 GAIUS Caligula AD 12–41

Gaius Julius Caesar Germanicus was born on 31 August (**A38r**; Suet. *Cal.* 8), the third surviving son of Agrippina and Germanicus. He was widely known as 'Caligula' ('Little-boots') see **J19a** below. He survives the fall of mother and elder brothers, living with Tiberius on Capri (*Ann.* 6.20.1; Suet. *Cal.* 10). Shortly after the death of Tiberius his great-uncle and grandfather by adoption he eliminates his rival and cousin Gemellus. Rome had been ruled by men over 50 for the previous 48 years. This, and Germanicus' posthumous popularity, ensured a 'honeymoon period' for Gaius' reign (Suet. *Cal.* 13–15; Philo *Emb.* 8–13 = D1), quickly ended, perhaps after an illness (Suet. *Cal.* 14.2; Philo *Emb.* 14–18 = **D2**). The rest of his reign is, in Suetonius' phrase (*Cal.* 22.1) 'the story of a monster', ended by his assassination (Jos. *JA* = **E1–E16**). Tacitus' account (in *Annals* 7–8) is completely lost, but the Acts of the Arval Brothers preserves the official account for much of his reign (**A37c – A40c**). He married 4 times between AD 33 and 39 (Suet. *Cal.* 25).

Lollia Paulina, perhaps *c.* AD 20–49, was, for a very brief period, Caligula's third wife (Suet. *Cal.* 25.2; Dio 59.12.1). Tacitus gives an 'obituary notice' at her death in AD 49, engineered by Agrippina against an unsuccessful rival as Claudius' wife (Tac. *Ann.* 12.22.2, 12.1.1). For Caesonia, see **J15**.

Modern treatment: Barrett, *Caligula* (London 1989).

J19a Gaius' nickname, 'Little Boots'

[4] Gaius himself, however, would take every comment as an insult. This is typical: those who are the most willing to dish out insults are usually the very ones least able to tolerate the same treatment from others. He had a grudge against Herennius Macer because he greeted him as Gaius; he never forgave a senior centurion for having referred to him as "Little Boots" (*Caligula*). Gaius, of course, had been born and brought up amongst the legionaries, and this was the soldiers' favourite nickname for him. But now that he had graduated to the boots of an actor not a soldier, he regarded "Little Boots" as a shameful insult.

[Seneca, *On Firmness of Purpose* 18.4]

Nothing else is known of Herennius Macer. Gaius was reputed to be born in a legionary camp but was actually born to Germanicus and Agrippina at Antium (Suet. *Cal* .8). He was, however, brought up among the soldiers and he earned the nickname while his father was serving on the Rhine (Tac. *Ann.* 1.41.2; Suet. *Cal.* 9).

J19b Gaius Caligula's personal appearance

Gaius Caesar had a multitude of vices, among them his capacity for offensive personal insult. He seemed to be obsessed with an extraordinary desire to draw attention to everyone else's peculiarities, even though he himself was by far the richest possible source of amusement. He was hideously ugly, with a pallid countenance suggestive of insanity; he had wild eyes set deep within their sockets, like those of an old witch; his head was misshapen, bald, but with a sprinkling of stubble like that of an old beggar; his neck, similarly, was besieged by bristles, his legs were spindly, and his feet enormous.

[Seneca, *On Firmness of Purpose* 18.1]

On Caligula's appearance, see Suet. *Cal.* 50.1. This and other such passages need to be read in the light of the ancient belief in physiognomy (a person's character being reflected in their appearance).

J19c Honoured at Vienne before his accession, AD 33–37

To Gaius Caesar Germanicus, son of Germanicus, grandson of Tiberius Augustus, great-grandson of Divus Augustus, pontiff and quaestor.

[*CIL* 12.1848–49 = *ILS* 189 = LACTOR 8 no.18 = EJ 97]

Two squared limestone blocks from Vienna in Narbonensis (mod. Vienne), inscribed with the same text in honour of Gaius, probably belonged to a single monument. The text illustrates Gaius' credentials to become emperor, namely his descent from Augustus. It also illustrates how he had very little experience of public life before becoming emperor; he became quaestor in 33 or 34 (Dio 58.23). Few inscriptions of Caligula survive because many monuments in his honour were destroyed in the aftermath of his assassination.

J19d Oath of allegiance, 11 May AD 37, Aritium (Lusitania)

An oath of the citizens of Aritium to Gaius Ummidius Durmius Quadratus, propraetorian legate of Gaius Caesar Germanicus Imperator: from the deepest conviction, as truly as I shall be the enemy of those whom I learn to be the enemies of Gaius Caesar Germanicus, so I shall not cease to pursue by land and sea with armed force in bitter warfare anyone who endangers or shall endanger him and his safety, until he has paid the penalty to him; I shall consider neither myself nor my children dearer than his safety, and shall regard those who show hostile intentions towards him as my enemies. If I knowingly break my oath now or in the future, then may Jupiter Best and Greatest and Divus Augustus and all the rest of the immortal gods deprive me and my children of my country, my safety and all my possessions. Dated 11 May in the old town of Aritium, in the consulship of Gnaeus Acerronius Proculus and Gaius Petronius Pontius Nigrinus, in the magistracy of Vegetus, son of Tallicus, and [*name lost*].

[*CIL* 2.172 = *ILS* 190 = SG 32 = LACTOR 8 no.26 = LACTOR 18 no.182 = Sherk 41]

This is the text of an oath of allegiance for Gaius (inscribed on bronze), taken fifty-two days after the death of Tiberius at Aritium in Lusitania (Portugal). It continues the tradition of oaths of loyalty seen earlier in the case of both Augustus and Tiberius (**J2b**). A similar oath of loyalty to Gaius (in Greek) has also been found at Assus, in the Troad (Smallwood 33).

J19e Gifts of Gaius, AD 37

June 1: a gift of 75 sesterces given.
August 1: another 75 sesterces.

[Fasti from Ostia, fragment Ch = Smallwood 31]

J19f Letter from Gaius to the League in Achaia, AD 37

Imperator Augustus Caesar, descendant of the god Augustus, grandson of Tiberius Caesar, *pontifex maximus*, with tribunician power, consul, to the league of Achaians and Boeotians and Locrians and Phocians and Euboeans, greetings.

I have read the decree given to me by your envoys and have noted that you have spared no extravagance in your zeal and piety towards me, in that you have each personally offered sacrifice for my welfare and have joined in a common festival and have decreed the greatest honours you could. For all this I commend you and give my approval and, mindful of the brilliance of each of the Greek peoples from ancient times, I permit you to meet as a league. But as for the statues you decreed for me, set aside the greater part, if you would, and be satisfied with those to be set up at Olympia and Nemea and Delphi and the Isthmus, so that you… and you burden yourselves with less costs. The envoys whose names are written below [delivered] the decree to me. [Farewell.] Head of the embassy … [names of the envoys follow, fragments]

Given on 19 August, in Rome.

[Greek: *ILS* 8792 = *IG* VII 2711 = Smallwood 361]

This letter from the emperor dates from 19 August AD 37, and was found inscribed at Acraephia in Boeotia. It belongs to a dossier of nine related documents all inscribed together on a large stone monument. It is third in the sequence, being preceded by a letter from the strategos of the league of Achaians to the magistrates of Acraephia concerning an embassy sent to congratulate Gaius on his accession (compare a similar embassy at Tiberius' accession **J2c**) and a decree honouring its leader. The emperor's letter is followed by further decrees concerning honours to the leader of the embassy, Epaminondas. This illustrates the way in which Roman official documents might in effect be transformed into honorific inscriptions for members of the local élite. Gaius allows statues to himself at the four famous venues of the traditional 'circuit games' (compare Nero's tour, **Q17–Q18**, Dio 63.10.1, Suet. *Nero* 24.2).

J19g Dedication to Gaius in Egypt

To Gaius Caesar Augustus Germanicus, great grandson of Divus Augustus, grandson of Tiberius Caesar Augustus, son of Germanicus Caesar, consul twice, with tribunician power, *pontifex maximus*, hailed as victorious commander, father of his country, through Gaius Vitrasius Pollio, prefect of Egypt, the cohort of Ituraeans which is commanded by Lucius Eienus Saturninus, son of Lucius, of the tribe Falerna, in year 3 of Gaius Caesar Augustus Germanicus, 28 April m ndh 3.

[*ILS* 8899 = Smallwood 277]

28 April 39. Syene, Egypt. Ituraeans, a Bedouin Arab people were famed as archers and provided several cohorts to Rome's armies. The ending is unintelligible.

J19h Caligula's tax remission, *quadrans*, AD 39, Rome

Obv: *pileus* (cap worn by freed slaves) between S C

C CAESAR DIVI AVG PRON AVG (Gaius Caesar Augustus, grandson of Augustus, by decree of the senate

Rev: RCC (Remission of the 1/200 tax)

PON M TR P III P P COS DES III (*pontifex maximus,* in his 3rd year of tribunician power, father of the fatherland, designated consul for the 3rd time)

[*BMC* Gaius 57; *RIC* Gaius 39]

Suetonius, *Caligula* 16.3 reports the abolition of the 0.5% auction tax. Public disturbances over this tax at 1% had caused Tiberius to reduce it to 0.5% (Tac. *Ann.* 1.78.2 and 2.42.4; see also Dio 59.9.6, apparently in error). So this was clearly a popular move, though hardly the freedom from slavery claimed by the coin. Variations in his imperial titulature show that this coin was minted three times between AD 39 and 40/1 (*RIC* 39, 45, 52) each time on the quadrans (lowest value coin (Petronius (*Satyricon* 45) defines a really mean man as one who would pick a *quadrans* out of a dung-heap with his teeth!).

J20 Marcus Aemilius Lepidus (after AD 12–39)

The last descendant of a famous, patrician family. Great-great-nephew of the triumvir, he was also great-grandson of Scribonia and a descendant of the equally aristocratic Cornelius Scipio family. His uncle married Julia the Younger (**J6**, Augustus' granddaughter). His father (cos AD 6) was described by Tacitus as 'capable of becoming emperor, but thinking it beneath him' (*Annals* 1.13.2) and died in 33 (obituary, Tac. *Ann.* 6.27.4). M. Aemilius Lepidus' sister married Drusus Caesar (**J18**), and he married Drusilla (**J22**), Gaius' sister. Dio 59.22.6 says that Gaius marked Lepidus out as his potential successor, but had him killed for conspiracy with Gaetulicus and Gaius' other sisters in 39 (Dio 59.22.5–8; Suet. *Cal.* 24.3; *Claud.* 9.1).

Modern treatment: Syme, *Augustan Aristocracy,* ch.8 and 10 and table 4.

J20a Statue from a family group at Aphrodisias

Marcus Lepidus

[Greek: *IAph2007* 9.33]

This marble statue base was part of a series found near the theatre in Aphrodisias (Caria), inscribed with texts identifying members of the imperial family, see **L36c** and note. Given that no dedicator is mentioned, they were presumably set up by the city.

J21 Agrippina the Younger AD 15–59

Julia Agrippina, or 'the younger Agrippina' was born on 6 November (**A56b**), almost certainly a year after the death of Augustus. The eldest daughter of Agrippina and Germanicus, she was great-granddaughter of both Augustus (through her mother, Agrippina) and Livia (through her father, Germanicus). She was betrothed to Gnaeus Domitius Ahenobarbus in AD 28 (Tac. *Ann.* 4.75). Their only surviving child, Nero was born in 37. Later that year, her brother became emperor. As such she was included in prayers for the emperor (**A38c**), but exiled the following year on charge of conspiracy (**D7**; Suet. *Cal.* 29.1; Dio 59.22.8;). Recalled by her uncle, Claudius, she became his fourth wife in AD 49, by special law of the senate (**J12e** and note). Tacitus presents a detailed picture of her ruthless manipulation of Claudius and destruction of anyone she opposed, for her personal pleasure, power, wealth, and promotion of her son (Tac. *Ann.* 12.22, 25, 26, 41–2, 57, 59, 64). Almost all sources hold her responsible for murdering her husband (**P9**, **J21d**). Tacitus portrays the rapid waning of her initially dominant influence over her son in *Annals* 13.2, 13–19, 21, despite official honours recorded by the Arval Brothers (**A57c**, **A58e** with note). Their records also provide the official version of Nero's murder of Agrippina (**A59f–g** and **i**; Tac. *Ann.* 14.10–13; Dio 62.16; **P10**). For the likely truth, apparently widely known (Suet. *Nero* 39.2–3, 46.3) see *Octavia* **H6, H15**; Tac. *Ann.* 14.1–9; Suet. *Nero* 34.2–3.

Modern treatment: Barrett, *Agrippina: Sex, Power and Politics in the Early Empire,* (London 1996); Ginsburg, *Representing Agrippina* (Oxford 2006). Portraits: German Archaeological Institute, Rome; British Museum sardonyx cameo of Agrippina the Younger (BM Gem 3946).

J21a Birthday of Agrippina the Younger

November 6: Birthday of Agrippina Julia.

[Fasti at Antium, = EJ p.54]

J21b Nero & Agrippina on *aureus* of AD 54 (mint of Rome)

Obv: Heads of Nero and Agrippina facing each other

AGRIPP AVG DIVI CLAVD NERONIS CAES MATER (Agrippina Augusta, wife of Divus Claudius, mother of Nero Caesar)

Rev: EX S C in oak-wreath

NERONI CLAVD DIVI F CAES AVG GERM IMP TR P (By decree of the senate [this oak-wreath is awarded to] Nero Caesar Augustus Germanicus, son of Divus Claudius hailed victorious commander, with tribunician power)

[*BMC* Nero 1; *RIC* Nero 1]

The coin can be dated to within months of Nero's accession, as he is not yet consul. Denarii with the same obverse and reverse were also issued (*RIC* 2, *BMC* 3).

J21c Birthday poem for Agrippina

This man will send you crystal, that one silver, topaz the others,
All of them birthday gifts of rich men for their queen.
But look, for Agrippina I have merely penned two isopsephic couplets:
Enough for me a gift that envy can't demean.

[Leonides 8 = Palatine Anthology 6.329]

This epigram is isopsephic (see on Leonides, **R27**).

J21d Josephus on Agrippina

[148] There followed the death of Claudius Caesar, after a reign of thirteen years, eight months, and twenty days. Some accounts have it that he was poisoned by his wife, Agrippina. Her father was Germanicus, the emperor's brother, and her first husband Domitius Ahenobarbus, one of the most distinguished of Rome's citizens. [149] After his death, she remained a widow for a long time until Claudius married her. She had a son, named Domitius after his father, whom she brought with her when she re-married.

[Josephus, *Jewish Antiquities* 20.148–9]

J22 Drusilla AD 16–38

Julia Drusilla, second daughter of Germanicus and Agrippina, born AD 16, Tiberius married her to L. Cassius Longinus (cos. 30) in 33 (Tac. *Ann.* 6.15.1), and then to M. Aemilius Lepidus (**J20**). As favourite sister of Gaius (Suet. *Cal.* 24.1–2) she is included in vows for the imperial family (**A38c; Suet. *Cal.* 15.2**), and apparently named as his heir in 37 (Suet. *Cal.* 24.1; Dio 59.22.6). Incest was rumoured (Suet. *Cal.* 24.1; 36.1), fuelled by Gaius' extravagant reaction to her death in 38; public mourning; deification (**A38t**; Sen. *Apocol.* = **F1.2**).

Modern treatment: Barrett, *Caligula* (London 1989), pages 85–9.

J22a Caligula's three sisters, brass *sestertius*, AD 37–8 (Rome)

Obv: Laureate head of Caligula, left

C CAESAR AVG GERMANICVS PON M TR POT (Gaius Caesar, Augustus, Germanicus, *pontifex maximus*, with tribunician power).

Rev. Agripinna stands on the left (in the form of *Securitas*), resting on a column, holding a cornucopia and placing hand on shoulder of Drusilla; Drusilla (in the form of Concordia) holds a cornucopia and *patera* (dish used for sacrifice); Julia (in the form of Fortuna) holds a cornucopia and rudder.

AGRIPPINA, DRVSILLA, IVLIA; Gaius Caligula's three sisters standing facing, draped. S C (by decree of the senate).

[*BMC* Gaius 37; *RIC* Gaius 33]

On these coins, Gaius' three sisters are shown as virtues associated with the imperial house – Security, Concord and good Fortune. The cornucopia represents an abundance of good things.

J22b Drusilla honoured at Mytilene, Lesbos

To Nero, Drusus, Agrippina, and Drusilla new Aphrodite, the siblings of Imperator Gaius Caesar.

[Greek: Smallwood 128b = *IGRRP* IV 78b]

This dedication offers an idealised picture of Gaius' family: it includes his two elder brothers who had once looked likely heirs of Tiberius – Nero, who had been exiled and executed in 31, and Drusus, who had been imprisoned and died in 33 – and two of his three younger sisters – Drusilla, who died in 38, and Agrippina the Younger (thus excluding Livilla, who was exiled in 39).

J22c Death of Drusilla, AD 38

10 June: Drusilla passed away.

[Fasti from Ostia, fragment Ch = Smallwood 31]

J22d Dedication at Tibur

Sacred to Diva Drusilla. [Gaius] Rubellius Blandus, son of Gaius, quaestor of Divus Augustus, tribune of the plebs, praetor, consul, proconsul, pontiff.

[Smallwood 128a = *ILS* 196 = *CIL* XIV 3576]

C. Rubellius Blandus, consul in 18, had married Tiberius' granddaughter in 33 and so was honouring his wife's first cousin. His undistinguished family came from Tibur (modern Tivoli) (Tac. *Ann.* 6.27.1).

J22e Gaius' behaviour after Drusilla's death

[3] I have gone through the whole catalogue of Caesars from whom Fortune stole brothers and sisters. But I cannot leave out the one Caesar from all their number whose name deserves to be obliterated from that list. He was one whom Nature

spawned to be the ruin and disgrace of all humanity; he brought fire and utter destruction to an empire, which is now being restored by the clemency of our most kindly emperor.

[4] Gaius Caesar lost his sister, Drusilla. He was a man incapable of expressing grief or pleasure in a manner fit for an emperor. He shunned all sight of or converse with his fellow citizens, and did not even attend his own sister's funeral rites or pay the respect and honour due to her remains. Instead, in his Alban villa he sought to lighten the distress of that most bitter loss by gambling with dice and indulging in other such occupations better suited to the vulgarities of the public squares. What a disgrace to our empire that its emperor, in mourning for his sister, should find solace in the dice board.

[5] This was the selfsame Gaius who, with an inconsistency born of madness, would at one moment let his hair and beard grow long and then the next proceed to shave them off. Meanwhile he wandered aimlessly along the shores of Italy and Sicily, unable to make up his mind whether he wanted his sister to be mourned as a mortal or worshipped as a goddess. And all this time, while he was setting up temples and shrines to her memory, he inflicted the most savage punishments on those whose grief he deemed inadequate. In all this he bore the hammer blows of misfortune with that same lack of decency and restraint as he had shown when, in the elation of moments of good fortune, he had swollen with an arrogance beyond all human propriety.

[Seneca, *On Consolation, to Polybius* 17.3–5]

Dio similarly describes Gaius' excessive grief for his sister, alleging incest (59.11), as does Suetonius (*Cal.* 24.1).

J23 Julia Livilla / Livilla AD 18–42

Daughter of Germanicus and Agrippina, born AD 18, while they were on the Greek island of Lesbos, on Germanicus' command in the East (Tac. *Ann.* 2.54.1). Known as Julia (Tacitus and Dio) and Livilla (Dio and her epitaph). Tiberius marries her to M. Vinicius (cos. 30 and 45) in 33 (Tac. *Ann.* 6.15.1). As sister of Gaius she is included in vows for the imperial family (**A38c**) but is exiled for adultery/conspiracy (**D7**; Suet. *Cal.* 29.1; Dio 59.22.8). Recalled by Claudius (Suet. *Claud.* 12.1), but almost immediately banished and killed at the instigation of Messallina (Dio 60.4.8; Sen. *Apocol.* = **F10.4**; *Octavia* 944–6 = **H15**; main narrative in lost part of *Annals*, referred to at 14.63.2).

J23a Epitaph of Livilla, Mausoleum of Augustus.

Here lies Livilla, [wife of M. Vinicius], daughter of Germanicus Caesar.

[Rome: *ILS* 188 = *CIL* 6.891 = Smallwood 87]

Found near Mausoleum of Augustus with **J9c**, **J17d** and **J24c.**

J24 Tiberius Gemellus AD 19–37

Tiberius Julius Caesar Nero 'Gemellus' was one of twin sons of Drusus (**J10**), son of Tiberius, and Livilla (**J11**), born in AD 19 to much rejoicing (Tac. *Ann.* 2.84.1). The other twin (Drusus Gemellus) died the same year as his father (AD 23: Tac. *Ann.* 4.15.1; Velleius = **C130.3**). Gemellus, seven years younger than his cousin, Gaius, was 17 at the time of Tiberius' death, and was named as co-heir in the will drawn up two years before (Suet. *Tib.* 76; Philo = **D4**.23), but the senate set aside the will (Dio 59.1.1–2). Tacitus has Tiberius leaving the decision to fate (*Ann.* 6.46.3). Instead Gemellus was adopted by Gaius (Philo = **D4.**26–9; Dio 59.1.3; Suet. *Cal.* 15.2) and eliminated soon afterwards (Philo = **D4.**23–31; Dio 59.1.3; Suet Cal 23.3; 29.1).

Modern treatment: Levick, *Tiberius* (London 1976), chapter XII.

J24a Tiberius' twin grandsons: *sestertius*, AD 22–3 (Rome)

Obv: Confronting heads of two little boys on crossed cornucopiae, with caduceus between.
No inscription

Rev: Large SC (by decree of the senate)
DRVSVS CAESAR TI AVG F DIVI AVG N PONT TR POT II (Drusus Caesar, son of Tiberius Augustus, grandson of Divus Augustus, pontiff, in his 2nd year of tribunician power.

[*BMC* Tiberius 95; *RIC* Tiberius 42]

The cornucopiae and caduceus symbolise fertility and good fortune, reflecting Tiberius' pleasure at the birth of his twin grandsons in AD 19.

J24b Tiberius Gemellus honoured in Samnium

To Tiberius Caesar, son of Drusus Caesar, grandson of Tiberius Caesar Augustus, by decree of the decurions.

[Cavuoto (1975) 223 no.3]

This marble slab shows Gemellus being honoured by the town council at Telesia in Samnium.

J24c Epitaph of Tiberius Gemellus, Mausoleum of Augustus.

Here lies Tiberius Caesar, son of Drusus Caesar.

[Rome: *ILS* 172 = *CIL* 6.892 = Smallwood 88]

Found near Mausoleum of Augustus. No mention is made of his adoption by Gaius.

J25 Messalina (before AD 20 – 48)

Valeria Messal(l)ina was great-granddaughter of Augustus' sister, Octavia on mother's and father's sides of the family (Sen. *Apocol.* = **F11.1**). She married her second cousin Claudius early in Gaius' reign, bearing Octavia and then Britannicus (born Feb 41 – Suet. *Claud.* 27.2). Tacitus and other sources depict her as often keeping Claudius in complete ignorance of her crimes (e.g. Tac. *Ann.* 11.1–3; Suet. *Claud.* 26.2, 29, 37.2). Her adulterous affairs were notorious (see below, **P8a**, **R41**) culminating in her bigamous marriage to Gaius Silius (see **H5**; **P8b**, Tac. *Ann.* 11.12–13, 11.26–31; Suet. *Claud.* 26.2, 29.3; Dio 60.31.3–4) and death (**H5**; **H15**; **P8c**; Tac. *Ann.* 11.34–38; Dio 60.31.4–5).

Modern treatment: Levick, *Claudius* (London 1990), chapter 6.

J25a Claudius' wife and children, silver *didrachm*, Caesarea in Cappadocia

Obv: Draped bust of Messallina, right, with hair-curls and pigtail
MESSALLINA AVGVSTA

Rev: Britannicus standing, clasping hands with Octavia on the left; to their right, Antonia holding cornucopia
OCTAVIA, BRITANNICVS, ANTONIA

[*RIC* Claudius 124; *BMC* Claudius 242]

This coin has to pre-date Messallina's execution for adultery in AD 48. It shows her children by Claudius, Octavia (**J31**) and Britannicus (**J32**), and Claudius' daughter from an earlier marriage, Antonia (**J26**).

J25b Juvenal on Messallina

Do you bother about private misdeeds, misconduct at home?
Do you care what Eppia did? Take a look at the emperors' households,
Those rivals of gods. Let me tell you what Claudius
Had to put up with.
As soon as his wife knew her husband
Was sleeping, that whore of an empress would dare
To dress like some night-prowling hoodie; by choice
She exchanged for her comfortable bed in the Palace
The cheapest of mattresses; out she would creep
With only one maid to escort her; to hide her black hair
She pulled on a flax-coloured wig, hurried into a brothel
That steamed with the smell of stale blankets; in a cell,
Kept empty, reserved for her personal use, she offered her services.
Stark naked she stood there, her tits tipped with gold,
Conducting her trade as "Lycisca", the She-Wolf,
Displaying for clients to ogle the belly that once bore
Britannicus, scion of emperors. With welcome seductive
As each client entered, she asked for their money – in cash.
Then flat on her back, without respite, she sustained their assaults.
All too soon, when the pimp was already dismissing his girls,
With regret she departed, and closed up her bedroom for business
As late as she possibly could. Still aroused, with her fanny on fire,
Her pussy still panting for more, though exhausted, she went off
Unsatisfied; filthy, her cheeks stained with lamp-smoke, disgusting,
She brought back her foul brothel-smells to her bedroom.
Aphrodisiacs, love-spells and poison, so carefully stewed

As a gift for your stepson – why mention them all? Womankind,
Compelled by their sex-drive, commit much more serious crimes.
Sins of lust are the least of their failings.

[Juvenal, *Satires* 6.113–135]

Punch magazine in 1845 famously gave 'Advice to those about to marry: Don't.' Juvenal's sixth *Satire* gives similar advice at infinitely greater length (661 lines) and with far more vitriol aimed at wives, especially ones of the upper class. Postumus is advised to commit suicide rather than marry (28–32) and a lengthy tirade follows.

Eppia (114) was allegedly the wife of a senator, and ran off with a gladiator (80–112).

J26 Antonia (daughter of Claudius) *c.* AD 28 – 65

Daughter of Claudius by his second wife, Aelia Paetina (Suet. *Claud* 27.1). She was married to Faustus Cornelius Sulla Felix (see **B52**) in AD 41 (Suet. *Claud.* 12.1 and Tac. *Ann.* 13.23.1). After Claudius' death, her husband is banished to Marseilles by Nero (Tac. *Ann.* 13.47) in AD 58 and murdered four years later (*Ann.* 14.57). Antonia survives until implicated in the Piso conspiracy of AD 65 (Tac. *Ann.* 15.53.3–4, Suet. *Nero* 35.4).

J26a Antonia, victim of Nero

Nero, however, killed his mother and his aunt and his wife and Antonia, daughter of Claudius, who refused to marry him after the deaths of these women.

[Scholia on Juvenal, 8.213]

The commentator on Juvenal follows Suetonius, *Nero* 35.4 or a common source. The version is plausible in that any husband of Antonia could have been a threat to the heirless Nero.

J27 Poppaea (before AD 31–65)

Poppaea Sabina's background and first marriages are given by Tacitus *Annals* 13.45–46 (variant accounts of the Otho-Poppaea-Nero relationship in Tac. *Hist.* 1.13.3; Plutarch, *Galba* 19.2–20.2; Suet. *Otho* 3; Dio 61.11.2–4). Nero may have divorced Octavia in AD 62 to marry Poppaea (*Octavia* 780–805 = **H13**; Tac. *Ann.* 14.61–62), or even to have killed his mother to achieve this (Tac. *Ann.* 14.1.1). Poppaea bore him a daughter, **Claudia** on 21 January 63 (A63c; Tac. *Ann.* 15.23). Poppaea herself died in AD 65 (Suet. *Nero* 35.3; Tac. *Ann.* 16.6) and like her baby daughter, was deified (**A66e**, **L34–L35**). Poppaea's first husband, Rufrius Crispinus and their son both also fall victim to Nero (*Octavia* 728–33 = H12; Tac. *Ann.* 15.71.4; 16.17.1–2; Suet Nero 35.5). Her second husband Otho was emperor 15 January – 16 April AD 69 (Tac. *Hist.* 1.27 – 2.50).

Modern treatment: Griffin, *Nero* (London 1984), pages 100–4.

J27a Nero and Poppaea, base-silver tetradrachm of Alexandria, AD 64–65

Obv: Head of Nero with radiate crown, right

ΝΕΡΩ ΚΛΑΥ ΚΑΙΣ ΣΕΒ ΓΕΡ ΑΥ (Nero Claudius Caesar Augustus, Imperator)

Rev: Bust of Poppaea, right
ΠΟΠΠΑΙΑ ΣΕΒΑΣΤΗ ΛΑ (Poppaea Augusta; Year 11)

[*BMC* 124]

For radiate crowns, see L32 and L33a with note.

J27b Poppaea helps Jews

Nero gave the Jewish delegation a full hearing and then not only endorsed their actions, but also agreed that they could leave the disputed building as it was. He allowed this as a favour to his wife, Poppaea, who was a god-fearer, and pleaded with him on behalf of the Jews.

[Josephus, *Jewish Antiquities* 20.195]

Dio (62.11–12) and Tacitus (e.g. *Ann.* 13.45–46, 14.1) depict Poppaea as duplicitous and manipulative; Josephus here presents a different picture of a deeply religious woman. Empresses frequently involved themselves in these cases – compare Agrippina in *JA* 20.125–136.

J27c A birthday present for Poppaea

On this your birthday, pray receive this gift, a map of heaven;
Nile-born Leonides has sent you it,
Poppaea, Augusta, Zeus' Consort-Queen. For you delight
In gifts that match your marriage and your wit.

[Leonides 32 (Page) = Palatine Anthology 9.355]

This epigram is isopsephic (see on Leonides, **R27**).

J27d Poppaea's amber-coloured hair

Domitius Nero, amongst other monstrous deeds in his life, adopted the term for the hair-colour of his wife, Poppaea, calling it amber in one of his poems, since a positive term can be applied to any vice. From that time this third hair-colour became fashionable for upper-class women.

[Pliny, *Natural History* 37.50]

This shows some of Pliny's hatred for Nero in regarding a poem praising the colour of her hair as one of his monstrous deeds. The other two fashionable hair-colours were obviously fair and dark.

J28 Statilia Messallina *c.* AD 32 – after AD 69

Nero's third wife was great-great-granddaughter of Augustus' important commander, T. Statilius Taurus (Suet. *Nero* 35.1), and probably daughter of the consul of AD 44 (**B44**). She had had four husbands (for her fourth, see Tac. *Ann.* 15.68.3) before marrying Nero by June 66 (**A66e**), and accompanied him on his tour of Greece (**M14–M17**). She outlived Nero, even contemplating a sixth husband, Otho (Suet. *Otho* 10.2).

J28a Statilia Messallina's marriages and talents

Statilia Messalina, who after four marriages had ended in various ways finally wedded Nero, is being satirised [for being a literary bore]. After his destruction she maintained her pre-eminence in wealth, beauty and talent. She continued putting her eloquence into practice even to the point of an eagerness for public speaking.

[Scholia on Juvenal 6.434]

J28b Bronze coin of Nero and Messalina struck at Hypaepa (Lydia), AD 66–8

Obv: Draped bust of Messalina facing right, and laureate head of Nero facing left
ΝΕΡΩΝ ΜΕΣΣΑΛ(Ε)ΙΝΑ (Nero and Messalina)

Rev: Cult statue of Artemis
ΥΠΑ(Ι) ΙΟΥ ΓΡ ΗΓΗΣΙΠΠΟΣ (Gaios Ioulios Hegesippos, Grammateus [senior magistrate])

[*BMC* 21; *RPC* 2543/3]

Three cities in the Empire honoured Messalina on their coins. The imperial *aurei* of Rome with the inscription AVGVSTVS AVGVSTA appear to date to AD 64–6 so probably refer to Nero and Poppaea (cf. *BMC* Nero 52; *RIC* Nero 44).

J29 Rubellius Plautus *c.* AD 35–62

Tacitus hints at his pedigree in *Annals* 14.22.1: he was son of Tiberius' granddaughter Julia, by her *mésalliance* with Rubellius Blandus (*Ann.* 6.27.1): thus (doubly) the great-great-grandson of Livia, and also of Octavia & Antony. He was thus a potential rival to Nero with or without a marriage to Agrippina (*Annals* 13.19.3 and 14.22.1, 14.57–59) and was killed (**H7**, Tac. *Ann.* 14.57–59).

J30 NERO AD 37–68

Nero Claudius Caesar was born on 15 December (**A57f**; Suet. *Nero* 6.1) to Agrippina (the Younger) and Cn. Domitius Ahenobarbus. He was the great-great-grandson of Augustus, though entirely through the female line. Soon after his mother's marriage to Claudius in AD 49, he is betrothed to Octavia, adopted as Claudius' son (A59c; Tac. *Ann.* 12.25–26; Suet. *Nero* 7.1) and marked out for succession as *princeps iuventutis* (leader of the younger generation: **A54a**; Tac. *Ann.* 12.41). Tacitus gives a detailed account of his accession (*Ann.* 12.64–69) and reign until AD 66 (*Annals* 13–16: the rest of the text is lost). Dio's account only survives in epitome (books 61–63). Suetonius divides his biography into two parts: an account of bad (20–57) and reasonably good (6–19) deeds. Other significant material can be found in Seneca (*Apocol* = **Section F**; *on Clemency* = **Section G**); in 'silver age' poetry, but Nero, as the last of the dynasty is particularly susceptible to the twin dangers of historiographical tradition as expressed by Tacitus **R3**.

Modern treatment: Griffin, *Nero* (London 1984).

J30a Nero, *princeps iuventutis* on *aureus* of Claudius, AD 50–54 (Rome)

Obv: Draped bust of Nero right

NERO CLAVD CAES DRVSVS GERM PRINC IVVENT (Nero Claudius Caesar Drusus Germanicus, leader of the younger generation)

Rev: *simpulum* (ladle) above tripod to left; *lituus* (augur's wand) above *patera* (dish used in sacrifices) to right

SACERD COOPT IN OMN CONL SVPRA NVM, EX S C (Coopted as an additional member of every college of priests, by decree of the senate)

[*BMC* Claudius 84; *RIC* Claudius 76]

This coin commemorates Nero's admission into the four great colleges of priests: the pontiffs, the augurs, the *quindecimviri sacris faciendis*, (Board of Fifteen for the performance of sacred rites) and the *septemviri epulones* (seven-man board for the management of feasts). Augustus had issued a *denarius* in 16 BC with the same symbols (LACTOR 17, L1).

J30b Nero's acclamation in Egypt, AD 54

Paying his dues to his forefathers and as manifest god, Caesar has gone to them, whilst the expected and hoped for *imperator* of the world has revealed himself: the good spirit of the world, who is the origin of all good things, ~~greatest~~, Nero Caesar has revealed himself. For this reason, all of us ought to wear wreaths and sacrifice oxen, to show gratitude to all the gods. Year 1 of Nero Claudius Caesar Augustus Germanicus, on the 21st of the month New Augustus.

[Greek: Smallwood 47 = Sherk 61 = *P.Oxy.* 1021]

This appears to be a draft on papyrus of the proclamation of Nero's accession on 17 Nov. 54, thirty-five days after Claudius' death on 13 Oct.

J30c Coins (aurei) of Nero going to seed, AD 54 to *c.* 68

Obverses of *aurei* of AD 54, *c.* 65, and *c.* 68 (*BMC* 1, 103, and 68)

The coins show a good-looking young man who became emperor shortly before his 17th birthday turning into a grossly obese man who died when still only 30. It is strange that he should have been happy for the change to be so vividly documented.

J30d Nero's voice

"What about that voice, Musonius, which made him mad about music and in love with the Olympic and Pythian Games? What is the tyrant's voice like? When people sailed over to Lemnos some thought it wonderful, some ridiculous."
"Actually, Menecrates, he has a voice that is neither wonderful nor ridiculous: nature has made him a competent and reasonable musician. His voice is naturally resonant and deep as his throat is set back, giving a sort of buzzing sound to his singing. But the pitch of his voice 'smoothes this over' when he does not rely so much on vocal quality as on mild ornamentation, catchy melody, supportive accompaniment on the lyre, in knowing the right time to walk, stand still and move, and in swaying his head in time to the music. The only disgrace is that a king should think perfecting these things important."

[Philostratos? *Nero* 6]

This dialogue features Musonius Rufus, a stoic philosopher of Nero's own day, who shared the exile of Rubellius Plautus AD 60–62 and was exiled in the wake of the Pisonian conspiracy in AD 65. But despite the circumstantial detail, the author of this dialogue, probably written over 100 years after Nero's death is unlikely to have any evidence of Nero's voice. For his salutations as Olympic and Pythian victor see Suet. *Nero* 25, Dio [Xiphilinus] 63.10.1 and 63.20.5.

J30e Nero's quinquennium (five years)

Though only a young man, he was absolute ruler for as long as his step-father and for five years he was such a great emperor, especially in improving Rome that Trajan was right to say seriously and on many occasions that other emperors fell far short of Nero's 'quinquennium'. In this period too he reduced Pontus to the status of a province, with Polemo's permission, and named it Polemonian Pontus, and similarly the Cottian Alps on the death of King Cottius. Therefore it is amply proven that youth is no impediment to excellence; but this can easily be changed when talent is corrupted by lack of self-control, and a lack of rules, as it were, governing youth results is very dangerous. For Nero spent the rest of his life so appallingly that it is disgraceful and displeasing to have to record such behaviour in anyone, let alone the ruler of an empire.

[Aurelius Victor, *Book on the Emperors,* 5.2–4]

Trajan's opinion (also recorded in the anonymous *Summary of the Emperors*, 5.2–5) clearly referred to an early period of Nero's reign, though both historians, in searching to explain the remark, choose examples from the latter years of his reign. For Polemo, see **M48**.

J31 Octavia AD 40–62

Claudia Octavia, daughter of Claudius and Messalina was betrothed in infancy to L. Junius Silanus (see **J33a**), an engagement broken by Agrippina's machinations (*Octavia 145–9* = **H1**; Sen. *Apocol.*= **F10.4**; Tac. *Ann.* 12.3–4 and 8; Suet. *Claud.* 29.1–2). Instead she married Nero in AD 53 (Tac. *Ann.* 12.58.1). To get rid of her, Nero accuses her of adultery, exiles, and finally murders her in AD 62 (Tac. *Ann.* 14.60–64; *Octavia* = **H13**, **H16**; Suet. *Nero* 35). Nero died on the 6th anniversary of her death (9 June: Suet. *Nero* 57.1).

J32 Britannicus AD 41–55

Tiberius Claudius Caesar Britannicus was born on 22nd day of Claudius' reign (Suet. *Claud.* 27.2 – probably 12 Feb), the son of Claudius and Messallina. Initially called Germanicus, but Britannicus after Claudius' invasion of Britain (Suet. *Claud.* 27.1). Aged 8 at his mother's death, he is soon supplanted as heir by the adoption of his step-brother (Tac. *Ann.* 12.25) and the removal of potential supporters (Tac. *Ann.* 12.26, 12.41–42). Popular despite this (Tac. *Ann.* 12.69, 13.15) and perhaps attaining Agrippina's support, he is murdered (Tac. *Ann.* 13.15–17; Suet. *Nero* 33.2–3; *Octavia* 166–73 = **H3**; Dio 61.7.4).

Modern treatment: Levick, *Claudius* (London 1990), chapter 7.

J32a Britannicus honoured at Acmonia (Phrygia)

To Tiberius Claudius Caesar Britannicus, son of New Zeus Claudius Caesar Augustus.

[Greek: Smallwood 138 = *MAMA* VI 250]

J32b Britannicus honoured at Rome

To [Tiberius] Claudius C[aesar Bri]tannicus, [brother] of Nero Claudius Caesar.

[Smallwood 108 = *CIL* VI 922]

J32c Nero, Poppaea and Britannicus honoured at Amisus (Pontus), 63/65

Nero Claudius Caesar Augustus Germanicus, Augusta Poppaea, Tiberius Claudius Britannicus: the people, through the agency of Lucius Jutius Potitus and his fellow-magistrates (set this up).

[Greek: Smallwood 112 = SEG XVI 748]

Mention of Poppaea establishes the date, but mention of Britannicus, up to 10 years after his death is very odd, presumably reflecting popular acceptance of the official cause of his death (epilepsy).

J33 Junius Silanus Family

The Junii Silani are a family very prominent under the Julio-Claudian emperors. Two distinct branches share a common ancestor, M. Silanus, praetor in 77 BC. **M. Junius Silanus (cos AD 19)** married Aemilia Lepida, the great-granddaughter of Augustus. They had 5 surviving children, the first, **M. Junius Silanus (cos 46)**, born in the last year of Augustus' life. Mockingly described by Caligula as 'the golden sheep' he was the first victim of Nero's reign (Tac. *Ann.* 13.1). His youngest brother, **L. Junius Silanus**, was betrothed to Octavia and ruined by Agrippina's false charge of incest with his sister (Tac. *Ann.* 12.3–4). He committed suicide on the day Octavia married Nero (12.8). His sister, **Junia Calvina** was banished, though she survived to be recalled by Vespasian and was buried in Augustus' Mausoleum around AD 79, as Augustus' last descendant (Suet. *Vesp.* 23.4). Another brother, **D. Junius Silanus Torquatus** was consul in AD 53, and survived until his suicide in AD 65 when facing flimsy treason charges (Tac. *Ann.* 15.35.3). **Junia Lepida**, the other great-great-grandchild of Augustus was also falsely charged by Nero in the wake of the Pisonian conspiracy of AD 65, along with her husband, Gaius Cassius Longinus and nephew, **L. Silanus** who was killed (Tac. *Ann.* 16.7–9).

A fairly distant cousin of these descendants of Augustus was **M. Junius Silanus (cos suff. AD 15)**. His daughter, **Junia Claudilla** married Caligula in AD 33 (Tac. *Ann.* 6.20.1; Suet. *Cal.* 12.1; Dio 58.25.2). She died in childbirth before Caligula's accession, and Caligula drove his father-in-law to suicide (Philo, *Embassy* 62–5 = **D6**; Suet. *Cal.* 23.3; **A38j** replaced as Arval; Sen. *Apocol.* = F11.2). Other members of this branch of the Junii Silani were two brothers of Caligula's father-in-law, **Gaius Silanus (cos AD 10)** and **Decimus Junius Silanus** disgraced by his adultery with the younger Julia (Tac. *Ann.* 3.24.3); also and a nephew, **C. Appius Junius Silanus** (cos 28) whom Claudius thought a suitably aristocratic husband for Domitia Lepida (his mother-in-law, also Nero's aunt) in AD 54 (Dio 60.14.3) but who is done to death by Messalina/Claudius soon afterwards (Suet. *Claud.* 37.2) and Appius' son, **M. Junius Silanus (cos AD 54)**.

Modern treatment: Syme, *The Augustan Aristocracy,* Oxford 1986 – chapter XIV – The Julii Silani.

J33a Claudius' (would-be) son-in-law

Lucius Junius Silanus Torquatus, son of Marcus, grandson of Marcus, honoured at age 18 with triumphal ornaments, quaestor, praetor for cases between citizens and foreigners, son-in-law of Tiberius Claudius Caesar Augustus.

[Tusculum: Smallwood 236]

Statue from Tusculum. See J33 above and Tac. *Ann.* 12.3–4.

SECTION K

Rome and Italy

'In architecture too we have conquered the world.' (Pliny, *NH*)

Introduction: Augustus boasted of having found Rome made of brick and left it made of marble (Suet. *Aug.* 28.3). His huge building programme, vaunted in *Res Gestae* 19–21, brought large-scale employment, and huge political value (explored by Zanker, *The Power of Images in the Age of Augustus* (1988)), and is still visible all round Rome today. The modern tourist in Rome will see less evidence of his immediate successors, though there are important archaeological remains (see A. Claridge, *Rome: an Oxford Archaeological Guide* (2nd edition, Oxford 2010)). Strabo and Pliny provide descriptions of Rome from just before and just after this period: see LACTOR 17, K4 and K29 (Strabo 5.3.8) and K3 (Pliny, *NH* 36.101–4, including the quotation above). Pliny also gives a general account of Rome in AD 73 (*NH* 3.66–67) which concentrates on its overall dimensions and roads. The sources here are given in approximate chronological order.

TIBERIUS: K1–K7

Despite Velleius' praise of Tiberius' wonderful buildings (**C6**), Tacitus (*Ann.* 6.45.1) and Suetonius (*Tib.* 47) seem right that Tiberius' building work amounted to little. The quantity of Augustus' work and perhaps Tiberius' own temperament left him little beyond restorations of previous buildings (Dio 57.10.1–3).

K1 *Aureus* showing *castra praetoria*, AD 41–2 (Rome)

Obv. Laureate head of Claudius, right

TI CLAVD CAESAR AVG P M TR P (Tiberius Claudius Caesar, Augustus, *pontifex maximus*, with tribunician power)

Rev. Battlements of the praetorian camp at Rome in which a soldier stands holding a spear and next to a legionary eagle (*aquila*).

IMPER RECEPT (the victorious commander welcomed)

[*BMC* Claudius 37; *RIC* Claudius 7]

The *castra praetoria* (praetorian camp) was built by Tiberius to accommodate all the cohorts which had previously been deliberately kept in temporary quarters in Rome or billeted in towns outside Rome (Suet. *Aug* 49.1). The change probably happened in AD 20 (Dio 57.19.6), with the main instigator and beneficiary being the praetorian prefect, Sejanus. Tacitus puts the change right at the start of his 'Sejanus narrative' – *Annals* 4.2. It was just outside the ancient, Servian Walls of Rome, and was later built into the third-century, Aurelianic Walls. Significant parts of the walls of the camp survive from Tiberius' original building and Aurelian's additions, and it was clearly arranged on the traditional 'playing card' design of Roman camps.

This coin refers to Claudius' accession when he was taken to the camp by the Praetorian Guard and there hailed as emperor (**E25**). Thereafter the camp becomes the crucial stage for bids for power on the part of emperors or aspirants to the throne, e.g. Tac. *Ann.* 11.31, 12.69, 13.14, 15.53.3, 15.59.1; *Hist.* 3.84.

K2 Tiberius' bridge at Ariminum, AD 21

Imperator Caesar Augustus, son of Divus, *pontifex maximus*, consul 13 times, hailed victorious commander 20 times, in his 37th year of tribunician power, father of the fatherland, and Tiberius Caesar Augustus, son of Divus Augustus, grandson of Divus Julius, *pontifex maximus*, consul 4 times, hailed victorious commander 8 times, in his 22nd year of tribunician power, gave this.

[EJ 82 = *ILS* 113]

The bridge at Ariminium (modern Rimini, Italy) was started by Augustus in 14 and completed by Tiberius in 21 originally spanning the River Marecchia. It still carries road and foot traffic across a modern canal.

K3 Statue to Divus Augustus by Livia and Tiberius

23 April: Julia Augusta and Tiberius Augustus dedicated a statue to Divus Augustus their father at the Theatre of Marcellus

[Fasti at Praeneste = EJ page 48]

Tacitus, *Annals* 3.64.2 (AD 22) suggests that Tiberius felt slighted that his mother's name was placed first. Augustus is 'their' father because Livia had been adopted in Augustus' will (Tac. *Ann.* 1.8.1) as Julia Augusta.

K4 Statue of Divus Augustus on *sestertius* of Tiberius, Rome, AD 34/5

Obv: Chariot drawn left by four elephants with riders; statue of Augustus, radiate in chariot holding laurel-branch and long sceptre

DIVO AVGVSTO, S P Q R (to Divus Augustus, the Senate and People of Rome)

Rev: S C (by decree of the senate)

TI CAESAR DIVI AVG F AVGVST P M TR POT XXXVI (Tiberius Caesar Augustus, son of Divus Augustus, *pontifex maximus,* in his 36th year of tribunician power)

[*BMC* Tiberius 102; *RIC* Tiberius 56]

This *sestertius* of AD 34/5 from Rome was also issued with tribunician power numbers for AD 35/6 and 36/7. No coins with tribunician power numbers for AD 24 to AD 34 seems to have been issued by the mint at Rome, though it is not known why.

K5 Fire at Rome, AD 36

1 November: part of the Circus around the basket-makers district burnt. Tiberius Caesar gave (100 million sesterces) to the public fund.

[Fasti at Ostia, fragment Ch = EJ p.43]

Tacitus, *Annals* 6.45.1 confirms the year and location, describing it as the Circus bordering the Aventine, and the amount spent on rebuilding. Major fires in Rome also occurred in AD 27 (Tac. *Ann*. 4.64.1; **C6**) and well as the Great Fire of AD 64 Tac. *Ann* 15.38–41 and **K38–K40**.

Temple of Augustus, K6–7

A temple to Augustus was voted by the senate immediately after Augustus' funeral (Tac. *Ann.* 1.10.8, Dio 56.43.3 and Livia). It is mentioned in decrees honouring Germanicus (late 19, **J8o**) as being built. Tiberius completed the temple but failed to dedicate it, according to Tacitus, *Annals* 6.45.2, while Suetonius believes Tiberius did not even complete it (*Tib.* 47) though in a context which suggests that he may have been fooled by Tiberius' traditional reluctance to put his name to the many buildings he restored (Dio 57.10.1–3). The Arval Brothers regularly held sacrifices there, in what was called 'the new temple' (e.g. **A38g**, **A66e, U2**). The temple was on the Palatine or its lower slopes (**K7**; Suet. *Cal.* 22.2). It is depicted on coins of Caligula (see below) and of Antoninus Pius (reflecting its rebuilding, probably by Domitian).

K6 Temple of Augustus on *sestertius* of Gaius, AD 37/8

Obv: Pietas, seated facing left, veiled and draped, with *patera* (bowl for libation) in right hand, left arm resting on samll draped figure

C CAESAR AVG GERMANICVS P M TR POT, below PIETAS (Gaius Caesar Augustus Germanicus, *pontifex maximus*, with tribunician power, Piety.

Rev: In background: garlanded temple façade of six ionic columns, with statues of four-horse chariot and other figures on top of pediment. In foreground: Gaius with folds of toga over his head, holding a *patera* (bowl for libations), prepares to sacrifice a bull at an altar, helped by two attendants, one leading the bull, the other holding another *patera.*

DIVO AVG, S C (To Divus Augustus, by decree of the senate)

[*BMC* Gaius 41; *RIC* Gaius 36]

Sestertii of this design were minted at Rome in AD 37/8 and then again in 39/40 and 40/1 as shown by Gaius' tribunician power numbers (*RIC* 44 and 51). *Pietas* 'piety', claimed by Gaius, represents duty to one's gods, but also one's ancestors and country (as exemplified by *pius* Aeneas in Virgil's *Aeneid*). [Images of this coin copyright Andreas Pangert, www.romancoins.info]

K7 The Temple of Divus Augustus in Pliny's time

In the temple of Divus Augustus on the Palatine built by his wife, Augusta, I have seen a cinnamon root of great weight, placed on a golden bowl. Each year, until the shrine was destroyed by fire, droplets seeped from it and hardened into drops of resin.

[Pliny, *Natural History* 12.94]

The fire must have been between AD 66 and Pliny's own death in the eruption of Vesuvius (AD 79). The resin is a compound of cinnamaldehyde from the bark oil.

GAIUS CALIGULA: K8–9

Gaius' short and ultimately unpopular reign results in little positive information on building works. For work on his palace, see **K42**, **L13**. Claudius completed aqueducts started by Gaius (**K24**).

K8 The Vatican obelisk

(Pliny is discussing exceptional trees)

A most amazing fir-tree was seen on the ship which on the emperor Gaius' orders brought from Egypt the obelisk in the Vatican Circus and four blocks of the same stone as its base. Certainly nothing more amazing than this ship has been seen at sea. It carried 200 gallons of lentils as ballast. In length was almost that of the left side of Ostia's harbour, since under Claudius it was sunk there, with three moles the height of towers built there on top of it, specially made of Puteoli cement and transported there.

[Pliny, *Natural History* 16.201–2]

This is the famous obelisk that now stands in St Peter's Square. It is a red granite monolith, 25.36 metres tall (hence the huge ship required – see also Suet. *Claud.* 20.3; Dio 60.11). In 1586 it took one year and 900 men under Giovanni Fontana to move the obelisk 275m to its present position, an endeavour commemorated by a fresco in the Vatican Library. For Claudius' harbour at Ostia, see **K14–K17**. Puteoli cement and its property of hardening underwater had been described, early in Augustus' reign by Vitruvius, *On Architecture* 2.6.1.

K9 The Vatican obelisk inscription

Sacred to Divus Caesar Augustus, son of Divus Julius, and to Tiberius Caesar Augustus, son of Divus Augustus.

[*CIL* 6.882 = Smallwood 306]

CLAUDIUS AND THE SUPPLY OF GRAIN: K10–K21

By the time of Augustus, the population of Rome was up to a million people, with 200,000 in receipt of a free corn dole. With the great majority of corn being imported from northern Africa (**N1j** and **N1k**), often by canal from Puteoli on the Bay of Naples (**K10** and **K11**) rather than to Rome's difficult harbour (**K14**), shortages could and did happen, Tac. *Ann.* 2.87 (prices fixed in AD 19); 4.6.4 (Tiberius exonerated in AD 23). Amongst the first officials to swear loyalty to Tiberius in AD 14 was the prefect of the corn supply (Tac. *Ann.* 1.7.2). Claudius came to power during a grain crisis (**K12**) and took various measures in short and long term (**K13–K19**; Suet. *Claud.* 18–19) to improve supply, though shortages still occurred, *e.g.* in AD 51 (Tac. *Ann.* 12.43). For Claudius' efforts, see Levick, *Claudius,* 109–111.

Business affairs at Puteoli, K10–11

The 127 'Murecine tablets' were found abandoned in a building just outside Pompeii. These wax tablets offer a picture of economic activities pursued by the bankers C. Sulpicius Faustus, C. Sulpicius Cinnamus, and C. Sulpicius Onirus in Puteoli between AD 26 and AD 61, with texts relating to loans, accounts, auctions, rents, and various judicial proceedings. The two tablets given as examples below, both of which record loans made on the security of foodstuffs, reflect the importance of Alexandrian wheat for Rome, which at this date was imported via Puteoli. They also give a lively impression of the financial wheelings and dealings of imperial slaves and freedmen. [G. Camodeca, Tabulae Pompeianae Sulpiciorum. *Edizione critica dell'archivio puteolano dei Sulpicii* (1999: Vetera 12, Quasar: Rome) = TPSulp]

K10 Money-lending by imperial agents, AD 37

Hand-written document of Gaius Novius Eunus relating to a loan of 10,000 sesterces at Puetoli on 18 June.

In the consulship of Procullus and Nigrinus.

In the consulship of Gnaeus Acceronius Proculus and Gaius Petronius Pontius, on 18 June, I, Gaius Novius Eunus, have written that I received on loan from Evenus

Primianus, freedman of Tiberius Caesar Augustus, in his absence through Hessychus, his slave, and that I owe him 10,000 sesterces, which I will return to him upon demand. These 10,000 sesterces, mentioned above, are to be given back according to the law and without error as stipulated by Hessychus, slave of Evenus Primianus, freedman of Tiberius Caesar Augustus, as I, Gaius Novius Eunus, have promised. As security or pledge for these 10,000 sesterces I have put up: [----] Alexandrian wheat, 7,000 *modii*, more or less, as well as chick-peas, wheat, monocopium, and lentils in 200 sacks: 4,000 *modii*, more or less. I have all these in my possession and stored in the Bassian Warehouse, under my complete legal authority and at my own risk, as I declare. Transacted at Puteoli.

[TPSulp 51 = Sherk 176]

The modius is the Roman measure of capacity = 8.62 litres. 7,000 *modii* of corn would be *c.* 27 tonnes.

K11 A loan secured by grain, 13 March AD 40

[Handwritten document of Nardus, slave of Publius Annius Seleucus], on the hiring of Granary 26 [---] Publius Annius [Seleucus].

In the consulship of Gaius Laecanius [Bassus and Quintus Terentius Culle]o, [on 13 March]. I, Nardus, [the slave of] Publius [Annius Seleucus, have written this out] in the presence of and on the command of [Publius Annius Seleucus] my [master], because [he declared] that he [did not know his alphabet]: that [I hired out] to Gaius Sulpicius [Faustus] Granary [26, which is] in the upper [Barbatian estate of Domitia] Lepida; in [this granary is deposited thirteen] thousand [*modii* of Alexandrian wheat which] my [master] will measure out with [his slaves] for a fee: 100 sesterces each month. Transacted at Puteoli. Seals of Publius Annius Seleucus, Gnaeus Pollio Rufus, son of Gnaeus, Gaius Julius Felix, Nardus, slave of Publius Annius Seleucus, Publius Annius Seleucus.

[TPSulp 46]

This loan document incidentally reveals that Nero's aunt, Domitia Lepida, owned the Barbatian Granaries at Puteoli, which were managed for her by P. Annius Seleucus.

K12 Only 8 days' grain supply left at Claudius' accession

[5] Consider how much anxiety you bring upon yourself by the massive burden of high office. Your whole existence is tied up with the belly of the human animal. A starving population is intolerant of reason, cannot be mollified by justice, and is indifferent to any form of entreaty. Just recently, within a few days of the death of Gaius Caesar, while his spirit was still outraged (if the dead are capable of feelings) by the knowledge that the Roman people were alive with some seven or eight days' food supplies yet remaining, we were entering upon the worst of all disasters which can happen to the inhabitants of a city, even under siege – a shortage of supplies.

(Seneca blames the shortage on Gaius building a bridge of boats – see ***T10****)*

[6] Imagine then the anxieties of those responsible for the public food supply when confronted by rioters with rocks, weapons, and arson – and to cap it all, with Gaius himself. By a masterpiece of misinformation, they concealed the desperate calamity lurking in the entrails of the state – most certainly with excellent reasons. There are some afflictions that must be cured without the patient's knowledge, since, for many, a knowledge of the nature of their illness has been the cause of their deaths.

[Seneca, *On the Shortness of Life,* 18.5–6]

This essay is addressed to Pompeius Paulinus, the father of Seneca's second wife, who had succeeded C. Turranius in 48 as *praefectus annonae*, one of the top equestrian posts, responsible for managing the supply of corn to the city of Rome. He retired from the post in 55. The building of the bridge of boats across the Bay of Naples from Puteoli to the vicinity of Baiae is associated by Seneca with a famine in the last days of Gaius. Dio also mention famine as a result of the requisition of so many ships for this purpose (59.17.2), but Seneca's dating is questionable as Dio dates the bridge episode to 39.

K13 Goddess of Corn on *dupondius* of Claudius

Obv: Head of Claudius, left

TI CLAVDIVS CAESAR AVG P M TR P IMP (Tiberius Claudius Caesar Augustus, *pontifex maximus,* with tribunician power, hailed as victorious commander)

Rev: Ceres, veiled and draped, sitting sideways on an ornamental throne, facing left, holding two ears of corn in right hand, long torch in left

CERES AVGVSTA (Augustan Goddess of Corn)

[*BMC* Claudius 140; *RIC* Claudius 94]

This coin from the mint of Rome cannot be firmly dated. It is part of a series with this portrait of Claudius on the obverse and personifications of imperial deities on the reverse: *Constantia Augusti* ('Determination of Augustus' – *RIC* 95), *Libertas Augusta* ('Augustan Liberty' – *RIC* 97), and *Spes Augusta* ('Augustan Hope' – *RIC* 99, with a different portrait). Another later series portrayed Claudius and the same four Augustan deities (*RIC* 110, 111, 113, 115).

K14 Ostia/Portus before Claudius

Ostia is a city without a harbour because of the silting-up caused by the Tiber being fed by many tributaries. Therefore it is hazardous for merchant ships to anchor on the high sea, but desire for profits wins out. In addition the good supply of smaller vessels to unload one lot of cargo and bring others aboard enables the speedy departure of the ships before they reach the river. Or else, when some of their load has been taken off, they sail up the river to reach Rome, a distance of 25 miles.

[Strabo, *Geography,* 5.3.5]

Strabo shows something of the difficulty of supplying Rome by sea at the start of Tiberius' reign, pointing out elsewhere (3.2.6) that large vessels from Spain would sail to Puteoli (on the Bay of Naples, with cargo transported on the canal alongside the Appian Way (Strabo 5.3.6, compare Horace, *Sat.* 1.5) or Ostia (in that order). This explains the real need for a better harbour at Ostia or Portus (2 miles away, though sources use the names indiscriminately). Even *c.* AD 62 St Paul gets to Rome via Puteoli and the Appian Way (or canal) (*Acts* 28.13–15).

K15 The harbour at Ostia

(Pliny is writing about obelisks.)

Divus Claudius preserved for several years the ship used by Gaius Caesar for importing his obelisk: it was the most remarkable ship ever to have set sail. Towers made of volcanic soil were built on its deck at Puteoli and it was then towed to Ostia and sunk to form part of the harbour.

[Pliny, *Natural History,* 36.70]

K16 Claudius' harbour AD 46

Tiberius Claudius Caesar Augustus Germanicus, son of Drusus, *pontifex maximus*, in his 6th year of tribunician power, consul designate for the 4th time, hailed victorious commander 12 times, father of the fatherland, liberated the city from the danger of flooding once ditches had been dug from the Tiber and extended into the sea on account of the harbour project.

[Smallwood 312b = *ILS* 207]

As commemorated in this monumental inscription found near Ostia, Claudius created a new harbour roughly two miles to the north of Ostia (in the area of the modern airport at Fiumicino) to serve the needs of the capital. This involved extensive engineering works creating two curving moles and canals linking the new harbour basin to the Tiber, along with a lighthouse. The harbour was not a complete success, given the wreckage of 200 ships there in 62 (Tac. *Ann.*15.18.3), and was perhaps not completed until 64, when commemorative coins were issued under Nero (**K37**). Trajan constructed an artificial hexagonal basin there as a safer haven.

K17 Claudian freedman, procurator of Ostia

Of Claudius Optatus, freedman of the emperor, procurator of the port at Ostia.

[*ILS* 1533 = Smallwood 173]

This text is upon a circular bronze plaque, of uncertain purpose and origin, but it records the involvement of a member of the imperial household in the running of Claudius' new harbour to the north of Ostia.

K18 Collecting corn-dole

Tiberius Claudius Januarius, freedman of Augustus, curator, from the Minucian portico on day 14, from gate 42, and Avonia Tyche, his wife, Pituaniani, built the terraces (…) at their own expense.

[*ILS* 6071 = Smallwood 174]

This inscription was found at Rome. The corn-dole to the plebs of Rome was distributed from the portico Minucia. Not all members of the plebs were entitled to the corn-dole, and so membership of the *plebs frumentaria* could be considered worthy of commemoration, as here, which records the details of when and where Januarius received his monthly distribution of public corn.

K19 Full citizenship offered by Claudius for shipowners importing corn

Again, by an edict of Claudius, Latin freedmen attain full citizenship if they build a sea-going ship with a capacity of not less than ten thousand bushels of corn, and that ship, or any which replaces it, carries corn to Rome for six years.

[Gaius, *Institutes,* 1.32c]

For Latin freedmen see Gaius, *Institutes* 1.22–24, 28–29 = LACTOR 17, S34. Suetonius *Claudius* 19 reports this and other incentives for shipowners, which could have included **K20**.

K20 Increased penalties for wreckers

In the time of Claudius, a senatorial decree was enacted that if anyone, in a shipwreck, should remove nails of a ship, or one of them, he will be held liable for taking the whole ship. Furthermore it was provided by another decree of the senate that those by whose fraud or strategy shipwrecked persons were overcome by force, in order to prevent help being given to the ship, or to those in danger on board, would be subject to the penalties of the Cornelian Law on murder. And, moreover, that those who seized anything from the wretched fortunes of the shipwrecked person, or profited by some trick, should have to pay as much into the Treasury as could be recovered by a lawsuit under the Edict of the Praetor.

[Digest 47.9.3.8 = Ulpian, *Commentary on the Praetor's Edict* 56]

K21 Claudius and the Fucine Lake (AD 41–52)

[124] One of the most important achievements of Claudius, at least in my opinion, though abandoned by his hated successor, was tunnelling through a mountain to drain the Fucine Lake. This was, of course, a task of indescribable expense and of many years' duration even for a huge labour-force. This was because where the mountain was composed of earth, this had to be carried to the top on pulleys; while everywhere else it was a case of cutting through solid rock to form the drainage canal.

[Pliny, *Natural History* 36.124]

The Fucine Lake in Central Italy originally had an area of about 140 km². A 6.3 km-long canal built between 1862 and 1875, along the route of Roman works, drained the lake, the resulting plain being one of Italy's most fertile regions. This was the aim of Claudius' three mile outlet, which according to Suetonius took 30,000 men 11 years to dig (Suet. *Claud.* 20.2; Tac. *Ann.* 12.56), and reduced the area of the lake.

CLAUDIUS' ROADS IN ITALY: K22–K23

Claudius was responsible for the building or improvement of roads throughout Italy and also in Gaul, Spain and the Alps. See **M24**, and Levick, *Claudius* 167–177 for maps and analysis, suggesting practical responses to existing conditions, making use of British slaves, rather than a policy of innovation or that of an historian wanting to complete previous schemes.

K22 Via Claudia Nova, AD 47/48

Tiberius Claudius Caesar Augustus Germanicus, son of Drusus, *pontifex maximus*, in his 7th year of tribunician power, consul 4 times, hailed victorious commander 11 times, father of the fatherland, censor designate, saw to it that the via Claudia Nova was paved from Foruli to the confluence of the Atternus and Tirinus, over a distance of 47 miles, 192 paces.

[Smallwood 329 = *ILS* 209]

This is inscribed upon a boundary marker at Foruli (Sabinum). Claudius' road in modern Abruzzo (central Italy) linked Amiternum to the Via Claudia Valeria (see below).

K23 Via Claudia Valeria, AD 48/49, Teate Marrucinorum

Tiberius Claudius Caesar Augustus Germanicus, *pontifex maximus*, in his 8th year of tribunician power, hailed victorious commander 16 times, consul 4 times, father of the fatherland, censor, built the Via Claudia Valeria from Cerfennia to Ostia Aterni and also built 43 bridges.

[Smallwood 330 = *CIL* IX 5973]

This inscription from Teate (modern Chieti in Abruzzo, N. Italy) uses the digamma, one of the obsolete letters revived by Claudius, at the start of the words via and Valeria. This road extended the ancient via

Valeria from Cerfennia (Collarmele) to the mouth of the Aternus (modern Pescara), providing the shortest route from Rome to the Adriatic. Claudius' road was around 50 miles long, descending 300m overall and crossing the main ridge of the Appennines.

CLAUDIUS AND AQUEDUCTS: K24–K31

'How can we withhold our respect from a water system that, in the first century AD, supplied the city of Rome with substantially more water than was supplied in 1985 to New York City?' (Hodge, *Roman Aqueducts and Water Systems*). Claudius' aqueducts formed a major part of this system. His rejection of private building projects in favour of ones of large-scale public benefit is typified by his British triumphal arch being incorporated into arches of the *aqua Virgo* (**N25**). His works included restoration (**K25**) and two completely new aqueducts (**K26–29**).

K24 Aqueducts of Gaius and Claudius

[122] The very recent spending on the work begun by Gaius Caesar and completed by Claudius has surpassed previous aqueducts. Starting at the 40th milestone, the Curtian and Caerulean springs and the *Anio novus* have been made to flow into the city at a height sufficient to all seven of her hills, at a total cost of 350 million sesterces. [123] Careful consideration of the abundant supply of water to public buildings, baths, fish-ponds, water-features, houses, private parks, and suburban villas; the distant source of the water; the arches built; the mountains tunnelled through; the valleys bridged, will make anyone admit that there has been no more remarkable achievement in the whole world.

[Pliny, *Natural History* 36.122–3]

Pliny in discussing Rome's buildings (36.101–123) greatly approves of practical, public buildings, and roundly condemns luxurious private buildings. The culmination of his account is 'marvels unsurpassed for their genuine worth' (36.121), i.e. aqueducts: compare Frontinus, *Aqueducts* 16 = **K29**.

K25 Claudius restores *aqua Virgo*, AD 46

Tiberius Claudius Caesar Augustus Germanicus, son of Drusus, *pontifex maximus*, in his 5th year of tribunician power, hailed victorious commander 11 times, father of the fatherland, designated consul for the 4th time, renovated from the foundations and restored the arches of the *aqua Virgo* disturbed by Gaius Caesar.

[*ILS* 205 = Smallwood 308b: Rome, on *aqua Virgo*]

The *aqua Virgo* was built by Agrippa in 19 BC (Front., *Aq.* 10). Caligula disturbed it in starting work on an amphitheatre (Suet. *Cal.* 21; Dio 59.10.5). The inscription is still on an archway in the modern *Via del Nazareno* (Claridge, *Rome*², page 222). Another arch of the aqueduct formed Claudius' triumphal arch over the Britons, see **N25** and possibly **N22**.

K26 Aqueducts of Claudius

[13] After these aqueducts, Gaius Caesar who succeeded Tiberius began two others, since the seven aqueducts seemed insufficient for public amenities and private luxury. This was in the second year of his reign, when Marcus Aquila Iulianus and Publius Nonius Asprenas were consuls, the seven hundred and ninety-first year after the foundation of Rome [AD 38]. Claudius completed these works on a most lavish scale, and dedicated them on 1 August, when Sulla and Titianus were consuls, the eight hundred and third year after the foundation of Rome [AD 50]. One aqueduct, whose source was the Caerulean and Curtian springs, was called the *aqua Claudia*. The quality of this is second only to the *aqua Marcia*. The second, since two Anio

aqueducts had now begun to flow into the city, became known as the *Anio novus* (New Anio): the earlier Anio was now called the Old Anio.

[Frontinus, *On Aqueducts* 13]

Claudius' two new aqueducts almost doubled the supply of water to Rome, according to Frontinus' various methods of calculation (chapters 65–73). The aqueducts brought supplies to all of the fourteen regions of Rome (86). See also Tac. *Ann.* 11.13 (dating the work to AD 47); Suet. Claud. 20.1.

K27 Inscription on *aqua Claudia*, AD 52/53

Tiberius Claudius, son of Drusus, Caesar Augustus Germanicus, *pontifex maximus*, in his 12th year of tribunician power, consul for the 5th time, hailed victorious commander 27 times, father of the fatherland, saw to it that the *aqua Claudia* was brought into the city from the springs which are called Caeruleus and Curtius from the 45th milestone, and also the *Anio novus* from the 62nd milestone, at his own expense.

[*ILS* 218 = Smallwood 309: Rome, Porta Maggiore]

This inscription is repeated on both sides of the higher aqueduct channel at Rome's Praenestine Gate – modern Porta Maggiore (Vespasian and Titus added inscriptions on the lower level). The arches carried the *aqua Claudia* and *aqua Anio* in separate channels over two Roman roads and a series of other aqueducts at ground level. The 19m high structure is typical of Claudius' 'rusticated' style of exaggeratedly unpolished blocks of marble. See Claridge, *Rome*², 383–5 for description and drawing. The arches actually became a gateway when the city walls of Aurelian were built on either side, AD 271–5. The arches were not just for display. As Frontinus notes (*Aq.* 18) Claudius' aqueducts reached Rome at a height which allowed water supply to all of Rome, even the hillier areas.

K28 The *aqua Claudia*

[14] The *aqua Claudia* begins on the Via Sublacensis, on its thirty-eighth milestone, less than 300 paces to the left of a crossroads. It is supplied by two very plentiful and beautiful springs, the Caerulean which gets its name from its dark blue appearance, and the Curtian. The *aqua Claudia* is forty-six thousand, four hundred and six paces long. 36,230 in a channel underground, 10,176 above ground, including 3,076 paces on arches in several locations near its source, and near the city, from the seventh milestone, 609 paces on substructures and 6,491 on arches.

[Frontinus, *On Aqueducts* 14]

K29 The *Anio novus*

[15] The *Anio novus* takes its water from a river at the forty-second milestone of the Via Sublacensis in the area of Simbruvium. The *Anio novus* aqueduct is 58,700 paces long. 49,300 in a channel underground, 9,400 above ground, including 3,076 paces in several locations near its source on substructures or arches, and near the city, from the seventh milestone, 609 paces on substructures and 6,491 on arches. These are the highest arches, raised at certain points to 109 feet.

[16] How favourably all these indispensable water works compare with the pointless pyramids or the useless though famous works of the Greeks!

[Frontinus, *On Aqueducts* 15–6]

Frontinus goes on to explain that the details of lengths and structures of the aqueducts given in **K28–29** are important for him in his role as Aqueducts Commissioner.

K30 Private water as a gift from the emperor

[105] Anyone wishing to draw off water for private use must make a request and bring a letter to the Aqueducts Commissioner from the *princeps*. The Commissioner must quickly act upon this favour granted by Caesar and appoint in writing one of Caesar's freedmen as his deputy in this matter. Claudius seems to have been the first to engage people in this capacity after introducing the *Anio novus* and the *aqua Claudia*. The contents of the letter must also be known to the foremen, so that they cannot cover up incompetence or fraud by pleading ignorance.

[Frontinus, *On Aqueducts* 105]

The emperor might be expected to provide water for the public fountains of Rome, but a private supply of water remained a *beneficium* – or personal favour granted by the emperor.

K31 Maintenance of water supply

[116] Maintenance of the aqueducts is still to be discussed, but before I begin to do so, a word of explanation should be given about the workforces set up for this task. There are two, one answerable to the state, the other to the emperor. That answerable to the state was established first, as we have described, and was left by Agrippa to Augustus and transferred to the state by him. It has around 240 men. The emperor's workforce numbers 460: Claudius established it when he brought his aqueducts into the Rome.

[Frontinus, *On Aqueducts* 116]

K32 Frontinus' list of Aqueducts Commisioners (*curatores aquarum*)

Year	Commissioner	Consulship
11 BC	(M. Valerius) Messala (Corvinus)	31 BC
AD 13	C. Ateius Capito †	AD 5
AD 23	L. Tarius Rufus †	16 BC
AD 24	M. Cocceius Nerva †	AD 21?
AD 34	C. Octavius Laenas †	AD 33
AD 38	M. Porcius Cato †	AD 36
AD 38	A. Didius Gallus •	AD 39
AD 49	Cn. Domitius Afer †	AD 39
AD 60	L. (Calpurnius) Piso •	AD 57
AD 63	P. Petronius Turpilius •	AD 61
AD 64	P. Marius	AD 62
AD 66	C. Fonteius Agrippa •	AD 58
AD 68	Q. Vibius Crispus •	AD 61?, 74, 83
AD 71	M. Pompeius Silvanus •	AD 45
AD 73	L. Tampius Flavianus •	Under Claudius
AD 74	M'. Acilius Aviola	AD 54
AD 97	S. Julius Frontinus	AD 73?

† = likely or certain to have died in office: • = known not to have died in office
Consular dates in **bold** indicate a consul *ordinarius*: others a suffect consul.

The table on the previous page represents the information given by Frontinus, 102. Due to the standard use of dating by giving the names of the consuls of the year, Frontinus' text is little more than a list of names, and it is more than likely that some names have been omitted or mistaken in the transmission of the text over the centuries. This may explain why Didius Gallus appears, uniquely, to have been Commissioner before holding the consulship.

BUILDING REGULATIONS: K33–K34

A bronze tablet containing two related senatorial decrees from the reigns of Claudius and Nero was found at Herculaneum. It is unclear why they had been inscribed there, but we might suppose that local circumstances had made the issue of property speculation a source of some anxiety there. The decrees give some insight into imperial ideology, with the expectation that the emperor should take the lead in promoting building-projects not just in Rome, but in the towns of Italy as well.

K33 Senatorial decree on building, Herculaneum, 22 September, AD 47

A decree of the senate on 22 September in the consulship of Gnaeus Hosidius Geta and Lucius Vagellius.

"Since the forethought of our excellent emperor has made provision for the buildings of our city and the whole of Italy for their permanence, which he himself aided not only by his most august instruction but also by his own example; and since it was appropriate to the happiness of the coming age to protect public and private buildings in due measure; and since everyone ought to refrain from the most savage kind of business and ought not to be bringing about the scene that is most incompatible with peace through the ruins of houses and villas; the senate decrees:

If anyone for the sake of business buys a building so that he may by demolishing it gain more than the price he paid for it, then twice the sum at which he bought the property is paid into the treasury, and the matter shall nonetheless be referred to the senate. And since equally people ought not to sell rather than buy through bad example, that sellers should also be compelled, who wittingly and with bad intent sell contrary to this will of the senate, it is decreed that such sales shall be invalid. The senate, however, affirms that nothing is decreed for owners who, intending to remain in possession of their own properties, change some parts of them, provided that this is not done for the sake of business."

Approved. 383 senators were present.

K34 Senatorial decree on building, Herculaneum, 2 March, AD 56

A decree of the senate on 2 March in the consulship of Quintus Volusius and Publius Cornelius:

"Seeing as Quintus Volusius and Publius Cornelius spoke on the request of the relatives of Alliatoria Celsilla, with regard to what it might please the senate to be done with regard to this matter, concerning this matter they have decided as follows:

Since the decree of the senate which was passed on 22 September during the consulship of Hosidius Geta and Lucius Vagellius, most distinguished senators, on the motion of Divus Claudius forbade anyone from demolishing a house or a villa so as to gain more for himself, and forbade anyone for the sake of business from buying or selling any property, and established a penalty for any buyer who acted contrary to this decree of the senate, namely that anyone who bought a property should be compelled to pay twice the price at which he had bought it to the treasury, and that the sale of the person who sold it should be invalid, but concerning those who intending to remain in possession of their own properties, changed some parts of them, provided that they did not change them for the sake of business, nothing new was introduced;

And since the relatives of Alliatoria Celsilla, wife of the most honourable Atilius Lupercus, explained to this body that her father, Alliatorius Celsus, had bought lands with buildings in the region of Mutina which is called Macer's Fields, where in earlier times a market had regularly been held, but which now for some years had ceased to be held, and these buildings were becoming dilapidated because they were old and would not be of any use if repaired because nobody lived in them nor would anyone wish to go and live in buildings that were solitary and collapsing:

That Celsilla should not be liable to any punishment, fine or penalty if these buildings, which were discussed in this body, should be either demolished, or on this condition if someone sells them whether on their own or with the lands) that the buyer should be permitted to destroy or remove them without punishment. In future, however, everyone else should be advised to refrain from such a disgraceful kind of business, especially in this age in which it is more fitting that new buildings should be erected and all of them embellished by which the happiness of the world might shine forth, rather than that any part of Italy should be made ugly by the ruins of buildings, and that the [irresponsibility] of earlier times [which had its effect on everything] should still be continued so that it could be said that by old age [...]"

Approved. Present in the senate [were...]

[Smallwood 365 = *ILS* 6043]

NERO: K35–45

Tacitus expresses clear admiration for Nero's rebuilding of Rome after the Great Fire of AD 64, commenting on 'the great beauty of the city as it was rebuilt'(*Annals* 15.41.1); 'practical measures which also improved the appearance of the new city' (15.43.5), and reports of actions taken by Nero to improve the situation (15.39.2, 15.43.2) . These authorial comments, however, are typically surrounded by rumours of Nero's responsibility (15.38.1, 15.44.2), reported grumbling (15.41.1, 15.43.5), and criticism of the luxury of the golden house (15.421–2). Other literary sources are almost entirely critical (Suet. *Nero* 31–32, 39.2; Pliny **K38**, **K42**; Martial **K45**), reflecting Vespasian's clever propaganda of turning Nero's private lake into the Flavian Amphitheatre (Colosseum – **K45**).

K35 Temple of Claudius: archaeological evidence

Begun by Agrippina, but neglected by Nero and completed by Vespasian (Suet. *Vesp.* 9) the remains of its massive podium (175 x 205m) built out from the Caelian Hill survive (Claridge, *Rome*[2] 349–50) Nero converted part of the podium into a monumental fountain within the grounds of his Golden House (on modern Via Claudia, near the Flavian Amphitheatre, see Claridge, *Rome*[2] 343–4). Nothing survives of the temple itself or its surrounding porticoes (see Martial, **K45** below).

K36 Nero's market on brass *dupondius* of Nero, struck at Rome, *c.* AD 63

Obv: Head of Nero with radiate crown, left

NERO CLAVD CAESAR AVG GERM P M TR P IMP P P (Nero Claudius Caesar Augustus Germanicus, *pontifex maximus,* with tribunician power, hailed as victorious commander, father of the fatherland)

Rev: Frontal view of *macellum magnum*, a two-storey building. Central section is domed, approached by steps and contains a statue. Wings on either side are two-storied porticoies, decorated and deliberately asymmetrical.

MAC AVG S C (Augustan Market-place, by decree of the senate)

[*BMC* Nero 196; *RIC* Nero 110]

Dio 62.18.3 mentions the dedication of a *macellum* in AD 59 in the context of celebrations of Nero surviving Agrippina's 'assassination attempt' (though Tacitus' account does not (*Ann.* 14.12–15)). Modern conservation work on the wonderful fifth-century church, San Stefano Rotondo, has shown that it is not a conversion of Nero's *macellum* as was previously thought.

K37 Harbour of Ostia on brass *sestertius* of Nero *c.* AD 64 (Rome)

Obv. Laureate head of Nero, right

NERO CLAVD CAESAR AVG GER P M TR P IMP P P (Nero Claudius Caesar, Augustus, Germanicus, *pontifex maximus*, with tribunician power, victorious commander, father of the fatherland).

Rev. Bird's-eye view of harbour of Ostia showing a crescent-shaped pier, sceptred statue on a column, a variety of ships and a reclining Neptune. At one end of the pier is a very small detail showing a sacrifice.

AVGVSTI POR OST, S C (The imperial port of Ostia, by decree of the senate)

[*RIC* Nero 178; *BMC* Nero 131]

The new harbour at Ostia was started by Claudius around AD 42 and completed by AD 47 (see **K16**). It is probable that this coin commemorates further refurbishments made in Nero's reign. Several series of *sestertii* of Ostia's harbour were minted at Rome and Lugdunum (*RIC* 178–183, 440–1, 513–4, 586–9).

K38 Nero's fire of AD 64

These hackberry trees / nettle trees (*Celtis australis*) had an abundant canopy of densely spreading branches. In my youth, Caecina Largus one of the leading figures in Rome, used to point them out in his house. They lasted (we have already mentioned how very long trees can live) until the fires of the emperor Nero, green and flourishing through careful husbandry, until that emperor hastened the death even of trees.

[Pliny, *Natural History* 17.5]

Pliny, talking about the longevity of trees had recounted how greatly Lucius Licinius Crassus (censor 92 BC) had valued these trees in his house. For Caecina Largus see **B42**. Pliny here blames Nero for the great fire of AD 64. Tacitus' account insinuates blame, while in reality giving plenty of evidence that Nero was not responsible (*Annals* 15.39.1).

K39 Full citizenship offered by Nero for housebuilding in Rome

Moreover, it was established by Nero that if a Latin freedman worth 200,000 sesterces or more builds a house in Rome on which he spends more than half what he is worth, he is to attain full citizenship.

[Gaius, *Institutes,* 1.32c]

For Latin freedmen see Gaius, *Institutes* 1.22–24, 28–29 = LACTOR 17, S34. This law cannot be dated, but would make sense after the Great Fire.

K40 Temple of Vesta on *aureus* of Nero, *c.* AD 65/6

Obv: Nero, bearded with laurel wreath, right
NERO CAESAR AVGVSTVS

Rev: Round, domed, temple on steps, with draped figure of Vesta, seated, facing the entrance, holding *patera* (libation bowl) and long sceptre
VESTA

[*BMC* Nero 103; *RIC* Nero 61]

Romans believed this to be one of the oldest and most important temples in Rome, honouring the goddess of hearth and home, and housing the sacred flame, which the Vestal Virgins were charged with keeping alive, on pain of death. The temple is known to have burnt down several times in the republic. The Augustan temple (*RIC* Tiberius 74, *BMC* Tiberius 142) was burnt in the Great Fire of AD 64 (Tac. *Ann.* 15.41.1), prompting Nero's rebuilding.

K41 Nero's Golden House: archaeological evidence

Part of Nero's Golden House is buried on the Esquiline Hill. This wing of the palace measures 220m and contains 142 rooms with immensely high ceilings of 10–11m. Even so, it is clear from the symmetrical structure that only just over half the original length has been preserved and that the wing would have been almost 400m in length and with perhaps 250 rooms. (The famous façade of Buckingham Palace opposite The Mall is about 100m in length.) The entire wing seems to have been designed for banquets, with multiple suites of dining-rooms in many shapes and sizes. These main rooms would have been covered in marble and adorned with statuary. The wall paintings (see **R29**) which so impressed Renaissance artists and modern visitors decorated mere service corridors. Finally, what really seems to have impressed or offended Romans were the vast, private landscape gardens of the palace, containing lakes, groves and parklands (Suet. *Nero* 31; Tac. *Ann.* 15.42.1; **K42**; **K45**). For the considerable remains of the Golden House, see Claridge, *Rome*[2] 301–5 and 326–8 and Griffin, *Nero* 133–142).

K42 Imperial palaces

(Pliny has discussed remarkable public and private buildings)

But two houses have dwarfed all of these. We have twice seen the whole city encircled by the palaces of the *principes* Gaius and Nero, the latter's being nothing less than a house of gold.

[Pliny, *Natural History* 36.111]

For Gaius' palace, see L13. Nero had already built a *domus transitoria* ('a linking house') to join the Palatine palace to the imperial Gardens of Maecenas on the Esquiline Hill (Tac. *Ann.* 15.39.1, Suet. *Nero* 31.1).

K43 Statues in Nero's Golden House

Out of all these works which I have mentioned, the most famous have now been dedicated in Rome by the *princeps* Vespasian in his Temple of Peace and other buildings. Nero had stolen them by force and arranged them in the lounges of his Golden House.

[Pliny, *Natural History* 34.84]

Golden House: **K41**. Pliny on working gold (*NH* 33.61f) notes that an ounce of gold can be worked into over 750 leaves four inches square (giving a thickness of 0.00034mm. A gold-beater today can produce a book of 256 gold leaves of about 3 inches square (80mm) weighing only 1/3 gramme). J. F. Healy, *Pliny the Elder on Science and Technology,* Oxford 1999, 288–9.

K44 The Colossus of Nero

But for sheer size, all statues of this sort have been surpassed in our lifetime by Zenodorus' *Mercury.* He produced this over ten years in the settlement of Averni in Gaul and was paid 40 million sesterces. Once he had given proof of his skill there, he was summoned to Rome by Nero where he made the colossus, over 100 feet tall, intended as a statue of the emperor, but now dedicated to the Sun, after condemnation of that *princeps'* crimes. In his studio we used to look with wonder not only at the remarkable clay model, but also at the frame of withes which formed the first stage of the work. That statue shows that the art of casting bronze has now died out, since Nero would have been prepared to meet the expense of silver or gold, though Zenodorus was second to none of the old masters in casting and engraving bronze.'

[Pliny, *Natural History* 34.45–6]

The exact reading of the number (given in Roman feet) in the texts is not certain. Possible figures are 90, 106½, 119, 119½ Roman feet (about 3% shorter than the imperial measurement). Suetonius gives the height as 120 feet. (Suet. *Nero* 31.1). Trajan's column is 128 Roman feet, and was surmounted by a 16 foot statue of Trajan. Casting a statue in metal involves making an exact model, covering it with a layer of wax and another layer of clay. The wax was melted and drained away. Molten metal was poured into the gap and allowed to set. The outer layer of clay could then be broken off leaving the metal statue.

Pliny shows Nero as exemplifying extravagance in the size of the statue and his willingness to pay for it to be cast in silver or gold. This contrasts with the ideal portraits as far as Pliny is concerned, the *imagines* – wax masks, taken from the features of a dead ancestor and proudly preserved by his family – which form the subject of *NH* 35. See Carey, *Pliny's Catalogue of Culture,* Oxford 2003, 156–165.

Martial (1.70.7 = **L32**) described the statue as 'radiate' (i.e. wearing a crown decorated with rays of sun – an attribute of the gods). It is not clear whether the statue was 'radiate' originally or as a result of its rededication to the Sun-God by Vespasian in 75 (Suet. *Vesp.* 18; Dio 66.15.1). See Carey, above.

K45 What the Flavian Amphitheatre replaced

Here where Colossus, heaven's neighbour, more closely sees the stars,
    And lofty scaffolding the central highway bars,
The hated palace of a savage king once gleamed,
    The entire city his one single dwelling seemed.
Where upward soars the Amphitheatre's great, prodigious mass,
    An emperor's ornamental lakes we used to pass;
Where now we marvel, when on the Baths' instant blessings we have gazed,
    The hovels of hapless poverty Nero's proud acres razed.

Where now the portico of Claudius spreads its generous shade,
    A palace's final footprints were once laid.
Now, Rome is restored to Romans. By Great Caesar's patronage we see
    A tyrant's pleasure-domes belong to you and me.

[Martial, *On the Shows,* 2]

Colossus, see **K44**. The Baths of Titus probably remodelled Nero's private baths for public use. Claudius' portico presumably stood on the vast podium built for his temple, see **K35** above.

SECTION L
RELIGION AND IMPERIAL CULT

Oh dear, I think I'm becoming a god!
[Vespasian's dying words – Suet. *Vesp.* 23.4]

Introduction: Material in this section is arranged chronologically, with notes on each emperor, but with some of the most important evidence, from the Sebasteion at Aphrodisias (modern Turkey), built *c.* AD 20 – 60 being placed at the end (**L36**). Latin uses the word *divus*, or its feminine form, *diva* to refer to those deified, rather than the related word for a god/goddess, *deus/dea.* Greek however uses the same word, θεός (feminine = θέα) for deified mortals and Olympians gods. Throughout the volume, the forms 'Divus Augustus' or 'Diva Augusta' are used for Latin documents, while 'God Augustus' renders the Greek 'θεός Σεβαστός'.

AUGUSTUS: L1–L3

In his (lost) biography, Augustus expressed his delight at the appearance of the comet at his games in honour of his adoptive father being taken by the common people as a sign of Julius Caesar's deification (Pliny, NH 2.94 = LACTOR 17, H3). Thereafter his official name included *Divi filius* – 'Son of Divus', treating *divus* (= deity, god) as if it were Julius Caesar's first name (e.g **K2**).

The poets referred to him as a present and future god, even from his time as triumvir (e.g. Virgil, *Ecl.* 1.6; Horace, *Odes* 1.2.41–52; Ovid, *Fasti* 4.949–954, (= LACTOR 17, G1, G21, H31). Prayers and sacrifices were made at altars to his divinity at Rome and in Spain and Gaul (LACTOR 17, C10, L17–18, M19–21). Abstract divinities were given an Augustan identity: the famous *Ara Pacis Augustae* – Altar of Augustan Peace (see **A38p**); The Temple of Concordia Augusta – Augustan Concord (**A39c**). Augustus' *genius* (roughly 'divine spirit') was worshipped at Rome (LACTOR 17, L12, L13). The many parts of the empire used to worshipping a living ruler, do so for Augustus, and there is even evidence for direct worship of Augustus in Italy in his lifetime (temples at Fanum and Puteoli – LACTOR 17, L14, L15). The senate officially decreed divine cult for Augustus just under a month after his death (**L1**). Building of his temple in Rome started soon after this but was only finally completed by Gaius (see **K6–K7**, with further references). In the meantime a statue to Divus Augustus was dedicated near the Theatre of Marcellus (**K3–K4**).

L1 Augustus decreed heavenly honours

17 September: Public holiday by decree of the senate because on this day heavenly honours were decreed to Divus Augustus by the senate in the consulships of Pompeius and Appuleius.

[Calendars at Amiternum and Rome, Oppian Hill = EJ page 52]

Amiternum: 60 miles north-east of Rome. Deification: Tac. *Ann.* 1.10.8, Dio 56.46.2, **C1** (124.3).

L2 Priest-list from the temple of Rome and Augustus, Ancyra

The [Ga]latians who were priests of the god Augustus and of the goddess Roma.
[When … was governor, …], son of King Brigatos, gave a public banquet, provided olive oil for four months, presented spectacles, including thirty pairs of gladiators and a hunt of bulls and wild animals. Rufus gave a public banquet and spectacles and a hunt.

When Metilius was governor, Pylaimenes, son of King Amyntas, twice gave a public banquet, twice presented spectacles, gave a gymnastic competition, a chariot race and a horse race, and also a bull-fight and animal-hunt. He provided the city with oil, he presented (the city with) the places where the Sebasteion is located and where the festival and horse racing take place. Albiorix, (son) of Ateporix, gave a public banquet and set up statues of Caesar and Julia Augusta. Amyntas, (son) of Gaizatodiastos, twice gave a public banquet, sacrificed 100 oxen, presented spectacles, gave a distribution of grain of 33 kilograms per capita. [When …, son] of Diognetos was [priest], Albiorix, (son) of Ateporix, for a second time gave a public banquet.

When Fronto was governor. Metrodorus, (son) of Menemachos, natural son of [Do]rylaos, gave a public banquet, provided [olive oil] for four months. Mousanos, (son) of Artiknos, gave a public banquet. […] (son) of Seleukos, gave a public banquet and provided olive oil for four months. Pylaimenes, son of King Amyntas, gave a public banquet to the three tribes and [sacrificed] 10 oxen in Ancyra, presented shows and a parade, and also a bull-fight and bull-fighters and 50 pairs of gladiators. He provided the three tribes with olive oil for the whole year and gave an animal-hunt.

When Silvanus [was governor]. [Ga(?)]llios gave a public banquet in Pessinus, 25 pairs of gladiators (in Ancyra) and 10 (pairs) in Pessinus. He provided two tribes with oil for the whole year and set up a statue in Pessinus. [Se]leukos, (son) of Philodamos, twice gave public banquets to the two cities, provided two tribes with oil for the whole year, and presented shows. Julius Pontikos gave a public banquet, sacrificed 100 oxen, and provided oil for the whole year. Aristokles, (son) of Al[biorix,] gave [a public banquet,] and provided oil for the whole year.

[Greek: Sherk no.38 = OGIS 533; EJ 109]

The temple of Rome and Augustus (possibly consecrated *c*.5 BC) at Ancyra, the provincial capital of Galatia, was the headquarters for the provincial cult administered by the council (*koinon*) of the Galatians. This inscription on the left wall of the temple records the annually appointed priests of the cult and their benefactions. It seems likely that the opening lines of the inscription were added to the temple in AD 14, but record the priests in post from 5/4 BC. The text of the *Res Gestae divi Augusti* was subsequently added to its walls in both a Latin and Greek version in around AD 19 (see A.E. Cooley, *RGDA Commentary,* 7–13). This juxtaposition invites comparison of the local benefactors with Augustus. The benefactions given by the priests combine characteristics of the mixed society in Galatia, with elements that are Celtic (public banquet), Greek (distribution of olive-oil, gymnastics), and Roman (gladiatorial combat). In particular, Amyntas' gift of a grain-distribution is unusual, and is reminiscent of Augustus' handouts in the city of Rome: this comparison is implicit also in the use of a Latin word to describe the measures of grain distributed. The names of the priests also reflect the cultural mix in Galatia, with Celtic names appearing alongside Hellenistic, Seleucid, and Roman names. The earlier priests in the list include several members of the local élite descended from the last kings of Galatia, before it was annexed as a province under Augustus in the mid-20s BC, and show how the existing élite expressed its new allegiance to Rome via this cult of Rome and Augustus.

L3 Decree from Forum Clodii (Italy), AD 18

In the consulship of Tiberius Caesar for the third time and Germanicus Caesar for the second time, when Gnaeus Acceius Rufus Lutatius, son of Gnaeus, of the Arnensis tribe, and Titus Petillius, son of Publius, of the Quirina tribe, were chief magistrates, the following were decreed:

a shrine and these statues, and a sacrificial victim for the dedication;

the two sacrificial victims which have been in perpetuity usually sacrificed at the altar which is dedicated to the Augustan divinity to commemorate the birthday of Augustus on 24 September, should be sacrificed on 23 and 24 September;

likewise, on the birthday of Tiberius Caesar in perpetuity, the town councillors about to take up office and people should hold a banquet; this expense Quintus Caescellius Labeo promises to fund in perpetuity: thanks should be given for his generosity;

on his birthday each year a calf should be sacrificed;

and on the birthdays of Augustus and Tiberius Caesar, before the town councillors go to eat, their spirits should be invited with incense and wine to feast at the altar of the Augustan divinity.

We have supervised the construction of the altar to the Augustan divinity at our own expense; we have supervised shows on six days from the 13 August at our own expense. On the birthday of Augusta we have given honeyed wine and pastries to the women of the district at the shrine of the Good Goddess at our own expense; likewise, at the dedication of the statues of the Caesars and of Augusta, we have given honeyed wine and pastries at our own expense to the town councillors and people, and we have solemnly declared that we will give these in perpetuity on the anniversary of this dedication. In order to make that day more crowded each year, we will observe 10 March, the day upon which Tiberius Caesar was so happily made *pontifex maximus*.

[*CIL* XI 3303 = *ILS* 154 = EJ 101 = LACTOR 8 no.4]

This decree, inscribed upon a small marble plaque, gives an unusually detailed picture of rituals linked to a shrine associated with the imperial family. It shows how the town of Forum Clodii in Etruria added to existing honours for Augustus in AD 18, to include Tiberius and Julia Augusta. The rites are probably similar to those paid by most Roman families at the tombs of their family members on notable anniversaries. The singling out of women who lived in a rural district at a sanctuary of the Good Goddess probably reflects long-standing links of the Claudii with the town and with this cult. The town's name suggests that it was founded by a Clodius, whilst Julia Augusta promoted the cult of the Good Goddess, restoring her temple on the Aventine at Rome. She may have been partly motivated by the key-role played by a Claudia in bringing the goddess to Rome, as well as by the appropriateness of sponsoring this cult reserved for female devotees. Augustus' birthday was celebrated over a two-day period, 23–24 September according to entries in the inscribed calendars (and **A45b**).

TIBERIUS: L4–L12

Tiberius, it is very clear, was personally disinclined to see any expansion of emperor-worship. Suetonius, *Tiberius* 26.1 states quite categorically that he refused decrees allowing temples and priests for himself; and only allowed statues and portrait-bust of himself to be set up with explicit permission; and then only as part of the decoration of the temple, not among statues of the gods. In the context of Tiberius refusing permission in AD 25 for Further Spain to build a shrine to Tiberius and Augusta, Tacitus gives Tiberius a speech (*Annals* 4.37–8) in which he apologises for allowing the communities of Asia Minor to start a temple to Tiberius, Augusta, and the Senate in AD 23 (Tacitus, *Annals* 4.15.3 (and 4.55–56 – Smyrna chosen as the site)), and insists that he is mortal and content with mortal honours. Tacitus goes on to assert that after this speech, Tiberius continued to reject worship, even in private conversations. This can be shown in Tiberius' own letter to the people of Gytheion (**L4b** below). Therefore religious honours continue to take the established forms of vows for the *princeps* (**L5**), worship of his divine spirit (**L6**).

In the Greek East, however, either following the precedent set by Augustus (itself modelled on that set by Hellenistic Kings), or because several cities in the Greek East were technically free cities, Tiberius allowed himself to be worshipped as a god in his lifetime (**L7**–**L9**).

L4 Emperor-worship at Gytheion (Laconia), AD 15

... let him (i.e. the market clerk) set up ...[on the first base a statue of god Augustus Caesar] the father, and on the second from the right of Julia Augusta, and on the third of *imperator* Tiberius Caesar Augustus, the city providing the statues for him. [5] And let a table also be set out by him in the middle of the theatre and let an incense-burner be placed there, and let all the councillors and magistrates make sacrifices before the performances commence, on behalf of the safety of the leaders. And let him observe the first day in honour of god Caesar Augustus, son of a god, Saviour and Deliverer; the second day in honour of Imperator Tiberius Caesar Augustus and father of the fatherland; and the third day of Julia Augusta, [10] the Fortune of our nation and city; and the fourth day of Germanicus Caesar, of Victory; and the fifth day as of Drusus Caesar, of Aphrodite; and the sixth day as of Titus Quinctius Flamininus; and let him see to the good order of the competitors.

[The next five lines, omitted here, detail punishments for misappropriation of the funds]

After the completion of the days of the gods and the leaders, let the market clerk introduce two further days for performances of the thymelic contests, one to the memory of Gaius Julius Eurykles, [20] who has been benefactor of our nation and city in many ways, and a second for the honour of Gaius Julius Laco, who is protector of our nation and our city's security and safety. Let him observe the contests of the goddess on whatever days he can; and whenever he leaves office, let the city hand over to the one who happens to be the next market clerk, by public document, all the sacrificial victims for the contests, and let the city obtain a hand-written receipt from the one who receives them. When the market clerk [25] celebrates the thymelic games, he shall conduct a procession from the temple of Asklepios and Health, including in it all the ephebes and young men and other citizens wearing garlands of bay leaves, and in white clothing. They shall be accompanied in the procession by the sacred maidens and the women in their sacred clothing. And when the procession comes to the Caesareion (temple of Caesar), the ephors shall sacrifice a bull on behalf of the safety of our rulers and gods and the eternal continuance of their rule, and, [30] after their sacrifice, they shall constrain the common messes and the collective magistracies to sacrifice in the agora. And if they do not conduct the procession or do not sacrifice or after sacrificing do not constrain the common messes and collective magistracies to sacrifice in the agora, they shall pay to the gods 2,000 sacred drachmas. Permission shall be given to any citizen of Gytheion who wishes to accuse them.

While Chairon is strategos and priest of god Augustus Caesar, the ephors who are colleagues of Terentius Biades shall deliver three painted images of the god [35] Augustus and Julia Augusta and Tiberius Caesar Augustus, and for the theatre (they shall deliver) the platform for the chorus and four doors for stage performances and footstools for the musicians. And they shall erect a stele of stone with an inscription on it of this sacred law, and they shall deposit in the public archives a copy of the sacred law, in order that, reposing in a public place and in the open air for everyone to see, this law may continuously display the gratitude of the People of Gytheion toward their rulers for all men (to see). [40] And if they do not inscribe this law or do not erect the stele in front of the temple or do not write up [a copy ---]

L4b Tiberius' reply

[Letter of Tiber]ius

[Tiberius Caesar] Augustus, son of [the god] Augustus, *pontifex maximus*, in his [16th] year of tribunician power, to the superintendents and city of Gytheion, greeting. Decimus Turranius Nicanor, the envoy sent by you to me and my mother, gave me your letter to which were appended the measures passed by you in veneration of my father and in our honour. I commend you for this and accept that it is fitting for all men in general and for your city in particular to reserve special honours befitting the gods in keeping with the greatness of the services of my father to the whole world; but I myself am satisfied with more moderate honours suitable for men. My mother, however, will reply to you when she hears your decision about honours for her.

[Greek: LACTOR 8 no.3: EJ 102a/b = *SEG* 11.922–23 = Sherk 31–32]

These texts (March/June AD 15) were inscribed in Greek upon a stone stele at Gytheion in Laconia (south-east Peloponnese), a harbour-town associated with Sparta. The first document contains a record of the regulations for an eight-day civic festival celebrating members of the imperial family alongside other benefactors. The term thymelic contests refers to musical performances with dancing and declamation. The festival includes a procession from the temple of Asklepios and Hygeia (deities associated with health) to the Caesareion, where a bull – the animal typically used in emperor-worship – is sacrificed. It is worth emphasising, however, that the sacrifice is not actually to the emperor, but for his welfare. The choice of this temple as a starting-point reflects the people's hopes for health and a long rule by Tiberius. Again, we see a certain degree of confusion over imperial titulature, since Gytheion here wrongly gives Tiberius the title 'father of the fatherland', which he never actually assumed (compare **L7**). Titus Quinctius Flamininus (consul 198 BC) was a Roman general famous for having liberated Achaia from Philip V of Macedon (see **M15**), and was celebrated throughout the province. Furthermore, he also freed Gytheion from the rule of Spartan King Nabis, in thanks for which Gytheion set up a festival in his honour. Gaius Julius Eurykles and Gaius Julius Laco were members of a prominent family in Sparta itself. Julius Eurykles had been given Roman citizenship and control of Sparta by Augustus, having helped him at Actium, but had later been disgraced and banished. After his death, his memory was honoured once again and cult established in his honour. He is honoured here as benefactor of the city of Gytheion and of the League of Free Laconians (a league of Laconian towns excluding Sparta). Julius Laco was his son, who eventually inherited his father's power in Sparta. Although the beginning and end of this sacred law are both damaged, we still have a remarkably detailed record of Gytheion's response to the accession of Tiberius a few months earlier. Given that the family of Claudii to which Tiberius belonged were hereditary patrons of Sparta, which had sheltered Livia and infant Tiberius during the upheavals of the civil wars, the town clearly considered this a good opportunity to strengthen these ties further. By inscribing the sacred law and setting up a system of penalties for non-compliance with it, Gytheion tries to ensure the continuation of the cult in future years.

The second document is a letter from Tiberius to the town, in response to Gytheion's decree communicated to him by an ambassador. In it he declines for himself any honours associated with the gods, and makes a distinction between the honours appropriate for himself and Augustus. His sentiments here closely match a speech given to him by Tacitus in declining cult in Spain (*Annals* 4.38). He leaves his mother Julia Augusta to reply to the town for herself.

L5 Fulfilment of a vow for Tiberius' safety, Roman Forum

For the safety of Tiberius Caesar Augustus, *pontifex maximus*, [best] and most just *princeps*, in accordance with a vow which he had undertaken. Gaius Fulvius [...]us proconsul, [praetor], prefect for the distribution of grain by decree of the senate, propraetorian legate [...], propraetorian quaestor, military tribune of legion IX Hispana. To Concord. 5 pounds of gold, 23 pounds of silver.

[*ILS* 3783 = *CIL* VI 30856 = EJ 215]

This inscribed marble base records the fulfilment of a vow by a leading senator. The choice of context is deliberate, since Tiberius had restored the Temple of Concord with the spoils of war from Germany, dedicating it on 16 January AD 10 (see LACTOR 17, K40–2).

L6 Worship of Tiberius' *genius* at Rome, AD 27

To the *genius* of Tiberius Caesar Augustus, son of Divus Augustus. Gaius Fulvius Chryses, president of the lesser Amentine district, gave (this) as a gift on 28 May, in the consulship of Lucius Calpurnius Piso and Marcus Crassus Frugi.

[*ILS* 6080 = *CIL* VI 251 = EJ 133]

This dedication is inscribed twice, on both sides of the stone.

L7 Emperor-worship on Cyprus, AD 29

To Tiberius Caesar Augustus, god, son of god Augustus, hailed victorious commander, *pontifex maximus*, in his 31st year of tribunician power, when Lucius Axius Naso was proconsul and Marcus Etrilius Lupercus was legate and Gaius Flavius Figulus was quaestor, Adrastus Philocaesar, son of Adrastus, the hereditary priest of the temple and statue of Tiberius Caesar Augustus, set up by him in the gymnasium at his own expense, patriotic, model of all virtue, free, voluntary gymnasiarch and priest of the gods in the gymnasium, set up the temple and the statue for his own god at his own expense, when the ephebarch was Dionysius, son of Dionysius, also the son of Apollodotus Philocaesar. Adrastus Philocaesar, son of Adrastus, dedicated (this), with his son, Adrastus Philocaesar, joining in the dedication, who is himself the free and voluntary gymnasiarch of the boys, on the birthday of Tiberius. Year 16, Apogonicus 24.

[Greek: *OGIS* 583 = LACTOR 8 no.5 = EJ 134]

This inscription (November 16, AD 29) from Lapethus, Cyprus, shows the eagerness of a local benefactor, Adrastus Philocaesar ('emperor-loving') to set up cult for Tiberius. He appears to have paid for and established the cult in the gymnasium, and to have taken upon himself the role of priest of the new cult, and to have associated his son in the dedication too. The cult of Tiberius appears added to that of the traditional gods in the gymnasium, Mercury and Hercules. Year 16 refers to Tiberius' regnal year, whilst Apogonicus corresponds to a month in the local calendar. Tiberius' birthday fell on 16 November (**A35b**).

L8 Tiberius honoured at Myra (Lycia)

Tiberius Caesar, god Augustus, son of Augustan gods, imperator of land and sea, the benefactor and saviour of the whole world, the people of Myra.

[Greek: *IGRRP* III 721 = EJ 88]

L9 Julia Augusta (Livia) honoured at Myra (Lycia)

Julia, goddess Augusta, wife of god Augustus Caesar, mother of Tiberius god Augustus Caesar, the people of Myra.

[Greek: *IGRRP* III 720]

The people of Myra had earlier honoured Augustus in similar terms (EJ 72).

L10 Julia Augusta the new Demeter at Lampsacus (Asia Minor)

The council of elders honours Julia Augusta Hestia, new Demeter. The cost of the statue, its base and its erection is borne, at his own expense, out of piety towards the crowns, by the priest of the Augusti and crown-wearer of their whole house, the treasurer of the people for the second time, Dionysius, son of Apollonotimos.

[Greek: *IGRRP* IV 180 = EJ 129]

Julia Augusta is here associated with Hestia (Vesta) and Demeter (Ceres).

L11 Ceres Julia Augusta, Malta

To Ceres Julia Augusta, wife of Divus Augustus, mother of Tiberius Caesar Augustus. Lutatia, daughter of Gaius, priestess of Augusta <in perpetuity>, wife of Marcus Livius Optatus, son of Marcus, of the Quirina voting-tribe, *flamen* on Gaulus, to Julia, wife of Augustus, <in perpetuity>, together with her five children consecrated (this) at her own expense.

[*ILS* 121 = *CIL* X 7501 = EJ 126]

This short marble inscription shows the cult of Ceres Julia Augusta on the island of Gaulus (modern Gozo), part of the Maltese archipelago. The words within < > have been inscribed on top of an erasure, and have to be emended to make sense in both instances. Furthermore, the abbreviated Latin of the final clause could mean 'together with her husband and children' or 'together with her five children'.

L12 Dedication to Tiberius, Nasium (Gallia Belgica)

To Tiberius Caesar Augustus, son [of Augustus], and for the eternal safety of the divine household.

[*CIL* XIII 4635 = EJ 137]

This dedication appears on an architectural fragment (h.28 cm., w. 46 cm.) from a frieze, and so suggests the dedication of a building on behalf of Tiberius and the *divina domus*, 'divine household', an expression which only became common much later. Unusually, to judge by the limited space available for restoring letters at the end of line 1, Augustus' status as deified god is not mentioned.

GAIUS CALIGULA: L13–L16

Despite his short reign, and problems with sources (the lack of Tacitus, and the tendency to portray Caligula as mad or bad), Gaius does seem to have moved well beyond the careful formulas established by Augustus and Tiberius. Suetonius castigates Caligula's divine pretensions at *Caligula* 22.2–4 as does Dio 59.26.5 – 27.1 (charges essentially concerned with dressing-up as gods, compare Suet. *Cal.* 52) and 59.28.1–8 (some perhaps supported by archaeology, see **L14**). For his deification of Drusilla, see **L16**.

Gaius clearly made suggestions connected with his worship that deeply offended the Jews. Two of our main sources for Gaius are Jewish authors, Philo and Josephus (see Sections **D** and **E**). Given his close acquaintance with Agrippa (**J5c**), it is hard to excuse Gaius through ignorance of Jewish customs. Quite possibly he was simply showing his authority or was corrupted by the sort of adulation shown in embassy from Cyzicus describing him as the new Sun-God, **M46**. Barrett, *Caligula – The Corruption of Power* chapter 9 gives a good summary of the situation before Caligula before moving on to Caligula himself.

L13 Temple of Gaius at Didyma (Caria), AD 40/41

[Imperator Gaius Ca]esar Germanicus, son [of Germanicus,] god Augustus: those who were his first temple-curators, when Gnaeus Vergilius Capito was high-priest of the temple of Gaius Caesar in Miletos for the first time, and of Asia for the third time, and when Tiberius Julius Menogenes, son of Demetrios the law-giver, was high-priest for the second time and warden of the temple in Miletos, and when Protomachos, son of Glycon, of Iulia, was the chief temple-curator, *sebastoneos*, and emperor-eulogiser – they, out of their own funds dedicated (this):

(The names of twelve individuals from Iulia, Miletus, Pergamum, Antioch, Cyzicus, Apamea, Laodicea, Caesarea, Adramyttion, Philomelion, Halicarnassus, Smyrna, Sardis, are omitted here).

These are the emperor-lovers whose names have been written in an order determined by lot.

[Greek: Sherk 43 = Smallwood 127 = Inscr. Didyma 148; Magie RRAM II 1366–7]

This inscription in Greek upon a base of white marble, found in the temple of Gaius at Didyma in Caria, records the dedication of a statue of Gaius by various cult officials. It shows a variety of official positions associated with the cult of Gaius; the precise meaning of *sebastoneos* is unclear. The emperor-eulogiser declaimed eulogies of the emperor on ceremonial occasions. The temple-curators listed by name here are representatives from every judicial district in the province of Asia. In contrast to Dio's account of Gaius insisting on a sactuary at Miletus (Dio 59.18.1), the inscription implies a picture of the cities of Asia Minor themselves competing to honour Gaius, each district in the province insisting on sending a 'temple-builder' from the district centres, and even having to decide the order of names and towns by lot. This fits the debate on setting up a temple to honour Tiberius (or actually, Tiberius, Livia and the Senate), won by Smyrna (Tac. *Ann.* 4.15, 4.55–56).

L14 Caligula and the Temple of Castor and Pollux: an archaeological note

The question of Caligula's association of himself with the gods through topography is complex. Caligula is said to have encircled the whole city with his palaces (**K42**). More specifically, Suetonius describes him 'converting the temple of Castor and Pollux into the vestibule of his palace' (Suet. *Cal.* 22.2). Dio (59.28.2–5) agrees, adding that he created an entrance to the palace right through the middle of the statues, saying later that Claudius gave their temple back to the Dioscuri (Dio 60.6.8). Archaeology supports, or perhaps explains, the Castor and Pollux episode: the corner of the Palatine Hill overlooks the temple. Massive building work by Domitian seems to overlie the remains of a massive atrium building, with some evidence pointing to Caligula (a fragmentary inscription possibly naming the 'SON OF GERMANICUS') and none ruling out this period. Thus his new palace may have been built right behind the temple, and may have been approached by a slope from the forum, near the temple, or even through the temple with a door cut in the back wall and a short bridge across to the Palatine, as suggested by Hurst 'domus Gai' in *Lexicon Topographicum Urbis Romae* II. D–G ed. Steinby, 1995 (the definitive work on Roman topography).

L15 Caligula as Zeus, silver three-drachma, struck on Crete (possibly at Gortyn)

Obv: Head of Gaius, right, with drapery at back of neck; sceptre carried over left shoulder
ΓΑΙΟΣ ΚΑΙΣΑΡ ΣΕΒ ΓΕΡ ΑΡΧ ΜΕΓ ΔΗΜ ΕΞΟΥ ΥΠΑ (Gaius Caesar Augustus Germanicus, *pontifex maximus*, with tribunician power)

Rev: Statue of Divus Augustus, wearing a toga, seated on throne, with long sceptre in left hand and *patera* (libation bowl) in right. His feet rest on a stool. In field, seven stars.

[*BMC* Crete 1; *RPC* 964/1]

This three-drachma silver coin, minted on the island of Crete, was one of a series struck to commemorate the accession of Caligula, emphasising his connection with the founder of the dynasty, Augustus. The seven stars represent the Septentriones or Great Bear. This constellation had a particular connection with Crete, as in mythology, the nurses of Zeus, Helice and Kynosoura, were placed heavens as the Great and Little Bear. In this way, the seven stars linked with the cult image of Augustus brought him into a close relationship with 'Crete-born' Zeus.

Suetonius accuses Caligula of sharing Jupiter's Temple on the Capitol by building a bridge from Palatine to Capitoline and starting to build a new house within the Capitol precincts – (Suet. *Cal.* 22.4, Dio 59.28.2). The bridge would have had to have been about 250m long and 30m high. London's Millenium Footbridge (a steel suspension bridge) is about 330m long, but only 12m above the river. Its alarming wobble took two years to correct.

L16 Death and deification of Drusilla

Drusilla was the first Roman woman to be deified, though a precedent of sorts had been set by Livia/Augusta who had been worshipped while alive alongside Tiberius and the Senate in Asia Minor and whose deification had been suggested by the senate. Tiberius' rejection, as reported by Tacitus, *Annals* 5.2.1 was not on the grounds of gender but of her personal wishes. What makes Drusilla's case more striking is that she, unlike Livia/Julia Augusta (later deified: **L22**) or Antonia Augusta (not deified), was of no political significance whatsoever. She was deified simply for being the emperor's sister. Her ascent to heaven was 'witnessed' (Dio 59.11.4: Sen, *Apocol.* 1.2 = **F1**) and her deification was decreed on 23 Sept, AD 38 also the date of official celebrations to mark Augustus' birthday (**A38t**).

CLAUDIUS: L17–L25

Claudius seems, unsurprisingly, to have followed the policies of Augustus and Tiberius rather than Gaius, in declining direct worship (**L17**, **L18**; Dio 60.5.3–5 – Claudius sounds as if he meant it!) while accepting traditional forms of religion, such as vows for his safety in Rome (**L19**), but worship elsewhere (**L20**, **L21**). Though he did deify his grandmother, Augusta, he could claim the support of the senate for this (**L22**). For his own deification, see **L25**.

L17 The letter of Claudius to the Alexandrians

Lucius Aemilius Rectus announces:

Since all the populace, owing to its numbers, was unable to be present at the reading of the most sacred and most beneficent letter to the city, I have thought it necessary to publish the letter in order that reading it each one of you may admire the greatness of our god Caesar and feel gratitude for his goodwill towards the city. The second year of the emperor Tiberius Claudius Caesar Augustus Germanicus, 14th of New Augustus.

Tiberius Claudius Caesar Augustus Germanicus, Imperator, *pontifex maximus*, with tribunician power, consul designate, to the City of the Alexandrians, greeting.

[16] Tiberius Claudius Barbillus, Apollonius son of Artemidorus, Chaeremon son of Leonidas, Marcus Julius Asclepiades, Gaius Julius Dionysius, Tiberius Claudius Phanias, Pasion son of Potamon, Dionysios son of Sabbion, Tiberius Claudius Archibius, Apollonius son of Ariston, Gaius Julius Apollonius, Hermaiscus son of Apollonius, your ambassadors, delivered your decree to me and spoke at length concerning the city, directing my attention to your goodwill towards us, which, you may be sure, has been long stored up to your advantage in my memory; since you are by nature reverent towards the emperors, as I know from many proofs, and in particular have taken a warm interest in my own family, which is warmly reciprocated. Of this (to mention the latest and pass over the other instances) the best witness is my brother Germanicus Caesar, who addressed you in the most sincere language. For this reason I have gladly accepted the honours given to me by you, although I have no great desire for such things.

[30] Firstly I allow you to keep my birthday as a sacred day, as you have yourselves proposed; and I agree to the erection of statues of myself and my family in several places; for I see that you are anxious to establish on every side memorials of your reverence for my family. Of the two golden statues, the one made to represent Augustan Claudian Peace, as my most honoured Barbillus suggested and entreated, which I was inclined to refuse since it appeared rather excessive, shall be erected at Rome; and the other according to your request shall be carried in procession on the name-days in your city, and it shall be accompanied by a throne in the manner which you think best.

[40] It would perhaps be foolish, while accepting such great honours, to refuse the institution of a Claudian Tribe and the establishment of groves after the Egyptian custom; and so I grant these requests to you as well. If you wish, you may also erect

the equestrian statues of Vitrasius Pollio my procurator. I also allow you to erect the four-horse chariots which you wish to set up at the entrances to your country, one placed at Taposiris, the Libyan town of that name, another at Pharos in Alexandria, and a third at Pelusium in Egypt. But I decline the appointment of a High Priest to me and the building of temples for myself, for I do not wish to be offensive to my contemporaries, and it is my opinion that temples and such forms of honour have been granted by all ages to the gods alone.

[*P. Lond (Greek Papyri in the British Museum)* VI 1912 = Smallwood 370]

The letter from Claudius is introduced by an edict by the prefect of Egypt, Aemilius Rectus, who is concerned with ensuring the publication of the imperial edict. The date 10 Nov. 41 falls into the second year of Claudius' rule by the Egyptian system, which started its new year on 29 August. The envoys are high-ranking representatives from the city, including six Roman citizens, led by Tiberius Claudius Barbillus/Balbillus, see **U21**: most of them were associated with the Museum; none was a Jew. For Germanicus' visit to Alexandria, see **J7d**, **J7e**, **M59**, **M60**. The letter was copied onto papyrus by a wealthy local. The letter answered an embassy sent to Claudius about the long running dispute between Greek and Jewish communities of Alexandria (see Philo, *Embassy* – Section **D**), left unresolved at Gaius' death. For the rest of the letter, dealing with the main reasons for the embassy, see **M6**. In introducing their request, the Alexandrians clearly petitioned the emperor as a god. Claudius however, while willing to acknowledge that he was related to Divus Augustus, and accept some honours, was not prepared openly to declare himself a god, compare **L18** and **L4.**

L18 Letter to Thasos, rejecting a temple, AD 42

Tiberius Claudius Caesar Germanicus, *pontifex maximus*, in his 2nd year of tribunician power, consul designate for the third time, Imperator, father of the fatherland, to the magistrates, council, and people of the Thasians, greetings.

With regard to what I plainly declared [to the envoys] sent [by you], I say this to you too, that I accept all the [...] of your zeal and piety alike, but I reject the temple, judging it to be for the gods alone, whilst accepting the other honours, which befit the best leaders. Moreover, I maintain for you, in accordance with the decrees of god Augustus, all the honours from him and those which [...] belong to you, and being careful of the export of grain [...] to the prefect [...]. If nothing [...] in the province, I am writing so that [...] when these have been given to you, may show to me. And as to the other matters, you may be quite sure that I am taking care of the city. Those who gave me the decree were... [a fragmentary list of names follows...]

[Greek: Smallwood 371]

For a similar rejection of divine honours by a new emperor, compare Tiberius above (**L4b**). It is typical of Claudius to cite Augustus as a precedent.

L19 Vow for the safety of Claudius and his family, Rome, 47/48

For the safety of Tiberius Claudius Caesar Augustus Germanicus, *pontifex maximus*, in his 7th year of tribunician power, consul four times, hailed victorious commander 15 times, father of his country, censor, ~~and of Valeria Messalina wife of Augustus~~ and ~~their~~ children, in fulfillment of a vow, Gaius Julius Postumus, son of Sextus, of the Cornelia voting-tribe, prefect of Egypt of Tiberius Claudius Caesar Augustus Germanicus, from sixteen pounds of gold.

[Smallwood 99 = *ILS* 210 = CIL VI 918]

The name of Messalina was later deleted from this inscription (compare Tacitus, *Annals* 11.38). The word *Aegypti* ('Egypt') is inscribed here with one of the letters revived by Claudius, Ⱶ in place of Y (compare **R24**; Tac. *Ann.* 11.14; Suet. *Claud.* 41.3).

L20 Claudius honoured at Athens

Tiberius Claudius Caesar [Augustus] Germanicus, Imperator, Ancestral [Apollo]: the priest of him and [of his family] for life and [military] *strategos* for the third time, Dionysodoros, son of So[phocles], of Sounion, (honoured) one who is the saviour and benefactor of himself and his whole house. Euboulides of Piraeus made it.

[Greek: Smallwood 137 = *SEG* XXII 153]

L21 Possible Worship in Britain

It is possible that Claudius was celebrated as a god in Britain in his lifetime. Certainly the Temple of Claudius was one of the targets for Boudicca's revolt in AD 61 (see Tac. *Ann.* 14.31.3 and the famous bronze head of Claudius (**J12i**)). Seneca's *Apocolocyntosis* 8.3 = **F8** refers to a temple in Britain, where barbarians worship him and pray to him as a god. The dramatic context of the *Apocolocyntosis* – immediately after Claudius' death – should imply that it was built in his lifetime and it is also more likely that a local should wish to show loyalty to the current emperor than to one held in dubious honour by his successor (see Suet, *Claud.* 45). If so, however, Claudius is simply doing the same as Augustus in Gaul (LACTOR 17, M18–20) who had a temple at Lugdunum.

L22 Livia deified, on brass *dupondius* of *c.* AD 41–50 (mint of Rome)

Obv: Augustus with radiate crown, facing left
DIVVS AVGVSTVS, SC (Divus Augustus, by decree of the senate)

Rev: Livia seated, looking left, holding ears of corn in right hand and long torch in left
DIVA AVGVSTA (Diva Augusta)

[*BMC* Claudius 224; *RIC* Claudius 101]

Claudius saw to the deification of his grandmother, Livia (Julia Augusta). A temple to Tiberius, Augusta and the Senate had been allowed in Smyrna (Asia Minor) in AD 23 (Tacitus, *Annals* 4.15.3). Soon after her death in AD 29 her deification had been proposed by the senate, but denied by Tiberius, apparently stating that that had been her preference (Tac. *Ann.* 5.2.1; Suet. *Tib.* 51.2; Dio 58.2.1). Claudius was the first *princeps* not to have been a member of the Julian clan by blood or adoption and not therefore able to claim descent from Divus Julius or Divus Augustus. But he was grandson of Livia/Augusta, and her deification and the accompanying issue of coins will have reminded people of Claudius' very close links to her. She was deified on 17 Jan, AD 42, the anniversary of her marriage to Augustus (Suet. *Claud.* 11.2; **A44b**; Dio 60.5.2).

L23 Fake Phoenix at Claudius' *ludi saeculares*

Cornelius Valerianus records that a phoenix flew down into Egypt when Plautius and Papinius were consuls (AD 36). The official records show that it was brought to Rome when the emperor Claudius was censor in the 800th year of the city (AD 47), and displayed in the Comitium, but everyone realises that it was a fake.

[Pliny, *Natural History* 10.5]

Pliny is talking about phoenixes and Tacitus unexpectedly devotes a whole chapter (*Annals* 6.28.1–6) to the phoenix, whose appearance he places in AD 34 (see Syme, *Tacitus* 771–4 on the dating). Dio agrees with AD 36, making it portend Tiberius' death. The phoenix will have been displayed as part of Claudius' celebrations of the Centennial Games in AD 47 (Tac. *Ann.* 11.11; Suet. *Claud.* 21.2).

L24 Records of the *Sodales Augustales Claudiales*, Rome, AD 51 and 68

Division 27

Adlected into the number by decree of the senate was Nero Claudius Caesar Germanicus, son of Augustus, in the consulship of Tiberius Claudius Caesar Augustus Germanicus for the fifth time and Servius Cornelius Orfitus, year 804 after the foundation of Rome.

[Gaius] Rutilius G[all]icus was co-opted, in the consulship of [Publius G]alerius Trachalus and Tiberius Catius Silius Italicus, year 821 after the foundation of Rome.

[Smallwood 132 = *ILS* 5025]

This record shows the adlection of Nero shortly after his adoption by Claudius into the prestigious priesthood of the *Sodales Augustales*, established in AD 14 – Tac. *Ann.* 1.54.1. The second entry shows the successor in the priesthood to Nero.

L25 Claudius' deification on *aureus* of AD 54

Obv: Laureate head of Claudius, left

DIVVS CLAVDIVS AVGVSTVS (Divus Claudius Augustus)

Rev: ornamental four-horse chariot surmounted by miniature set of four horses flanked by Victories

EX S C (by decree of the senate)

[*BMC* Nero 4; *RIC* Nero 4]

This took place soon after his death on 13 Oct AD 54 (Tac. *Ann.* 12.69). It was useful for Nero to be Divi filius, but also dangerous, since Britannicus was also, so the legend appears only briefly on his coins (*RIC* Nero 6,7,10), but still appears in dedications such as **L28**, **L35**. Even at the eulogy, written by Seneca, delivered by Nero, references to Claudius' foresight and wisdom were greeted by laughter (Tac. *Ann.* 13.3.2). Soon this was to be the court line, as famously in Seneca's *Apocolocyntosis* (Section **F**). Similarly, the Temple to Claudius on the Caelian hill is started by Agrippina, abandoned by Nero, and podium reused as nymphaeum (See Claridge, *Rome*[2], 342–4) and completed by Vespasian (Suet. *Claud.* 45). See **K35**.

NERO: L26–L35

The standard biography of Nero notes, 'There is little evidence for the notion that Nero introduced important innovations in ruler cult.' (M.T. Griffin, *Nero,* pages 215–220, 'The Notion of a Divine Monarchy'). Nero rejected excessive honours (**L26**; Tac. *Ann.* 13.10, 15.74.3) and neither Suetonius nor the surviving parts of Tacitus' *Annals* really complain about Nero usurping divine honours. Poets of Nero's court are doing no more than Virgil or Horace in praising the *princeps* as a god on earth (**L27**).

L26 Refusal of divine honours in Egypt

(Col. 1) [----] of the two remaining, I declined your temple because to gods alone is this honour granted rightly by men, and the gold crown I sent back so as to give it up, since I did not wish at the beginning of my rule to be a burden to you. Whatever you, the 6,475, hold, having received them from the rulers before me [I wish to be securely yours,] (col. 2) of all of you in common and each according to his share, to keep yourselves free from insult and unmolested, just as the god my father wished. As to what you have given testimony about as regards everything he granted both to the city and to the 6,475 of you, I approve and accept. The envoys were [Ai]akidas son of Ptolemaois, Antenor [---]ethos, Nibitas son of Nibitas, Po[lykra]tes son of Didymos, [----]

[Sherk no.62 = P. Med. Inv. 70.01 verso = Montevecchi (1970) 6–7]

This text is preserved in Greek on a papyrus from the Arsinoite nome in Egypt. Its reference to previous emperors and a deified father fits the profile of Nero. The 6,475 refers to the military colonists of the Arsinoite nome. [O. Montevecchi, 'Nerone e una polis e ai 6475', *Aegyptus* 50 (1970) 5–33].

L27 Calpurnius Siculus, *Eclogue* 4, praise of the god Nero

In Calpurnius Siculus, *Eclogue* 4, the shepherd Corydon explains to his friend, Meliboeus, that he is meditating verses to praise the golden age and the god who rules over nations, cities and a toga-wearing peace (5–8). He recants his previous advice to give up pipe-playing, and thanks Meliboeus for saving him from exile and instead bringing his verses to the ear of the god (29–50). Corydon and his brother Amyntas then begin to exchange verses praising Caesar for having brought every divine blessing possible on the countryside (82–136), their prayers culminating in the lines below. The whole eclogue is thoroughly modelled on Virgil's *Eclogues* (quoted directly at 4.82), and of course invites an allegorical reading, with Corydon as Calpurnius, thanking Meliboeus as Calpurnius' (unknown) patron for bringing his verse to the notice of the god, the emperor. Though the praise may seem extravagant, Virgil's *Eclogues* of 100 years before had also featured rustics praising a young man (Octavian) as a god.

Amyntas
Ye gods, I pray you, only recall to heaven this youth, whom (I well know)
You sent us from the ethereal realms above, when he has enjoyed
Long years of life. Or better, unwind the spindles of the Fates
And thus exchange his mortal, allotted span, and grant to him instead
Some heavenly thread of life, forged in the everlasting metal of eternity.
Grant him divinity, but make him loath to trade his earthly palace for heaven.
Corydon
You also, Caesar, whether you dwell among us in changed form
As Jupiter himself, or, as some other of the gods above, you lurk
Concealed in false resemblance of some mortal shape, (for you are god),
I beg you rule this world, govern the nations as our king for ever, and regard
Your love for heaven as valueless. Never desert this peace you have begun.

[Calpurnius Siculus, *Eclogue* 4.136–146]

Calpurnius uses, perhaps consciously, the same image as *Apocolocyntosis* 4.1 where the thread of Nero's life spun by the fates is magically turned to gold. Other poetry of the time (as perhaps of all imperial Roman times) praises the emperor as a god: Seneca, *Apocol.* 4.1 = **F4**; Calpurnius Siculus = **T15**; Lucan, *Civil War* = **T16**; the anonymous 'Einsiedeln Eclogues'; Antiphilus = **M13**).

L28 Honoured on the Parthenon, Athens, *c.* AD 61

The council of the Areopagus and the council of the 600 and the People of Athens: the greatest Imperator Nero Caesar Claudius Augustus Germanicus, son of a god, when Tiberius [Cl]audius Novius, son of Philinos, was general of the hoplites for the eighth time, curator, and lawgiver, and when the priestess was Paullina, daughter of Kapito.

[Greek: Sherk no.78A = Carroll (1982) 16]

This text has been reconstructed from the remains of cuttings for the placement of bronze letters on the east architrave of the Parthenon, beneath twelve groups of triglyphs. It seems that the inscription was removed shortly after it had been put in place. The Athenians have chosen a non-standard form of nomenclature for Nero as a form of flattery. The exact function of the inscription remains unclear; it perhaps rededicated the Parthenon to Nero, and is perhaps to be associated with Corbulo's victories over Armenia (**N45–N51**), given the longstanding association of the Parthenon with victories in the East. Tiberius Claudius Novius was the most important magistrate in the city at the time (datable to 60/1 or 61/2 by another inscription, *IG* II^2 1990); Paullina was priestess of Athena Polias. [K.K. Carroll, *The Parthenon Inscription* (1982): http://www.duke.edu/web/classics/grbs/FTexts/monogr/Carroll.pdf]. For Nero plundering works of art from the Acropolis, see **R33**.

L29 Honoured as New Sun, Sagalassus (Pamphylia)

To New Sun, Nero Tiberius Claudius Caesar Germanicus: [Tiberius C]laudius Darius and his sons have made this dedication.

[Greek: Smallwood 146 = *IGRRP* III 345]

Nero was also honoured as Apollo in Athens, see **Q19**.

L30 Novel honours for Nero, Aezani (Phrygia)

From Rome. Nero to Menophilos, greetings. Menecles and Metrodoros, your sons, came to me and revealed all the ways in which you yourself have been eager to honour us and also all the things you have proposed to the city concerning our honours. In addition to this, I was exceedingly satisfied with the certainty of your goodwill towards me and your constant intention to devise something extra [in my honour?... *3 lines missing*...] may your eagerness to honour us be without expense to you, who have already given ample proof that you do not choose to spare your own resources. Menecles, your son, was also prepared to stay with me as long as I might wish [...*15 fragmentary lines follow*...].

[Greek: Smallwood 390 = *IGRRP* IV 561]

L31 Nero and Poppaea honour Venus at Pompeii

Poppaea sent as gifts to most holy Venus a beryl, and ear-drop pearl, and a large single pearl.

When Caesar came to most holy Venus and when your heavenly feet brought you there, Augustus, there was a countless weight of gold.

[*AE* 1985 283–4 = Cooley and Cooley (2004) E19–20]

It is unclear whether these two graffiti texts in the House of Julius Polybius (IX.xiii.1–3) preserve a memory of a real visit of Poppaea and Nero to the town, but the imperial couple was certainly popular there, possibly because Poppaea's family originated in the region. At any rate, she owned property near Pompeii. Venus was the tutelary goddess of the town.

L32 Radiate crown a symbol of the gods

Civil war shall make *Divi* the equals of the gods above.
Rome shall decorate their spirits with thunderbolts, radiate crown, and stars,
And in their temples shall swear by their ghosts.

[Lucan, *Civil War* 7.457–9]

Divus Augustus is shown with radiate crown on the coin shown in **L22**. For Lucan's *Civil War*, written under Nero, see **T16**.

L33 Silver four-drachma coin struck at Alexandria

Obv: Head of Nero with radiate crown
ΝΕΡΩ ΚΛΑΥΔ ΚΑΙΣ ΣΕΒ ΓΕΡ ΑΥ (Nero Claudius Caesar Augustus Germanicus, victorious commander)

Rev: Bust of Olympian Zeus, laureate, right
ΔΙΟΣ ΟΛΥΜΠΙΟΥ (of Olympian Zeus)

[*BMC* Alexandria 127; *RPC* 5297]

The appearance of Nero with radiate crown on coinage offers some evidence of an association with divinity, since a passage of Lucan's contemporary *Civil War* makes the connection explicit The type of crown appears for the first time on Nero (but not the last – Vespasian and Titus used it, presumably without any overtones of divinity). And these four-drachma coins, minted at Alexandria would have circulated in the East. For other coins in this series, minted to celebrate Nero's tour of Greece, see **Q18**.

L34 Deification of Nero's wife and baby daughter

Obv: Female figure seated, holding cornucopia, between two columns of a temple
DIVA POPPAEA AVG (Diva Poppaea Augusta)

Rev: Female figure standing within circular temple
DIVA CLAVD NER F (Diva Claudia, daughter of Nero)

[*RPC* 4846 = Smallwood 148]

Nero exceeded Caligula's deification of Drusilla (**L16** above) by deifying his baby daughter, Octavia Claudia, who died aged 4 months (Tac. *Ann.* 15.23.4, with mention of a temple), and his second wife, Poppaea (Tac. *Ann.* 16.21.2; temple attested by Dio 63.26.3).

L35 Nero and Diva Poppaea at Luna (Etruria), 66/67

To Imperator Nero Claudius Caesar Augustus Germanicus, son of Divus Claudius, grandson of Germanicus Caesar, great-grandson of Tiberius Caesar Augustus, great-great-grandson of Divus Augustus, *pontifex maximus*, in his 13th year of tribunician power, hailed victorious commander 11 times, consul four times: Lucius Titinius

Glaucus Lucretianus, son of Lucius, of the Galerian voting-tribe, priest of Rome and Augustus, *duumvir* for the fourth time, patron of the colony, *sevir*, Roman equestrian, *curio*, staff officer of a consul, military tribune of legion XXII Primigenia, prefect in place of a legate of the Balearic islands, military tribune of legion VI Victrix, in fulfilment of a vow undertaken for the health of Imperator Nero, which he had vowed at the Balearics in the year when Aulus Licinius Nerva was consul; when the duumvirs were Lucius Saufeius Vegetus and Quintus Aburius Nepos; he should set it up wherever he wants, his vow having been fulfilled, he set it up to Jupiter, Juno, Minerva, Happiness of Rome, Divus Augustus.

To Diva Poppaea Augusta, wife of Imperator Nero Caesar Augustus:
(*this inscription then repeats exactly the dedicator's name, titles and reason for the dedication to Nero given above*)

[Smallwood 149 = *ILS* 233]

These dedications were inscribed together on a marble plaque in fulfilment of a vow made by Titinius Glaucus Lucretianus for the health of Nero during the year of the Pisonian conspiracy. The consul Licinius Nerva is mentioned on his own here to indicate the year 65, because his consular colleague M. Vestinus Atticus had been forced to commit suicide by Nero, on a false charge of conspiracy, according to Tacitus.

Inscriptions at the Sebasteion, Aphrosdisias (Caria)

These inscriptions are all believed to have been displayed originally in a temple and sanctuary complex dedicated to Aphrodite and the Augustan gods (i.e. the Julio-Claudian imperial family) by members of two families from the local élite. The complex – consisting of a monumental gateway, two long porticoes framing a processional route, and temple – was established under Tiberius, further developed under Claudius, and completed under Nero. One family built the gateway and north portico, the other family the temple and south portico. The gateway displayed statues of the Julio-Claudians and their legendary ancestors Aeneas and Aphrodite, with some rather obscure members of the imperial family being represented, alongside those more commonly honoured. About eighty relief panels from the processional way have been found, depicting mythological, allegorical, and imperial scenes, as well as personifications of peoples and provinces conquered by Rome (see below for Claudius and Britain, Nero and Armenia). The overall programme appears to have been to represent the Roman empire as without end in time or space. This is just one example of how the people of Aphrodisias emphasised their special connections to Rome, via the founding ancestress, Aphrodite / Venus Genetrix, shared by the town and by the Julio-Claudians. In return, the town received privileged status from Rome. [R.R.R. Smith, 'The Imperial Reliefs from the Sebasteion at Aphrodisias', *JRS* 77 (1987) 88–138 and 'Simulacra Gentium: The Ethne from the Sebasteion at Aphrodisias', *JRS* 78 (1988) 50–77; *IAph2007* = J. Reynolds, C. Roueché, G. Bodard, *Inscriptions of Aphrodisias* (2007): http://insaph.kcl.ac.uk/iaph2007 and R.R.R. Smith, The Marble Reliefs from the Julio-Claudian Sebasteion at Aphrodisias (forthcoming)]. The photographs below appear by very kind permission of Professor R.R.R. Smith.

L36a Aphrodite and Augustus/Augusta

To Aphrodite, to the God[.] August[.], to Tiberius Claudius Caesar, to the People. Tiberius Claudius Diogenes, friend of the citizens, restored what Diogenes his father promised, and Attalis, and also on behalf of his uncle Attalos his part.

[Greek: *IAph2007* 9.25]

This text is inscribed upon the architrave blocks of white marble from the south portico of the Sebasteion. Because the inscription is left intentionally incomplete and is also damaged, it is unclear whether the dedication is to the God Augustus or to the Goddess Augusta (i.e. Livia). It can be dated to the reign of Claudius.

L36b Antonia Augusta

Antonia Augusta: Hermias, priest, dedicated this.

[Greek: *IAph2007* 9.26]

Antonia had declined the title Augusta when offered it by Caligula, but was granted it posthumously by her son Claudius after he came to power (Dio Cassius 59.3.4; Suet. *Claud.*11.2). Hermias is possibly priest of the cult of Antonia.

L36c Agrippina the Elder

Agrippina, daughter of Marcus Agrippa, wife of Germanicus Caesar, mother of Gaius Imperator Augustus Caesar.

[Greek: *IAph2007* 9.37]

Unusually, Gaius' name was not erased from his mother's statue base after his assassination. This statue base belongs to a series honouring members of the imperial family in the Sebasteion. The close similarity of their lettering suggests that they were all set up over a short space of time, probably early under Caligula, when the Julian part of the imperial family was re-emphasised once again, playing a crucial role in legitimising the new emperor. Others honour Atia, Augustus' mother (*IAph2007* 9.40); Gaius Caesar (*IAph2007* 9.29); Lucius Caesar (*IAph2007* 9.27); Germanicus (*IAph2007* 9.38); Tiberius' son, Drusus (**J10**: *IAph2007* 9.28); Julia (see **J16a**), daughter of Drusus (*IAph2007* 9.31); Agrippina (**J21**), daughter of Germanicus (*IAph2007* 9.32); Marcus Lepidus (*IAph2007* 9.33) – see **J20a**; Claudius' son, Drusus (*IAph2007* 9.30); Aemilia Lepida, daughter of Marcus Lepidus (*IAph2007* 9.36), – this was the sister of Gaius' potential heir, M. (Aemilius) Lepidus.

L36d Aphrodite as Venus Genetrix

Aphrodite, ancestral mother of the Augustan gods.

[Greek: *IAph2007* 9.34]

This statue base honours Aphrodite in her guise as Venus Genetrix.

L36e Aeneas

Aeneas, son of Anchises.

[Greek: *IAph2007* 9.35]

This statue honours the legendary founder of the Julian family.

L36f Nero as Sun

~~Nero~~ Claudius Drusus Caesar Augustus
Sun

[Greek: *IAph2007* 9.42]

Nero's personal name was erased after 68.

L36g Claudius

Claudius is nude as appropriate to a god or hero, though with a mantle billowing behind him, suggesting movement as he strides across the heavens. The figure on the right with tail of a sea creature presents him with an oar, while that on the left gives a cornucopia (horn of plenty), symbolising his power over land and sea.

Photo: New York University Excavations at Aphrodisias

L36h Claudius and Britannia

This inscribed base (**N28**) labels Claudius and Britannia while the relief depicts a heroic Claudius, nude and with swirling cloak, on the point of delivering a death-blow to a hapless Britannia.

Photo: New York University Excavations at Aphrodisias

L36i Nero and Agrippina

A realistically youthful Nero is crowned by Agrippina. She carries a cornucopia. He wears breastplate and cloak, and a helmet is at his feet. In contrast an earlier panel showed Agrippina grasping the hand of a Claudius portrayed essentially as a nude, with a mantle covering only his left shoulder and arm.

Photo: New York University Excavations at Aphrodisias

L36j Nero and Armenia

This inscribed base (**N53**) labels Nero and Armenia on a scene of Nero's conquest of Armenia that parallels that of Claudius' conquest of Britain. It shows that the complex was incomplete on Claudius' death, and that later victories were subsequently incorporated into its design. Nero's personal name was erased following his suicide in 68. The relief shows signs that Nero's head was also deliberately removed.

Photo: New York University Excavations at Aphrodisias

SECTION M
ADMINISTRATION OF EMPIRE

You have appealed to Caesar: to Caesar you shall go! (Acts, 25.12)

F. Millar remarks of this passage (**M37**) that though it does not show much about exact legal procedure, it does say a lot about the power of the emperor's name, and about the assumption that the emperor would hear in person a case involving a relatively unimportant provincial (*ERW*, page 511). Fifty years later we have Pliny the Younger's detailed correspondence with the emperor Trajan (*Letters,* book 10) in which we can see the governor of a public province referring all matters of doubt directly to the emperor (but see *Letters* 10.31.1 and 10.32.1 for the suggestion that Pliny had special permission to refer so much to Trajan) who replies in full. The 'petition and response' model of how the empire operated can be seen from early in Augustus' reign when a fisherman travels to Corinth to ask Octavian/Augustus for remission of tax (LACTOR 17, M68). Philo provides a written account of his embassy to Gaius (Section **D**), while a town in Lycia sees fit to carve on marble a template of how to approach an emperor (**M10**). Direct interventions of an emperor can be seen in **M1**–**M19**, with intervention in the form of building projects in **M20**–**M27**.

IMPERIAL INTERVENTION: M1–M19

M1 Tiberius, a master of procrastination

[170] Tiberius made no effort to receive embassies quickly, and when he sent governors and procurators out to the provinces, he failed to appoint successors, unless they died prematurely while in office. He was no less dilatory about hearing the cases of arrested prisoners. [171] When his friends asked why he was so inclined to drag his feet in such matters, he explained that he deliberately slowed the reception of embassies, because if they settled their business too quickly, another lot would be appointed and he would have all the bother of receiving and dismissing them as well. [172] As for the officials, once they were appointed he allowed them to remain in office out of sensitivity for the anxieties of their subjects. It was natural that every governor was inclined to maximise his profits, but if the length of their tenure was curtailed, being either temporary or liable to unexpected cancellation, then those holding such posts would have a far greater incentive to extortion. [173] If, on the other hand, they remained in office for longer periods, they would have enjoyed such a surfeit of robberies that the sheer weight of their profits would diminish the compulsion to further extortion in the future. If successive appointments came too thick and fast, there was no way in which their subjects, who were destined to be the source of profit for their rulers, could possibly satisfy them. There would be no period of respite for them, during which those who had already gorged themselves on profits might relax their appetite for extortion. They would be moved on before it could happen.

[Josephus, *Jewish Antiquities* 18.170–173]

Embassies were a crucial route of communication between emperors and cities and emperors could expect a large number of embassies on important occasions, such as an accession, the adoption of an heir, or when an imperial judgement was required. Ideally emperors would meet embassies swiftly and respond to them promptly, (compare Pliny the Younger praising Trajan for this in *Pan.* 79.6–7), yet in practice few emperors did so; as Josephus says this simply led to another being sent. Tiberius delegated some ambassadorial business to the senate (Tac. *Ann.* 3.60–63) and he was renowned for leaving governors in office for longer periods (Tac. *Ann.* 1.80 and 6.27.2–3 – Aelius Lamia and L. Arruntius, governors of Asia and Spain for 10 years, but kept by Tiberius in Rome). However this was probably more due to efficiency and continuity than to limit embezzlement as Josephus suggests.

M2 Tiberius suffers from colitis

Tiberius Caesar was *princeps* when this disease [colitis] reached Rome, and as the Emperor was the very first to suffer from it, great confusion was caused when the public read this unfamiliar term in an edict of Tiberius apologising for his indisposition.

[Pliny, *Natural History* 26.9]

Colitis (inflammation of the colon) will not have been a new disease: the confusion will rather have been caused by a new and unfamiliar term (albeit one used by Cornelius Celsus, *On Medicine*, 1.7, 2.12.2, (written under Tiberius)). This piece of information suggests, incidentally, Tiberius' conscientiousness in carrying out his duties.

M3 Asian earthquake relief on *sestertius* of AD 22/3

Obv: Tiberius, with laurel crown, seated with feet on stool to left, holding *patera* (libation bowl) in right hand, long sceptre in left

CIVITATIBVS ASIAE RESTITVTIS (the cities of Asia restored)

Rev: S C (by decree of the senate)

TI CAESAR DIVI AVG F AVGVST P M TR POT XXIIII (Tiberius Claudius Augustus, son of Divus Augustus, *pontifex maximus,* in his 24th year of tribunician power

[*BMC* Tiberius 70; *RIC* Tiberius 48]

Pliny, *NH* 2.200 records 'the greatest earthquake in the memory of mankind occurred in the principate of Tiberius Caesar, when twelve cities in Asia were destroyed in one night.' This devastating earthquake of AD 17 and Tiberius' response is described in Tacitus, *Annals* 2.47. Contemporary accounts of various sorts are provided by an epigram by Bianor (Gow & Page, no.16 = Greek Anthology 9.423); Strabo 13.4.8; Phlegon, *Fragments of Greek Historians*, 257 F36 – 'he restored them again at his private expense.'; *OGIS* 471; and in the two inscription below. The coin is interesting in that it was minted in Rome, perhaps a deliberate attempt to rebut persistent accusations about Tiberius' meanness, preserved, *e.g.* by Suetonius 48–49.1 'no act of generosity ever eased the burden on the provinces, except when the cities of Asia were torn apart by the earthquake'. For disaster-relief becoming a function of the emperor see Millar, *ERW* 422–3.

M4 Tiberius' support for cities in Asia Minor, Puteoli, AD 30

To Tiberius Caesar Augustus, son of Divus Augustus, grandson of Divus Julius, *pontifex maximus*, four times consul, hailed victorious commander 8 times, in his thirty-second year of tribunician power. The *Augustales*. Restoration by the community.

[Henia?] Sardes, [?ulloron] Magnesia, Philadelphia, Tmolus, Cyme, Temnos, Cibyra, Myrina, Ephesos, Apollonidea, Hyrcania, Mostene, Aegae, Hierocaesarea.

[EJ 50 = *ILS* 156]

This large block is engraved on its four sides with representations of the fourteen cities of Asia (each labelled with its name) which received imperial financial aid following extensive damage caused by earthquakes in 17, 23, and 29. The dedicatory inscription to Tiberius appears on the front of the monument. It seems that the *Augustales* of Puteoli set this base up (probably to support a colossal statue of the emperor) in imitation of a monument set up by the cities of Asia in the *Forum Iulium* at Rome, and that it was also subsequently restored by the town of Puteoli.

M5 Thanks to Tiberius at Mostene, AD 31/32

[Tiberius Caesar] Augustus, [son] of god Augustus, [grandson of god] Julius, *pontifex maximus*, in his 33rd year of tribunician power, hailed victorious commander 8 times, consul five times, founder of twelve cities simultaneously, founded the city.

[Greek: *ILS* 8785]

This dedication also relates to Tiberius' financial aid following the earthquakes in Asia Minor (see above). A similar dedication has also been found at another of the damaged cities, Aegae (*CIL* III 7096).

M6 Claudius' letter to the Alexandrians, 10 November AD 41

One of the problems which Claudius inherited from his predecessor was continuing unrest at Alexandria, amid tensions between the Jewish and Greek inhabitants of that city. At the time, the community of Jews there was probably the most significant one in the diaspora, but the city was itself Greek in character, and Greeks enjoyed privileged status there. In turn, the Jews existed there as a virtually autonomous civic unit, with the right to live in the city and to administer their own internal affairs via their own independent officials, but they did not in general hold Greek citizenship (**M6b**, line 95). Both parties had sent embassies to Gaius, but had failed to reach a resolution (see Philo, Section **D**). Early on in his reign, therefore, Claudius attempted to defuse the situation by sending a letter to the Alexandrians. In doing so, he was responding to an embassy sent to him, but he took the opportunity to deal with a whole range of matters, such as the honours voted for him (**L17**) and local administrative arrangements, but ending with a stern warning to Jews and Greeks alike to settle their differences. He thus attempted to settle the unrest by reasserting the religious freedom for the Jews granted to them by Augustus, but at the same time warning the Jews not to try to over-stretch themselves in intruding into the life of the Greek city and seeking further privileges.

M6a Claudius accepts some honours and rejects others

This part of the letter is given as ***L17***

M6b Claudius' decision on rights of the Alexandrian Greeks

[52] Concerning the requests which you have made to me, I decide as follows. All those who have been registered as *ephebes* up to the time of my principate I confirm and guarantee their Alexandrian citizenship with all the privileges and benefits enjoyed by the city, excepting those who have made their way into your number as *ephebes* though born of slave mothers. And it is also my will that all the other privileges which were granted to you by former emperors, kings and prefects shall be confirmed, as Divus Augustus also confirmed them. [60] It is also my will that the wardens of the Temple of Divus Augustus in Alexandria shall be chosen by lot in the same way as those of Divus Augustus in Canopus are. With regard to the civic magistracies holding their offices for three years, your proposal seems to me to be very good; for through fear of being called to account for any abuse of power, your magistrates will behave with greater moderation during their term of office. Concerning the council, what your custom may have been under the ancient kings I

cannot say, but you are well aware that you had no council under the emperors. [69] As this is a new matter bought before me for the first time, and it is not certain whether it will be of benefit to the city and to my government, I have written to Aemilius Rectus to hold an inquiry and inform me whether in the first place it is right that a council should be constituted, and, if it should be right to create one, what form it should take.

M6c Claudius' threat to those creating trouble in Alexandria

[73] With regard to the responsibility for the disturbances and civil strife, or rather, if I must speak the truth, the war against the Jews, I have decided not to conduct a detailed investigation, although your ambassadors, particularly Dionysius son of Theon, in a spirited confrontation made many efforts on your behalf, but I am storing up an unyielding indignation against those who renewed the conflict. [79] I tell you plainly that, unless you immediately put a stop to this destructive and mutual enmity, I shall be forced to show what it is like when a benevolent ruler is moved to righteous indignation. Therefore I once again ask that the Alexandrians behave gently and kindly towards the Jews who have dwelt in the same city for many years, [85] and not to dishonour any of their customs in their worship of their god, but to permit them to observe their customs, as they did in the time of Divus Augustus and as I too have confirmed, after hearing both sides. On the other hand I order the Jews not to aim at more than they have previously had and not to send – as if they lived in two cities – two embassies in future, something which has never been done before, and not to pour into the games presided over by the *gymnasiarchs* and the administrators since they enjoy what is theirs and possess an abundance of all good things in a city which is not their own. [96] Nor are they to bring in or admit Jews coming from Syria or Egypt, a practice which I shall be forced to view with notably greater suspicion. If they disobey, I shall proceed against them in every way as fomenting a common plague for the whole world. [100] If both sides change their present ways and are willing to live in gentleness and kindness with one another, I for my part will do my utmost for the city, as one which has long been closely connected to the house of my ancestors. I testify that Balbillus my friend has always exercised the greatest care for you in his dealings with me and has now conducted your case with the greatest zeal as has my friend Tiberius Claudius Archibius. Farewell.

[P. Lond (Greek Papyri in the British Museum) VI 1912 = Smallwood 370]

The gymnasiarch was the official in charge of the gymnasium, where *ephebes* trained – the young men entitled to enter the Greek gymnasium for education – which might lead to their acquiring Roman citizenship. For Balbillus, Claudius' friend, and the leader of the embassy (**L17**), see **U21**.

M7 The trial of Isidorus

The trial of Isidorus is presented in four papyri from different parts of Roman Egypt. The precise date and the location of the trial are unknown, but the participants can all be placed in Rome in AD 41, and this is the most likely date. These copies of the stories were made late in the second century AD, long after the events they purport to describe. They have the form of the minutes made at the trial, but even if the original versions of the trial came from minutes made by participants, they have been heavily embellished and fictionalised by later writers. It is difficult, for example, to see how Isidorus could have played a part in the death of Gaius' Praetorian Prefect Macro.

The trial, part of a series of texts called the *Acta Alexandrinorum*, presents the heroes Isidorus and Lampon as bravely striving to protect the rights of the Alexandrian Greeks, their clear loyalty demonstrated by Isidorus' desire to die in the robes of a gymnasiarch – the chief magistrate of the city. They are judged by Claudius, portrayed here as a stereotypical tyrant who will not even listen to their arguments. The bitter exchanges between the emperor and the Alexandrians are likely to be later additions to the story; such insolence would not be tolerated in the imperial court. The background to the story is severe tensions between Greeks and Jews in Alexandria (see introduction to **M6** above). The ill-feeling towards the Jews is evident here – Agrippa is described as 'three-obol Jew' ('worthless' or 'cheap'), the Jews are described as being not of the same nature as the Alexandrians, and Isidorus quips that Claudius is the cast-off son of the Jewess Salome in response to being called the son of an actress (i.e. prostitute), implying that the latter is preferable.

M7a The setting of the trial of Isidorus

The Alexandrian envoys were summoned and the emperor postponed their hearing until the following day. The fifth day of Pachon in the (?) year of Claudius Caesar Augustus.

The sixth day of Pachon: the second day. Claudius Caesar hears the case of Isidorus, gymnasiarch of Alexandria against King Agrippa in the [?Servi]lian Gardens. With him sat twenty senators and also sixteen men of consular rank, with the women of the court also attending the trial of Isidorus.

Isidorus was the first to speak: 'My Lord Caesar, I beg you to listen to my account of the sufferings of my fatherland.'

The emperor: 'I grant you this day [to put your case].'

All the senators who were sitting as assessors agree with this, knowing the kind of man Isidorus was.

5 Pachon = 1 May. For Agrippa see **J5c**. The detail of Claudius sitting with advisers is likely, but 36 seems a great many, perhaps an attempt to increase the significance of the trial (Tiberius' *consilium* was twenty-strong (Suet. *Tib.* 55), Domitian's *consilium* numbered 12: see note on **U8**), while the reference to women of the court, could also be invented detail.

M7b Claudius resents Isidorus' abuse of Agrippa

Claudius Caesar: 'Do not, by the Gods, say anything against my friend. For you have killed two other friends of mine. You have already killed Theon the religious advisor and Naevius the prefect of Egypt and the prefect of the Praetorian Guard at Rome; and now you prosecute this man.'

Isidorus: 'My Lord Caesar, what do you care for a three-obol Jew like Agrippa?'

Claudius Caesar: 'What? You are the most insolent of men to speak ...'

Isidorus: '... I will not deny ... be quiet ... beaten ... Olympian Caesar ... about Augustus ... I am brought here (or 'led away to death'?), a gymnasiarch of Alexandria, fifty-six years old, a Greek ... an orator ...' and with his right hand ... he threw off his cloak ... and said: 'one must not ...'

Claudius Caesar: '... Isidorus, against Theon ... neither Rome nor Alexandria ...'

Isidorus: '... a gymnasiarch of Alexandria ... by nature ... seven temples of Augustus ... not allow me ...' ... being taken away in the robes of a gymnasiarch.

Claudius Caesar: 'Do not say anything, Isidorus, Isidorus (by the Gods!) anything against my friend ...'

Agrippa was a friend of Antonia, mother of Claudius (**J5c**), and, also, according to the Jewish Josephus, instrumental in securing the throne for Claudius (**E27** and **E31**).

M7c Isidorus cross-examines Agrippa

Isidorus: 'My Lord Augustus, with regard to your interests, Balbillus indeed speaks well. But to you, Agrippa, I wish to oppose the points you bring up about the Jews. I

accuse them of wishing to stir up the entire world...We must consider every detail in order to judge the whole people. They are not of the same nature as the Alexandrians, but live rather in the same manner as the Egyptians. Are they not equal to those who pay the poll-tax?'
Agrippa: 'The Egyptians have had taxes levied on them by their rulers...But no one has imposed tributes on the Jews.'
Balbillus: 'Look to what extremes of insolence either his god or...'

By 'Alexandrians', Isidorus means the Greek citizens, not Egyptians, the local inhabitants.

M7d Isidorus continues to abuse Claudius

Lampon to Isidorus: 'I have looked upon my death...'
Claudius Caesar: 'Isidorus, you have killed many friends of mine.'
Isidorus: 'I merely obeyed the orders of the king who was then ruling. So too I should be willing to denounce anyone you wish.'
Claudius Caesar: 'Isidorus, you really are the son of an actress!'
Isidorus: 'I am neither a slave nor the son of an actress, but a gymnasiarch of the glorious city of Alexandria. But you are a cast-off son of the Jewess Salome! Therefore...'
Lampon to Isidorus: 'We might as well give in to a crazy emperor.'
Claudius Caesar: 'To those whom I ordered (to carry out) the execution of Isidorus and Lampon...'

[*Corpus Papyrorum Judaicarum* II 156a, b, c and d]

M8 Speech of Claudius(?) to the senate on judicial reform

It should be noted that this speech nowhere actually identifies its speaker, but it is generally accepted that this fragmentary speech preserved on papyrus was delivered by Claudius to the senate, possibly at some point between 42 and 47. Claudius was noted for his high level of involvement in court cases at Rome, but his interventions were represented as arbitrary and inconsistent (For this Claudian habit, compare Seneca, *Apocol.* **F12.3**, v. 21, **F14.2–3**; Suet. *Claud.* 15.2; Dio 60.28.5.). In this speech, he appears to be attempting to reduce the number of malicious prosecutions in the lawcourts, particularly when prosecutors fail to continue with cases which they have brought. Claudius here urges the senate to decide cases against them if litigants are absent. This speech also gives insight into the relationship between emperor and senate, with Claudius being concerned for the senate's *maiestas* ('dignity' – compare similar concerns in **Q1**), and urging senators to engage in meaningful debate. For Tiberius' contempt for 'men ready to be slaves' see Tac. *Ann.* 3.65.3.

M8a Jurors in cases of slavery and freedom

[*Column* I.1] [...] it seems troublesome (for them) to be attached to five jury-panels. For sure, see to it that you take care that no one of 24 years [is given as] an assessor: for it is not unjust, in my opinion, that these men make judgements about slavery and freedom, [who] in pursuing their own affairs [use the help] of the Plaetorian law in no respect. In my opinion, gentlemen of the senate, I have indeed often noticed at other times too, but especially at this time, the incredible skills of those who are engaged in lawsuits, who once an indictment has been signed [...]

M8b Malicious prosecutions

[*Column* II.1] [...] [so that] it may be profitable for the plaintiff to have won the case. So that these skills do not bring advantage to those acting maliciously, if you agree, gentlemen of the senate, let us decree that the necessity of judging, even in court recesses, should be imposed on those judges who have not made judgements once they have been begun within the days allotted for the case. Nor am I unaware that many ploys will be attempted by those acting monstrously: I hope we have thought of remedies against these. [II. 9] Meanwhile it is sufficient to have blocked this abuse which is too widespead amongst those making malicious prosecutions. For I cannot bear at all the tyranny of prosecutors, who have brought their enemies as defendants before a panel of inquiry, then leave them hanging on the charge-sheet while they themselves go on their holidays as if they have done nothing, though natural justice rather than the laws holds that the prosecutor should be as much bound and restrained as the defendant. The fastidiousness of defendants who choose not to put on mourning clothes and let hair and beards grow so as to make their plight seem more pitiful, helps make such acts by the prosecutors seem less offensive.

[*Column* III.1] Nonetheless they themselves may see what gifts given by [nature may benefit them] in achieving sympathy. But as for the prosecutors, [let us remove] their ill-defined tyranny in such a way that we allow the praetor, once the days for collecting evidence have elapsed, to summon the prosecutor; and if he neither comes nor offers any excuse, it should be judged that the prosecution was undertaken wrongly and maliciously.

Claudius extended the law terms (Suet. *Claud.* 23.1). For his tendency to penalise absent litigants, see Suet. *Claud.* 15.2; Dio 60.28.6).

M8c Claudius encourages proper senatorial discussion

[III.10] Gentlemen of the senate, if these things please you, show as much at once, straightforwardly and sincerely. If not, find other solutions, but here, within this sacred space, or if you wish to take time to consider this at greater leisure, take the time, while in whatever order you are called upon, remember to give your [own] opinion. [III.17] For it goes completely against the dignity of this senatorial order for only one, the consul designate, to express the opinion written down in the report of the consuls and for all the others simply to say, 'I agree' and then, on leaving 'we have spoken'.

[Smallwood 367 = *BGU* 611]

M9 Claudius' edict, Tridentum, AD 46

This bronze tablet was found near Tridentum (modern Trento) in the Alps. Claudius' edict deals with two separate issues, namely controversy between the people of Comum and the Bergaleians, and the improper assumption of Roman citizenship by the Anauni and other tribes, who incorrectly assumed that they were permitted to adopt citizenship on being assigned to the authority of the city of Tridentum. The extension of Roman citizenship was one of the features of Claudius' reign, but this particular example seems to have been an ad hoc response to a particular situation rather than the result of a particular policy to extend citizenship. Claudius criticises his two predecessors, alluding to Tiberius' prolonged absence from Rome on Capri. In referring to names in the final paragraph, Claudius means the *tria nomina* of Roman citizens. The translation may seem rather rambling and incoherent, but so is Claudius' edict!

M9a Preamble

[1] In the consulship of Marcus Junius Silanus and Quintus Sulpicius Camerinus [AD 46], on 15 March, the edict of Tiberius Claudius Caesar Augustus Germanicus which is written below was published at the imperial residence at Baiae.

Tiberius Claudius Caesar Augustus Germanicus, *pontifex maximus*, holding tribunician power for the 6th time, hailed as victorious commander 11 times, father of the fatherland, designated to be consul for the fourth time, declares:

M9b Claudius criticises his predecessors

[7] "Since, as a result of the old disputes which were in the air for some considerable time even in the times of Tiberius Caesar my uncle, to settle which disputes he had sent Pinarius Apollinaris (disputes which were only between the people of Comum, as far as I remember, and the Bergaleians), and he, first because of the prolonged absence of my uncle and then also in the principate of Gaius because he was not being required by him to make a report, he did not do so (rather cannily), and afterwards Camurius Statutus has informed me that very many fields and woodlands are under my jurisdiction; to deal with this pressing matter I have sent Julius Planta, my friend and associate, who, after he had summoned my procurators both in another area and in the neighbourhood, he has investigated the matter with the greatest care and has made an inquiry; as for the other matters, as explained to me in the report which he has made, I grant him permission to decide and make a pronouncement.

M9c Claudius' decision on the status of Anaunians and others

[21] As far as relates to the status of the Anaunians, the Tulliassians and the Sindunians, part of whom an informer is said to have proved to have been assigned to the Tridentines, and part of them not even assigned, although I note that this type of persons does not have a very strong basis for their Roman citizenship, nevertheless, since they are said to have been in possession of it for a long time and to be so intermingled with the Tridentines that they could not be separated from them without serious harm to that distinguished *municipium*, I permit them to remain in that right which they believed they had through my favour, the more willingly because a very many of this type of persons are said to be in my praetorian guard, some indeed as centurions, and that some of them have been appointed to juries in Rome to decide lawsuits.

[34] I grant this favour to them on condition that I order that whatever they have done and transacted as if they were Roman citizens either among themselves or with the Tridentines or with others should be ratified, and as for their names, which they had previously as if they were Roman citizens, that I permit them to keep them.

[Smallwood 368 = *ILS* 206 = Sherk no.52]

M10 Regulations concerning embassies from Maroneia to Rome (after AD 45/6)

Two inscribed decrees upon a stele of Thasian marble, found reused at Samothrace, appear to have been brought there from Maroneia as ballast or building-material. They relate to the relationship between Maroneia and Rome. Maroneia had been granted valuable privileges in a treaty with Rome, perhaps around 167 BC. These appear to have been threatened or overlooked shortly after Claudius became emperor, perhaps as a result of the creation of the new province of Thrace in AD 45–46. The inscription relates how Claudius has confirmed their privileges in response to an embassy sent to him, and establishes a procedure for sending future embassies to whomever happens to be emperor at the time in an attempt to protect the city's interests. It also alludes to the troubles experienced by Maroneia in response to their support of Rome during the Mithridatic war in 88–87 BC. The inscription's opening formula documents the take-over of real power in Maroneia by an interest group of the leading inhabitants and the marginalising of the majority of citizens. It is this group which devises a procedure for choosing future ambassadors, in an anti-democratic scheme. The second decree is a template for how to send an embassy to the emperor.

M10a Traditional privileges of Maroneia confirmed by Claudius

Decree of the town councilors, priests, magistrates, Romans living in the city, and all the remaining citizens. The council decided: since the most conspicuous god of the universe and creator of new blessings for all men, Tiberius Claudius Caes[ar Augu]stus Germanicus, after we sent an embassy to him and made clear the support of the city towards the people of Rome and the misfortunes which the people of Maroneia formerly endured because of its friendship towards the Romans, since it became friend and ally straightaway at the same time as their rule was established, and since after this it endured seeing the destruction of the city across a perimeter of eight miles, the loss of children, and plundering and taking prisoner and the other misfortunes in turn, so that none of the rights of the Romans should be broken, in return for which it was judged ally and friend by the senate through decrees, and partner in a treaty and alliance, it received freedom and laws with other privileges which were made clear by the senate through decrees and by emperors through their responses, it replied that such a city was deserving of being adorned with everlasting thanks, with none of the privileges granted to it being diminished, because of which in fact it restored its ancient right, confirming its freedom and all its privileges, having promised through its reply an undertaking that is appropriate and possible for such a god, and that we should be kept for the future free from injury.

M10b Procedure established for future embassies

But it is very necessary for all of us too to take care that it happens not now nor at any other time, the rights of the city being forgotten, that in any way our freedom and privileges are diminished. It will be on this condition if, thanks to these things and through a decree considered as an everlasting law, the embassy to the Augusti is ready at every critical moment, with no way being possible to trouble those who wish to undertake the contest for their fatherland. It was decided by the council and people for the decree concerning such an embassy, which is written at the end of the decree, to be inscribed and ratified, and that it be secured beforehand for ever, so that if any emergency compels the need for such an embassy, our freedom being shattered or the rest of our privileges in any way, all those who so desire have the power through a public document to register themselves as envoys in the decree, having sworn the oath written below this decree to register themselves as envoys and having sealed the decree with a seal which has the face of Dionysos, as those judged best who were in this way established as envoys according to the decree by the leader of the empire, Imperator god Augustus Caesar, no one having the power to write nor say the opposite of this, nor to put forward another envoy, nor for anyone to serve as an envoy according to a temporary decree containing the opposite to what had previously been decreed, nor to hinder the embassy or to make anything fighting against the decree passed as law in any way.

[...*further fragmentary lines follow concerning the envoys*...]

[......] is considered worthy of being friend and ally and of [receiving the freedom] decided upon [through] decrees of the senate and the laws with the city and territory and all the privileges which are clear from the decrees and responses of emperors.

It is supremely necessary to neglect no opportunity to recall each point about our rights so that everything may be kept unbroken and safe by the leaders of the empire. It was decided by the council and people to choose an embassy which, having come to Imperator god Augustus Caesar should greet him on behalf of the city, and having joined in celebrating the fact that his household and affairs are strong and that things are going as well as possible for the people of Rome, having set out all the rights of the city to him and to the holy senate, shall ask with every petition and prayer to preserve our freedom and laws and city and territory and all the other privileges which our ancestors and ourselves have received from them and possess, so that we who on every occasion and without interruption have kept goodwill and good faith towards the Romans may have the benefit of their gratitude because of this at all times. Envoys were chosen who are most truly enthusiastic for their fatherland.

M10c Oath for ambassadors and other citizens

Oath for envoys through a public document will be as follows:

Someone, son of someone made an undertaking in front of the archons at a meeting offering to be an envoy to the Augustus and senate concerning the freedom of the city of Maroneia and all their privileges, just as the decrees which have been written about this contain on three *stelai*, striving with all strength and not executing the embassy in bad faith, nor compromising it, nor being bribed by anyone in any way, and I swear by god [Augustus] Caesar and Tiberius Caesar god Augustus and Tiberius Claudius Cae[sar Augus]tus Germanicus and by the holy senate and by all the other gods that I shall observe all that is written above. If I remain true to my oath, may things go well for me, but the opposite if I swear falsely.

Oath to be sworn by everyone: I swear by all the gods and all the goddesses and by god Augu[stus Caesar and by Tiberius Caesa]r god Augustus and Tiberius Claudius Caesar [Augustus Germanicus and] by the holy senate that I shall do everything, striving with all [my strength…] for the freedom of the fatherland and for all [the privileges] which we have received from the senate and people [of Rome and the emperors] and not to conduct an embassy against these things […. nor to write anything against] the common interest in any way nor to say nor [do anything … for the] destruction, or repeal or cancellation […If I remain true to my oath, may things go well for me,] but if I swear falsely, total and utter destruction [for all my descendants].

[Greek: *AE* (2003) 1559]

M11 Claudius' speech on admitting the Gauls to the senate, AD 48

In this speech, preserved as an inscription in two columns upon a bronze tablet found at Lugdunum (modern Lyons), Claudius advocates admitting Gauls from the province of Gallia Comata to membership of the senate. This formed part of his activities as censor that year, a post whose duties included revising membership of the senate. According to Tacitus, a request had come from leading-men in Gallia Comata that they should be allowed to hold public office at Rome. Although Claudius could just have acted of his own accord, he chose to try to persuade the senate to incline towards his way of thinking on the subject. The speech displays Claudius' love of antiquarian scholarship, and gives a vivid impression of his style of speech-making, complete with feeble jokes, weak arguments, rambling digressions, and self-apostrophe. The version of the speech in Tacitus (*Ann.* 11.23–25, **M12**) is a great improvement upon the original, lending it more authority and coherence, and arguing with the benefit of hindsight in favour of the higher profile of provincials at Rome (by Tacitus' day, of course, even the emperor could be of provincial origin: Trajan was from Spain).

M11a Claudius' introduction

[Column 1] [*The first line is fragmentary*]. Indeed I beg you not to show that reaction which tends to occur first of all, one which I foresee will be the very first obstacle to my new proposal, of being horrified as if it is something revolutionary being introduced. I ask you instead to consider how many innovations have been made in this state, how many different forms of constitution have been established, right from the foundation of our City.

something revolutionary: Claudius is aware that the Romans generally and doubtless senators in particular were very conservative. The Latin for 'revolution' is *res novae*, literally 'new things'. Claudius himself describes his new proposal as *res nova* – 'a new thing'.

M11b Claudius on the Kings of Rome

[1.8] In ancient times kings governed this city, but they did not happen to hand it down to successors within their own house. Other families took over power, sometimes even foreigners. Examples of this are Numa, Romulus' successor, who was a Sabine, a neighbouring people, admittedly, but at that time foreign, and Tarquinius Priscus who came after Ancus Martius. When he was refused any opportunity of winning an honourable position at home because of his impure blood – because he was the son of a father, Demarathus, who was a Corinthian, and his mother, although from Tarquinii, was noble but impoverished and so had no option but to sink to marrying such a husband – after he migrated to Rome, he gained the throne.

[1.16] Between the first Tarquin and his son or grandson (our sources differ on this) came Servius Tullius. If we follow Roman authors, he was the son of a woman prisoner of war, Ocresia. But if we follow Etruscan ones, originally he was the most loyal of Caelius Vivenna's companions, who had been with him in all his adventures: forced to leave Etruria after various escapades with all that was left of Caelius' army, he seized the Caelian Hill, which he named after his own leader Caelius. Having changed his own name (his Tuscan name had been Mastarna) to Servius Tullius, as I have mentioned, his reign was of greatest benefit to the state. Then after the behaviour of Tarquin the Proud became intolerable to the citizens of Rome, and not only his own, but that of his sons, public opinion was thoroughly disgusted with the monarchy, and the government was therefore entrusted to consuls, magistrates elected annually.

Numa: Livy 1.18 says that the senators voted unanimously for him as king despite fearing a consequent increase in Sabine influence (compare Dionysius of Halicarnassus, *Roman Antiquities,* 2.58).

Tarquinius Priscus: Livy 1.34 and 35 describes how in canvassing for the kingship he cited two previous foreign kings of Rome (compare Dio. Hal. 3.46–48).

our sources differ: Livy 1.46.4 notes the same uncertainty. Dionysius of Halicarnassus (4.6–7) goes to great lengths to show they must have been grandsons, citing the annalist L. Piso Frugi as the only historian to suggest this.

Ocresia: compare Livy 1.39, although he does not give the name Ocresia (compare Dio. Hal, 4.1 for 'Ocrisia').

Caelian Hill: compare Dio. Hal. 2.36.2; Varro, *Latin Language* 5.46.

Etruscan ones: None of this Etruscan version is mentioned by Livy or Dionysius Halicarnassus, and reflects Claudius' own antiquarian researches.

Servius Tullius: compare Livy 1.41–48, with 'republican' tribute to his reign (1.48.8–9) and Dionysius of Halicarnassus *Ant. Rom.* 4.13–26 for details of the new institutions he established for Rome.

Tarquin the Proud: compare Livy 1.46–60, Dio. Hal. 4.28–48 and 4.64–85.

M11c Claudius on the Republic

[1.28] Why should I now refer to the dictatorial powers, established by our ancestors as stronger than those of the consuls, which were called into operation in times of crisis whether in wars or in civil unrest? Or to the tribunes of the people, appointed to help the people? Or the transference of supreme power from the consuls to the decemvirs, and then back again to the consuls after the reign of the decemvirs had been brought to an end? Or, further, to the fact that consular power was divided among a larger number of men, called military tribunes with consular authority, who were appointed six and often eight at a time. Or, finally, to the sharing by plebeians in the priesthoods as well as in positions of power.

If I were now to speak of the wars from which our ancestors began and how far we have advanced, I fear I should seem too arrogant. You would think I was trying to boast of the glory of extending our Empire beyond Ocean. But I shall instead return to the point. The citizenship … *(rest of paragraph lost)*

A very similar brief sweep through the various constitutions of the Roman Republic is in Tac. *Ann.* 1.1.2.

dictatorial powers: The first dictatorship was established in 501 BC (Livy 2.18; Dionysius of Halicarnassus, *Roman Antiquities*, 5.70–73).

tribunes of the people: first tribunate of the plebs in 494/3 BC (Livy 2.33; Dio.Hal. 6.87–89).

decemvirs: The decemvirate began in 451 BC (Livy 3.33/36) and 449 (Livy 3.54; Dio. Hal, 10.75–76). During this period, Appius Claudius Crassus Inregillensis Sabinus helped to consolidate the Claudian tribe's reputation for arrogance and hostility towards the *plebs* (Suet. *Tib.* 1–3).

military tribunes: established in 444–367 BC (Livy 4.6).

extending our Empire beyond Ocean: Claudius alludes here to his conquest of Britain.

citizenship: Given that the text breaks off at this point, it is impossible to judge whether or not Claudius went on to elucidate his attitude towards granting Roman citizenship, generosity in doing which is one of the features of his reign.

M11d Claudius on Gaul

[*The start of column II is lost …*] can be. It was, of course, an innovation when both my great-uncle, Divus Augustus, and my uncle, Tiberius Caesar, wanted all the best men from colonies and municipalities everywhere to be in this senate, provided they had the necessary qualifications of character and wealth. [2.5] You may object that an Italian senator is preferable to a provincial one. Well, I soon shall make clear my opinion on this when I begin to ask you to ratify that part of my censorship. But in my opinion not even provincials should be rejected, provided that they can be of value to the senate.

[2.9] Just look at the extremely distinguished and wealthy colony of Vienne. How long is it now that it has provided this senate house with members? From this colony has come, amongst others, Lucius Vestinus, that excellent and outstanding member of the equestrian order, whom I number among my closest friends and whom today I am employing in my private affairs. And I beg that his children may enjoy the first rank of priesthoods and later, as the years go by, advance to further honours. I shall not mention the ill-omened name of a certain rogue. [2.15] And I dislike intensely that monstrosity of the wrestling-ring who brought the consulship into his family before his colony had received the full benefit of Roman citizenship. I could say the same about his brother who, because of this very unfortunate and disgraceful circumstance cannot be a useful member of the senate.

[2.20] Now is the time, Tiberius Caesar Germanicus, to reveal to the gentlemen of the senate the direction of your speech; for you have already reached the extreme edge of Narbonese Gaul. [2.23] Look – all those noble young men whom I am looking at would cause us no more shame if they became senators than my friend Persicus, that most aristocratic of men, is ashamed to read the name of Allobrogicus among the busts of his ancestors. If you agree that this is so, what further argument do you require, than that I point out that the very land beyond the frontiers of Narbonese Gaul is already sending us senators, when we have senators from Lyons whom we are not ashamed to welcome into our order? [2.30] I am apprehensive, gentlemen of the senate, of going beyond the provincial frontiers you are accustomed to and familiar with; but the case of Gallia Comata must now be rigorously argued. If anyone is concerned about the fact that the people there plagued Divus Julius for ten years in war, let him set against that one hundred years of resolute loyalty, an allegiance which has more than stood the test of many difficult crises in the Empire. [2.35] It was they who ensured that my father, Drusus, when engaged in the conquest of Germany, had behind him a province that was safe, quiet, reliable and peaceful, even though he was called away to war while conducting the census, which was something new and unaccustomed for the Gauls. The difficulty of this task we are at this time particularly discovering ourselves [2.40] by all too bitter experience, although we are trying merely to publish the state of our resources.

[Smallwood 369 = *ILS* 212]

Vienne: in Gallia Narbonensis.

Lucius Vestinus: a member of the imperial council and imperial procurator; later prefect of Egypt.

ill-omened name of a certain rogue: Claudius is referring obliquely to Valerius Asiaticus, from Vienne. He was consul in 35 and 46, but was forced to commit suicide in 47, when he was accused of a plan to start a revolt (compare Tac., *Annals* 11.1–3).

my friend Persicus: Paullus Fabius Persicus (consul in 34), was a descendant of Quintus Fabius Maximus, who as consul in 121 BC defeated the Arverni and Allobroges tribes of central Gaul, winning for himself the unique name 'Allobrogicus'. This is Claudius' point: the new Gauls will have strange names, but so did some of Rome's aristocrats. But we may wonder if senators would not have found this a rather flawed argument: after all, Fabius Maximus was called Allobrogicus not because he belonged to the Allobroges, but because he had conquered them. This may be a rather feeble attempt at a joke on Claudius' part.

senators from Lyons: possibly another feeble joke, alluding to the fact that Claudius himself had been born in Lyons (ancient Lugdunum), at a time when his mother Antonia had accompanied her husband, Drusus, who was effectively governing Gaul.

Gallia Comata: This refers to the whole area we think of as Gaul, i.e. modern France. But the term, meaning 'Long-Haired Gaul' is usually insulting.

one hundred years of resolute loyalty: Claudius chooses to ignore the serious revolt of Florus and Sacrovir under Tiberius (Tac. *Ann.* 3.40ff).

my father, Drusus: Claudius puts a positive spin on history here. The summary of Livy (LACTOR 17, D6) says: 'The states of Germany on both sides of the Rhine were attacked by Drusus, and a revolt which arose in Gaul over the census was settled.' Dio Cassius (54.32.1) suggests that Drusus took pre-emptive action to prevent a German tribe exploiting Gallic unrest.

M12 Tacitus' version

My own ancestors, the first of whom, Clausus was of Sabine origin but was made a Roman citizen and a patrician at one and the same time, encourage me to adopt the same policy for the nation, by bringing outstanding talent to Rome, wherever it is found. For I do not forget that the Julii are from Alba Longa, the Coruncanii from Camerium, the Porcii from Tusculum; and, to leave antiquity aside, that men from Etruria, Lucania, and all Italy have been brought into the senate; and that finally Italy herself has been extended to the Alps, so that not only single individuals but whole areas and races have been united as Romans.

Then we prospered with long periods of peace at home and success abroad. We admitted those living beyond the Po to the citizenship; and the strongest of the provincials were added to settlements of legionaries all over the world as a means of reinvigorating the tired empire. Is it shameful that the Balbi immigrated from Spain, and other equally distinguished men from Narbonese Gaul? Their descendants are with us; and they love their country no less than we do. What else brought about the fall of Sparta and Athens, despite their military strength, but failing to integrate conquered peoples as foreigners? Whereas our founder, Romulus, was wise enough to regard several peoples as enemies one day and Roman citizens the next. Even foreigners have been kings among us. Nor is it a recent innovation, as most people wrongly believe, for the sons of freedmen to hold elected office: it often happened in ancient times.

'But we fought Gauls from Senonia.' Yes, and Italians often were arrayed in battle against us – the Vulsci and Aequi. 'We were captured by Gauls.' And we surrendered hostages to the Etruscans and were enslaved by the Samnites. Yet if you look back over all our wars, none was over so quickly as that against the Gauls: and from that time peace and loyalty have been unbroken. Now that they have been assimilated into our customs, culture and even our families, they should contribute their gold and wealth, not keep it to themselves. Members of the senate, even the most hallowed institutions were once new. Plebeians followed patricians into elected office; Latins followed plebeians; other Italian peoples followed the Latins. This change too will become long-established; and what we look for precedents to justify will itself become a precedent.

[Tacitus, *Annals* 11.24]

Attus (later Appius) *Clausus*: (cos. 495) – Livy 2.16 and Suet. *Tib.* 1.1 ('Atta Claudius'). The *Sabines* were one of Rome's earliest rivals and enemies, with the 'Abduction of the Sabine Women' being one of the most famous stories (myths?) of Ancient Rome, e.g. Livy 1.9–13.

Iulii – Iulus/Ascanius, son of Aeneas, founder of Alba Longa – Livy 1.3; Virgil, *Aeneid* 1.268–272.

Coruncanii: Tiberius Coruncanius, cos 280 BC, first plebeian *pontifex maximus* (Livy, *Epitome* 18).

Porcii: family famous for M. Porcius Cato 'the Censor', 'a dominant figure of political and cultural life in the first half of the 2nd century BC.' (*OCD*) and his grandson, M. Porcius Cato 'of Utica', opponent of Julius Caesar in the civil war.

Po: river in area now Northern Italy, but originally known to Romans as Cisapline Gaul. Conquest was completed in 191 BC; a province after 87 BC, the inhabitants were first given Latin rights, then full citizenship by Julius Caesar in 49 BC. As 'Transpadania' 1 of 11 regions of Italy in Augustus' division of Italy (LACTOR 17, K64, K65).

Balbi: L. Cornelius Balbus, from Cadiz in Baetica (S. Spain) became Rome's first non-Italian consul in 40 BC. He built a theatre in Rome in 13 BC.

Narbonese Gaul: now known as 'Provence' because it was the first Latin *provincia* in 121 BC. Prominent men from Narbonensis included Duvius Avitus, *cos suff.* 56 and Burrus, praetorian prefect AD 51–62.

foreigners ... kings: Tacitus makes very briefly the same point as Claudius (**M10b**).

Gauls: Rome was captured and sacked by Gauls in 390 BC (Livy 5.40–49).

Vulsci, Aequi, Etruscans, Samnites: native Italic peoples who fought against Rome at various points.

M13 Epigram on Nero, the saviour of Rhodes

Rhodes is my name, the isle of Helios, now Caesar's own.
From each alike I boast an equal light.
My old fire died; a new sun brought fresh radiance;
Nero outshone you, Helios, with beams more bright.
Where lies my greater debt, I cannot tell. When I arose from sea
Helios revealed me; but when I sank, 'twas Nero rescued me.

[Antiphilus 6 (Gow & Page) = *Palatine Anthology* 9.178]

Antiphilus wrote around 50 Greek epigrams on varied, but commonplace themes. The epigram above is the only one on political events and provides our only evidence for the poet's dates. Rhodes was deprived of its liberties by Claudius in AD 44. In AD 53, Nero as *princeps iuventutis* made a speech to the senate in Greek successfully asking for their restoration (Tac. *Ann.* 12.58). The Rhodians celebrated Nero on a public inscription (*IG* 12 1.2.12) and on a coin (Eckhel *Doctrina Numorum Veterum* 2.605). In mythology, when the gods initially claims lands for themselves, Helios was away and Rhodes underwater. So Helios claimed the island when it emerged (Pindar, *Olympian Odes* 7.54–71).

NERO FREES GREECE: M14–M17

Nero spent sixteen months travelling in Greece during 66/67. The major panhellenic games were rescheduled so as to allow him to 'compete' in them. The province of Achaia had experienced various misfortunes, as the battle-ground for Mithridates, Sulla, and Brutus and Cassius in turn. Nero's itinerary focused upon the Roman province of Achaia, with its provincial capital at Corinth, rather than upon classical Athens and Sparta. He embarked upon excavating a canal across the isthmus at Corinth (**M18**; Suet. *Nero* 19), an ambitious project that remained incomplete until the end of the nineteenth century. The climax to his visit was his grant of 'freedom' to the province at the Isthmian games of 67, whereby it was made exempt from Roman rule and taxation, but this grant was rescinded a few years later by Vespasian (**M16**). The relevant part of Tacitus' *Annals* is lost, but Dio Cassius 63.8–11 gives an account possibly derived from the senator and historian Cluvius Rufus who was forced to act as Nero's herald, and full of outrage at a Roman emperor competing in artistic competitions.

M14a Edict of Nero

Imperator Caesar says: "Wishing to repay the noblest land of Hellas for her goodwill and reverence towards me, I order as many as possible from this province to be present at Corinth on the 28th day of November."

M14b Speech of Nero

When the crowds came together in the assembly, he addressed them in the following words:

"It is an unexpected gift, men of Hellas, that I grant you – although nothing is beyond expectation from my generosity – a gift so great that you were incapable of asking for it. All you Hellenes, who inhabit Achaia and what was till now the Peloponnese, receive your freedom and immunity from taxation, which you did not enjoy even in your most fortunate days. For you were enslaved either to foreigners or to one another. I wish that I were offering this gift when Hellas was in its heyday, so that more might benefit from this favour. For this reason, I blame time for squandering already the extent of my favour. Even now it is not through pity so much as goodwill that I grant this benefit to you, and I make repayment to your gods, whose consideration for me I have always experienced both by land and sea, because they have allowed me to bestow so great a favour. Other leaders have liberated cities, [[but only Nero]] has liberated a province."

M14c Decree of Acraephia, commemorating the liberation of Achaia

Epaminondas, son of Epaminondas, high priest of the Augusti for life, and of Nero Claudius Caesar Augustus, spoke as follows, declaring that he had proposed this decree to the council and people:

"Since Nero, lord of the whole world, mightiest imperator, in the 13th year of tribunician power, father of the fatherland, new Sun-god shining upon the Hellenes, having chosen to show kindness to Hellas and at the same time repaying and reverencing our gods for always standing by him in providence and protection, since he alone throughout all time mightiest imperator, philhellene, ~~Nero~~ Zeus Liberator, has given, granted and re-established in its ancient state of autonomy and freedom, the freedom which was indigenous and innate from all time which had formerly been removed, granting in addition to this great, unexpected gift immunity from taxation as well, which no one of the former Augusti granted in full; for all these reasons it has been decided by rulers and councillors and people to dedicate at this present time the altar to Zeus the Saviour with the inscription

'To Zeus Liberator ~~Nero~~ for ever'

and to set up alongside our own ancestral gods in the temple of Apollo Ptoios statues of ~~Nero~~ Zeus Liberator and of goddess Augusta ~~Messalina~~, so that when this work is completed our city also may be seen to have rendered in full all honour and reverence to the ~~House of Nero~~ lord Augustus. And it is proposed that the decree be inscribed on a stele alongside the temple of Zeus the Saviour in the market-place and in the temple of Apollo Ptoios."

[Greek: Smallwood 64 = *ILS* 8794]

This inscription is preserved upon a marble stele, found at Acraephia in Boeotia. It was displayed in the Temple of Apollo Ptoios. The stele contains an edict and speech delivered by Nero at the Isthmian Games at Corinth (Suet. *Nero* 24.2; Pliny *NH* 4.22; Pausanias 7.17.2), in which he liberated the province of Achaia, followed by an honorific decree by the town of Acraephia. The authentic voice of Nero may be detected in the first part, with its rather pompous self-reference and self-glorification. The reference to 'what was till now the Peloponnese' hints that perhaps plans were underfoot to rename the Peloponnese, possibly as the Neronese. This is followed by a decree put forward by a member of the local élite, proposing that the town honour Nero as Zeus Eleutherios ('the Liberator'). The people and council grant divine honours to Nero, including the setting up of statues of Nero and his wife Messalina Statilia in the temple. Like the grant of freedom itself, these honours were also shortlived: the names of Nero and Messalina were later erased, after the emperor's downfall.

M15 Freedom granted to Greece twice

So, in the city of Corinth, the same event, concerning the Greeks, has now happened twice. For Titus Flaminius before, and Nero again in our own times, on both occasions at Corinth and during the Isthmian Games, made the Greeks free and independent. Titus is said to have used a herald, but Nero spoke in public to a large crowd from a platform in the *agora*. But this was later.

[Plutarch, *Life of Titus Flaminius* 12.8]

Titus Quinctius Flaminius (*c.* 229–174 BC) was a patrician politician and general. In charge of the war against Philip V of Macedon, he proclaimed the freedom of Achaia in 196 BC and was showered with honours, including, in Greece, divine honours. Livy gives an account of the announcement at 33.32–3. Plutarch (*c.* AD 50–120) introduces this digression on Nero into his biography of Titus Flaminius. Plutarch rightly presents Nero making the announcement in the *agora* (Greek equivalent of a Roman forum, and where the assembly would be) as against Suetonius who has it in the middle of the stadium (*Nero* 24.2). Philostratos, *Life of Apollonius of Tyana* 5.41 gives a later and much more rose-tinted view of freed Greece achieving a renaissance and a unity greater than in the past.

M16 Pausanias' *Guide to Greece*: Nero frees Greece

Some time later Roman kingship passed to Nero, and he released Achaia from all duties. He thus made a change in regard to the Roman people, by giving them the very prosperous island of Sardinia in exchange for Greece. When I consider this action of Nero, it seems to me that the philosopher Plato got it exactly right in saying that the most significant crimes in terms of size and scope are not those of the man on the street, but come from a noble spirit ruined by a corrupt education. However the Greeks were not to benefit from this gift: in the reign of Vespasian, who followed Nero, they fell into civil war, and Vespasian ordered them to pay taxes once more and to obey a governor, saying that the Greek nation had forgotten freedom.

[Pausanias, 7.17.3–4]

Elsewhere Pausanias links Nero stealing works of art from Greek temples with killing his mother and wives (9.27.4). Provinces were 'imperial' (governed by prefects or procurators, appointed by the emperor) or 'public' (governed by senators) – see Strabo 17.3.25 = LACTOR 17, M2. Nero's changes were reversed by Vespasian (Suet. *Vesp.* 8.4) who made Achaia a public province once more but assigned Sardinia to an imperial prefect (Levick, *Vesp.* 138).

M17 Aftermath of grant of freedom to Achaia, Epidaurus, AD 67

Achaians, Boeotians, Phocians, Euboeans, Locrians, and Dorians (honoured) Titus Statilius Timocrates, who had been their secretary, for his merit. Since Titus Statilius Timocrates, a man of distinction and of the first rank, who has in every way lived a dignified and admirable life, pursued an excellent political course and, when elected secretary after our grant of freedom [in] times that involved crises that were very troublesome and on occasion also dangerous, undertook tasks and responsibilities that were too great for a single man and too numerous for one year, by means of which he often put us in an advantageous position and set the conditions of our freedom, which were still undirected, on a firm basis. On account of all these things the Assembly of the Panachaians decided to praise this man and set up bronze statues of him in the assembly places of the Panachaians and [in the] sacred enclosure [of Amarios] and at Epidauros in the shrine of Asclepius, [with] the following inscription: Achaians, Boeotians, Phocians, Euboeans, Locrians, and Dorians (honoured) Titus Statilius Timocrates who was [their secretary], for his merit.

[Greek: Smallwood 65 = *SIG*^{3} 796A]

This inscribed marble base from Epidauros attests to problems following the grant of freedom to Achaia. Poverty and depopulation were probably underlying problems ('practically two thirds of Euboea is infertile because of neglect and depopulation' according to Dio Chrysostom, *Orations* 7.34, writing around thirty years later). Local rivalries of the sort which provided Vespasian with the excuse for revoking Nero's grant of freedom were presumably another source of difficulty.

M18a Nero and the Corinthian Canal: the good

You can be assured, Menecrates, that Nero's plans were genuinely good: for he would have put an end to seafarers having to make the voyage round the Peloponnese, past Cape Malea, by breaking through the two and a half miles of the isthmus. This would have helped trade as well as cities on the coast. Cities inland would have benefited too since they are self-sufficient when the coastline is prosperous.

[Philostratus I? *Nero* 1]

Cape Malea is the easternmost cape of the Peloponnese, with proverbially dangerous waters (Virgil, *Aeneid* 5.193; Livy 21.44). The voyage all the way round the coast of the Peloponnese is around 250 miles. Julius Caesar and Gaius had both had plans for a canal at Corinth according to Suetonius (Julius 44.3 and Gaius 21; and **T11**). The isthmus is indeed only 2½ miles at the cutting attempted by Nero. His works were still visible until the modern canal (1881–93) was cut on the same line.

M18b Nero and the Corinthian Canal: the bad

[3] Nero came forward onto a stage and sang a hymn to Amphitrite and Poseidon and a song to Melicerta and Leucothea. The governor of Achaia handed him a golden pickaxe and he went at the digging to the sound of applause and chanting. When he had struck the ground three times, I think, he exhorted those charged with starting the job to engage with their task enthusiastically. Then he went up to Corinth thinking that he had surpassed all the labours of Heracles. Men from the prison began to work away at the solid rock and difficult ground while the army tackled flat areas and those where there was soil. [4] When we had been chained to the isthmus for some seventy-five days, word came from Corinth that Nero had changed his mind about the cutting, though this was not confirmed.

[Philostratus I? *Nero* 3–4]

Nero's songs were in honour of various sea deities: Melicerta was possibly honoured by the Isthmian Games. Amphitrite was also worshipped at Corinth. Suetonius, *Nero* 19 and Dio [Xiphilinus] 63.16.1–2 also mention Nero starting the project. All accounts probably derive from the (lost) historian Cluvius Rufus who was there. Josephus, *Jewish War* 3.10.10 mentions 6,000 Jewish prisoners being used on this project. The army contingent was apparently the praetorian guard (Suet. *Nero* 19). Nero's change of mind is linked either to worries about the levels of sea on either side being different, or to Vindex's uprising.

M19 Nero restores land on Crete

~~Nero~~ Claudius Caesar Augustus Germanicus restored to Aesculapius three acres which had been given by Divus Augustus and confirmed by Divus Claudius for the Julian colony of noble(?) Cnossus, through Publius Licinius Secundus(?), procurator.

[Smallwood 385 = *ILS* 8901]

Nero's name is erased in the first line of this inscription from Cnossus on Crete. An alternative reading of the inscription suggests the name of the procurator is P. Licinius Caecina.

IMPERIAL SPONSORSHIP: M20–M27

M20 Milestone on road in *Africa Proconsularis* (Tunisia) AD 14

Imperator Caesar Augustus, son of Augustus, in his 16th year of tribunician power. Asprenas, consul, proconsul, one of the Board of Seven for the management of feasts, saw to the construction of the road from the winter camp of Tacape. Legion III Augusta. 10[. miles].

[EJ 290 = *ILS* 151]

This is one of three milestones found along this road between Tacape and Capsa (modern Gabès and Gafsa) (compare *AE* (2006) 1670; *CIL* VIII 10018), set up during the early autumn in AD 14, shortly after Augustus' death and the accession of Tiberius. They all show some uncertainty about imperial titulature: Augustus is not mentioned as deified, whilst Tiberius is titled as Imperator Caesar Augustus, although he did not immediately accept the title Augustus. The last number refers to the distance along the road, 101–104 or 109 miles. L. Nonius Asprenas (cos suff. AD 6) was governor (Tac. *Ann.* 1.53.6).

M21 Aqueduct at Nicopolis in Syria, under Tiberius, *c.* AD 21

[Tiberius Caesar] Augustus, hailed victorious commander, son of Divus Augustus, grandson of Divus Julius, [*pontifex*] *maximus*, consul four times, with tribunician power, saw to the [Aqua] Augusta being brought to Nicopolis [under the supervision of Gnaeus] Saturninus, legate of Caesar Augustus.

[EJ 284 = *CIL* III 6703]

This can be dated from imperial titulature to AD 21/30. Cn. Sentius Saturninus (cos suff AD 4) became governor of Syria following Piso's recall in AD 19 (Tac. *Ann.* 2.74.1). He must have been replaced shortly after AD 21 if Tacitus is right in recording Aelius Lamia's 10-year official tenure (*Ann.* 6.27.2).

M22 Road-building in Dalmatia under Tiberius, AD 19–20

[Tiberius C]aesar [Au]gustus, son of Divus Augustus, hailed victorious commander, *pontifex maximus*, in his 21st year of tribunician power, consul three times, built the road from Salonae to [...] the fort of the Daesitiates over a distance of 156 miles, and he also built a road from Salona to the River Ba[...] which divides [... from...] 158 miles.

[EJ 293 = *ILS* 5829a]

This inscription from Salona (modern Solin in Croatia) records Tiberius' road-building activities in the area of Dalmatia in AD 19–20, the natural consolidation of his military campaigns in the area some years earlier. Another inscription (EJ 292 = *ILS* 5829) commemorates Tiberius's earlier road-building in the same region in AD 16/17.

M23 Road-building in Hispania (Baetica) under Gaius, AD 39

Gaius Caesar Germanicus Augustus, son of Germanicus Caesar, grandson of Tiberius Augustus, great-grandson of Divus Augustus, great-great-grandson of Divus Julius, father of the fatherland, consul twice, hailed victorious commander, in his 2nd year of tribunician power, *pontifex maximus*, from the Baetis and Augustan Janus to Ocean, 62.

[Smallwood 333 = *CIL* II 6208 = *CIL* II^2/7, p.65 n.2]

This is a cylindrical milestone of AD 39 from the Via Augusta at Corduba (modern Córdoba).

M24 Road-building in the Alps under Claudius, AD 47

Tiberius Claudius Caesar Augustus Germanicus, son of Drusus, *pontifex maximus*, in his 6th year of tribunician power, consul for the 4th time, hailed victorious commander 11 times, censor, father of the fatherland, repaired the Via Claudia Augusta which his father Drusus had built, once the Alps had been opened up by war, from Altinum to the river Danube over 350 miles.

[*ILS* 208]

Although resembling a milestone in its appearance, this monument was not a means of measuring distance, but commemorated Claudius' repairs to the road first built through the Alps by his father, the Elder Drusus, following his victory over the Raeti in 15 BC. It dates from the beginning of 47 (for a similar monument, see *CIL* V 8003 = Smallwood 328).

M25 An aqueduct for Sardis under Claudius, AD 52–54

[Tiberius Claudi]us Caesar Augustus [Germanicus], son of Drusus, [*pontifex maximus*, in his ? year of tribunician power, consul five times, hailed victorious commander] 27 times, [father of the fatherland, brought] an aqueduct [from the source] to the city of the Sardians; Tiberius Claudius Apollophanes, son of Demetrius, of the Quirina voting-tribe, [supervised the work].

[Bilingual, Greek and Latin: Smallwood 318 = *IGRRP* IV 1505]

The translation above is of the Latin version of the inscription. Claudius' titles dates it to AD 52–54.

M26 Communications in Thrace under Nero, AD 61/62

~~Nero~~ Claudius Caesar Augustus Germanicus, son of Divus Claudius, grandson of Germanicus Caesar, great-grandson of Tiberius Caesar Augustus, great-great-grandson of Divus Augustus, *pontifex maximus*, in his 8th year of tribunician power, hailed victorious commander 8 times, consul four times, father of the fatherland, ordered eating-houses and rest-houses to be constructed along the military roads by Tiberius Julius Ustus, procurator of the province of Thrace.

[Smallwood 351 = *ILS* 231]

This inscription upon a marble plaque was found about 35 km. from Philippopolis in Thrace, at the foot of the Haemus Mountains. Thrace had only recently been incorporated into the empire as a province, and was particularly important geographically, as the region which linked the western to the eastern part of the empire. Nero's name was later erased.

M27 Lighthouse at Patara (Lycia) under Nero, AD 64/65

Nero Claudius Caesar Augustus Germanicus, son of god Claudius, grandson of Tiberius Caesar Augustus and Germanicus Caesar, great-grandson of god Augustus, *pontifex maximus*, in his 11th year of tribunician power, consul [four times], imperator of land and sea [...], the father of the fatherland, set up the lighthouse for the safety of sailors by the agency of Sextus Marcius Priscus, legate of Caesar with propraetorian rank who had founded the work.

[Greek: C.P. Jones, *ZPE* 166 (2008) 153–54; compare Eck et al. *ZPE* 164 (2008) 91–121]

This inscription originally consisted of gilded bronze letters, whose outlines alone now survive. Nero was credited with building a pair of lighthouses at Patara (Lycia) in 64/65 via his legate Marcius Priscus, who governed Lycia for eight years, spanning the reigns of Nero and Vespasian. The city also set up an inscription in 71/72 honouring the governor for his just governance and for having constructed the two lighthouses. His name also appears on a building-inscription commemorating Vespasian's repair of an aqueduct. The phrase 'imperator of land and sea' appears to be a formula distinctive to imperial dedications in Lycia.

PROVINCIAL OFFICIALS: M28–M38

Augustus had divided the empire between imperial provinces (less long-established; with legions stationed there; run by an equestrian or senatorial *legatus,* prefect or procurator directly appointed by the emperor) and public provinces (longer-established; without significant military presence; run by annually appointed proconsul or propraetor (former consul or praetor)). Governors would also have various officials to help them. Provinces might change status, e.g. Achaia and Macedonia become 'imperial' between AD 15 and 44 (Tac. *Ann.* 1.76.2, Dio 60.24.1). But since consuls might be chosen by the emperor (**B1**, **N36b**, **U9**) the main difference as far as provincials were concerned may have been length of tenure (see **M1**).

M28 Building project by Pontius Pilate in Judaea, AD 26–36

[Marcus?] Pontius Pilatus, prefect of Judaea, rebuilt the Tiberieum [?for sailors].

[*AE* (1999) 1681]

This limestone block was found reused in the theatre at Caesarea Maritima. It is badly damaged, and its text is hotly debated. It seems originally to have commemorated a building project. On the interpretation proposed here, the structure known as 'Tiberieum' refers to one of two lighthouses at the entrance to the city's harbour originally built by King Herod the Great (and now apparently rebuilt by Pontius Pilate), the other being known as the Druseum. This is in stark contrast to earlier interpretations of the inscription as referring to some sort of shrine for emperor-worship. What it does show for certain, however, is that Pontius Pilate was a prefect, not procurator, a title given to him in error by literary texts on analogy with later administrative titles in the province.

M29 Honours for a governor of the Maritime Alps, Iulium Carnicum

To Gaius Baebius Atticus, son of Publius, of the voting-tribe Claudia, duumvir with judicial powers, senior centurion of the legion V Macedonica, prefect of the communities of Moesia and Treballia, prefect of the communities in the Maritime Alps, military tribune of the 8th praetorian cohort, senior centurion for a second time, procurator of Tiberius Claudius Caesar Augustus Germanicus in Noricum; the community of the Saevates and Laeanci (set this up).

[EJ 243 = *ILS* 1349]

This bronze tablet was found at Iulium Carnicum (modern Zuglio). It illustrates how equestrian governors of minor provinces were first known as prefects, and only later from the time of Claudius as procurator (compare Pontius Pilate, **M28**). Baebius Atticus' career includes a municipal magistracy, then military service as centurion in a legion stationed on the Danube at Oescus. He was appointed to take charge of communities to the south of the Danube and then in Alps. He ended up as the first known governor of Noricum, which had previously been a dependent kingdom, and was organised as a province under Claudius. The Saevates and Laeanci were tribes in Noricum.

M30 Governor of Africa as civic patron, AD 42 (Hippo Regius)

[When Tiberius Claudius Caesar] Augustus Germanicus, [son of Drusus, was *pontifex maximus*,] in his 2nd year of [tribunician] power, hailed victorious commander [3 times, consul twice, father of the fatherland,] the senate and people of [Hippo Regi]us, at [public] expense, to Quintus Marcius Barea, son of Gaius, consul, one of the Board of Fifteen in charge of sacrifices, *fetialis* priest, proconsul for two years, patron. Quintus Allius Maximus, propraetorian legate for two years, made this dedication to the patron.

[Smallwood 405 = *AE* (1935) 32]

This is inscribed upon a fragmentary statue base.

M31 Edict of the proconsul of Asia, Ephesos, AD *c*.44

This edict, found at Ephesos, covers a variety of related topics dealing with sacred finances at Ephesos. It was issued by the proconsul of Asia, Paullus Fabius Persicus, who enjoyed a distinguished career, as son of Marcia (Augustus' cousin) and Paullus Fabius Maximus. He is concerned here with stemming financial abuses in the cult of Artemis (whose temple at Ephesos was regarded as one of the Wonders of the Ancient World) whilst also maintaining the dignity of emperor-worship at the cheapest possible price. Julia Augusta (Livia) was deified by Claudius in 42. Fragments of a Latin version of the same edict also survive.

M31a Introduction and praise of Claudius

[*Column* 1] Pa[ullus Fabius Pe]rsicus, pont[ifex, *sodalis Augustalis*, Arval brother, quaestor of Imperator] Tiberius Caesar [Augustus, praetor… consul… proconsul of Asia proclaimed, at the instigation of Imperator] [*Column* 2] Tiberius Claudius Caesar Augustus Germanicus himself, an edict beneficial [both to the city of the Ephesians and] to the whole province, which he published at Ephesos [and] saw to it that it was inscribed on a stele [*before 28*] March. Starting out consistently [above all] in this assumption that those put in charge of provinces ought to take care of the magistracy entrusted to them [with all] steadfastness and good faith, so that they think ahead about what is useful continually and throughout life both throughout the whole province and [2.10] city by city, but not only for his own year of office, nevertheless I am happy to admit to having been directed towards this opinion by the example of the greatest and most truly just leader, who having declared the whole race of men to be in his personal care, has conferred this favour among the foremost and most pleasing to all men that his own property should be restored to each man.

M31b Problems of Ephesos

Because of this I have taken a decision which is burdensome but necessary for the most illustrious city of the Ephesians [*Column* 3] [... *9 lines lost* ...] for many houses [...] have been destroyed by fire or [*Column* 4] have fallen down into a heap of rubble by collapse; and the temple of Artemis herself, which is the glory of the whole province on account of the grandeur of the building and the antiquity of the cult of the goddess and because of the abundance of funds which have been restored to the goddess by Augustus, is being deprived of its own money which could have sufficed for the care and decoration of the dedications. For this money is being siphoned off to the corrupt desires of those [4.10] who lead the league in such a way that they consider to be to their own profit. For whenever good news comes from Rome, they exploit it for their own profit: using the condition of the divine house as a smoke-screen, they sell priesthoods as if at public auction and they call together men of every kind to buy them; then they do not choose those most suitable to have the appropriate crown placed on their heads. They allot to the priests as much of the revenues as they are willing to take, [4.20] so that they themselves may purloin as much as possible [*Column* 5] [... *11 lines lost*...] [It seems necessary to me that the city] bear these expenses so that [*Column* 6] the most suitable man may be thought to deserve the honour from the people. It is my resolution to cut off the excessive [burden] by means of this decree. Since I know the payment of the huge sum of money to be completely impossible for the city, if it were forced to pay out now what they took from the purchases, it is my resolution that the city give the priests no more than 1% of the price then paid, [6.10] in accordance with the arrangement of Vedius Pollio, which was confirmed by the god Augustus. But it is not my resolution that the priests give anything to the council or take anything back from it in turn.

M31c Cuts in expenditure

Likewise, all those free men who do the jobs of public slaves and burden the league with excessive expense ought to be dismissed and replaced in their jobs by public slaves.

Likewise, in respect of public slaves, it is my resolution that any of those slaves said to buy infants at any old price and dedicate them to Artemis [6.20] so that their slaves may be kept at the expense of her funds should themselves provide upkeep for their own slaves.

Likewise, in respect of victors at the sacred games who are said to be priests of Artemis [*Column* 7] with regard to the prize-account, [it is not my resolution that they be supported by] Artemis, [but that they receive only so much] as has been decreed under the arrangement of Vedius Pollio.

[Likewise, it is my resolution that none of the priests of Artemis or annual magistrates] borrow money on behalf of the public, unless [he is able] to repay the loan from the income of that year. But if anyone pledges the revenue of the following year, the recovery of the money loaned should be given to the moneylender [from him].

Likewise, whatever money is bequeathed to the city or to some part or organisation of citizens in it, it is my resolution [*Column* 8] that it be lent out according to the regulation by which it was bound and not be diverted by the magistrates for other uses and expenses.

Likewise, that no more than 4,500 denarii be expended on the quinquennial games, in accordance with the arrangement of Vedius Pollio.

Likewise, it is my resolution that the hymnodes, upon whom no small part of the city's income is spent, be released from this service, and that the ephebes, whose age and reputation and aptitude for learning them better suited for such a public duty, perform this function without payment. [8.10] However, in order that I shall not appear to have made this pronouncement with regard to all hymnodes everywhere, I exempt those who hymn the god Augustus himself at Pergamum in the sanctuary dedicated by Asia, whose first gathering was convened not for payment, but voluntarily and without payment, for which reason too the god Augustus confirmed the privileges thereafter decreed to them and their successors, and ordered their expenses to be paid not by the Pergamenes alone, but by the whole of Asia, reckoning it such an expense as to be burdensome for one city. [8.20] However, it will be necessary for the city of the Ephesians, which has been freed from this expense, and once the service has been transfrerred to the ephebes in accordance with this decree, to ensure that the ephebes perform this function with care and due attention, as befits those who hymn the divine house.

M31d Divine honours for Julia Augusta

Furthermore, since the long-due divine honour has been conferred upon Julia Augusta [*Column* 9] by [the emperor, our most pious imperator and greatest] leader, it is [necessary] for her hymnodes [to be deemed worthy] of the same rights as those who hymn the Augustan gods, since [the senate] and god Augustus – after she had been [honoured with sacred] laws before her immortality – considered her worthy of divinity and conferred it upon her. Likewise, it is also [right] for others [to ratify] the honours, which the person who went up onto the rostrum [proposed, the main gist] of which has been appended to this edict:

[The Greeks of Asia have resolved], Alexander having proposed on the rostrum [...] in Asia, when Gaius Julius [...] was high priest. A pious act [...]

[Greek: Smallwood 380]

M32 Decree against the falsification of public documents, Lycia, AD 43–48

Decree of Quintus [Ve]ranius, legate of T[ibe]r[ius Cla]udius Caesar Augustus, with propraetorian power.

T[ry]phon, public slave of the city of Tlos, has [not] learned his lesson either from my edicts or threats nor from the punishment of slaves who have committed errors of a similar nature, that one must not accept documents of public administrators that have interpolations and erasures. I have introduced him to the [realisation] of my vexation at such practices by having him lashed with the whip, and I have demonstrated to him by such a sign that [if] he is once more careless of my edict concerning public records, not only by beatings but also by the supreme punishment will I force the rest of the public slaves to forget their former indifference. The man who exposed Tryphon, Apollonius, son of Diopeithes, from Patara is to receive from the city of Tlos, through the incumbent treasurers, 300 drachmas, for I have set this as the reward for the service done by those who expose public slaves.

But in order also that those who issue documents – on whose behalf it has been my concern to order investigations about these matters – should stop acting contrary to their own security, I make it clear that every transaction of any type will be invalid from today if it is written [on] a palimpsest or has interpolations or erasures, whether it is a contract or a handwritten note or a covenant or a clarification or a notice or an account rendered or an appeal or a disclosure about a legal situation or a legal process involving a dowry or a decision of arbitrators or judges. And if, through some such transaction, a fixed period of time is required, in such a way as to add the fixed period later, the one who does not follow my orders will disrupt the administration. For, as for documents which in their delivery are open to suspicion, after being subject to forgetfulness after the passage of much time, [how] can they not appear unreliable when the reason why the interpolations and the erasures were made can no longer be clear to those who intend to review the documents? In no less a manner will also those public slaves who accept such documents be punished. Throughout the whole province which is entrusted to me the local officials in post in the month of Artemision shall publish this decree.

[Greek: *AE* (1976) 673 = Sherk no.48]

This edict concerning the proper upkeep of civic archives was issued by the provincial governor to the city of Tlos, and was found inscribed upon a limestone stele at Myra in Lycia. Q. Veranius was the first governor of the new province, and perhaps the concerns here were particularly pertinent in establishing order in the new province. It dates from the period 43/48.

M33 Corbulo, governor of Asia, on appeals to the emperor

[Gnaeus Dom]itius Corbulo, proconsul, sends greetings to the magistrates, council and people of the [Coa]ns; I have often considered it [not without profit] to show [even to cities], especially with regard to whatever is in my remit, [that] instructions have been given in letters that [whatever] is considered to be worthy of the divine [judgement] of the emperor should [first be sent to] those in charge of the provinces. [Now a certain individual has, on the basis of] a decree issued by you, made an appeal to [the emperor, and] I perceived that he had done this abusively. Well then, it will be necessary, if the appeal to the emperor takes place, first that I investigate the reason, but if the appeal comes to me, that the [quaestor] takes sufficient pledges of 2,500 denarii, according to the edict laid down by me on account of those who fail to show up for trial. But if [...]

[Greek: Oliver, *AJPhil* 100 (1979) 551ff]

This fragmentary inscription from Cos gives us a rare glimpse of the practice of emperors giving regular instructions to governors of public as well as of imperial provinces, and into the requirement that provincials should approach their governors first before petitioning the emperor himself (Paul's appeal (**M37**) was against the procurator). At this time, under Claudius, Corbulo was serving as proconsul of Asia.

M34 Honours for the procurator of Galatia

The people of [C]laud[iconium] honoured [L]ucius Pupius [P]raesens, son of Lucius, of the voting-tribe Sabatina, military tribune, prefect of the Picentine cavalry squadron, procurator of Caesar in charge of the Tiber's banks, procurator of Tiberius Claudius [C]aesar Augustus Ger[m]anicus and of Nero [C]laudius Caesar Augustus Germanicus of the province of Galatia, their benefactor and founder.

[Greek: Smallwood 265 = *ILS* 8848]

This inscription comes from Iconium, on the border of Phyrgia and Lycaonia. Honouring Praesens as benefactor and founder implies substantial involvement in sponsoring public buildings.

M35 Governor of Syria hears cases and refers them to Rome

Ummidius Quadratus was governor of Syria from *c.*AD 50 – 60. He adjudicated a dispute between Jews and Samaritans following an outbreak of violence in AD 52. The Jews accused the procurator of Syria, Ventidius Cumanus, of favouring the Samaritans. Quadratus suppressed the violence, crucifying the instigators. The leaders of both sides, along with Cumanus and a tribune named Celer were all sent to Rome to seek Claudius' judgement. Claudius, influenced by the intervention of his wife, Agrippina and his friend, King Agrippa II, found in favour of the Jews, executing the Samaritan delegates and exiling Cumanus. Tacitus' version of events (*Annals* 12.45, 54) differs in several ways.

[20.125] The leading Samaritans met with Ummidius Quadratus, the governor of Syria, who happened to be in Tyre at the time, and denounced the Jews for burning down and sacking their villages. [126] They claimed that their grievance was not so much about what they had themselves actually suffered as for the fact that Jewish actions were an insult to Rome. All disputes were supposed to be referred to the Roman authorities, and if the Jews had a complaint against the Samaritans, they should not have invaded their country as they did, as if they were not subject to Roman governance. They had come to him, therefore, to demand justice. [127] That was the gist of the Samaritans' case.

The Jewish response laid the blame for current factional disorder and violence firmly at the door of the Samaritans, focusing in particular on Cumanus, whom they alleged to have been corrupted by bribes and therefore to have failed to report the assassination of the Jewish victims. [128] Quadratus listened to the arguments and then reserved his judgement, promising to make it public when he had reached Judaea and investigated the facts of the case more thoroughly. [129] So the Samaritans went away empty-handed.

Soon afterwards, Quadratus arrived in Samaria and held a detailed hearing of the case. Having decided that it was in fact the Samaritans who had been the cause of the troubles, he crucified all those Samaritans and Jews who had been identified as having taking part in the disorders and arrested by Cumanus. [130] From there he moved on to Lydda, a village that was in fact little smaller than a city. There he set up his judgement seat and held a second full-scale hearing of the Samaritans' complaint. One of the Samaritans told him that a Jewish leader called Doetus and four other trouble-makers had encouraged the mob to stage a riot against the Romans. [131] So Quadratus had them put to death as well. As for Ananias, the High Priest, and Ananus, the Temple Superintendant, together with their associates, he put them all in chains and sent them off to Rome to give an account of their actions before the emperor, Claudius Caesar. [132] In addition, he instructed the leaders of both Jews and

Samaritans, together with the procurator, Cumanus, and Celer, the military tribune, to go to Rome and seek a judgement from the emperor himself on the matters in dispute between them. [133] He himself was worried that there might be further trouble brewing among the Jewish masses, and so he made his way to Jerusalem. He found all quiet in the city and the celebration of a religious festival in full swing. Confident that he need fear no further trouble from that quarter, he left them to celebrate the festival and returned to Antioch.

[134] Cumanus and the Samaritan leaders, together with their delegations, having been duly sent off to Rome, were allocated a day for them to make their case before the emperor on the matters under dispute between them. [135] There was a strong prejudice in favour of Cumanus and the Samaritans on the part of Caesar's freedmen and friends. In fact the Jews would probably have lost their case, had not Agrippa the Younger happened to be in Rome at the time. He realised that the Jewish leaders were in danger of losing the contest, so he begged the emperor's wife, Agrippina, to persuade her husband to hear the case carefully in a manner that befitted his own principles of justice, and to punish those responsible for the riots. [136] Claudius was won over by her entreaties, and having listened to the case in detail he decided that it was the Samaritans who had been the initial source of the disorders. So he ordered the Samaritans in front of him to be executed, condemned Cumanus to exile, and the tribune Celer to be taken back to Jerusalem and there to be dragged publicly round the whole city before being put to death.

[Josephus, *Jewish Antiquities,* 20.125–36]

M36 Praise for a prefect of Egypt, AD 55/9

With good fortune. Since ~~Nero~~ Claudius Caesar Augustus Germanicus Imperator, the good spirit of the inhabited world, along with all the good deeds with which he has acted a benefactor towards Egypt, with the most manifest foresight sent to us Tiberius Claudius Balbillus as governor. Because of this man's favours and benefactions, Egypt is full of all good things, sees the gifts of the Nile growing greater year by year, and now enjoyed even more the well-balanced rising of the god (i.e. the Nile), it has been decided by the people from the village of Bouseiris of the Letopolite district who live near the pyramids and by the district secretaries and village secretaries who dwell in it to pass a decree and to set up a stele of stone near [the greatest god,] the Sun Harmachis. This will show from the good things engraved on it his benefactions from which [everyone will] know his excellent conduct towards the whole of Egypt. For it is [fitting] that his god-like favours, recorded by sacred writings, shall forever be remembered. He came into our district and performed an act of adoration of the Sun Harmachis, overseer and saviour, having been delighted with the greatness and magnificence of the pyramids. And when he had seen the great quantity of sand because of the length of time [... *(8 lines lost)*]

[Greek: Smallwood 418 = *IGRRP* I 1110]

This is inscribed upon a stone stele found at Memphis in Egypt, near the pyramid of Chephren. Nero's name has been erased at the start. Egypt's prosperity was largely dependent upon the annual flooding of the river Nile, which was worshipped as a god, to irrigate the fields. For Ti. Claudius Balbillus, see also **U21**.

M37 Paul on trial before Festus, procurator of Judaea, appeals to Caesar

[6] When Festus had stayed among them not more than eight or ten days, he went down to Caesarea; and the next day he took his seat on the tribunal and ordered Paul to be brought. [7] And when he had come, the Jews who had gone down from Jerusalem stood about him, bringing against him many serious charges which they could not prove. [8] Paul said in his defence, "Neither against the law of the Jews, nor against the temple, nor against Caesar have I offended at all." [9] But Festus, wishing to do the Jews a favour, said to Paul, "Do you wish to go up to Jerusalem, and there be tried on these charges before me?" [10] But Paul said, "I am standing before Caesar's tribunal, where I ought to be tried; to the Jews I have done no wrong, as you know very well. [11] If then I am a wrongdoer, and have committed anything for which I deserve to die, I do not seek to escape death; but if there is nothing in their charges against me, no one can give me up to them. I appeal to Caesar." [12] Then Festus, when he had conferred with his council, answered, "You have appealed to Caesar; to Caesar you shall go."

[Acts. 25.6–12 (Revised Standard Version)]

Porcius Festus was procurator of Judaea, and Paul had been sent to him by Claudius Lysias (see **M76**) after being accused of causing a disturbance in Jerusalem. Paul invokes the long-standing right of a Roman citizen of appeal against summary punishment, torture without trial, or actual trial outside Italy. See Sherwin-White, *Roman Society and Roman Law in the New Testament* (Oxford 1963), pages 48–70, and Millar, *ERW* page 511.

M38 Procurator of Britain

To departed spirits of [Gaius Julius] Alpinus Classicianus, [son of Gaius, of the voting-tribe Fabia …] procurator of the province of Britain; Julia Pacata I[nduta], daughter of Indus, his wife (set this up).

[Smallwood 268 = *RIB* I 12]

This epitaph is very fragmentary. It belongs to an immensely grand funerary altar (2.18 m. high by 2.3 m. wide, now in the British Museum), fragments of which were found reused in one of the bastions of London's defences constructed in the fourth century. A provincial from Gaul, he was married to a daughter of Indus, who, according to Tacitus (*Ann.* 3.42), had opposed the Gallic revolt led by Florus in 21. Classicianus succeeded Decianus Catus as procurator in Britain following the Boudiccan revolt in 61 (Tac. *Ann.* 14.38). See Birley, *Roman Government of Britain,* (Oxford 2005) 1.14.3.

FRIENDLY KINGDOMS: M39 – M51

From quite early in the development of the Roman empire, Rome seems to have realised that friendly relationships with kings whose territories lay on the margins of the empire could be established to mutual advantage: the king could expect Roman military support against internal and external enemies; Rome might call on troops in return, and was spared the trouble of garrisoning and administering a province, though the kingdom might later become formally part of the empire, when a king died or when a region became easier and more profitable to govern directly. For Tacitus' cynical comment on Romans employing kings to enslave others, see **N31**. After Actium, Octavian/Augustus was happy to allow most friendly kings to continue in power despite their support for Antony. Ironically by the reign of Tiberius, many of these friendly monarchs were direct descendants of Antony (see **M39**)! Even after he divorced her, Octavia had brought up in her household all of Antony's children by other wives (Plut. *Ant.* 57), and their daughter Antonia (Augusta), in turn gave home to the three sons of Antony's great-granddaughter, Antonia Tryphaena (**M44**); to Agrippa I (Jos. *JA* 18.143, 164–7); to Ptolemy of Mauretania, another grandson of Antony (Suet. *Cal.* 26.1 and **M40**); as well as to her son Claudius and grandson Caligula (Suet. *Cal.* 10.1); and quite probably to other friendly kings known to have been in Rome in this period ((see Kokkinos, *Antonia Augusta,* 1992, page 25 and notes).

M39 Family tree showing friendly monarchs related to Mark Antony

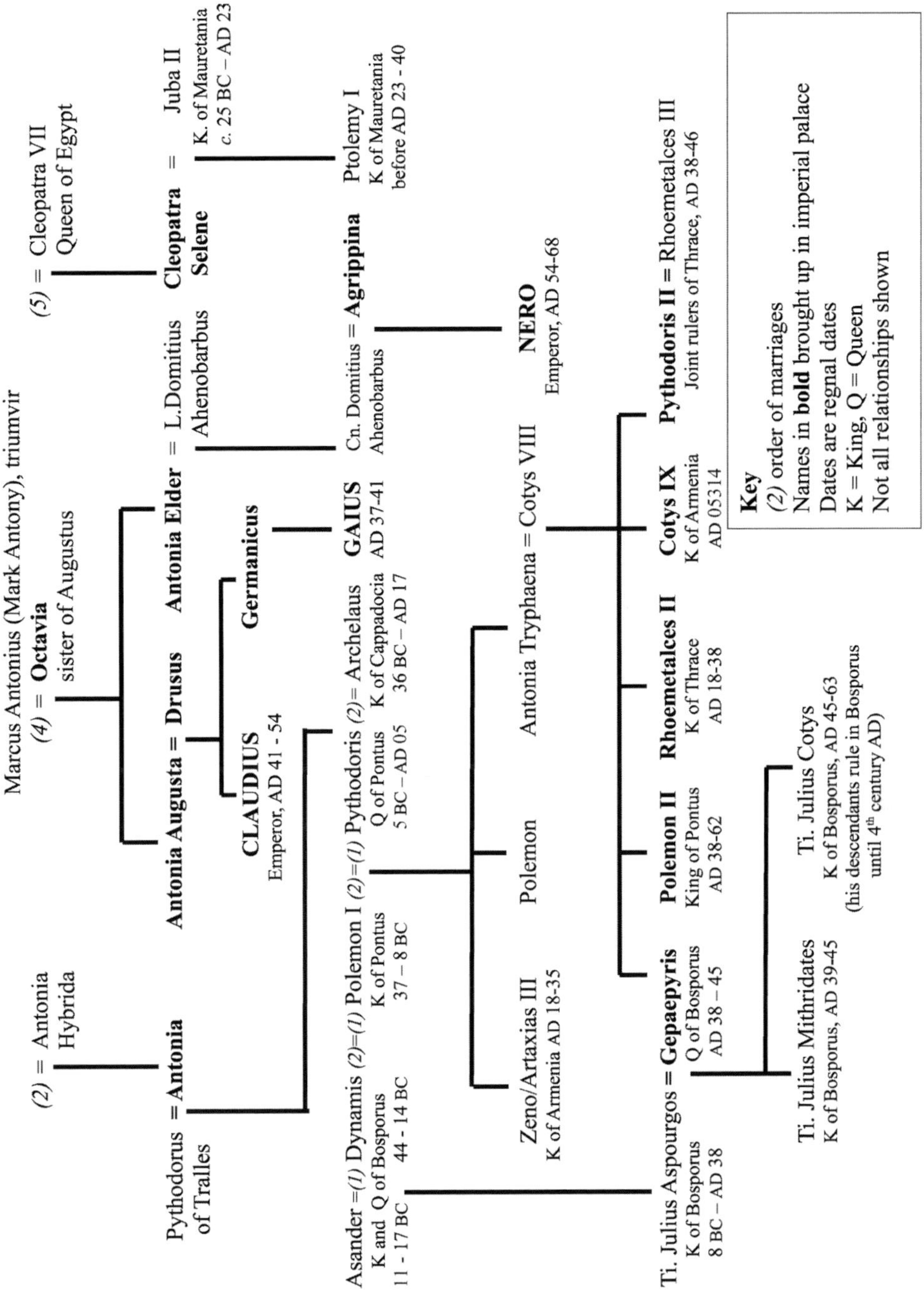

M40 Ptolemy of Mauretania

Shortly before my own time the kings of the house of Bogud and Bocchus, who were well-disposed to Rome, ruled Mauretania. When they died, Juba succeeded to the throne, having been given the kingdom to add to his father's dominions by Caesar Augustus. His father had fought with Scipio against the god Caesar. Juba recently died and has been succeeded on the throne by his son, Ptolemy, whose mother was the daughter of Antony and Cleopatra.

[Strabo, *Geography* 17.3.7]

For Ptolemy's fate under his cousin and childhood friend, Caligula, see Suet. *Cal.* 26.1 and **N8**).

M40a King Ptolemy on silver *denarius* struck in AD 24/5

Obv: Diademed and draped bust of Ptolemy, right
REX PTOLEMAEVS (King Ptolemy)

Rev: Palm-tree
R – A [V] (Regis Anno V (Year 5 of the King))

[BM Collection 1853.0716.224; Alexandropoulos 224]

M41 King Ptolemy, AD 29–30

[For the welfare] of King Ptolemy, son of King Juba, in the 10th year of his reign; I, Antistia Galla, willingly and deservedly fulfilled my vow to Saturn, once the sacrificial offering was received from Julia Vitalis, daughter of Respectus, of Rusguniae.

[EJ 163 = *AE* (1938) 149]

This inscription from Caesarea Mauretania (modern Cherchel) commemorates the fulfilment of a vow to Saturn, who was a popular deity in north Africa by virtue of being assimilated with the indigenous god Baal. King Ptolemy was the son of Juba II and Cleopatra Selene (daughter of the famous Cleopatra). For his fate and that of his kingdom, see **N8–N12**. Rusguniae was a coastal colony.

M42 The family of Pythodoris

Pythodoris rules the Tibarenians, the Chaldaeans as far as Colchis, Pharnacia and Trapezus. She is wise and well capable of ruling over affairs of state. She is the daughter of Pythodoros of Tralles, and became the wife of Polemon, reigning jointly with him for a period before succeeding him in power on his death in the territory of the Aspurgiani – the name of one of the barbarian tribes around Sindice. She has two sons by Polemon and one daughter who was married to Cotys of Thrace who was treacherously killed, leaving her a widow with children by him. The eldest of these is in power. As for the sons of Pythodoris, one is a private citizen, helping his mother rule, the other has recently been installed as king of Greater Armenia. Pythodoris herself married Archelaus and stayed with him until his death. Now widowed, she possesses the places mentioned above and other lands more beautiful, which I shall describe in turn.

[Strabo, *Geography* 12.3.29]

Strabo is well-informed. Pythodoris ruled parts of Pontus very close to his own home town, Amasia (12.3.39). She was the daughter of Pythodoros and Antonia, daughter of Mark Antony's second marriage to his cousin Antonia Hybrida. Antony made Polemon, his grandson-in-law king of Pontus and Lesser Armenia. After Actium, Augustus removed him from Armenia, but later awarded him the Bosporan kingdom. Their daughter was Antonia Tryphaena who further strengthened links to other friendly kings and to Rome by marrying Cotys of Thrace and after his death (Tac. *Ann.* 2.64–67) bringing up her three sons in the household of her great-aunt Antonia, alongside Claudius and Gaius (see **M46**). Pythodoris' son Zeno was installed as King Artaxias III of Armenia by his second cousin, Germanicus in AD 18 (**M46**, Tac. *Ann.* 2.56)

M43 Germanicus crowns Artaxias on silver didrachm of AD 37–38, Cappadocia

Obv: Head of Germanicus, right

GERMANICVS CAESAR TI AVG F COS II (Germanicus Caesar, son of Tiberius Augustus, twice consul)

Rev: Germanicus standing on right, holding spear in left hand, turning to place diadem on head of Artaxias who stands to left, facing forwards, with right hand raised

ARTAXIAS, GERMANICUS

[*BMC* Gaius 104; *RIC* Gaius 59]

This is a two-drachma silver coin from the mint in Cappadocia. Tacitus, *Annals* 2.56 gives a brief account of the ceremony to crown Zeno, son of Polemon king of Pontus, as King Artaxias of Armenia, taking the name from Artaxata, the capital city. It should be noted that the coin was minted to celebrate Caligula's father, around 18 years after the event and the death of Germanicus and 2 years after the death of Artaxias III in 34/5 (Tac. *Ann.* 6.31.1) and the installation of Arsaces, son of King Artabanus II of Parthia on the throne of Armenia.

M44 Antonia Tryphaena in Cyzicus

When Pausanias, son of Eumenes, was chief magistrate for the second time, in the month of Calamaion, the council and people adopted the following resolution: Pausanias, son of Eumenes, of the tribe Aegicoreis, at the second assembly, under the presidency of Demetrius, made the proposal:

Antonia Tryphaena, daughter of King Polemo and Queen Pythodoris, in her complete piety towards the eternal house of the greatest of gods, Tiberius Augustus Caesar, and his immortal principate, joined in dedicating to Athene the City Guardian the statue of his mother Augusta Victrix. And when she accepted from the city the priesthood of Augusta at the Panathenaic festival held last year, she perfectly fulfilled for the Imperial Family every possible respect for the gods, as befits her nature, carrying out many sacrifices. She displayed her natural generosity towards locals and visitors so that in return she was greatly admired by foreign visitors for her piety, holiness and good reputation. The following year, even though she was away, all the rituals were carried out in full, in accordance with her piety, and traders from the whole region and visitors who had come to the festival wishing to dedicate a gilded shield with her image, approached the council and people determined to begranted permission to put up this dedication. For all these reasons, the council and the people resolved:

That they be permitted to dedicate the shield in the temple of the City Guardian and to inscribe on it: "The businessmen of Asia, who came to the celebration and the festival conducted at Cyzicus for the Imperial Family and Athene the City Guardian, honoured Antonia Tryphaena, daughter of King Polemo and Queen Pythodoris Philometor, priestess of Augusta Victrix, for her piety towards the house of the greatest of gods, Tiberius Augustus Caesar, and for her reverence in all things and her generosity towards themselves."

[EJ 352, Cyzicus]

For Antonia Tryphaena, see **M42** and note. Cyzicus was an important port on the south side of the Sea of Marmara (modern NW Turkey), founded by Greeks. Situated near Thrace but part of the Roman province of Asia it was a convenient and safe place for her to live in as a patron. Antonia Tryphaena had every reason to be grateful to Tiberius, who avenged the death of her husband, Cotys VIII, and restored the kingdom of Thrace to her son (Tac. *Ann.* 2.64–67, **C5**).

M45 King Aspourgos of Bosporus

Great King Aspourgos, Friend of the Romans, son of King Asandrochos, Friend of Caesar and Friend of the Romans, king of all the Bosporos, of Theodosia, of the Sindoi, of the Maitai, of the Tarpeites, of the Toretai, of the Psesoi, and of the Tanaeitai. He subjugated the Scythians and the Taurians. Menestratos II, in charge of the island, (dedicated this statue) to his saviour and benefactor.

[Sherk 42A – IGRR I 879, EJ 172]

Base of white marble inscribed in Greek, from Panticapaeum in the Bosporan kingdom (north side of the Black Sea). Aspourgos succeeded his step-father in inheriting the Bosporan kingdom of his father, the very long-lived Asander. He was given citizenship by Tiberius, and issued coins with his portrait on one side and that of the Roman emperor, Tiberius (*RPC* 1903) and then Gaius (*RPC* 1904) on the other. Other coins also feature his wife, Gypaepyris, daughter of Antonia Tryphaena.

M46 Decree expressing devotion to Gaius, Cyzicus, AD 37

While Gaius Caesar was chief magistrate, on the 9th of the month of Thargelion. The people decided the following, on the proposal of all the archons. The secretary of the council, Aeolos, son of Aeolos, of the tribe Oinops, spoke as follows in the central session under the presidency of Menophon:

"After the new Sun-God Gaius Caesar Augustus Germanicus was willing to shine forth with his rays at the same time also upon the kings who are the bodyguards of his leadership, so that the greatness of his immortality should be more revered in that respect also, [5] while the kings, even though they have been forming many plans with regard to giving thanks to so great a deity, have been unable to discover repayments equal to the benefits received, he reinstated the sons of Cotys – Rhoemetalces, Polemon and Cotys – who were brought up with him and had become his companions, into the kingdoms owed to them from their fathers and forbears. Those who are enjoying the liberality of his immortal favour are greater in this respect than their predecessors, because whereas their predecessors held onto the succession from their fathers, these have become kings through the favour of Gaius Caesar so as to share the rule with such great deities, and the favours of deities differ [10] from inheritances from human beings by the same degree as sunshine from night and immortal from mortal nature. Having then become greater than the great and more marvellous than the illustrious, Rhoemetalces and Polemon have come to our city to join in the sacrifices and join in the festivals with their mother, who will celebrate the games of the goddess, new Aphrodite Drusilla, not only in respect of a fatherland that is friendly, but also one that hers by birthright, because she who is both daughter of kings and mother of kings, their mother Tryphaena, considering this her fatherland, has settled her home's hearth and the good fortune of her life there [15] where she will be fortunate in her childrens' kingdoms which are free from the jealousy of the gods. For its part the people, since it considers their residence a source of the greatest pleasure, has with all enthusiasm instructed the archons to propose a decree of welcome for them, through which they will thank their mother Tryphaena on their account for the benefits that she has wished to confer on the city, and through which they will make clear also the disposition of the people towards them.

The people has decided to praise the kings Rhoemetalces, Polemon, and Cotys, and their mother Tryphaena. At the time of their entry, the priests and priestesses, having opened up the sacred enclosures and added more adornment to the images of the gods, are to pray for the everlasting life of Gaius Caesar and for their well-being. Moreover all the people of Cyzicus, displaying their goodwill towards them, going to meet them with the archons and the crown-wearers, are to welcome them, rejoice with them, and invite them to consider the city as their own fatherland and to become responsible for all its good; the magistrate in charge of youth is also to lead the youths to the greeting, and the supervisor of education is to lead the free boys. The decree is about both devotion to Augustus and honour to the kings.

[Greek: *IGRRP* IV 145 = Smallwood 401 = LACTOR 18 no.71 = Sherk 42B]

For Cyzicus see **M42**. Cotys of Thrace had been killed in 14/15 (**M42**, **C5**, Tac. *Ann.* 2.64–67) and his sons by Antonia Tryphaena had been brought up the household of Antonia Augusta with Gaius. On accession Gaius awarded them all kingdoms in a ceremony in Rome: Rhoemetalces III, King of Thrace; Polemon II, King of Pontus and Bosporus, and Cotys IX, King of Armenia Minor (Dio 59.12.2 = LACTOR 15, B10).

The inscription shows the high hopes and aspirations of Cyzicus in claiming to be the fatherland of client kings brought up with Gaius. The level of adulation of Gaius is still striking, especially given that they are not addressing him directly.

M47 Gaius and Rhoemetalces of Thrace, bronze coin from Thrace

Obv: Laureate head of Gaius
ΓΑΙΩ ΚΑΙΣΑΡΙ ΣΕΒΑΣΤΩ (To Gaius Caesar Augustus)

Rev: Head of Rhoemetalces
ΒΑΣΙΛΕΥΣ ΡΟΙΜΗΤΑΛΚΑΣ (King Rhoemetalces)

[*BMC* Thrace p210, no 2 = Smallwood 201]

For Rhoemetalces III and Gaius see note on **M46**.

M48 Claudius and Polemon II of Pontus, silver drachma, Pontus AD 52–53

Obv: Head of Polemon
ΒΑCΙΛΕΩC ΠΟΛΕΜΩΝΟC (of King Polemon)

Rev: Laureate head of Claudius
ΕΤΟΥC ΙΕ (in year 15 = AD 52–3)

[*BMC* Pontus p46, no 3 = Smallwood 206]

M48b Nero and Polemon II of Pontus, silver drachma, Pontus AD 55–6

Obv: Diademed head of Polemon, right
ΒΑCΙΛΕωC ΠΟΛΕΜωΝΟC (of King Polemon)

Rev: Laureate head of Nero, right

ETOYC IH (in year 18 = AD 55/6)

[*BMC* Coll. 1931.0601.40; *RPC* 3830/3]

Coins were struck by Polemon II in the Kingdom of Pontus during the reigns of Claudius and Nero, until the kingdom was annexed in AD 62 (Suet. *Nero* 18). The most common coins were struck in the years AD 55–58 and it is reckoned that they were connected with the help Polemo was giving Corbulo and Corbulo's use of Pontus as a base.

M49 Antiochus and Polemon put on games in honour of Claudius

[Tiberius C]laudius Caesar Augustus Germanicus Sarmaticus, *pontifex* [*maximus*], in his 7th year of tribunician power, consul for the 6th time, hailed victorious commander 18 times, father of the fatherland, greets the Heraclean association of travelling athletes.

In two [decrees] given to me at the same time you [kindly told] me how Gaius Julius Antiochus, the king [of Commagene], and Julius Polemon, the king of Pontus, men honoured by me [and] friends, acted with all enthusiasm and benevolently towards you at the time when they held the games established by them in my name. I welcomed your gratitude towards them and recognised rather than was surprised at their goodwill towards myself and their benevolence in your regard. Those mentioned in the decrees were Diogenes, son of Miccalus, of Antioch, who was the high-priest nearest to the association and whom I thought deserving of Roman citizenship, together with his two daughters, Sandogenes [...] son of Miccalus, of Antioch. Farewell.

[Greek: Smallwood 374]

This is the second of two letters of Claudius from AD 46 and 47 to an association of travelling athletes which are preserved on papyrus (for the first, see **N21**). Claudius did not take the victory-title 'Sarmaticus': its repetition here is most peculiar, and is perhaps in error for Britannicus. This letter contains errors in imperial titulature: it should be consul four times, not six; the imperatorial number is also too high. Antiochus IV of Commagene had been established as client king by Gaius, and reigned until 72. For Polemon II see **M46**, **M48**.

M50 King Togidubnus of Britain

To Neptune and Minerva for the welfare of the Divine House, by authority of Tiberius Claudius Togidubnus, great king of Britain, the guild of smiths and those who belong to it gave this temple from their own resources, the site having been given by [...]ens, son of Pudentinus.

[*RIB* 91 = Smallwood 197 = Sherk 56 = LACTOR 4.137]

Different manuscripts of Tacitus give Cogidumnus and Togidumnus, and the first two letters of his name on the inscription are lost, but Togidubnus is a more likely Celtic name. The marble inscription from a dedication to a temple shows he was given Roman citizenship by Claudius and, like Aspourgos above **M45**, the grandiloquent title *rex magnus,* great king (compare Tacitus' description of 'certain communities' in his comment on Togidubnus in *Agricola* in **N31**). It was found in 1723 in Chichester, the centre of Togidubnus' friendly kingdom.

M51 Tiberius Julius Cotys, King of Bosporus, AD 58

Imperator Nero Caesar Augustus, son of Claudius, consul three times, in his 5th year of tribunician power, father of the fatherland, his own saviour and benefactor; Cotys, son of Aspourgos, king, Friend of Caesar and Friend of the Romans, pious, high-priest of the Imperial Family for life, dedicated this.

[Greek, Panticapaeum: Smallwood 203b]

Aspourgos was succeeded by his elder son, Mithridates, by the time of Gaius (as shown by a gold coin of Gaius and Mithridates, dated 39/40, Smallwood 202); Claudius confirmed him (Dio 60.8.2) but in AD 46 replaced him with his younger brother, Tiberius Julius Cotys (Dio 60.28.7, confusing kings called Mithridates). Mithridates' attempts to get his kingdom back end in 49 (Tac. *Ann.* 12.15–21).

IMPERIAL ESTATES: M52–M54

The census qualification required for a senator to be, or remain a senator depended essentially on wealth in the form of land. Most will have had several estates in Italy and the provinces and these might well be bequeathed to an emperor (Augustus received legacies worth 1.4 billion sesterces in his last 20 years (Suet. *Aug.* 101.3) and legacies to the emperor become effectively an inheritance tax: **T18–T20**) or simply confiscated (**M54**). The result is vast estates run by imperial slaves or freedmen. For imperial estates, see Millar, *ERW* 175–189).

M52 A wealthy procurator (Teate Marrucinorum – Samnium), AD 36–37

To Tiberius Caesar Augustus, son of Divus Augustus, *pontifex maximus*, in his 38th year of tribunician power, consul five times, according to the will of Marcus Pulfennius, son of Sextus, of the voting-tribe Arnensis, centurion of legion VI Ferrata; Gaius Herennius Capito, son of Titus, of the voting-tribe Arnensis, military tribune three times, prefect of cavalry, prefect of veterans, procurator of Julia Augusta, procurator of Tiberius Caesar Augustus, procurator of Gaius Caesar Augustus Germanicus, with ten pounds of silver.

[EJ 225 = *AE* (1941) 105]

This inscription records the dedication of a silver bust of Tiberius. Having served in the army, Herennius Capito became manager of imperial estates in Jamnia in Judaea, bequeathed to Julia Augusta by Salome, sister of Herod the Great (Jos. *JA* 18.158). As with Burrus (**U25**), his career illustrates continuity in imperial estate management.

M53 A boundary dispute in Pisidia

In accordance with a letter of god Augustus Germanicus Caesar, Quintus Petronius Umber, propraetorian legate of Nero Claudius Caesar Augustus Germanicus, and Lucius Pupius Praesens, procurator of Nero Claudius Caesar Augustus Germanicus, fixed the boundaries, the territory on the right to belong to the people of Sagalassos, that on the left to the village of the people of Tymbrianassus, the property of Nero Claudius Caesar Augustus Germanicus, in which one fifth is to belong to the people of Sagalassos.

[Greek: Smallwood 387 = *IGRRP* III 335]

This inscription was carved three times on rectangular blocks of stone set at various points on a disputed boundary, along a stream, between an imperial estate (including the village of Tymbrianassus) and the territory of Sagalassos the major city of Pisidia (S. Turkey), part of the province of Galatia. Claudius (here = god Augustus Germanicus Caesar) had written to the provincial governor and imperial procurator but had then died. Pupius is also honoured as procurator of Galatia (**M34**).

M54 Huge estates

To confess the truth, huge estates have ruined Italy, and even the provinces too – six landlords owned half the province of Africa before the emperor Nero put them to death.

[Pliny, *Natural History* 18.35]

Huge estates were thought to have driven the traditional small-holdings farmer to the city. It is mentioned as a problem in Tac. *Ann.* 3.53.4 (speech of Tiberius), Sen. *Ep.* 89.20–1 and 87.7 and Sen. *Benefits* 7.10.5.

THE BURDEN ON THE PROVINCES: M55–M63

Dio reports a story, which he places early in Tiberius' reign (57.10.5), that the prefect of Egypt sent him more money from taxes than had been agreed. Tiberius' response was "I want my sheep shorn not skinned alive." A slightly different version is given by Suetonius, *Tiberius* 32.2. Tacitus regards the principate as bringing an improvement in the lot of the provincials by removing some of the potential for extortion at the hands of governors who had, under the republic, expected to recoup their election expenses in their year governing a province (Tac. *Ann.* 1.2.2). The system remained exploitative (**M56**), since 'tax-farmers' (*publicani*) would bid for an area's tax contract, and be personally responsible for any shortfall in the amount actually collected, while making their profits from any surplus. The earliest 'petition and response' story (LACTOR 17, M68) concerns a tax-burden. **M55** shows how a city achieved the required amount.

Another burden on provincials was requisitioning **(M59–M63).** In order to ensure the smooth functioning of public transport and the communications system in the empire, local communities were required to provide facilities for official travellers, such as accommodation, and road-repairs. This system is known as requisitioning, and in principle strict limits were placed upon who could claim what facilities at the local level, but it was in reality open to abuse by Romans and local grandees. Repeated efforts were made by Roman emperors and their representatives to stem such abuse, but without apparent effect (**M63**).

M55 A city's tax burden

[23] Whereas Aristocles, on taking over as secretary of the councillors the office entrusted to him by the magistrates and councillors took prompt care to protect properly both the city and its inhabitants, as far as it lay within his power, and first of all he made sure that all the financial administration of the city was clearly written up on the wall on a daily basis by those who control it, setting an example to worthy men as regards integrity and justice in the conduct of office. He himself, however, desiring to be above suspicion in everything before the citizens, as to the fact that he conducts himself faultlessly, has not engaged in any financial transaction for himself nor fraudulently through other persons, but has appointed men of sound character as collectors for each civic duty and financial transaction, and secures for the city everything satisfactory. [30] Even when many large taxes were being imposed, he achieved many important advantages to the benefit of the city at the hands of the governors, some here in the city, and others as an envoy. Further, in entertaining both governors and numerous other Romans, he sets down his own resources to the advantage of the city. And he has paid attention to the just and equitable administration of all the other affairs of its inhabitants, proving worthy of the offices that it had previously put into his charge. On account of this and his excellent conduct he was honoured with statues by the city. And on account of all the merits inscribed above, Memmius the proconsul and Vibius the praetorian legate have each in recognition of his conduct given him the right to wear the gold ring, as have the councillors also, while all with one accord declared that it was right that Aristocles should be given honours worthy of him for all the merits inscribed above, and all the citizens have been eager to accord him the honour of a statue and two carved portraits; [40] and it is fitting that good patriotic men who show care with complete impartiality for the common interest should be commended and honoured with the appropriate honours.

The councillors and people have decreed as followed: To commend Aristocles, the son of Callicrates, secretary of the councillors, on his care in matters of public interest and for his integrity and his impartiality with which [he continues toward the] citizens, [and likewise] too for the many substantial things [he has done for the advantage of the city …]

[Greek: *IG* 5, 1, 1432, lines 23–44]

This is an extract from a lengthy inscription in Greek from Messene in the Peloponnese, roughly datable from the reference to P. Memmius Regulus, governor of Achaia around the death of Gaius (**E3**). It records praise for the way in which Aristocles has handled public finances. After this extract ends, there follow details of the tax burden imposed upon Messene by Rome, and how the town had arranged for it to be paid. The sum of 100,000 denarii had been imposed on Messene as its land-tax contribution, and this burden was then divided up among different constituencies, including tribes, Olympic victors, and Romans. The inscription gives details of the value of property owned by Messenians and aliens, subtracts the assessments of those exempt from having to pay the tax, and then calculates the total of taxable property.

M56 Abusive behaviour by a tax collector

To Tiberius Claudius Pasion, *strategos*, from Sarapio, son of Theon, of the weavers from the city of Oxyrhynchus, of the district of Gymnasium Avenue.

Apollophanes, having become collector of the weavers' tax in the first year of Tiberius Claudius Caesar Augustus Germanicus, imperator, very violently seized a linen cloak that I was wearing, worth 8 drachmas; and he extorted from me a further 4 drachmas, and 2 drachmas per month in the six months from the month of New Augustus in the ninth year of Tiberius Claudius Caesar Augustus Germanicus, imperator, up until *Pharmouthi*: in total 24 drachmas. I therefore request that you take action against him as you think fit. Farewell.

[Greek: Smallwood 438 = *POxy* 285]

This papyrus records a petition made to the *strategos* (district governor) of Oxyrhynchus *c*.50. Complaint is made about the same tax-collector in another papyrus (*POxy* 284). *Pharmouthi* is the Egyptian month starting on 27 March.

M57 An appeal from tax-collectors in Egypt

To Tiberius Claudius Balbillus, from Nemesion, collector of the poll-tax of Philadelphia [names of five other poll-tax collectors in different villages], the six collectors ~~of the poll-tax~~ of the aforementioned villages of the Heraclides region of the Arsinoite *nome*.

The previously numerous inhabitants in the aforementioned villages have now reduced to only a few, because some have withdrawn through poverty, whilst others have died without heirs, and for this reason, there is a danger of us abandoning tax-collection because of its paltriness. Turning to you for these reasons, ~~with a view to not abandoning tax-collection,~~ we ask you, the saviour and benefactor of all, to write, if you think fit, to the strategos of the *nome*, Asianus, for him to protect us so that we are undisturbed, and to wait until your decision at the assize of the upper *nome*, so that we may receive your beneficence. Farewell.

[Greek: Smallwood 439 = A.S. Hunt & C.C. Edgar, *Select Papyri* II (1977) no. 281]

This papyrus contains a petition from a group of tax-collectors to the prefect of Egypt, Balbillus (see **U21**). A *nome* is an administrative district of Egypt. Two phrases are deleted, presumably as redundant.

M58 The Customs Law of Asia, Ephesos, AD 62

This inscription from Ephesos preserves a copy of a series of regulations governing the collection of customs dues on imports and exports in the province of Asia. The stone had been re-cut and was found reused in the Church of St John in Selçuk in 1976: as a result the document is only partially preserved. Its preface makes clear that the text is an official copy made in AD 62 of a document archived at Rome, which has been translated into Greek. Instead of updating the regulations, the inscription transcribes a series of modifications made to them from 75 BC down to AD 62. Customs dues were collected by contractors, who would make a bid promising to pay a certain sum of money to the state, and would then attempt to make a profit by collecting more in dues. The publication of these regulations at this particular time perhaps relates to the concerns about corrupt practices among tax-collectors on the part of the emperor Nero and the senate recorded for AD 58 by Tacitus (*Ann.* 15.18.2–4). The three special commissioners named by Tacitus as appointed to take charge of public revenues appear in the final fragmentary lines of this inscription.

M58a Prescript

[1] When [Quintus Manlius Tarquitius Sat]urninus and Publius Petronius Niger were consuls, on 9 July, [copied and checked, at Rome, on the first floor (?)] of the Basilica Julia, in the record office of the keepers of the public revenues, from the records [of the keepers of the public revenues, in which there was written] what is written below:

When A. Pompeius Paulinus, L. Calpurnius Piso and A. Ducenius [Geminus were keepers of the public revenues, from the regulations (?)] of the contract, year one, revenue register (?) one, in tablet one, under the authority of Nero Claudius Caesar Augustus [Germanicus, *pontifex maximus*, consul for the fourth time, in his] 8th year of [tribunician power], hailed victorious commander 9 times, father of the fatherland, and by senatorial decree, the regular revenues for the dues of Asia were ex[tracted and checked at the discretion] of the same keepers, on 15 April, from the regular revenues of T. Domitius Decidianus, [quaestor of the treasury, in respect of year one of the tax and years] two, three, four, five of the tax.

M58b Scope of the regulations

[7] The regulation for the dues of Asia on import and export by land and sea, [where it lies beside the coast of Asia and where the boundaries] of Cappadocia, Galatia, and Bithynia girdle Asia, and where the lands of the Chalcedonians or Byzantines within the [same boundaries have customs stations for the sake of the dues on] import or export by sea at the mouth of the Black Sea; in whatever places by senatorial decree or by statute [or by plebiscite it is obligatory for a censor or consul] to lease out the customs duties, in those places, whatever is imported by sea or exported overseas, [whatever is conveyed in or driven in by land], and whatever is conveyed out, driven out, or exported by land, is to give the fortieth part to the collector.

[*There follows a detailed series of customs regulations designed to curb tax avoidance. They include information relating to the rates of duty on different commodities (e.g. slaves, purple dye, grain, wine, oil, minerals) and exemptions (for some communities), methods of payment, and penalties for evasion. The inscription records a whole series of emendations made to the regulations between 75* BC *and* AD *62, before breaking off where the stone is damaged.*]

[Greek: M. Cottier, et al., *The Customs Law of Asia* (2008) lines 1–11]

M59 Edict of Germanicus against abuse of requisitioning, AD 19

[Germanicus Caesar, son of Augustus, grandson of god Augustus, proconsul, says: "Hearing that now already for my visit] requisitions [of boats] and animals are being made, and that lodgings are being seized as quarters by force and private citizens intimidated, I considered it necessary to make clear that I want neither boat nor baggage animal to be taken over by anyone, nor lodgings to be seized, except on the command of Baebius, my friend and secretary. For if it is necessary, Baebius himself will distribute the lodgings fairly and justly. And I order that payments are duly made according to my scheme for the boats or animals that are being requisitioned. I want those who object to be brought before my secretary, who will either himself prevent private persons from being wronged or will report to me. I forbid baggage animals which are passing through the city to be forcibly taken away by those who happen to meet them. For this is actually an act of confessed robbery."

[Greek: *Select Papyri* II no.211 = LACTOR 8 no.7a = EJ 320(a) = Braund 558]

This is one of two edicts of Germanicus preserved, in Greek, on papyrus (see **J7d**). It shows that Germanicus tried to ensure that his visit did not become over-burdensome upon the locals.

M60 Supplies for the visit of Germanicus, 25 Jan. AD 19

Phatres, son of Psenthotes, has made a payment into the bank at Great Diospolis for the price of the wheat from the granary [--- | ---] for the visit of Germanicus Caesar base-metal drachmas [---]. Year 5 of Tiberius Caesar Augustus. Tybe 30. Menedoros.

[Greek: Sherk 34c = Wilcken no.413]

This text is preserved on an ostrakon (pottery fragment) from Diospolis Magna, Thebes in Egypt. It is dated by regnal year of Tiberius and by local calendar month, with Tybe 30 equating to 25 January. It acted as a receipt given to Phatres by Menedoros for the sum of money which he was required to deposit in place of a quantity of wheat which was demanded from him to supply Germanicus and his entourage. [L. Mitteis & U. Wilcken, *Grundzüge und Chrestomathie der Papyruskunde* (1912)]

M61 Edict by a provincial governor of Galatia

Sextus Sotidius Strabo Libuscidianus, propraetorian legate of Tiberius Caesar Augustus declares: "It is certainly the most unjust thing of all for me in my edict to tighten up that which the Augusti – one the greatest of gods, the other of leaders – have most carefully decreed against, namely that no one may use transport facilities without payment. But since the lack of discipline of some persons requires a punishment here and now, I have published in individual towns and villages a list of the services that I judge ought to be provided, with the object of seeing it observed, or, if it is disregarded, of exacting punishment not only with my own power but with the majesty of the best leader from whom I received instructions on this very point. The people of Sagalassus must provide a service of ten carts and the same number of mules for the necessary purposes of persons passing through, and receive from those who use them ten asses per hour for each cart and four asses per hour for each mule; but if they prefer to provide donkeys, they are to give at the same price two donkeys in place of each mule. Alternatively, if they prefer, they should be responsible for giving to members of another town or village who actually perform the service, for each mule and each cart what they were going to receive if they were providing them themselves, so they take it on in the same way. They shall be obliged to provide transport as far as Cormasa and Conana.

However, the right to use this service shall not belong to everybody, but to the procurator of the best leader and (?) to his son, a right to use them which extends to ten carts, or three mules in place of each cart, or two donkeys in place of each mule, which they may use at the same time, for which they are to pay the price established by me. In addition, the right to use this service shall belong to men on military service, both those who have a permit, and those who travel through from other provinces on military service, on the following terms: that to a senator of the Roman people not more than ten carts, or three mules in place of each cart, or two donkeys in place of each mule, are to be supplied, for which they are to pay what I have laid down; to a Roman equestrian whose service the best leader is using, three carts, or three mules in place of each, or in place of each mule two donkeys, must be given on the same condition; if anyone requires more, he should hire them at the rate decided by the person who is hiring them out; to a centurion a cart or three mules or six donkeys, on the same condition. To those who are transporting grain or anything else of the kind for their own profit or use, I wish nothing to be supplied, nor anything for a man's baggage animals or those of his freedmen or slaves. Board and lodging ought to be supplied free of charge to all who are members of my own staff and to persons on military service from all provinces and to freedmen and slaves of the best leader and their baggage animals, on condition that they do not demand other services free of charge from those who are unwilling."

[Bilingual, Latin & Greek: *AE* (1976) 653 + Mitchell, *ZPE* 45 (1982) 99–100]

This bilingual edict was found inscribed in Latin and Greek upon a marble stele, with pediments and acroteria, at Burdur in Pisidia (S. Turkey). It probably dates from the early years of Tiberius' rule, given the emphasis upon Augustus (now deceased and deified) alongside Tiberius. The list of those entitled to use the requisitioning system includes the procurator (and, unexpectedly, his son – perhaps as a result of a linguistic error), the governor's retinue, military personnel, and imperial freedmen and slaves. He explicitly excludes claims from private individuals involved in trading. Distances are measured by the hour because of the mountainous terrain in the district. It also alludes to the permits (*diplomata*) issued by the emperor for use on the imperial post service (*cursus publicus*).

M62 Edict by prefect of Egypt against illegal requisitioning, AD 42

Lucius Aemilius Rectus declares: "Nobody is permitted to press into service the people in the countryside or to demand provisions for travel or any other gift without my permit, and each of those people who have my permit may take sufficient necessities and pay the price of them. If there is any report either of soldiers or men under arms or any of the attendants in public service having acted contrary to my order or having used force against any of those from the countryside or having levied money, against such a person I will administer the highest penalty. Year 2 of Tiberius Claudius Caesar Augustus Imperator, on the 4th day of Germanicus."

[Greek: Smallwood 381 = *P. London* 1171 verso, col. III]

This edict is preserved upon papyrus. L. Aemilius Rectus was prefect during 41–42 (**M6**). The dating formula shows that the Egyptian month Pachon (26 April to 26 May) was renamed 'Germanicus'.

M63 Edict of Claudius, AD 49/50

Tiberius Claudius Caesar Augustus G[erm]anicus, *pontifex maximus*, in his 9th year of tribunician power, hailed victorious commander 16 times, father of the fatherland, declares: "Although I had often attempted to relieve both colonies and municipalities not only of Italy but also of the provinces, likewise the towns of each province, from the burdens of supplying transport, and although I thought that I had found a sufficiently large number of remedies, it has nevertheless proved [impossible to cope adequately] with the evil of men [...]"

[Smallwood 375 = *ILS* 214]

This edict from Tegea (Arcadia) gives an impression of Claudius' exasperation at not having managed to solve the problem of the abuse of the transport system.

PROVINCIAL CITY LIFE: M64–M73

Beyond paying taxes, cities in the provinces were usually free to run their own affairs, electing their own local officials (**M70–M73**). They might seek imperial favour and attention by sending embassies; by giving the emperor an honorary local magistracy (**M46**, **U29**); or making a prominent Roman their patron (**M64**, **M65**, **M72**); or by buildings embellishing the town, but dedicated to the imperial family (**M66–M70**).

M64 Patronal agreement, AD 28

On 5 December in the consulship of Lucius Silanus, *flamen* of Mars, and Gaius Vellaeus Tutor, the senate and people of Siagu formed a friendship with Gaius Silius Aviola, son of Gaius, of the voting-tribe Fabia, military tribune of the legion III Augusta, prefect of the engineers and chose him and his descendants as patron for themselves and their descendants. Gaius Silius Aviola, son of Gaius, of the voting-tribe Fabia, received them and their descendants into allegiance and client-relationship. Transacted by Celer, son of Imilcho Gulalsa, *sufet*.

[EJ 354 = *ILS* 6099]

This is one of three bronze patronal tablets found near Brixia (modern Brescia), in northern Italy, and were probably all originally on display in the house of Silius Aviola. This particular agreement is between Silius Aviola and Siagu in Tunisia. It seems likely that this patronal agreement arose out of Aviola's office as military tribune of legion III Augusta, since that legion was stationed in that area of North Africa. Aviola was also patron of other communities in north Africa. The final word – sufet – alludes to the office of chief magistrate in towns of Punic background.

M65 Guest-friendship pact, AD 31

In the consulship of Tiberius Caesar for the fifth time, and Lucius Aelius Sejanus, 21 January. Quintus Stertinius Bassus, son of Quintus, Quintus Stertinius Rufus, son of Quintus, and Lucius Stertinius Rufinus, son of Quintus, made guest-friendship with Lucius Fulcinius Trio, legate of Tiberius Caesar, and his children and descendants. Lucius Fulcinius Trio, legate of Tiberius Caesar, received Quintus Stertinius Bassus, son of Quintus, Quintus Stertinius Rufus, son of Quintus, and Lucius Stertinius Rufinus, son of Quintus, and their children and descendants into the good faith and client-relationship of himself, his children and his descendants.

[*AE* (1953) 88 = EJ 358a]

This inscription comes from Juromenha in Lusitania (modern Portugal). It illustrates the formal friendships established between some representatives of Roman imperial government and their families, and provincials and their families. Fulcinius Trio became suffect consul from 1 July in 31 (see **B31**).

M66 Arch at Mediolanum Santonum (Aquitania), AD 19

To Germanicus [Caesa]r son of Tiberius Augustus, grandson of Divus Augustus, great-grandson of Divus Julius, augur, *flamen Augustalis*, consul twice, hailed victorious commander twice.

To Tiberius Caesar [Augustus, son of Divus Augustus, grandson of Divus Julius,] *pontifex maximus*, [consul three times], hailed victorious commander 8 times, [in his 21st year of tribunician] power.

To Drusus Caesar, son [of Tiberius Augustus], grandson [of Divus Augustus], [great-grandson] of Divus Julius, [consul], pontifex, augur.

Gaius Julius Rufus, son of Gaius Julius Catuaneunus, grandson of Gaius Julius Agedomopas, great-grandson of Epotsorovis, of the voting-tribe Voltinia, priest of Rome and Augustus at the altar which is located at the Confluence, prefect of the engineers, constructed this at his own expense.

[*CIL* XIII 1036]

This is the dedicatory inscription on an imposing double-bayed arch built at Mediolanum Santonum (modern Saintes), the provincial capital of Aquitania, in AD 19 by a member of the local élite C. Iulius Rufus, who records the fact of his priesthood of Rome and Augustus at the altar of the Three Gauls at the confluence of the Rhône and Saône rivers at Lugdunum (modern Lyon). It seems likely that his family was given citizenship by Julius Caesar himself: he proudly records his ancestry back to his great-grandfather, who was not himself a Roman citizen. He also paid for the amphitheatre of the Tres Galliae sanctuary at Lyon.

M67 Building-work in Dalmatia under Tiberius

To Tiberius Caesar Augustus, son of Augustus, *pontifex maximus*, Gaius Aemilius Oca, son of Volso, and Lucius Fonteius Rufus, son of Quintus, duumvirs, saw to the construction of the portico and senate-house, by decree of the decurions, and also approved them.

[EJ 348 = *ILS* 5516]

This building-inscription from Chersus, an island in the region of Dalmatia, illustrates how local magistrates begin to include the emperor on building-inscriptions in a purely honorific capacity. In this instance, the magistrates have not paid for the buildings themselves, but have been in charge of supervising the contract for the work to be done.

M68 Embellishing the forum at Dougga, AD 36–37

To Imperator Tiberius Caesar Augustus, son of Divus Augustus, *pontifex maximus*, in his 38th year of tribunician power, consul five times; Lucius Manilius Bucco, son of Lucius, of the voting-tribe Arnensis, duumvir, dedicated this. Lucius Postumius Chius, son of Gaius, of the voting-tribe Arnensis, patron of the district, in his own name and that of his sons Firmus and Rufus, paved the forum and the open space in front of the temple of Caesar, and also saw to the construction at his own expense of an altar of Augustus, a temple of Saturn, and an arch.

[EJ 345 = *AE* (1914) 172]

This inscription from Dougga (modern Thugga), northern Tunisia, illustrates the inclusion of the emperor in a building-inscription for purely honorific purposes, with the cost of the building being met by a member of the local élite. There was a dual community at Dougga – the indigenous *civitas*, whose inhabitants continued to be administered by ancient local institutions, and a *pagus* of Roman citizens (here translated as 'the district'). Saturn was a popular deity in North Africa, being associated with Baal.

M69 Embellishing Lepcis Magna (Tripolitana)

Pompeius Silvanus (cos 45, **B45**) the governor and Cassius Gratus, his deputy are attested as dedicating buildings in Lepcis to Claudius and Nero over a three-year tenure (though in reality, members of the local élite paid for the buildings).

M69a The forum at Lepcis Magna, AD 53

To Tiberius Claudius Caesar Augustus Germanicus, son of Drusus, *pontifex maximus*, in his 13th year of tribuncian power, hailed victorious commander 17 times, consul five times, censor, father of the fatherland. Marcus Pompeius Silvanus, consul, one of the Board of Fifteen in charge of sacrifices, proconsul, patron, dedicated this, when Quintus Cassius Gratus, praetor, proconsul of Crete and Cyrene, was propraetorian legate of Africa. Gaius son of Anno, in the name of Gaius son of Gaius, his grandson, gave at his own expense the columns with their superstructure and the forum; Balitho Commodus, son of Anno Macer, having been adopted in his will, saw to it that this was carried out.

[Smallwood 320 = *IRT2009* 338]

This limestone stele (236 cm high, 85.5 cm wide, 30 cm deep) is one of four set up to commemorate the dedication of the Old Forum at Lepcis to Claudius. The lettering of the inscription was in metal. This Latin text is followed by four lines in neo-Punic: this omits reference to the Roman authorities, and simply commemorates the benefaction of the local family.

M69b Dedication of the amphitheatre at Lepcis AD 56

To ~~Nero~~ Claudius Caesar Augustus Germanicus, son of Divus Claudius, grandson of Germanicus Caesar, great-grandson of Tiberius Caesar Augustus, great-great-grandson of Divus Augustus, *pontifex maximus*, with tribunician power, hailed victorious commander, designated consul for the second time, father of the fatherland. M. Pompeius Silvanus Staberius Flavinus, one of the Board of Fifteen in charge of sacrifices, proconsul for the 3rd time, dedicated this, when Q. Cassius Gratus, praetor, proconsul of Crete and Cyrene, was propraetorian legate of Africa for the 3rd time.

[*AE* 1968.549]

M70 An efficient strategos in Egypt, AD 22–23

Ninth year of Tiberius Caesar Augustus [...] the men of Bousiris in the Letopolite *nome* met and unanimously decreed the following:

[Whereas] Gnaeus Pompeius Sabinus, our strategos, does not cease being energetically and generously disposed towards the inhabitants of the *nome*, and especially in continually advancing the inhabitants of the village in addition to his beneficence, he both gives out justice in his judgements always fairly, correctly, and without bribery in accordance with the will of the most divine prefect Gaius Galerius, and he handles the work on the dykes at the required times with every care impartially, undertaking hard toil both night and day until he has finished the job, [with the result that] the flatlands have been completely flooded and an exceptional crop produced; and whereas he has brought it about that crops are paid to those working on the dykes [of the village] beyond past practice, in addition to their being free from slanders and accusations; and whereas, moreover, he farms out public taxes with complete fairness, without any force and abuse – and this is the greatest contribution to the prosperity and endurance of villages – and by paying what the village owed to other officials of the administration he keeps the farmers free from suspicion and liability, just as it was fitting. Because of [these things], we ourselves, wishing to repay him with honours, decided to honour the aforementioned Gnaeus Pompeius Sabinus, the strategos, with a stone stele bearing this decree, and to set it up in the most prominent place in the village, and also to present him with a copy, signed by as many people as possible, and this copy will be valid.

[Greek: EJ 320a = *SEG* VIII 527]

M71 A useful envoy, Cibyra (Caria)

[The people honoured] Quintus V[er]anius Philagrus, son of [T]roi[l]us, of the voting-tribe Clustumina, [priest] of Virtue for life, who has undertaken embassies four times, at no cost to the state, to the Augusti at Rome, and who was successful and acted as public advocate concerning many important affairs in many important public lawsuits, as a result of which sufficient money accrued for the foundation of the city, and brought under control 107 public slaves and possession of land, and became priest of Caesar Augustus, and gave to the city in due years a distribution of 54,000 Rhodian drachmas for the celebration of Caesarean games, and loans amounting to 100,000 Rhodian drachmas he bestowed upon those chosen by the people, and he broke a great conspiracy which was doing the greatest harm to the city. And, as for the most pressing things he gained in his embassies, he asked Tiberius Claudius Caesar to get rid of Tiberius Nicephorus, who was exacting 3,000 denarii from the city each year and keeping it, and that the sale of grain should take place in the market-place, of 75 *modii* (500kg) per acre over the whole territory. For these reasons the city gave him the honours of a heroic leader.

[Greek: Smallwood 408 = *IGRRP* IV 914]

This inscription is from the theatre at Cibyra. The honorand's achievements should be placed in the context of the refoundation of the town following a severe earthquake in 23.

M72 Imperial priest/doctor, Thasos

The people (honoured) Paramonus, son of Nicades, who has piously been priest to Tiberius Claudius Caesar Germanicus Augustus and to Imperator Caesar god Augustus, and who has conducted his magistracy fairly, justly and generously and who is skilled in medicine to the well-being of all.

[Greek: Smallwood 133]

M73 Leading-magistrate at Athens

[The] council of the Areopagus and [the] council of the 600 and the people honoured Tiberius Claudius Novius, son of Philinus, general of the hoplites for the fourth time and priest of Delian Apollo for life and president of the great Augustan Panathenaea and the Augustan Caesarea and high-priest of Antonia Augusta, friend of Caesar and friend of his country, for his virtue. When Junia Megiste, wife of Zeno, of Sounion, was priestess. Made by Epagathus, son of Aristodemus, of Thriasia.

[Greek: Smallwood 414 =*IG* II/III^2 3535]

Novius' career spanned the reigns of Claudius and Nero. Hoplite general, the most important magistrate at Athens at the time was in charge of the grain supply and markets, and empowered to propose decrees in the council and assembly. He went on to hold the post on at least four more occasions, ensuring honours for Nero (**L28**, **Q12**). This inscription probably belongs to the latter years of Claudius.

MILITARY PERSONNEL: M74–M77b

Except for the praetorian guard, soldiers were not stationed in Italy, and many veterans would settle in colonies in the provinces on discharge. In addition, soldiers, as well as auxiliaries, come increasingly to be recruited from the provinces.

M74 Discharge diploma for a sailor, AD 52

[Exterior of first tablet]

Tiberius Claudius Caesar Augustus Germanicus, *pontifex maximus*, in his 12th year of tribunician power, hailed victorious commander 27 times, father of the fatherland, censor, consul five times: to the trireme-commanders and rowers who have served in the fleet which is at Misenum under the command of Tiberius Julius Optatus, freedman of Augustus, and who have been discharged honourably, whose names are written below; to them, to their children, and their descendants he has given citizenship and legal marriage with the wives which they had at the time when citizenship was given to them, or, if any were unmarried, with those women whom afterwards they married, provided only one each. On 11 December, when Faustus Cornelius Sulla Felix and Lucius Salvidienus Rufus Salvianus were consuls.

To ordinary sailor: Sparticus Dipscurtus, son of Diuzenus, of the Bessi.

Copied and certified from the tablet of bronze which is attached at Rome on the Capitol on the right side of the temple of Good Faith of the Roman People.

[*ILS* 1986 = Smallwood 295 = Sherk 58]

So-called 'diplomas' (a modern term for this type of inscription) were official extracts copied from the imperial constitutions displayed as inscriptions upon large bronze tablets on the Capitol at Rome, granting citizenship and other rights to auxiliary veterans at the end of their terms of service (possibly after 26 years in service). These constitutions could relate to several hundred soldiers in different units at the same time, but the diploma was a personalised version issued to an individual, and was kept by him as proof of his status and legal rights. A diploma consisted of two rectangular bronze tablets, tied together with copper thread, and sealed by seven witnesses, who verified that the text was an authentic and accurate copy of the original constitution. A diploma contained two texts, with the exterior text reproducing the interior one, and the authenticity of the whole was guaranteed by being sealed by the seals of seven witnesses (in this case individuals from Macedonia). The interior text was intended to be consulted only in case of dispute, and was not read in ordinary circumstances: it acted simply as a legal safeguard. This is the earliest surviving discharge diploma, from 11 Dec AD 52. It was found at Stabiae, near Misenum on the Bay of Naples. The Bessi were Thracians. The document incidentally reveals an imperial freedman in charge of the fleet, later commanded by Anicetus, Nero's freedman (Tac. *Ann.* 14.3.3) and Pliny the Elder (Pliny the Younger, *Letters* 6.16). The coincidence of our earliest diploma belonging to the Claudian period supports our picture of that emperor taking steps to promote citizenship grants.

M75 Imperial bodyguard

Indus, bodyguard of Nero Claudius Caesar Augustus, in the squad of Secundus, by nationality a Batavian, lived 36 years, is buried here. Erected by Eumenes, his brother and heir, from the fraternity of Germans.

[*AE* (1952) 148 = Smallwood 293 = Sherk 76]

This is inscribed upon a substantial decorated funerary stele from Rome.

M76 St Paul and the military tribune

[22] Up to this word they listened to him; then they lifted up their voices and said, "Away with such a fellow from the earth! For he ought not to live." [23] And as they cried out and waved their garments and threw dust into the air, [24] the tribune commanded him to be brought into the barracks, and ordered him to be examined by scourging, to find out why they shouted thus against him. [25] But when they had tied him up with the thongs, Paul said to the centurion who was standing by, "Is it lawful for you to scourge a man who is a Roman citizen, and uncondemned?" [26] When the centurion heard that, he went to the tribune and said to him, "What are you about to do? For this man is a Roman citizen." [27] So the tribune came and said to him, "Tell me, are you a Roman citizen?" And he said, "Yes." [28] The tribune answered, "I bought this citizenship for a large sum." Paul said, "But I was born a citizen." [29] So those who were about to examine him withdrew from him instantly; and the tribune also was afraid, for he realised that Paul was a Roman citizen and that he had bound him.

[Acts, 22.22–29 (Revised Standard Version)]

Paul was a citizen of Tarsus in Cilicia (Acts 21.39, 22.3). The author of *Acts* can be trusted for his picture of the Roman empire since he was writing for a contemporary, non-Jewish audience within the Roman empire, who would have been quick to spot any mistakes, which in turn would have undermined the rest of his narrative.

Paul's question is clearly rhetorical: all concerned are clearly aware of the rights of a Roman citizen. The tribune is later named as Claudius Lysias (*Acts* 23.26). He thus acquired his citizenship from the emperor Claudius. The great sum he paid will have been a bribe to intermediaries in imperial or provincial administration for putting his name on the lists of candidates for enfranchisement to be approved by

Claudius. Compare Dio 60.17.5–6. As a military tribune, Claudius Lysias held an equestrian position, though he may have risen through the ranks to this position. See Sherwin-White, *Roman Society and Roman Law in the New Testament* (Oxford 1963), pages 149–156.

M77 The rights of veterans: meetings with the prefect of Egypt, AD 63

These two accounts on papyrus of the same meeting at Alexandria between veteran soldiers and the prefect of Egypt offer interesting differences of perspective. The first – the official report – only records the final meeting between the two, whereas the soldiers' version shows that the process was actually more drawn out than this, covering several days. The prefect in question is C. Caecina Tuscus (AD 63–?66).

M77a The official version

Transcript of official record.

Year 10 of Nero Claudius Caesar Augustus Germanicus Imperator, in the month Sebastos 7, in the Great Hall at the tribunal. Present on his Advisory Board were Norbanus Ptolemaios the *iuridicus* and the *idiologos*, Avilius Quadratus and Tennius Vetus, [...] Atticus, Papirius Pastor and Baebius Iuncinus the military tribunes (?), Iulius Lysimachus, Claudius Herakleides the chief financial official, [Clau]dius Euktemon, Claudius Secundus.

[In] the matter of the discharged soldiers, on the subject of citizenship.

[Tuscus:] "I told you also previously that the case for [each] of you is not similar nor the same; for some of you are veterans of the legions, others of the *alae*, others again of the cohorts, and still others of the rowers, [with the result that] the legal right of all of you is not the same. I will take care of this matter, and I have written to the *strategoi* nome by nome in order that the grant in its entirety may be preserved for [each] of you according to each one's legal right."

[In different handwriting]: I [...] have written.

[Greek: Smallwood 297a = Sherk 67 A = *FIRA* III (1943) 171a]

This is the official report on the meeting between veterans of different military units and the prefect, concerned about their rights to Roman citizenship. It is preserved on papyrus. It reveals the workings and composition of of the prefect's *consilium* (advisory board), whose members include leading civil administrators, representatives of the two legions stationed in Egypt, and members of the local élite. The *iuridicus* is the Roman equestrian appointed by emperor, with judicial power; the *idiologos* is the equestrian in charge of irregular and occasional sources of revenue in the province. Here both posts are held by the same individual. The Greek includes several loan-words from Latin to refer to specific military ranks.

M77b The legionaries' version

Transcript of a meeting.

The legionaries made their approach, on the road of the camp by the temple of Isis.

Tuscus the prefect replied to us: "Do not speak impiously. Nobody is troubling you. Write on tablets where each of you is staying and I will write to the *strategoi* so that nobody may give you trouble."

On the 4th of the month Sebastos we gave him the tablets in the camp headquarters and he said to us: "Did you give them separately and one by one?" And the legionaries said to him, "We gave them separately."

On the 5th of the same month we greeted him near the Paliourus and he greeted us in return, and on the [6th] of the same month we greeted him in the Hall, as he sat upon the tribunal. Tuscus said to us: "I told you also in the camp and now I tell you the same thing. There is one procedure for legionaries, another for the cohorts, still another for rowers. Go, each of you, back to your own places and do not become idle".

[Greek: Smallwood 297b = Sherk 67B = *FIRA* III (1943) 171b]

This account gives the impression that the soldiers at first approached the prefect informally, but that their meetings with him gradually became more formal in character.

LAWS: M78–M82

The emperor could make laws for Rome and the provinces by edicts, but laws could also be made by decree of the senate, and emperors sometimes chose to make laws through the senate. The huge *Digest of Roman Law*, commissioned by Justinian on his accession in AD 527 often contains details, sometimes even wording of earlier laws. Claudius took his legal responsibilities especially seriously (Suet. *Claud.* 14–16, 21, but with criticism of his inconsistency, also attacked by Seneca, *Apocol.* F12.2, F12.3 verses 18–26, F14.2–3, F15.2). On Claudius' other legislation, see Tacitus, *Annals* 11.7 (AD 47: limiting payment to lawyers); 11.13 (AD 47 as censor: stopping lending of money to young men repayable on their fathers' deaths); 12.53 (punishment for women having sexual relationships with slaves); Suetonius, *Claudius* 23: praetors for trusts, changes to marriage laws; 25.1: punishments for freedmen, freeing of abandoned slaves.

M78 Women not allowed to act as guarantors for a debtor

Later a decree of the senate was enacted which was of the greatest benefit to all women. These are the words of the decree: "Inasmuch as Marcus Silanus and Vellaeus Tutor, the consuls, have made a statement about the obligations of women who guarantee the debts of others. As to what should happen in this situation, they have decided as follows: In regard to guarantees and loans given for others, in which women might have been involved. The law seems to have been previously established that no claim nor legal proceedings may be made against them in this case, since it would not be fair for them to perform male duties or be bound by obligations of this sort. The senate believes that those who have such cases brought before them will be acting rightly and properly in ensuring that the wish of the senate in this matter is maintained."

[Digest 16.1.2.1 = Ulpian, *Commentary on the Praetor's edict* 29]

This decree reinforced one made by Augustus (*Digest* 16.1.2 preface). See Levick, *Claudius* page 124, no. 5. The decree protected women freed from legal guardianship by legislation of Augustus and Claudius from having to offer surety for their husband's debts, but perhaps more simply reflected concerns that such matters of business were a male concern.

M79 Claudius rules a son's property not be confiscated along with his father's

We are not persuaded that it is of benefit to a son to have personal property; it is of more benefit to the father than to the son, although in any case personal property is relevant for the son. Think what happens if a father's estate is seized by the state treasury for unpaid debt: the son's personal property is kept separate under a regulation of Claudius.

[Digest 4.4.3.4 = Ulpian, *Commentary on Praetor's Edict* 11 = Smallwood 363]

M80 Claudius allows mothers to inherit property from their children

But the rigidity of this rule [of inheritance being only in the male line] was later relaxed. Divus Claudius was the first to give a mother some solace for the loss of her children by their estates coming to her.

[*Justinian's Institutes*, 3.3.1]

The *Institutes* is discussing the rule of property being inherited only by and through male members of a family. See Levick, *Claudius* 125 no.9.

M81 Claudius releases women from guardianship of male relations

In the past women also had male relatives on their father's side as legal guardians. But later the Act of Claudius was passed, which abolished the guardianship of male relations as far as it applies to women.

[Gaius, *Institutes*, 1.157]

Roman women without a living father had needed a legal guardian (nearest male relative on their father's side or other person appointed in the father's will) to give or withhold authorisation for certain legal transactions affecting their property. Augustan family legislation had released women with three children from this (see LACTOR 17, S7). Claudius' legislation now removed this restriction from other women. See further B.M. Levick, *Claudius* page 125, no. 8, J.F. Gardner, *Women in Roman Law and Society* (1986) 14–22.

M82 Decree under Nero protecting trustees from being sued

[1] Under Nero, a senatorial decree was enacted on 25 August in the consulship of Annaeus Seneca and Trebellius Maximus [AD 56] in the following words: [2] "It is entirely fair in all matters of inheritance through trusts, that if any lawsuits are pending regarding the properties concerned, they should be taken against those to whom the legal right and benefit has been transferred, rather than that someone should be endangered by his good faith. Therefore it has been decided that actions which are usually brought against or by heirs should not be brought against or by people who have fulfilled their trust in passing on property as they were asked to do. Instead actions should be brought against or by those to whom property has been given under the terms of trust in the will. Thus in future the last wishes of the deceased will be strengthened."

[3] This senatorial decree removed hesitancy on the part of those who thought to refuse to act as heir either through fear of litigiation, or by offering such fear as an excuse.

[Digest 36.1.1.1–3 = Ulpian, *Trusts* 3]

The 'trusts' (*fideicommissa*) were essentially a less formal version of a will, allowing the testator greater flexibility in avoiding restrictions on who could legally inherit. So, for example, if someone wished to make Gaius Seius his heir, but he could not legally inherit, he might make Lucius Titius his heir, adding 'and I ask you, Lucius Titius, as soon as you can accept the estate, to give it to Seius.' Originally the trusts were unenforceable, relying instead on the honour of the beneficiary to pass on the legacy. Augustus gave responsibility for enforcing them to the consuls. Claudius created an extra two praetors each year to deal with trusts (**U13**). Nero's reform was designed to protect trustees from being sued. For more on trusts, see Justinian's Institutes, 2.23; *OCD* under '*fideicommissa*'. Despite this obviously sensible provision, official heirs, seeing no profit in trusts, began to refuse such inheritances, until under Vespasian a decree allotted the trustee a quarter of the value of the property passed on (*Justinian's Institutes*, 2.23.4–5)

SECTION N

WAR AND EXPANSION

'The empire should not be extended beyond its current boundaries.' (Augustus)

Augustus' list of the empire's resources, including this recommendation was read out in the senate on Tiberius' orders in the first meeting after Augustus' funeral (Tacitus, *Annals* 1.11.4). Tacitus suggests jealousy as a possible motive: Augustus himself had hugely expanded the Roman empire, or, in his own words 'subjected the world to the empire of the Roman people' (*RG, title*). In fact, expansion of the empire, whether through invasion or annexation continues throughout the period, as emperors (especially those without military credentials themselves) see the benefit of attaining military glory.

This section begins with the general account provided by Josephus' *Jewish War* of Rome's resources in AD 66, and then deals with wars by region and chronologically, so Germany, the setting of campaigns from the first years of Tiberius comes first; and the Caucasus, Nero's target towards the end of his reign comes last.

N1a The Might of Rome in AD 66

Josephus provides a comprehensive account of the Roman empire and its manpower in AD 66 in his *Jewish War,* 2.363–387. Although its literary context is entirely implausible (a lengthy speech of Agrippa II urging the Jews against the revolt which led to the destruction of the Temple in Jerusalem), Josephus seems to have used a very accurate source. Josephus himself provides a unique perspective in having himself commanded forces against Rome (for Josephus, see Section **E**).

[363] Having conquered that world, they are still greedy for more. They are not satisfied that to the east their frontiers have reached the Euphrates, to the north the Danube, to the south Libya, whose uninhabited deserts they have explored, and Cadiz to the west; for now they seek another empire beyond the Ocean, and already they have carried their arms as far as the Britons, peoples hitherto unknown to history. [364] Face reality, I beg you. Are you richer than the Gauls, stronger than the Germans, cleverer than the Greeks, more numerous that the population of the whole wide world? What crazy optimism makes you think you can take on the Romans?

N1b Achaia (Greece) & Macedonia

[365] I suppose someone is going to tell me that you "cannot endure your slavery." Well, slavery is far worse for the Greeks, the noblest of all nations under the sun, and theirs is a very big country. Yet they yield obedience to the *fasces* of a Roman governor and his six lictors; so too the Macedonians, who have a better right than you to demand their liberty.

N1c Asia Minor & The Black Sea

[366] What about the five hundred cities of Asia? They have no garrison, and yet they cringe before a single governor and the rods, which symbolise his consular rank. Need I remind you of the Heniochi and the Colchians, the Taurian tribesmen, the peoples of the Bosporus, and those who dwell along the shores of the Black Sea and the Sea of Azov. [367] None of them until now had ever recognised being subject to one of their own people; but now three thousand legionaries are enough to keep them all in order, while a mere forty triremes have sufficed to impose peace on their wild and hitherto un-traversed sea. [368] Bithynia, Cappadocia, Pamphylia, the Lycians and the

Cilicians all have powerful arguments for their liberty; yet all pay their taxes without the need for an army to compel them.

N1d Thrace

But then consider this. The Thracians possess a country one hundred and twenty-five miles wide and a hundred and seventy-five long, with a terrain far more savage than your own and more easily defended; its penetrating cold strikes terror into those who campaign against them. Yet even they obey a garrison which is a mere two thousand strong.

N1e The Danube region

[369] As for the neighbouring Illyrians, who inhabit a territory stretching from Dalmatia to the Danube, they are controlled by just two legions, and even join with them to drive back Dacian raiders. [370] The Dalmatians themselves in pursuit of liberty have raised the standards of revolt often enough; and every time they have been defeated they have gathered their forces for a fresh challenge. Yet now they live in peace under the control of a single legion.

Josephus is confused here by the various names of the region (still not fixed at this period – see *OCD* 'Illyricum') and omits two legions – either in Pannonia or Moesia (depending on what he means by 'Illyrians').

N1f Gaul

[371] But if there is one nation whose great resources should encourage them above all others to revolt, it is the Gauls. Nature has provided them with such massive defences: to the east the Alps; to the north the river Rhine; to the south the Pyrenees; and to the west the Atlantic Ocean. [372] And yet, despite such formidable defences, despite their enormous population of some three hundred and five different tribes, despite the fact that their own lands provide them with what one might describe as well-springs of prosperity so abundant that their produce almost swamps the whole world, despite all this they tolerate the fact that the Romans treat them simply as a source of revenue – and then assign them an allowance from their own prosperity. [373] All this they put up with, not because they are effeminate cowards or racially degenerate – after all they fought for their freedom for some eighty years – but because they have been shattered by the sheer might of Rome's armies and the hand of Fate, which has brought her more success than even her armies. And that is why they submit, like slaves, to the control of some twelve hundred soldiers, though they almost match them in the number of their cities.

1,200 soldiers: two urban cohorts were stationed at Lugdunum (Lyons), cohort XVIII (Tac. *Hist.* 1.64.3) and XIII? (Tac. *Ann.* 3.41.2). In AD 66 Nero raised another legion for his planned Caspian expedition. Instead, this was sent to Gaul in AD 68 and also stationed at Lugdunum.

N1g Spain

[374] As for the peoples of Spain, not even the gold which their lands produce was sufficient to finance a war for freedom; the vast distance of land and sea which separates them from Rome, the fighting spirit of the Lusitanians and Cantabrians, the adjacent ocean whose tidal flows bring terror even to the native peoples, none of these could preserve their liberty. [375] Even they were reduced to slavery by Rome, whose military might reached beyond the Straits of Gibraltar, and whose armies marched

across the cloud-capped Pyrenees. One legion is now sufficient garrison for these doughty fighters, dwelling in such a distant land.

N1h Germany

[376] Which of you has not heard of the Germans with their massive population? You surely must have seen them often enough, with their brute strength and muscular physique, since everywhere the Romans possess German captives as their slaves. [377] Theirs is a territory boundless in extent, a fighting spirit even more formidable than their bodies, hearts that are contemptuous of death, and a battle-rage that is fiercer than the wildest of wild animals. And yet the Rhine has placed a curb on their aggression, they have been tamed by the might of eight Roman legions, reduced to slavery as captives, while the remainder of their nation has sought safety in flight.

N1i Britain

[378] You now put your trust in the walls of Jerusalem. But look at what a wall the British had. Yes, for they are surrounded by the Ocean, and inhabit an island at least as large as our own territories. Yet the Romans sailed across and reduced them to slavery, and now four legions guard that enormous island.

N1j Parthia

[379] Need I say more? Even the Parthians, the most warlike of all nations, rulers of innumerable tribes, and defended by such mighty armies, even they send hostages to Rome. There you can see them, the aristocrats of the East, on Italian soil, going through the motions of negotiating peace, while in reality they are but slaves.

See **N54** on the crowing of Tiridates in AD 66.

N1k North Africa

[380] That is the stark truth. Almost every nation under the sun pays homage to the armies of Rome. Are you then going to be the only ones to make war upon them? Will you not spare a thought for what happened to the Carthaginians? For all their pride in Hannibal the Great and their glorious Phoenician lineage, they fell before the mighty hand of Scipio. [381] Neither the Cyrenians, for all their Spartan origins, nor the Libyans, whose tribal boundaries stretch to the very edges of the desert, nor the Syrtes (Gulf of Sidra), whose very reputation is a source of terror, nor yet the Nasamonians, the Moors, nor the numberless Numidians: not one of these could defeat the military might of Rome. [382] Rome now controls the whole of Africa, that is one third of all the inhabited world, whose tribes cannot easily be counted, and whose boundaries stretch from the Atlantic Ocean and the Straits of Gibraltar as far as the Red Sea, where dwell the uncountable peoples of Ethiopia. [383] For eight months of the year its annual produce feeds the population of Rome; as well as that, they pay taxes of every kind, and meet the empire's needs by willingly submitting to additional impositions. And though they are only garrisoned by one single legion, they do not regard such demands as outrageous insults, as you do.

N1m Egypt

[384] But why should I look for proofs of Roman power from far away, when they are to be found in your next-door neighbour, Egypt? [385] Her lands extend from Arabia Felix (the port for trade with India) to Aethiopia; on the evidence of individual census

returns, her population numbers some seven million five hundred thousand (excluding the population of Alexandria). Yet she tolerates Roman domination, even though she has a potent source of encouragement to revolt in Alexandria's teeming population, its wealth, as well as its size. [386] That city is nearly four miles long, and over a mile wide. The tax revenues which she pays to Rome every month exceed what you pay for a whole year; and quite apart from those financial revenues, she sends to Rome sufficient corn to feed its population for four months. She is defended on all sides by impassable deserts, a coastline without harbours, or by rivers and marshes. [387] Yet none of these features proved sufficient to protect her from the imperial destiny of Rome. Two legions form the city's garrison, and are sufficient to control even the outer reaches of Egypt and her Macedonian aristocracy.

[Josephus, *Jewish War* 2.363–387]

N2 Legions of the empire, tabulated according to Tacitus and Josephus

Area	AD 23 Tac. *Ann.* 4.5	AD 66 Jos. *JW* 2.363–87	AD 69 (start) Legions	Tac. *Hist.*
Britain	N/A	**4**	**3**	3.22.2
Lower Germany	**4**	**4**	**4**	1.55.1–2
Upper Germany	**4**	**4**	**3**	1.55.3, 1.61.2
Gaul	**0**	1,200 men	**1**	1.59.2
Spain	**3**	**1**	**2**	2.58.2
Pannonia	**2**	**(2)**	**3**	2.86
Dalmatia	**2**	**1**	**1**	3.50
Moesia	**2**	**2**	**3***	2.85
Thrace	Rhoemetalces	2,000 men	minor	1.11.2
Mauretania	Juba	**0**	19 cohorts	2.58
Africa	**2**	**1**	**1**	1.11.2
Egypt	**2**	**2**	**2**	2.76
Judaea	(under Syria)	(under Syria)	**3**	1.10.3
Syria	**4**	**(4)** not in *JW*	**4***	1.10.1
Black Sea		3,000 men		
Cappadocia?	N/A	(2)	**0**	
Rome			**1**	1.6.2
Total of Legions	**25**	**27**	**30**	

Tacitus gives his survey under AD 23. For Josephus, see above, **N1**. Tacitus' survey at the start of his *Histories* (1.8–11) does not give full details, but these can often be filled out by his later narrative.

Pannonia AD 69: it is not clear where legion XIV, recalled from Britain to be sent to the East was: it was later stationed in Pannonia.

Cappadocia AD 66: legions V Macedonica and XV Apollinaris were moved to Corbulo's overall command (Tac. *Ann.* 15.26.2). Corbulo was still in the East in autumn 66. Titus brought XV Apollinaris to join V Macedonica commanded by his father in Ptolemais in early spring 67. It is likely that these legions had not gone back to their normal bases in Moesia and Pannonia (Jos. *JW* 7.117). Jos. *JW* 7.18 implies that the disgraced XII Fulminata is sent to Melitene in Cappadocia, the temporary camp of one or both of legions V and XV.

*Tacitus counts legion III Gallica twice, as Nero moved it to Moesia just before his death, but it could still counts as a legion loyal to Mucianus' army in Syria. Tacitus gives an explanation of several of the changes between AD 66 and 69 at *Hist.* 1.6.2.

Total: The increase in total number of legions came about as follows: XV Primigenia and XXII Primigenia were created under Caligula (Suet. *Cal.* 45.1; Dio 59.22.1) for a German campaign, or under Claudius to release experienced legions for the invasion of Britain. I Italica was formed for Nero's planned expedition to the Caucasus (Suet. *Nero* 19). The raising of I Adiutrix and VII Galbiana (later Gemina) was begun by Nero and completed by Galba. (Tac. *Hist.* 1.6.2; Suet. *Galba* 10.2).

Germany: N3–N4

Germany was the scene of the most difficult, prolonged and unsuccessful campaigns of Augustus' reign, culminating in the loss of three legions in the Varus disaster of AD 9 (Vell. 2.117–122; Suet. *Aug.* 23). Germanicus' campaigns across the Rhine AD 14–16 attempted to restore or improve the position lost by the Varus disaster and are recounted briefly by Velleius (2.129.2) and in detail by Tacitus (*Ann.* 1.49–51 (AD 14); 55–71 (AD 15); 2.5–26 (AD 16) and see Goodyear, *Commentary Volume 2,* pages 65–8, 198–9). After Germanicus' recall the Rhine continues to mark the boundary of Roman territory, with 8 legions still deployed. Caligula's campaigns are dismissed in the sources (Suet. *Cal.* 45; Dio 59.21.2–3) and he issues coins celebrating his father's victories and recovery of the legionary standards (*RIC* Gaius 57 = *BMC* 94). Corbulo campaigns in the area in AD 47 (Tac. *Ann.* 11.16–20).

N3 Germanicus Caesar across the Rhine

In a coastal area of Germany on the far side of the Rhine, where Germanicus Caesar had moved his camp, there was only a single spring of fresh water. Drinking from it resulted in teeth falling out and knee-joints being weakened within two years.

[Pliny, *Natural History* 25.20]

Pliny is discussing plants as remedies for certain diseases. Germanicus' expeditions quickly become the stuff of epic poetry (see Albinovanus Pedo, **J7b**), with consequent exaggerations of the strangeness of the lands he had tried (heroically or rashly) to conquer.

N4 Amber found in islands of N Ocean under Germanicus

It has been established that amber occurs naturally in the islands of the Northern Ocean. The Germans call it 'glaesum', and, as a result, one of the islands there, which the locals call Austeravia, was known by our men as Glaesaria when Germanicus Caesar was operating in that area with his fleet.

[Pliny, *Natural History* 37.42]

Pliny reflects the fascination of the ancients with the formation and properties of amber (37.31–48; Tac. *Germ.* 45) and see J. F. Healy, *Pliny the Elder on Science and Technology,* Oxford 1999, 250–3.

ASIA MINOR: N5

From AD 17 to 20, Drusus Caesar, Tiberius' son, held a special commission in the Balkans, with proconsular *imperium.* He helped bring about the fall of the formidable King Maroboduus of the Marcomanni and eventually placed the remains of the kingdom in the hands of the Quadian Vannius (Tacitus, *Ann.* 2.44–46; 3.7.1, 3.11.1). Drusus' officers also dealt with pirates operating in the Dardanelles. On his return to Rome, Drusus was awarded an ovation.

N5 Drusus' campaigns against pirates, Ilium, Asia

The council and people honoured Titus Valerius Proculus, procurator of Drusus Caesar, who destroyed the pirate vessels in the Hellespont and kept the city in every respect free of burdens.

[Greek: EJ 227 = *IGRRP* IV 219]

AFRICA: N6–N7

Under Augustus, Africa (roughly Tunisia and Western Libya) became a public province governed by a proconsul, though with a legion. Between AD 17 and 23 a former Roman auxiliary, Tacfarinas, led fighting against Rome which Tacitus presents as a revolt (*Annals* 2.52 (AD 17), 3.20–21 (AD 20); 3.32.1 (AD 21); 3.73–74 (AD 22); 4.23–26 (AD 24) though it may really have been continuation of war against the Gaetulians (AD 3–6, see LACTOR 17, N10 and further references).

N6 Celebrating the defeat of Tacfarinas at Lepcis Magna

To Augustan Victory. Publius Cornelius Dolabella, consul, one of the Board of Seven for the management of feasts, *sodalis Titiensis*, proconsul, set this up after Tacfarinas was killed.

[*AE* (1961) 107]

On Dolabella's victory over Tacfarinas, see Tac., *Ann.* 4.23–26.

N7 Aftermath of the Gaetulian revolt, AD 35–36

To Tiberius Caesar Augustus, son of Divus Augustus, grandson of Divus Julius, *pontifex maximus*, consul five times, hailed victorious commander 8 times, in his 37th year of tribunician power. Gaius Rubellius Blandus, quaestor of Divus Augustus, plebeian tribune, praetor, consul, proconsul, pontiff, patron; from the revenues of the lands which he restored to the people of Lepcis, he [saw to] the paving in stone of all the roads of the community of Lepcis. Marcus Etrilius Lupercus, propraetorian legate, patron, [let the contracts for the work].

[EJ 218a = *IRT2009* 330]

This monumental inscription appears on each of the two faces of a plain arch of grey limestone set up on the main street (decumanus maximus) at Lepcis Magna (compare *IRT2009* 331). Etrilius had previously been a legate in Cyprus (**L7**).

MAURETANIA: N8–N12

Mauretania represents the area of the Atlas Mountains: modern Morocco and North-West Algeria. In 25 BC, Augustus had installed Juba II as client king over this area with Ptolemy, his son by Cleopatra Selene (thus grandson of Mark Antony – see **M39**) eventually ruling alongside his father before succeeding him in AD 23 (Tac. *Ann.* 4.5.2 and 4.23.1; **M40**, **M41**). Early in his reign he helped Cornelius Dolabella finally defeat Tacfarinas of Numidia (Tac. *Ann.* 4.23–26; **N6**). In AD 39/40, his cousin Caligula summoned him Rome and had him executed (**N8**; Suet. *Cal.*26.1, 35.1; Dio 59.25.1). Gaius annexed Mauretania and divided it into two provinces (**N9**), each under an equestrian governor, prompting a revolt (Dio 60.8.6–9.5). The execution of Ptolemy probably followed from the decision to annexe and the consequent revolt rather than the trivial reasons adduced by Suetonius and Dio, see Barrett, *Caligula* chapter 7. The revolt was ended by Claudius.

N8 Ptolemy arrested by Caligula

In our own lifetime we have seen Ptolemy, king of Africa, and Mithridates, king of Armenia, arrested by the guards of Gaius Caligula. The latter was sent into exile; the former wished that he really was being sent into exile.

[Seneca, *On Tranquillity of Mind*, 11.12]

Seneca is making the (Stoic) philosophical point to his pupil, Serenus, that even kings can fall, but that one should be prepared to bear misfortune.

N9 Mauretania divided into provinces by Caligula

The first countries in Africa are called the Mauretanias: right up to the time of Gaius Caesar, son of Germanicus, these were kingdoms, but were divided into two provinces through his cruelty.

[Pliny, *Natural History* 5.2]

The geography of Mauretania is the subject of Pliny *NH* 5.1–22. The two provinces were Mauretania Caesarensis and Mauretania Tingitana.

N10 Aedemon's revolt in Mauretania and its subsequent government

A Roman army first waged war in Mauretania in the principate of Claudius, when Aedemon attempted to avenge the death of his former master, King Ptolemy, at the hands of Gaius Caesar. When the local tribes were routed the pursuit certainly reached Mount Atlas. The glory of having penetrated into the Atlas range belongs not only to the former consuls and generals drawn from the senate, but also to the equestrians who then governed there. There are, as we have mentioned, five Roman colonies in that province.

[Pliny, *Natural History* 5.11–12]

Pliny had described the marvels of Mount Atlas at *NH* 5.6–7 and gives further information about it, obtained from Suetonius Paulinus, propraetor in Mauretania in AD 42, 'consul in our own day [AD 66] and the first Roman general to cross the Atlas range and go some distance beyond it' – *NH* 5.14–15.

N11 Rewards for Volubilis, AD 44 (Mauretania Tingitana)

To Tiberius Claudius Caesar Augustus Germanicus, son of Divus, *pontifex maximus*, in his 4th year of tribunician power, consul for the third time, designated consul for a fourth time, hailed as victorious commander 8 times, father of his fatherland, the town of Volubilis dedicated this by decree of the town councillors, when it had acquired Roman citizenship, the right of intermarriage, and freedom from compulsory public burdens. Marcus Fadius Celer Flavianus Maximus, imperial procurator with the authority of a legate, dedicated it.

[Smallwood 407a = *AE* (1924) 66= Sherk 50]

The town of Volubilis (modern Walili in Morocco (a UNESCO World Heritage site)) dates from the 4th or 3rd century BC, and flourished under Carthage and as the western capital of Juba II. This ornate statue base is dated to AD 44, shortly after Mauretania had been annexed as a province. Volubilis had supported Rome against the revolt of Ptolemy's freedman Aedemon after Gaius had executed King Ptolemy (**N8–N10** above). The first rebellion led by Aedemon had been suppressed in AD 40/41, and a further revolt among Moorish tribesmen in 41/42 (Dio Cass. 60.9). Volubilis had remained loyal throughout this period of unrest, apparently enduring attack by the rebels, and the inscription below implies that whole families had been wiped out. Claudius subsequently rewarded Volubilis for its loyalty by granting Roman citizenship and other privileges to the whole *municipium*. Claudius is here wrongly entitled 'son of a god'. The granting of the authority of a legate to the imperial procurator reflects steps taken to deal with the emergency, putting him in command of legionary troops.

N12 Volubilis honours its leading citizen.

To Marcus Valerius Severus, son of Bostar, of the tribe Galeria, aedile, *sufes*, duumvir, first priest of the imperial cult in his town, commander of the auxiliary troops against Aedemon who was defeated in the war; to him the council of the town of Volubilis, because of his services towards the state and an embassy completed successfully, during which he gained for his fellow-citizens from Divus Claudius Roman citizenship and the right of marriage to non-Roman women, freedom from taxation for ten years, the right of including others as residents, and the ownership of the goods of citizens killed in war who had no heirs. Fabia Bira, the daughter of Izelta, his wife, to the kindest of husbands accepted the honour but remitted the cost and dedicated it at her own expense.

[Smallwood 407b = *AE* (1916) 42]

This inscribed statue base belongs to a later date, some time after AD 54 (given that Claudius is now deified), but relates to the same episode as that celebrated upon Claudius' statue base (**N11** above). It illustrates the key role played by one of the town's leading citizens in securing privileges for the town from Claudius via an embassy. His filiation reveals his Punic origins, and his career spans the period when Volubilis was independent (*sufes* being a Punic magistracy) and then incorporated into the Roman empire (when the chief magistracy changed to duumvir). His wife's names are of Libyan origin. Property without heirs would normally revert to the Roman treasury rather than to the local city.

BRITAIN: N13–N30

Claudius needed a military triumph to establish his rule, especially after Scribonianus' revolt in AD 42 (**P7**). Britain provided the perfect opportunity for Claudius to surpass the expeditions in 55 and 54 BC of Julius Caesar, and the propaganda of Augustus (e.g. *RG* 32.1; Horace, *Odes* 3.5). The death of King Cunobelin, and his succession by two sons, Togodumnus and Cara(c)tacus, less friendly to Rome also provided an opportunity.

N13 Pomponius Mela's *Geography*

[3.49] What sort of place Britannia is and the sort of men it produces will soon be stated with more certainty and based on better information. For, lo and behold!, the greatest *princeps* has opened an island for so long closed. The conqueror of peoples, previously not merely undefeated but actually unknown, carries the tangible proofs of what he set out to achieve in war to be proclaimed in his triumph.

[3.50] Otherwise, as we have thought before, with a corner at an obtuse angle overlooking the harbours of the Rhine, Britannia stretches out towards the north and west, then the sloping side slants back. Thus the island faces Gaul on one side, Germany on the other; then again on the uninterrupted edge of the straight shoreline, sloping down from its back, it forms an irregular triangle, three-sided and very similar in shape to Sicily. Britannia is flat, large and fertile, especially for those raising flocks rather than men.

[3.51] Britannia provides forests and glades, huge rivers which, with changing tides sometimes flow into the sea, sometimes back, and some which produce gemstones and pearls. There are tribes and kings of tribes, but all are uncivilised. The further away from the mainland they are, the more ignorant of finer resources; rich only in sheep and territory, their bodies painted with woad, whether to make them look better or for some other purpose.

[3.52] However they stir up causes of war and wars themselves, and frequently attack each other, especially in desire to be in command and out of eagerness to extend the lands they possess. They fight not only on horseback or on foot, but also from chariots and vehicles armed in the Gallic fashion: they call these 'covinni' which use blades on the axles.

[3.53] Beyond Britannia is Iuverna (Hibernia / Ireland), almost equal in size, but oblong in shape with an equal length of shore on each side. Its climate is not suitable for crops to ripen, but the island is so luxuriant with grasses which are sweet as well as juicy, that flocks eat their fill in only a short part of the day, and would burst from grazing too long unless kept away from fodder. The inhabitants are rough and ignorant of virtues to an even greater degree than other tribes, and completely lacking in religious piety.

[Pomponius Mela, *Geography* 3.49–53]

Pomponius Mela came from Tingentera (near Gibraltar) in Baetica, as he proudly declares (2.86). His *de chorographia* was the first work on geography to be written in Latin. The date of his work is shown by his reference to Claudius' forthcoming triumph. Mela's information derives from earlier Greek geographers, now lost, and from accounts of Britain by Caesar, *Gallic Wars* 4.20–38; 5.1–23, Diodorus Siculus 5.21.3–6, and Strabo 4.5.1–4. (e.g. chariots: Caesar 4.33; 5.16; Kent relatively civilised: Caesar 5.14; Irish lack of piety: Strabo 4.5.4; woad: Caesar 5.14). These three authors had all described Britain as triangular in shape (for other comparisons see **R12**. Mela follows Diodorus' comparison with Sicily and more accurate orientation. The unlikely tradition of axle-blades (as on Boudicca's famous statue in London) seems to originate with Mela. Nonetheless, his account gives an excellent idea of what an informed Roman, might have thought of Britain at the time of the Claudian invasion, and may have been written to celebrate the invasion of Britain.

N14 Sketch of the shape and orientation of Britain as given by Pomponius Mela

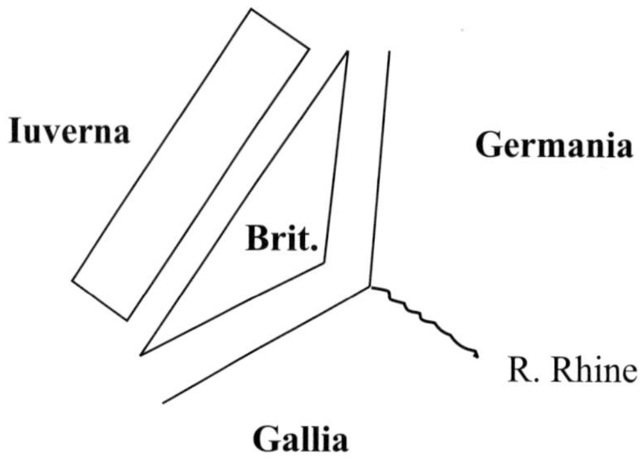

N15 The invasion of Britain

Claudius waged war on Britain, where no Roman had set foot since the days of C. Caesar, and when the country had been vanquished by Cn. Sentius and A. Plautius, distinguished members of noble families, he held a magnificent triumph.

[Eutropius, 7.13.2]

The account in Tacitus' *Annals* is lost, and that in *Agricola* 13 is very brief. Suetonius' accounts (*Claud.* 17.1–2 and *Vesp.* 4.1) concentrate on the deeds of the respective emperors. Dio 60.19–22 provides a narrative. The preparations were meticulous, and in 43, three legions under Aulus Plautius began the conquest, landing either at Richborough in Kent, or possibly near the later palace of Fishbourne in Sussex. When the general claimed to need imperial help, Claudius advanced with elephants towards Camulodunum (Colchester, in Essex), where a council of chieftains ready to swear allegiance was assembled. For a modern account, see Webster, *The Roman Invasion of Britain* (1980).

N16 Verses in praise of Claudius Caesar

A land inviolate before to triumphs of Italia,
Has fallen, great Caesar, to your lightning strike.
And now beyond itself the Ocean sees
Your altars blazing on its further side.
The limit of the world was not the limit of your empire.

Romulus, once the Tiber was your kingdom's boundary.
This too, most Holy Numa, was the limit of your land.

Your power, sanctioned by heaven that is your own,
Stopped, Divine One, only at the Ocean's furthest bounds.
But now Ocean's waters flow between two worlds;
Now of your empire it is part, where once
It was the boundary.

[Bucheler & Riese eds *Anthologia Latina i*^{2} (1894) no 419 and 423]

The author of these undistinguished verses in unknown. Romulus and Numa, Rome's first two kings, could be thought of as representing military might and justice (e.g. Livy 1.19.1). The 'Divine One' (*Divus*) referred to could be either Julius Caesar or Augustus.

N17 Claudius' triumphant return

Claudius Caesar sailed out into the Adriatic in a great palace rather than a mere ship, from this harbour, known as the Harbour of Vatrenus, when celebrating his triumph over Britain.

[Pliny, *Natural History* 3.119]

Claudius presumably took a detour on his journey back from Britain to include areas associated with his father Nero Drusus (Levick, *Claudius* 143).

N18 Claudius' triumph

Claudius, his successor, in the celebration of his triumph over Britain, had placards stating that among the crowns of gold, that sent by Nearer Spain weighed 7,000 pounds, and that from Gallia Comata, 9,000 pounds.

[Pliny, *Natural History* 33.54]

After five or six months away from Rome, and apparently only 16 days in Britain, Claudius returned to Rome to celebrate, in 44, the first triumph since Augustus' triple triumph of 29 BC (Dio 60.23.1 = LACTOR 15.98; Suet. *Claud.* 17.2). Two triumphal arches were erected, one in Gaul, one in Rome (Dio 60.22.1 = LACTOR 15.98; **N25**).

N19 Vows for victory in Britain, AD 45–46, Etruria

Having undertaken a vow for the safety and return and victory in Britain of Tiberius Claudius Caesar Augustus Germanicus, *pontifex maximus*, in his 5th year of tribunician power, hailed victorious commander 10 times, father of his fatherland, *pontifex maximus*, consul designate for the fourth time, Aulus Vicirius Proculus, *flamen Augustalis* and military tribune, has fulfilled his vow for the victory in Britain.

[*Année Epigraphique* (1980) 457 = Sherk 51]

This inscription on a block of white marble was found at Rusellae in Etruria. The same individual also fulfilled a similar vow there on behalf of Claudius' safety (*AE* (1980) 458). The cult of *Victoria Britannica* appears in a number of inscribed dedications made in fulfilment of vows by individuals in many parts of the empire, from Narbonne to Corinth.

N20 Vows for victory in Britain, AD 45–46, Pisidia Antioch

To Tiberius Claudius Caesar Augustus Germanicus, *pontifex maximus*, consul three times, in his 5th year of tribunician power, father of his fatherland, on behalf of his safety and victory in Britain. In accordance with the vow which he had undertaken with his children, Gaius Caristanius Fronto Caisianus Iullus duumvir three times, pontiff, tribune of legion XII Fulminata, prefect of the cohort of the Bosporani, prefect of the engineers six times, gave a statue, games for the youth, sacrifices and a hunt.

[*Année Epigraphique* (2001) 1918]

This dedication from Pisidian Antioch (Galatia) is inscribed upon a tall statue base (over 2.5 m.) honouring Claudius, which, to judge from its dimensions, must have borne an over-lifesized statue of the emperor. It shows how a member of the colony's magisterial élite had made a vow on behalf of Claudius as he embarked upon his conquest of Britain. Subsequently, he fulfilled this vow in celebration of the emperor's victory in Britain by providing games, sacrifices, and a beast hunt, as well as by setting up this statue. It dates from AD 45–46.

CLAUDIUS CONTINUES TO CELEBRATE HIS VICTORY

While campaigning continued in Britain, earning Claudius a series of acclamations as *imperator* (victorious commander), he also found other ways of keeping success in Britain in people's minds. A series of coins was minted between 46 and 50, depicting the triumphal arch actually completed in 51 (**N25**). Plautius returned to receive an ovation in 47 (Suet. *Claud.* 24.3). British gladiators were displayed (Dio 60.30.2–3). Claudius enlarged the *pomerium* in 49 (**N23**, **N24**). King Caratacus was paraded in 50 (Tac. *Ann.* 12.36–38).

N21 Claudius to the athletes, AD 46

Tiberius Claudius Caesar Augustus Germanicus Sarmaticus, *pontifex maximus*, in his 6th year of tribunician power, designated consul for the 4th time, hailed victorious commander 12 times, father of the fatherland, greets the association of touring athletes. I received with pleasure the gold crown which you sent me on account of the victory over the Britons, as a perpetual symbol of your loyalty to me. The delegates were Tiberius Claudius Hermas; Tiberius Claudius Cyrus; Dio, son of Mykkalos, from Antioch.

[Papyrus of London 3.215]

For a second letter of Claudius to the athletes on the same papyrus, and giving Claudius the same erroneous title 'Sarmaticus', see **M49**.

N22 Claudius celebrates his victory: *aureus* of Claudius, AD 46–7

Obv: Laureate head of Claudius, right
TI CLAVD CAESAR AVG P M TR P VI IMP XI (Tiberius Claudius Caesar, Augustus, *pontifex maximus*, in his 6th year of tribunician power, hailed as victorious commander 11 times)

Rev. DE BRITANN (over Britain) on the architrave of a triumphal arch surmounted by an equestrian statue facing left, between two trophies

[*BMC* Claudius 32, *RIC* Claudius 33]

This coin celebrating Claudius' invasion of Britain and his triumph of AD 44 was first struck earlier in AD 46/7 when Claudius was 'imperator' 10 times (*RIC* 29), and was further 'updated' to 'imperator' 16 times (AD 49/50: *RIC* 44). For the actual arch, completed in AD 51–2, see **N26**.

N23 Claudius extends the *pomerium* (city boundary)

[3] The most ancient *pomerium*, which was established by Romulus ended at the foot of the Palatine Hill. But that *pomerium* was extended on several occasions in keeping with expansion of the state and embraces many of the high hills. In addition whoever provided the Roman people with territory captured from the enemy has the right to extend the *pomerium.*

> *(Gellius now mentions extensions of the* pomerium *by King Servius Tullius (reigned c. 578–534* BC*) and Sulla (dictator 82–1* BC*), and suggests why Julius Caesar did not include the Aventine Hill.)*

[7] But regarding the Aventine Hill, I thought I should not omit something I came across recently in the *Commentary* of an early grammarian Elys in which he wrote that the Aventine was previously excluded from the *pomerium*, just as we said, but under Divus Claudius it was included and admitted within the boundaries of the *pomerium.*

[Aulus Gellius, *Nights in Attica,* 13.14.3–7]

Tacitus, *Annals* 12.23–24 (= LACTOR 17 K10) also discusses the *pomerium*, mentioning Claudius' extension as being within the right of someone who had extended the empire, but only exercised by Sulla and Augustus. Tacitus is probably wrong about Augustus whose extension is nowhere else mentioned. The *Law on the power of Vespasian* of AD 69/70 (see LACTOR 17, H52) cites only Claudius as precedent for the emperor extending the *pomerium*. Its new limits were marked out by a series of boundary stones, of which **N24** is one example.

N24 Extension of the *pomerium* at Rome, AD 49

Tiberius Claudius Caisar Augustus Germanicus, son of Drusus, *pontifex maximus*, in his 9th year of tribunician power, hailed victorious commander 16 times, consul four times, censor, father of the fatherland, having expanded the boundaries of the Roman people, has extended and delimited the *pomerium.*

[On the top] *Pomerium*
[On the side] 8

[Smallwood 44 = *ILS* 213]

This *cippus* (boundary stone) was found to the south-east of Monte Testaccio in Rome. It includes archaising spelling (Caisar) and the obsolete digamma typical of Claudius.

N25 Arch of Claudius at Rome celebrating victory in Britain, AD 51–52

To Tiberius Clau[dius Cai]sar Augu[stus Germani]cus, [son of Drusus], *pontifex maximus*, in his 11th year of tribunician power, consul five times, hailed victorious commander [22? times, censor, father] of the fatherland: the senate and people of Rome (set this up) because he received the submission of eleven kings of the Britons, [conquered without] any loss and because he was the first to bring barbarian tribes [beyond Ocean] into the dominion [of the Roman people].

[*ILS* 216 = Smallwood 43b]

This is most probably the dedicatory inscription from the triumphal arch on the Field of Mars on the Via Lata (modern Corso), appropriately for a victorious return from the north. The arch also formed part of the structure of the aqua Virgo. The arch was mirrored by another dedicated at Gesoriacum (modern Boulogne), the point of embarkation to Britain. The arch was also decorated with reliefs of combat between Romans and Celtic barbarians. The Latin includes archaising spelling. The arch displayed statues of members of the imperial family (**N26** below).

N26 Statues from the triumphal arch at Rome, AD 51–52

To Germanicus Caisar, son of Tiberius Augustus, grandson of Divus Augustus, great-grandson of Divus Julius, augur, *flamen Augustalis*, consul twice, hailed victorious commander twice.

To Antonia Augusta, wife of Drusus, priestess of Divus Augustus, mother of Tiberius Claudius Caisar Augustus, father of his country.

To Julia Augusta Agrippina, daughter of Germanicus Caisar, wife of Tiberius Claudius Caisar Augustus, father of his country.

To Nero Claudius Caisar Drusus Germanicus, son of Augustus, pontiff, augur, one of the Board of Fifteen in charge of sacrifices, one of the Board of Seven for the management of feasts, consul designate, leader of the youth.

To Octavia, daughter of Tiberius Claudius Caisar Augustus, father of his country.

[To Tiberius] Claudius C[aisar] [Bri]tannicus, [brother] of Nero [Claudius] Caisar.
[Smallwood 100 = *ILS* 222 + *CIL* VI 922]

These inscriptions include archaising spelling and one of the obsolete letters revived by Claudius, the digamma (**R24**, Tac. *Ann.* 11.13–14). The members of Claudius' family represented include his brother Germanicus (long deceased), his mother (also deceased), his wife Agrippina, his adopted son Nero ('son of Augustus' refers to Claudius as Augustus), son Britannicus (granted an honorific name in honour of his father's victory), and daughter Octavia. It is likely that his father Drusus was also originally part of the group. It is possible that the statues were duplicated on both sides of the arch.

N27 Claudius' victory celebrated at Cyzicus, Asia

To Divus Augustus Caesar; to Tiberius Augustus [son of Divus Augustus]; to Imperator Tiberius Claudius [Caesar Augustus Ger]manicus, son of Drusus, *pontifex maximus*, [in his 11th year of tribunician power, consul five times, hailed victorious commander 22(?) times], father of his country, champion of freedom, conqueror [of eleven kings] of Britain: the Roman citizens who [reside] in Cyzicus and the Cyzicenes [set up] the ar[ch], under the supervision of [---]
[Smallwood 45 = *ILS* 217]

This dedicatory inscription on a triumphal arch set up at Cyzicus is restored on analogy with the arch at Rome. It perhaps dates from AD 51/2. For the city of Cyzicus and its connections to the imperial family see **M44**, **M46**.

N28 Relief at Aphrodisias

Tiberius Claudius Caesar
Britannia

[Greek: *IAph2007* 41]

This inscription accompanies a depiction of a heroic Claudius, nude and with swirling cloak, on the point of delivering a death-blow to a hapless Britannia. For picture, See **L36h**.

N29 Veterans of the conquest: Gavius Silvanus

To Gaius Gavius Silvanus, son of Lucius, of the voting-tribe Stellatina, senior centurion of legion VIII Augusta, tribune of the 2nd cohort of city watchmen, tribune of the 13th urban cohort, tribune of the 12th praetorian cohort, decorated by Divus

Claudius in the British War with collars, armbands, discs, and a golden wreath, patron of the colony, by decree of the town councilors.

[Smallwood 282 = Sherk 49A = *ILS* 2701]

This honorific statue base (set up after Claudius' deification) shows the successful career of a veteran of the campaigns in Britain at Colonia Iulia Augusta Taurinorum (modern Turin). When tribune of the 12th Praetorian cohort, Silvanus was involved in the Pisonian conspiracy against Nero, and ended up committing suicide in AD 65 (Tac. *Ann.* 15.50.3, 15.60.4, 15.61.4, 15.71.2).

N30 Veterans of the conquest: Anicius Maximus

To Publius Anicius Maximus, son of Publius, of the voting-tribe Sergia, prefect of Gnaeus Domitius Ahenobarbus, senior centurion of legion XII Fulminata, prefect of the camp of legion II Augusta in Britain, prefect of the army which is in Egypt, decorated by the emperor with military decorations because of the expedition, honoured with a mural crown and a parade-spear because of the war in Britain. The city of Alexandria which is in Egypt (set this up) to honour him.

[Smallwood 281 = Sherk 49C = *ILS* 2696]

This inscription is from the colony of Pisidian Antioch (Galatia). The first three lines are inscribed in large letters. The post of prefect was a prestigious position within the colony, whereby Maximus acted as the representative of Nero's father Domitius Ahenobarbus, who had been elected as magistrate in the town at some point before his death in AD 40, but who held the position as a token of honour only, with a local deputy then actually doing the work involved in the office.

CONTINUED OPERATIONS IN BRITAIN AD 43–68: N31–32

Accounts of the first few years of conquest are in the lost books of the *Annals*. Tacitus breaks his annalistic principles by putting together accounts of campaigns under Ostorius and Didius (AD 47–54) in one section, *Annals* 12.31–40. Tacitus provides a very detailed account of Boudicca's revolt in *Annals* 14.29–39. His *Agricola* provides briefer accounts. Gnaeus Julius Agricola was Tacitus' father-in-law and had served under Suetonius Paullinus during Boudicca's revolt (see **N37**).

N31 Continued conquest: Tacitus' summary of AD 43–60

Aulus Plautius was the first ex-consul to be placed in charge of Britain, followed by Ostorius Scapula, both of them outstanding in war; the nearest part of Britain was gradually reduced to the form of a province, with a colony of veterans superimposed. In accordance with the long-established tradition of Rome of making even kings the means of imposing slavery, certain communities were given to Togidumnus who remained unswervingly loyal right down to our own times. [2] Soon Didius Gallus maintained what he had received from his predecessors with not more than a handful of fortresses pushed into advanced positions to obtain the reputation of success in his period of office. Veranius took over from Didius and died within a year. [3] Then Suetonius Paulinus had two years of success, subduing tribes and strengthening garrisons; relying on this, he attacked the island of Anglesey which was providing support for the rebels, exposing himself to attack from behind.

[Tacitus, *Agricola* 14.1–3]

N32 The Revolt of Boudicca: Tacitus' summary

Spurred on by the exchange of such comments, they all began a war, under the leadership of Boudicca, a woman of the royal family (for they allow both sexes to command). Soldiers in their scattered fortresses were hunted down; garrisons taken by storm; the colony itself, being seen as the base of their slavery was assaulted, and there was no form of atrocity which these people, by nature barbarous, did not commit in their anger and triumph. [2] Had not Paullinus brought rapid help on hearing of the revolt of the province, Britannia would have been lost. As it was, he restored it to its former submission by winning a single battle. But many still kept their weapons, prompted by guilt at their rebellion and personal fear that the governor, though excellent in other respects, would abuse prisoners, and take measures that were too harsh in punishing, as it were, a personal insult. [3] Therefore Petronius Turpilianus was sent out as someone more conciliatory and sympathetic to claims of repentance, being without personal knowledge of the enemy's crimes. He restored the situation but took no further risks before handing the province over to Trebellius Maximus. Trebellius was rather inactive and without experience of military life, and governed the province with a light administrative touch. The barbarians now also learned to condone tempting immorality, and the intervention of civil war offered a good excuse for inactivity.

[Tacitus, *Agricola* 16.1–3]

GOVERNORS OF ROMAN BRITAIN: N33–N39

For full details of these, see A.R. Birley, *The Government of Roman Britain,* 2005.

N33 Aulus Plautius (cos. 29: governor 43–47)

Plautii had achieved prominence under the Julio-Claudians, as well as a large family mausoleum (see **U3**). Urganalia, the mother of M. Plautius Silvanus, was a very good friend of Livia (Tac. *Ann.* 2.34.2). He gained the consulship with Augustus in 2 BC and his daughter, Urgulanilla, was the young Claudius' first wife. Plautius Silvanus' cousin, the father of the conqueror of Britain, was suffect the following year. The young Aulus Plautius is almost certainly the quaestor of Tiberius who wrote down the text of the decree on Piso (**P3q**) in AD 20, he then progressed to being suffect consul for the second half of 29. He probably became governor of Pannonia in 39 and will have gained Claudius' gratitude by not joining the rebellion of Scribonianus based in the neighbouring province of Dalmatia. Tacitus' presumed account of his governorship of Britain is lost, and nothing further is known about his career after his return to Rome in 47 to celebrate an ovation.

N34 Publius Ostorius Scapula (cos. ? governor 47–52)

Tacitus gives a detailed description of his governorship (Tac. *Ann.* 12.31–40) but very little is known about his previous career: even the date of his consulship is unknown.

N35 Aulus Didius Gallus (cos. 39, governor 52–57)

Tacitus, *Annals* 12.40.1–5 gives a brief account of his governorship, further summarised at 14.29.1 as 'Aulus Didius, as I have mentioned, simply held what had been acquired'. His career, known from a variety of sources, included quaestor in AD 19 (thus born around 7 BC), Aqueducts Commissioner, AD 38–49 (**K32**), a post unusually undertaken before his consulship in 39 (attested by a wax-tablet from Pompeii). He also held a priesthood with special responsibilities for celebrating Centennial Games held by Claudius in AD 47, and was governor of Sicily and Asia (**N35a**). He was known to have canvassed for governorship of a province (Quintilian, 6.3.38 – see **U10**).

N35a Didius Gallus, inscription from Olympia

A. Didius Gallus, legate of Tiberius Claudius Caesar Augustus Germanicus, awarded triumphal decorations, consul, one of the Board of Fifteen in charge of sacrifices, governor of Asia and Sicily, cavalry commander [...]

[*ILS* 970 = Smallwood 226a]

Fragmentary inscription in Latin at Olympia erected by Didius Gallus, perhaps on his way to govern Asia.

N36 Quintus Veranius (cos. 49, governor 57–58)

Veranius' father was companion of Germanicus in the East, appointed governor of newly annexed Cappadocia (Tac. *Ann.* 2.56.4) and helped prosecute Piso (Tac. *Ann.* 2.74.2, 3.10.1, 3.13.2, 3.19.1). His grandfather had been guardian for Drusus, Tiberius' brother (*AE* 1981.824). He had experience of another newly created province – Lycia – see **M32**, **N36b**, **N40–N42**). Tacitus, *Annals* 14.29.1 gives a brief evaluation of the man and his short period in Britain.

N36a Veranius' early career

Quintus Veranius, son of Quintus, member of the board of three in charge of the mint, tribune of legion IV Scythica, quaestor of Tiberius and Gaius, tribune [of the people ...]

[Greek: *IGRRP* 3.703 = Smallwood 231b]

This fragmentary inscription in Greek from Cyanaeae in Lycia (N. Turkey) shows the start of Veranius' career. The particular privilege of being quaestor of the emperor arises from the strong links between Veranius' family and that of the emperor (see above).

N36b Epitaph of Q. Veranius

... he was governor of the province of Lycia with Pamphylia for five years ... he reduced ... to submission to Tiberius Claudius Caesar Augustus Germanicus and stormed and destroyed [the fortress of] Tracheotae; [on the written instructions of the senate and people of Rome and of] Tiberius Claudius Caesar Augustus Germanicus [he completed] the restoration of [the city walls of Cibyra] which had been interrupted and pacified ... Because of these services, on the proposal of Tiberius Claudius Augustus Germanicus, he was appointed consul and in his consulship he was elected augur on the nomination [of the same (emperor)], in place of [...]nus and was raised to the rank of patrician. [On the decision of Tiberius Claudius Caesar Augustus Germ]anicus the equestrian class and the Roman people with the agreement of the senate entrusted to him the [care] of sacred buildings and [public works] and places. He was [put in charge of the Great] Games by the *princeps* Augustus, of whose generosity he was the agent, [though he had not sought this honour?] He was made governor of Britain [under Nero Augustus Germanicus] in which province he died. Verania, daughter of Quintus Veranius, lived six years and ten months.

[Smallwood 231c]

Inscription found 6 miles east of Rome.

N37 Gaius Suetonius Paullinus (cos in unknown year, *c.* 45, governor 58–61)

Tacitus will have had a great deal of knowledge about Paullinus' governorship in Britain, since his father-in-law, Julius Agricola (later governor of Britannia AD 78–84) had served as military tribune in Britain under Paullinus (Tac. *Agr.* 5.1), and so will have witnessed and participated in many of the events described in this section. Tacitus married Agricola's daughter in AD 77. Agricola died in AD 93 and Tacitus published his biography in AD 98. This provides a summary of Paullinus' governorship praising Paullinus for preventing the loss of Britain and for restoring Roman authority in a single battle (Tac. *Agr.* 15.1–16.2). A much longer account, embellished with set-piece speeches is *Annals* 14.29–39.

N38 P. Petronius Turpilianus (cos. ord. 61, governor 61–63)

Petronius was probably the son of P. Petronius, cos. 19 (see **B19**) and an experienced governor (see notes on **D8** and Philo, *Embassy* 243), and nephew of A. Plautius the first governor of Britannia. Both connections may well have been a recommendation and Petronius' governorship was short and uneventful (Tac. *Agr.* 16.3; *Ann.* 14.39.3). He returned to Rome as Aqueducts Commissioner (**K32**). A Nero loyalist in the Pisonian conspiracy (Tac. *Ann.* 15.72.1 and **P11**) he was given charge of an army to put down Vindex's rebellion (Dio 63.27.1a). He was put to death under Galba when an old man (Plut. *Galba* 15.2, 17.3 ; Tac. *Hist.* 1.6.1, 1.37.3).

N39 M. Trebellius Maximus (cos. 55, governor 63–69)

He was legionary legate in Syria in AD 36 (Tac. Ann. 6.41.1). A senator in AD 41 (Jos. *JA* 19.185 = Section **E**), he was suffect consul in AD 55 with Seneca, despite having no known senatorial ancestry and being despised by his two noble colleagues in conducting a census in Gaul in AD 61 (Tac. *Ann.* 14.46). Tacitus condemns his governorship *Agr.* 16.3–4 and *Hist.* 1.60, in particular a mutiny during the civil war which led to Trebellius' fleeing into hiding, and returning as a puppet figure. Nonetheless he had been appointed to the Arval Brotherhood by AD 72.

LYCIA: N40–N43

Claudius annexed Lycia as a province in AD 43, following disturbances and judicial irregularities in the region. This group of monuments gives the official version of the circumstances and rationale for the Roman annexation of Lycia as a province. They complement passages in Suetonius and Cassius Dio, and the epitaph from the tomb of the Veranii outside Rome (**N36b**; Suet. *Claud.* 25.3; Dio Cass. 60.17.3), particularly in their common emphasis upon the fact that Lycia needed Roman intervention to help it to achieve peace and stability against the background of severe internal discord in the region. The local response, while clearly directed by the Roman authorities, may effectively have taken the form of a colossal 'team-building' enterprise by the inhabitants of the new province.

N40 Central milestone of Lycia, Patara, AD 45/46

[Face A] To Tiberius [Cl]audius Caesar Augustus Germanicus, son of Drusus, *pontifex maximus*, in his 5th year of tribunician power, hailed victorious commander 11 times, father of his fatherland, designated as consul for the fourth time, the saviour of their nation: the Lycians, Rome-loving and Caesar-loving, faithful allies, set free from faction, lawlessness and brigandage through his divine foresight, having recovered concord, the fair administration of justice and the ancestral(?) laws, the conduct of affairs having been entrusted to councilors drawn from among the aristocracy by the incompetent majority, [in return for the many benefits they have received from him through Quintus] Veranius, propraetorian legate of Tiberius Claudius Caesar Augustus.

[Face B, opening lines only] Tiberius Claudius Caesar Augustus Germanicus, son of Drusus, Imperator of the world, built roads throughout the whole of Lycia through the agency of Quintus Veranius his own propraetorian legate, of which (roads) the distance is written below.

[Greek: *AE* 2001, 1931–32]

This inscription commemorates the construction of the road-network that was an integral part of Claudius' pacification and reconstruction of the new province. It consists of blocks that originally formed a rectangular pillar that stood approximately 6m. tall, 1.6m. wide, and 2.3m. deep, overlooking the quayside of the ancient harbour. The monument may have supported an equestrian statue of Claudius and bore two texts, inscribed in Greek over three of its sides. Face A presents a dedicatory text (above) by the Lycians in honour of Claudius who has freed them 'from faction, lawlessness and brigandage through his divine foresight' through the agency of his propraetorian legate in Lycia, AD *c*.43–47, Q. Veranius. They also celebrate an anti-democratic reform of the constitution of the Lycian commonwealth. The second text (only the beginning of which is included above) commemorates Claudius' road-building programme. The overwhelming bulk of this second text comprises the listing of the distances between at least fifty places across the entirety of Lycia. This is preceded by an eight-line preface, proclaiming that Claudius, 'emperor of the world', has constructed roads throughout the whole of Lycia, through the agency of his legate Q. Veranius. The last lines of Face C herald a shift in emphasis and geography, and mention roads in Asia too. The monument's similarity to Augustus' *miliarium aureum* (Golden central milestone) at Rome may further illustrate Claudius' emulation of his predecessor.

N41 Altar near Limyra, AD 45

[To Tiberius Claudi]us [Caesar A]ugu[stus G]ermanicus, son of Dr[us]us, [*pontifex maximus*], in his 5th year of tribunician power, hailed victorious commander 11 times, father of the fatherland, consul three times: the Caesar-loving and Rome-loving Lycians (set this up) in thanks for the peace and the building of the roads; under the supervision of Quintus Veranius propraetorian legate of Tiberius Claudius [Ge]rma[nicus Caesar Au]gustus.

[Greek: *AE* (2002) 1472]

This is the dedicatory inscription on a substantial altar found by the roadside in the territory of Limyra in Lycia. It celebrates the same road-building programme as is recorded at Patara (**N40**). The Lycians describe themselves in the same way as at Patara, and give a positive picture of their enthusiasm for their new Roman rulers, and the the road-building programme.

N42 Dedication to Claudius, Gagai (Lycia), AD *c*.43

Tiberius Claudius Caesar Augustus, the most conspicuous saviour god: the ? councillors chosen according to his divine foresight, through(?) his propraetorian legate Quintus Veranius: Harpalos son of Synmachos (…*a list of names follows*…)

[Greek: *SEG* 50 [2000] 1350]

This dedication to Claudius on a round altar of white marble reflects the same enthusiastic response to Roman authority as is found elsewhere in the new province.

N43 Silver *drachma* of Claudius struck in Lycia

Obv: Laureate head of Claudius, right
ΤΙΒΕΡΙΟϹ ΚΛΑΥΔΙΟϹ ΚΑΙϹΑΡ ϹΕΒΑϹΤΟϹ (Tiberius Claudius Caesar Augustus)

Rev: Lyre. ΛΥ (Lycia)
ΓΕΡΜΑΝΙΚΟϹ ΑΥΤΟΚΡΑΤѠΡ (Germanicus, victorious commander)

[BM Collection 1979.0101.1982; *RPC* 3334/1]

The lyre had long been a symbol of the federation of Lycian city-states. It was the symbol of Apollo who was often given the title 'Lycian' Apollo (e.g. Aeschylus, *Agamemnon* 1257), and who was Lycia's patron god (*Homeric Hymn to Apollo,* 179). It is possible that these coins were struck for use in a closed currency in Lycia. It is also possible that they were struck before the annexation of the province in AD 43.

THRACE: N44

Thrace had been a friendly kingdom since the time of Augustus, ruled by Rhoemetalces I, supported by various Roman campaigns (see LACTOR 17, N50–51). After his death in AD 12, internecine strife amongst the royal family resulted in repeated intervention by Roman legions in Moesia (AD 19 – Tac. *Ann.* 2.64–67; AD 21 – Tac. *Ann.* 3.38–39; AD 26 – Tac. *Ann.* 4.46–51). Gaius installed Rhoemetalces II, a member of the ruling family and his own distant cousin, who had been brought up with him (**M39**, **M42**; **M46**, **M47**). He is soon succeeded by his cousin and brother-in-law Rhoemetalces III, but after his murder at the hands of his wife, Claudius annexed the province in AD 46 (**N44**).

N44 Thrace reduced to a Roman province.

[AD 46] Hitherto having been under kings, Thrace is reduced to a Roman province.

[Jerome, *Chronicle,* p.180 H]

ARMENIA: N45–N54

Armenia was a buffer state between the Roman and Parthian empires. The policy of Augustus and Tiberius was to support the rule of client kings who were from dynasties independent of Parthia. For Germanicus' installation of his cousin Zeno see **M43**. Gaius removed Mithridates from the throne (**N8** above) while Claudius sent him home to recover the Armenian throne in 41 (Tac. *Ann.* 11.8–9; Dio 60.8.1). When the king of Parthia installs his brother on the throne of Armenia (Tac. *Ann.* 12.50), a Roman army is eventually sent under Corbulo (*Ann.* 13.6–8) with serious fighting from AD 58 (*Ann.* 13.34). Eventually a diplomatic solution is reached with Tiridates travelling to Rome to allow himself to be crowned as king of Armenia by Nero in AD 66.

Domitius Corbulo in the East: N45–N50

Gnaeus Domitius Corbulo was the most prominent and greatest general of his time. He was extremely well-connected, not least through one of his step-sisters marrying Gaius (see **J15a**). Corbulo first appears in Tacitus' extant narrative as the new governor of Lower Germany in AD 47 (*Annals* 11.18 – but the lack of full name shows he had been mentioned earlier). Tacitus uses Corbulo for great literary and moral ends, with accounts of campaigns in the East perhaps taking up space disproportionate to what was actually achieved: 13.6–9, 34–41; 14.23–26; 15.1–17, 25–32. Corbulo is immediately portrayed as a disciplinarian of the old school at a time when the discipline of the Roman soldier has been corrupted (11.18, 13.56–7). Once trained, his armies are ready for great conquests, comparable to those achieved in the past: but now emperors are jealous of military glory – 'Lucky the generals of the past' he is reported to have said on being ordered to withdraw by Claudius (Tac. *Ann.* 11.20). The culmination of the story is lost in Tacitus. But Nero, on his tour of Greece in 66/7 summoned Corbulo and ordered him to commit suicide which he promptly did (Dio 63.17.5–6). Corbulo had presumably incurred Nero's suspicion, perhaps for alleged involvement in the 'conspiracy' of Annius Vinicius, Corbulo's son-in-law (see **P12**; Griffin, *Nero* 177–9). Corbulo's reputation as a disciplinarian is confirmed by Frontinus who may possibly have served under him (Birley, *Roman Government of Britain* 2005). Corbulo himself wrote memoirs (Pliny *NH* 1 – contents, citing him as a source for books 5 and 6; Tac. *Ann.* 15.16.1; Syme, *Tacitus* 297).

N45 Corbulo's old-fashioned discipline I

By improving discipline, Domitius Corbulo withstood the Parthians with two legions and very few auxiliaries.

[Frontinus, *Strategems* 4.2.3]

Tacitus, *Annals* 13.8 confirms the small forces: the two legions assigned to Corbulo's command were part of the standard garrison of four for the province of Syria. He was also to be helped by auxiliary infantry and cavalry wintering in Cappadocia and by forces of allied kings.

N46 Corbulo's old-fashioned discipline II

Domitius Corbulo in Armenia ordered two squadrons and three cohorts who had retreated from the enemy near the fort of Initia to remain outside the ramparts of the camp until they had made up for their disgrace by hard work and successful raids.

[Frontinus, *Strategems* 4.1.21]

N47 Corbulo's old-fashioned discipline III

In Armenia, Aemilius Rufus, a cavalry prefect had retreated from the enemy and kept his squadron with insufficient weapons. Domitius Corbulo had a lictor tear his clothes and made him stand at the headquarters as he was in his wrecked uniform until he was released.

[Frontinus, *Strategems* 4.1.28]

Tacitus, *Annals* 13.35–36 gives details of the poor discipline Corbulo found and his remedies, including a version of **N46** (Corbulo disciplines squadrons) in which the commander of these units is named as *primipilus* Paccius Orfitus. Tacitus suggests that the punishment of the units was ended by petition of the whole army.

N48 Corbulo records an eclipse in Armenia, AD 59

An eclipse of the sun which happened a few years ago on April 30, in the consulship of Vipstanus and Fonteius (AD 59), was observed in Campania between the seventh and eighth hours of daylight but reported by the general Corbulo in Armenia between the eleventh and twelfth hours of daylight. This is because the roundness of the globe displays and hides different phenomena in different places. If the earth were flat, everything would be visible to everyone at the same time, and nights would not vary in length.

[Pliny, *Natural History* 2.180]

The writings of Corbulo are cited by Pliny at 5.83 (source of Euphrates in Armenia) and 6.23 (recent events and royal family of Armenia), and by Tacitus, *Annals* 15.16.1 for information on his own campaigns.

N49 Corbulo besieging Tigranocerta, AD 60

Domitius Corbulo, when he was besieging Tigranocerta and the Armenians seemed likely to make every effort to withstand the siege, executed Vadandus one of the grandees he had captured and shot his head from a *ballista* into the enemy fortifications. It landed in the middle of a meeting which the barbarians were just holding, and at the sight of it, they hurriedly surrendered as if it had been a sign from heaven.

[Frontinus, *Strategems* 2.9.5]

Tacitus' account of Corbulo's capture of Tigranocerta is 14.24, where surrender of the town quickly follows the discovery of a plot to kill Corbulo and execution of plotters, including an enemy nobleman.

N50 Corbulo's command under Nero, AD 64–65

Nero Claudius Caesar Augustus Germanicus, Imperator, *pontifex maximus*, in his 11th year of tribunician power, consul four times, hailed victorious commander 9 times, father of his country, under the supervision of Gnaeus Domitius Corbulo, imperial propraetorian legate, and Titus Aurelius Fulvus, imperial legate of the legion III Gallica.

[Smallwood 51b = *ILS* 232]

Dating from 64/65, this inscription was found – together with another similar one – at Ziata (modern Harput) in the province of Cappadocia. In 63, Corbulo arranged the agreement to recognise Tiridates as king of Armenia, and appears to have stayed in the region until at least the time of Tiridates' visit to Rome in 66. Titus Aurelius Fulvus was the grandfather of the future emperor Antoninus Pius.

N51 Triumphal arch of Nero, on *sestertius* of *c.* AD 64

Obv: Head of Nero (obese), with laurel wreath, right

NERO CLAVDIVS CAESAR AVG GER P M TR P IMP P P (Nero Claudius Caesar Augustus Germanicus, *pontifex maximus*, with tribunician power, victorious commander, father of the fatherland)

Rev: Ornate triumphal arch, seen from left. Nero in four-horse chariot on top, accompanied by Victory (right) and Peace (left). Figure of Mars in niche on side of arch, holding spear and shield

S C (by decree of the senate)

[*RIC* Nero 147, *BMC* Nero 187]

The arch was erected on the Capitol between AD 58 and 62 for Corbulo's victories over the Parthians (Tac. *Ann.* 13.41 and 15.18).

N52 Gates of Janus on brass *sestertius* of Nero, struck at Rome, *c.* AD 65

Obv: Laureate head of Nero right, wearing *aegis*

NERO CLAVDIVS CAESAR AVG GER P M TR P IMP P P (Nero Claudius Caesar, Augustus, Germanicus, *pontifex maximus*, with tribunician power, victorious commander, father of the fatherland)

Rev: Rectangular building with flat roof, at front, twin closed gates in arch with garland; at side, lattice windows above panels.

PACE P R TERRA MARIQ PARTA IANUM CLUSIT S C (After obtaining peace for the Roman People by land and sea, he closed [the gates of] Janus, by decree of the senate)

[*BMC* Nero 164; *RIC* Nero 270]

Augustus had set great store by closing the gates of Janus to indicate peace throughout the Roman empire (*RG* 13; Livy 1.19; Ovid, *Fasti* 1.277–281 = LACTOR 17, A13, K47, K48). Nero claimed he had done the same after claiming victory in Armenia, with the coronation of Tiridates in Rome. Nero's coins show a small rectangular structure. They have been found in a variety of denominations (*sestertius*, *dupondius*, *as*) in issues from AD 65, 66 and 67 and from the mints at Rome and Lugdunum.

N53 Nero's conquest

Armenia
~~Nero~~ Claudius Drusus Caesar Augustus Germanicus

IAph2007 9.14

This inscribed base from the Sebasteion at Aphrodisias (**L36j**) identifies a scene of Nero's conquest of Armenia that parallels that of Claudius' conquest of Britain (**L36h** and **N28**). It shows that the complex was incomplete on Claudius' death, and that later victories were subsequently incorporated into its design. Nero's personal name was erased following his suicide in 68.

N54 Tiridates as *magus* and Nero

Tiridates the Magus had come to Nero, at heavy expense for the provinces, bringing with him all that would be needed for Nero's Armenian triumph over him. [17] He had refused to travel by sea, as the Magi think it wrong to spit into the sea or to pollute its essence with any other natural bodily function. He had brought Magi with him, and initiated Nero into their banquets. He, however, could not acquire skill in magic from Tiridates, even though Nero was giving him a kingdom.

[Pliny, *Natural History* 30.16–7]

The war in Armenia was to be settled by Tiridates travelling to Rome to be ceremonially given the crown of Armenia by Nero (Tac. *Ann.* 15.29). The ceremony took place in AD 66 (Tac. *Ann.* 16.24.1, though Tacitus' account is lost). Suetonius *Nero* 13 and 30.2 and Dio 63.1–7 stress the splendour and the theatricality of his reception, as does *NH* 33.53 (**Q13**). Herodotus (1.138.2) attributed care not to pollute rivers with spit or urine to all Persians.

SUDAN: N55–N56

The potential expedition is mentioned by Dio (63.8.1 – AD 66/7) and supported by the contemporary evidence of Pliny and Seneca below (but Griffin, *Nero* 229 is sceptical). Any Tacitean narrative is lost, while Suetonius typically underplays military matters (*Nero* 18).

N55 Nero's planned expedition to Sudan

Recently, when the emperor Nero was contemplating, amongst other wars, one against Aethiopia, he certainly sent praetorian troops under a tribune on reconnaissance. They reported only deserts.

[Pliny, *Natural History* 6.181]

Pliny is writing about the geography of Africa and repeats similar information at 12.19 about a lack of any trees except palm trees. Aethiopia is the area we would call (Northern) Sudan, with the new state of Southern Sudan being fertile and modern Ethiopia being further South and East.

N56 Reconnaissance of the Nile

[8.3] Nero is a great enthusiast for all man's finest qualities, but above all he is dedicated to the pursuit of truth. I even heard the report of two centurions, whom he sent to explore the source of the Nile. They said that they had been given assistance by the king of Aethiopia, who had commended them to the neighbouring kings. But they described it as an immensely long journey, during which they had penetrated remote regions.

[Seneca, *Natural Questions* 6.8.3]

Seneca wrote this work between AD 62 and 64.

THE CAUCASUS: N57

Nero planned an expedition to the Caucasus in AD 66/7: Tac. *Hist.* 1.6.2; Suet. *Nero* 19.2; Dio 63.8.1. All these sources describe the objective as the Caspian Gates. Pliny's evidence shows that he was not aiming at the area normally called the Caspian Gates – the narrow stretch of land between the Caucusus mountains and the Caspian Sea in the area of modern Derbent in Russia, just north of Azerbaijan. Instead he aimed at the Duriel pass, right in the middle of the Caucusus, and at taking action against the Rhoxolani, one of the main groups of the Sarmatae tribe. See Griffin, *Nero,* 228-9.

N57 Nero's planned expedition to the Caucasus, AD 66/7

We must here correct a common error, made even by people who recently campaigned with Corbulo in Armenia. They gave the name Caspian Gates to that pass in Iberia which we have said [*NH* 6.30] is called the Caucasus Gates, and plans of the region sent from Armenia are labelled as 'Caspian Gates'. Now the threatened expedition of emperor Nero was said to have been aimed at the Caspian Gates when in fact it was aimed at the passes leading through Iberia to Sarmatia as the mountains between scarcely offer any access to the Caspian sea.

[Pliny, *Natural History* 6.40]

SECTION P
CONSPIRACIES, REVOLTS AND SCANDALS

'An emperor's lot is greatly to be pitied since only when he is killed does anyone believe there really was a conspiracy.' (Domitian)

Whilst there may be some truth in this remark, attributed by Suetonius (*Dom.* 21) to Domitian (assassinated AD 96) it is also the case that emperors were quick to claim as conspiracy anything and anyone which they could conceive as a threat to their own position. It is also probable that all six emperors from Caligula to Vitellius died unnatural deaths arising from revolt or conspiracy. This chapter arranges sources on various conspiracies, scandals, and revolts by their date.

P1 M. Scribonius Libo Drusus, AD 16

For the trial of M. Scribonius Libo Drusus, see Tacitus, *Annals* 2.27–31; Dio 57.15.4f; Vell. 2.129.2; Suet., *Tib* 25.1 and 25.3. This trial is highlighted as the first major case of *maiestas* under Tiberius by Tacitus in his *Annals*. Tacitus sees its importance as signalling the evils of *maiestas* trials. The charges of dabbling in astrology made against Libo Drusus were serious in their political implications. The official line (**P1a**) was a conspiracy (Levick, *Tib.,* 149–52). One of Scribonius' great-grandfathers was Scribonius Libo the father of Scribonia, first wife of Augustus. Scribonius was thus second cousin to Agrippina the Elder. Pompey the Great was another great-grandfather.

P1a Conspiracy's suppression celebrated in the *Fasti Amiterni*, 13 September, AD 16

Holiday in accordance with a decree of the senate, because on this day the wicked plans begun by Marcus Libo concerning the safety of Tiberius Caesar and his children and the other leaders of the state and concerning the republic, were exposed.

[Sherk no.28A = EJ p.52]

P1b Scribonius Libo – suicide after *maiestas* AD 16

Scribonia, a strait-laced lady, was aunt of Libo Drusus, a young man as stupid as he was aristocratic. His ambitions were greater than anyone could entertain in that age; greater indeed than he could have entertained in any age. He had been carried away from the senate, unwell and in a litter, with no great crowd of mourners, since all his close friends had disgracefully deserted him as being dead rather than on trial. He then began to consider whether to commit suicide or await his death. Scribonia asked him, "Why would you wish to do what someone else wants done?" She failed to persuade him; he took his own life. And he was right, for it is the person who lives on when an enemy has decided that he will die in two or three days who 'does what someone else wants done'.

[Seneca, *Epistles* 70.10]

Seneca expounds the Stoic view of suicide, according to which it is acceptable when the decision is made on rational grounds, including, usually, discussion with others. Despite his stupidity, the young aristocrat, in Seneca's view, made the right decision and made it properly. The death is less edifying in Tacitus (*Ann.* 2.31).

P1c Dedication in the Temple of Concord

Quintus Coelius Primus, son of Lucius, plebeian aedile of Ceres, in accordance with a decree of the senate, who as a result of the fulfilment of his vow for the safety of

Tiberius Caesar Augustus, son of Divus Augustus, *pontifex maximus*, gave a gift of his own to Concord, weighing 25 pounds of gold.

[*ILS* 153]

This is one of several inscriptions found in the forum at Rome, among the ruins of the temple of Concord, recording offerings made on behalf of Tiberius' safety. It commemorates the fact that Coelius had made a promise to dedicate something to Concord in return for the emperor's safety, and that, once the conspiracy of Libo Drusus had been suppressed, it was considered the right moment to regard that prayer as having been granted. No trace remains of the golden object originally dedicated with it. Concord is a significant choice of deity: not only was she considered representative of Concord at the level of state affairs, but her temple had recently been rebuilt by Tiberius himself. According to Tacitus, the senate vowed dedications to Jupiter, Mars, and Concord (*Ann.* 2.32.2).

GNAEUS CALPURNIUS PISO, AD 19–20: P2–P3

Cn. Calpurnius Piso seems to have inherited his outspokenness and general severity of character from his father, a die-hard Republican during the civil wars, who only entered public life under the principate when offered the consulship by Augustus (Tac. *Ann.* 2.43.2). The son was consul in 7 BC and went on to at least three provincial governorships, becoming *legatus Augusti pro praetore* of Hispania Tarraconensis (attested by an inscription in AD 9–10) and proconsul of Africa (*CIL* 2703) at an unknown date before his appointment as *legatus Augusti pro praetore* of Syria and *adiutor* (assistant) to Germanicus in AD 17. The incident in Seneca (**P2b**) is probably to be ascribed to his time in Africa, on the assumption that Seneca refers back to Piso at 19.3 when he speaks of an angry proconsul. He was condemned for treason by the senate in AD 20, though the charge for murdering Germanicus failed (Tac. *Ann.* 3.12–15). In his last letter to Tiberius, he described himself as having been a trusted friend of Augustus and then Tiberius for forty-five years (Tac. *Ann.* 3.16.4).

P2a Piso consul with Tiberius, 7 BC

Tiberius Claudius Nero, son of Tiberius, pontiff, consul for the 2nd time, hailed victorious commander twice, celebrated votive games to Jupiter Best and Greatest, in accordance with a decree of the senate, in honour of the return of Imperator Caesar Augustus, son of Divus, *pontifex maximus*, ~~with his colleague in the consulship, Gnaeus Calpurnius Piso~~.

[EJ 39 = *ILS* 95]

This marble base was found in Rome in the Field of Mars. Piso's name has been erased from the inscription. Although his name was not erased consistently from all inscriptions, it was erased from inscriptions connecting him closely with members of the imperial family. Similarly, the *SCPP* prescribes that his name should be erased from the base of a statue of Germanicus (lines 83–84 = **P3f**).

P2b Piso as vengeful commander

[3] I well remember Gnaeus Piso as a man free from many vices but possessing one serious deficiency, in that he could not tell the difference between inflexibility and firmness of purpose. Once he lost his temper and ordered the execution of a soldier who had returned from leave without his comrade, insisting that if he could not produce the man he must have murdered him. When the accused asked for a little time to search for the missing man, he refused. The condemned man was led outside the defences and was already offering his neck to the executioner, when the comrade whom he was supposed to have killed suddenly appeared. [4] So the centurion in charge of the execution immediately ordered the general's assistant to sheathe his sword, and led the condemned man back to Piso, so as to free Piso from blame, just as Chance had now freed the soldier. With their arms around each other's shoulders the two comrades were accompanied by a huge crowd of delighted soldiers from their garrison. But Piso in a blazing temper mounted the tribunal and gave orders for both

of them to be executed, both the soldier who had not murdered his companion and the one who had not been murdered.

[5] Could anything have been more disgraceful? Because one man had proved innocent, two men were condemned to death. But Piso added a third by ordering the centurion, who had brought the condemned man back to him, to be executed as well! So because one man was innocent, three were condemned to die on the same spot. [6] Rage certainly shows a certain genius for contriving excuses for its outrageous conduct. "You there!" it exclaims to the first victim. "I order you to be executed, because you were found guilty. You," to the second, "must die, because you were the cause of your comrade's condemnation. And as for you," to the third; "you must die for failure to obey your general's order for their execution." Thus rage contrived three criminal accusations, because it was unable to justify any.

[Seneca the Younger, *on Anger* 1.18.3–6]

P2c Evidence from the trial of Piso

It is said that in cremating those who have died from heart disease, the heart does not burn, and that the same is true of victims of poisoning. There certainly exists a speech of Vitellius which uses this argument to prove Gnaeus Piso guilty of this crime, openly citing as evidence that Germanicus Caesar's heart could not be cremated because of poison. In reply, Piso's defence was based on the nature of Germanicus' illness.

[Pliny, *Natural History* 11.187]

Pliny is discussing the heart. The idea that the heart does not burn is repeated by Suetonius, *Caligula* 1. Publius Vitellius, uncle of the future emperor, was a close friend of Germanicus, prominent in prosecuting Piso (Tac. Ann. 2.74.2, 3.10.1, 3.13.2, 3.19.1).

P3 The senatorial decree concerning Cn. Calpurnius Piso, AD 20

This decree, usually abbreviated to *SCPP* (*senatus consultum de Pisone patre* = senatorial decree concerning Piso senior) was found by metal detectorists in different places in Spain (Roman province of Baetica), in the form of two main copies inscribed upon bronze and a handful of fragments from other copies. The extant fragments must have originated from at least six places in Baetica. This translation is a composite version of the different inscriptions. The account of Piso's trial and punishment in Tacitus is quite different in its emphasis and aims, focusing upon the charge of poisoning Germanicus (Tacitus, *Annals* 3.10–18, also 2.43, 53–84; 3.1–9). In the light of the senate's vitriolic attack on Piso here, Tacitus emerges as comparatively objective.

P3a Heading of SCPP

DECREE OF THE SENATE CONCERNING GNAEUS PISO SENIOR, PUBLISHED IN THE PROCONSULSHIP OF NUMERIUS VIBIUS SERENUS.

This heading (on Copy A only) draws attention in large letters to the person of N. Vibius Serenus, governor of Baetica, who is otherwise unmentioned in the inscription. Far more copies of the inscription have been discovered in Baetica than the single copy required by the senate to be set up in each province's capital (compare lines 170–71). The heading raises the possibility that the provincial governor may himself have had a hand in publishing the decree rather over-enthusiastically. Vibius Serenus had prosecuted Libo Drusus in AD 16 (Tac., *Ann.* 2.30.1), and had subsequently complained that he had been insufficiently rewarded by Tiberius for so doing (Tac., *Ann.* 4.29.3). His over-zealous promotion of this loyal document may perhaps represent his attempt to maintain imperial favour. If so, he failed, since he was exiled in AD 23 for abusive behaviour (*vis publica*) towards Roman citizens whilst governor in Baetica (Tac., *Ann.* 4.13.2).

P3b Preamble

[1] On 10 December on the Palatine in the portico which is by the temple of Apollo. There were present at the drafting of the decree Marcus Valerius Messallinus, son of Marcus, of the voting-tribe Lemonia; Gaius Ateius Capito, son of Lucius, of the voting-tribe Aniensis; Sextus Pompeius, son of Sextus, of the voting-tribe Arnensis; Marcus Pompeius Priscus, son of Marcus, of the voting-tribe Teretina; Gaius Arrenus Gallus, son of Gaius, of the voting-tribe Galeria; Lucius Nonius Asprenas, son of Lucius, of the voting-tribe Pomptina, quaestor; Marcus Vinucius, son of Publius, of the voting-tribe Poblilia, quaestor.

[*SCPP* lines 1–4]

The dating of this decree to 10 December has raised questions about the structure and chronology of Tacitus' account of the same events. Tacitus (*Ann.* 3.19.3), by contrast, implies that the trial was concluded before Drusus' triumphal entry into Rome, which is independently dated by the *fasti Ostienses* to 28 May (**J10c**). Tacitus perhaps changes the order of events within the year AD 20; possibly the trial itself did not actually take place until November, after Piso had travelled back to Rome. Alternatively, this decree was issued several months after the conclusion of the trial, in response to continuing unease at Rome and in the provinces. In support of this view is the fact that this decree is not a record of the trial itself, but a summary of the senate's view of Piso following his suicide.

The choice of meeting-place is significant, given the proximity of the temple of Apollo to the House of Augustus. The senate had also earlier met in the same location when debating honours for the deceased Germanicus (**J8j**). The document inscribed here does not consist simply of minutes of the meeting, but a report on proceedings compiled by the individuals named. These include three men of consular rank, two probably of praetorian rank, and two quaestors. Sex Pompeius was one of those who had refused to undertake Piso's defence (Tac., *Ann.* 3.11.2).

P3c Four items for discussion in the senate, introduced by Tiberius

Whereas Tiberius Caesar Augustus, son of Divus Augustus, [5] *pontifex maximus*, in his 22nd year of tribunician power, consul 3 times, designated for the fourth time, referred to the senate for decision:

how the case of Gnaeus Piso Senior was regarded and whether in their view he took his own life deservedly;

and how the case of Marcus Piso was regarded, to which item he added that this House should be mindful of his pleas on behalf of the young man;

<and> how the case of Plancina was regarded for whom he had presented earlier his pleas and the reasons for them

[10] and what the senate's judgment was concerning Visellius Karus and Sempronius Bassus, members of the staff of Gnaeus Piso Senior.

Concerning these matters the senate decreed as follows:

[*SCPP* lines 4–11]

This makes clear that it was Tiberius himself who introduced the matter before the senate, in a process known technically as the *relatio*. This decree does not concern the original trial, but comes as a response to Piso's suicide. Four cases are raised separately here: of Piso himself; of his younger son Marcus; of his wife Plancina; and of his two associates Visellius Karus and Sempronius Bassus. Domitius Celer, named by Tacitus as on Piso's staff and as having encouraged Piso's seditious activities in the East, is not mentioned in the decree: possibly he had already committed suicide by this point (*Ann.* 2.77.1). No mention is made here of Piso's elder son, Gnaeus, who appears not to have been implicated in his fathers' actions: he probably did not accompany him to Syria, but was serving at the time as Tiberius' quaestor at Rome (line 94 = **P3g**). It also reveals that Tiberius himself had intervened personally for Plancina (see below for the involvement of Julia Augusta).

P3d Thanks to the gods for thwarting Piso, and to Tiberius for facilitating his trial

That the senate and the Roman people give thanks above all to the immortal gods because they did not allow the wicked plans of Gnaeus Piso Senior to disturb the present tranquil condition of the commonwealth, than which no better could be desired and which the beneficence of our *princeps* has made it possible to enjoy; [15] then to Tiberius Caesar Augustus their *princeps* for making available to the senate everything necessary to determining the truth – the senate admires his fairness and patience on this count too, that, although the crimes of Gnaeus Piso Senior could not be more apparent and he had inflicted the death penalty on himself, nonetheless he (Tiberius) wanted a formal enquiry into his (Piso's) case to be held [20] and summoning his sons, urged them to defend their father's case, to the extent that he wished even the son who was not yet a member of the senate to be brought into the senate for that purpose and that he gave them both the opportunity to speak for their father, for their mother, and for Marcus Piso.

[*SCPP* lines 12–22]

P3e The circumstances that led to Piso's prosecution: his behaviour in Syria

That accordingly, inasmuch as the case has been pleaded over a number of days by the prosecutors of Gnaeus Piso Senior and by Gnaeus Piso Senior himself, letters have been read out as well as copies of the memoranda which [25] Germanicus Caesar had written to Gnaeus Piso Senior, witnesses of every order have been brought before the court, <the senate> is convinced that the exceptional restraint and patience of Germanicus Caesar was exhausted by the brutish behaviour of Gnaeus Piso Senior and that for this reason, when dying, Germanicus Caesar, who himself bore witness that Gnaeus Piso was the cause of his death, renounced his friendship with the man, not without good cause: this man (Piso), although he should have kept in mind that he was assigned [30] as an assistant to Germanicus Caesar, who had been dispatched by our *princeps* with the authority of this House to put overseas affairs in order, affairs which called for the presence either of Tiberius Caesar Augustus himself or of one of his two sons, without regard even for the majesty of the house of Augustus, without regard even for public law in that he, when he had been attached to a proconsul, and indeed to a proconsul for whom a law had actually been passed by the people to the effect that in whatever province he entered he would have greater *imperium* [35] than the person who was governing that province as proconsul, with the proviso that in every respect Tiberius Caesar Augustus was to have greater *imperium* than Germanicus Caesar, conducted himself while he was in the province of Syria as if everything ought to be a matter for his decision and authority; (this man) stirred up war with Armenia and Parthia, as far as lay within his power, in that he was unwilling, despite the instructions of our *princeps* and the many letters which Germanicus Caesar wrote when he was away, for Vonones, who was an object of [40] suspicion to the Parthian king, to be moved farther away so that he might be unable to escape from custody (which he did), and in that he allowed some evil and reckless persons in the ranks of the Armenians to converse with Vonones to the end that disorder might be provoked in Armenia and that once the king of Armenia, whom Germanicus Caesar had assigned as king to that people in accordance with the wishes of his father and of the senate, had been killed or expelled, [45] Vonones might take his place and these things he did, corrupted by large bribes from Vonones. He also tried to foment civil war, when all the evils of civil war had long since been buried through the divine power of Divus Augustus and the virtues of Tiberius Caesar Augustus, by trying to regain, after the death of Germanicus, the province of Syria which he had abandoned while Germanicus was still alive – a deed wicked both in its intent and in the example it provided, and on that account Roman soldiers were forced into conflict with each other, when he had also [50] manifested his unparalleled cruelty by inflicting the death penalty on many without hearing their cases, without consulting his council, and by crucifying not only foreigners but also a centurion, a Roman citizen; he had destroyed the military discipline established by Divus Augustus and maintained by Tiberius Caesar Augustus, not only by allowing soldiers not to obey in the traditional manner those in command of them, but also by giving donatives [55] in his own name from the treasury of our *princeps*, a deed which, he was pleased to see, led to some soldiers being called 'Pisonians', others 'Caesarians', and by going on to confer distinctions on those who, after usurping such a name, had shown him obedience; he dared, after the death of Germanicus Caesar, whose loss not only the Roman people but foreign nations as well mourned, to send to his most excellent and forbearing parent, a document accusing him (Germanicus), forgetting not [60] only the respect and affection due to a son of the *princeps*, but even common humanity which does not permit feuds to be carried on after death; that he rejoiced in his death was obvious to the senate from the following evidence: that wicked sacrifices were offered by him, that the ships in which he sailed were decorated, that he reopened the temples of the immortal gods which the unwavering devotion of the whole Roman [65] empire had closed; evidence of the same attitude was to be found in the fact that he had given a present of money to the man who informed him of the death of Germanicus Caesar; and it was also proven that on several occasions he had held banquets during those very days in which he had been informed of the death of Germanicus Caesar; it was also the opinion of the senate that the divine spirit of Divus Augustus was violated by him in that he removed every sign of honour that had been accorded to his memory or to those portraits [70] which were [dedicated] to him before he was included in the number of the gods.

[*SCPP* lines 23–70]

The senate constantly contrasts the dignified behaviour of Germanicus with the cruel and inhuman actions of Piso. By describing Piso's cruelty as unique and unparalleled, the senate is perhaps trying to give the impression that Piso was unrepresentative of any wider opposition to Germanicus. Consequently, once Piso himself is removed, the harmony and concord of the rest of Roman society, at Rome and abroad, in honouring the imperial family is restored. The only mention of the murder charge, which is so prominent in Tacitus' account, is here represented as reflecting the suspicions of the dying Germanicus himself. Renouncing friendship was a formal act.

The decree offers us the official wording used to describe both Germanicus' mission,'to put overseas affairs in order' (compare **J7e** and **J8b**) and Piso's subordinate position to him. In describing Germanicus' powers in the provinces as being greater than those of other Roman officials but inferior to Tiberius', it is clear that so-called *maius imperium* was not a fixed set of powers, but expressed the hierarchical relationship of different holders of official power (*imperium*). The point of this, however, seems to be to make clear that Piso was not equal to Germanicus in authority.

Armenia and Parthia had long been a bone of contention – Augustus had tried to impose a solution, with only patchy success. Vonones, son of the Parthian king Phraates IV, had spent many years in Rome as a hostage, and had been educated according to a Roman lifestyle. He was nominated by Augustus at the Parthians' request as their king, but was then deposed because of his Roman outlook, becoming instead king of Greater Armenia in AD *c*.12 (Tac., *Ann.* 2.1–4). By AD *c*.15, however, he fled to Syria, where he was imprisoned by the Roman governor, whilst Germanicus handed over the kingdom to Artaxias III (**M43**; Tac. *Ann.* 2.56; *RIC Gaius* 59 = *BMC Gaius* 104). Piso' s alleged collusion with Vonones is downplayed by Tacitus (Tac., *Ann.* 2.58.2).

Piso is accused of fomenting civil war by returning to Syria with his army after Germanicus' death. In referring to Tiberius' suppression of civil war, the senate is probably alluding to the mutinies that broke out in AD 14 on the Rhine and in the Balkans. It seems likely that the real reason for Piso's downfall was his meddling in the army, something which Tiberius would not tolerate, and the details of which recorded here are pretty damning. Augustus had taken pains to establish a personal loyalty towards himself on the part of the army, and this was not something that Tiberius would wish to see undermined. The senate, however, has to tread carefully so as not to imply that the army had been disloyal to Tiberius, and does so by loading Piso with sole responsibility.

Piso is accused here of a curious combination of real crimes (such as crucifying a citizen) with other 'crimes' that are presented as indicative of his bad character, but which in themselves are not actually offences in law (such as giving a tip to the messenger bringing news of Germanicus' death). For mourning at Germanicus' death, see **J8f**. The final statement here seems to be an attempt by the senate to implicate Piso in a charge of *maiestas*.

P3f Verdict of the senate: postumous punishments for Piso

That for these reasons the senate believes that he did not undergo the punishment he deserved but saved himself from the harsher one which he inferred from the devotion to duty and the strictness of the judges was threatening him; therefore it adds to the punishments which he inflicted on himself: that no mourning for his death be undertaken by the women by whom he should have been mourned, in accordance with ancestral custom, had this decree of the senate [75] not been passed; and that the statues and portraits of Gnaeus Piso Senior, wherever they may have been placed, be removed; that whoever shall at any time belong to the Calpurnian family or be connected to the family by blood or marriage will have acted rightly and properly if they take care, when anyone who belongs to that *gens* or who is one of those who is connected by blood or marriage to the Calpurnian family has died and is [80] to be mourned, that the portrait of Gnaeus Piso Senior shall not be brought out with the rest of the portraits <with which> they customarily solemnise the processions at their funerals nor placed among the portraits of the Calpurnian family; and that the name of Gnaeus Piso Senior be removed from the inscription on the statue of Germanicus Caesar which the *sodales Augustales* had erected to him in the Field of Mars next to the Altar of Providence; and that the property of Gnaeus Piso Senior be declared public property [85] with the exception of the woodland which is in Illyricum. This woodland, it has been decided, should be returned to Tiberius Caesar Augustus our *princeps*, by whose father Divus Augustus it was given to Gnaeus Piso Senior, since he (Tiberius) had expressed the wish that it be given to him because <the communities> whose territory borders that of the woodland have often complained of injuries from Gnaeus Piso Senior, his freedmen and slaves, and for this reason he thinks care should be taken that [90] the allies of the Roman people should no longer be able to complain with just cause.

[*SCPP* lines 71–90]

This section of the decree prescribes additional punishments for Piso after he had committed suicide. The senate's aim is to remove any memory of him within his family: his wax mask is not to be paraded at family funerals nor displayed in family homes. Furthermore, his name is to be erased from a specific inscription, on the base of a statue of Germanicus. Although not mentioned here, Piso's name is also erased from another inscription associating him with the imperial family, a base which he had dedicated jointly with Tiberius in 7 BC (**P2a**). This is not a blanket punishment affecting all inscriptions, and is a relatively early example in the evolution of the practice of erasure, but is designed to remove Piso from the proximity of members of the imperial family. In short, what we see here is an attack upon traditional forms of honour among the Roman aristocracy. It reveals incidentally that Piso was a member of the priestly college of the *sodales Augustales*, the priesthood established in AD 14 to honour Augustus (**L24**). This is another sign of imperial favour towards him and his high social status (Tac., *Ann.* 1.54.1). The Altar of Providence was a dynastic monument on the Field of Mars, possibly dedicated in AD 4 in connection with the adoption of Tiberius by Augustus and of Germanicus by Tiberius on 26 May, thus securing the dynastic succession (or so it seemed). The confiscation of woodland in Illyricum which had been given to Piso by Augustus is another reflection of the close relationship between the two men.

P3g Verdict of the senate: modifications to the punishments; pardon for M. Piso

Likewise the senate, mindful of its clemency, justice and generosity of spirit, virtues which it has inherited from its ancestors and also learned in particular from Divus Augustus and Tiberius Caesar Augustus, its *principes*, deems it fair and humane that from the confiscated goods of Gnaeus Piso Senior half of the property be given, in the name of the *princeps* and the senate, to his elder son Piso, about whom nothing had been said (sc. during the hearing), who had served as quaestor of our *princeps*, whom Germanicus also had honoured with his liberality, and who had given many indications of his restraint which made it possible to hope that he would turn out very different from his father; and that he, under the obligation of so great a favour, would be behaving rightly and appropriately if he changed his first name, that of his father; and that to Marcus Piso, to whom the senate, in agreement with the humanity and restraint of its *princeps*, thought impunity should be given, so that the favour of the senate might more easily accrue to him unspoiled, the other half of his father's property should be given, and in such a way that from the whole of the estate which had been declared public property by senatorial decree and conceded to them, one million sesterces be given to Calpurnia, the daughter of Gnaeus Piso, as dowry and likewise four million sesterces as her *peculium*. Likewise the senate has decided that the officials responsible for jurisdiction over public places should see to it that the structure which Gnaeus Piso Senior built above the Fontinal Gate to connect private residences be removed and destroyed.

[*SCPP* lines 90–109]

Piso's elder son, Gnaeus, had perhaps served as military tribune during Germanicus' campaigns on the Rhine, and during the critical period of his father's rebellion had been serving as quaestor to the emperor at Rome. Despite being completely exonerated of involvement in his father's misdeeds, he was advised to change his praenomen. Accordingly, he abandoned his name of Gnaeus in favour of Lucius. This followed the precedent of the praenomen Marcus being banned from the family of Marcus Antonius. His political career did not suffer because of his father's disgrace, however, and he went on to become consul shortly afterwards, in AD 27. Marcus Piso had been with his father in Syria, but is pardoned for any part in his insurrection. Piso's daughter, Calpurnia, receives a substantial sum as dowry and *peculium*, a personal fund: 5 million sesterces is a significant sum. Piso's house at the Fontinal Gate appears to have spanned the *clivus Argentarius* on the east side of Capitol. This must have been a conspicuous structure, partly explaining why it was considered right to demolish it, but it may also be the case that Piso had transgressed more fundamentally by even having a house on the Capitol, an area from which patricians were banned.

P3h Verdict of the senate: pardon for Piso's wife, Plancina

That as regards the case of Plancina, against whom many extremely serious charges had been brought, since she was now admitting that she placed all her hope in the mercy of our *princeps* and the senate, and our *princeps* has often and pressingly requested from this House that the senate be satisfied with the punishment of Gnaeus Piso Senior and spare his wife as it spared his son Marcus, and pleaded himself for

Plancina at the request of his mother and had very just reasons presented to him by her for wanting to secure her [115] request, the senate believes that to Julia Augusta, who had served the commonwealth superlatively not only in giving birth to our *princeps* but also through her many great favours towards men of every rank, and who rightly and deservedly could have supreme influence in what she asked from the senate, but who used that influence sparingly, and to the supreme piety of our *princeps* towards his mother, support and indulgence should be accorded and has decided [120] that the punishment of Plancina should be waived.

[*SCPP* lines 109–120]

Piso's wife Plancina was, like her husband, of aristocratic lineage, as the granddaughter of L. Munatius Plancus (consul in 42 BC). This is probably the most extraordinary part of this startling document, since there is no attempt to claim that Plancina is innocent: her pardon is simply secured in response to a plea on her behalf by her friend Julia Augusta, via Tiberius. It is unexpected to find the senate publicising the fact of Julia Augusta's intervention and indeed even praising her restraint in intervening infrequently in public affairs. Plancina eventually committed suicide when the case against her was resumed in 33, after her protetctor Julia Augusta had died (Tac., *Ann.* 6.26.3).

P3i Verdict of the senate: penalties for members of Piso's staff

On Visellius Karus and Sempronius Bassus, members of the staff of Gnaeus Piso Senior and his associates and allies in all his misdeeds, the senate has decided that the penalty of interdiction from water and fire should be imposed by the praetor who presides over cases under the law of *maiestas,* and that their goods should be sold and the profits consigned to the public treasury by the praetors in charge of the public treasury.

[*SCPP* lines 120–123]

Piso's associates here suffer the standard penalties for *maiestas*, namely exile (*interdictio aquae et ignis*) and property confiscation. This indicates that the death penalty was not the standard penalty at this date.

P3j Praise for members of the imperial family

Likewise, since it is the view of the senate that Tiberius Caesar Augustus our *princeps* has surpassed all parties in his [125] devotion to duty, after witnessing so often <the signs> of his grief, so great and so enduring, by which the senate also been deeply moved, it makes a strong plea and request that he devote all the care that he previously divided between his two sons to the one whom he still has, and the senate hopes that the immortal gods will devote all the more care to the one who remains, the more they realise that all hope for the post which his father holds, to [130] the benefit of the commonwealth, rests for the future on one person alone; for which reason he (Tiberius) should end his grief and regain for his country, not only the frame of mind, but even the appearance appropriate to public rejoicing; likewise the senate offers abundant praise of the restraint of Julia Augusta and Drusus Caesar who, in imitation of the justice of our *princeps*, as this House recognises, equalled their devotion to the memory of [135] Germanicus with their fairness in reserving their own judgement until the case of Gnaeus Piso Senior was tried; likewise of the others related by kinship to Germanicus Caesar, the senate expresses its great admiration: of Agrippina, commended to the senate by the memory of Divus Augustus, who greatly esteemed her; and by the memory of her husband Germanicus, with whom she lived in unique harmony; and by the many children born of their most fortunate union and who survive; [140] and further the senate expresses its great admiration of Antonia the mother of Germanicus Caesar, whose only marriage was to Drusus the father of Germanicus, and who, through the excellence of her moral character, proved herself to Divus Augustus worthy of so close a relationship; and of Livia the sister of Germanicus Caesar whom her grandmother and her father-in-law, who is also her uncle, our *princeps*, hold in the highest esteem, whose esteem, even if she did not belong to their family, she could deservedly vaunt and can do so [145] all the more as she is a lady attached by such family ties: the senate greatly admires these ladies in equal measure for their most loyal grief and their moderation in that grief. Likewise the fact that the child's grief felt by the sons of Germanicus at the loss of such a father and especially the grief which is, in the case of Nero Caesar, already that of a young man, and similarly the grief of his brother Tiberius Germanicus Caesar has not exceeded the proper limits, the senate attributes primarily to the training of [150] their grandfather and uncle and of Julia Augusta, but nonetheless accords them praise in their own right.

[*SCPP* lines 123–150]

We find here an explicit statement of the senate's expectation of dynastic succession, with Drusus now in line to succeed his father. The order in which the senate praises different members of the Augustan family indicates the pecking-order, namely Tiberius, followed by his mother and son, followed by Germanicus' wife, mother, sister, children, and brother. The way in which the future emperor Claudius is tacked on at the end following Germanicus' infant children clearly shows his marginalisation in the imperial family at this time (compare *Ann.* 3.18.3). The prominence of imperial women in this list is striking, and reflects their new importance in creating the dynastic chain.

P3k Praise for the equestrian order

Likewise the senate particularly commends the conscientious efforts of the equestrian order in that it has loyally understood how important a matter and how relevant to the safety and devotion of all was at stake, and because it declared with repeated acclamations its sentiments and its grief for the wrongs of our *princeps* and of his son and did this to the advantage of the commonwealth.

[*SCPP* lines 151–154]

Under Augustus, the equestrian order had taken on a new importance, playing a prominent part in public life and developing a corporate identity. In particular, it was associated with Augustus' heirs, Gaius and Lucius, hailing them as *principes iuventutis* and presenting them with silver shields and spears (*Res Gestae* 14.2). This association was continued under Tiberius (see **J8p** for the specific role played by the equestrian order in honouring Germanicus after his death).

P3m Praise for the plebs of Rome

[155] That the senate praises the *plebs* as well because it joined with the equestrian order in demonstrating its devotion towards our *princeps* and the memory of his son and, although with its unrestrained enthusiasm it roused itself to the point of itself carrying out the punishment of Gnaeus Piso Senior, it allowed itself to follow the example of the equestrian order and be governed by our *princeps*.

[*SCPP* lines 155–158]

This hints at the rioting that broke at in Rome at the time of Piso's trial, as the plebs dragged statues of Piso off their pedestals and into the Tiber. This was a demonstration of the popular support for Agrippina (compare *Ann.* 3.4.2).

P3n Praise for the army

That likewise the senate commends the loyalty of those [160] soldiers whose hearts were tempted in vain by the criminal activity of Gnaeus Piso Senior and hopes that all who were soldiers in the service of our *princeps* will continue to manifest the same loyalty and devotion to the Imperial House, since they know that the safety of our empire depends on the protection of that House. The senate believes that it belongs to their concern and duty that, among those who command them at any time, the greatest authority with them should belong to those who have with the most devoted loyalty [165] honoured the name of the Caesars, which gives protection to this city and to the empire of the Roman people.

[*SCPP* lines 159–165]

This section of praise for the legions again reflects the importance of army loyalty to Tiberius, and the threat posed to this by Piso.

P3o Instructions for publication of the decree

And in order that the course of the proceedings as a whole may be more easily transmitted to the memory of future generations and that they may know what the senate's judgment was concerning the exceptional restraint of Germanicus Caesar and the crimes of Gnaeus Piso Senior, the senate has decided that the speech which our *princeps* delivered and also these decrees of the senate, inscribed on bronze, should be set up in whatever place seems best to Tiberius [170] Caesar Augustus and that likewise this decree of the senate, inscribed on bronze, should be set up in the most frequented city of each province and in the most frequented place in that city, and that likewise this decree of the senate should be set up in the winter quarters of each legion where the standards are kept.

[*SCPP* lines 165–173]

Having issued instructions roughly a year earlier for the senatorial decrees concerning honours for the dead Germanicus to be published, the senate follows these up with similar instructions for publication of this decree too. The fact that the two main copies found in Baetica were found in relatively minor places indicates that publication in Baetica exceeded the senate's requirements. The phrasing referring to 'these decrees of the senate' is either a mistake, or reveals that the current document is in fact a composite document consisting of several decrees. It is worth noting the significant addition that the decree concerning Piso is to be set up at army headquarters. This is once again indicative of concerns to cement army loyalty following Piso's insurrection.

P3p Senatorial procedure

Decree passed. They passed the decree. There were 301 present in the senate. This senatorial decree was passed by proposal only.

[*SCPP* lines 173–174]

301 senators represent about half the total senate of the time. By alluding to the fact that the decree was 'passed by proposal only', it emphasises the senate's unanimity: no amendments had to be made.

P3q Addendum by Tiberius

Tiberius Caesar Augustus, in my 22nd year of tribunician power, wrote this with my own hand: it is my wish that this senatorial decree, which was [175] passed on 10 December in the year when Cotta and Messalla were consuls on the basis of my proposal and was copied by the hand of my quaestor Aulus on 14 tablets, should be placed in the public archives.

[*SCPP* lines 174–176]

Tiberius alludes only to his tribunician power, suggesting that it was in virtue of that power that he had brought the matter before the senate. Note that Tiberius here uses the *cognomen* Augustus of himself: this contrasts with Suetonius' claim that Tiberius used it only in letters to kings and dynasts (*Tib.* 26.2). His reference to 'my quaestor Aulus' is strikingly casual in tone, in using only the praenomen for identification; it is thought that the man in question is A. Plautius (**N33**).

P4 LUCIUS AELIUS SEIANUS

Sejanus was appointed joint praetorian prefect with his father on Tiberius' accession (Tac. *Ann.* 1.24.2) and then sole command after his father was made prefect of Egypt (**P4a**). He achieved a power base by establishing the praetorian camp within the city (Tac. *Ann.* 4.2.2) and his prime influence after the death of Drusus, later alleged as murder (Tac. *Ann.* 4.10), is consolidated by prosecution of supporters of Agrippina (**P4c**, Tac. *Ann.* 4.18–21) and by Tiberius' withdrawal to Capri in AD 26 (Tac. *Ann.* 4.67). By AD 30 and the elaborate praise offered by Velleius (**C4**), he had eliminated Agrippina and her two sons, Nero and Drusus (**C7**), and was, quite irregularly, elected as consul for AD 31 (B31, P4d). He may have hoped to receive tribunician power, but instead was denounced in the senate by a letter from Tiberius and executed (Dio 58.8–12, **P4f, j–k**). He was vilified (**R5, P4i, P4m**) and suffered official *damnatio memoriae*.

Most of Tacitus, *Annals* 4–6 is devoted to the rise of Sejanus, but with the loss of crucial parts of books 5 and 6 (some narrative supplied by Dio 58.2–12 = LACTOR 15, A1–7), some problems remain unsolved, especially about his ultimate goals (despite Tac. *Ann.* 4.1.2 – 'to seize absolute power (*dominatio*)) and his 'conspiracy' – see e.g. Syme, *Tacitus,* appendix 65. The case of Sejanus perfectly illustrates the twin dangers of historiography: gross sycophancy while he was in power; vitriolic attack after his fall (compare **C4** and **R3–R5**).

P4a Sejanus' family background

[Lucius Seius Strabo,] prefect of Egypt, and Terentia, his mother, daughter of Aulus, and Cosconia Galitta, his wife, daughter of Lentulus Maluginensis, having bought the buildings and razed them to the ground, gave the baths with all their [adornment] to the people of [Volsinii] for public use.

[EJ 220 = *ILS* 8996]

This marble tablet was found in Volsinii (modern Bolsena). Tacitus (*Ann.* 4.1.3) records that Sejanus was born at Volsinii to a Roman equestrian. His father, Seius Strabo, was preeminent among the equestrian order. He had married into the noble family of the Cornelii Lentuli his wife's father was consul in AD 10. His son Sejanus was perhaps adopted by Aelius Gallus, his mother's first husband, hence his full name Lucius Aelius Seianus. Strabo was sole praetorian prefect by 14, and was among the first to swear loyalty to Tiberius (Tac., *Ann.* 1.7.2). Later that year he was joined by his son Sejanus (Tac. *Ann.* 1.24.2) before being made prefect of Egypt in 17.

P4b Tiberius and Seius, prefect of Egypt

Tiberius Caesar returned an obsidian statue of Menelaus to be used in the religious rites at Heliopolis which had been found in the legacy of that Seius who was prefect of Egypt.

[Pliny the Elder, *Natural History* 36.197]

Obsidian is a dark, glassy volcanic stone. Heliopolis, modern Baalbek in Eastern Lebanon. Though the name Seius has been garbled in the manuscripts, this is likely to refer to the father of Sejanus.

P4c Cremutius Cordus pays the price for mocking Sejanus (AD 25)

[4] Think back to what for you were the most bitter of times, when Sejanus handed over your father like a politician's bribe to his client, Satrius Secundus. He was angry with him for one or two outspokenly critical comments. Your father had felt unable to endure the fact that someone like Sejanus was not merely being set like a yoke upon our necks, but actually climbing up there of his own accord.

A motion was being debated, which proposed that a statue of Sejanus should be set up in Pompey's Theatre, which Tiberius Caesar was in process of restoring after it was damaged by fire. Cordus had exclaimed that such a decision really would be tantamount to the theatre's total destruction. What else could he say? [5] Should he not have exploded with fury to think of the statue of Sejanus being erected upon the ashes of Gnaeus Pompey, a treacherous soldier being honoured with a place within the monument to Rome's greatest general? But Sejanus' signature was holy writ. So his attack dogs, those fearsome beasts whom he kept savage towards all others on a diet of human blood but tame towards himself alone, they all began to bay around the noble Cordus, who was by now well and truly trapped. [6] What could he do? If he wanted to live, he had to plead with Sejanus; if to die, he had to plead with his daughter. Both were adamant in their refusal.

So he decided to deceive his daughter. He took a bath and then to weaken himself further he retired to his bedroom as if intending to take his meal there. He dismissed his slaves and then threw some of the food out of the window, so as to give the appearance of having eaten it. He then failed to appear for dinner, thus giving the impression that he had dined adequately in his bedroom. On the second and third days he did the same, but on the fourth day the manifest weakness of his condition revealed what was really happening. At this point he embraced you, Marcia, and said, "My darling daughter, in all my life this is the only secret I have ever kept from you. But I am now on my way to death and am almost half way there. You cannot and should not call me back." He then ordered all light to be excluded from the room and consigned himself to darkness.

[7] Once his intentions became known, there was general delight that their quarry had escaped from the jaws of those ravening wolves, the informers. Instigated by Sejanus, accusers appeared before the consuls' tribunal to complain that Cordus was dying, and to urge them to prevent the very action that they had themselves compelled him to take. Clearly they felt strongly that Cordus was slipping through their clutches. The crux of the matter was the issue of whether a defendant had forfeited his right to die. While the debate still raged and the accusers were making a second appeal to the consuls, Cordus had already gained his freedom. Can you see, Marcia, what great and unexpected changes of fortune can overtake us in evil days like those? Are you shedding tears because one of your loved ones felt compelled to die? He was very nearly denied that privilege!

[Seneca, *On Consolation, to Marcia,* 22.4–7]

Cremutius Cordus committed suicide by voluntary starvation in 25, anticipating his condemnation by the senate. Though the formal charges concerned his history (Tac. *Ann.* 4.34–35; Dio 57.24.3), Seneca explains the real reason for the prosecution in terms of Sejanus' resentment of Cremutius' hostile remarks about him. Tacitus names his accusers as Satrius Secundus and Pinarius Natta, the second being unmentioned by Seneca, perhaps because he knew him (*Ep.* 122.11). Seneca's expression of extreme hostility here to Sejanus, the favourable remarks about Tiberius (3.2; 15.3), and the lack of any reference to Gaius may point to the work being written during Gaius' reign after 39 when Gaius decided that Sejanus (and the senate), not Tiberius, bore responsibility for the deaths of his mother and brothers and other innocent people (Dio 59.16.4; Suet. *Cal.* 30.2).

P4d Sejanus' election as consul

[...] now(?) since [...] of sixty years, of wicked Sejanus [...] and improper assembly, which took place on the Aventine hill, when Sejanus was made consul, and I – weak, useless, a walking stick's companion – that I might become a suppliant now I earnestly(?) ask you, fellow-tribesmen, if I have always appeared to you a good and useful fellow-tribesman, if I have never been unmindful of my duty nor [...]

[EJ 53 = *ILS* 6044 = Sherk no.40A]

This fragmentary text was found at Rome elegantly inscribed upon a large marble slab with a cornice, broken on all sides except the right. Its exact genre and context is unclear, but it clearly refers to Sejanus' election as consul together with Tiberius for AD 31, 'a startling and flagrant anomaly' (Syme, *AA,* 311) since he was only an equestrian. Another extraordinary feature seems to have been that Sejanus was elected on the Aventine Hill, rather than, as normal, the Field of Mars. The Aventine was traditionally the centre of plebeian support (it was where the *plebs* withdrew in Roman history as a protest against oppression by the upper classes). It makes sense if Sejanus was hoping to enlist popular support (perhaps especially as against the traditional senatorial aristocracy who will have been especially opposed to Sejanus' consulship). Although it has been suggested that the speaker here is Tiberius himself (Levick, *Tiberius* 119–120), the text is too fragmentary to exclude other possibilities.

P4e Antonia exposes Sejanus

[181] Antonia had discreetly done Tiberius a very great favour. There had been a major conspiracy against him, instigated by his friend Sejanus, at that time the most powerful man in Rome, because he held the post of Prefect of the Praetorian Guard. A majority of the senators and the freedmen had joined the conspiracy, the military were corrupted by bribery, and the plot was developing very successfully. Indeed, Sejanus would have succeeded in his plan, had not Antonia displayed a combination of courage and cunning, which proved more than a match for his wickedness. [182] When she learned of the plot against him, she wrote a long and detailed account of the matter in a letter to Tiberius, which she gave to Pallas, her most trusted slave, and sent it to him on Capri. On the basis of her information, Tiberius put Sejanus and the other conspirators to death. He had always had a high regard for Antonia, but he now admired her more than ever and had complete faith in her.

[Josephus, *Jewish Antiquities* 18.181–2]

Sejanus' coup ended in October AD 31 when he was summoned to a meeting of the senate by a letter of Tiberius and subsequently arrested and executed. Tacitus' account of this is not extant, so Josephus' account complements that of Suetonius and Dio (Suet. *Tib.* 65; Dio 58.10.1–8). Antonia was a niece of Augustus, a daughter of Mark Antony and his sister Octavia. She had been married to Tiberius brother, Drusus, which led to the high regard which Tiberius felt for her.

P4f Sejanus' family wiped out: *Fasti* from Ostia, AD 31:

18 October:	Sejanus s[trangled]
24 October:	Strabo, son of [Seianus] strangled
26 October:	[Apicata,] wife of Sejanus killed herself [...] Decimus Capito Aelia[nus and] Iunilla, daughter of Sejanus, lay [on the Gemonian Steps]

[EJ, p.42 = *Fasti* at Ostia, fragment Cb right, 23–29]

P4g Coin of Sejanus from Bilbilis in Spain, AD 31

Obv: Head of Tiberius with laurel wreath, right

TI CAESAR DIVI AVGVSTI F AVGVSTVS (Tiberius Claudius Augustus, son of Divus Augustus)

Rev: Laurel wreath, surrounding large CoS (consul(s))

MVN AVGVSTA BILBILIS TI CAESARE V L AELIO SEIANO (The Augustan *municipium* of Bilbilis, when Tiberius Caesar for the 5th time, and Lucius Aelius Sejanus were consuls

[BM 1951, 1006.20; *RPC* 398/8]

This copper-alloy coin (29mm) celebrating the consulship of Tiberius and Sejanus, was struck at Bilbilis (E. Tarraconensis, Spain) in AD 31. The copy above, in the British Museum, shows his name, but on other copies (*e.g. RPC* 399/5; Naples Museum 131) his name has deliberately been removed either by filing or stamping. The exact links between the town and Sejanus are not clear, but it appears that it took pains to prevent association of its name with that of Sejanus.

Sejanus suffered *damnatio memoriae* – the pulling down of his statues, removal of his name from public records (e.g. the consular fasti (see **B31**)). Where he is mentioned, it is by allusion – 'most dangerous enemy of the Roman people' (**P4h**) or 'whose vicious savagery exceeds that of uncivilised barbarians' **(R5).** More informally anyone who had been punished by Sejanus would be guaranteed public sympathy (**P4m**).

P4h Inscription from Interamna Nahars (Umbria) celebrating Sejanus' fall, AD 32

To the everlasting Augustan safety and to the public freedom of the Roman people. To the divine spirit of the town in the 704th year after the foundation of Interamna down to the consulship of Cn. Domitius Ahenobarbus and ~~L. Arruntius Camillus Scribonianus~~. To the foresight of Tiberius Caesar Augustus, born for the eternity of the Roman name, on the occasion of the removal of the most dangerous enemy of the Roman people. Faustus Titius Liberalis, *sevir Augustalis* for the second time, saw to the setting up (of this) at his own expense.

[EJ 51 = *ILS* 157 = Sherk 40C]

This dedication, inscribed in three parts upon a substantial marble plaque in large lettering, was set up in AD 32 at Interamna Nahars (modern Terni, Umbria) to celebrate the downfall of Sejanus. The dedicator of the inscription identifies himself as a *sevir Augustalis*, in virtue of which he may have regarded himself as particularly well qualified to celebrate the emperor's successful suppression of Sejanus, who is carefully not named in the inscription. Ironically, the name of the consul Scribonianus was erased at a later date, after he led an unsuccessful revolt against Claudius in AD 42 (**P7**; Dio Cass. 60.15, Suet., *Claud.* 13.2).

P4i Governor of Crete celebrating Sejanus' fall

To the divine spirit and providence [of Tiberius Ca]esar Augustus and of the senate, [in memory] of the day of 18 October. [Publius] Viriasius Naso, in his third year as proconsul, dedicated this at his own expense.

[EJ 52 = *ILS* 158 = Sherk 40B]

This dedication was found at Gortyn in Crete, where the governor of the island was based. According to Tacitus (*Ann.* 6.25.3) 18 October was the date of Sejanus' death (and also that of Agrippina the Elder two years later). Gifts to Jupiter were to be dedicated each year.

P4j "The Vanity of Human Wishes": Juvenal on Sejanus

For some, it's their power, source of unlimited envy,
Which topples them, that and their list, long and glorious,
Of honours that sinks them, lost without trace. Dragged down by the heave
Of the rope come their statues; broken up by the axe-blows,
Off come the wheels of their triumphal chariots; and shattered
Now are the legs of their innocent horses. Listen! The fires are roaring.
Now furnace and bellows combine to consume that same head
That once was the toast of all Rome; he's toasting all right. Sejanus,
The Great, goes snap-crackle-pop in the flames. And out of his face,
That was formerly second only to one in the whole wide world,
They are fashioning toby-jugs, frying-pans, basins, and piss-pots.
Deck your doorposts with laurel; lead an ox to the Capitol's altar,
White with chalk and enormous. But see! It's Sejanus they're leading,
Dragged off on the end of a hook, such a sight for sore eyes; and the crowd
Are all cheering with joy. "Just look at those lips! What an ugly mug!
Believe me, I hated his guts." "But what was he charged with?
What did for him? Who was it grassed on him? What
Was the evidence? Who were the witnesses?" "Oh! It was nothing like that.
Just a long rigmarole of a letter that came from Capri." "OK. No more questions."
But what about Remus' rabble? As always, they wait for the roll of the dice
And then bet on the winners. For them losers are damned – and they hate them.
If Tuscany's Lady of Luck had but smiled on Sejanus,
If the emperor's careless old age had been taken off guard and suppressed,
That very same mob at this same very hour would be hailing Sejanus
"Augustus." Long ago, when we all stopped selling our votes,
They ditched any duty to Rome. There once was a time when the people
Made generals and consuls, raised legions, you name it – they did it.
But now aspiration is dead; only two anxious thoughts can compel
Their earnest attention: Bread and Circuses.

"I hear there's a danger that massive reprisals are coming."
"It's an absolute certainty. There's room in the emperor's oven for hundreds."
"That explains it. Bruttidius, my friend, was white as a sheet
When I met him just now, at the altar of Mars in the City.
I am rather afraid that our emperor, like Ajax defeated, is out for revenge
On those who so failed to defend him. Quick, let's make a dash for it.
While the corpse is still lying exposed down there by the river,
We'll put the boot hard into Caesar's opponent. But always make sure

That we're seen by the slaves, in case one should deny that we did it,
And drag his poor master in terror off to the law courts
With a rope round his neck."

So much for the talk of Sejanus – the so secret whispers of popular comment.
Do you really want to greeted by clients each morning, as he was?
Do you want wealth to match his? The power to award high office to one,
And Army commands to another? Do you want to be called
The Emperor's Guardian, as perched on Capri's narrow precipice
He communes with his Chaldaean counsellors? Of course you would
Like to have javelins and cohorts, young equestrians, specially chosen,
A personal bodyguard camped on your doorstep? And why should you not?
Even those with no longing to kill would still like the capacity.
But tell me, what fame and success is so precious that you would equate
Its worth with the price of disaster? Would you rather assume
The purple-edged robe of Sejanus, even now being dragged on a hook,
Or be Lord of some village, Fidenae or Gabii perhaps,
Giving judgement on trivial issues, such as measures and weights,
Or as down-at-heels *aedile* of tiny Ulubrae, condemn for destruction
Some sub-standard pots, whose measures were false?

So then, you admit it? Sejanus was simply a fool; he had no idea
Of what was a worthwhile ambition. There he was, seeking endless
High honours, and asking for more and more wealth. But all he was doing
Was building yet more and more storeys to add to his pinnacled tower.
And so its last downfall was greater; its headlong destruction extreme.

[Juvenal, *Satires* 10.56–108]

58–64: equestrian statues of Sejanus pulled down, as a spontaneous gesture (compare **H13**) or as part of *damnatio memoriae* (see **P4g**). Bronze statues were more expensive and therefore prestigious, but could also be melted down.

65: *lead an ox*: for celebrations of Sejanus' fall, see **P4h**, **P4i**; for public holidays and sacrifices following the removal of opponents of the emperor, see **P1a**, **P3d**, **P5a**, **P11e**, **P12a**.

67: *end of a hook*: this was how dead gladiators or condemned criminals were dragged out of the arena.

72–81: *Remus' rabble*: the *plebs.* Remus and Romulus were joint founders of Rome. Under the republic, consuls were elected annually (though actually in a form of voting heavily weighted against the lower classes). Juvenal has it both ways, complaining about the loss of democracy and the loss of electoral corruption (bribery of voters was almost universal).

81: *Bread and Circuses*: for exactly the same sentiment from a serious scholar, see **Q17**.

83: *Bruttidius*: Bruttidius Niger prosecuted C. Silanus in AD 22 (Tac. *Ann.* 3.66.1) in a case designed to curry favour with Tiberius. He can be assumed to have been one of Sejanus' 'attack dogs' (**P4c**) prosecuting Sejanus' opponents. Juvenal also mentions him to get a joke out of his *cognomen* being Niger (Latin for 'black') but the man being white with fear.

84: Ajax was a hero of the Trojan war, and subject of a play by Sophocles, who tried to kill the Greek commanders when they awarded Achilles' armour to Odysseus rather than to him.

93: *Chaldaean counsellors*: Chaldaea in Assyria became a byword for astologers, and Tiberius was a devotee (Suet. *Tib.* 69).

100–2: Juvenal names three small towns in Latium. Democracy might have died at Rome, but local elections were fierce at Pompeii, where visitors can still see the official measuring table erected by two local officials (Cooley, *Pompeii,* H64a, H64b). Aediles at Herculaneum had also standardised weights there (*CIL* X 8067.1–2).

P4k Ancient scholar explains who Sejanus was

Sejanus was such a close friend of Tiberius that nothing he asked for from Tiberius was refused. Yet he was so ungrateful as even to contemplate his murder and put in place accomplices of his plot so that he could reign once Tiberius was killed. When Tiberius discovered this he sent a letter to the senate about Sejanus' title, and he was thus condemned by the consuls together with all his children, with the senate even ordering that his young daughter should be raped by the executioner and then killed so that the killing might seem legal.

[*Scholia on Juvenal, Satires* 10.63]

P4m Phaedrus, writer of fables prosecuted by Sejanus

To start with, let me briefly help you see
How Fables as a genre came to be.
The hapless breed of slaves was once the source;
Their fear of punishment the likely cause.
About their real feelings to complain
They never dared; in fables hid their pain,
And so, the charge of malice to evade,
Fictitious jokes of it they often made.
In Aesop's footsteps now a path I tread,
Inventing fables, more than can be read
In all that Master's works which now remain.
And some have brought me no reward but pain.

Yet if complaints against me should be laid
By any but Sejanus, if arrayed
As witness and as judge were any but he,
Then surely at my trial, believe you me,
I would admit how gravely I transgress,
And so, deserving punishment, confess:
Not seek like this to make my blame the less.

But if, in error, some become suspicious
And think my moral lessons are malicious,
Then such suspicious souls have only sealed
Their own conviction, for they have revealed
Stark naked to the world, the guilt that lies
Within their consciences, before our eyes.
But though they're fools, I'll ask them, all the same,
For their forgiveness, since my only aim
Is not to pillory the folk I know;
Rather men's lives and morals here to show.

[Phaedrus 3. Prologue 33–50]

Gaius Julius Phaedrus (*c.* 15 BC – AD 50) was a freedman of Augustus. He composed five books of verse fables in Latin, modelled on the collection of Aesop. The extract below is from the prologue to the third book. From it, Phaedrus would seem to have offended Sejanus through suspected allusions in his earlier fables and to have suffered some sort of punishment.

P5 Conspiracy against Gaius, AD 40

A conspiracy is merely mentioned by Dio 59.22.5, and Suetonius, *Claudius* 9.1. Both these sources mention Gaetulicus and Marcus Lepidus as the main leaders (or victims) of the conspiracy. Gaetulicus (Cn. Cornelius Lentulus Gaetulicus, see **B26**) had commanded the four legions of the army in Upper Germany since AD 29, and presumably had the personal loyalty of his men. Marcus Aemilius Lepidus was Gaius' brother-in-law and apparent successor (**J20**). Josephus suggests Lepidus' death was a motive for Gaius' assassination (**E2**). For a modern interpretation of the conspiracy, see Barrett, *Caligula* 101–113.

P5a The official version

27 October. On account of the uncovering of wicked plots against Gaius Germanicus by Cn. Lentulus Gaetulicus … L. Salvius Otho, priest and vice-president on behalf of the [college of] Arval Brothers sacrificed …

[*AFA* AD 39 = A39e]

P5b Sextus Papinius, AD 40

[3] Gaius Caesar recently flogged and tortured Sextus Papinius, whose father had been a consul, and Betilienus Bassus, his quaestor and the son of his own procurator, together with other Roman senators and equestrians, all in a single day, simply for fun, and with no desire to extract information from them. [4] And then, because he was incapable of deferring any pleasure, especially one so great as this which demanded immediate gratification, while enjoying an evening stroll by lamplight with some senior Roman ladies and senators, he chopped off their heads right there on the walkway in his mother's gardens, which runs between the portico and the river Tiber. Why the hurry? What possible danger, public or private, was increased by a single night's delay? It would have been such a trivial matter to wait until dawn, so as to avoid executing Roman senators and ruining his best sandals.

[Seneca, *On Anger* 3.18.3–4]

Sextus Papinius was the son of Sextus Papinius Allenius, consul under Tiberius in AD 36 and the stepson of Anicius Cerialis (cos. suff. 65). His mother was accused before the senate in 37 of driving her elder son to suicide by her persistent sexual advances and was denied access to the city for ten years in order to protect Sextus, her younger son (Tac. *Ann.* 6.49). According to Dio 59.25.5b Sextus Papinius, Cerialis and Bassus were accused of conspiring against Gaius in 40, and Papinius gave information about others in the plot when promised pardon; but Gaius killed him and those he named. Tacitus, in describing his death in AD 66, mentions Cerialis having given away a plot against Gaius (*Ann.* 16.17 end). Betilienus Bassus was the son of Gaius' procurator Betilienus Capito and in 40 one of the two *quaestores Caesaris* who read out the Emperor's speeches and otherwise served him, a notable honour for a man of non-senatorial origin. His father was summoned to his execution for conspiracy and, when he asked if he could shut his eyes, was put to death too (Dio 59.25.6, compare Suet. *Cal.* 27.4). Seneca portrays the killing as an example of wanton cruelty on the part of Gaius.

P6 The assassination of Gaius, AD 41

For a very full account of Gaius' assassination, quite possibly based on an eye-witness account, see Josephus, Section **E**.

P6a A portent of Gaius' assassination

We can remember a fish holding back the ship of the *princeps* Gaius who was sailing back from Astura to Antium. As events proved, the fish was an omen since very soon after that return to Rome the emperor was stabbed by his own men.

[Pliny, *Natural History,* 32.4–5]

P6b Even an Emperor must pay for his excesses in the end

[3] By contrast the military tribune, Chaerea had a limp manner of speech, which belied his outstanding military record; his voice was quiet and, if you did not know his record, you might have had your doubts about him. When on duty he had to ask Gaius for the password, to which Gaius (himself dressed in see-through dress, sandals, and gold accessories) would give him "Venus" or "Priapus", as if seeking to suggest in one way or another that this military hero was a lecherous effeminate. Rather than having to go on asking for the password in this way, Chaerea was driven by him to employ cold steel. He was the first of the conspirators to strike, with one blow cutting off the emperor's head. After that, from every side sword thrusts rained in upon him from men seeking vengeance for past insults, public and private. But the first to strike had been the man who seemed least likely of all to do it.

[Seneca, *On Firmness of Purpose* 18.3]

Cassius Chaerea was a tribune of the praetorian guard, having previously served as a centurion in the army of Lower Germany (Tac. *Ann.* 1.32.2). Gaius' insults drove him to lead the conspiracy against him (Jos. *JA* 19.28ff = **E7–E31**; Suet. *Cal.* 56.2; 58.2; Dio 59.29). He was put to death by Claudius (Suet. *Claud.* 11.1; Dio 60.3), whose elevation he had opposed (**E28**). Seneca draws the conclusion that the arrogant will be punished for their insults.

P7 Scribonianus revolt, AD 42

L. Arruntius Camillus Scribonianus, governor of Dalmatia, led a revolt against Claudius in AD 42. Tacitus gives the briefest summaries (the full account is lost) at *Annals* 12.52; *Histories* 1.89; 2.75 (assassinated by Volaginius, a member of his own army). Suetonius, *Claudius* 13.2 and 35.2 provides some further details. Dio provides the clearest account (60.15–16 = LACTOR 15 C8) of the revolt. It apparently aimed to put on the throne L. Annius Vinicianus, part of the successful plot against Gaius (**E2**) but failed for lack of support even among the two legions which Scribonianus commanded, and which were given the honorific titles *Claudia pia fidelis* 'Claudius' own, loyal and faithful'. Scribonianus suffers *damnatio memoriae* (see **P4h**), but his son was spared (Tac. *Ann.* 12.52.1). Calpurnius Siculus 1.49–53 (**T15b**) may refer exaggeratedly to this revolt in praising Nero for banishing civil wars. For discussion, see Levick, *Claudius* 59–60.

P7a 'Stoic opposition': Caecina Paetus, Arria, and the Scribonianus revolt

[6] Arria's actions when her husband was condemned to death were indeed remarkable. She drew a dagger, plunged it into her breast, pulled it out and handed it to her husband with the immortal, almost inspired words, "Paetus, it does not hurt." But on that occasion, even as she did the deed and spoke those words, she had before her eyes the prospect of glory for ever after. But wasn't her previous action even more remarkable? On that occasion [*just described by Pliny: her husband and son were both ill; and then her son died*] there was no hope of the reward of glorious immortality to spur her on, but she masked her tears and hid her grief, and carried on playing out a mother's role, even though her son was already dead.

[7] Scribonianus had been the leader of a revolt against Claudius in Illyricum. Paetus had supported him and when Scribonianus was killed, Paetus was dragged back to Rome as a prisoner. [8] Just as he was about to embark, Arria begged his escort to allow her to sail with him. "Surely," she said, "you are going to allow a man of consular rank a few slaves to feed him, dress him, and put on his shoes? I can do all those jobs on my own. [9] When her request was refused, she hired a small fishing boat and followed that enormous ship in her own tiny vessel.

At the trial before the emperor Claudius himself, Scribonianus' widow was offering to give evidence for the prosecution. Arria said to her, "Am I going to have to listen to you, when you still cling to life after your husband Scribonianus died in your arms?" This makes it quite clear that her plan to die a glorious death was no spur of the moment decision. [10] Further proof of this lies in the fact that, when her son-in-law, Thrasea Paetus, was trying to persuade her not to go through with her plan to commit suicide, he asked her (among other things) whether she would wish her own daughter to die with him, if he himself faced a similar death. "If," she replied, "she lives as long and harmoniously with you as I have done with Paetus, my answer is 'Yes!'" [11] Her reply greatly increased her family's anxiety for her and they kept an increasingly careful eye on her. She became aware of this and told them that they were simply wasting their time. "You may be able to force me to die shamefully," she said. "But you can't stop me dying." [12] With these words she leapt out of her chair and struck her head against the wall in front of her with such violence that she collapsed. Once she had been revived she said to them, "I told you that I would find a thoroughly unpleasant way to die, if you denied me an easy way out."

[13] Don't you think that these words were even more remarkable than her more famous saying, "It doesn't hurt, Paetus," which marked the end of her story? Yet this remark is known all over the world, while no-one has even heard of the earlier ones. This simply illustrates the point I made at the start of my letter that fame and greatness are not necessarily identical.

[Pliny the Younger, *Letters* 3.16.6–13]

Arria was somehow connected to the satirist Persius who wrote her biography (Probus, *Life of Persius*). Her name becomes proverbial. Almost all that is known about her husband, Caecina Paetus (suffect consul in AD 37) is contained in this letter. His son-in-law, P. Clodius Thrasea Paetus was a Stoic, famous for his belief in senatorial freedom (see Tacitus, *Annals* 13.49, 14.12.1, 14.48.3, 15.20.2–4, 15.23.4, 16.21–22; but Tacitus' description of his death is lost.)

P7b Claudius' own, loyal and faithful legion

Publius Palpellius Clodius Quirinalis, son of Publius, of the Maecian voting-tribe, *primipilus* of legion XX, military tribune of legion VII, *Claudia Pia Fidelis*, procurator of the emperor, prefect of the fleet, gave [this].

[*ILS* 2702 = Smallwood 291]

This inscription is from from Tergeste (modern Trieste, NE Italy). Quirinalis is mentioned by Tacitus (*Ann.* 13.30) as committing suicide in AD 56. The title of the legion granted after the revolt (Dio 60.15.4) is regularly abbreviated to C.p.f as here, but sometimes given in full (*ILS* 2655 (centurion of Antoninus Pius) or, for legion XI, *ILS* 2339). The title means 'legion of Claudius, loyal and faithful'.

P7c Claudius pardons the wife of a rebel

Other events can also be referred to, which is what Domitius Afer did when he was defending Cloatilla. She had been charged with having buried her husband, who had taken part in a rebellion, but Claudius had pardoned her. At the end of his speech, Afer said to her sons, 'But you boys will have to bury your mother!'

[Quintilian, *The Orator's Education* 8.5.16]

Afer's defence speech, for Cloatilla against her own sons on an unknown charge, was clearly famous – Quintilian gives 3 other quotations from it. The historical point is that *maiestas* (treason) was not defined: burying someone guilty of rebellion *could* have led to charge or conviction. Claudius exercised common sense and mercy, and this is the literary point: Cloatilla had previously behaved honourably and bravely to the boys' father and been pardoned by the emperor, but was then facing prosecution by her sons.

P8 MESSALINA AND GAIUS SILIUS, AD 48

Tacitus admits that his account of Messalina's marriage to Gaius Silius (AD 48, *Annals* 11.26–38) will appear fictional (*fabulosum* – 11.27.1) but insists that he is following earlier sources. Other accounts include Suetonius, *Claudius* 26.2, 29.3, 36 (all with different emphases) and Dio 61.31. The *Octavia* 257–269 = **H5** attributes Messalina's behaviour to the power of Venus. All our (male) sources agree in blaming Messalina for outrageous sexual license (see also **R41**). It remains unclear whether the episode was really a plot against Claudius (for discussion, see Levick, *Claudius* 64–7).

P8a Messalina's 'world-record' for sex

Pliny is discussing mating habits in the natural world

All other animals have fixed mating seasons in the year. Mankind, as has been said, mates at every hour of day and night. Other animals have enough of intercourse, mankind is almost insatiable. Messalina, the wife of Claudius Caesar, thinking this would be a crowning victory, selected as an opponent in this contest the highest ranking slave-girl of the prostitutes who provide their services for a fee. Messalina beat her in a twenty-four hour contest, having sexual intercourse twenty-five times.

[Pliny, *Natural History* 10.171–2]

Similar attacks on Valeria Messalina are found in Juvenal 6.115–35; 10.329–42 (below). The literary record, rightly or wrongly, consistently blames Claudius' wives and freedmen for failings in his reign.

P8b Messalina marries Silius

A woman shamed is deadliest of her kind. What advice would you give
To young Silius, Messalina's own target of choice for the "marriage" she planned,
Messalina, the emperor's wife? This admirable youth, this handsome patrician,
Poor lad, he is raped and seduced by an empress' eyes, and doomed to destruction.
There she sits, has been sitting for ages, bridal veil at the ready, marriage bed
Decked in purple and openly made up, right there in her gardens to gawp at.
There's a dowry as well, worth a million, as old custom decrees; with a priest
In attendance, an augur, of course, with witnesses ready and waiting –
Well surely you didn't expect something secret, confined to a few?
It's got to be legally done – or else she won't do it. So how do you want it?
Refuse her demands and you're bound to be dead before nightfall.
Accept, and the crime you commit will allow you the briefest delay,
Till the "secret" now shared by the city and people of Rome comes at last
To the emperor's ears, the last one to hear of his household's disgrace.
So decide; accept her demands, if you crave just a few final days for your life.
Whichever you think is the quickest and easiest, choose it. Whatever,
That pretty white neck must be bared to the sword of the state's executioner.

[Juvenal, *Satires* 10.328–345]

Juvenal's main target in *Satire* 10 is ambition for unworthwhile objects: wealth, power, eloquence, military glory, long life, and finally (here) good looks. Juvenal gives various examples from Roman and Greek mythology, before ending with that of Silius. (Samuel Johnson's famous *Vanity of Human Wishes* (1749) took this satire as its model, ending this theme 'Now Beauty falls betrayed, despised, distressed, / And hissing Infamy proclaims the rest.' (lines 341–2)).

P8c Narcissus tells Claudius to order Messalina's execution

If you ask how much wealth is enough, I'll give you my answer:
Enough to keep hunger and thirst at bay, and to ward off the cold....

...But if that's not enough to pour into your lap, if you're looking for more,
Then for your appetite, nothing will do: not the wealth of a Croesus,
Not the kingdoms of Persia, not even the wealth of Narcissus, the freedman.
The emperor Claudius granted him anything that he requested;
Followed whatever Narcissus demanded: so killed his own wife.

[Juvenal, *Satires* 14.327–332]

These lines form the 'bitterly despondent climax' (Ferguson) to *Satire* 14, in which Juvenal is attacking a greed so institutional within Roman society that parents teach it to their children. For Narcissus and other freedmen of Claudius, see **S23–S30**. Tacitus describes Narcissus as ordering Messalina's execution (*Annals* 11.37).

P9 Death of Claudius, AD 54

Claudius' death on 13 October AD 54 is widely attributed in our sources to poisoning at the instigation of Agrippina. In the absence of a modern *post mortem* examination, or indeed modern standards of food hygiene, we cannot rule out disease or accidental food-poisoning, but we can see that the timing of the death was fortunate for Nero and Agrippina, in that Britannicus had turned thirteen in February 54, the age at which Nero had been allowed to assume the *toga virilis* (come of age). Though Claudius had not hastened his own son's advancement, he had made a will (later suppressed by Nero – Tac. *Ann.* 12.69; Dio 61.1–2; Suet. *Claud.* 44.1).

The official version seems to have been that Claudius' death was caused by a fever (Sen. *Apocol.* 6 = **F6**). Poisoning is alleged by mushroom – Pliny, **P9c**; Dio 60.34.2; 60.35.4; Mart. 1.20; Juvenal **P9d**; unspecified poisoning *Octavia* 164–5; Pliny **P9b**, *NH* 11.189; Tac. *Ann.* 12.67–8 and Suet. *Claud.* 44.2 both mention mushrooms as one possible means of administering the poison. Josephus alone implies there were other versions (**P9a**). Nero's apparent joking quotation about mushrooms being 'the food of the gods' (Suet. *Nero* 33.1, Dio 60.35.4) could simply mock Claudius' favourite food (Suet. *Claud.* 44.2) and his deification rather than the means of his death.

P9a Josephus' account

[148] There followed the death of Claudius Caesar, after a reign of thirteen years, eight months, and twenty days. Some accounts have it that he was poisoned by his wife, Agrippina.

(Josephus then gives a brief account of Claudius and his family – see **J12h**)

[151] Agrippina was afraid that Britannicus might inherit the empire from his father once he came of age, and was determined to make a pre-emptive strike to gain the empire for her own child. So, according to the general account, she contrived to murder Claudius. [152] She then immediately sent Burrus, the praetorian prefect, to escort Nero to their camp accompanied by his military tribunes and all the most powerful freedmen, and there to proclaim him emperor. [153] Having acquired the empire in this way, Nero did away with Britannicus by poison secretly, but very soon afterwards quite openly murdered his mother. That was his method of thanking her, not only for giving birth to him, but also contriving to win for him the office of emperor. He also put his wife Octavia to death together with a large number of distinguished Romans, on the grounds that they had plotted against him.

[Josephus, *Jewish Antiquities* 20.148 and 151–2]

P9b Comet marks Claudius' poisoning

Pliny is talking about comets appearing as terrifying portents

As in the civil unrest in the consulship of Octavius (43 BC); and again in the war between Pompey and Caesar; or, indeed, in our age, around the time of the poisoning which resulted in Claudius Caesar leaving the empire to Domitius Nero, with the comet shining almost throughout his principate with glaring light.

[Pliny, *Natural History* 2.92]

A comet appearing at the time of Claudius' death is mentioned by Suetonius, *Claudius* 46; Dio 60.35.1; Seneca, *Natural Questions* 7.17.2; Calpurnius Siculus 1.78. Tacitus mentions comets in AD 60 (*Ann.* 14.22.1) and 64 (*Ann.* 15.47.1). Suetonius, *Nero* 36.1 also mentions a comet. Halley's comet was due around AD 66. Pliny exaggerates in keeping with his great dislike of Nero. Pliny explicitly blames Agrippina **P9c** below.

P9c Claudius poisoned by mushrooms

Mushrooms should be classed amongst foods which are eaten rashly. Though delicacies, they are associated with the most notorious murder, having been the means by which Agrippina poisoned her husband, the emperor Claudius, and by so doing, gave the whole world, and especially herself another poison – her son, Nero.

[Pliny, *Natural History* 22.92]

P9d Claudius' last food

(*Juvenal's satirical target here is hosts who serve cheaper food to their less valued guests.*)

Some dodgy helping of toadstools is what's set in front of his guests
Of low grade. For the master, *porcini*, as eaten by Claudius,
Until they were served by his wife as the last things he ever would eat.

[Juvenal *Satires* 5.146–8]

P10 NERO AND AGRIPPINA, AD 59

In AD 59 Nero attempted to disguise the murder of his mother in a contrived shipwreck. When she escaped this, Agrippina was killed by hitmen. The official version was that she had plotted to kill Nero, and had then committed suicide. Tacitus gives a very full account of the whole episode and Nero's motives – *Annals* 14.3–9; a more contemporary dramatic account comes in *Octavia* **H6**. Suetonius, *Nero* 34.1–5 and Dio 62.12–16 provide similar details and Suetonius suggests at 34.4 that earlier historians had provided embellished accounts. The records of the Arval Brothers confirm the official version of Nero surviving an attempt on his life: **A59f–g**, **A59i–j**. But both at the time, and throughout history Nero has been a byword for matricide (e.g. Suet. *Nero* 39.2; Dio 62.16.2; Chaucer, *The Canterbury Tales,* The Monk's Tale; Shakespeare, *Hamlet* Act III sc.2).

P10a Remark to Nero on death of Agrippina

Africanus famously said to Nero on the death of his mother, "Your Gallic provinces beg you, Caesar, to bear your happiness bravely."

[Quintilian, *The Orator's Education* 8.5.15]

Julius Africanus was a well-known orator (alongside Domitius Afer the greatest orator heard by Quintilian (10.1.118)), originally from Gaul. Quintilian gives this as an example of a witty saying based on the unexpected. It must have been intended as a compliment – that Nero was right to be happy at the death of a mother who, in the official version, plotted against him.

P10b Nero's remark on death of Agrippina composed by Seneca

Mere repetition can create a memorable saying, such as that of Seneca in the statement which Nero sent to the senate after his mother was killed, when he wanted to show that he had been in danger, "I neither believe nor rejoice that I am still alive."

[Quintilian, *The Orator's Education* 8.5.18]

P11 THE PISONIAN CONSPIRACY, AD 65

Tacitus' account of the conspiracy is Annals 15.48–74. Within this account he cites the Elder Pliny (15.53.3–4) and Fabius Rusticus (15.61.3) as well as participants (15.73.2) whom he could have spoken to after their return from exile. Fabius Rusticus could well have witnessed Seneca's death (13.20). Gaius Calpurnius Piso, the figurehead of the conspiracy was a member of the famous Calpurnii clan, though his exact relationship to other members of the clan is unclear. He had been exiled by Caligula who had stolen his wife, Livia Orestilla (Suet. *Cal.* 25.1) and had incurred suspicion under Nero by AD 62 (*Ann.* 14.65). The account in the summaries of Dio give far fewer details, ascribing the plot to Seneca and Faenius Rufus (Dio 62.24–27). Tacitus suggests that Nero used the discovery of the plot to conduct a purge of his enemies (*Ann.* 15.60.2, 15.68.2, 15.71.3). An inscription from Etruria (**L35**) records a vow for Nero's safety in response to this conspiracy.

For modern discussion, Griffin, *Nero*, 166–170.

P11a Careless talk costs lives: Pisonian conspiracy betrayed

The careless talk of one man prevented Rome from removing Nero and becoming free. Everything had been prepared, and there was only one night left until the tyrant was to be killed. But when the intended assassin was on his way to the theatre he saw at the gates a prisoner about to be led before Nero and lamenting his misfortune. So he came up to him and whispered, "Just pray, my friend, to get through this day, and tomorrow you will be grateful to me." The prisoner grasped the meaning of this riddle, and realising, I suppose, that 'A bird in hand is worth two in the bush' chose the safer means of escape rather than the more just, and informed Nero of what the man had said. He was immediately seized and tortured by being beaten and burnt when he denied in the face of violence what he had freely revealed.

[Plutarch, *Moralia – On Talkativeness,* 505C]

Plutarch is writing about the dangers of talkativeness before moving on to talk about those who heroically remained silent under interrogation. This account is very different from the later version of Tacitus – *Annals* 15.54–55.

P11b Lucan's suicide, *Life of Lucan*

He satirised viciously not only the emperor himself, but his most powerful friends, in a lampoon. Finally he emerged as virtually the standard-bearer of Piso's conspiracy, saying a great deal publicly about the glory of tyrannicides, and making many threats, including being so rash as to boast of offering Caesar's head to his closest friends. But in fact when the conspiracy was uncovered he displayed no such resolve of spirit. Rather he confessed readily and descended to the most abject pleas, even naming his own mother, innocent though she was, as one of the guilty parties. This was in the hope that a *princeps* who had killed his own mother would give him credit for a lack of family feeling. However when granted freedom to choose his own death, he wrote to his father with corrections for some of his poetry, dined in style, and offered his arms for his veins to be cut by a doctor.

[Suetonius? *Lives of Famous Men, On Poets – Lucan*]

Tacitus agrees that the motive was poetic rivalry (15.49.3), and that Lucan denounced his own mother, though not immediately (15.56.4); he adds that Lucan recited a passage from his poem about a soldier bleeding to death as he died (15.70.1). Tyrannicides was a term applied to Brutus, Cassius and others invloved in the assassination of Julius Caesar.

P11c Martial in Praise of Lucan

This is a famous day, witness of glorious birth. To Lucan it gave life,
 To Rome it gave Lucan, a husband to Polla, his wife;

Alas, Nero, none of your murders made you more loathed than his;
The gods above at least should not have allowed you this.

[Martial, *Epigrams* 7.21]

P11d Caesonius Maximus, banished by Nero

Here, you see, is the bust of famous Maximus,
Mighty friend of Seneca the eloquent;
Close, indeed, even closer than Serenus,
Whom he greets in his endless correspondence.
This, Ovidius, is the man you followed to
Exile, far across the seas of Sicily,
Spurning tantrums of a raging tyrant.
In your praise let no mortal tongue be silent.
Let past ages wonder at their Pylades,
He who stuck by the friend his mother exiled.
Who could make between you both comparison?
You stuck close to a friend that Nero exiled!

[Martial, *Epigrams,* 7.45]

Martial wrote several epigrams to his friend and neighbour Quintus Ovidius. In this and 7.44, he praises him for his loyalty to Caesonius (or Caesennius) Maximus, a friend of Seneca (Epistles, 87.2 – a wealthy Roman's camping expedition!), exiled by Nero (Tac. *Ann.* 15.71.4).

P11e Egypt sacrifices 100 oxen in Rome for Caesar's Preservation

Beside the Tiber's sacred waters Egypt makes festival,
For Caesar's preservation, to heaven thanks men render;
One hundred axes bloody the altars of Olympian Zeus,
As oxen in willing sacrifice their necks surrender.

[Leonides 29 = AP 9.352]

This epigram probably marked the Pisonian conspiracy: less likely the death of Agrippina. For Leonides as a court poet, see **R27**.

P11f Coin celebrating Nero's safety

Obv: Nero, bearded, with laurel wreath, right
NERO CAESAR AVGVSTVS

Rev: Jupiter seated on a stool, holding lightning bolt and sceptre, with drapery over legs
IVPPITER CVSTOS (Jupiter the Guardian)

[*BMC* Nero 68; compare *RIC* Nero 68 obv and 52 rev]

The coin can be dated by its weight to after Nero's reform of currency in AD 64, and by Nero's portrait. Tacitus, *Annals* 15.74 tells us that official celebrations of the failure of the Pisonian conspiracy included Nero dedicating the dagger on the Capitol with an inscription 'To Jupiter the Avenger' and erecting a temple to Salus (Health & Safety) and coins with the same obverse as above show named Salus seated on a throne with a bowl for a libation (*RIC* 59–60). Both reverse types reappear on aurei and denarii with a different, obese portrait of Nero (*RIC* 63–64 and 66–67), and, on denarii only, on a third, grossly obese portrait (*RIC* 69 and 71–72). The likely conclusion is that the coins celebrate failure of the Pisonian conspiracy, with reissues celebrating that of Vinicianus (below, **P12**).

P11g Statue to Silanus, victim of Nero

[17.1] So loyalty and a sense of duty are not dead; men still care about them. Indeed there are some whose loyalty to their friends remains intact, even after they are dead. Titinius Capito has persuaded our emperor to allow him to put up a statue to Lucius Silanus in the forum..... [4] .... He has paid to Silanus an honour that was his due, and in so doing Capito has ensured his own as well as his friend's immortality. For it is no more a mark of outstanding distinction to have one's own statue in the Roman forum than to set one up to someone else.

[Pliny the Younger, *Letters* 1.17.1, 4]

Cn. Octavius Titinius Capito was the first *ab epistulis* (imperial secretary) to be an equestrian rather than an imperial freedman. He served under Domitian, Nerva and Trajan, but must, as a young man, have been helped by the aristocratic Junii Silani family (**J33**). Nero used the aftermath of the Piso conspiracy to get rid of a potential rival Lucius Junius Silanus Torquatus, great-great-great-grandson of Augustus (Tac. *Ann.* 15.52.3 and 16.7–9).

P12 VINICIANUS CONSPIRACY, AD 66

Suetonius merely mentions a conspiracy of Vinicianus at Beneventum after that of Piso at Rome (*Nero* 36.1). Tacitus' account is lost. This conspiracy is probably that whose detection was celebrated by the Arval Brothers in the summer of AD 66 (**A66g** = **P12a**), and the leader was probably L. Annius Vinicianus. His father had conspired against Claudius (**P7**); his brother Annius Pollio was wrongly accused and exiled in the Piso conspiracy (Tac. *Ann.* 15.56.4, 15.71.3); his father-in-law was Domitius Corbulo, Nero's general (Tac. *Ann.* 15.28.3). Vinicianus' conspiracy probably led to Corbulo being summoned to Greece in AD 66/7 to commit suicide. Coins may also celebrate Nero's escape from this conspiracy (see above on **P11f**).

P12a Records of the Arval Brothers, between 19 June and 25 September, AD 66

When M. Arruntius and M. Vettius Bolanus were consuls, on *(date lost),* having carried out the sacrifices which the Arval Brethren had vowed to do in honour of the detection of evil conspiracies, in the second presidency of Emperor Nero Claudius Caesar Augustus, father of the fatherland, Saturninus on behalf of the college of Arval Brothers in fulfilment of the vows sacrificed a male ox to Jupiter, a cow to Juno, a cow to Minerva, *(one other sacrifice),* a cow to Providence, an ox to Mars.

[*AFA* 30, column II, cef, lines 20–26]

P13 THE REVOLTS AGAINST NERO, AD 68

Gaius Julius Vindex was a Romanised Gaul from a leading Aquitanian family granted citizenship by Julius Caesar. His father had probably been admitted into the senate by Claudius in 48 (see **M11**). Vindex was a senator and governor probably of Gallia Lugdunensis (Tac. *Hist.* 1.16). Plutarch alone mentions the sending of letters (**P13a** compare Suet. *Galba* 9.2), but this shows that Vindex launched a senatorial revolt against Nero (as also shown by his coinage, **P13b**) of a province, not some Gallic uprising as portrayed by Nero (Suet. *Nero* 41.2, 43.2) and suggested by Dio's summarisers (63.22.1–2). The relevant portion of Tacitus' *Annals* is lost.

Servius Sulpicius Galba was from an ancient patrician family and was favoured by Livia (Suet. *Galba* 5.2). Consul in 33, he governed Aquitania, Upper Germany, Africa and finally Spain from AD 60. After Vindex's revolt, he had his troops hail him as representative of the senate and people of Rome, issuing coins with traditional republican or Augustan types (**P13f**, **P13g**). He enrolled a new legion (VII Gemina) and after Nero's suicide, marched on Rome, initially supported by the praetorians.

Verginius Rufus was consul in AD 63 and governor of Upper Germany in AD 67, thus in charge of 4 legions, and with responsibility for Gaul. It is unclear whether he was complicit with Vindex' rising and forced to battle against him by the troops (as Plut. *Galba* 6.3; Dio 63.24). At any rate he conspicuously failed to back Nero after his victory, though also refusing to be proclaimed emperor himself after the battle (**P13c**, **P13h**, **P13j**) and again after Otho's death in 69 (Tac. *Hist.* 2.51; Plut. *Otho* 18.3–4). Verginius became consul for a second time under Otho, lived quietly under the Flavians, but was given the great honour of a third consulship, shared with Nerva in 97. Rufus is completely ignored by Suetonius.

L. Clodius Macer commanded the single legion stationed in Africa. After Vindex's revolt, he launched an independent rebellion against Nero. Details are unclear, since the relevant portions of Tacitus' *Annals* are lost, Dio's summarisers ignore him and Suetonius only mentions him as a threat to Galba (*Galba* 11). References in Tacitus' *Histories* show that he threatened grain supplies (1.73) and raised troops (2.97). Plutarch's description of Macer (**P13d**) is too much the stereotypical explanation for revolts to be believed. A sequence of coins issued by him offers another perspective (**P13e** and *RIC* Clodius Macer 1–42. After Nero's fall, Galba moved quickly to eliminate him (Tac. *Hist.* 1.7, 1.11).

P13a Vindex urges provincial governors to revolt

Galba was in the eighth year as governor when Julius Vindex, a governor of Gaul rebelled against Nero. It is said that even before the open rebellion, letters reached him from Vindex: Galba neither put any trust in them nor reported what they said. Other provincial governors forwarded their letters to Nero and did their best to destroy Vindex's enterprise which they later took part in, demonstrating that they had betrayed themselves as well as Vindex.

[Plutarch, *Galba* 4.2]

P13b Denarius of Vindex, struck in Gaul, AD 68, showing Victory and legend 'SPQR'

Obv: Victory standing on a globe, facing left, with wreath in right hand and palm in left

SALVS GENERIS HVMANI (Salvation of the human race)

Rev: Oak wreath

SPQR (Senate and People of Rome)

[*BMC* Civil Wars 34; *RIC* Civil Wars 72]

A Roman of this period would have been as surprised to see a coin without an imperial portrait on the obverse as we would be to see a British coin without 'heads'. Coinage of the republic had traditionally not carried portraits of people, and this feature together with the traditional SPQR legend, common to many of the coins thought to have been issued by Vindex, suggests that his revolt was about system of government, not nationality. The oak wreath, traditionally referring to saving a citizen's life in battle, corrupted by

Augustus into an award for ending the civil wars, and adopted by other emperors, here suggests lives to be saved by a victory of the senate and people.

P13c Verginius refuses to be hailed as emperor during the Vindex revolt

Verginius commanded the strongest legions who often hailed him as emperor and put great pressure on him to accept. He said that he would not take imperial power himself, nor allow it to be given to anyone else unless chosen by the senate.

[Plutarch, *Galba* 6.2]

P13d Clodius Macer's revolt

Many were now defecting from Nero, with pretty well all joining Galba, except for Clodius Macer in Libya, and Verginius Rufus in Gaul, who was in command of the German armies. They both acted independently but with different motives. Clodius had, through savagery and greed, plundered property and murdered men, and had clearly reached a situation in which he could neither retain nor resign his command.

[Plutarch, *Galba* 6.1–2]

P13e Denarius of L. Clodius Macer

Obv: Lion's head, right

L CLODI MACRI, SC ([legion] of Lucius Clodius Macer, by decree of the senate)

Rev: *aquila* (legionary eagle) between two *vexilla* (legionary standards)

LIB AUG LEG III (the liberating Augustan legion III)

[*RIC* L. Clodius Macer 8]

Legion III Augsta was the established legion stationed in Africa, here given the new title 'Liberatrix' – 'Liberating'. Much of the coinage minted by Macer will have been needed to pay his troops. Forty-two different denarius types have been identified for Macer's short rebellion. All carry his name somewhere. Half depict one or the other of his legions. Other images or legends are of Africa, Sicily, warships, Victory or Liberty. (*RIC* volume I, pages 188–196).

P13f Denarius of Galba: liberty restored

Obv: Female bust with hair in small knot above neck, facing right
LIBERTAS (Liberty …) P R

Rev: *pileus* (cap worn by freed slaves) between two daggers
RESTITVTA (… restored to the Roman People)

[*BMC* Civil Wars 7/8; *RIC* Civil Wars 24/5]

This denarius was issued in Spain where Galba was governor of Tarraconensis. The reverse of this coin consciously imitates the famous 'Ides of March denarius' issued by Brutus to celebrate the assassination of Julius Caesar (Dio 47.25.3, BM CM 1855.5–12.40). But Galba avoided putting his own portrait on the obverse as Brutus had done. For Gaius' use of the cap of liberty idea, see **J19h**.

P13g Denarius of Galba as the new Augustus

Obv: Head of Augustus, right
AVGVSTVS DIVI F (Augustus, son of Divus (Julius))

Rev: Victory advancing to left, holding shield inscribed CL V (shield of virtue)
SENAT P Q R (Senate and People of Rome)

[*BMC* Civil Wars 57; *RIC* Civil Wars 110]

This denarius was issued in Spain or Gaul (*RIC* pages 199–200) and is part of an 'Augustus' series (*RIC* Civil Wars 81–111) which depict and name Augustus, and often imitate actual Augustan coin types (e.g. the Capricorn (*RIC* Civil Wars 81–85, compare *RIC* Augustus 125–130 = LACTOR 17, L8), or even one showing Gaius and Lucius Caesar as *principes iuventutis* (*RIC* Civil Wars 87, compare *RIC* Augustus 205 = LACTOR 17, J58). Galba's message was clearly that he intended to model himself on the first *princeps.* Here Galba claims for himself Augustus' golden shield of virtue, set up in the senate house as part of his package of honours of 28/7 BC (*Res Gestae* 34.2; EJ 22; *RIC* Augustus 42b = LACTOR 17, A34.2; H24, H25).

P13h Verginius still refuses to be hailed as emperor after Nero's death

No name was greater than that of Verginius, and no one had a reputation to equal his, since he had been the decisive factor in ridding the Roman state of a repressive tyrant and of Gallic wars. But he still remained true to what he had argued initially in maintaining that the choice of emperor lay with the senate. Yet when Nero's death was confirmed, the mass of his troops again put pressure on him, and one of the military tribunes in his tent drew his sword and ordered Verginius to accept imperial power or the sword.

[Plutarch, *Galba* 10.2]

Verginius was again urged to become emperor after Otho's death in 69 (Tac. *Hist.* 2.51.1; Plut. *Otho* 18.3–4).

P13i The Public Funeral of Verginius Rufus

[1] Verginius Rufus' state funeral has given the people of Rome the finest and most memorable spectacle that they have enjoyed for many years. He was one of our greatest and most outstanding citizens – but he was lucky as well. [2] He had a glorious career, and yet managed to survive for a further thirty years. So he was able to read poems composed about himself and histories of his own achievements – in fact he became a legend in his own time. Three times he held the consulship, thus reaching the highest pinnacle of achievement for an ordinary citizen, since he had refused the position of emperor. [3] His admirable qualities were such that some of the emperors suspected and even hated him, but he survived intact, until he left the best and kindest of them all safely installed upon the throne. It was almost as if fate had preserved him to enjoy this very act of public recognition in his public funeral. [4] He died at the age of eighty three, living in profoundly peaceful seclusion and universally admired.

(Pliny gives some details, here omitted, of his death as a result of a fall in his home).

[6] This was a man whose funeral brings the utmost credit to our emperor and a touch of glory to our times; to public life and the speakers from the rostrum it brings the highest honour. The memorial address was given by the consul, Cornelius Tacitus, the most outstanding orator of our day, and his words marked the culmination of Verginius' good fortune.

[Pliny the Younger, *Letters* 2.1.1–4 & 6]

P13j Pliny's comments on the tomb of Verginius Rufus and its inscription

[1] You say that you read in one of my letters (VI.10) that Verginius Rufus left instructions for the following inscription to be placed upon his tomb:

Here lies Rufus, who once defeated Vindex, and not for his own
But for his country's sake, kept safe the imperial throne.

You feel that such instructions were somewhat reprehensible, adding that you find rather more appropriate and dignified the decision of Frontinus to forbid any sort of monument to be erected to himself. And then at the end you ask me what I think of both men.

(Pliny's praise of Verginius and musings on immortality are here omitted)

[4] I cannot readily think of anyone except Verginius whose modesty in describing his achievement is matched by the glory of the achievement itself. [5] In this I offer myself as witness for the defence. We were great friends and he trusted me implicitly. Yet only once in my hearing did he ever go so far as to make any mention whatsoever

of what he had done. He was having a conversation with Cluvius Rufus, the historian, who remarked to him, "You must understand, Verginius, that historians have a duty to tell the truth. So, if you find anything in my histories which offends you in any way, I trust you will forgive me." Verginius replied, "And don't *you* understand, Cluvius, that I did what I did so that all of you historians would be free to write whatever you like."

[Pliny the Younger, *Letters* 9.19.1–5]

The inscription offers the deliberate ambiguity of whether Verginius saved Rome from Vindex (unlikely in reality but perhaps the official version of why his armies defeated Vindex's forces) or whether he simply left to Rome the choice of new emperor rather than claiming it for himself. For Cluvius Rufus the historian, see **R11**. Verginius (not Pliny the Elder) was appointed as Pliny the Younger's guardian by his father's will (Pliny, Letters 2.1.8).

SECTION Q
POPULAR ENTERTAINMENT

The people of Rome were kept in check by two things: the corn dole and shows.
[Fronto, *Principles of History,* 20]

Introduction: Suetonius regularly includes a section in his *Lives* on each emperor's attitude to entertainments. Augustus learnt from criticism of Julius Caesar for working during shows (*Aug.* 45.1) and listed his many shows among his achievements (*RG* 22–23). Augustus' marriage law of 18 BC had banned marriages between members of senatorial families and actors or children of actors (*Digest* 23.2.44 = LACTOR 17, S1). Indeed, the *SC Larinum* (**Q1**) represents the traditional upper-class Roman view of participants in entertainment of all kinds. Tiberius did not bother to pretend an interest (*Tib.* 47 and Tac. *Ann.* 1.54.2; **Q2**).

Yet the young Caligula (and later Nero) could possibly point to Olympic victories of both Tiberius and Germanicus in the four-horse chariot race (**J7c** (though winners were owners, not charioteers)) as justification for his interest in chariot-racing, not to mention the political aspect of 'bread and shows' (**Q20**). For Caligula's interest in various sorts of popular entertainment, see **Q4–7**; Suet. *Cal.* 18–20, 26.4–27.4, 30.2–3, 32.2, 35.2–3, 54–55; Dio 59.7.2–9 = LACTOR 15.B5, Dio 59.14 = LACTOR 15.B11; D2.12. It is appropriate that his assassination took place in the context of the Palatine Games (**E13, E14**). Claudius was enthusiastic too, sometimes naively so, exposing himself to ridicule: Suet. *Claud.* 21, 34.2; Centennial Games: Tac. *Ann.* 11.11, **L23**; Fucine Lake: Tac. *Ann.* 12.56. Claudius' enthusiasm for actors (see **Q8**) is shown by comic actors being called for to cover up his death (Suet. *Claud.* 45, **F4**).

Nero seems to have combined a genuine interest from youth in all forms of performing (Suet. *Nero* 7.1, 20.1, 22.1) together with an appreciation of the political advantages (Tac. *Ann.* 14.21.1; Suet. *Nero* 57; **Q10**), however much the upper classes may have disapproved (Tac. *Ann.* 14.14–16, 14.20; Suet. *Nero* 20–25). A young man of infinite power and resources, living in a court, surrounded by sycophants is not, of course, living in the real world, but 'on stage' (compare Seneca's advice 'You can no more hide yourself than can the sun. You live in the bright glare of public observation.' – **G7**). The sources exaggerate, but do not invent the idea of almost everything being turned into a show: Tiridates' coronation, (Suet. *Nero* 13; **Q16**); the Great Fire (Suet. *Nero* 38, Tac. *Ann.* 15.39); the tour of Greece (Suet. *Nero* 22–24; Dio 63.8–10); the melodramatic plots to murder his mother (Suet. *Nero* 34.2; Tac. *Ann.* 14.3–5; **H6**); even news of the revolt (Suet. *Nero* 42.2) and his sex-life (Tac. *Ann.* 15.37.4). Nero's final words are fitting: 'Dead – and so great a star!' (Suet. *Nero* 49.1).

Q1 SC Larinum, AD 19: upper-class participation in performances prohibited

Decree of the senate.

[...] on the Palatine in the portico which is next to the temple of Apollo. Present at the drafting were: Gaius Ateius Capito, son of Lucius, of the voting-tribe Aniensis; Sextus Pomp[eius, son of Sextus, of the voting-tribe ...; ...] Octavius Fronto, son of Gaius, of the voting-tribe Stellatina; Marcus Asinius Mamilianus, son of Curtius, of the voting-tribe Arnensis; Gaius Gavius Macer, son of Gaius, of the voting-tribe Poblilia, quaestor; Aulus Did[ius] Gallus [son of ..., of the voting-tribe ...], quaestor.

[Whereas Marcus Silan]us and Lucius Norbanus Balbus, the consuls, said that they had composed a memorandum, just as they had been commissioned to do, [on matters] relating to [...] or to those who, contrary to the dignity of their order, [were appearing in public performances] on the stage or at the games [or were hiring themselves out as gladiators,] as is punishable by decrees of the senate, which had been passed on that subject in earlier years, employing fraudulent evasion so as to [diminish] the majesty of the senate, [with regard to what it might please the senate to be done with regard to this matter, concerning this matter the senate has decided as follows:]

It pleased the senate that no one should bring on to the stage a senator's son, daughter, grandson, granddaughter, great-grandson, great-granddaughter, nor any man [whose father or grandfather,] whether paternal or maternal, or brother, or any woman whose husband or father or grandfather, whether paternal or [maternal, or brother ever had the right] of watching performances in the seats reserved for equestrians, or [ask them to fight in the arena] for a fee or to snatch the plumes of gladiators or take away a sword or to offer any other similar service; [nor] should anyone hire someone, if any should offer [himself;] and it is for this reason that more diligent care must be exercised in preventing that; in the case of those who had the right to sit in the seats reserved for equestrians [some have persisted in fraudulent intent who] for the purpose of evading the authority of their order because there have been some (?)] who had taken pains either to incur [public disgrace] or to be condemned in a notorious court-case, and after they had [voluntarily withdrawn from] their equestrian seats, they had hired themselves out as gladiators or had appeared on stage; nor should any of those persons [mentioned above, if doing something contrary to the dignity of his order (?),] have proper burial, unless any of them had already appeared on the stage or [had hired out their] services [for the arena] or were the offspring – whether male or female – an actor or gladiator or gladiatorial manager or a procurer.

[And with regard to what was] written or [provided for (?) in the senatorial] decree which was passed on the motion of the consuls Manius Lepidus and Titus Statilius Taurus, [that no free-born female who was less than] twenty years old or that no free-born male who was less than twenty-five years old should be permitted to hire out his services [for the arena or stage (?) …] except for any of them who by Divus Augustus or by Tiberius Caesar Aug[ustus had been consigned?...]

[*AE* (1983) 210 = Sherk 35]

This senatorial decree is preserved on a bronze tablet from Larinum, in Samnium (Region IV of Italy), which was recut for reuse as a patronal tablet. The precise date of the decree is missing from the beginning of the text, but it can be dated to the first six months of AD 19. Some of the crucial details in the decree have been lost through damage to the bronze, but its general gist is clear. The senate is concerned with protecting the dignity of the upper classes in Roman society by prohibiting their participation on the stage or in the arena. This extended the ban on such behaviour in decrees passed by the senate under Augustus, and continued his attempts to reinforce the hierarchical nature of Roman society (compare *Digest* 23.2.44 = LACTOR 17, S1). Some of the gaps in the text have sometimes been restored with references to the fraudulent behaviour of upper-class women in registering themselves as prostitutes in order to escape punishment for adultery, but this is far from secure. The consuls mentioned in the final paragraph held office in AD 11. The ending of the decree is too damaged to allow for secure reconstruction.

Q2 Few Gladiatorial Shows Under Tiberius

I once heard a gladiator in the time of Tiberius Caesar called Triumphus lamenting the rarity of gladiatorial spectacles. "What a glorious era has come to an end," he complained.

[Seneca, *On Providence* 4.4]

Seneca has two main criticisms of Tiberius: that he was stingy and that he encouraged treason charges. This anecdote fits with what Suetonius says about the Emperor's reluctance to spend money on entertainments (*Tib.* 47). The glorious era here is, of course, the age of Augustus, who boasts of the number of his gladiatorial shows in *Res Gestae* 22.1. The people too resented the contrast and tried to turn Tiberius' funeral into a show (Suet. 75.3).

Q3 A successful charioteer, Rome AD 15

In the consulship of Drusus Caesar and Gaius Norbanus Flaccus, Menander, slave of Gaius Cominius Macer and of Gaius Cornelius Crispus, was victorious as driver of a two-horse chariot at the Games of Mars which the consuls put on, with the horses Basiliscus and Rusticus; and at the Games of the Victory of Caesar, which Publius Cornelius Scipio and Quintus Pompeius Macer, the praetors, put on, with the horses Hister and Corax.

[EJ 362 = *ILS* 9349]

This curious inscription upon a slab of white marble was reported found outside the Aurelianic Walls of Rome in the area of the *via Salaria*. It is the earliest known dated inscription relating to a charioteer. The Games of Mars occurred on 12 May, whilst those of the Victory of Caesar took place 20–30 July.

Q4 Obelisk in Gaius' circus

The third obelisk in Rome is in the Vatican chariot-track of the *principes* Gaius and Nero, and was made by Nencoreus, son of Sesosis. This was the only one of the obelisks to have been broken during the efforts to transport it.

[Pliny, *Natural History,* 36.74]

On this obelisk, see also NH 16.201–2 and 36.70. It shows no sign of having been broken. The pharaohs mentioned may have been Nubkaura (reigned as Amenemhat II, 1911–1877 BC), son of Senusret I (names and dates from *The Oxford History of Ancient Egypt*).

Q5 Epitaph of a 'green' charioteer

To Tiberius Claudius Epaphroditus, freedman of the emperor, charioteer of the Faction of the Greens. Anicetus, charioteer of the same Faction to his master.

[*CIL* VI 10061 = Sherk 168E]

This epitaph of a charioteer belonging to the imperial household was found at Rome.

Q6 Gaius' theatrical show with silver

Gaius when *princeps* had a temporary stage brought into the circus with on it silver weighing 124,000 pounds.

[Pliny, *Natural History* 33.53]

Q7a Letter of Claudius to the Dionysiac performers, January AD 43

[Tiberius Claudius Caesar Augustus Germanicus, *pontifex maximus*, in his] 2nd year [of tribunician power], consul 3 times, hailed victorious commander 4 times, father of the fatherland, greets those crowned with laurel world-wide as victors in the sacred contests of Dionysus and their fellow competitors. The statues by which means we are being revered with proper honour I allow to be set up, and the legal privileges and benefits granted to you by deified Augustus, I preserve. The envoys were Claudius Pho[..]s, Claudius Epagathus, C[la]udius Dionysius, Claudius Thamyris [.... was written] in Rome in the consulships of Tiberius Claudius Caesar Augustus for the third time and Vitellius for the second time.

[Greek: Smallwood 373a]

Performers in Greek musical and dramatic festivals had since the third century BC grouped themselves into professional associations, known as the performers or artists of Dionysos. These associations then approached kings and emperors in order to try to secure privileges, such as personal inviolability, exemption from public burdens, and the right to wear honorific costume. This is a copy on papyrus of a letter from the emperor Claudius confirming the privileges granted earlier by Augustus. It shows that a worldwide association of Dionysiac artists had been established by this date. For letters of Claudius to association of athletes, see **N21** and **M49**.

Q7b Letter of Claudius to the Dionysiac performers, AD 48/49, Miletus

[Ti]berius Claudius Caesar Augustus Germ[anic]us, in his 6th year of tribunician power, consul [4] times, hailed victorious commander 15 times, father of the fatherland, censor, greets the victors in the sacred contests of Dionysus and the artists. As you recalled my grants in which I preserved the rights given you by the Augusti before me and by the senate, I approve them and shall endeavour to enhance them, seeing that you are loyally disposed towards my house. This was made known to me by my close friend Marcus Valerius Junianus, whom I also commend for his disposition towards you. Farewell.

[Greek: Smallwood 373b = Sherk 54]

This letter is preserved inscribed upon a marble block at Miletus.

Q8 Freedman of Claudius: in charge of theatrical costumes under Nero

To the departed spirits. Tiberius Claudius [Di]pterus, freedman of Divus Claudius, costume-maker of Caesar in charge of theatrical costume. Claudia Lycoris made (this) for her husband and herself and her family.

[Smallwood 186 = *ILS* 1765]

This epitaph from Rome illustrates the use of the digamma (one of the obsolete letters revived by Claudius) by the family of an imperial freedman even after Claudius' death, showing a close sense of affiliation to the deceased emperor's ideals, even under the new Neronian regime. At the same time, his nature of his employment under Nero shows his versatility in accommodating to the tastes of the new ruler too.

Q9 Nero's games of AD 57

Tacitus refers sneeringly to events of AD 57 and their reporting: 'little that is worthy of historical record, except for those like filling whole volumes praising the foundations and wood-work employed by Caesar in building his massive amphitheatre on the Campus Martius.' Suetonius (*Nero* 12.1) reports a wooden theatre built in under a year, while Pliny (*NH* 16.200) mentions a larchwood beam, 120 feet long, being used. Calpurnius Siculus' *Eclogue* 7 pretends to be a dialogue between two rustics one of whom has just visited the games at Rome. As with Calpurnius' other eclogues (see **T15**) gross flattery of Nero is perhaps inevitable from a would-be court-poet near the start of his reign. But details of the amphitheatre and games must have stood recitation in front of an audience who had all been there.

Q9a Nero's temporary amphitheatre

CORYDON:
I saw an amphitheatre towering skywards from its
Network of interwoven beams, so tall it almost could look down
On the Tarpeian rock. We climbed its steps and gently sloping terraces
Until we reached the seats where, in their drab clothes, the vulgar sort
Would sit to watch the spectacle among the women's benches.
But all such seats as lie uncovered and open to the skies above
Were with equestrians packed, or tribunes in their whitened togas dressed.
It's like this valley here, which gradually recedes to form an expanding bowl,
While its flanks and their spreading woods to left and right bend round
With hollow curves enfolded in the bosom of that chain of hills.
So too in Rome the amphitheatre's curved embrace enfolds its central plain, while

The arena's sandy oval is defined by massive twin structures of spectators' seats.
How can I now begin to tell you of those sights, whose individual details I,
With my own eyes, could scarce take in, so dumbstruck was I by such
Glittering wonderlands on every side? I stood there, flabbergasted,
Gawping at all I saw in wonderment, as yet unable to absorb it all.
And then as it chanced, my neighbour on my left, a man well on in years,
Remarked to me, "Up from the country are you? Well, it's no surprise
That you're dumbfounded by such opulence. I expect you've only known
Those grubby hovels, huts, and cottages of yours; gold must be new to you.
Look at me! I am old; I've got the shakes; my hair's all white; and in this city
I've spent all my days – yet even I am stupefied to see it all. Believe you me,
The wonders that we saw in earlier days I count as nothing, and those early shows
We watched were mere frivolity compared to these."

[Calpurnius Siculus, *Eclogue* 7.23–46]

25: The Tarpeian rock formed the south-west part of the Capitoline Hill, and is about 38 metres above the level of the river Tiber.

26–29: Corydon's description coincides exactly with Augustus' reforms to seating at games (the 'Julian Theatre Law' of *c.* 22 BC), as described by Suetonius (*Aug.* 44), which restricted those dressed in dark tunics and women to the upper sections and strengthened a previous law (the 'Roscian Law' of 67 BC) in keeping the front seats for the upper classes. (See LACTOR 17, pages 382–3). The equestrian seats were presumably 'open to the skies above' in not being shaded by awnings (see **Q10**).

34: Twin structure because amphi-theatre literally means double-theatre, and the first amphitheatre of Scribonius Curio in 52 BC was apparently two theatres back to back which swivelled round to form an amphitheatre (Pliny, *NH* 36.117).

Q9b The entertainments

Lycotas, look! And in your mind's eye see the dividing gangways, studded with gems;
See how the colonnaded galleries compete for brilliance. Then the arena's sandy edge,
Offers exciting viewing right up close to the surrounding marble wall.
Ivory panels wonderfully decorate the interlocking beams, round cylinders
All fashioned to rotate as smoothly as a wheel upon its well-made axle.
Thus they will swivel suddenly and cheat the claws of such wild beasts
As strive to climb upon them, simply shaking them off. See also how the nets,
Woven from twisted gold, gleam with reflected light, and stretch their lines
Across the arena's sands suspended from whole tusks, and all of equal size.
And (trust me Lycotas, I'm not kidding you!) every tusk is bigger than our plough.
You don't want a catalogue, but I tell you I saw wild animals of every kind.
For here I saw snow-white hares, wild boars with tusks, also an elk,
A beast but rarely seen even within the forests where it dwells.
Bulls we saw also, one breed from whose outsized neck a hump projects
Misshapen and ugly; another kind tossing a shaggy mane along its neck,
With bristling beard lying along its chin, as frozen stiff with cold
The bristles hang rigid from its shaking dewlap. My luck was really in.
It was not only granted me to see those monsters of the forests I've described,
But sea calves I saw, fighting it out with bears, and river-horses too,
The hippopotami, such ugly brutes, their very name an insult to the horse.
They breed along the er …, that river which with its waters every spring
Sustains the crops that grow about its banks. Ah, how we trembled then,
As often as we saw the arena split in twain, its floor turned upside down,

While from the ruptured earth's crevasses wild beasts leapt; and yet,
How often, also, from those self-same sundered clefts quite suddenly there sprang
Wild strawberry trees, wrought all in gold, and vessels pouring watery showers out.
LYCOTAS:
Corydon, what a lucky man you are! For tremulous old age has not, as yet,
Hampered your youthful limbs. Lucky too, that an indulgent god
Has granted you in such a century as this to spend your earliest years.
Now tell me this, did fortune let you see more closely our revered divinity,
The emperor? Were you close enough yourself to see his face and bearing?
Come on, come on, and tell me, Corydon. Help me imagine how a god appears.
CORYDON:
How I could wish I had been more smartly dressed, not in my peasant's clothes.
For then I might well have seen my god more closely. But my dismal poverty
And humble clothing held by a simple brooch with twisted pin, prevented me.
But all the same, I thought I saw him in his very self, though some way off;
And if I'm not mistaken, there I saw in that one face two faces there combined,
Those of the gods Apollo and of Mars.

[Calpurnius Siculus, *Eclogue* 7.46–84]

67: Calpurnius Siculus jokingly makes his shepherd forget the name of the Nile!

68–72: Excavations in the Roman Forum uncovered a complex network of underground passages (*hypogea*) and even wooden sockets for winches to enable animals to be lifted into the arena, see Welch, *The Roman Amphitheatre* 38–42. The Flavian Amphitheatre was built with an extremely sophisticated network of underground passages, cages, ramps and pulleys.

Q10 Awnings in Nero's amphitheatres

Recently awnings the colour of the sky and decorated with stars have been stretched on ropes in the emperor Nero's amphitheatres.

[Pliny, *Natural History* 19.24]

Pliny has been talking about cloth, especially awnings. These are regularly advertised at Pompeii, see Cooley & Cooley, *Pompeii* D11–23.

Q11 Gold-solder sprinkled in the circus

(Pliny is talking about a substance known by the Greek name, literally gold-solder.)
Gold-solder has been seen before now at shows of the *princeps* Nero, sprinkled on the sand of the circus when he himself was to race chariots in an outfit of the same colour.

[Pliny, *Natural History* 33.90]

For his public appearances as charioteer, Suet, *Nero* 22.2; Tac. *Ann.* 14.14.1; Dio 61.6.1; 62.15.1; 63.6.3.

Q12 Nero honoured in the Theatre of Dionysus at Athens, AD 54–60

Tiberius Claudius [Herodes of Marathon, priest and high-priest of ~~Nero~~ Caesar August]us for life, made this dedication to [Dionysus] the Liberator and to ~~Nero~~ Claudius Caesar Au[gustus Ger]man[icus and to the council of the Areopagus and the council of the 600 and to the people of the Athenians at] his own expense, when C[laudius Novius] was general of the hoplites for the seventh time.

[Greek: Smallwood 415]

This dedication was set up in the Theatre of Dionysus at Athens. For hoplite general (the most important magistracy in Athens at the time, and Claudius Novius, see **M73** and **L28**. This inscription predates Novius' eighth magistracy of AD 60/1 or 61/2 (see **L28**).

Q13 Nero as Apollo the Lyre-Player on copper-alloy *as* struck at Rome, *c.* AD 62

Obv: Bare head of Nero, left

NERO CLAVDIVS CAESAR AVG GERMA (Nero Claudius Caesar, Augustus, Germanicus)

Rev: Nero, as Apollo Citharoedus, advancing right playing lyre

PONTIF MAX TR P IMP P P (*pontifex maximus,* with tribunician power, victorious commander, father of the fatherland)

[*BMC* Nero 236; *RIC* Nero 79]

Suetonius, *Nero* 25.2 mentions Nero erecting statues of himself in the dress of a lyre-player and even minting coins with this design. The association with Apollo is certain given that Augustus had frequently minted coins with reverses of Actian Apollo, his patron god, including many of Apollo playing the lyre (e.g. *RIC* Augustus 170–171b, 179–180, 190–193, 365).

Q14 Nero giving a hand-out to the people, *sestertius, c.* AD 64

Obv: Bust of Nero, wearing laurel wreath and aegis, right

NERO CLAVDIVS CAESAR AVG GERM P M TR P IMP P P (Nero Claudius Caesar Augustus Germanicus, *pontifex maximus,* with tribunician power, victorious commander, father of the fatherland)

Rev: Nero, dressed in a toga, sits on a platform, with *praefectus annonae* (prefect of the corn-dole) behind him. Attendant standing in centre hands token to citizen standing, dressed in toga on left of coin. Minerva stands behind (top centre of coin) with owl and spear in hand, beside flat roof of a building.

DAT POP CONG II S C (he gives a second hand-out to the people)

[*BMC* Nero 140; *RIC* Nero 161]

The *congiarium* could be a single distribution of food or money.

Q15 Nero's games, on *semis* of *c*. AD 64

Obv: Laureate head of Nero, right
NERO CAES AVG IMP

Rev: Urn and wreath on table with lion's paw legs. On front panel, relief of two gryphons or sphinxes. Below, shield.
CER QVINQ ROM CO, S C (Quinquennial games established at Rome, by decree of the Senate')

[*BMC* Nero 261; *RIC* Nero 233]

In AD 60, Nero established quinquennial games at Rome (Tac. *Ann.* 14.20.1). These were modelled on the Greek 'circuit' games (Olympic, Pythian etc.) but every five years (Tac. *Ann.* 16.4–5, despite Suet. *Nero* 21.1). Suetonius refers to them as the *Neronia* (*Nero* 12.3–4) as does Dio (61.21). All accounts agree that the contests were held for Nero's benefit as a performer. Brass *semis* were coins of low value, and therefore high circulation. This type were minted at Rome, and also Lugdunum (*RIC* 427, 486–8, 559).

Q16 Tiridates' coronation, AD 66

Next, his successor, Nero, covered the Theatre of Pompey in gold for a single day, to show it to Tiridates, King of Armenia, though it was only a fraction of the size of his Golden House which surrounds the city.

[Pliny, *Natural History* 33.54]

This passage continues **N18**. The first permanent theatre in Rome was built by Pompey the Great in 55 BC. For Nero's decoration of it, also including a purple awning, see Dio 63.6.1–2 = LACTOR 15, 103–4.

Nero's victories at the Greek 'circuit' games, AD 66/7: Q17–Q18

The Olympic Games were the oldest and most prestigious of the 'circuit' games, which also included the Pythian Games at Delphi in honour of Apollo, the Isthmian Games at Corinth in honour of Poseidon, and the Games at Nemea in honour of Zeus. Augustus had given the same status to games in honour of Actian Apollo at Nikopolis established to celebrate his victory at Actium (Strabo 7.7.6 = LACTOR 17, H11). Olympic and Pythian Games were on a four-year cycle, two years apart, with Nemean and Isthmian Games on a two-year cycle in the other years. Nero forced the Olympic Games to be held out of sequence (they had been held in AD 65 (Philostratos, *Apollonius of Tyana* 5.7.2). 'Nero's Olympic Games was later omitted from the official records.' (Pausanias 10.36.9). They did include musical contests, though naturally not as many as the Pythian Games at Delphi in honour of Apollo. Suetonius, however, describes Nero's introduction of musical contests as 'breaking tradition' (*Nero* 23; Dio 63.8.3; 63.14; Griffin, *Nero* 162–3).

Q17 Nero's victories on tour of Greece, AD 66/7

Nero left his palace and came to Greece to make himself subject to the rules of the Olympic and Pythian Games, though he also won at Corinth. He won victories in competitions for lyre-players and for heralds, and at tragedy at Olympia.

[Philostratos, *Life of Apollonius of Tyana,* 4.24.2]

Philostratos also mentions three Olympic victories (5.7.4) and constant sacrifices in Spain (Baetica) on reports of his Pythian victories (5.9).

Q18 Coins of Alexandria celebrate Nero's victories

Alexandria minted a series of five base-silver four-drachma coins to celebrate Nero's association with each of the circuit games. Each obverse shows a bust of Nero with radiate crown (possibly associated with divinity – see **L32**) and *aegis* (a scaly device worn round the neck, associated with Zeus, most clearly seen in **Q18c**). The legend reads NERΩ KLAV KAIΣ ΣEB ΓEP AV (Nero Claudius Caesar, Augustus, Germanicus, Commander). The reverses show the god worshipped at the respective games, named. For Nero and the Olympic Games, see **L33**.

Q18a Nero and Nemean Zeus

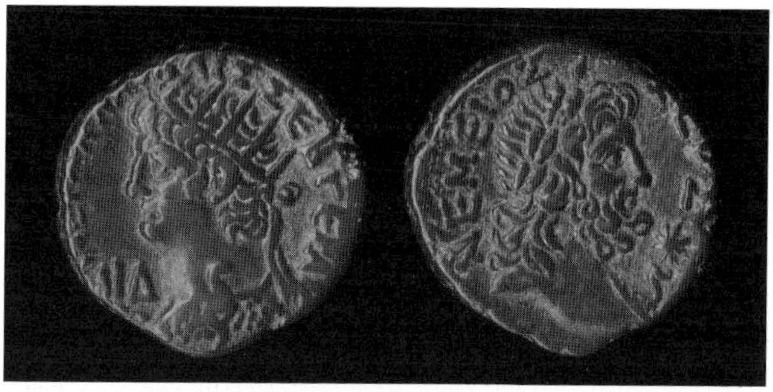

Rev: Bust of Nemean Zeus with parsley crown and *aegis*
ΝΕΜΕΙΟΣ ΖΕΥΣ (Nemean Zeus)

[*BMC* Alexandria 130; *RPC* 5298]

Q18b Nero and Isthmian Poseidon

Rev: Bust of Poseidon right, with trident
ΠΟΣΕΙΔΩΝ ΙΣΘΜΙΟΣ (Isthmian Poseidon)

[BM Coll. 2671 ; *RPC* 5300]

Q18c Nero and Pythian Apollo

Rev: Laureate bust of Pythian Apollo with quiver right
ΠΥΘΙΟΣ ΑΠΟΛΛΩΝ (Pythian Apollo)

[*BMC* Alexandria 141; *RPC* 5302]

Q18d Nero and Actian Apollo

Rev: Bust of Actian Apollo with quiver right
ΑΚΤΙΟΣ ΑΠΟΛΛΩΝ (Actian Apollo)

[BM Coll. 2683 ; *RPC* 5301]

Q19 Nero as New Apollo at Athens

To Imperator ~~Nero~~ Caesar Augustus new Apollo.

[Greek: Smallwood 145 = *IG* II/III^2 3278 = Sherk 78B]

This inscribed altar perhaps alludes to Nero's musical performances during his tour of Greece in 66. Nero's name was later erased.

Q20 Trajan keeps the people happy

From an excellent assessment of the art of politics, Trajan took on board that the emperor should not ignore even actors or other stars of stage, circus or arena, since he knew that the people of Rome were kept in check by two things especially: the corn dole and shows.

[Fronto, *Principles of History,* 20]

Marcus Cornelius Fronto, *c.* AD 95–166 was a distinguished orator and tutor to Marcus Aurelius. His sober assessment of the policy of the 'best *princeps*' echoes Juvenal's more famous and disparaging comment about the *plebs* of Rome caring only about *panem et circenses* – 'bread and chariot-racing' (**P4j** line 81).

SECTION R

LEARNING, LITERATURE, ARTS AND CULTURE

The Caesars of the first dynasty, though apart from Augustus they might be called monsters, were all men of high culture and uncommon intelligence.

This summary of the Julio-Claudian emperors by Aurelius Victor (*On the Caesars* 8.7, paraphrased by Syme *AA* 441) can easily be justified. Claudius is well-known as a scholar; Nero as a poet and artist. But Suetonius includes chapters on the culture of all the Julio-Claudian emperors: *Augustus* 84–89, *Tiberius* 70–71, *Caligula* 53, *Claudius* 41–42, *Nero* 52. From this and other sources, many members of the imperial family are known to have published poems or more substantial works (**R16**, **R17**, **R25**, **R26**, **R37**, **R38**). In addition the emperors maintained the traditional role of wealthy Roman families, by acting as patrons of art and literature. Tacitus is scathing about Nero's circle of court poets (*Ann.* 14.16.1), but the list of writers in all genres of literature operating under the Julio-Claudians is lengthy and includes subjects from medicine (**R40**) to epic poetry (**R38**). The writing of contemporary history, however, forms a separate category, with Tacitus' important statement of the dangers history-writing (*Annals* 1.1.2) being only one of many (see **R1–R3**, **R8**). This section provides evidence for the dangers of history turning into panegyric or invective (**R1–R8**), then considers what we know about some of the contemporary historians of the period whose works do not survive, but were the sources for Tacitus and others (**R9–R16**). Remaining documents of various aspects of literary and artistic culture, as they relate to the imperial family, are then arranged in roughly chronological order. Finally **R40–R45** illustrate aspects of learning in medicine and law.

FREEDOM OF SPEECH: R1–R8

For examples of freedom of speech being upheld or denied under Augustus, see LACTOR 17, P19–P24. Syme, *RR* 486–489 provides an excellent, brief summary of freedom of speech in the writing of contemporary history under the Julio-Claudians.

R1 Livy on dangers of contemporary history

I shall thus spare myself the anxieties which may well distract the historian of contemporary events, even if they fail to divert him from the truth.

[Livy, Preface 5]

Livy (57 BC – AD 17) here excuses his decision to write *From the Foundation of the City*. Though he did go on to cover Augustan history, his account stopped in 9 BC.

R2 Cremutius Cordus' *History*

[1.2] For as long as you could, you strove to prevent the suicide of your father Aulus Cremutius Cordus. Once it became obvious that death was his only escape from slavery, hemmed in as he was by the acolytes of Sejanus, you acknowledged defeat and held up your hands in surrender, even though you deplored his decision. In public, you put your tears to flight, choking down your sobs, without concealing your feelings behind a mask of cheerfulness – all this in an era when the highest act of filial devotion was to avoid any overt act of filial disloyalty.

[1.3] But as soon as changed times gave you the opportunity, you restored to the public arena a recognition of your father's genius, which had cost him his life, thus rescuing him from the only real death by restoring to the nation's archives the very books which that bravest of men had written in his own blood. By this deed you have earned the utmost gratitude of every scholar of Roman history, since a high proportion of his writings had been burned; you have earned the thanks of all posterity, since the integrity of those books as sources will be reinforced by the high price their author paid; you have earned the thanks of your father himself, since his fame now lives on, and will endure – so long as men place high value upon the knowledge of Rome's history; so long as any man alive still yearns to be reminded of the great deeds of our ancestors; so long as any seek to know what it means to be a true Roman, what it means to remain indomitable, when all men's necks are bowed in servitude and crushed beneath the yoke of a Sejanus, and what it means to be a free man in mind, in spirit, and in conduct.

[4] How vast was the loss to Rome, by Heaven, had you not rescued your father from an oblivion, into which he had been cast by two of man's noblest qualities – eloquence and the love of freedom of speech. But now he is read, he thrives, and held in the hands and heart of humanity, he need not fear the advance of decrepitude. As for those butchers who slew him, their crimes, which are their only fit memorial, will swiftly be forgotten.

[Seneca, To Marcia, On Consolation 1.2–4]

Aulus Cremutius Cordus wrote under Augustus and Tiberius a history of Rome from the civil wars to at least 18 BC (Suet. *Aug.* 35.2, *Tib.* 61.3), in which he showed no particular regard for Caesar and Augustus, praised Brutus, and called Cassius 'the last of the Romans' (Dio 57.24.3; Tac. *Ann.* 4.34). A senatorial decree ordered the burning of his books by the aediles in AD 25. Contrary to the impression given by Seneca, not only Marcia but others also had kept copies (Tac. *Ann.* 4.35; Dio 57.24.4) and, when the works were republished early in Gaius' reign (Suet. *Gaius* 16.1), some of the most provocative passages were removed (Quintilian 10.1.104), though the frankness was still there.

R3 Tacitus, *Histories*

After the battle of Actium had been won and all power had been conferred upon one man in the interest of peace, those great talents ceased. Truth came under attack from many directions at once: first ignorance because there was no experience of public life; then an appetite for sycophancy; or hatred of those in power: neither group, the flatterers or the bitter opponents cared about posterity. But though one can easily shun time-serving writers, disparagement or spite find a ready audience. Adulation gives rise to the unpleasant charge of servility; unjust criticism to the false impression of independence.

[Tacitus, *Histories* 1.1]

Compare similar comments at the start of Tacitus, *Annals* (1.1.2). For servility and spite from the same Tiberian author, see the next two passages.

R4 Valerius Maximus invokes Tiberius in place of gods/muses

I pray for your help in this enterprise, Caesar, our fatherland's surest safeguard, into whose hands the unanimous wish of men and gods has entrusted rule over land and sea. Your heavenly foresight most generously nurtures the virtues which I shall narrate, and punishes most severely the vices. For if the orators of old were right to start from Jupiter the Best and Greatest, if the finest bards took their first lines from some deity, then my humble work will have recourse all the more properly to your support, since other divinity is a matter of belief, but yours can be seen, a present help, equal to the star of your father and grandfather, whose matchless radiance has brought much glory and renown to our religious worship. The other gods we have received; the Caesars we have given.

[Valerius Maximus, *Memorable Deeds and Saying, Preface*]

Valerius Maximus has set out the theme of his work, a selection from Rome and elsewhere of memorable deeds and sayings. He then invokes, not a god or muse, as was traditional, but the emperor Tiberius. The stars of his father and grandfather refer to the deification of Julius and Augustus, the former secured by the comet (see LACTOR 17, H3, K44–5), the latter apparently witnessed by a senator (Dio 56.46.2; Suet. *Aug.* 100.4; parodied by Sen. *Apocol.* 1.2).

R5 Valerius Maximus inveighs against Sejanus

But why do I pursue these crimes or dwell on others when I see all wrongs surpassed by the thought of a single act of parricide. So, with the greatest possible indignation, I am seized by feelings more of righteous anger than of strong reason to tear apart that deed. For who could find words of deserved execration strong enough to condemn an attempt to abolish loyal friendship and bury the human race in bloody darkness? Or could you, perhaps, whose vicious savagery exceeds that of uncivilised barbarians, have seized the reins of the Roman empire which our leader and parent keeps safe in his hand. Or would the world have stayed as it is, if you had achieved your mad desire?

Rome captured by the Gauls; the river Cremera stained by the slaughter of three hundred heroes from a famous family; the day of the Allia; the Scipios crushed in Spain; Lake Trasimene; Cannae; swords dripping with Roman blood shed in civil wars: all these catastrophes would have been recreated and surpassed by the insane designs of your madness.

But the eyes of the gods were watching, the stars kept their power, the altars, couches of the gods, and temples were strong with divine presence. Nothing charged with keeping watch over the august life or the fatherland allowed itself to slacken. Above all the author and guarantor of our safety saw to it with his divine providence that his excellent benefactions should not buried in the destruction of the whole world. Therefore peace abides, the laws are upheld, the course of public and private duty is preserved intact. But the man who tried to subvert all this, breaking the sanctity of friendship, together with his whole family, has been crushed by the weight of the Roman people, and even in the underworld, if he is let in there, he suffers the punishment he deserves.

[Valerius Maximus, *Memorable Doings and Sayings*, 9.11 ext 4]

Though not named explicitly, there is no doubt about the subject of this denunciation (for more on Sejanus, see **P3**. This passage contains more rhetoric than real information but does convey the feeling of hostility. The episodes mentioned in the second paragraph refer to some of Rome's worst military defeats.

R6 Josephus on Nero

But I shall leave off writing more about these matters: for many writers have put together histories of Nero. Some of these in gratitude for having been well-treated by him neglected the truth, while others through hatred and enmity towards him have so shamelessly behaved in a drunken fashion with their lies that they deserve condemnation.

[Josephus, *Jewish Antiquities,* 20.154]

No works or even names of pro-Neronian historians are known.

R7 Books about Nero's victims.

[2] Another feature of Gaius Fannius' death which upset me is that he died without making a new will: his previous one leaves out many people he was very fond of, but benefits others who were no longer friends. But this can be borne. More serious is the fact that he has left his finest work unfinished. [3] Although he was much preoccupied by his legal commitments, he was writing an account of the deaths of those who were executed or exiled by Nero. He had completed the first three volumes, which were masterpieces of solid research and Latinity, striking a nice balance between unpretentious narrative and academic historiography. The wider the readership of those early volumes grew, the more eager he became to complete the rest.

[Pliny the Younger, *Letters,* 5.5.2–3]

The letter probably dates from 105–6. Gaius Fannius is otherwise unknown, but could be related to Thrasea Paetus (suicide AD 66) whose daughter was called Fannia, see Syme, *Tacitus* 92.

R8 Pliny the Elder on the publication of his *History*

We have written about your father, your brother and you yourself in a proper work, a history of our own day, a continuation of Aufidius Bassus. Where is this work, you will ask. It is already finished and kept safely; and anyway I had decided to entrust it to my heir, so that my lifetime should not be judged to have made any concessions to ambition.

[Pliny, *Natural History*, preface 20]

Pliny dedicated his *Natural History* to Titus in his sixth consulship (*preface* 3) in AD 77. For more on Pliny's history, see **R14, R15**.

LOST JULIO-CLAUDIAN HISTORIANS: R9 – R15

Most of the contemporary histories of the Julio-Claudian emperors mentioned by Tacitus have not survived. Like all ancient historians, Tacitus very rarely mentions his sources, and though at *Annals* 13.20 he promises to name his sources where they disagree, 'he did not carry out his promise' according to the greatest modern scholar of Tacitus (Syme, *Tacitus,* 291).

R9 Servilius Nonianus

A man of notable talent, full of clever sayings, but less concise than an authoritative historian should be.

[Quintilian, *The Orator's Education,* 10.1.102]

Tacitus' 'obituary' (*Ann.* 14.19) records 'a famous man, with distinguished career; a great orator, for a long time in the courts, then in recording Roman history; a man of discriminating taste.' For the popularity of his recitals, see **R23**. His history probably covered the reign of Tiberius and quite possibly Caligula. Servilius was consul in AD 35. Suetonius, *Tiberius* 61.6 refers to an ex-consul who wrote *Annals*: this may be Servilius. He was probably a major source for Tacitus writing on Tiberius. See further: Syme, *Tacitus*, 274–7, 287–8.

R10 Aufidius Bassus

Authority was a notable quality of Aufidius Bassus, a slightly earlier writer [than Servilius Nonianus], especially in his books of *The German War*.

[Quintilian, *Orator's Education* 10.1.103]

Tacitus, *Dialogus* 23 also praises his eloquence (and that of Servilius). Aufidius also wrote a general history, which includes an account of Cicero's murder in 43 BC (preserved by Seneca, *Suasoriae* 6.18.23). This work was famous enough for Pliny the Elder simply to entitle his historical work '*a fine Aufidii Bassi' – A Continuation of Aufidius Bassus* (**R8**), but this end-date of Aufidius' history is not known – perhaps AD 31, perhaps later. Aufidius is not known to have held public office and was terminally ill around AD 60 (Seneca, *Letters* 30). See further: Syme, *Tacitus*, 274–6, 287–9 and 697–700.

R11 Cluvius Rufus

Prominent historian and senator, consul before AD 41. He is cited as a writer on Nero by Tacitus, *Annals* 13.20, 14.2, and Plutarch, *Life of Otho*, 3. He also wrote about Verginius Rufus according to an anecdote related by the Younger Pliny (see **P13j**). Cluvius Rufus was required to be Nero's herald on his tour of Greece (Dio 63.14.3), so can be presumed to have provided a first-hand and hostile account of Nero's reign. The fact that Tacitus refers to him at *Annals* 13.20 as simply Cluvius indicates that Tacitus had cited him previously in a lost part of the *Annals*. In fact he had witnessed Caligula's assassination (Jos. *JA* 19.91f) and is probably the source for Josephus' detailed account (**Section E**). See further: Wiseman, *Death of an Emperor*, 111–118.

R12 Fabius Rusticus

Livy and Fabius Rusticus, the most eloquent of ancient and recent authors have likened the overall shape of Britannia to an elongated rhombus or an axe head.

[Tacitus, *Agr.* 10.3]

Fabius was an historian originally from Spain, not known to have held public office. He may or may not be the writer mentioned by Quintilian below. Tacitus cites Fabius Rusticus as one of his three main sources for Nero's reign at 13.20, where the full version of his name shows that he had not been cited earlier in *Annals*. He is also mentioned at 14.2 and at 15.61 for a detail relevant to Seneca's execution. As Seneca was patron to Fabius we may reasonably suppose that the whole scene 15.60–4, and many other details about Seneca derive from Fabius' history. See further Syme, *Tacitus*, 289–94.

R13 A great writer, possibly Fabius Rusticus

One writer is still alive and adds to the glory of our times, a man who deserves to be remembered by future ages; he will be named one day; we know who he is.

[Quintilian, *Orator's Education* 10.1.104]

We *don't* know who this writer is, but Fabius Rusticus is the most likely candidate.

R14 List of the Pliny the Elder's books by his nephew

Gaius Pliny to Baebius Macro, greetings!

I am delighted that you have read my uncle's books so carefully as to wish to have all of them and ask for a complete list. …

On Throwing the Javelin from Horseback: one volume. He wrote this with both style and careful research when serving in command of a cavalry squadron.

Biography of Pomponius Secundus: two volumes. This served as a tribute owed to the memory of a friend who loved him dearly.

German Wars: twenty volumes. Containing accounts of all the wars we have waged against the Germans. He started this work while serving in Germany, prompted by a dream: there came to him in his sleep the ghost of Nero Drusus, who, after victories all over Germany had died there, charging him to preserve his memory and begging him to free him from undeserved oblivion.

Scholarship: three long volumes, divided into six chapters, in which he provides the perfect education for an orator right from the cradle.

Grammatical Problems: in eight volumes. He wrote this in the final years of Nero, when tyranny had made dangerous any literary pursuit of an even slightly more independent or distinguished genre.

Continuation of Aufidius Bassus: thirty-one volumes.

Natural History: thirty-seven volumes: a scholarly and comprehensive work, no less wide-ranging than nature herself.

[Pliny the Younger, *Letters* 3.5.1–6]

For the last two works mentioned, see **R8** above. Pliny's letter goes on to describe how his uncle managed such a phenomenal output, notably the last two works, composed between AD 69 and 79, while holding a succession of imperial posts. NB a 'volume' or 'book' represents what fitted on an ancient scroll – perhaps 40 pages of a modern paperback book.

Gaius Plinius Secundus or The Elder Pliny, a Roman equestrian, was commander of the fleet at Misenum, and met his death trying to rescue people from the eruption of Mt. Vesuvius (Younger Pliny, *Letters* 6.16). Tacitus cites Pliny three times in his *Annals*: 1.69 (his *German Wars*), 13.20 (one of three main sources for Nero), and 15.53 (for a story dismissed as 'absurd'). Also once at *Histories* 3.28 regarding the second battle of Cremona in AD 69. So Pliny's history, starting wherever Aufidius Bassus stopped, covered at least part of Claudius, all of Nero, and at least the accession of Vespasian. From occasional historical references in his *Natural History*, Pliny the Elder can be seen to have been hostile to Nero and comparatively indulgent to Claudius (Syme, *Tacitus* 292). See further Syme, *Tacitus* 60–63.

R15 Pliny's history of Nero's reign

Our own age experienced a no less remarkable earthquake, in the last year of Nero's principate, as we have described in our history of his reign.

[Pliny, *Natural History* 2.199]

At *NH* 17.245 Pliny describes this earthquake as a portent happening 'at the fall of Nero'. Suetonius (*Nero* 48.2) and Dio (63.28.1) record an earthquake occurring when Nero had already fled the palace.

THE IMPERIAL FAMILY AS PATRONS AND PRACTITIONERS: R16–R35

Neither side of this represented a new venture. Julius Caesar wrote *commentarii* on his campaigns in Gaul and in the civil war. Augustus wrote many works in a large variety of genres (Suet. *Aug.* 85) as well as the *Res Gestae*, and was a great patron of the arts (see *e.g.* LACTOR 17, R14–R22). See also Wallace-Hadrill, *Suetonius* 83–86.

R16 Tiberius Caesar, *On the City of Troy*

Hector, scion of Mars, though far beneath the earth you lie,
If Fate permits you, hearken to my words, and at their sound
Draw breath once more – an heir and your avenger has arisen
To spread your country's glory to earth's utmost bound.
Lo, far-famed Troy arises once again; is furrowed by the plough,
By a nation dear to Mars, though less in war than thou.
Tell fierce Achilles, Hector, that his Myrmidons all are dead,
His Thessaly conquered, and great Aeneas' sons rule in his stead.

[*Palatine Anthology,* 9.387 = Tiberius I, Page, *Further Greek Epigrams*]

The Greek version of this epigram is ascribed in the Greek Anthology to Hadrian, Tiberius or Germanicus. The Latin version (= Page, Further Greek Epigrams, p559), far more likely to be the translation than the original version is listed in the Latin Anthology as by Germanicus. Tiberius wrote poems in Greek (Suet. Tib. 70), so he probably wrote the Greek version and his adopted son, Germanicus, produced a Latin version.

R17 Germanicus' poetry

You cannot, Germanicus, despise the tribute of a poet
For you are one yourself.

[Ovid, *ex Ponto* 4.8.67]

Ovid fourth book of poems, *From Pontus*, his place of exile on the Black Sea contains an appeal to Germanicus (4.8.63–88), datable by reference to Augustus' deification. Germanicus' translation of the Hellenistic poet, Aratus' *Phaenomena* still survives.

R18 Epitaph to imperial librarian

To the departed spirits of Tiberius Julius Pappus, son of Zoilus, of the Fabian tribe, companion of the Emperor Tiberius, superintendent of all the imperial libraries from the time of the Emperor Tiberius to that of the Emperor Claudius. Set up by his heir Tiberius Julius Nico, also inheritor of one quarter of the estate, and by Julia Fortunata.

[*American Journal of Archaeology,* 63 (1959), p.384 = Dudley p158]

R19 Tiberius' liking of a statue

Lysippus, a prolific artist, as we have said, made more statues than anyone else, including the *Apoxyomenos* (Bather using a strigil) which Agrippa dedicated in front of his Baths and which Tiberius so liked. He could not resist his feelings for it, even though he kept control of himself at the start of his principate, and had it moved to his bedroom and replaced by another statue. The people of Rome were so determined that they chanted in the theatre for the *Apoxyomenos* to be replaced, and the *princeps*, though greatly in love with it, replaced it.

[Pliny, *Natural History* 34.62]

Lysippus: Pliny's discussion of Lysippus of Sikyon (34.61–7) links his career to Philip of Macedon and Alexander the Great. Several probable copies of Lysippus' *Apoxyomenos* have survived. Most 'bad' emperors were accused of lusting after works of classical art (which could be consciously erotic, e.g. the 'Barberini Faun') – Suet. *Tib.* 43.2 (pictures, statuary, books of pornography), and **R20, R21**.

R20 Tiberius lusts after a painting

Parrhasios painted a *High Priest of Cybele*, a picture which the *princeps* Tiberius loved and kept in his bedroom.

[Pliny, *Natural History* 35.70]

Priests of Cybele were eunuchs, sometimes thought to castrate themselves. Suet. *Tib.* 44.2 tells of another obscene 'old master' by Parrhasios of Ephesos (4th century BC: *NH* 35.67–72) which Tiberius kept in his bedroom.

R21 Caligula lusts after paintings

Similarly at Lanuvium, Atlanta and Helen are painted close together by the same artist. They are nude and both outstandingly lovely, the former depicted as a girl. They had not been damaged by the collapse of the temple. The *princeps* Gaius, driven by lust, tried to remove them but the type of plaster prevented it.

[Pliny, *Natural History* 35.18]

Pliny has been talking about early Italian painting. A $4^{th}/3^{rd}$ century BC temple of Juno is known at Lanuvium in Latium, on the site of an earlier temple. The artist is not known.

R22 Claudian paper

Claudius improved the best quality paper. For thin Augustan paper was not strong enough for the pens used; in addition writing showed through, leading to the risk of illegibility because of what was on the other side, and in other respects the great transparency looked unattractive. … For these reasons, Claudian paper is superior to other types, with Augustan still being used most in letters.

[Pliny, *Natural History* 13.79–80]

Pliny had explained (13.74) that the best quality paper had been renamed after Augustus and the second best after Livia. For paper in the ancient world, see J. F. Healy, *Pliny the Elder on Science and Technology*, Oxford 1999, 358–9.

R23 Claudius at a Recitation

Nowadays no-one stays very long at a recitation. They assemble slowly and reluctantly, and leave before the finish, some discreetly and on tiptoe, others quite openly and without embarrassment. [3] What a contrast with the good old days! We are told how in our parents' day the emperor Claudius was taking a stroll on the Palatine, when he became aware of a disturbance. When he asked what was going on, he was told that the orator Nonianus was giving a recital. On the spur of the moment and much to the speaker's surprise, Claudius joined the audience

[Pliny the Younger, *Letters* 1.13.2–3]

The Elder Seneca ascribes the invention of the recitation as a means of an author publishing his works to Asinius Pollio in the time of Augustus (*Controversiae* 4.pr.2). For M. Servilius Nonianus see **R9.**

R24 Claudius adds letters to the Roman alphabet

Claudius' addition of that Greek letter for these sounds (in *servus* and *cervus*) was quite useful.

[Quintilian, *The Orator's Education* 1.7.26]

Quintilian had earlier commented, 'But all *grammatici* (experts on grammar) will certainly go into points of detail, such as whether our alphabet is missing some letters necessary for writing Latin itself. For example *servus* and *vulgus* require a Greek digamma, and there is a sound between U and I (for we do not pronounce *optimus* like *opimus*).' (Quint. 1.4.11). Suetonius tells us that Claudius had written a book before becoming emperor about three extra letters required in Latin, and that he introduced them on accession (*Claud.* 41.3). They were the inverted digamma Ⅎ for the V/W sound; Ⱶ for the U/I; and Ↄ for BS. The first is quite often found in Claudian inscriptions, the second very rarely, the third not at all.

R25 Claudius' *Histories*

Pliny on six occasions cites Claudius as his source for information in *Natural History*, as well as mentioning him in his 'index' – book 1 as a source in books 5, 6, 12, 13.

a) Lake Mareotis' (on the south side of Alexandria) 'is 30 miles across and 250 in circumference, according to Claudius Caesar. (*NH* 5.63).
b) Claudius Caesar gives the length [of Armenia] from Dascusa to the shore of the Caspian Sea as 1,300 miles, and its breadth from Tigranocerta to Iberia as half that distance. (*NH* 6.27)
c) Claudius Caesar gives the distance as 150 miles from the Cimmerian Bosphorus to the Caspian Sea, and says that Seleucus Nicator was contemplating cutting a canal through the area at the time when he was killed by Ptolemy Ceraunus. (*NH* 6.31)
d) Claudius Caesar writes that the Tigris flows so close to the Arsanias in the region of Archene that when they flood they flow together but that their waters do not mix. The lighter waters of the Arsanias float on the top for almost 4 miles, then diverts and flows into the Euphrates. (*NH* 6.128)
e) (*Pliny is talking about abnormal births.*) Claudius Caesar writes that a hippocentaur was born in Thessaly (central Greece) and died on the same day. In his reign we saw one brought to him from Egypt, preserved in honey. (*NH* 7.35)
f) (*Pliny is talking about the most sought-after trees.*) So they search, amongst the Elymaei tribe, for the *bratus* – a tree like the spreading cypress, but with very white branches, which gives off a pleasant smell when burnt. In his histories

> Claudius Caesar also ascribes to it a marvellous property: he writes that the Parthians sprinkle leaves on their drinks; that is scent is very like that of the cedar; and that its smoke provides an antidote against effects of other types of wood (*NH* 12.78).

Suetonius, *Claudius* 41–2 gives us evidence of Claudius' works as a scholar: in Latin, *Histories* (2 books starting with Julius Caesar's assassination, then a gap, then 41 books resuming at the end of the civil wars), *Autobiography*, a defence of Cicero's style, a book on the Roman alphabet; in Greek, *Etruscan History, Carthaginian History.* None of these passages give us anything approaching the political history of his own times that we would most like to have. Like most ancient geographers, the distances given by Claudius are inaccurate. Syme, *Tacitus,* appendixes 40–1 traces Tacitus' use in the *Annals* of Claudius' speeches and histories.

R26 Agrippina's writings (*commentarii*)

Agrippina wrote that her son Nero, emperor a short while ago, and enemy of the human race throughout his reign, was born feet first.

[Pliny, *Natural History* 7.45]

Pliny is writing about 'breech' births. Agrippina, wife of Claudius is mentioned as a source for Book 7 in Pliny's 'Index' – book 1. Tacitus also cites Agrippina's *commentarii* at *Annals* 4.53.2. For other information probably derived from this work and its likely purpose, see Barrett, *Agrippina* 198–9. On Pliny's dislike of Nero (he makes the point that a breach birth is unnatural and therefore ill-omened) see Beagon *Roman Nature,* 117–18.

R27 Leonides of Alexandria, isopsephic epigrams

a Caesar, this little birthday sacrifice comes as a dainty dish
For you, from the Nile-born Muse of Leonides.
The Muse's sacrifices e'er lack altar-smoke; but if you wish,
Next year she'll make a better sacrifice than these.

[Palatine Anthology, 6.321 = Leonides I in Page, *Further Greek Epigrams*]

b Caesar, I pray, accept from me another book – it's Volume Three
Of isopsephic elegance, a sample of my poetry.
The Nile, in any case, will send back (via Greece direct) these words
To you in Rome – a gift more tuneful than the birds.

[Palatine Anthology, 6.328 = Leonides VII in Page, *Further Greek Epigrams*]

Greek used its alphabet to represent numbers as well as letters (α–ε = 1–5; ζ–θ = 7–9; ι–π = 10–80; ρ–ω = 100–800). Leonides of Alexandria invented a type of epigram, 'isopsephic', in which the letters of the first 'distich' (pair of lines), when converted to numerical values and added together equals the values of the second. That this sort of game had a fairly wide appeal is shown by a Greek lampoon quoted by Suetonius (*Nero* 39.2) noting that his name in Greek, Νέρων = 1,005 = ἰδίαν μητέρα ἀπέκτεινε. The effect is obviously impossible to render in translation. 42 isopsephic epigrams survive, several of which are described as birthday-presents for members of the imperial family (see **J21c, J27c**). Leonides clearly was a court-poet, apparently retained by Vespasian, since epigram 26 is very probably addressed to him. One of his own poems (21 = *AP* 9.344) describes himself as 'everybody's favourite'. For more on Leonides, see Page, *Further Greek Epigrams* 503–540.

R28 Lucillius

"Let us begin our song with the Muses of Helicon."
Wrote Hesiod, it's said while shepherding.
"Sing, goddess, of the wrath" and "Tell me, muse, of the man"
Said Calliope, through the mouth of Homer.
I too have to write a first line. But what shall I write

As I attempt to make money from my second book?
"Muses of Olympus, daughters of Zeus, I was saved
Only because Nero Caesar gave me money."

[Lucillius in Greek Anthology 9.572]

Lucillius' epigram quotes the opening words of the three most famous Greek epic poems: Hesiod, *Theogony*, and Homer's, *Iliad* and *Odyssey*. For knowledge of Hesiod and Homer as essential for an educated Roman, see **R39**.

R29 Famulus, painter of the Golden House

There was recently a painter, Famulus who was dignified and stately, yet also ornate and florid in style. He only painted for a few hours each day, and did so with dignity, dressed always in a toga even when on scaffolding. The Golden House was the prison for his paintings so that few examples of his work can be found elsewhere.

[Pliny, *Natural History* 35.120]

The rediscovery of the Golden House and Famulus' paintings *c.* 1500 was hugely influential on the Renaissance. For the Golden House, see **K41–K43**.

R30 Nero commissions a colossal painting of himself

I shall also mention one contemporary crazy venture in painting. The *princeps* Nero had ordered a colossal, 120-foot portrait of himself, to be painted on linen. When finished, this unprecedented painting was struck by lightning in the Gardens of Maius and burnt together with the best part of the Gardens.

[Pliny, *Natural History* 35.51]

R31 Sculptures in Nero's Gardens of Servilius

[23] The works of Praxiteles at Rome are a *Flora*, a *Triptolemus*, and a *Ceres* in the Gardens of Servilius. … [25] Scopas made the celebrated *Vesta Seated* in the Gardens of Servilius and the two turning-posts on either side of her … [36] in the Gardens of Servilius, famous works are, I find, *Apollo* by Calamis the well-known engraver; *the Boxers* of Dercylides; *Callisthenes the Historian* by Amphistratos.

[Pliny, *Natural History* 36.23, 25, 36]

Gardens of Servilius: probably in the south of Rome. Nero was there when brought news of the Pisonian conspiracy (Tac. *Ann.* 15.55). The artists mentioned were all Greek and active in the 4th century BC.

R32 Laocoon

Some outstanding works of art bring their creators too little renown because they are the work of several hands, so no single individual takes the credit, but neither can all the artists be named together. This is the case with *Laocoon* in the palace of the Imperator Titus, a greater work of art than any painting or statue. Laocoon and his children and the marvelous coils of the snakes are all carved from a single block to a design worked out by the great masters from Rhodes, Hagesander, Polydorus and Athenodorus.

[Pliny, *Natural History* 36.37]

This famous work is now in the Vatican Museum. 'Its dramatic rediscovery in 1506 made a great impression, particularly on Michelangelo.' (Oxford Companion to Art, 1970). The same artists are named on sculpture groups of Odysseus, Polyphemus and Scylla in a cave at Sperlonga, site of a luxurious villa of Tiberius (Suet. *Tib.* 39; Tac. *Ann.* 4.59). On Laocoon and Sperlonga groups see Boardman, Oxford History of Classical Art, (Oxford 1993) items 201–2; Beard & Henderson, *Classical Art* (Oxford 2001) 72–82 on the severe problems of dating works and artists.

R33 Nero and his Freedmen as Art "Collectors"

Dio Cocceianus, later called Chrysostom ('Golden-Mouth' for his skill at speaking) lived *c.* AD 40/50 – 110. Born at Prusa in Bithynia (Turkey) he travelled widely through Rome and the Greek East. *Oration* 31, purportedly delivered at Rhodes, condemns their habit of honouring someone with a statue merely by changing the name and titles on the inscribed base of an existing statue. Dio's account fits in well with other evidence of Nero's depredations, but favourable treatment of Rhodes (**M13**; Tac. *Ann.* 12.58.2; Suet. *Claud.* 25.3, *Nero* 7.2), *IGRRP* 4.1123–4).

[148] Nero had such an enthusiastic lust for art that he could not even keep his hands off the treasures of Olympia or Delphi. And yet these were the two shrines which he honoured above all others. As for the Acropolis at Athens, he carried off most of the art treasures from there and a large number from Pergamum as well, even though its sanctuary belonged to him. I could go on, but what is the point of listing all his thefts from other places? But despite this, yours, people of Rhodes, is the only city whose treasures he left untouched, and indeed he showed you such goodwill and admiration that he regarded your whole city as more sacred than any of the leading sanctuaries.

[149] You know, too, that Nero's freedman, the notorious Acratus, who scoured virtually all the inhabited world in his quest for loot, and left barely even a village unscathed – he even came here. You were all, naturally, appalled, but he insisted that he had only come as a simple tourist, since he had no authority to lay so much as a finger on any of your treasures. But your vast collection of statues brings you another kind of fame, quite apart from the fact that the whole world flocks to see them. They are visible symbols of your goodwill towards your rulers, and of their high esteem for yourselves.

[150] And so, given that Rome and Nero showed such concern to protect your treasures and regarded them as sacrosanct, are you yourselves going to fail to protect them? Of all our emperors, Nero was the most extreme of autocrats, regarding everything as his own property and his powers in every sphere as unlimited and absolute; yet he failed to remove a single statue of anyone who had been honoured by the people of Rhodes. And this is the only known example of such restraint by him.

[Dio Chrysostom, *Orations* 31.148–150]

[148] Pergamum: in Mysia, Asia Minor, now Bergama in W. Turkey, near Aegean. Capital of the Hellenistic Attalid kings from *c.* 300 BC. Much of its superb sculpture is now in Berlin's 'Pergamon Museum'. The sanctuary could be said, albeit with exaggeration, to belong to Nero because Augustus had allowed a precinct at Pergamum to be consecrated in his honour (Dio 51.20.7 and 59.28.1).

[149] For Acrastus' search through Asia and Achaia for loot to replenish the treasuries in AD 64, see Tac. *Ann.* 15.45. Also 16.23 where Adrastus was forcibly prevented. Barea Soranus, then governor of Asia did not punish Pergamum, so was in turn prosecuted and forced to suicide in AD 66.

R34 Nero's poem on Troy

This Paris, according to Nero's *Troica* was the strongest, defeating everyone in athletic contests at Troy, including Hector himself. When Hector angrily drew his sword on him, Paris said that he was his brother, and proved it by bringing tokens of his childhood while still disguised by his shepherd's clothes.

[Servius, *Commentary on Virgil's Aeneid* 5.370 = Courtney, *Fragmentary Latin Poets,* Nero 8]

This version, in which the baby Paris is predicted to cause Troy's destruction, and saved from death by his mother secretly giving him to a shepherd to be brought up, was a recognised variant, used by both

Sophocles and Euripides in their lost plays, *Alexander* (itself another traditional name for Paris). Nero's poem was an epic version, in Latin. It is probably referred to by Dio 62.29.1 and Suet. *Nero* 10.2, and presumably provided the lines on the burning of Troy which Nero allegedly sang while watching the Great Fire of Rome (Tac. *Ann.* 15.39.3; Suet. *Nero* 38.2; Dio 62.18.1) or even the whole foundation for the allegation. A few lines survive in quotations by other authors (**R36**, and see Griffin, *Nero* 150–3 for an assessment of Nero's verse, and page 276 for the three-line fragments quoted by a commentator on Lucan 3.261; Courtney, *FLP* pages 357–9 for other possible fragments). For the allegation that Nero used 'ghost-writers' see Tac. *Ann.* 14.16 and Suet. *Nero* 52 (refuting it).

R35 Verses written by Julio-Claudian politicians and emperors

[5] I would not dream of citing any living author in my defence, lest I seem to be indulging in a kind of self-serving flattery. But surely I have nothing to be ashamed of in imitating Marcus Cicero (*and 13 others named*), Annaeus Seneca, and Verginius Rufus among our contemporaries. And if such exemplary figures seem inadequate, what about Divus Julius Caesar, Divus Augustus, Divus Nerva and the emperor Tiberius? [6] I deliberately make no mention of Nero, since I realise that activities which are occasionally practised by wicked men are not thereby invalidated; rather their merits are confirmed by the fact that they are more often practised by the virtuous.

[Pliny the Younger, *Letters* 5.3.5–6]

Pliny is justifying his own attempts at writing light verse. For Seneca, see Index of Names; for Verginius Rufus, see **P13h–j**.

THE ARTS AS A MEANS TO SELF-ADVANCEMENT: R36–R39

R36–R38 suggest that engagement with the arts, especially poetry could be viewed as a clear means to imperial favour. The identification of Titus Petronius, Nero's 'arbiter of style' (Tac. *Ann.* 16.18) with the famous author of *Satyricon* would also support this (and **R39** supports the picture painted in *Satyricon* of wealthy freemen trying to appear cultured). Seneca has proved far more influential for his tragedies than his philosophy or politics, though his influence in the Renaissance.

R36 Lucan's poetry

Marcus Annaeus Lucan from Corduba first displayed his talent with a poem 'In Praise of Nero' in his quinquennial competition. Later he gave a public reading of his 'Civil War' on the conflict between Pompey and Caesar. In a sort of preface to this poem, comparing his age and first works with those of Virgil, he was bold enough to say,

"*How far short am I of his* 'Culex'?"

[*The part of the work dealing with Lucan's family and education is lost*]

Recalled from Athens by Nero and added to the ranks of his friends, he was further honoured by being made *quaestor*, but did not long remain in favour. For being offended that while he was giving a public reading Nero had suddenly called a meeting of the senate simply in order to pour cold water on the event, he did not refrain from words and deeds insulting to Nero which are still famous. So, for example, in the public toilets, he cleared his bowels rather loudly and declaimed a verse of the emperor's

'You would have thought that there was thunder underground'

while most of those using the toilets at the same time fled.

[Suetonius, *Lives of Famous Men, On Poets* – Lucan]

For the *Neronia* see **Q15.** *Culex* is a 414-line mini-epic poem on the death of a gnat (*culex*). It includes a dedication to Octavian and was widely thought to be a youthful work of Virgil, (written at 16 according to Donatus, *Life of Virgil*). For the rest of this short biography on Lucan's involvement in the Pisonian conspiracy and suicide, see **P11b**, and for a Martial epigram in praise of Lucan, see **P11c**.

R37 Panegyric on Calpurnius Piso

It is uncertain whether this is L. Calpurnius Piso, cos. AD 57, or Calpurnius Piso, the conspirator against Nero, who was executed in AD 65. The author is also unknown, but the style is very similar to that of other writers of the Neronian period. The panegyric is interesting as indicative of how aristocratic Romans might wish to see themselves.

*(**1–24**: The poem begins by lavishing praise on the nobility of the* gens Calpurnia *(Calpurnian clan), including military achievements, and on the excellence of the subject in every walk of life.)*

R37a Forensic oratory (25–40)

We, too, (like bards of old) can match the peaceful glories of our modern Piso
To warlike deeds accomplished by his ancestors. Warfare may now be dead,
But courage never dies. And in our courts brave men in lawyers' gowns
May still wage war like soldiers and, with no taste of blood,
Before a judge appointed by the Law may fight their gentler battles.
Glory now is won by other means, no less legitimate: he who saves
A citizen's life may deck his lofty doorposts with victorious palms.

Come now, young orator, and with your eloquence yet higher rise
Than all the honours of your forefathers, above the glories of ancestral praise,
And by your courage in the courts outshine the lustre of their military deeds.
So too in days of yore, when mighty Cicero was in his prime,
The laurels of victorious arms were forced to yield to toga'd eloquence.
But those same crowds, which once in dense array would pack the streets
To see the glorious triumphs of the Pisos' clan, are now the self-same crowds
Whose massed ranks pack the forum, when to protect the woe-begone defendants
Your voice sends out the arrows of its eloquence – and sets them free.

25–6: *peaceful glories ... warlike deeds*: a tacit admission that this Piso had no military accomplishments that could be praised.

30–1: *saves a citizen's life*: a crown made of oak leaves (*corona* civica) was traditionally awarded to a soldier who saved a comrade's life in battle. In 28/7 Augustus claimed the honour for saving lives by ending the civil wars and put the decoration on his door-posts. See Valerius Maximus, 2.8.7 (= LACTOR 17, H20). The honour is claimed by Gaius (coin – Sm 81), Claudius (coin – Sm 93/4), Nero (coin – Sm 106) all on accession. Also Sen, *de clem.* 1.26.5 = **G19**.

32: *young orator*: this may deliberately recall Nero who at 14 thanked Claudius in the senate for honours (Suet. *de rhet.* 1.6–7, *Nero* 7.2); two years later he represented Bononia (Tac. *Ann.* 12.58).

35: *Cicero*: (106–43 BC) Roman orator whose name was a byword for eloquence (Juvenal, *Satire* 10.114), and whose speeches were the subject of several commentaries by Asconius, a well-known writer under Nero.

36: *arms ... yield to toga'd eloquence*: echoes a frequently quoted (and ridiculed) line of Cicero's own poem on his consulship (Courtney, *Fragmentary Latin Poets,* Cicero 12 = Cic., *in Pis* 72–4).

*(**41–80**: The poet continues to praise Piso's ability to sway the feelings of judge and jury by his oratory in the law-courts. His speech in praise of the emperor, customary*

on attaining the consulship (an example survives in the form of Pliny's Panegyric), is also recalled and the poet protests his inability to do justice to Piso's eloquence!)

R37b Private eloquence (81–92)

So come, Calliope, and set aside his grave solemnity of rhetoric
And with me make your way to Piso's doors. For much there still remains
Amidst his household gods for you to find worthy of yet more praise.
For to that house the youth of Rome converges eagerly
To hearken to his words, when judges are weary of their tasks and Law's
Business ceases and the dreary quarrels of the courts fall silent.
For then he seems to exercise his mind with lighter weaponry,
And practises his skills by settling legal disputes artificially contrived.
Here, too, from Roman lips there flows an eloquence derived
From Greece, as in his speech Cecrops' Athens meets a worthy rival.
Naples, herself so eloquent, to this bears witness, she that built her walls
With auspices blessed by the Acidalian doves of Venus, while nearby
Cumae still reminds us of the Euboean arts of Chalcis.

90: Nero's eloquence in Greek, at age of 16, is attested by Tacitus (*Ann.* 12.58).

91: *Naples*: Nero's favourite venue for his artistic performances (Suet. *Nero* 20, 25.1). Chalcis, the chief city of the Greek island of Euboea had sent a colony to Cumae in Campania *c.* 740 BC. Cumae in turn had founded Naples (Neapolis) *c.* 600 BC.

***(93–108**: The poet continues to praise Piso's eloquence, style of delivery and personal qualities)*

R37c Piso's generosity as a *patronus* (109–119)

Most eloquent youth, pray tell me this: does any client steeped in poverty
Ever approach your threshold to receive a welcome less than generous,
Or by your kind indulgence fail to be delighted by an unexpected subsidy?
You honour and respect them all as equals, which is a gift more precious
Than any other gift that you could give. Your clients' fortunes move you not;
You are indifferent to their pedigree. One test alone applies to all – integrity.
Your clients do not suffer from the mocking innuendos of the proud;
Their grievances invite no snide and sudden sniggers from your friends.
Your friendship's single standard will embrace both high and low alike.
Rare is that house indeed, which does not spurn a friend fallen on evil days;
Rare is that house, where arrogance will not humiliate the humblest client.

109 *client*: a Roman *cliens* would be expected to pay his daily respects (*salutatio*) to his *patronus,* receiving *sportula* – a basket of food, later converted to a standard sum of money. Juvenal complains about the indignity felt by a client, *Satire* 1.94–128. Martial, 6.88, implies that a patron would expect to be called '*dominus*' (master).

***(120–132:** The poet elaborates on this theme by giving the contrasting picture of a client providing a target for ridicule)*

R37d The Piso household's range of pleasures and pastimes (133–39)

Everywhere the house echoes with varied sounds of its accomplished visitors;
The love of learning is its driving force. A crowd of crass and ignorant boors

Brings you no pleasure in a clientele, whose only skill (a wretched one at that)
Consists in processions to escort their patron, when once the riff-raff are removed.
Your pleasure lies in virtues varied and numerous; your own enthusiasm
Turns your heart to every kind of interest, whether the summons comes
From grave affairs of state or mere frivolities of lighter kinds.

***(140–161:** The poet defends recreational activities with a variety of parallels from life, nature, and the gods)*

R37e Playing the lyre (162–177)

A grave demeanour, wondrous to behold, attends you in public duties. Yet,
When gravity is briefly laid aside, your lighter charms are no less wonderful.
If it amuses you perhaps to improvise light-hearted songs with loose-knit verse,
How quickly and easily for your audience your page will draw down an Aonian song.
But if on the lyre or harp with fingers and ivory-fashioned plectrum you perform,
How sweet the song that follows, as if it flowed from Apollo's own tortoise-shell
And you had truly learned your skills from Phoebus himself, the master of musicians.
There is no need for shame to play the lyre, while peace reigns serene and public harmony
Prevails, and all the world is free from fear. There is no need for shame.
For so, men say, Apollo's instruments are played by those same hands
By which in fiercer times the bow is also drawn by that same god.
So, too, the story goes, savage Achilles was wont to play the lyre
Even while Hector, Priam's hero son, was bringing torches to a thousand ships
And war's grim trumpets shattered the beauty of those well-tuned strings.
The hero scion of Nereus plucked out sweet melodies with that same thumb
As that from which his spear, fashioned from Pelion's oaks, flew at his enemies.

166: *lyre*: for Nero's lyre-playing, see **Q13, Q17, T17** and, e.g. Suet, *Nero* 12.3–4, 21.1; 22.3; Dio 61.21; statues and coins *Nero* 25.2.

173: *Achilles*: Homer, *Iliad* 9.186–7.

R37f Other pastimes – boxing, ball games, board games etc. (178–194)

Sometimes, perhaps, your pleasure is to hurl a discus spinning from your shoulders,
Or in single combat you stand with limbs compacted to face your opponent's charge,
Now dodging his assault, now striving for an opening as he attacks. But then
With such nimble footwork you contrive to circle him, hither and thither
Weaving your manoeuvres, pressing upon him with oblique assaults as he withdraws.
Now with your right arm's lightning thrusts you test his defences to the front,
And then with an unexpected blow you strike him on the unprotected flank.

And yet the quickness of your footwork is no less, if it should please you
To return the flying ball or with a brilliant diving movement save it as it falls
And with an unexpected shot recover it and keep the ball in play.
Spectators are transfixed to watch the game, and suddenly the crowd of other players,
All sweating at their sports, as one abandon their own matches to observe the spectacle.
But if perhaps, when wearied by the weight of serious studies, you should choose
Instead of aimless idleness to turn your mind to intellectual games of skill,

Then on the open battlefield of the board a piece is moved with greater subtlety
And war is waged to the death with soldiers made of glass, in such a way that
White's pieces at first trap Black, but then Black turns the tables and in turn traps White.

179: *single combat*: the description could be of fencing, or boxing, a traditional part of Greek athletic festivals (and even public games at Pompeii – Cooley, *Pompeii* D8). Tacitus' moralising attack on the *Neronia* festival (*Annals* 14.20) decries the idea that Roman noblemen were forced to 'pollute the stage in performing speeches and songs. All that is left is for them to strip off and put on boxing gloves and train in that sort of combat rather than in military service and arms.'

186: *flying ball*: for contemporary references to various sorts of ball games, see Seneca, *Benefits* 2.17.3–4, using a sporting analogy; Petronius, *Satyricon* 27, satirising Trimalchio who gets a new ball each time it falls to the ground.

191: *games of skill*: the poet refers to the Roman equivalent of chess/draughts, *ludus latrunculorum*. Seneca, *Epistles* 106.11 and 117.30 treats 'playing with pawns' as the ultimately trivial pastime, but see also *Tranquillity* 14.7 = **T8**. Ovid claims that poetry had been written on the game's tactics (*Tristia* 2.477–80)

(195–261: *The poet provides further details of Piso's skill at 'chess' (195–208), before again protesting his inability to do justice to his subject's excellent qualities (209–215). Finally the poet begs for Piso's artistic patronage, or, as he absurdly puts it, to be Maecenas to the poet's Virgil or Horace (216–261)).*

[*Laus Pisonis – Panegyric on Piso* (in Duff, *Minor Latin Poets*)]

R38 The Death of Silius Italicus (AD *c.* 25–101)

[1] The news has just come through that Silius Italicus is dead, by voluntary starvation. [2] The cause of death was his own ill-health, since he had developed an incurable tumour, which became increasingly intolerable until he finally and irrevocably decided to end his life. That life had been entirely happy and successful right up till his final days, except for the loss of the younger of his two sons. But he left the elder and more talented one getting on very well and already of consular rank. [3] He had done some damage to his reputation under Nero, since it was believed that he had volunteered to act as an informer. But as a friend of Vitellius he always conducted himself with a genial discretion; as proconsul of Asia he won a great reputation, and in a distinguished retirement he fully purged the disgrace he had earned by his previous indiscretion. [4] He was a pillar of the establishment, whose lack of power spared him the jealousy of detractors. He became a centre of attention, a much respected figure, who spent many hours reclining on his couch, in a room always crowded with visitors, who did not visit out of deference to his position. Whenever he could spare the time from his writing, his days were occupied with intellectual discussions.

[5] His poems were the product of a meticulous attention to detail rather than poetic talent; indeed he sometimes gave readings of them so as to assess the public reaction. [6] More recently his increasing age persuaded him to leave Rome and retire to Campania, and nothing thereafter persuaded him to leave it – not even the arrival of a new emperor, [7] a fact which is greatly to the credit of the emperor for allowing such a liberty, and no less credit on Silius for having the nerve to take advantage of it. [8] He was an avid art collector, spending with an extravagance bordering on the offensive. He owned a number of properties in the same area, but grew rapidly bored with each of his previous purchases in his enthusiasm for the latest acquisition. But all of them were packed with books, statues, and portraits, which to him were not merely

possessions but cherished objects of veneration. This was true, above all, of his busts of Virgil, whose birthday he would celebrate with even more devotion than his own, especially at Naples, where he would visit his tomb as if it were a shrine.

[9] Amid such peaceful surrounding he died, at the age of seventy five, cosseted rather than genuinely frail. He was Nero's last appointment to the consulship, and appropriately enough, he was the last to die of all the consuls appointed by Nero.

[Pliny the Younger, *Letters* 3.7.1–9]

Titus Catius Asconius Silius Italicus is known as the author of the longest surviving Latin epic poem , the *Punica* or (Second) *Punic War.* Despite being a *novus homo* he was *consul ordinarius* for AD 68. Pliny's letter allows us to attribute this to services as a prosecutor and, perhaps, to his artistic interests. Martial *Epigrams* 7.63 also mentions his consulship in AD 68. He played a role in negotiations between Vitellius and Vespasian's agents in 69 (Tac. *Hist.* 3.75).

R39 Calivisius Sabinus buys educated slaves to seem educated himself

Seneca exhorts Lucilius to continue to strive for (Stoic) virtue, work that allows no delegation.

Calvisius Sabinus was a rich man of our own times. He had the inheritance and the intellect of a freedman. I have never seen a man who less deserved his prosperity. His memory was so bad that he would sometimes forget the names of Odysseus, or Achilles, or Priam … nevertheless he wanted to appear well-educated. [6] So he devised this short-cut: he bought slaves at huge expense, one who knew Homer by heart, another for Hesiod; in addition he assigned one slave to each of the nine lyric poets. It is no surprise that he paid a lot of money for them: if he did not find them, he had them specially made. After this household was ready, he began to annoy his guests. He would keep them at the foot of his couch and from time to time ask them for verses for him to repeat, but then forget them in the middle of a word. [7] When he remarked that each slave cost him one hundred thousand sesterces, Satellius replied, "You could have bought as many bookcases for less."

[Seneca, *Moral Epistles* 27.5–7]

Calvisius Sabinus is clearly a rich man, not a freedman, given Seneca's insulting comparison of his wealth and culture to that of rich and vulgar freedmen. Similarities with Petronius' portrait of Trimalchio in the *Cena Trimalchionis* show what Seneca's readers would have understood by the comparison. (For the resentment felt towards rich and powerful imperial freedmen in particular, see *Ep.* 47.9.) Roman education commonly started with Greek authors and was bilingual. Not being able to remember characters in Homer, a staple of ancient education at all levels, shows his inadequacy at its worst. The nine lyric poets are Alcaeus, Sappho, Stesichorus, Ibycus, Bacchylides, Simonides, Alcman, Anacreon, and Pindar. The cost of these slaves can be compared to the capital of 400,000 sesterces required of a Roman of equestrian status.

MEDICINE AND LAW: R40–R45

Medical writings from Cornelius Celsus, Pedanius Dioscorides and Scribonius Largus survive from this period. Much of Pliny's *Natural History*, books 20–32 is concerned with medicinal uses of natural products.

R40 Scribonius Largus

For as soon as you could, you did not allow your sense of loyalty to me to lapse, but passed my Latin writings on medicine to our god Caesar; I had offered these to you, so that you might read them first and tell me, in sincerity, what you thought.

[Scribonius Largus, *Compositiones,* prologue]

Scribonius Largus is here dedicating his *Compositiones* (Prescriptions) to Callistus, freedman of Claudius, who had secured the emperor's patronage for his protégé, including Scribonius accompanying Claudius to Britain in AD 43 (*Compositiones* 163). Despite the mockery of Petronius, *Satyricon,* freedmen did become patrons of writers such as Statius (*e.g.* **S32**).

R41 Prominent doctors

I shall not mention many very famous doctors including the likes of Cassius, Calpetanus, Arruntius, and Rubrius. Their annual salaries from the *principes* were two hundred and fifty thousand sesterces. Quintus Stertinius regarded being satisfied with five hundred thousand sesterces *per annum* as a special favour to the *principes*, since a count of his town houses showed that his city practice was worth six hundred thousand. Claudius Caesar lavished the same fees on Stertinius' brother, whose estate, though severely reduced by public works beautifying Naples, was still worth 300 million sesterces to his heir. Of his contemporaries, only Arruntius was worth as much. Then Vettius Valens rose to prominence, famed equally for his adultery with Messalina, wife of Claudius Caesar, and his eloquence. His followers and power enabled him to found a new movement. That same generation switched over to Thessalus in the principate of Nero. He abolished all received wisdom, feverishly denouncing doctors of every age, with the sort of good sense and temperament perfectly exemplified by his monument on the Appian Way commemorating himself as 'Champion Physician'.

[Pliny, *Natural History* 29.7–8]

Cassius is mentioned by Cornelius Celsus, who wrote under Tiberius as 'the most talented doctor of our age, who died recently' *On Medicine, proem* 69. The next 3 are unknown. Stertinius of Cos: **R42–R44**.

R42 Stertinius Xenophon, imperial physician, honoured by Cos

[... Gaius Stertinius] Xenophon, son of Heraclitus, of the voting-tribe Cornelia, chief physician of the gods Augusti and in charge of Greek correspondence; he had been military tribune and prefect of engineers and was decorated with a golden crown and spear in the triumph over the Britons; son of his people, ~~devoted friend of Claudius devoted friend of Nero~~, devoted friend of Caesar, of Augustus, of Rome, and of his city, benefactor of his fatherland, chief priest of the gods and priest for life of the Augusti and of Asclepius, Hygeia and Epione; when Marcus Septicius Rufus, son of Marcus, and Ariston, son of Philocles, devoted friends of the Caesars, were temple treasurers.

[Greek: Smallwood 262 = *IGRRP* IV 1086]

This honour was set up by the people of Cos, and illustrates how those who served the emperor had to adapt to changing fortunes. The word in Greek meaning 'devoted friend of Nero' (*philonerona*), originally read 'devoted friend of Claudius' (*philoclaudion*), but this was erased and reinscribed. In turn, however, the word for 'devoted friend of Nero', was also subsequently erased. Xenophon must have derived some of his professional kudos as physician from his home of Cos, which was famous for its sanctuary of Asclepius and Hygeia. From other sources we know that Xenophon had petitioned Claudius successfully in 53 to gain exemption from taxation for the people of Cos (Tacitus, *Ann.* 12.61.2). He was reputedly involved in Claudius' murder (Tac., *Ann.* 12.67.2–4).

R43 Stertinius Xenophon's dedication to Asclepius, Cos

Gaius Stertinius Xenophon, benefactor of his fatherland and priest for life, dedicated this to Asclepius Caesar, good god.

[Greek: Smallwood 147 = *IGRRP* IV 1053]

R44 Xenophon's brother, Cos

Tiberius Claudius Cleonymus, son of Heraclitus, of the voting-tribe Quirina, the brother of Gaius Stertinius Xenophon, having served in Germany as military tribune of legion XXII Primigenia, having twice been 'monarch' and having often acted as ambassador on behalf of his fatherland to the Augusti; Claudia Phoebe honoured her husband and benefactor for his virtue and kindness.

[Greek: Smallwood 289 = *IGRRP* IV 1060]

The post of 'monarch' refers to the chief magistracy of Cos.

R45 Prominent jurists

Therefore Sabinus was allowed by Tiberius Caesar to state legal opinions in public. He was admitted to the equestrian order when quite old, in fact almost fifty. He had no great private means but was mostly supported by his pupils. Gaius Cassius Longinus succeeded him. He was the son of Tubero's daughter, who was grand-daughter to Servius Sulpicius. So he knew Servius Sulpicius as his great-grandfather. Cassius Longinus was consul with Surdinus under Tiberius, but was of the greatest influence in the state right until the emperor [Nero] exiled him from Rome. He was exiled to Sardinia, but recalled by Vespasian and died in his reign.

[Digest 1.2.2.50–2 = Pomponius, *Introduction to Law*]

Masurius Sabinus, see **A1** and *OCD*. Gaius Cassius Longinus, cos. AD 30, see B30 and Tac. *Ann.* 12.11–2, 13.41, 14.42–5, 16.7, 16.9. Servius Sulpicius Rufus (cos 51 BC), a leading lawyer of Cicero's day.

SECTION S

SLAVES AND FREEDMEN

'Slaves, obey your earthly masters with fear and trembling.' (St Paul)

Introduction

Roman society was completely dependent on slavery, especially so the upper classes, who provide the great majority of our evidence for treatment of slaves (including legal sources). Slaves who had saved hard to provide a tombstone for themselves did not waste money describing their treatment. Slaves were part of the Roman *familia*. Their treatment will have ranged from that of a 'living tool' (Aristotle, *Politics* 1.4) to a genuine member of the family, suckling on the same breast as imperial babies (**S7**). In most cases, the relationship was probably based on fear (on both sides). The quotation above comes from St Paul's *Letters to the Ephesians* 6.5. The murder of the city prefect, Pedanius Secundus in AD 61, produces a panic-stricken debate in the senate (Tac. *Ann.* 14.42–45, compare **S3**); arming one's slaves was the ultimate crime (*RG* 25.1 (on Sextus Pompey); Tac. *Ann.* 4.27). Seneca wrote (*Ben.* 1.24.1 = **G18**) that a proposal that would have made slaves wear clothes to mark them out was rejected out of fear that slaves would be aware of the comparatively low number of free people. Within Italy as a whole, there may have been about 1 slave for every 3 free people (a modern estimate, *OCD* under 'slavery: Roman').

Most Romans must consciously or unconsciously have justified their reliance on slavery by the idea that slaves were naturally inferior (Aristotle's justification in *Politics* 1). Hence their furious indignation that slaves (as literary writers often refer to freedmen) should achieve positions of wealth, influence and power in the imperial household. (The same reasons explain why they are indignant at the power of imperial women.) Injury is added to insult when imperial freedmen begin to hold positions to which members of the upper classes might aspire (e.g. Anicetus as Nero's prefect of the fleet: a position later held by Pliny).

This section deals with laws enacted concerning slaves (**S1–S4**), and then with some examples of imperial slaves, arranged roughly chronologically (**S5–S14**). The same pattern is then reproduced as regards freedmen: laws (**S15–S17**) and famous imperial freedmen (**S18–S32**). It will be seen that Claudius figures prominently throughout the section. He was notoriously fond of the courts (Suet. *Claud.* 14–15; **F12**), and spent a busy term as censor (Tac. *Ann.* 11.13, 11.15, Suet. *Claud.* 16). Levick sees in his legislation an advance in the treatment of slaves (Levick, *Claudius,* 123). Claudius, however, was more notorious for the power and wealth of freedmen during his reign. Freedmen had reached important positions under Augustus (e.g. Licinus in Gaul, see LACTOR 17, T40–T42; and freedmen get the last mention in Suetonius' biography of Augustus, *Aug.* 101.4), but it is clear that freedmen reached their greatest influence under Claudius. However exaggerated Suetonius' description 'most of what he did was at the instigation of his wives and freedmen' (*Claud.* 25.5), Dio 60.2.4 'He, more clearly than any other emperor, was dominated by slaves and by women' may be right, if only because by a generation later, equestrians were willing to take many of their positions. For a brief but definitive account, of imperial freedmen see Millar, *ERW* III.4.

S1 Claudius decrees that a sick, abandoned slave be given his freedom

By a decree of Divus Claudius, a slave, abandoned by his master because of a serious infirmity gains his freedom.

[Digest 40.8.2 = Modestinus, *Guidelines* 6]

S2 More details on freedom given to abandoned slaves

But we know that this was instituted in the former custom of Latin freedmen under an edict of Divus Claudius. That is, if anyone throws out of his home into a public place a slave of his, dangerously ill, taking no care of him nor entrusting him to anyone else, despite having the clear opportunity of sending him to a guest-house or helping him however he can, if he lacks the means to look after him himself; a slave of this sort retains the aforementioned Latin freedom, and the man who left him to die receives back his possessions when he does die.

[Justinian's Legal Code: CJ.7.6.1.3]

Suetonius, *Claud.* 25.2 adds the details that many sick slaves had been abandoned on the island of Aesculapius in the Tiber by owners wishing to avoid the costs of looking after them. See also Dio 60.29.7a. 'Latin freedmen' or 'Junian Latins' were originally slaves freed but without the full legal conditions of freedom (e.g. being over 30) being met. For further details, see LACTOR 17, pages 370–1.

S3 Slaves of a murdered master liable to torture and execution

Title: Concerning the senatorial decrees of Silanus and Claudius: about people whose wills should not be unsealed.

No house can otherwise be safe unless slaves be forced to take responsibility, under penalty of death, for guarding their masters from enemies both inside and outside the house. Therefore senatorial decrees were introduced concerning the public interrogation of the household of murder victims.

[Digest 29.5.0 and 29.5.1 preface = Ulpian, *Commentary on the Praetor's Edict* 50]

The relevance of the title in the *Digest* is that interrogation of slaves should take place before the wills of murder victims can be unsealed: in other words be given top priority. No such cases are known under Claudius, but 400 slaves were executed after the murder in AD 61 of city prefect Pedanius Secundus (Tac. *Ann.* 14.42–45). Claudius' edict reinforced an earlier senatorial decree.

S4 Claudian decree of the senate, AD 52

Tacitus describes Claudius raising discussion in the senate about punishing women involved in sexual relationships with slaves (*Annals* 12.53.1). Claudius attributed these proposals to Pallas: see **S29** for the senate's extravagant response. The decree remained in place until the time of Justinian who repealed it.

a) Look at the Claudian decree of the senate to see that a female Roman citizen who had intercourse with the slave of another person, and by the consent of that owner, would remain free herself as a result of that agreement, but the child would be a slave.

[Gaius, *Institutes* 1.84]

b) Loss of status is also suffered by women who become the slaves of the owners of slaves with whom they have had intercourse against the clearly stated wishes of the owner, under the Claudian decree of the senate.

[Gaius, *Institutes* 1.160]

c) There was, as a result of a Claudian decree of the senate, another pitiful way for an entire estate to change hands: a free woman, mad with love for a slave would, through the decree of the senate, lose her freedom, and her property as well.

[Justinian, *Institutes* 3.12.1]

S5 Slave-administrator of a provincial treasury

To Musicus Scurranus, slave of Tiberius Caesar Augustus, steward of the Gallic treasury of the province of Lugdunensis, from his slaves who were with him in Rome when he died, well-deserving man: Venustus, wholesale trader; Decimianus, in charge of household expenses; Dicaeus, secretary; Mutatus, secretary; Creticus, secretary; Agathopus, doctor; Epaphra, financial aide; Primio, in charge of clothing; Communis, personal attendant; Pothus, manservant; Tiasus, cook; Facilis, manservant; Anthus, financial aide; Hedylus, personal attendant; Firmus, cook; Secunda.

[*ILS* 1514 = Sherk no.178D]

This epitaph was found in a *columbarium* at Rome. Although slaves were prohibited by law from owning any possessions of their own, this imperial slave clearly amassed considerable wealth through serving as financial officer in Gallia Lugdunensis, so much so that his epitaph is set up by a whole sequence of his slaves, the range of which would not look out of place in the household of the emperor himself!

S6 Slave eye-doctor

Thyrius Celadianus, slave of Tiberius Caesar Augustus, eye-doctor, dutiful to his parents, lived 30 years, is buried here in perpetuity.

[*CIL* VI 8909]

This epitaph was found at Rome. Celadianus had only just reached the minimum age for manumission.

S7 Household slave of Antonia Minor

Communio household slave of Antonia Augusta, lived for two years, ten months, fellow-nursling of Drusus son of Blandus.

[*CIL* VI 16057 + *AE* (2005) 106]

This epitaph records that the household slave Communio shared a wet-nurse with Drusus, son of Rubellius Blandus and Tiberius' granddaughter Julia, who thus had the distinction of being great-grandson of both Antonia and Tiberius. The wet-nurse in question was probably Communio's mother, herself also likely to have been a slave in Antonia's household. The situation offers a rare glimpse of the links between two imperial households created through the sharing of staff. It may also illustrate Antonia's intervention in the affairs of junior members of the imperial family. The epitaph dates from AD *c*.37, when Antonia was named Augusta by Gaius.

S8 Slave librarian

Alexander Pylaemenianus, slave of Gaius Caesar Augustus Germanicus, in charge of the Greek library of the temple of Apollo, lived 30 years.

[*CIL* VI 5188]

This epitaph is from Rome. It commemorates the imperial slave who worked in the Greek library established by Augustus in the temple of Palatine Apollo. Pylaemenianus had only just reached the minimum age for manumission.

S9 Public slave at shrine of Divus Augustus

To the departed spirits. To Claudia Lachne, freedwoman of Antonia: Philippus Rustianus, public slave of the shrine of Divus Augustus, made (this) for his dearest wife and for himself.

[*ILS* 4992 = Smallwood 187]

This epitaph from Rome commemorates a freedwoman of Claudius' daughter, Claudia Antonia.

S10 Slave in charge of Messallina's jewels

Amoenus, slave of Messallina, wife of Tiberius Claudius Caesar, in charge of jewels.

[*ILS* 1781]

This epitaph is inscribed upon a columbarium plaque at Rome.

S11 Slave wet-nurse of Britannicus

To Claudia Pthonge, nurse of Britannicus. Aphnius, secretary of Caesar Augustus, to his 'wife', deserving the very best from him.

[Sherk no.47A = Smallwood 188]

This epitaph is inscribed upon a small marble slab from Rome. Slaves could not legally be married, and so Claudia Pthonge is named as *contubernalis* rather than full wife.

S12 Slave-seamstress

Extricata, slave of Octavia, daughter of Augustus, seamstress, lived 20 years.

[*ILS* 1788]

This epitaph was found in Rome and is now in Warwick Castle.

S13 A family of imperial slaves and freedmen

Of Tiberius Claudius Avitus, freedman of Augustus, invitations-officer, and of Titus Aelius Theodotus, freedman of Augustus, judicial-assistant, and of Scetasia, slave of Octavia: Antonia Rhodine, their mother, made (this) for her dearest children.

[*ILS* 1697 = Smallwood 180]

This epitaph from Rome shows the intertwining of imperial households in the distribution of one mother's children across different families.

S14 Slave in charge of furniture in Nero's Golden House

Eumolpus, slave of Caesar, in charge of the furniture of the Golden House, and Claudia Pallas, his daughter, set (this) up as a gift to Sun and Moon.

[*ILS* 1774]

This dedication is a marble altar, from Rome, with a portrait of Sun on the front (sometimes considered to bear the features of Nero himself), and a libation dish and jug carved on its sides. It is an expensive item for a slave to have afforded. Imperial slaves were very much in a superior class of their own. His daughter, by contrast, appears to have been given her freedom, to judge from her name.

S15 Claudius returns a freedman to slavery

Divus Claudius ordered that a freedman, who was proven to have sent informers to carry out an investigation for him of his patron's status, should become his patron's slave.

[Digest 37.14.5 preface = Marcianus 13 inst]

This single case seems to form the basis of Suetonius' statement (*Claud.* 25.1) that freedmen proving ungrateful to a former master reverted to slavery.

S16 Patron's rights over freedmen can be bequeathed to his heir

In a senatorial decree passed in the time of Claudius, when Vellaeus Rufus and Osterius Scapula were consuls, on assigning freedmen, it is stated in the following words: if anyone with two or more legitimate children under his authority, has indicated, with regard to his freedman or freedwoman, which of his children he wished to be patron of the freedman or freedwoman, then that child would be the sole patron or patroness, whenever the man who had manumitted the freedman or freedwoman – in his lifetime or by his will – had passed away, exactly as if freedom had been granted by him or her. Furthermore, if that child had passed away without leaving any children, then all the legal rights of the manumittor's other children would be preserved just as if the parent had made no indication as to the freedman or freedwoman.

[Digest 38.4.1 preface = Ulpian, *Commentary on Civil Law* 14]

For this reform see Levick, *Claudius* 123–4, number 4. Vellaeus and Osterius were consuls at an unknown date between AD 41 and 45.

S17 Freedman's property reverts to former master

Later, when Lupus and Largus were consuls [AD 42] the senate decided that the property of Latin freedmen should go the person who freed them; then, in order of proximity, to his descendants, unless specifically disinherited; then, as under the old law, to the heirs of the persons who had freed them.

[Gaius, *Institutes* 3.63]

S18 Honorific decree for a freedman of Augustus, Veii, AD 26

When the council of 100 of the *municipium* of Augustan Veii met in Rome at the temple of Venus the Ancestress, they decided unanimously that, until the decree should be written down, in the meantime, Gaius Julius Gelos, freedman of Divus Augustus, who has at all times not only helped the *municipium* of Veii with his advice and goodwill, but also wanted it to be celebrated because of his investment and through his son, be allowed to be decreed the most fitting honour: that he be included in the body of the *Augustales* just as if he enjoyed that honour, and be allowed to sit on an honorific seat of his own among the *Augustales* at all the games in our *municipium*, and to take part in all public feasts among the town councillors. They also decided that no tax imposed by the *municpium* of Augustan Veii should be exacted from him or his children.

There were present: Gaius Scaevius Curiatius, Lucius Peperna Priscus, duumvirs; Marcus Flavius Rufus, quaestor; Titus Vettius Rufus, quaestor; Marcus Tarquitius Saturninus, Lucius Maecilius Scrupus, Lucius Favonius Lucanus, Gnaeus Octavius Sabinus, Titus Sempronius Gracchus, Publius Acuvius, son of Publius, of the voting-tribe Tromentina, Gaius Veianius Maximus, Titus Tarquitius Rufus, Gaius Julius Merula. Transacted in the consulship of Gaetulicus and Calvisius Sabinus.

[EJ 333 = *ILS* 6579]

This marble tablet was found at Veii, and records honours decreed to an imperial freedman in AD 26. Given that freedmen were excluded from serving as town councillors, the decree has to find other ways of honouring someone who has in effect acted as the town's patron. It illustrates how an imperial freedman could continue to exercise influence even after his emperor's death. It is unclear why the councillors met at Rome, about 10 miles from Veii, but this may explain why only thirteen of them are listed as having participated in the meeting.

S19 Imperial freedman, sub-prefect of fleet at Alexandria

To Tiberius Julius Xanthus, freedman of the emperor, imperial official of Tiberius Caesar and of Divus Claudius, and sub-prefect of the fleet at Alexandria: Atellia Prisca his wife and Lamyrus his freedman, his heirs. He lived for 90 years.

[*ILS* 2816 = Sherk 48D]

This epitaph was found at Rome. It is possible that his life-span of ninety years reflects age-rounding, and may not be an entirely accurate representation of his real age.

S20 A freedmen gets 'adopted' by Claudius

From Cyprus, this type of plane tree was imported to Italy when Claudius was *princeps*, to the estate near Rome of an extremely rich eunuch from Thessaly. He had been the freedman of Marcellus Aeserninus, but had got himself adopted as a freedmen of the emperor for the power it gave him.

[Pliny, *Natural History* 12.12]

M. Claudius Marcellus Aeserninus: grandson of C. Asinius Pollio, friend of Augustus and patron of Virgil. Aeserninus was well-known as an orator. Praetor in AD 19, he refused to represent Piso on trial over the death of Germanicus (Tac. *Ann.* 3.11.2).

S21 Freedmen of Claudius, director of library studies

Tiberius Claudius Lemnius, freedman of Divus Claudius Augustus, director of library studies.

[Rome: *ILS* 1682 = Sherk 48E]

S22 Freedmen procurator

To the departed spirits of Tiberius Claudius Saturninus, freedman of Augustus, procurator of the Five-Percent Tax on Inheritances in the province of Achaia, Saturnina his wife made (this monument).

[*ILS* 1546 = Sherk 48F]

This epitaph from Rome illustrates the integration of imperial freedmen into important financial roles within the administration of the provinces. The advantage therein for the emperor was their absolute loyalty and dependency upon him.

S23 Wealth of Claudian freedman, treasurer in Spain

In the principate of Claudius, a slave of his, Drusillanus, called Rotundus, his treasurer of Nearer Spain, had a silver dish weighing five hundred pounds, which had required a special workshop to be built first, and eight other dishes in the set, each of 250 pounds. I wonder how many of his fellow slaves carried them in, and who ate off them.

[Pliny, *Natural History* 33.145]

The slave's name indicates he must have belonged to Julia Drusilla (Caligula's sister).

S24 The duties of an imperial freedman

[6.5] A great fortune is a form of extreme slavery. It deprives you of all freedom of choice. There are so many thousands of applicants to be given an audience, so many thousands of petitions to be dealt with. There is a vast pile of business pouring in from all over the world that must be examined carefully so that it may be brought to the attention of our illustrious emperor in due order. As I have said, you may not weep, so that you can be free to heed the lamentations of others, who are in danger and begging for the pity of our most beneficent Caesar. If you weep yourself, you must dry your own tears.

[Seneca, *On Consolation, to Polybius* 6.5]

Suetonius tells us that Polybius was one of Claudius' freedmen who exerted excessive influence, and was often to be seen walking between the consuls (*Claud.* 28). He gives his post as *a studiis* (presumably, a literary adviser), which makes sense, for Claudius wrote historical and antiquarian works and Polybius was the author, as Seneca tells us in this work (8.2–3; 11.5), of translations of Homer into Latin and of Virgil into Greek and other works. This passage seems to indicate that he was serving as *a libellis*, perhaps at the same time. This makes him a suitable recipient for what is a kind of plea by Seneca for recall from from his banishment in Corsica (13.2–4; compare 2.1; 18.9) in the guise of a consolation to Polybius on the death of his brother. The relation of this work to that mentioned by Dio 61.10.2 is disputed.

S25 The wealth of Claudius' freedmen

We have more recently known many freed slaves of even greater wealth [than Marcus Licinius Crassus], including three at once in the principate of Claudius a short while ago: Callistus, Pallas and Narcissus.

[Pliny, *Natural History* 33.134]

Pliny has been talking about the proverbial wealth of Marcus Licinius Crassus (mid-first century BC). Suetonius reports a joke that Claudius would be wealthy if Pallas and Narcissus took him into partnership (*Claud.*28). Pallas turned down a gift of 15 million sesterces from the senate – Pliny, *Letters* 8.6 = **S29**; Tac. *Ann.* 12.53, reporting his wealth as 300 million sesterces. He was allegedly killed by Nero for his wealth (Tac. *Ann.* 14.65). Callistus was freed by Caligula and became *a libellis* of Claudius in AD 47. Narcissus' fortune, according to Dio 60.34.6 was 400 million sesterces. These three all feature in Tac. *Ann.* 11.29 and 12.1–2 – the debate about Claudius' new wife.

S26 Callistus' luxury

Later use of onyx stone varied considerably: the four small columns which Cornelius Balbus placed in his theatre were regarded as marvels; yet we have seen 30 larger ones in the banqueting hall which Callistus, the freedman of Claudius, well-known for his influence, had built for himself.

[Pliny, *Natural History* 36.60]

Callistus, freedman of Gaius, then *a libellis* (in charge of petitions) under Claudius, and one of his three most influential freedmen, see **S25**. Cornelius Balbus (cos 40 BC) dedicated his theatre in Rome in 13 BC.

S27 Callistus refuses entry to his former master

(Seneca is encouraging Lucilius to continue to treat his slaves with humanity, not cruelty.)

I have seen standing on the doorstep of Callistus that man's former master: he who put a placard on him and who put him up for sale amongst his unwanted property being shut out while others were welcomed. That slave, thrown into the first batch on which the auctioneer warms up his voice, paid back his master, and in turn rejected his master, and judged him not good enough for his house. The master sold Callistus, but how Callistus paid him back!

[Seneca, *Epistles* 47.9]

C. Julius Callistus became a freedman of Gaius and then Claudius, after being sold off by an earlier master, who, as Seneca makes clear, did not think much of him. He was already politically influential under Gaius (Dio 59. 19.6), but joined the successful conspiracy against him. Under Claudius he succeeded Polybius as *a libellis* (in charge of petitions) and was one of the three most powerful freedman secretaries, along with Pallas and Narcissus (**S25**; Tac. *Ann.* 11.29, 12.1–2; Dio 60.30.6b). For his house, see above, **S26**.

S28 Pallas' honorary praetorship

(Discussion of white earth leads Pliny to the custom of feet being whitened with chalk at a slave auction and to freedmen.)

We have even seen such men (former slaves) reach such positions of power as to witness honorary praetorships being decreed by the senate at the command of Agrippina, wife of Claudius Caesar, and all but sent back with triumphal *fasces* to the place they came from with chalked feet.

[Pliny, *Natural History,* 35.201]

S29 The senate honours Pallas

Pliny had written to Montanus about seeing the monument to Pallas on the road to Tibur, less than a mile from Rome (*Letter* 7.29). There Pliny refers to Pallas as 'filth, dirt and a worthless slave' while insisting that he regards the monument as laughable rather than outrageous. This letter sees him working himself up into a fine state of snobbish indignation, shared by his uncle (**S28**) and Tacitus (*Annals* 12.53 – placed with deliberate irony immediately after a note about the emperor praising those who withdrew from the senatorial order because of financial difficulties). The occasion was Pallas drafting the legislation, **S4**. But Scipio's comments in Tacitus, and the decree itself (**S29d**) make it clear that it was Pallas' whole service which was being praised (the honour may have marked 10 years of service). Sherwin-White, *The Letters of Pliny,* Oxford 1965 suggests that Pliny's generation of senators was more afraid of competition from freedmen than the senators of Claudius' time. Narcissus had previously been given the insignia of a *quaestor* (a rank below a *praetor:* Tac. *Ann.* 11.38).

S29a Pallas' monument

[6.1] You should have learned from my last letter that I had been looking recently at a monument to Pallas, which has the following inscription.

To this man, in recognition of his loyalty and devotion to his patrons, the senate decreed the honour of praetorian insignia and a grant of 15 million sesterces. He was satisfied with the honour alone.

[2] After that I decided that it was worth researching the actual terms of the senate's decree. I found it so extravagantly effusive, that it made the utter arrogance of the inscription itself seem modestly restrained to the point of reticence. A combination of all the great heroes of the past, the heroes of the campaigns in Africa, Achaia, Numantia, and also more recent commanders like Marius, Sulla, and Pompey (to name but a few), all these together would not be a match for the fame of Pallas.

The praetorship was the elected magistracy ranking immediately below the consulship. A praetor would already have entered the senate and would be eligible after his year in office to govern a minor public province. Freedmen such as Pallas would, of course, not be eligible for the office: hence the offer of praetorian *insignia*. Pliny was praetor in AD 93 or 95. As a member of the senate, Pliny would have found the decree in the senatorial archives, mentioned by Tacitus, *Annals* 5.4.1, 15.74.3. Marius, Sulla, and Pompey were all very famous politicians and generals of the Roman republic.

S29b Pliny condemns the senate for their decree

[3] As for the senators who passed that decree, they must have been joking; or else they were simply pathetic – I am not sure which: joking, if that were fit and proper for the senate; pathetic, but no man could be so pathetic as to be forced to such indignity. So perhaps they were driven by ambition and a desire for promotion? But anyone who wants to win promotion at the price of his own and the state's dishonour must be off his head, given that it was a state where the greatest honour available for those in high office was to be first to offer compliments to Pallas.

[4] I shall say nothing of the fact that praetorian insignia were offered to Pallas, a slave – after all, the offer was made by slaves; I shall say nothing of the fact that they voted for him to be compelled, not just encouraged, to wear a gold ring, since it would not do at all for someone of praetorian rank to wear an iron ring, like a slave. [5] These are insignificant matters, which can safely be ignored. But what must never be forgotten and stands as an unexpurgated stain upon the senate's record to this very day, is this: that in the name of Pallas, I repeat, in the name of Pallas, our own senate passed a motion of thanks to the emperor for having selected him for such a signal honour, and for so graciously allowing the senate an opportunity to express their goodwill towards him. [6] Of course the senate could never find a more noble deed than to show their gratitude publicly to Pallas in an adequate manner!

On rings and associated ranks, see Pliny 33.32 = **U26**. Pliny exaggerates: the offer of *insignia* did not make Pallas actually of praetorian rank: nor, of course, was he a slave.

S29c The senate's decree I

The senate's motion continued as follows:

" ...that Pallas, to whom every member of this body acknowledges the utmost possible debt of gratitude, should receive a well-deserved reward for such outstanding loyalty and devotion to duty."

Anyone would think that he had expanded the boundaries of our empire, or brought our armies safely back to Rome. [7] It goes on:

"Whereas no more welcome occasion for generosity could be offered to the senate and people of Rome than the facility to enhance the resources of this prudent and loyal guardian of the imperial purse, ..."

So that was the senate's desire, the greatest possible source of delight for the people of Rome, the most popular basis for an outburst of public extravagance – to boost Pallas' private bank balances by draining the public purse.

[8] And what followed? It was the stated will of the senate that he should be voted a grant from the exchequer of 15 million sesterces. And, since everybody understood how unthinkable such an idea must be to Pallas, it begged the emperor all the more earnestly, as father of the state, to compel him to yield to the senate's wishes. [9] In fact the only thing missing was a decision to turn the whole thing into official business, with a delegation begging Pallas to accept the senate's proposal, and for Caesar himself to act as patron and spokesman, personally requesting Pallas to abandon such overweening self-restraint in rejecting that sum of 15 million sesterces. But reject it he did. It was the only possible way of expressing his contempt for such a vast offering of public money even more forcibly than by accepting it.

15 million sesterces: a man had to be worth at least one million sesterces to be a senator. Pliny spent 3 million on a single estate (*Letters* 3.19.7) and probably had an overall fortune of 20 million. Tacitus says Pallas was then worth 300 million: Dio that he was worth 400 million at his death (62.14.3).

S29d The senate's decree II

[10] The senate greeted even this rebuff with a kind of querulous flattery, complimenting him in the following terms.

"*Inasmuch as our most excellent emperor, the father of our state, has acceded to the request of Pallas, and consented to annul that section of the resolution pertaining to the grant of 15 million sesterces from the exchequer, the senate hereby declares that, notwithstanding its own voluntary and justifiable decision to vote this sum and other honours to the said Pallas in recognition of his outstanding loyalty and commitment, nevertheless, in this matter also it has deferred to the wishes of their emperor, whose will in this as in all matters it is blasphemy to resist."*

[11] Picture, if you will, Pallas in effect vetoing a decree of the senate by seeking to limit his own honours and refusing a grant of 15 million sesterces as excessive, while accepting the insignia of praetorian status, as if that were a somewhat lesser accolade. Picture, if you will, Caesar deferring to his own freedman's request, or rather his command, since when a freedman issues a request to his patron in the senate, it is surely tantamount to a command. [12] Picture, if you will, the senate tying itself up in knots to suggest that, amongst its other honours, it had voluntarily and justifiably decided on this supreme accolade to Pallas, and that it would have insisted upon it, had it not felt constrained to defer to the emperor's wishes because it would have been blasphemous to resist them. In short, to prevent Pallas carrying off his booty of 15 million sesterces from the treasury, required an act of massive self-restraint by Pallas combined with grovelling obsequiousness on the part of the senate, which would never have responded on this particular occasion if it had felt there was any way in which they could legitimately without blasphemy refuse.

S29e The senate's decree III

[13] Is that the end of it, do you think? Not a bit of it. Wait till you hear something even more extraordinary. The senate's motion goes on:

"Whereas it is in the public interest that the emperor's generous eagerness to lavish praise and rewards on deserving citizens should be widely publicised, especially in those places where the officials in charge of his affairs may be most effectively encouraged to match such dedication, and where the well established loyalty and integrity of Pallas may best inspire a zeal in them for honourable imitation, it is hereby resolved that those remarks made by our most excellent emperor at the meeting of this honourable house on 23 January last, together with those resolutions of the senate passed in pursuance of those aforementioned remarks, shall be inscribed upon a bronze plaque, and that same bronze plaque shall be affixed to the mail-clad statue of Divus Julius Caesar."

[14] So it was not deemed sufficient for the senate house to witness such shameful resolutions; instead they chose the most crowded place in Rome, where they were bound to be read by everyone alive today and by future generations for evermore. They passed a resolution that a bronze plaque should be inscribed with all the honours conferred upon this most disgusting slave, purchased in the market place, both the honours which he had spurned and those which he deigned to accept from a body whose power to confer them was uncertain. There, inscribed and chiselled onto a public monument for all eternity are the praetorian insignia of Pallas, recorded like some ancient treaty or the sacred tablets of the laws of our people.

The statue of Divus Julius was presumably outside his Temple in the Roman Forum. The base of an equestrian statue would have provided much room for bronze inscriptions.

S29f Pliny's moral indignation

[15] Words cannot express what I feel about such action by our emperor, by our senate, and by Pallas himself. It is as if they wanted to establish for the whole world to see a permanent reminder: Pallas of his insolence, the emperor of his sheer subjection, and the senate of its utter humiliation. They were not even ashamed to offer an egregiously specious pretext for their disreputable conduct: "by the example of the rewards granted to Pallas to inspire in others an eagerness to match his achievement." [16] Such was their contempt for the whole honours system – at least, such honours as even Pallas had condescended to accept. Yet they were expecting to find men of honourable birth to compete eagerly for rewards, which they saw given to a freedman and promised to slaves.

[17] Thank goodness I did not chance to live in those days, though I feel as ashamed of them as if indeed I did! I have no doubt you will feel the same. You have, I know, a quick intelligence and a sound sense of values, so I am sure you will appreciate that my sense of outrage is, if anything, understated rather than exaggerated. But I have found it all too easy to express that outrage rather more forcibly in certain places, perhaps, than is really appropriate in a personal letter.

[Pliny the Younger, *Letters* 8.6]

S30 Felix, brother of Pallas, procurator of Judaea

[137] Claudius then sent Felix, the brother of Pallas, to take charge of affairs in Judaea. ... [139] After receiving as a gift from the emperor <Philip's tetrarchy and Bataneia>, Agrippa gave his sister Drusilla in marriage to Azizus, king of Emesa, who had agreed to be circumcised...[141] But the marriage between Drusilla and Azizus had to be dissolved not long afterwards, for the following reasons. [142] While Felix was procurator of Judaea, he happened to catch sight of the lady on some occasion and became infatuated with her, because she was indeed supremely beautiful. One of his friends was a Cypriot Jew called Atomus, and Felix sent him to Drusilla posing as a magician to try and persuade her to leave her husband and marry him, promising her true felicity if she did not spurn his advances. [143] She was already very unhappy in her present situation and wanted to escape from the jealousy of her sister Berenice, so she was persuaded to break the traditional code of Jewish law and to marry Felix. She bore him a son to whom she gave the name Agrippa.

[Josephus, *Jewish Antiquities* 20.137–44 (excerpts)]

Felix was governor of Judaea from *c.* AD 52–58. He developed a reputation for abusing his power, as this extract exemplifies (compare Tac. *Ann.* 12.54.1; *Hist.* 5.9; Suet. *Claud.* 28). He used his brother Pallas' influence with Nero to escape censure for his licentious behaviour. Between 54–56 he married a Jewish princess, Drusilla, divorcing his wife of the same name to do so. Both (princess) Drusilla and her son, Marcus Antonius Agrippa were killed when Mt Vesuvius erupted in AD 79 (Jos. *JA* 20.144).

S31 Martial on Claudius Etruscus' father

Here lies the greybeard, famed in the imperial court;
Not cowed by Caesar's wrath, nor by his favour bought;
Beside his wife's sacred ashes his loving children laid him;
And with her now, Elysium's groves will shade him.
She died before him, of youth's first flowering too soon deprived;
But he thrice six Olympiads almost outlived.
And yet, Etruscus, he that beheld your tears, must surely
Have thought the hastening years had stolen him prematurely.

[Martial, *Epigrams* 7.40]

S32 Statius on Claudius Etruscus' father: freedman from Tiberius to Domitian

This lengthy poem was addressed to Claudius Etruscus, the son of the freedman, who is the subject of this poem but whose personal name is unknown.

S32a His career from Tiberius to Nero

Not from barbarian shores to Latium you came; Smyrna was your home.
You drank from Meles' holy spring, and the stream of Hermus where
Lydian Bacchus bathes, and with its gold-bearing mud renews his horns.
From there a happy line of duties and successive cares in office saw
Your honours increase. Always it was given you closely to tread
Near Caesar's side and in the footsteps of divinity, to share
The very secrets of the gods. For first Tiberius' palace opened up
Its doors to you, when your maturing youth had scarcely changed
The down upon its cheeks. Here freedom was granted you,
Your talent far outweighing your tender years. Nor could Caesar's heir
Expel you, savage though he was, and hounded by hell's own Furies.

As Caesar's companion you travelled far, even to Arctic frosts, and there
Endured the tyrant, terrible in looks and words, a monster to his own.
Like men who tame the terrifying hearts of beasts, compelling them
To render back from bloodstained jaws the very paws which they
Had plunged therein, thus teaching them to live deprived of prey.
Claudius it was, though old but not as yet translated to the stars
Of heaven, who raised you to the pinnacles of power, well deserved,
And then rich in your years of service to his descendant passed you on.
What god-respecting man can history show to us as one who served
So many altars or so many shrines as you? Jove has his messenger –
Mercury, the winged Arcadian; Juno is Iris' mistress, Thaumas' daughter,
She who brings the rain; Triton stands ready, swiftly to obey
Neptune's commands. Each serves one master. You endured the yoke
Of many masters and so often changed, yet lived to tell the tale.
How blessed your craft to sail on every sea (in every weather) and remain intact.

[Statius, *Silvae* 3.3.60–84]

60: Smyrna: Modern Izmir in Turkey. One of several cities to have claimed Homer. Famous in Roman period for wealth, fine buildings and scientific learning.

69: Caesar's heir: Caligula is not named, but allusions are made to his madness (Caesonia's aphrodisiac, see **J15b** and his expedition to Germany (Suet. *Cal.* 43).

76: Claudius made him an imperial procurator, with powers of taxation and jurisdiction.

78: Claudius' descendant: Nero, like Caligula is not named, and all that the poet, writing under Domtian can find to say is that Etruscus managed to survive under him.

S32b As 'minister of finance' under Vespasian

Then from on high upon your loyal house there shone a glorious light.
At full tilt, and at its loftiest, Fortune arrived. Now to one man was given
In trust the management of sacred treasures, riches from all nations
Harvested, the gross domestic product of the whole wide world.
All that Iberia spews from its golden mines; everything that shines
Among the high mountains of Dalmatia; all that from Africa is swept
Up in her harvests; all that the sweltering Nile produces from threshing floors;
All that the plunging divers of the eastern seas can gather; offspring too
Of Spartan Galaesus' carefully nurtured herds; transparent snow (rock crystals),
African timber, India's glory, tusks of ivory. All that the wild North Wind,
All that the raging East and cloud-filled South winds bring – all to one minister
Are now entrusted, all are obedient to his sole command. Swifter it were
To count the winter's raindrops or the summer's woodland leaves. But he,
Sagacious and sleepless, swiftly calculates the needed sums for every exercise
Of Roman arms in every clime, for distributing to the poor, for temples, how much
The lofty aqueducts demand, what sea-defences, the land's own battlements,
How much the far-flung reaches of our Roman roads, how much the gold
That gleams in the fretted ceilings of our emperor's home, the cost
Of gold which, melted in the fire, must take the shape of gods' own faces,
And how much jingle as coinage, stamped in the fires of Italy's Mint.
No wonder was it that you never learned to rest;
Pleasure remained an exile from your thoughts; fasting was feasting;
Never were cares beguiled by deep draughts of undiluted wine;

Dear to your heart were marriage bonds, and dear a mind
Bound in fidelity to the marriage bed, to marriage celebration,
And the joy of fathering servants faithful to your lord.

[Statius, *Silvae* 3.3.85–110]

86: Fortune arrived: Possibly at Vespasian's accession, he became *a rationibus* (in charge of financial accounts) or effectively chancellor of the exchequer.

Lines 86–96 give an interesting, if poetic, view of the empire's resources.

Lines 98–104 give an even more interesting, and possibly representative view of the main expenses of empire: the army; the dole; maintenance of buildings, especially temples, aqueducts, harbours, roads, imperial luxury, statues of gods; the mint.

110ff: Statius goes on to praise Etrusca, wife of Claudius Etruscus whose brother attained the consulship, but who died young. Finally he describes Etruscus as having been allowed to join in Titus' Jewish triumph, and as having been given equestrian status by Vespasian.

SECTION T

TYRANNY: PANEGYRIC OR INVECTIVE

'If only the people of Rome had one neck!' (Caligula (**T6**))

This chapter includes passages written by contemporaries, displaying fear or loathing or current or previous emperors. They display the twin dangers described by Tacitus (*Annals* 1.1.2 and **R3**), being sometimes in the form of savage condemnation, sometimes of gross flattery. Though none are from works of history, these sources and others of similar nature provided some of the primary material for later historians to use. Suetonius' biographies often appear schizophrenic in trying to reconcile positive and negative views of an emperor, leading to attempts to assign specific causes: temporal (*Tib.* 61.1; *Nero* 27.1; *Dom* 10.1); abandoning pretence (*Tib.* 42.1); personal (*Claud.* 29.1); medical (*Cal.* 51.1). Furthermore an historian's own experiences colour his views. Seneca writes of Claudius with cringing flattery (**T13–T14**) when he hoped that Claudius would revoke his exile, imposed, it seems in AD 41, for alleged adultery with Julia Livilla (Dio 60.8.5); then with equally unappealing mockery of Claudius and flattery of his new master, in the *Apocolocyntosis* (Section **F**). In a less obvious way, living through Domitian's reign surely influenced the way Tacitus, Suetonius and Pliny the Younger wrote about earlier young, 'bad' emperors.

Roman authors of this period are also, almost exclusively, from senatorial or equestrian backgrounds. They are therefore especially outraged at offences against their own class. They will also have been particularly aware of traditions in Greek and Roman history of heroic and successful resistance to tyranny. For the Romans this was exemplified in the early books of Livy (see, for example, the list given at Livy 4.14.7–4.15.4 of potential tyrants slain in the first 70 years of the republic). The Greeks too celebrated resistance to native and foreign (Persian) tyranny, (compare **T7–T10**).

TIBERIUS: T1–T2

Tacitus' account of Tiberius' reign charts the rise of the *maiestas* (treason) trials, 'the pernicious curse which crept in through Tiberius' cunning, was repressed and finally broke out to engulf everything' (*Ann.* 1.73.1). Tacitus reports eighty cases of treason trials, the majority in the second half of Tiberius' reign, see Goodyear, *Commentary* on 1.72.2. Other evidence of Tiberius' tyrannical rule is offered by Suetonius, *Tiberius* 55–66. Sejanus attracts his fair share of blame (**P4c**, **P4j**, **P4m**, **R5**). Flattery is offered by Velleius (Section **C**) and Valerius Maximus (**R4**).

T1 Charges of treason under Tiberius

[3.26.1] Under Tiberius Caesar treason charges became so commonplace that they amounted to a form of national madness and cost the lives of more Roman citizens than any civil war. Drunken conversations and light-hearted jokes became the targets for informers; nothing was safe; any excuse for brutality was welcome, and no-one waited to discover the fate of an accused – it was always the same.

A certain ex-praetor called Paulus happened to be attending a dinner party wearing a ring with a large central stone engraved with a portrait of Tiberius Caesar. [2] It would be a bit pathetic of me if I tried to put this politely: he was handed a chamber-pot, and this action was spotted simultaneously by Maro, one of the notorious informers of the day, and by one of the slaves of Paulus, the intended victim of this trap, who slipped the ring off the finger of his inebriated master. When Maro called his fellow banqueters to witness the fact that the emperor's portrait had been brought into contact with something disgusting, and was already putting together an indictment, the slave demonstrated to the company that the ring was in fact on his own finger. Anyone who could call such a man a slave would presumably have no difficulty in calling Maro a bosom-friend.

[Seneca, *Benefits*, 3.26.1–2]

Here Seneca speaks of the *maiestas* charges that Tacitus regards as a bad feature even of the early part of his reign (*Ann.* 1.72–74), though there were more acquittals early on than this suggests. Tacitus, like Seneca, emphasises the corrosive effect on society of such accusations being brought, especially as the charge could be tacked on to other charges and there was no fixed penalty in trials before the senate. Neither Paulus nor Maro are otherwise known.

T2 Execution of Titius Sabinus, AD 28

But the best example comes from our own age, as attested in the Public Records. In the consulship of Appius Junius and Publius Silanus (AD 28), the death penalty was being inflicted on Titius Sabinus and his household slaves after the trial concerning Nero, son of Germanicus. The dog of one of the slaves could not be driven away from him in prison and would not leave the body when it had been thrown out onto the Steps of Grief; howling sorrowfully to the large crowd gathered around, it took the food thrown to it by someone to the mouth of its dead master; and then swam to the corpse thrown into the Tiber, trying to keep it afloat, while a great crowd flooded out to see the animal's loyalty.

[Pliny, *Natural History* 8.145]

Pliny is discussing the loyalty of dogs. Dio 58.1.3 repeats the story of the dog. Tacitus omits the dog, but gives further details about the condemnation, engineered by Sejanus, of this loyal supporter of Germanicus' family in *Annals* 4.68–71. Steps of Grief: Pliny uses an alternative term for the 'Gemonian Steps' – steps on which bodies of executed criminals were exposed before being thrown into the Tiber. Victims thus treated included Sejanus (Dio 58.11.5) and his family (**P4f**).

GAIUS: T3–T12

Tacitus' account is completely lost: its flavour can be gained from Tiberius' prediction that Gaius would have all of Sulla's vices but none of his virtues (*Ann.* 6.46.4: for Sulla as archetypal tyrant see **G9**). Suetonius' account of 'the monster' rather than 'the *princeps*' begins with an anecdote about his wishing to be lord and king (*Cal.* 22.1) and goes on to catalogue every form of tyrannical behaviour (22–49). See also Dio 59 *passim*, especially 59.8.3–4, 59.10, 59.18.4–5, 59.20.6, 59.22.5, 59.25.5–26.2; Philo, *Embassy* (Section **D**); Josephus on his assassination (Section **E**); **J19a**, **J19b**, **L13–L16**, **P5**, **P6**. No works of literature flattering Gaius survive from his short reign, though Philo gives evidence of high hopes at his accession (**D2**). His assassination and Claudius' attitude to his nephew ensure that he is damned at the bar of history.

T3 Gaius mocks Valerius Asiaticus and his wife

[18.1] It would take me far too long to set out every one of the individual insults, which he heaped upon his parents and grand-parents as well as on others of every class and kind. So I shall confine myself to recording those which brought about his ultimate downfall. [2] Among his closest personal friends was one Asiaticus Valerius, a man of ferocious temper, who would certainly not take lying down the insults offered to himself by anyone else. In the middle of a dinner party, which is a very public occasion, Gaius mocked him at the top of his voice for his wife's sexual inadequacies. Ye gods! What a thing for a husband to be told or for an emperor to know about! How utterly disgusting for an emperor to announce his own adultery so publicly and his disappointment with the experience – and all this to one who was of consular status, a personal friend, and worst of all, the woman's own husband.

[Seneca, *On Firmness of Purpose,* 18.1–2]

This passage follows on from Seneca's description of Caligula's personal appearance (**J19b**) and continues with his mockery of Chaerea who eventually killed him (**P6b**). Suet. *Cal.* 23.1–2 records his insulting remarks about his maternal grandfather Agrippa, his mother Agrippina, his maternal great-grandfather Augustus, his paternal great-grandmother Livia, and his paternal grandmother Antonia. Valerius Asiaticus (cos. suff. 35; cos.II 46) was the first senator from Gallia Narbonensis. In 47 he was accused of being in the plot to murder Gaius and of boasting of it, (see **E21**). Messallina and her associates had him tried *in camera* and condemned to commit suicide (Tac. *Ann.* 11.1–3).

T4 Gaius likens himself to Jove

[20.7] Human greatness finds its source and foundation in goodness; evil men are capable of terrible, violent, and destructive deeds. But greatness they will never possess. They may try to give the impression of such greatness by speech, action, and every sort of external contrivance; [8] they may even make a speech, perhaps, which you feel to be expressive of greatness of soul. But take Gaius Caesar for example. He lost his temper with heaven, because its thunder interrupted a pantomime, whose actors he was more eager to imitate than to watch, and then because his dinner guests were terrified by thunderbolts, which obviously missed their intended target! So he challenged Jupiter to a duel to the death, shouting at the top of his voice, quoting in Greek Homer's Ajax wrestling with Odysseus, "Either lift me off my feet or I will lift you off yours." [9] He must have been utterly mad to imagine that he could do any harm to Jupiter, or that Jupiter could do no harm to him. I have little doubt that this sort of comment reinforced the determination of the conspirators to get rid of him. It seems like the supreme test of human endurance to put up with a man who himself could not put up with Jupiter.

[Seneca, *On Anger* 1.20.7–9]

Suet. *Cal.* 22 discusses Gaius' claim to equal status with the gods, especially Jupiter, including the same quotation from Homer (*Iliad* 23.724). Augustus and Tiberius had prohibited worship of themselves in Rome during their lifetimes (**L4b**).

T5 Gaius executes a son then forces his father to enjoy a dinner party

[2] There is a famous saying by one who had grown old in the service of kings. They asked him once how he had achieved that rarest of a courtier's achievements, old age. "By accepting injuries," he replied, "and saying 'thank you,' for them." Very often it is more expedient not just to forego vengeance for an injury, but to avoid even acknowledging that the injury has occurred.

[3] Gaius Caesar clapped the son of the distinguished equestrian, Pastor, into prison because he was outraged by his extravagant dress and elaborate hairstyle. When the boy's father begged for his life, Gaius ordered his immediate execution, almost as if he had just been reminded of his intention to punish him. But to avoid treating the father with total inhumanity he asked him to dinner on the same day. [4] Pastor arrived, his expression giving nothing away of his true feelings. Caesar drank his health in half a pint of wine and placed him under observation. The poor man put up with the ordeal, even though it felt as if he was drinking his own son's blood. Caesar then sent him perfumes and garlands and gave orders for him to be watched to see if he used them. He did. On the day on which his son was taken out for burial, indeed before the burial had taken place, he attended a dinner as one of a hundred guests and despite his age and his gout he drank more than would have really been appropriate at the birthday of his children. In all this he never shed a tear nor did he allow any sign of his grief to be seen. He dined as if he had gained the pardon he had sought for his son. How could he do it, you ask? Answer: he had another son. [5] Look at Priam of Troy. He too concealed his anger and embraced the knees of prince Achilles. He raised to his

lips the murderous hand which was stained with his son's blood, and then took dinner with the one who slew him. But his savage enemy used no perfumes, no garlands to persuade him to dine; instead he pressed him to do so with gentle words, and never compelled him to drain vast drinking vessels with a spy set over him to watch him.

[6] If that Roman father had feared for his own safety, you would have rightly despised him; but on this occasion love for his own son cooled his anger. He should have been allowed to leave the dinner to make the ritual gathering of his son's bones after cremation. But our teenage prince, so kind, so charming all the while, refused permission even for this. He tormented that old man with endless toasts, urging him to lay aside his woes; and in return the father affected a mask of happiness and indifference to all that had been done that day. If the guest had displeased the executioner in any way, that other son was dead.

[Seneca, *On Anger* 1.33.2–6]

This Pastor is not otherwise known.

T6 The wanton cruelties of Gaius

[1] In this context it is worth considering the arrogance which accompanied his cruelty. Some may regard this as an irrelevance, a digression from the subject in hand. But this characteristic will be seen to be typical of an anger whose rage has got out of hand. He had flogged a number of senators; but he was the one who made it possible to describe this as an everyday occurrence. He tortured them in every conceivably painful way known to nature – by garrotte, ankle-pins, the rack, fire, and even having to look upon his face. [2] But here's the answer. Why all this fuss about three senators being cut to pieces by fire and flogging like insignificant slaves by a man who had seriously considered butchering the whole senate. This was the same man who used to wish that the whole Roman people had one single neck, so that he could have concentrated all his crimes, spread over so many times and places, into one single stroke on one single day.

No-one had ever heard of an execution by night. Robberies certainly are usually concealed by darkness; but public sanctions serve all the more effectively as exemplary sources of improvement when they are attended by the maximum publicity of daylight. [3] But here too there is an answer. There is nothing surprising in all this. Gaius was a mad beast, and such brutalities were his daily bread and butter. This is what he lived for, stayed awake for, and for which he worked long hours. No-one else has ever been known to give instructions that all those condemned to death should have a sponge forced down their throats to gag them so that they could not even cry out. No dying man was ever before denied the right to utter even a groan. Caesar was afraid that in the last extremity of pain his victim might say something he would rather not have heard; he knew all too well that there were innumerable crimes which only a dying man would dare denounce him for. [4] When sponges were in short supply, he ordered his wretched victims' clothes to be torn off them and the pieces rammed into their mouths. That is the most depraved of savage acts. A man should be allowed to draw his last breath, to leave an exit for his departing soul, and not to force it to depart through his wounds. [5] I could add a long catalogue to this list of crimes, but it would be tedious. I could tell you how he used to send his centurions to the homes of his victims' parents to put an end to them on the same night as their son's execution – an act of pity, of course, from this merciful emperor, to spare them the agonies of grief.

But it is no part of my plan to describe the savagery of a Gaius; my subject is the savagery of anger generally, which does not confine its rage to individual victims, but tears whole nations to pieces, and like Xerxes at the Hellespont in its fury lashes whole cities and rivers, and all inanimate things insensible to pain.

[Seneca, *On Anger* 3.19.1–5]

This passage continues **P5b**. The anecdote about wishing the Roman people had only one neck is also in Suet. *Cal.* 30.2. Gaius' cruelty takes particularly shocking forms because Roman citizens were not supposed to be condemned on capital charges without a proper trial, usually before the senate for senators and high-ranking equestrians. Seneca alludes to Herodotus' account of Xerxes' rage against the Hellespont (7.35).

T7 A philosopher's indifference to a tyrant's cruelty

[4] Julius Canus, one of the finest of men, for whom one's admiration is in no way diluted by the fact that he is one of our own contemporaries, had a long argument with Gaius, a latter-day Phalaris. As he was leaving, Gaius said to him, 'I don't want you to indulge yourself in any false optimism. I have ordered your execution.' 'For that,' replied Canus, 'I must indeed thank you, most generous of emperors.'

[5] Quite what he meant by that, I cannot really tell, since a number of possibilities occur to me. Was it, perhaps, a calculated insult by which he sought to suggest how extreme must be the emperor's savagery, when death itself was a boon? Or was he throwing back in his teeth a reminder of his daily acts of madness? For those whose children had been murdered by him, or their possessions confiscated, used to thank him in a similar fashion. Or was he happy to accept death as a release from slavery? Whatever his intentions, it was a truly noble response.

[Seneca, *On Tranquillity of Mind*, 14.4–5]

Calling Gaius a Phalaris, the cruel sixth century BC tyrant of Agrigentum who roasted his enemies alive in a bronze bull, prepares us for his conventional despotic behaviour. Tacitus has Seneca himself, at the end of the interview in which he requests permission to retire into private life, thank Nero, 'the end of all conversations with despots' (*Ann.* 14.56.3), and Agricola's interview with Domitian ends the same way (*Agr.* 42.2, compare *Hist.* 2.71).

T8 A philosopher's execution

[6] You might think that after such a reply Gaius would have ordered him to stay alive instead. Canus had no fear of that, since Gaius was notorious for sticking to his word when he issued such orders. It is hard to believe that he spent the ten remaining days leading up to his execution without a care in the world. It is truly incredible how imperturbable he showed himself in all that he said or did. [7] He was playing a game of chess when the centurion in charge of the mass murders for that day ordered him to be summoned. Having heard the summons, he counted up the pieces and said to his opponent, "Now don't you go around after my death fibbing to everyone that you were winning." He then nodded to the centurion and said, "You will be my witness that I was one piece up." Do you think that Canus was simply playing a game on that occasion? He wasn't. He was enjoying his irony.

[8] His friends were lamenting the fact that they were about to lose a great man. But he demanded to know why they were so sad. "After all," he said, "you were discussing the immortality of the soul; I am now about to find out the answer." And to the very end he never ceased to explore the nature of reality and to make the subject of his own death part of those investigations. [9] His own philosophy tutor went with him to the place of execution, and as they were passing the low hill where daily sacrifices were made to our divine emperor, he asked Canus what was on his mind at that moment and how he was feeling. "I have decided," he replied, "to make exact observations of that very brief moment when the soul leaves the body. I want to know if it is actually aware of the process. I promise you that if I make any discoveries I shall go round all my friends and explain to them the true nature of the human soul."

[10] That is real tranquillity of mind in the very heart of the storm, that is a soul truly worthy of immortality. To think that he could examine his own death to test the truth of an hypothesis, and when he found himself at that final moment of extremity, he was ready to cross-question his own spirit as it departed, and was still seeking knowledge not only up to his death, but even from the very moment of death itself. No man has ever prolonged his study of philosophy further. He was a great man and shall not easily be forgotten; we must speak of him always with reverence. Canus, of all the victims of Gaius' butcheries the greatest, noblest of Romans, I hereby dedicate your memory to all eternity.

[Seneca, *On Tranquillity of Mind*, 14.6–10]

Julius Canus is elsewhere mentioned by Plutarch (*Mor.* frag. 211S) as a Stoic philosopher about whom the Greeks invented a story about prophecies he made as he was being led to execution, which were both fulfilled. One predicted the murder of his friend Rectus by Gaius; the other Canus' return from the dead to report on the nature of the soul, as he promises in Seneca: he reported that the soul survived. Stoic philosophers differed among themselves on the question.

In this anecdote Seneca combines two motifs associated with noble deaths under the principate: the bravado of Valerius Asiaticus, concerned with his trees, and of Petronius, dining as usual (Tac. *Ann.* 11.3; 16.19), and the nobility of Seneca and Thrasea Paetus, concerning themselves with the question of the soul's survival after death (Tac. *Ann.* 15.63; 16.34).

T9 Caligula makes a senator kiss his foot

[2.12.1] Gaius Caesar gave his life back to Pompeius Pennus, if you can call a failure to remove a man's life giving it back to him. And then, when the reprieved man was offering his thanks, Gaius extended his left foot for him to kiss. Those who want to make excuses for such behaviour and claim that it was not a calculated insult, maintain that he wanted to show off his gilt – or rather golden – slipper with its decorative motif of pearls. But that is the whole point: there could be no greater insult for an ex-consul than to kiss gold and pearls, when to kiss any other part of the emperor's person would have been less demeaning than that.

[Seneca, *On Benefits*, 2.12.1–2]

The story of Pompeius Pennus may or may not be the sequel to the story in Dio 59.26.4 and Jos. *AJ* 19.32ff., who call the senator 'Pomponius' and 'Pompedius' respectively and report his pardon after involvement in a conspiracy against Caligula. Prostrating oneself (proskynesis) was the sign of subjection traditionally associated with Persia and abhorred by the Greeks. Caligula's footwear is luxurious and effeminate and not suited for public business like a trial (**P5b**); the left (Lat. *sinister*) was thought to be adverse, harmful, even immoral.

T10 Caligula's Bridge at Baiae

The shortage of supplies had occurred while Gaius was building his bridge of boats [from Baiae to Puteoli] and playing with the resources of the empire like a child with its toys. He had played the role of a mad, barbarian king, arrogant to the point of disaster, and the price we almost paid was death by starvation and the revolution, which is its inevitable consequence.

[Seneca, *On the Shortness of Life,* 18.5]

Seneca is Gaius rode over the pontoon bridge on horseback and then in a chariot during a pageant that lasted several days (Suet. *Cal.* 19; Dio 59.17). The rivalry with Xerxes' bridging of the narrower Hellespont (the 'barbarian king') was overt, especially as a Parthian hostage called Darius rode with Gaius in his chariot. This was the name of Xerxes' father and also of the Persian king defeated by Alexander , whose breastplate Gaius claimed to be wearing (Dio 59 17.3).

T11 The Corinthian Canal

Therefore attempts have been made to dig a ship-canal through the narrowest part, by King Demetrius, Caesar the *dictator*, the emperor Gaius and Domitius Nero. But the deaths of all these men shows that the project was sacrilegious.

[Pliny, *Natural History* 4.10]

Suetonius mentions Gaius' attempt (*Cal.* 21). For Nero's, see **M18**.

T12 Lollia Paulina, consort of Gaius

I have seen Lollia Paulina, the wife of the emperor Gaius covered in emeralds and pearls, intertwined and glittering all over her head, hair, ears, neck and fingers, worth altogether forty million sesterces, as she was ready to prove on the spot with documentary evidence. Yet this was not even at some important or solemn ceremony, but at an ordinary engagement party. Nor were they gifts from an extravagant emperor, but family heirlooms, or at least ones plundered from the provinces: the result of spoils for which Marcus Lollius disgraced himself, taking bribes from kings across the East, but losing the friendship of Gaius Caesar, son of Augustus, and taking poison. So his granddaughter can be seen by lamplight, covered in forty million sesterces!

[Pliny, *Natural History* 9.117–8]

Lollia Paulina became Gaius' third wife at some point in AD 38. At the time she was married to P. Memmius Regulus (**B31**) Suet, *Cal.* 25.2. Her grandfather, *Marcus Lollius*, a prominent supporter of Augustus, was consul as *novus homo* in 21 BC.

Forty million sesterces: Pliny goes on to value at ten million Cleopatra's pearls, subject of her famous wager with Mark Antony that she could provide a meal costing that amount (she swallowed the pearl!). Complaints about the expenditure of the consorts of tyrants are frequent through history, e.g. Marie Antoinette or Imelda Marcos. See also **T22** on Poppaea.

CLAUDIUS: T13–T14

The tyrannical aspects of Claudius' reign are usually blamed on his wives and freedmen: typical is the first surviving episode of Tacitus' account: Messalina prompts the *maiestas* accusation (*Ann.* 11.1.1), while Claudius is unaware of Poppaea's suicide (11.2.2). See also Suet. *Claud.* 25.5, Dio 60.2.4 and introduction to Section **S**. Overall Claudius' reputation is helped by that of the emperors immediately before and after him. And while Nero's court encouraged mockery of Claudius (Seneca, *Apocolocyntosis* = Section **F, T15b**), Nero also honoured him, at least initially (**K35**, **L25**, and Seneca wrote the official eulogy for Claudius, delivered by Nero (Tac. *Ann.* 13.3.1)). Vespasian rehabilitated Claudius' reputation (*e.g.* Suet. *Claud.* 45; *Law on the power of Vespasian*, repeatedly citing Claudius as a precedent (LACTOR 17, H52).

T13 Don't worry: your brother is dead, but the emperor is alive!

[12.3] I shall go on and on, again and again, reminding you to keep Caesar in your mind. While he rules the earth, while he shows how much better it is to govern the empire by generosity than by force of arms, while he presides over all human destinies, there is no danger, no need for you to feel at risk of any loss; on Caesar alone is founded all the protection you need, all your sources of comfort. Lift up your heart, and as often as the tears well up in your eyes, fix those eyes on Caesar. They will soon be dried, when you contemplate the greatness and the glory of his divinity; they will be dazzled by his brightness, their gaze transfixed always by his presence. [4] By night and day Caesar is always in your sight and from him your thoughts never stray. Keep him always in your mind; summon him to your help against misfortune. His kindness towards all his people is so boundless, his generosity so abundant, that I feel certain he has already assuaged your present wound with many forms of solace, and heaped upon you many sources of comfort for your sorrow. Indeed, even if he has done none of these things, surely the very sight, the very thought of Caesar will be your most immediate and utmost source of consolation?

[Seneca, *On Consolation, to Polybius,* 12.3–4]

Polybius was an important freedman of Claudius, at some time concerned with patronage (*a studiis* – Suet. *Claud.* 28), and at the time of the essay, possibly concerned with petitions (*a libellis* – 6.5).

T14 Seneca praises Claudius for exiling him

[5] May the gods and goddesses grant him long to live upon the earth. May he match the deeds of Divus Augustus; may he surpass him in length of days. For as long as he shall dwell among mortal men, may he never see any of his household touched with mortality. May he by long years of faithful service test and approve his son Britannicus as ruler to the Roman Empire, and may the gods grant that he may see him first as his father's helper, before he becomes his successor. May the day come late, seen only by our grandchildren, when his family reclaim him into heaven. [13.1] Goddess of Fortune, lay not your hands upon him; give no proof of your power over him, save where you can give benefit! Grant him to bring healing to the human race so long stricken and afflicted; grant him to rebuild and restore to their rightful places all that the madness of our former emperor struck down. Grant that his star, which has cast its light over a world hurled headlong to the depths and buried in the darkness of night, may shine on for ever.

[2] May he tame Germany, open up the lands of Britain, and as well as the triumphs of his ancestors, may he celebrate fresh triumphs of his own. And that I shall live to see such triumphs is a promise granted to me by that virtue which holds the highest place in all his virtues, his clemency. He has not cast me so far down as to refuse to raise me up again. Indeed he never humbled me at all, but rather when I was laid low by misfortune, he caught me as I fell and when I was tumbling headlong to destruction with heavenly gentleness his blessed hand set me in my place once more. On my behalf he pleaded with the senate, and not only gave me back my life but even begged for it. [3] Let him be the judge; let him assess my cause whatever way he wishes. Either let his justice adjudge it good; or else, let his clemency ordain it so. Either judgement will be of equal benefit for me, whether he decides that I am innocent, or merely wishes it so. In the meanwhile the mighty solace for my own woes is to see his mercy spreading through the whole wide world. And since even here, in this small

corner of my fixed abode, his mercy has rescued many who were overwhelmed by the ruins of many years and restored them to the light, I have no fear that I shall be the only one his mercy will ignore. For he alone knows the perfect moment at which he should bring succour to each victim; I shall simply labour with all my might to see that he shall not be ashamed to succour me.

[4] How blessed is your clemency, Caesar, which enables exiles to live more peacefully under your sway than once kings lived beneath the rule of Gaius. Men are now free from fear; no more do they live from hour to hour in terror of the sword, nor cringe at the sight of every passing ship. Thanks to you, they recognise a limit to the cruelty of fortune, and hope at least for nothing worse at present and something even better in the future. For one must recognise that thunderbolts which are worshipped even by those they have struck are the most just of all.

[Seneca, *On Consolation, to Polybius* 12.5–13.4]

Seneca wrote the official eulogy for Claudius, delivered by Nero (Tac. *Ann.* 13.3.1) as well as the vitriolic attack on Claudius, *Apocolocyntosis* (see Section **F**). Seneca had been relegated to Corsica on a charge of adultery with Gaius' sister Julia Livilla in 41 (Dio 60.8.5). He indicates here that the trial was before the senate which voted for conviction and the death penalty, but that Claudius asked that his life be spared, perhaps at the request of Agrippina (Tac. *Ann.* 12.8). Seneca does not prejudice his plea here by asserting his innocence but, by asking that Claudius exercise either justice or clemency in recalling him, he leaves open the possibility that the Emperor did not think him guilty. The hope expressed of being at Rome to witness Claudius' triumph, which took place in 44 (Dio 60.23.1), suggests that the work was written not long before that event. Other exiles were recalled then (Suet. *Claud.* 17.3), but Seneca had to wait until Agrippina married Claudius and wanted Seneca recalled to teach her son rhetoric (Tac. *Ann.* 12.8).

NERO: T15–T22

Sources on Nero amply demonstrate panegyric and invective. Literature flourished under his reign: as often under new regimes happy to be told how much better they were than the previous one. Sections **G** and **H** fully illustrate this. Tacitus pointedly begins his Neronian books 'First in the new principate to die …' (*Ann.* 13.1.1). Suetonius lists Nero's vices at *Nero* 27–40. See also **K38**, **K41–K45**, **P9–P13**, **R33**. For praise by contemporaries, see **L27–L36**, **N56**, **Q9**, **R27–R28**.

T15 A pastoral poet predicts a new Golden Age under Nero.

In this eclogue by Calpurnius Siculus, the shepherd Ornytus is reading to Corydon a god's prophecy carved upon a sacred beech tree. The name Corydon is used by Virgil in his second and seventh eclogues, while in *Eclogue 5*, another shepherd recites verses carved on a beech tree. But the most obvious model for this eclogue is Virgil, *Eclogue* 4 (= LACTOR 17, G2) in which the poet, writing in 40 BC, predicts another Golden Age, ushered in by the birth of a child (identity unclear). Nothing is known of Calpurnius Siculus aside of his seven pastoral poems. But from references within his poems he can fairly securely be said to be a member of Nero's circle of court poets (disparaged by Tacitus *Annals* 14.16.1). For other excerpts from Calpurnius, see **L27** and **Q9**.

T15a A Golden Age for the countryside

"I, Faunus, offspring of the heavens, guardian of hills and woods,
To all the nations prophesy these things that are to come. Here
On this sacred tree it is my joy to carve glad tidings and lay bare the fates.

Rejoice especially all you, my people, dwellers within these woods,
Rejoice, I say. For every herd may wander far and wide,
Its herdsmen all untroubled; untroubled, too, the shepherd who
By night neglects to close with ashen hurdles the enclosing sheepfolds.

For no more shall the robber bring his thieving plots against these pens,
Nor the cattle-rustler loose your bullocks' halters as he drives them off.
The Age of Gold comes round once more,[1] reborn with carefree peace,
While Righteousness returns again to earth and sets aside
The squalor and neglect of mourning garb, and blessed centuries attend
The youth, whose cause brought victory for his mother's Julian clan.[2]

T15b A Golden Age for Rome

So long as he, a god in very truth,[3] shall rule the nations, to him Bellona,
War's unholy goddess shall give way, her conquered hands
Tethered behind her back, stripped of her weapons, while her jaws
In madness twisted, gnawing her own entrails, wage against herself
That civil strife with which of late she tore apart the world. No more
Shall Rome lament Philippi's battles, nor captive lead in triumph her captivity.[4]
All wars shall be consigned to Tartarus, in whose hellish dungeons they shall hide
Their heads in everlasting darkness and forever after shun the light of day.
Fair Peace shall dwell among us,[5] Peace not fair in outward countenance alone
As oft she was when, freed from warfare openly declared, once foreign foes
In far off lands were tamed, with frenzied weaponry and hidden blades
She spread domestic violence. For now Clemency[6] is queen and has ordained
For every vice which masquerades as peace a distant exile, while she beats
War's maddened weaponry into tools of peace. No more shall senators un-numbered
March to their death in fetters, exhausting our state's executioners;
Nor shall the Curia, with prisons full of senators, call its diminished roll.[7]
Abundant Peace will everywhere surround us, Peace that nothing knows
Of drawn swords. She will restore throughout the length and breadth
Of Latium old Saturn's second kingdom, and great Numa's second rule.
Numa it was who first taught arts of peace to legions revelling in slaughter

1 Age of Gold: Greco-Roman mythology (like the biblical Garden of Eden) had the idea of an initial Golden Age of peace and prosperity in which mankind did not need to work, followed by a 'fall from grace'. See Hesiod, *Works and Days* 106–120; Ovid, *Metamorphoses* 1.89–112; Virgil, *Eclogue* 4; Sen. *Apocol*. 4 = **F4**.

2 Nero's mother, Julia Agrippina (= 'Agrippina the Younger') was a Julian, while Claudius was not. There might also be an allusion to Nero speaking on behalf of Troy (Suet. *Nero* 7.2), since the Julian clan traced their ancestry back to Aeneas.

3 Though Augustus and Claudius were officially deified only after their deaths, the shepherds in Virgil, *Eclogue* 1 had already spoken of the young Octavian/Augustus as a god.

4 *Bellona*: an Italian goddess of war. Virgil pictures her involvement in the battle of Actium (*Aeneid* 8.703 – LACTOR 17, G38). *Philippi* in Greece was the scene of two battles in 42 BC between Mark Antony and the republicans under Brutus and Cassius. Though *triumphs* were only properly allowed for victories over foreign enemies, Julius Caesar celebrated a triumph for winning the civil war against Pompey, as did Octavian/Augustus against Mark Antony.

5 In AD 63 (after the presumed date of the poem), Nero made great play of closing the Gates of Janus, indicative of peace throughout the Roman empire, see **N52**.

6 For 'clemency' as the key virtue of an emperor, see Seneca's *de clementia* – Section **G**.

7 Various Senators fell victim to the greed, jealousy, and justified or unjustified suspicion of various emperors. Seneca, claims that 35 senators were killed by Claudius, and names 10 (F13–14). Suetonius gives the same number (*Claud.* 29.2).

And still all ablaze with savage ardour from the wars of Romulus.[8] He it was
That ordered weapons to fall silent, and amid sacred rites instead of wars
Commanded the trumpets to sound forth. No more shall the consul purchase
By sleaze the shady, outward form of government position, or sell his silence
For empty status symbols and the pointless power of high position.
The rule of Law returns; Right shall everywhere prevail; and now a better god
Shall bring us back the Forum's former customs and its ancient look;
He'll banish too the cruel afflictions of our present age.

T15c A Golden Age for the world

Let the nations rejoice,
All such as dwell far down towards the south, or high above us in the lofty north,
All such as lie open to the rising sun or to its setting beams, or again those
That lying between the two must boil and swelter now beneath its fiery rays.
Can you not see how in a cloudless sky our twentieth successive night glows bright,
Offering a comet's radiance to our gaze, shining with peaceful light?
See how its glory blazes in its fullness, promising no hint of ill foreboding.
See how it scorns a comet's usual signs, and neither burns the poles with bloody fire,
Nor yet allows its torches to blaze out with flames of blood-red hue.[9]
It was not always thus. For once, when Caesar fell by assassins' hands,
To hapless citizens the comet declared a cruel destiny of civil wars.[10]

But now, in truth, a god himself shall take upon his mighty shoulders
The massive burden of our Roman state, to carry it unshaken, undisturbed,
In such a way that none shall hear the thunder-crash of war
When next our world dominion passes to another's hands. For Rome
Shall never reckon that her household gods have to the full discharged
Their duty, till that day when a new ruler's dawn can safely backwards look
To the last sunset of the one that went before."

[Calpurnius Siculus, *Eclogue* 1.33–90]

T16 Lucan's panegyric on Nero

Marcus Annaeus Lucanus, AD 39–65 came from the hugely wealthy, cultured and influencial Annaeus family from Corduba in S. Spain. His grandfather was Seneca the Elder, his uncle Seneca the Younger. His *Civil War* (sometimes misleadingly called 'Pharsalia') is an epic poem on the Civil War between Julius Caesar and Pompey the Great (49–45 BC). The poem was unfinished in AD 65 when Lucan was forced to commit suicide, along with other relations, as a result of the Pisonian conspiracy against Nero (Tacitus, *Annals* 15.48–74, especially 49, 56, 57, 70, 71). Poetical jealousy was said to be a major factor by Tacitus and the *Life of Lucan* (see **R36**).

Lucan's *Civil War* begins with an introduction to the poem's theme followed by an extraordinary panegyric to Nero. Scholarship is divided as to whether this is to be taken literally, as the sort of thing a poet might

---

[8] The age of Saturn was another way of refering to the golden age. Romulus and Numa were traditionally the first two kings of Rome. Romulus' killing of his brother Remus over which should give their name to Rome was taken by later writers to explain Rome's tendency to civil war.

[9] A comet appeared around the time of Claudius' death (13 October 54) – Suet. *Claudius* 46; Pliny, *NH* 2.92; Dio 60.35.1. Seneca, *NQ* 7.17.2, of course agrees that the comet of Claudius/Nero was completely different from that of Julius Caesar). Seneca and Pliny agree that there are different types of comets, with different meanings (Pliny, *NH* 2.89, Sen. *NQ* 17.1.3).

[10] This was the comet sighted in 44 BC and taken to signify the deification of Julius Caesar after his assassination – Pliny *NH* 2.92–3

need to write under Nero, or whether the praise is so extreme as to undermine deliberately its own message. In favour of the second view is the fact that the introduction and the whole poem is all about the horrors of the civil war which brought about the 'Advent of Nero' (1.33) and Caesar (Julius) is throughout depicted as an anti-hero, with Pompey, the champion of liberty. But this section is full of panegyric undoubtedly meant seriously.

T16a Lucan's introduction

My song is a song of wars, worse than civil wars, wars fratricidal,
Waged over Pharsalus' plains,[11] giving crimes the veneer of legality,
As a powerful people turned with victorious hands its own weapons
Into its vitals, with brother aligned against brother, and tyranny's treaty now broken;
While a stricken world's armies united in one single crime, to fight in a war
Offensive to heaven itself. Legions' standards confronted the standards of legions;
Eagles faced confederate eagles; and Roman was menaced by javelins of Roman.

Men of Rome, what madness was this, whence such violence unbridled?
How could you endure to make gifts of Rome's blood to her most hated enemies?
How could you bear to wage war that was empty of triumphs for Rome,
While in far-away lands un-avenged there wandered the spirit of Crassus, where
Proud Parthia's Babylon stood, and our duty to win back our standards remained unfulfilled?[12]
Alas, what countries and oceans might once have been won with the blood,
Which from Romans themselves Roman hands, Roman weaponry, drained!
What conquests might have been made, in the east where the sunrise of Titan arises,
Or the west where Night hides all her stars; from the south where the breath of the sun
Blazes fiercely at mid-day, or north where the iron of winter, by spring never thawed,
Binds tight with shackles of ice all the waves of the Scythian sea!
By now distant China, Armenia's savages, all might have passed in surrender
Under our yoke; and the tribes, if any there be, that as guardians defend
The Nile's secret sources. O Romans, if such warfare obscene has become
Your obsession so deep, first conquer the world, bring all peoples under your laws,
And then, only then, make war on yourselves. Foreign foes still remain in their plenty.

Now in cities across all our land, buildings stand half-ruined, their walls
Are collapsed, and great rocks lie fallen, the scattered wreckage of ramparts;
No gatekeepers now guard the doors of the houses; in cities old as the hills
None but a remnant remains of a whole population, just aimlessly wandering.
Hesperia, Fate's promised land, now bristles with briars; not for years
Has plough turned her furrows; her fields vainly plead for the work of men's hands;[13]
But you, cruel Pyrrhus,[14] need shoulder no blame for such devastation; no blame need attach

[11] Pharsalus was a city in central Greece, where Julius Caesar finally defeated Pompey in 48 BC.

[12] Marcus Licinius Crassus in trying to emulate the military victories of Caesar and Pompey had led a disastrous expedition against Parthia, losing three legions and his own life at Carrhae (near the modern Turkey-Syria border) in 53 BC. The standards were those recovered by diplomatic triumph of Augustus.

[13] All fighting in the civil war took place in Greece or North Africa, not Hesperia (poetic name for Italy).

[14] Pyrrhus, 319–272 BC, of Epirus in Greece became ruler of a substantial kingdom in central Greece and attacked Rome in support of the Greek cities of Sicily and southern Italy winning at heavy cost the battle of Asculum in 279 BC (a Pyrrhic victory), but losing the war.

To Carthage's Hannibal.[15] For no enemy's sword could inflict so savage a blow
So deep in our vitals. Deepest by far are the wounds we receive from our kinsmen.

T16b Lucan's panegyric to Nero

But if Fate could not find an alternative way for the Advent of Nero,
If, even for gods, so high is the price of a kingdom eternal,
And the heavens themselves could not yield to Jupiter, Lord of the Thunder,
Unless first they warred against Giants, the fiercest of foemen,
Then, ye gods, our complaints must fall silent. Our blasphemous crimes
Are all part of the price of your blessings.
Pile up the corpses in heaps
There in Pharsalus; glut the ghosts of Carthage's dead with our blood;
Let Julius Caesar's last battle be joined in the holocaust horrors of Munda;
Add to these Caesar's rape of Perusia, add Mutina's ordeal,
The fleets savage Actium wrecked, and those wars fought out with our slaves
Beneath Etna's fiery summit.[16] So vast is Rome's debt to her own civil wars.
All for you Fate fashioned it, Caesar. And that was the cost of your Advent.

And at last, with your duty done, when you seek to ascend to the stars,
You will choose your own palace above, where they'll welcome you home
With shouts of rejoicing across heaven's vault. Then the choice will be yours:
To assume the great sceptre of Jove, or to mount Phoebus' chariot of fire
And encircle the earth with the flame of your passing – for Earth will not fear
The exchange of its Sun-Charioteer. To you pride of place will be ceded
By every divinity; Nature herself will concede jurisdiction, wherever you will,
Whatever the title your godhead desires, and the seat of your kingdom on high.
But choose not, we beg you, to establish that seat in the northern expanses,
Nor yet where the hot southern pole presses down with its opposite force.
For thence you would gaze down on Rome with a glance astigmatic.
Wherever you lean on one part of the vastness of heaven, its axis
Unbalanced will surely acknowledge your weight and incline. But rather
Retain at the centre of heaven your place, thus safely sustaining
The balance of all things. In that region of heaven we'll pray
For skies clear and serene, that no clouds may obscure our vision of Caesar.

On that day let the nations lay down their arms, seeking mutual blessings,
Then let nation love nation in brotherly love; let Peace take her flight

15 Hannibal 247–183/2 BC, the great Carthaginian general.

16 Lines 40–44: in the Latin, 'Caesar' is addressed once in line 41. This follows mention in line 40 of (Julius) Caesar's final battle at Munda (southern Spain) in 45 BC where he defeated an army raised by Pompey's sons. Line 41 includes references to (Octavian/Augustus) Caesar's victories against the 'Liberators', at Mutina (modern Modena, N. Italy) in 43 BC and against L. Antonius (Mark Antony's brother) at Perusia (modern Perugia, N. Italy) in 41 BC. The 'Slave War' was Octavian's defeat of Sextus Pompey in Sicily in 36 BC and Actium his naval victory against Antony and Cleopatra. By line 44, it is clear, however that the Caesar being addressed is, in fact, Nero.

All over the earth, and slam shut the war-loving Janus' grim, iron gates.[17]

Great Caesar, for *me* already a god – if my heart finds from you inspiration,
I need no more trouble Apollo, the source of the secrets of Delphi,
Nor summon great Bacchus down from the mountains of Nysa.
Caesar's own inspiration suffices for every poet of Rome.[18]

[Lucan, *Civil War* 1.1–66]

T17 Nero's devotion to magic

In our times, Nero as *princeps* discovered all these (magical ways of predicting the future) to be false lies, though in fact he had been just as enthusiastic about magic as about playing the lyre and tragic verse. Carried away by attaining the height of human prosperity to the depths of depravity in his mind, his greatest desire – and his noblest wish – was to command the gods. No one ever supported any other subject as forcefully. [15] There was no shortage of wealth, of strength, of aptitude for learning, or of anything that the world could allow! That Nero abandoned it is proof positive and undeniable that the subject is false. If only he had consulted the spirits of the dead and any divinities at all about his suspicions and not entrusted searches for evidence to brothels and prostitutes! Any religious rites, however barbarous and inhuman its practices, would have been less savage than Nero's judgement, so cruelly did he fill our nation with ghosts.

[Pliny, *Natural History* 30.14–5]

For lyre playing, see **R37e**, **Q13**, **Q17**.

T18 A fictional inheritance

My patron made me co-heir with the emperor and I gained a senator's fortune.

[Petronius, *Satyricon* 76]

Though Trimalchio is a fictional character, his inheritance as described by Petronius – probably Nero's 'judge of good taste' whose death is described at *Ann.* 16.18–19 – is entirely plausible. It was usual to make the emperor a major beneficiary of a will: Augustus received 1.4 billion sesterces in this way (Suet. *Aug.* 101.3). Claudius is praised for rules on inheritance (Dio 60.6.3; 60.17.7); Gaius and Nero greatly condemned (Suet. *Cal.* 38.2; *Nero* 32). The condemned L. Vetus was urged by friends to name Nero as his principal heir to protect the remaining inheritance for his grandchildren (Tac. *Ann.* 16.11.1). For the whole question see Millar, *Emperor in the Roman World,* 1992 pages 153–8.

T19 Nero legacies i

The amount of money wasted by this same man on other items of crystal can be gauged from their sheer quantity which was so great that when Nero stole them from the man's children and put them on display, they filled his private theatre in his gardens on the far side of the Tiber. This was large enough to satisfy even Nero's wish to prepare for his appearance in the Theatre of Pompey by singing to a full house.

[Pliny, *Natural History* 37.19]

[17] The gates of Janus were on a shrine of Janus Geminus in the forum and were closed when Rome was at peace and open when at war. Augustus made great play of closing these gates three times in his reign (*RG* 13 and Livy 1.19). Nero had the gates closed in AD 63 when the settlement with Tiridates in Armenia was proclaimed (Suet. *Nero* 13.2). The gates were frequently depicted on coins of Nero, see **N52**.

[18] Lucan thus explains why, unlike all previous classical epic poets, he has not called on muses or gods for poetic inspiration. (In fact his poem does not include the divine machinery traditional in epic either.)

The name of this man has been lost in a gap in the text just before this passage, though not his status as an ex-consul. The particular crystal mentioned here is fluorspar. The Crawford Vase, now in the British Museum, is an example of a fluorspar artefact. For its mining and working, see Healy, *Pliny the Elder on Science and Technology,* Oxford 1999, 228–235.

T20 Nero legacies ii

[20] Just before his death, Titus Petronius, an ex-consul, out of hatred for Nero, broke a crystal wine-ladle which he had bought for 300,000 sesterces, so as to disinherit the emperor's dining table: but Nero as you would expect of a *princeps* outdid everyone in paying 1 million sesterces for a single bowl.

[Pliny, *Natural History* 37.20]

For Petronius see **T18**. Shortly after this passage, Pliny (*NH* 37.29) mentions Nero's act of revenge on his whole generation by deliberately smashing two cups made of rock-crystal on receiving the news that all was lost in AD 68, as does Suetonius, *Nero* 47.

T21 Nero debased *denarii*

Later it was decided to mint 40 denarii from a [Roman] pound. The emperors gradually reduced the weight, with most recent reduction under Nero to 45 denarii from a pound.

[Pliny, *Natural History* 33.47]

Nero's coinage of all types shows evidence of a reduction in weight from early in AD 65. For more on Nero's coinage reform of AD 64, see page 14 and Griffin, *Nero* 122–3 and 238–9.

T22 Poppaea bathes in asses' milk

People think that asses' milk removes facial wrinkles, making the skin soft and white. It is well known that some women treat their cheeks exactly seven times a day. Poppaea, wife of the Emperor Nero, started this fashion even preparing baths of milk and therefore travelling with herds of asses.

[Pliny, *Natural History* 28.183]

NH book 28 is about medicinal uses of animal products. The asses were allegedly shod in silver (Suet. *Nero* 30.3). Cleopatra was also reported to have used asses' milk, which is still used in cosmetics.

T23 Pliny's panegyric on Emperor Trajan

[3.18.1] My office of consul imposed upon me the additional duty of proposing a vote of thanks to the emperor on behalf of the state. This I duly did in the senate in the traditional manner as time and place required. But then it occurred to me that it would be entirely appropriate for me, as a loyal citizen, to deal with the subject rather more fully and elaborately in a book. [2] My motives were twofold: first, by means of a genuinely sincere compliment to make our emperor aware of how profoundly his virtues are admired; and secondly, to offer future emperors a kind of handbook for the conduct of their office, based on the example of their predecessor rather than some pedagogue's instructions, and thus to show them how they could most readily aspire to the same degree of admiration. [3] For, of course, to seek to lay down the principles of conduct for an emperor would be a difficult, if not impertinent, undertaking, however helpful it might seem in theory. But to sing the praises of a wholly admirable emperor and thereby to offer a model of enlightened conduct for his successors to follow, seems to me to combine utility with discretion.

[3.18.4–5]: Pliny explains that he invited friends to hear a first reading of the book (equivalent to a modern publisher's book launch) and was delighted that, when the reading was not complete after two days, they all insisted on a third. He sees this as evidence of a revival of interest in the dying art of oratory.

[3.18.6] And what was the subject matter that generated such enthusiasm from my audience? Believe it or not, it was something which, even in the senate, used to bore us to tears after about thirty seconds, even though there we had no choice but to endure such tedium. And yet now here we have a reader and an audience willing to speak and to listen for three whole days on end. And the reason has nothing to do with any advance in standards of eloquence compared with earlier times, but simply because our greater freedom brings with it a greater pleasure in such literary exercises. [18.7] So this is yet another achievement to add to our emperor's credit: an activity, which used to be disliked intensely for its sheer hypocrisy, has suddenly become popular, because it is now possible to speak with sincerity.

[Pliny the Younger, *Letters* 3.18]

In their first speech in the senate after being elected, consuls designates were expected to make a proposal in honour of the emperor. Pliny was suffect consul for September-October AD 100, under Trajan. Tacitus' *Annals* occasionally shows this tradition (e.g. 12.9.1 – AD 49; 12.53 – AD 52; 15.74.3 – AD 65) which must have encouraged ever more sycophantic proposals. Pliny's *Panegyric* survives as do other later examples of this unattractive genre. In *Letter* 6.27, Pliny wrote to C. Vettenius Severus, suffect consul May-August 107, advising him on how to flatter the emperor in his first speech after being elected consul.

SECTION U
THE UPPER CLASSES

Legatus Senatus Populique Romani

Introduction: Galba initial description of his own position in revolt against Nero was as 'The representative of Senate and People of Rome' (Suet. *Galba* 10, Plut. *Galba* 5.2). In our period, **senators** were the wealthy, educated, male élite of the empire, drawn from either long-established Roman families or the Italian nobility. They had to own property in excess of 1,000,000 sesterces, and membership of the senate was hereditary. This system was not effective at maintaining numbers in the senate, so the emperor could bring into the senate equestrians and, increasingly, wealthy provincials (see **M11–M12**). Senators then had to climb a 'career ladder' known as the *cursus honorum* ('path of honours'), consisting of a series of magistracies: the stages are set out in the table below. Beyond this, an ex-consul might govern Africa or Asia, be put in charge of Rome's aqueducts (**K32**), achieve a second consulship, or become city prefect. For some examples of a senatorial *cursus*, see **N36a+b**, **U2**, **U4**, **U9**, **U18**.

Post	Responsibilities	Pre-requisites	Number
Vigintivir	Junior magistrates responsible for (one of) minting coins; executing criminals; judging legal cases; care of streets	Must be sons of senators, aged 18	20 *p.a.*
Military tribune	One of six assistants to the commander of a legion	Optional follow-up to vigintivirate	6 in each of 27 legions
Quaestor	Treasurer – often served in provinces	Followed vigintivirate. Candidate enters senate proper at this point: minimum age 25	20 *p.a.*
Aedile	In charge of city maintenance, markets and games in Rome	Optional follow-up to quaestorship	6 *p.a.*
Tribune of the *plebs*	A largely ceremonial post whose powers had passed to the emperor	Optional follow-up to quaestorship	10 *p.a.*
Praetor	Mainly responsible for the administration of justice	Followed quaestorship; usually also aedileship / tribunate: age 29	12 – 16 *p.a.*
Consul	Chief magistrates of Rome in the Republic; now second to the emperor	Must have completed praetorship: minimum age 42	2 (+ usually 2/4 suffects)

In Rome, the senate met once a fortnight, held debates and proposed legislation. Under the emperors, though, the issues they dealt with tended to be those which were unlikely to be controversial. More important issues, were now considered chiefly by the imperial court instead – i.e. the emperor, his household and a select group of senators (see *amici principis*, **U4–U8**). The senate also acted as a criminal court for cases of corruption and adultery committed by people within their own social class and as governors of provinces, and this is the aspect that looms large in Tacitus' *Annals.*

The **equestrian order** (*ordo equester*) is very much part of the ruling élite of the empire, but is distinct from and slightly less prestigious than the senatorial order. In the Republic, equestrians were essentially wealthy citizens who were not politically active but tended to involve themselves in trade and tax collection instead. They were also closely involved in the army – initially they had literally been 'knights' in the sense of cavalry, but by the late Republic were serving instead as army officers. However, from the Augustan period onwards, their role in both military and civilian administration increased.

Equestrians were distinguished from the senatorial order partly by wealth – the property qualification to be a senator was 400,000 *sestertii*, as compared to 1,000,000 for a senator. As entry into the equestrian order was not hereditary, members of local civic élites in Italy and the provinces could readily achieve equestrian status. Membership carried with it visible privileges (gold rings and toga with narrow purple stripe). Ambitious equestrians had a distinct career ladder for equestrians to climb (culminating in governing the richest province as prefect of Egypt or command of the élite military unit as praetorian prefect (see **M29**, **U25**, **U28**). These posts may have been designated to an equestrian on the grounds that an equestrian would be less of a threat to an emperor than a senator. The two groups shared similar values and could be united by ties of marriage, friendship and patronage (see **E2**).

PRAEFECTUS URBI – CITY PREFECT: U1–U3

Tacitus, *Annals* 6.11 (= LACTOR 17, K7) gives an account of this office, described as the peak of a senatorial career (Syme, *Roman Papers* 5, 608). Under Augustus the office was held in his absence by two of his most important assistants, Maecenas (Dio 49.16.2, 55.7.1) and Statilius Taurus (Dio 54.19.6), and very briefly by Messala Corvinus (**F10**, note 24). Holders of the post in this period are as follows (Syme, *RP* 5.608):

AD 13–32	L. Calpurnius Piso (Pontifex) – **U1**	cos 15 BC
AD 32–33	L. Aelius Lamia (Tac. *Ann.* 6.27.2)	cos AD 3
AD 33– ?36	Cossus Cornelius Lentulus – **U1**	cos 1 BC
AD ?36–39	L. Calpurnius Piso (Jos. *JA* 18.169, 235)	cos AD 27
AD ?39– ?41	Q. Sanquinius Maximus (Dio 59.13.2)	cos II suff. AD 39
AD ?41–56	L. Volusius Saturninus (**U2** and note)	cos suff. AD 3
AD 56–61	L. Pedanius Secundus (Tac. *Ann.* 14.42.1)	cos suff. AD 43
AD 61–68	T. Flavius Sabinus (Tac. *Hist.* 3.75.1)	cos suff. ? AD 47

U1 L. Piso and Cossus Cornelius Lentulus: city prefects and heavy drinkers

(Seneca is writing on drunkenness, trying to show that there is more wrong with it than Zeno's saying that no one entrusts secrets to a drunk.)

Lucius (Calpurnius) Piso, warden of the city, was drunk from the very moment he was appointed. He would spend most of the night at parties and then sleep till about midday. That was his morning routine. Nevertheless he discharged his duties, which included the security of the city, most conscientiously. Divus Augustus entrusted him with secret instructions when he put him in command of Thrace – which he conquered. Tiberius did likewise when he departed for Campania, leaving behind him in Rome a large number of suspicious activities and much unpopularity. Tiberius, I think because Piso's drunkenness had turned out well for him, afterwards made Cossus city prefect, a serious and restrained man, but so deep in his cups that on one occasion he went from a party to the senate house and was there overcome by sleep, could not be woken and was carried home. Nonetheless it was to this man that Tiberius gave many hand-written orders which he judged should not be entrusted even to his own secretaries. Cossus never leaked any secret, public or private.

[Younger Seneca, *Moral Epistles (to Lucilius)* 83.14–15]

Lucius Calpurnius Piso (cos. 15 BC) was known as 'the Pontifex' to distinguish him from Lucius Calprnius Piso (cos. 1 BC), known as 'the Augur', who was the younger brother of the Piso (cos. 7 BC) put on trial for the murder of Germanicus (see **P2, P3**). Before becoming *praefectus urbi* at the age of sixty, he had a distinguished career under Augustus. His three year campaign in Thrace against the Bessi (Dio 54.34.7; see Velleius 98.1–3 and note (LACTOR 17 Section **E**) belongs to 14 –11 or 12–10 BC and earned him triumphal honours. The secret instructions he received as *legatus Augusti*, probably of Galatia-Pamphylia, could have concerned dealings with vassal princes and using the army of the proconsul of Macedonia (Syme, *The Augustan Aristocracy* 332–5). He probably went on to be proconsul of Asia and governor of Syria from 4–1 BC, before being appointed Prefect of the City in AD 13, a post he held until his death twenty years later in AD 32, when he was in his 80th year (Tac. *Ann.* 6.10–11). He was thus appointed

while Augustus was alive, but Seneca, like the Elder Pliny (**J2d**) and Suetonius (*Tib.* 42.1), assumed that Tiberius had already succeeded Augustus when his long-serving Prefect took office. His responsibilities must have increased when Tiberius took up residence in Capri in AD 26, but we hear nothing of him during the crisis of Sejanus' fall and we know nothing of the secret instructions Seneca mention. What did he do to earn Velleius' testimony to his diligence and mildness or Tacitus' to his glory in the post? As Syme surmises, 'In short, the Prefect of the City kept his equilibrium all through and did nothing' (*AA* 343).
Less is known of **Cossus Cornelius Lentulus** (cos 1 BC), who, after the brief prefectship of L. Aelius Lamia (Tac. *Ann.* 6.27.2), held the post from AD 33 until his death in 36. He had won triumphal honours for his victory over the Gaetuli as proconsul of Africa in AD 6, and managed to block the prosecution of the excellent Lucius Arruntius, instigated by Sejanus in AD 31 (Dio 58.8.3; *Dig.* 48.2.12).

U2 Lucius Volusius Saturninus, city prefect

[To Lucius Volusius Sa]turninus, [son of Lucius, grandson of Quintus], consul, [augur, *sodalis Augustal]is*, *sodalis Titius*, pro[consul of Asia, legate of Divus Augustus and] propraetorian legate of [Tiberius Caesa]r Augsutus in the provinces and Dalmatia. He was prefect of the city [for sixteen years(?). During this magistracy], when he had died in his 93rd year of age, the senate [decreed on the proposal of Caesar Augustus German]icus that he be buried with a public funeral, whilst court proceedings were postponed for the sake of his burial, likewise that statues be set up for him: triumphal statues in the Forum of Augustus, a bronze one in the new temple of Divus Augustus, two marble consular statues – one in the temple of Divus Julius, a second on the Palatine within the Triple Gate, a third in the space of Apollo in sight of the senate house – an augural statue in the Regia, an equestrian statue close by the rostra and a statue seated on a curule chair by the Theatre of Pompey in the portico of the Lentuli.

[*AE* (1972) 174 + *AE* (1982) 268]

This inscription, along with **U12** were found at the villa belonging to the distinguished family of the Volusii Saturnini at Lucus Feroniae (modern Fiano Romano, Etruria), a few miles to the north of Rome. At least two generations were commemorated side-by-side at a single moment, when inscriptions were set up in the elaborate *lararium*, or household shrine. Firstly, we find L. Volusius Saturninus, consul in AD 3. His inscription records in detail the nine statues set up in his honour at various locations around Rome on his death aged ninety-three in AD 56, whilst prefect of the city of Rome (compare Tacitus, *Ann.* 13.30, 14.56.1). A fragmentary inscription (*AE* (1982) 63; *CIL* VI 41075a) found in the Roman Forum indicates that the inscription from the villa echoed the wording of the senatorial decree passed in his honour, which was also inscribed beneath the nine statues in Rome. Next to him was commemorated his son, Q. Volusius Saturninus, consul in AD 56 (**U12**). The layout of the shrine makes it likely that at least two other generations of the family were also represented (**U20**), and the inscriptions may have accompanied busts of the honorands. The inscriptions themselves belong to the final quarter of the first century AD, and we do not know what prompted these inscriptions to be set up so long after their honorands had died, but it clearly mattered to later generations of the family to create for their own consumption a particular, detailed picture of their ancestors' achievements. Members of the family remained prominent in Roman politics into the AD 90s, with two consuls in AD 92 and 95, but after that the family disappears from the historical record.

U3 Ti. Plautius Silvanus Aelianus

To Tiberius Plautius Silvanus Aelianus, son of Marcus, [of the voting-tribe Aniensis], pontiff, *sodalis Augustalis*, one of the board of three directors of the mint, quaestor of Tiberius Caesar, legate of legion V in Germany, urban praetor, legate and member of the staff of Claudius Caesar in Britain, consul, proconsul of Asia, propraetorian legate of Moesia, in which he transported more than 100,000 of the Trans-Danubians with their wives and children and chiefs or kings to be tribute-paying subjects; he crushed a revolt of Sarmatians at its outset, although he had sent a large part of his army to the expedition against Armenia; he transported kings hitherto unknown or hostile to the Roman People to the river bank which he was guarding, to pay homage to the Roman standards; he restored their sons to the kings of the Bastarnae and Rhoxolani, and to the king of the Dacians his brothers, who had been captured or seized from the enemy; from some of them he accepted hostages; by these means he both assured and extended the peace of the province, having also removed the king of the Scythians from the siege of the Chersonese, which lies beyond the Dnieper. He was the first to ease the corn-supply of the Roman people with a large amount of wheat from that province. While legate in Spain he was recalled to hold the city prefecture, and in his prefecture the senate honoured him with triumphal decorations, at the instigation of Imperator Caesar Augustus Vespasian in words from his speech which are written below:

"He governed Moesia so well that the honour of his triumphal decorations should not have been deferred to my time, except that by the delay a more distinguished title fell to his lot as city prefect." Imperator Caesar Augustus Vespasian made him consul for a second time during his post as city prefect.

[Smallwood 228 = *ILS* 986]

This epitaph is inscribed upon a marble tablet on the family mausoleum (see **U14**). The deceased's career spanned several reigns, from Tiberius to Vespasian. His name shows that he was adopted into the Plautii family. He participated in the conquest of Britain in 43/44; was governor of Moesia from about AD 57 to 67; and consul twice, in 45 and 74. He was possibly appointed by Vespasian early in his reign as a special commissioner in the Spanish peninsula, but then recalled to serve as City Prefect, the most prestigious post available to a senator who was not a member of the imperial family. The last post in his career was a repeated consulship, an unusual honour for someone not a member of the imperial family, and he held it alongside Titus himself. Given that Vespasian is not referred to as Divus, it seems likely that Plautius Silvanus pre-deceased that emperor some time before 79. Unusually, his epitaph ends with a quotation from a speech made by Vespasian himself in the course of awarding him triumphal decorations (perhaps in 73) for his service in Moesia. This speech contains implicit criticism of Nero for not having honoured him sooner, and reflects Vespasian's bid for popularity by representing himself as rectifying the injustices suffered under the last of the Julio-Claudians.

AMICI PRINCIPIS (FRIENDS OF THE PRINCEPS): U4–U8

This description becomes an increasingly official way of describing favoured senators and equestrians as friends and advisers of the emperor. See Millar, *ERW* 110–122 and **M11d** (Vestinus 'closest friend', Persicus 'friend'), **M35**.

U4 Publius Memmius Regulus, AD 31/37

To Publius Mem[mius] Reg[ulus, son of Publius], quaestor of [Tiberius] Caesar, [praetor], consul, one of the Board of Seven for the management of feasts, *sodalis Augustalis*, Arval Brother, legate of Caesar [Augustus, pat]ron.

[EJ 217 = *AE* (1914) 26]

This inscription has been reconstructed from nineteen marble fragments found in the area of the forum at Ruscino in Gallia Narbonensis (modern Castel Roussillon). It was originally part of a statue base, perhaps to be linked with a gilded bronze statue fragment found nearby. P. Memmius Regulus was consul at the end of AD 31, and was loyal supporter and probably chief confidant of Tiberius in removing Sejanus (Dio 58.9.3, 10.6–8). Arval from September 38–60, see **A38s–A60b.** He survives under Gaius (giving up his wife, Lollia Paulina to him (Suet. *Cal.* 25.2), but delays bringing statue of Olympian Zeus to him (**E3**). He retains influence under Claudius and Nero, dying a natural death in AD 61 (Tac. *Ann.* 14.47, with an 'obituary').

U5 Life of Passienus Crispus

Passienus Crispus, who came from the *municipium of* Vercellae began his maiden speech in the senate with the words: "Gentlemen of the senate and you, Caesar". As a result he was praised very highly, but insincerely, in a speech by Tiberius. He readily undertook very many cases in the centumviral court, and so his statue was set up in the Julian Basilica. He was twice consul. He married twice: first Domitia, then Agrippina, the former being the aunt and the latter the mother of the emperor Nero. He was worth two hundred million sesterces. He tried to curry favour with all the emperors, but especially Gaius whose journeys he accompanied on foot. When he was asked privately by Gaius when he had become intimate with his own sister, he answered, "Not yet", as cautious and proper answer as one could wish for, neither accusing the emperor by denial, nor disgracing himself by lying assent. He was killed by the treachery of Agrippina, whom he had made his heir, and was given the honour of a public funeral.

[Scholia on Juvenal, *Satire* 4.81]

This brief account is found in the ancient commentator on Juvenal who copied it out, thinking it referred to Vibius Crispus mentioned in Satire 4.81 (see below **U8**). In fact it is probably Suetonius' *Life of Gaius Sallustius Passienus Crispus*. He was the son of L. Passienus Rufus, cos 4 BC, adopted by Sallustius Crispus, 'successor' of Maecenas as minister of Augustus (Tac. *Ann.* 3.30 = LACTOR 17, R27). He died in AD 20, leaving his considerable fortune to Passienus who was famous as an orator and a wit, also responsible for the comment on Gaius, 'there has never been a better slave or a worse master' (Tac. *Ann.* 6.20.2; Suet. *Cal.* 10.2). He was consul in 27 (suffect) and 44 (ordinarius). See **B27**, **J12g** and Pliny, *NH* 16.242 for his eccentric behaviour hugging trees: also Barrett, *Agrippina* 84–86.

U6 Seneca on his experience as *amicus principis*

[1] Divus Augustus sent his own daughter into exile. She was immoral beyond any reproach for immorality and brought the scandals of the imperial household into the public domain. … [2] These were scandals which any emperor had a duty not only to punish but also to conceal, since there are some deeds whose sheer obscenity infects those who seek to punish them. But he could not contain his anger and he made them all public. As time went by, however, his anger turned to shame, and he came to lament the fact that he had not concealed her deeds and avoided public comment, since he had remained in ignorance of them for so long that comment could only bring disgrace. He would often exclaim that these things would not have happened, if Maecenas or Agrippa had been alive. Though he had thousands to command, such was the irreparable loss of these two men. [3] Yet when legions were destroyed, others were immediately enlisted; when a fleet was wrecked, a new one put to sea in a few days; when fire devastated public buildings, bigger and better ones arose upon their ruins. But nothing could fill the gap in his life left by the deaths of Maecenas and Agrippa.

Inevitably the question must be asked – must we seriously imagine that there were no other comparable figures, whom he could have recruited in their place? Or was it a flaw in his own make-up that he preferred to repine than to replace? [4] There is no reason to think that Agrippa and Maecenas made a habit of telling him the truth. Had they lived, they would have dissembled with the best of them. It is more that the very nature of a royal temperament is to glory in what is lost in order to demean what still remains, and to attribute the virtue of speaking the truth to those from whom there is no longer any danger of hearing it.

[Seneca, *On Benefits*, 6.32.1–4]

Both men had been close to Augustus from the period of the Triumvirate: M. Vipsanius Agrippa, his principal general, died in 12 BC; C. Cilnius Maecenas, diplomat and literary adviser, died in 8 BC. Had they been alive in 2 BC, they would both in fact, have found it very difficult to advise in this situation: Agrippa, as Julia's husband, Maecenas as the advocate of the marriage (Dio 54.6.5). Tacitus echoes Seneca's belief that no one really replaced Agrippa and Maecenas as close advisers to Augustus in the retirement dialogue he composed for Seneca and Nero (*Ann.* 14.53–56), where both think of these two as the precedents for Seneca's own position. Seneca seems to speak from personal experience here. Tacitus has him mention his exercise of free speech in his dealings with Nero when he was accused of involvement in the Pisonian conspiracy (*Ann.* 15.61), but the dialogue shows what Tacitus thought dealing with the *princeps* was really like.

U7 Seneca's property in Egypt

Psenamounis, son of Psenamounis and grandson of Thonis, and Dionysius, son of Ptollis and grandson of Orthonoos, inhabitants of the village of Sesphtha in the lower district, greet Tiberius Claudius Theon, lessee of the estate of Lucius Annaeus Seneca. Since we are unable to farm the three acres which we held in our own name in the lot of Diotimus on the same estate, we are leaving as from the ninth year of Nero Claudius Caesar Augustus Germanicus Imperator so as not to have any difficulties at all over the rents for the land. We therefore request that you assent to our leaving so that we may not be subject to false accusations. Farewell. Ninth year of Nero Claudius Caesar Augustus Germanicus Imperator, Phaophi 28.

[Second hand] I, Psenamounis, son of Psenamounis, am leaving the farm, as stated.

[Third hand] I, Dionysius, son of Ptollis, am leaving, as stated. The same date.

[Greek: *POxy* 2873]

Dating from 25 October (= Phaophi 28), AD 62, this papyrus demonstrates that Seneca owned property in Egypt, which he leased out to tenants. It complements the picture of his financial interests in Britain, as mentioned by Dio Cassius (62.2). Despite his reputation as a Stoic philosopher, Seneca had enormous wealth, a fact exploited in attacks by his enemies and rivals (Tac. *Ann.* 14.52–55).

U8 Vibius Crispus (cos. ? 61)

So the emperor convened a policy meeting, and summoned
His leading advisers. The subject was – Cooking a mullet….!

Along comes old Crispus, a dear, a master of eloquence, gifted
With morals to match, but a man with the mildest of manners,
Just the job as adviser to him that is ruler of nations,
The lord of the lands and the seas, were it but allowed
By that plague, that walking disaster that ruled us,
To denounce what is savage, and offer him honest advice.
But the ear of a tyrant spells danger – none more so. His friend,
Who was minded to talk of the weather, of rain, or the heat,
Or the storm-clouds of spring – he was probably putting
His neck on the line. But old Crispus was different. For he never swam
Against torrent or tide; no patriot he, such as dared to say freely
Whatever he thought, or risked his own life for the truth.
He survived, living on through his eightieth summer and winter.

Even there, in that court, and thus armed – he survived.

[Juvenal, *Satires*, 4.81–93]

Juvenal, *Satire* 4 is about Domitian's *consilium* or 'inner cabinet', called to discuss how to cook a fish too large for any pot. The 12 members included the emperor, the two praetorian prefects, the prefects of the city and eight other senior senators, of whom Q. Vibius Crispus, mentioned first, seems the most senior. He was consul three times under different emperors, probably in 61, then 74 and 83. Tacitus describes him as 'for his wealth, power, and talent, regarded as famous rather than virtuous' (*Hist.* 2.10), but others were more appreciative (Quintilian, 5.13.48 and Suet. *Dom.* 3.1). He was Aqueducts Commissioner 68–71 (**K32**).

CONSULS: U9–U12

For the list of consuls from this period, see Section **B**

U9 Consul appointed on Tiberius' recommendation

[To...] curator of roads(?) [... quaestor, tribune] of the plebs, praetor, [propraetorian] legate [of Imperator C]aesar Augustus for the second time, by commendation of Tiberius Caesar Augustus appointed consul by the senate, patron.

[EJ 213 = *ILS* 944]

This inscription is from Allifae, in Samnium. This reflects the new system of consular appointment, on the basis of imperial recommendation rather than popular election: now only as many candidates as there were vacancies were put forward for election (see introduction to Section **B** '*The consular election*' and **N36b**).

U10 Campaigning for a province to govern

What about irony? Even in its most severe form, is it not almost a type of joke? Afer used irony with sophistication when Didius Gallus who had campaigned very hard for a province, then complained when he had got one, as if he had been forced to: 'Well, do something for the public good, then!'

[Quintilian, *The Orator's Education* 6.3.68]

This is part of Quintilian's section on various sorts of jokes. We do not know the circumstances, but Didius may not have been expecting a posting to a theatre of war in Britain, when probably almost sixty. For Didius, see **N35**.

U11 Ghost story of Curtius Rufus

I personally am inclined to believe in the existence of ghosts by what I am told happened to Curtius Rufus. While he was very junior and still unknown, he served on the staff of the recently appointed governor of Africa. One afternoon he was taking a stroll in the portico of his house, when a woman appeared, larger than life and far more beautiful. He was scared out of his wits, but she told him that she was the Spirit of Africa, bringing him tidings of his own future. She said that he would go back to Rome and hold high office, and then return to that same province once again with supreme power as its governor. There he would meet his death. And that is exactly what happened.

[Pliny the Younger, *Letters* 7.27.2–3]

Tacitus tells the same story (*Annals* 11.20–21) to explain the rise to prominence (consulship AD 43, triumphal honours, governorship of Africa) of a man alleged to be the son of a gladiator and described by Tiberius as 'a self-made man' (Tac. *Ann.* 11.21). He is thought to be the same Curtius Rufus whose *History of Alexander* survives.

U12 Q. Volusius Saturninus

To Quintus Volusius Saturninus, son of Lucius, [grandson of Lucius], consul, *sodalis Augustalis, sodalis Titius*, Arval Brother, [legate] of Caesar for the census-receipts of the province of Belgica.

[*AE* (1972) 175]

For this man's father and the context of this inscription, see **U2** above. For his son, see **U18**.

OTHER SENATORS: U13–U20

For the senatorial *cursus* see the introduction.

U13 Claudius creates extra praetors to deal with law on trusts

Next the Divine Claudius added two praetors to administer the law on trusts. The Divine Titus abolished one of these.

[Digest 1.2.2.32 = Pomponius, *Introduction to Law*]

Pomponius is giving a summary of the number and responsibility of praetors. For trusts, see **M82**.

U14 Patrician Plautii: epitaph of the Plautii

Publius Plautius Pulcher, son of a *triumphalis*, augur, one of the board of three directors of the mint, quaestor of Tiberius Caesar Augustus in his fifth consulship, tribune of the plebs, praetor of the treasury, member of the staff of Drusus, son of Germanicus, uncle of Drusus, son of Tiberius Claudius Caesar Augustus, and appointed by him when censor among the patricians, appointed as curator for the paving of roads in the neighbourhood by authority of Tiberius Claudius Caesar Augustus Germanicus, proconsul of the province of Sicily.

Vibia, daughter of Marsus, born of Laelia, wife of Pulcher.

[Smallwood 227 = *ILS* 964]

This epitaph was inscribed upon an imposing family mausoleum – a large circular structure about 18 meters in diameter – just outside Tibur (modern Tivoli), near Rome. It illustrates the potential subjectivity that can sometimes be detected in the accounts of their lifetimes given by some members of the élite.

The honorand was Plautius Pulcher, the son of Plautius Silvanus (consul in 2 BC). His father was the founder of the mausoleum and had enjoyed a distinguished public career. In contrast, Pulcher's was lacklustre, but his epitaph endeavours to make it sound impressive. The formula 'son of a *triumphalis*' almost implies that being the son of someone who had celebrated a triumph was an achievement in itself. His various posts are of minor significance, but every opportunity is taken to mention various members of the imperial family in order to make Pulcher sound important. Close examination shows, however, that his association with members of the imperial family took place in rather ominous circumstances. As quaestor of Tiberius during his fifth consulship (AD 31), he must have been caught up in the downfall of Sejanus that year. He is described as member of the staff of Germanicus's son, Drusus, but Drusus was imprisoned and died of starvation in AD 33. In describing him as uncle of Drusus (who died by choking on a pear – Suet. *Claud.* 27.1), the inscription fails to mention the name of Drusus' mother, Claudius' disgraced first wife, and Pulcher's sister, Plautia Urgulanilla. Claudius' censorship in 47/8 saw the elevation of many prominent families to the patriciate, the highest level of nobility (Tac. *Ann.* 11.25.2). Aulus Plautius, conqueror of Britain (see **N33**), was probably Pulcher's brother.

U15 Tiberius grudgingly clears an ex-praetor of debt

[7.2] Tiberius Caesar was asked by Marius Nepos, an ex-praetor, to help him out with his debts. In response he ordered him to produce a list of his creditors. But this is not really an act of generosity; rather it is the act of convening a meeting of creditors. Once the list was supplied, Tiberius wrote to Nepos to say that he had ordered the debts to be settled, but added some offensive advice. The effect was that Nepos was certainly out of debt but had not received a genuine benefit. Tiberius had freed him from his creditors without establishing any ties of obligation between Nepos and himself. [3] But I assume that Tiberius had an ulterior motive. I suspect that he wanted to avoid a horde of others converging on him with similar requests. And I suppose that it is a perfectly effective way of curbing people's greed by exploiting their sense of shame. But for anyone wishing to bestow a genuine benefit, a totally different methodology is required. You must seek to make your gift more acceptable by increasing its attractions in every possible way. The above anecdote is not an example of a benefit, but an attempt to embarrass.

[8.1] But while I am on the subject, let me just make one observation on this point too. Even for an emperor, there is something not quite decent about offering a gift simply in order to humiliate. Indeed you may even observe that in fact Tiberius proved unable to achieve his objective by such methods. For a number of people subsequently emerged with similar requests, and he ordered them all to explain to the senate the reasons for their debt. Provided they did so, he granted them fixed sums of cash. [2] That is not generosity; it is the behaviour of a censor. It is help, it is a grant from the *princeps*. But a benefit it certainly is not, when the very recollection of it brings a blush to the recipient's face: he has been dragged into court, and to gain his request has had to plead his case like a common criminal.

[Seneca, *On Benefits*, 2.7.2–2.8.2]

Marius Nepos is not named in the accounts of Tiberius' behaviour in Tac. *Ann.* 1.75 and Suet. *Tib.* 47, but Tacitus names him in 2.48 among those indebted profligates removed from the senate or allowed to withdraw by the *princeps*. The historian regards Tiberius' conduct as correct, if severe. For this way of dealing with senators in debt, i.e. insisting that debtors make their case to the senate before helping them, Suetonius ascribes to Tiberius the same motive of discouraging requests for help as Seneca; Tacitus only mentions such discouragement as the result, not the motive, and he still applies the term *beneficium* to the emperor's assistance.

It is interesting to see Seneca, who, before retiring in the 60's, had been Nero's adviser as *amicus principis*, making this statement of policy in his own voice. Nero had in fact been generous with handouts to even dissolute nobles in 58, and Tacitus disapproved (*Ann.* 13.34.1). In interrogating the senators about their debts, Tiberius acted as a censor who had power to remove members from the senate for misconduct or failure to meet the property qualification. That Nepos was removed by Tiberius (Tac. *Ann.* 2.48.3) gives more point to the remark 'it is the behaviour of a censor', though no *princeps* formally held the censorship until Claudius.

U16 Tiberius rebukes a bankrupt

I can remember a time when many people adopted this lifestyle [living by night and sleeping by day], including an ex-praetor, Acilius Buta. After squandering a huge inheritance, he admitted being bankrupt to Tiberius, who replied, 'You've woken up too late!'

[Seneca, *Epistles* 122.10]

U17 Vatia – millionaire praetor who 'kept his head down'

As usual, however, I began to look around for anything I could find that would be useful. My eyes fell on a villa which had previously belonged to Vatia. That was where that rich ex-praetor grew old, famed simply for his life of leisure, the only reason for him to be considered fortunate. For whenever friendship with Asinius Gallus, whenever hatred or later affection for Sejanus, mired people (for to have offended him and to loved him were equally dangerous), men would exclaim, "Vatia, you alone know how to live." [4] In fact he knew how to hide, not how to live: for there is a great difference between a life of leisure and a life of idleness. So, even when he was alive, I never went past his villa, without saying to myself, 'Here lies Vatia'.

[Seneca, *Epistles* 55.3–4]

Seneca represents himself in *Epistles* 49 ff. as travelling in Campania in the spring of 64. This letter about the luxurious villa of Servilius Vatia, who was concerned to avoid trouble and enjoy total leisure, contrasts sharply with Seneca's description of the villa that had belonged to Scipio Africanus, the conqueror of Hannibal, who retreated there, according to Seneca for patriotic reasons (compare *Ep.* 51.11). There are strong hints that Vatia was an Epicurean, at least after he retired from his public career ('hide' recalls the Epicurean maxim '*lathe biōsas*' or 'live unnoticed'). It has been suggested (*PIR*[2] S 576, 602) that this ex-praetor is identical with P. Servilius, praetor in AD 25 who gave magnificent games (Dio 53.27.6): he was the son of P. Servilius Isauricus, consul in 48 and 41 BC. This date for Vatia's praetorship would fit the idea here that his retirement freed him from political danger, for Asinius Gallus was imprisoned in AD 30 and died in AD 33 (Tac. *Ann.* 6.23.1, 6.25.2; Dio 58.3) and Sejanus fell in 31.

U18 Senator from Cisalpine Gaul(?)

To Gaius Pontius Paelignus, [son] of Gaius [of the voting-tribe Fabia], military tribune of legion X Gemina, quaestor, curator of public places for a second time, curule aedile, [praetor], propraetorian legate for a second time by decree of the senate and by authority of Tiberius Caesar; by decree(?) [of the decurions].

[EJ 211 = *ILS* 942, with *AE* (1995) 604]

This inscription is from Brixia (modern Brescia), Cisalpine Gaul.

U19 Lucius Coiedius Candidus, Suasa (Umbria)

To Lucius Coiedius Candidus, son of Lucius, of the voting-tribe Aniensis, military tribune of legion VIII Augusta, triumvir for executions, quaestor of Tiberius Claudius Caesar Augustus Germanicus, quaestor of the treasury of Saturn, curator of the public records. This man, returned from military service, Tiberius Claudius Caesar Augustus presented with military gifts – a golden crown, a turreted crown, a rampart-crown, an untipped spear – since he had him amongst his quaestors, and in the same year ordered him to be quaestor of the treasury of Saturn. At public expense.

[Smallwood 234 = *ILS* 967]

This honorific dedication, set up by the town of Suasa, records how Coiedius Candidus was rewarded by Claudius for his brave military service within legion VIII Augusta, probably during operations in the Balkans in 41. He then continued to be selected for public offices directly by the emperor himself, showing Claudius' willingness to promote an individual of whose loyalty he felt assured.

U20 Q. Volusius Saturninus

To Quintus Volusius Saturninus, son of Quintus, grandson of Lucius, augur, priest of Mars on the Palatine, one of the board of three directors of the mint, prefect of the Latin festival, centurion of the first squadron of Roman equestrians. [Di]dymus, [freedman, set this up(?)].

[*AE* (1972) 176]

For this man's grandfather and the context of this inscription, see **U2** above. For his father, see **U12**.

PREFECTS OF EGYPT: U21–U23

For the special status of Egypt as the major provider of grain, and the bar on senators from even visiting Egypt without imperial permission see Tac. *Ann.* 2.59.3 and *Hist.* 1.11. The power of the person in control of Egypt can be seen from Clodius Macer's attempted revolt (**P13**) and from the role of Tiberius Claudius Alexander in securing Vespasian's accession (**U22–U23**).

U21 Ti. Claudius Balbillus honoured at Ephesos (Asia Minor)

[To Tiberius Claud]ius [Ba]lbillus, son of Tiberius Claudius [...], of the voting-tribe Quirina, [...] of the temples of Divus Augustus and [...] and of the groves and of [all] holy places which are at Alexandria [and in the whole of Egypt] and head of the museum and officer of the [Alexandrian] library and high-priest and officer of the temple of Hermes at Alexandria for [... years] and officer of embassies and replies [in Greek of Ca]esar Augustus Divus Claudius, and [military tribune] of legion XX and prefect of engineers of Divus Cla[udius and presented with gifts in his triumph by Divus] Claudius, [with a turreted crown and a banner and] an untipped [spear...]

[Smallwood 261a = *AE* (1924) 78]

[The council and the people] honoured [Tiberius Claudius] Balbillus, [the greatest] procurator of [Augustus], for his unremitting piety towards the goddess and his beneficence towards the city.

[Greek: Smallwood 261b]

Balbillus was born in Egypt, probably the son of the Tiberius' famous astrologer Tiberius Claudius Thrasyllus. He held posts in Egypt, Rome, and Asia Minor. His involvement in the Museum and Library at Alexandria reflect his intellectual reputation based upon astrological studies. He served as prefect of Egypt from 55 to 59 (**M6**, **M7**, **M36**, **M57**). After his death in 79, games were established in his honour at Ephesos, where both these inscriptions were found.

U22 Tiberius Julius Alexander

The successor to Fadus as procurator of Judaea was Tiberius Alexander. His father, also Alexander, had been the Alabarch (principal salt-tax collector) of Alexandria, and was its leading citizen by reason of his wealth and ancestry. In his scrupulous religious observance he also differed from his son, who showed little regard for his people's traditional practices.

[Josephus, *Jewish Antiquities,* 20.100]

Tiberius Julius Alexander was the son of an Alexandrian Jew who had been given Roman citizenship. He embarked on a career in the imperial service in the AD 40s. He held the post of epistrategos in Egypt in AD 42, the procuratorship of Judaea *c.* 46–48. Josephus' comment that he showed little regard for his people's practices probably refers to the fact that during his prefecture of Egypt he sent the legions to crush a Jewish revolt in Alexandria and later, serving under Titus, he participated in the siege of Jerusalem.

U23 Tiberius Julius Alexander satirised

Your whole day is a detailed diary of such smart occasions.
The dole first; then off to the forum to gawp at Apollo,
Of legal eagles the prince, and all those triumphal statues,
Where some bloody foreigner, an Arab official from Egypt,
Had the nerve to inscribe his CV. But as for his statue,
It's perfectly proper to piss on – and worse!

[Juvenal, *Satires*, 1.127–131]

The forum of Augustus had a statue of Apollo (Pliny, *NH* 7.183), described as a 'legal eagle' because of all the law-suits he heard standing there. Statues of generals to have won a triumph, together with inscriptions were set up under Augustus (see LACTOR 17 K20–25) and added to. The 'Arab official' is Juvenal's insulting reference to Tiberius Julius Alexander, who, as Prefect of Egypt from 66–69, made a timely and crucial intervention in favour of Vespasian (Tac. *Hist.* 1.11, 2.79). receiving an honorary triumph in return.

PRAETORIAN PREFECTS: U24–U25

This post was created by Augustus in 2 BC (Dio 55.10.10). In AD 14 the prefect, Seius Strabo, swears allegiance to Tiberius immediately after the consuls (Tac. *Ann.* 1.7.2) and the post continues to rise in importance of this post: Tacitus, *Annals* 4.2, and Millar, *ERW* 122–131, even though in this period it seems second to the prefectship of Egypt, as two praetorian prefects are promoted to that post. Prefects, sometimes joint in this period, are as follows:

? – AD 15	L. Seius Strabo (**P4a**, **P4b**, Tac. *Ann.* 1.7.2)
AD 14 – 31	L. Aelius Seianus (**C4**, **J10f**, **P4a–m**, **R2**, **R5**, Tac. *Ann.* 4, *passim,* esp. 4.1–2)
AD 31 – 38	Q. Naevius Sutorius Macro (**D5**, **D6**, **U24**, Dio 58.9.2–6; Tac. *Ann.* 6.45–50)
AD 38 – 41	M. Arrecinus Clemens (**E9**, **E10**, **E20**)
AD 38 – 41	L. Arruntius Stella (**E19**)
AD 41 – 43	Rufrius Pollio (**E30**; **F13**, Dio 60.23.2)
AD 41 – 43	Catonius Justus (**F13**, Dio 60.18.3)
AD 43 – 51	Rufrius Crispinus (**H12**, Tac. *Ann.* 11.1, 12.42.1, 16.17)
AD 47 – 51	L. Lusius Geta (Tac. *Ann.* 11.31, 12.42.1)
AD 51 – 62	Sex. Afranius Burrus (**G20**; Tac. *Ann.* 12.42.1)
AD 62 – 65	L. Faenius Rufus (Tac. *Ann.* 14.51.2, 15.50.3, 15.66)
AD 62 – 68	C. Ofonius Tigellinus (Tac. *Ann.* 14.51.2, *Hist.* 1.72)
AD 65 – 68	C. Nymphidius Sabinus (Tac. *Ann.* 15.72, *Hist.* 1.5)

U24 A legacy from the praetorian prefect, Macro

Quintus Naevius Cordus Sutorius Macro, son of Quintus, of the voting-tribe Fabia, prefect of the city watchmen, praetorian prefect of Tiberius Caesar Augustus, gave this in his will.

[EJ 370 = Smallwood 254 = *AE* (1957) 250]

Macro was involved in bringing about the downfall of Sejanus, whom he succeeded as praetorian prefect in 31, having previously been prefect of the watch. He was a supporter of Gaius, but was forced to commit suicide in 38. This building-inscription above one of the entrance ways into the amphitheatre at Alba Fucens (Samnium) shows that Macro donated substantial funds to his home-town in his will for building this structure.

U25 Honours for praetorian prefect Afranius Burrus

The Vocontii of Vaison to their patron Sextus Afranius Burrus, son of Sextus, of the voting-tribe Voltinia, military tribune, procurator of Augusta, procurator of Tiberius Caesar, procurator of Divus Claudius, prefect of the praetorian guard, honoured with the insignia of a consul.

[Smallwood 259 = *ILS* 1321]

This statue base from Vasio in Gallia Narbonensis (modern Vaison-la-Romaine) suggests that Burrus probably originated from that region. He was appointed as praetorian prefect by Claudius in 51, continuing under Nero until his death in 62. The inscription shows that he had served as financial agent of Livia, Tiberius, and Claudius, demonstrating continuous service under different emperors. The name of Gaius is omitted but probably reflects the desire not to mention the assassinated emperor rather than reflecting a break in Burrus' career. He played a key role in engineering Nero's acclamation as successor to Claudius (Tac. *Ann.* 12.69).

OTHER EQUESTRIANS: U26–U31

For the role and position of equestrians, see introduction to the section.

U26 Equestrian reforms under Tiberius

[32] Finally in the ninth year of the principate of Tiberius the equestrian order became a single entity. When Gaius Asinius Pollio and Gaius Antistius Vetus were consuls, in the 775th year since the foundation of Rome [AD 23], rules regulating the wearing

of rings were established. The reason behind it was surprisingly trivial. Gaius Sulpicius Galba had taken the opportunity of making his mark as a young politician with the *princeps* by levelling fines on fast food outlets. He complained in the senate that the owners would usually excuse themselves by displaying their rings. For this reason, it was established that the right to wear such a ring should be confined to men who were free-born; with free-born fathers and grandfathers; with a census rating of 400,000 sesterces; and entitled to sit in the front fourteen rows of seats under Augustus' Law on the Theatres. [33] Afterwards people began to apply for this status in droves. Because of these distinctions, Gaius as *princeps* added a fifth equestrian group, which has given rise to so much pride that panels that could not be filled under Divus Augustus are not big enough for that class, while everywhere there are men actually freed from slavery who make the leap over to these honours. This did not previously happen since both equestrians and judges were distinguished by an iron ring. The situation became so mixed up that when Claudius Caesar was censor, an equestrian, Flavius Proculus called for the investigation of 400 people for breaking the regulations. Thus a class, meant to be kept distinct from ordinary free-born men has been opened to slaves.

[Pliny, *Natural History,* 33.32–3]

Gaius Sulpicius Galba, brother of the emperor, was trying to follow Tiberius' order for aediles to impose restrictions on food for public sale (Suet. *Tib.* 34.1). Augustus had created four panels of 'judges' within those qualified as equestrians, the honour probably being a gift from the *princeps* (Suet. *Tib.* 41.1 on vacancies not being filled when Tiberius retired to Capri, and 51.1 on a candidate urged by Livia being enrolled with the words 'on the insistence of the emperor's mother'!). Gaius added a fifth panel (compare **M8**). For Claudius and the equestrians, see Suet. *Claud.* 16 and 25. His censorship was AD 47–48.

U27 Admission to Claudius' presence

During the principate of Claudius there was another unprecedented distinction, that of wearing a golden ring with the image of the *princeps*. This right was granted to those with free access to the *princeps* and provided great scope for accusations. The welcome rise to power of Vespasian put an end to all this by making the *princeps* accessible to all.

[Pliny, *Natural History*, 33.41]

The right of admission belonged to all senators, and also under Claudius to certain equestrians. Seneca, *On Benefits* mentions different levels of access to the *princeps* (6.33.4). The accusations that arose were presumably of forgery (Millar, *ERW* p.111). Vespasian extended this privilege to all equestrians.

U28 A distinguished family at Venafrum

Lusia Paullina, daughter of Marcus, wife of Sextus Vettulenus Cerialis, for herself and her father Marcus Vergilius Gallus Lusius, son of Marcus, of the voting-tribe Teretina, senior centurion of legion XI, prefect of the cohort of Ubian infantry and cavalry, presented with two untipped spears and golden crowns by Divus Augustus and Tiberius Caesar Augustus, prefect of the engineers three times, military tribune of the first praetorian cohort, imperial financial administrator in Egypt, duumvir twice, pontiff; and for her brother Aulus Lusius Gallus, son of Aulus of the voting-tribe Teretina, military tribune of legion XXII Cyrenaica, prefect of cavalry.

[EJ 245 = *ILS* 2690]

U29 Patron of Aquinum (Latium)

To Quintus Decius Saturninus, son of Quintus, grandson of Marcus, lesser priest at Rome, officiator at the *Tubilustrium* festival of the Roman people, the Quirites, staff officer of a consul three times, curator of the Labican and Latin roads, military tribune, staff officer for the administration of justice and for the selection of jurors by lot in Asia, quattuorvir for the administration of justice at Verona, quaestor twice, duumvir for the administration of justice, duumvir for a second time as quinquennalis, prefect quinquennalis of Tiberius Caesar Augustus, and for a second time of Drusus Caesar, son of Tiberius, and for a third time of Nero Caesar, son of Germanicus, pontiff, *flamen* of Rome and Divus Augustus in perpetuity by authority of Tiberius Caesar Augustus and by his permission chosen as patron of the colony; at public expense, by decree of the town councillors.

[EJ 229 = *ILS* 6286]

The post of prefect resulted when a member of the imperial family (here Tiberius, his son Drusus, and then Germanicus' son Nero) was elected to a town's local magistracy, in an honorific capacity. Saturninus must have derived considerable prestige from having in effect deputised for three different members of the imperial family. Holding a local magistracy as quinquennalis was also an especial honour, since it was a title borne by the magistrate charged with the taking of the census every five years. These titles indicate that Saturninus had an active career over at least a twenty-year period.

U30 An equestrian honoured at Pompeii, AD 47–54

Spurius Turranius Proculus Gellianus, son of Lucius, grandson of Spurius, great-grandson of Lucius, of the Fabian tribe; staff officer twice; prefect of the curators of the Tiber channel; prefect with the powers of a praetor in charge of jurisdiction in the city of Lavinium; 'father' of the deputation of the Laurentine people in charge of concluding the treaty with the Roman people in accordance with the Sibylline books, which relates to the rites concerned with the origins of the Roman people, the Quirites, and of the people of the Latin name, which are observed among the Laurentines; *flamen* of Jupiter; *flamen* of Mars; leading member of the Salii priesthood; augur and pontiff; prefect of the Gaetulian cohort; military tribune of legion X (dedicated this). Space granted by decree of the town councillors.

[Smallwood 257 = *ILS* 5004]

This small marble base originally supported a statue. It can be dated by its use of the digamma, a letter of the alphabet revived by the emperor Claudius for a short time. Its antiquarian flavour perhaps reflects the spirit of the times.

U31 A pre-eminent provincial in Achaia, *c.* AD 54/55?

To Gaius Julius Spartiaticus, son of Laco, grandson of Eurycles, of the voting-tribe Fabia, procurator of Caesar and of Augusta Agrippina, military tribune, honoured by Divus Claudius with the horse provided at public expense, *flamen* of Divus Julius, pontiff, twice quinquennial duumvir, president of the Isthmian and Caesarian Augustan games, first high priest of the Augustan House in perpetuity in the Achaian League, on account of his merit and for his keen and superlatively generous munificence towards the divine house and towards our colony. The tribesmen of the Calpurnian tribe, to their patron.

[Smallwood 264 = *AE* (1927) 2]

This inscription is carved upon a statue base of local limestone from Corinth, the provincial capital of Achaia. Spartiacus was a member of the ruling family at Sparta (for earlier generations, see **L4**). Spartiacus had inherited rule in Sparta from his father Laco, but fell from favour by 61. This inscription records how

Spartiacus was promoted to equestrian rank by Claudius, with the special honour of a 'public horse', and held priesthoods at both municipal and provincial level. His appointment by the Achaian League as first high priest in perpetuity for emperor-worship indicates his social pre-eminence at the time. The choice of Latin for this inscription reflects the emphasis in its content, upon Spartiacus as Roman military officer, imperial agent, equestrian, and priest of various cults for members of the imperial family. The phrase 'procurator of Caesar and of Augusta Agrippina' probably refers to Nero, and reflects Agrippina's dominance during Nero's early years in power. Members of the family acted as benefactors in other Greek cities, including Corinth. The Calpurnian tribe at the end refers to a local institution at Corinth.

CONCORDANCE

(By document number)

A: LITERARY SOURCES

Acts of the Apostles	
22.22-39	M76
25.6-12	M37
Albinovanus Pedo	
Fragment 1	J7b
Antiphilus (Gow & Page)	
6	M13
Anthologia Latina (Bucheler & Riese)	
419	N16
423	N16
Aurelius Victor	
Book on the Emperors	
5.2-4	J30e
8.7	intro to R
Bassus	
Epigram 5 (Gow & Page)	J7j
Calpurnius Siculus	
Eclogues	
1.33-90	T15
4.136-146	L27
7.23-46	Q9a
7.46-84	Q9b
Digest of Roman Law	
1.2.2.32	U13
1.2.2.50-2	R45
4.4.3.4	M79
16.1.2.1	M78
29.5.0-1 preface	S3
36.1.1.1-3	M80
37.14.5 preface	S15
38.4.1 preface	S16
40.8.2	S1
47.9.3.8	K20
Dio Chrysostom (= Dio of Prusa)	
Orations 31.148-150	R33
Eutropius	
7.13.2	N15
Frontinus	
On Aqueducts	
13	K26
14	K28
15-16	K29
102	K32
105	K30
116	K31
Strategems	
2.9.5	N49
4.2.3	N45
4.1.21	N46
4.1.28	N47
Fronto	
Principles of History 20	Q20
Gaius	
Institutes	
1.32c	K19
1.32c	K39
1.62	J2d
1.84	S4
1.157	M81
1.160	S4
3.63	S17
Gellius	
Nights in Attica	
7.7.8	A1
13.14.3-7	N23
Honestus	
Epigram 21 (Gow & Page)	J1a
Jerome	
Chronicle	
page 180	N44
Josephus	
Jewish Antiquities	
18.143	J5c
18.166	J5c
18.170-173	M1
18.181-2	P4e
18.205-211	J7k
18.257, 259	D1
19.1-273	Section E
20.100	U22
20.125-136	M35
20.137-144	S30
20.148	P9a
20.148-149	J21d
20.149-150	J12h
20.151-2	P9a
20.154	R6
20.195	J27b
20.259-260	E1a
20.263, 267	E1b-c
Jewish War	
2.363-387	N1-N2
Justinian's Institutes	
3.12.1	S4
Justinian's Digest	
3.3.1	M80
Justinian's Legal Code	
7.6.1.3	S2
Juvenal	
Satires	

8.145	T2
9.117-8	T12
10.5	L23
10.171-2	P8a
11.187	P2c
12.12	S20
12.78	R25f
12.94	K7
13.79-80	R22
14.143-6	J2d
16.201-2	K8
17.5	K38
18.6	A2
18.35	M54
19.24	Q10
22.92	P9c
25.20	N3
26.9	M2
28.183	T22
29.7-8	R41
30.14-15	T17
30.16-17	N54
32.4-5	P6a
33.32-33	U26
33.41	U27
33.47	T21
33.53	Q6
33.54	N18
33.54	Q16
33.90	Q11
33.134	S25
33.145	S23
34.45-6	K44
34.62	R19
34.84	K43
35.18	R21
35.51	R30
35.70	R20
35.120	R29
35.201	S28
36.23	R31
36.25	R31
36.36	R31
36.37	R32
36.60	S26
36.70	K15
36.74	Q4
36.101	K intro
36.111	K42
36.122-3	K24
36.124	K21
36.197	P4b
37.19	T19
37.20	T20
37.42	N4
37.50	J27d

Pliny (the Younger)	
Letters	
1.13.2-3	R23
1.17.1-4	P11g
2.1.1-6	P13i
3.5.1-6	R14
3.7.1-9	R38
3.16.6-13	P7a
3.18	T23
5.3.5-6	R35
5.5.2-3	R7
7.27.2-3	U11
8.6	S29
9.19.1-5	P13j
Plutarch	
Life of T. Flaminius	
12.8	M15
Life of Galba	
4.2	P13a
6.1-2	P13d
6.2	P13c
10.2	P13h
Moralia	
505C	P11a
Pomponius	
Introduction to Law	R45
Pomponius Mela	
Geography, 3.49-53	N13
Quintilian	
The Orator's Education	
1.7.26	R24
6.3.62	B1
6.3.68	U10
8.5.15	P10a
8.5.16	P7c
8.5.18	P10b
10.1.102	R9
10.1.103	R10
10.1.104	R13
Scholia on Juvenal	
4.81	U5
6.434	J28a
8.213	J26a
10.63	P4k
Scribonius Largus	
Prescriptions, prologue	R40
Seneca (the Elder)	
Suasoriae 1.15	J7b
Seneca (the Younger)	
Apocolocyntosis	Section F
Epistles	
47.9	S27
55.3-4	U17
70.10	P1b
83.14-15	U1
122.10	U16
Moral Epistles	

B: COINS

***BMC* Augustus**	
506	J2a
***BMC* Tiberius**	
70	M3
76	J1d
95	J24a
102	K4
***BMC* Gaius**	
7	J9b
13	J7n
37	J22a
41	K6
85	J9d
104	M43
***BMC* Claudius**	
8	J12b
32	N22
37	K1
104	J3b
140	K13
166	J5e
224	L22
242	J25a
***BMC* Nero**	
1	J21b
4	L25
68	P11f
84	J30a
103	K40
132	K37
140	Q14
187	N52
196	K36
236	Q13
261	Q15
405	N51
***BMC* Clodius Macer**	
3	P13e
***BMC* Civil Wars**	
8	P13f
34	P13b
57	P13g
BMC	
Alexandria 124	J27a
Alexandria 127	L33
Alexandria 130	Q18a
Alexandria 141	Q18c
Crete 1	L15
Lydia 21	J28b
Pontus 3	M48
Thrace 2	M47
1853.0716.224	M40a
1951.1006.20	P4g
1979.0101.1982	N43
2671	Q18b
***RIC* Augustus**	
225	J2a
***RIC* Tiberius**	
42	J24a
48	M3
51	J1d
56	K4
***RIC* Gaius**	
7	J9b
12	J7n
33	J22a
36	K6
55	J9d
59	M43
***RIC* Claudius**	
7	K1
11	J12b
33	N22
73	J3b
92	J5e
94	K13
101	L22
124	J25a
***RIC* Nero**	
1	J21b
4	L25
61	K40
76	J30a
79	Q13
110	K36
147	N52
161	Q14
178	K37
233	Q15
615	N51
***RIC* Clodius Macer**	
8	P13e
***RIC* Civil Wars**	
25	P13f
72	P13b
110	P13g
RPC	
5297	L33
964/1	L15
2367/2	J10b
865	J17e
2543/3	J28b
3334/1	N43
398/8	P4g
4846	L34
5298	Q18a
5300	Q18b
5302	Q18c
5301	Q18d
Alexandropoulos 224	M40a

C: INSCRIPTIONS

Acta Fratrum Arvalium	
ed. Scheid	Section A
***AE** (l'Année épigraphique)*	
1914.172	M68
1935.32	M30
1941.105	M52
1952.148	M75
1953.88	M65
1961.107	N6
1968.549	M69b
1972.174	U2
1972.175	U12
1972.176	U20
1976.653	M61
1976.673	M32
1980.457	N19
1982.268	U2
1983.210	Q1
1985.283-4	L31
1995.604	U18
1996.246a-d	J12f
1999.1681	M28
2001.1918	N20
2001.1931-2	N40
2002.1472	N41
2003.1559	M10
2005.106	S7
***AJA** (American Journal of Archaeology)*	
63 (1959).384	R18
***AJPhil** (American Journal of Philology)*	
100 (1979).551ff	M33
Carroll, *The Parthenon Inscription*	
16	L28
Cavuoto (1975)	
223 no.3	J24b
CIL	
VI 5188	S8
VI 8909	S6
XIII 1036	M66
Corpus Papyrorum Judaicarum	
2.156a-d	M7
Customs Law of Asia (Cottier, *et al.*)	
Lines 1-11	M58
Ehrenberg & Jones	
Pages 40-43	B14-B37
39	P2a
50	M4
51	P4h
52	P4i
53	P4d
82	K2
85	J2e
88	L8
89	J1b
90	J10d
92a/b	J10g
93	J5a
94	J7f
94a	J8j-q
95	J17b
96	J17c
97	J19c
101	L3
102a/b	L4
105*	J2b
109	L2
123	J1c
126	L11
129	L10
133	L6
134	L7
137	L12
163	M41
172	M45
211	U18
213	U9
215	L5
217	U4
218a	N7
220	P4a
225	M52
227	N5
243	M29
245	U28
284	M21
290	M20
293	M22
320a	M70
320(a)	M59
320(b)	J7d
333	S18
345	M68
348	M67
352	M44
354	M64
358a	M65
362	Q3
370	U24
Fasti at Amiternum	
17 Sep	L1
Fasti at Antium	
10 Oct	J7g
6 Nov	J21a
Fasti at Cumae	
24 May	J7a
5 Oct	J10a
Fasti Ostienses	
Cb	J10h
Cb r	P4f
Cd	J7h

Ce	J10c
Ce	J17a
Ch	J2g
Ch	J5d
Ch	J19e
Ch	J22c
Ch	K5
Fasti at Praeneste	
23 Apr	K3
Fasti Vallenses	
1 Aug	J12a
Feriale Duranum	
136	J7p
Hesberg & Panciera	
12	J7i
IAph2007	
9.14	N53
9.25	L36a
9.26	L36b
9.31	J16a
9.33	J20a
9.34	L36d
9.35	L36e
9.37	L36c
9.41	N28
9.42	L36f
IG	
II/III^2 3535	M73
V 1.1432	M55
XII 2.212	J17b
XII 2.540	J7f
IGRRP	
I 879	M45
I 1110	M36
III 335	M53
III 345	L29
III 703	N36a
III 720	L9
III 721	L8
IV 78b	J22b
IV 145	M46
IV 180	L10
IV 206	J5a
IV 208-9	J12e
IV 219	N5
IV 561	L30
IV 914	M71
IV 1053	R43
IV 1060	R44
IV 1086	R42
IV 1505	M25
ILS	
95	P2a
113	K2
121	L11
150	J5f
151	M20

153	P1c
154	L3
156	M4
157	P4h
158	P4i
159	J2e
164	J2h
168	J10g
172	J24c
176	J10g
180	J9c
181	J9a
182	J17c
183	J17d
185	J18a
188	J23a
189	J19c
190	J19d
196	J22d
205	K25
206	M9
207	K16
208	M24
209	K22
210	L19
212	M11
213	N24
214	M63
216	N25
217	N27
218	K27
222	N26
231	M26
232	N50
233	L35
942	U18
944	U9
964	U14
967	U19
970	N35a
986	U3
1349	M29
1321	U25
1514	S5
1533	K17
1546	S22
1682	S21
1697	S13
1765	Q8
1774	S14
1781	S10
1788	S12
1986	M74
2690	U28
2696	N30
2701	N29
2702	P7b

101	J12e
108	J32b
112	J32c
127	L13
128a	J22d
128b	J22b
132	L24
133	M72
136	J12c
137	L20
138	J32a
145	Q19
146	L29
147	R43
149	L35
173	K17
174	K18
180	S13
186	Q8
187	S9
188	S11
197	M50
201	M47
203b	M51
206	M48
226a	N35a
227	U14
228	U3
231a	N36a
231c	N36b
234	U19
236	J33a
254	U24
257	U29
259	U25
261a	U21
261b	U21
262	R42
264	U30
265	M34
268	M38
277	J19g
281	N30
282	N29
289	R44
291	P7b
293	M75
295	M74
297a	M77a
297b	M77b
306	K9
308b	K25
309	K27
312b	K16
318	M25
320	M69
329	K22
330	K23
333	M23
351	M26
361	J19f
363	M79
367	M8
368	M9
369	M11
370	L17, M6
371	L18
373a	Q7a
373b	Q7b
374	M49
375	M63
380	M31
381	M62
385	M19
387	M53
390	L30
401	M46
405	M30
407a	N11
407b	N12
408	M71
414	M73
415	Q12
418	M36
438	M56
439	M57
Tabula Hebana	J8j-q
Tabula Siarensis	J8a-i
Tabulae Pompeianae Sulpiciorum	
46	K11
51	K10
Wilcken, *Grundzüge und Chrestomathie der Papyruskunde* (1912)	
413	M60
ZPE	
45 (1982).99-100	M61
66 (2008).153-4	M27

Index of Persons

The following usual and ancient abbreviations for *praenomina* (first names) are used:

A.	Aulus	M.	Marcus
C.	Gaius	P.	Publius
Cn.	Gnaeus	Q.	Quintus
D.	Decimus	Sex.	Sextus
L.	Lucius	T.	Titus
M'.	Manius	Ti.	Tiberius

Other frequent abbreviations
cos = consul
cos ord = consul at start of year
cos suff = suffect consul

Ancient authors were inconsistent in how they referred to Romans. So too is modern usage. Well known figures are referred to by their usual names, other Romans by their family names. Consuls for AD 14–68 are listed in Section **B**. Entries for members of the imperial family appear in **bold**. Emperors appear in CAPITALS with regnal dates.

Acca Larentia: A1, A2
Cn. Acerronius Proculus (cos ord 37)
Acilia (mother of Lucan): P11b
M'. Acilius Aviola (cos ord 54); K32
Acilius Buta (praetor) : U17
Acratus (freedman of Nero) : R33
Acte (mistress of Nero): H4
Aedemon (rebel leader in Africa): N10, N12
Aelia Paetina (wife of Claudius): J12h
L. Aelius Lamia (city prefect): note to U1
L. Aelius Seianus *see Sejanus*
M. Aemilius Lepidus (cos ord 6)
commander in Spain: C2
M. Aemilius Lepidus (Gaius' brother-in-law) **J20**
& Gaius: E6, E10, J20
L. Aemilius Rectus
prefect of Egypt: L17, M6b, M62
Aemilius Regulus (conspirator): E6
Mamercus Aemilius Scaurus (cos suff AD 21)
Aeneas (founder of Rome): L36e
L. Afinius Gallus (cos ord 62)
Sex. Afranius Burrus (praet prefect): G20, U25
Agrippa (Herod Agrippa): M7a, S30
& imp family: J5d, E27, E30–1, M7b, M35
M. Agrippa (Aug's helper): C4, K31, R19, U6
Agrippina the Elder (wife of Germanicus) **J9**
birthday: A39d,
children: J9a, P3j
exile & death: C7, H15
'goddess': J17b
honoured: J9b, J9d, J20a, L36c, P3j
marriage: J8a, J8b, P3j
& Gaius: J9b–d
Agrippina the Younger (wife of Claudius, mother of Nero) **J21**
appointee of: U30
Augusta: A54a, A55a, N26, U30
birthday: A57c, A58e, J21a, J21c
damnatio memoriae: H10
death: H6, H15, P10a, P10b, P11b
family: J21d
honoured: J21a–b, J22b, L36i, N26
influence: M35
marriages: H1, J12d–f, K35, U5
shipwreck: H6, H15
words of: R26
& Britannicus: H3, H11
& Caligula: D7, J22a
& Claudius: H1–2, J12d–f, J21d, K35, P9a–c
& Nero: L36i, R26
& Pallas: S28
Albinovanus Pedo (poet): J7b
Alcyon (doctor): E20
Alexander of Alexandria (alabarch): D1
Q. Allius Maximus (cos suff 49): M30
Ananias (high priest of Jerusalem): M35
Ananus (temple superintendant Jerusalem): M35
Ancus Martius (4th King of Rome): M11b
Anicetus (freedman of Nero): H6
Anicetus (charioteer): Q5
C. Anicius Cerealis (cos suff 65)
P. Anicius Maximus (army prefect): N30
L. Annaeus Seneca (cos suff 55):
See also concordance of literary sources
Adviser of Nero: U6
exiled: T14
in *Octavia: H8, H9*
property of: U7
writer: P10b, P11b, R35,
M. Annius Afrinus (cos suff 67)
P. Annius Seleucus: K11
L. Annius Vinicianus

wife of Passienus Crispus U5
DOMITIAN (emperor 81–96): R8
Cn. Domitius Afer (cos suff 39); K32
Cn. Domitius Ahenobarbus (cos 16 BC,
arval: A15a
grandfather of Nero), J13a
Cn. Domitius Ahenobarbus (cos ord 32, father of Nero): J13, J21d, N30
arval: A27a, A37a, A37b, A38a, A38d, A38f, A38i, A38k, A38m, A38t, A39c, A39d
birthday celebrated: A55a, A57e, A58g, A59m
Cn. Domitius Corbulo (cos suff 39):
connection of Gaius: J15a
general in Armenia: N46–N51, N58
governor of Asia: M33
T. Domitius Decidianus (quaestor): M58a
Drusilla (sister of Caligula) **J22**
birthday: A40c
coin of Gaius: J22a
death: J22c, L16
deified: A38t; F1, J22d, J22e, L16
'goddess' (while alive): J22b, M46
honoured: J22b–c
Drusilla (Jewish princess): S30
Drusillanus (freedman): S23
Drusus (Nero Claudius Drusus, brother of Tiberius): **J3**
building: M25
family: J3a, J5a, J5c, P3j
in Germany: J3b, M11d, R14
& Livia: J1c
& Germanicus: J8b, J8d, J8j, P3j J1c, J3, J5a, J5c, J8b, J8d, J8j, M11d, M25, P3j
Drusus (Drusus Julius Caesar, son of Tib.) **J10**
Arval: A15a, A21b
birthday: J10a
commander: C5, N5
early death: C7, J7k, J10d, J10e
games: Q3
honours: J10a–d, J10f–h, L4, M66, U29
marriage: H15
Pannonia mutiny: C2
praised: P3j
triumph: J10c
& Germanicus: J8a, J8g, J10b, J10e, J10f, P3j
& Herod Agrippa: J5d
Drusus Caesar (1st son of Ger.& Agrippina) **J18**
death: H15
honoured: J18a, J22b
member of his staff: U14
A. Ducenius Geminus (cos unknown year):
tax commission: M58a
L. Duvius Avitus (cos suff 56)

Epaminondas: M14c
Epaphroditus (freedman of Gaius): Q5
M. Etrilius Lupercus: L7, N7
Eutychus ('green' charioteer): E29
Evenus Primianus (freedman of Tiberius): K10
Evodus (freedman of Tiberius): J7k

Fabia Bira: N12
Q. Fabius Barbarus Antonius Macer (cos suff 64)
P. Fabius Firmanus (cos suff 45)
A. Fabius Fortunatus (cos in uncertain year): J2e
Paullus Fabius Maximus (cos 11 BC): arval A15a
Paullus Fabius Persicus (cos ord 34):
Arval: A15a–A44b
friend of Claudius: M11d
governor of Asia: M31
Fabius Rusticus (historian): R12, R13
M. Fadius Celer Flavianus Maximus: procurator): N11
Fadus (procurator of Judaea): U22
Famulus (artist): R29
Felix (freedman of Claudius): S30
Flaminius (T. Quictius Flaminius, cos 197 BC):
liberated Achaia: L4, M15
C. Flavius Figulus (quaestor): L7
Flavius Proculus: U26
T. Flavius Sabinus (cos suff 47)
C. Fonteius Agrippa (cos suff 58); K32
C. Fonteius Capito (cos ord 59)
. . [Fonteius?] Capito (cos ord 67)
Fronto (governor of Galatia): L2
Fufius Geminus (cos ord AD 29)
L. Fulcinius Trio (cos suff 31): M65
C. Fulvius [...] us (proconsul): L5
M. Furius Camillus (cos ord 8, arval): A37c, A38a, A38d, A38f–g, A38i–s
M. Furrius Augurinus (cos suff 40); F3
Q. Futius (cos suff 50)
Q. Futius Lusius Saturninus (cos suff 41); F13

A. Gabinius Secundus (cos suff 43)
P. Gabinius Secundus (cos suff 35)
GAIUS (emperor), see **CALIGULA**
GALBA (emperor, 68/9 = Ser. Sulpicius Galba):
consul: B33
revolt: P13, P13a, P13d, P13f, P13g
L. Galba: B1
C. Galerius (prefect of Egypt): M70
P. Galerius Trachalus (cos ord 68)
C. Gavius Macer (senator): Q1
C. Gavius Silvanus (military tribune): N29
Germanicus (Germanicus Julius Caesar, Adopted son of Tiberius) **J7**
in Alexandria: J7d, M59, M60

Index of Places

Places are towns or settlements unless otherwise stated, and are followed by the Roman province they were in, in CAPITALS, and the modern country the town in is (as of 1 August, 2011, so Sudan now two countries, but Libya still one). Provinces are listed with approximate equivalent in terms of modern countries and are indexed to mention of the province in the texts, not to every town mentioned within the province. Information on the ancient sites relies on R.J.A. Talbert (ed.) *The Barrington Atlas of the Greek and Roman World,* (Princeton, 2000).

Index of Themes

Family Tree at Jan 1, AD 14

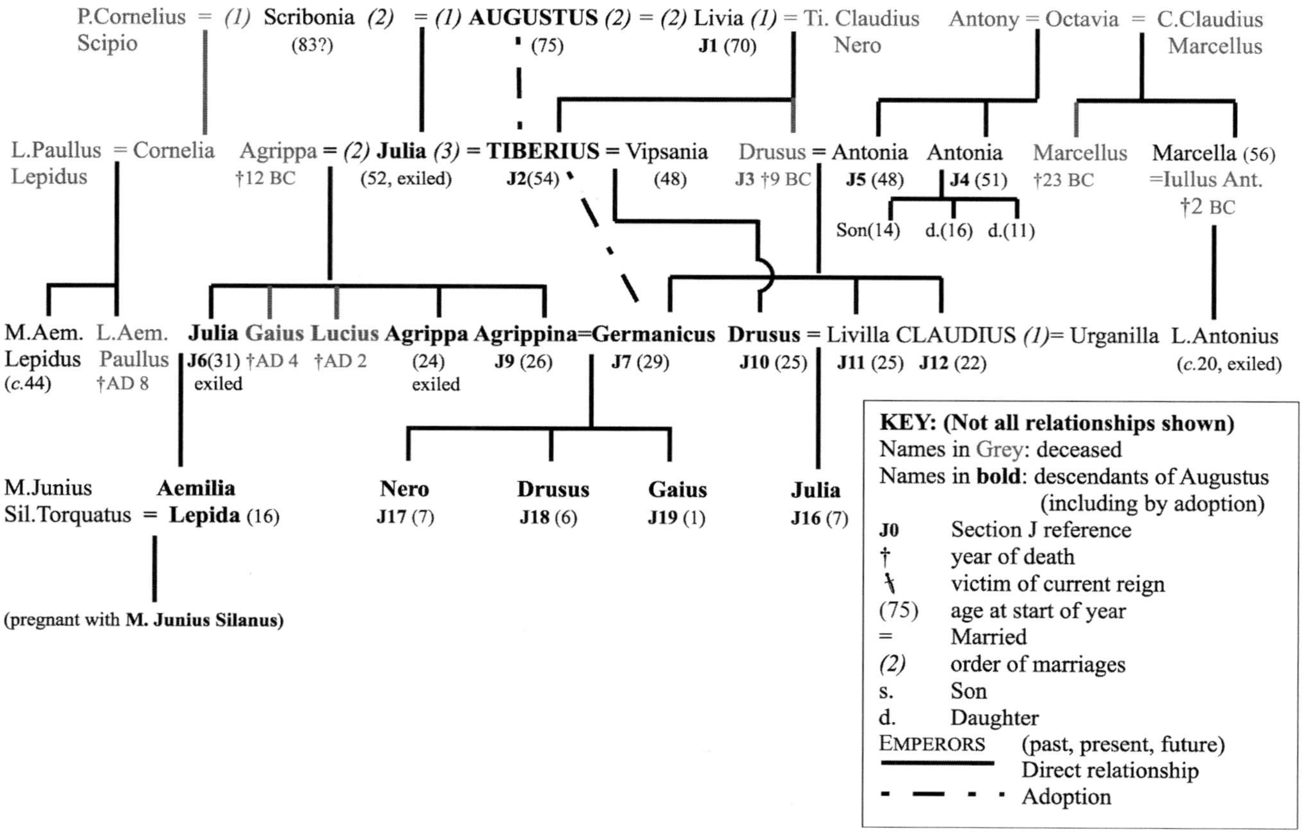

Family Tree at Jan 1, AD 30

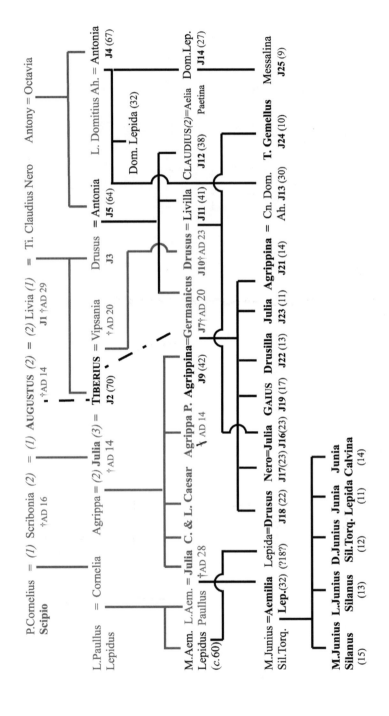

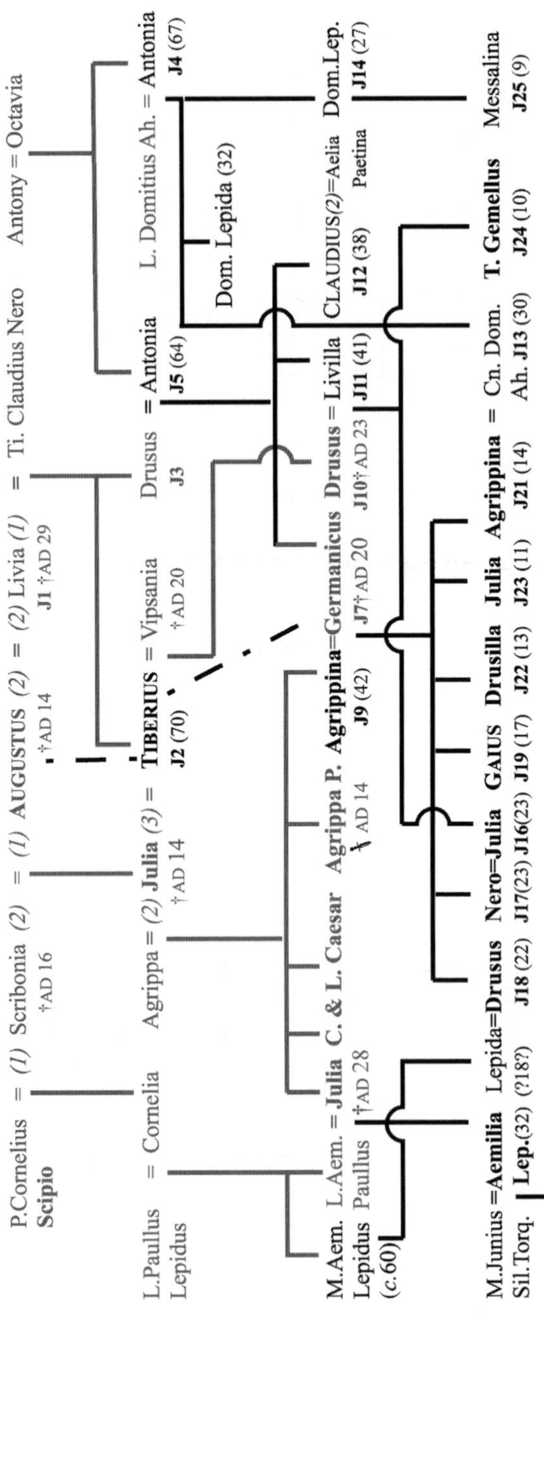

Family Tree in last year of Tiberius' reign (Jan 1, AD 37)

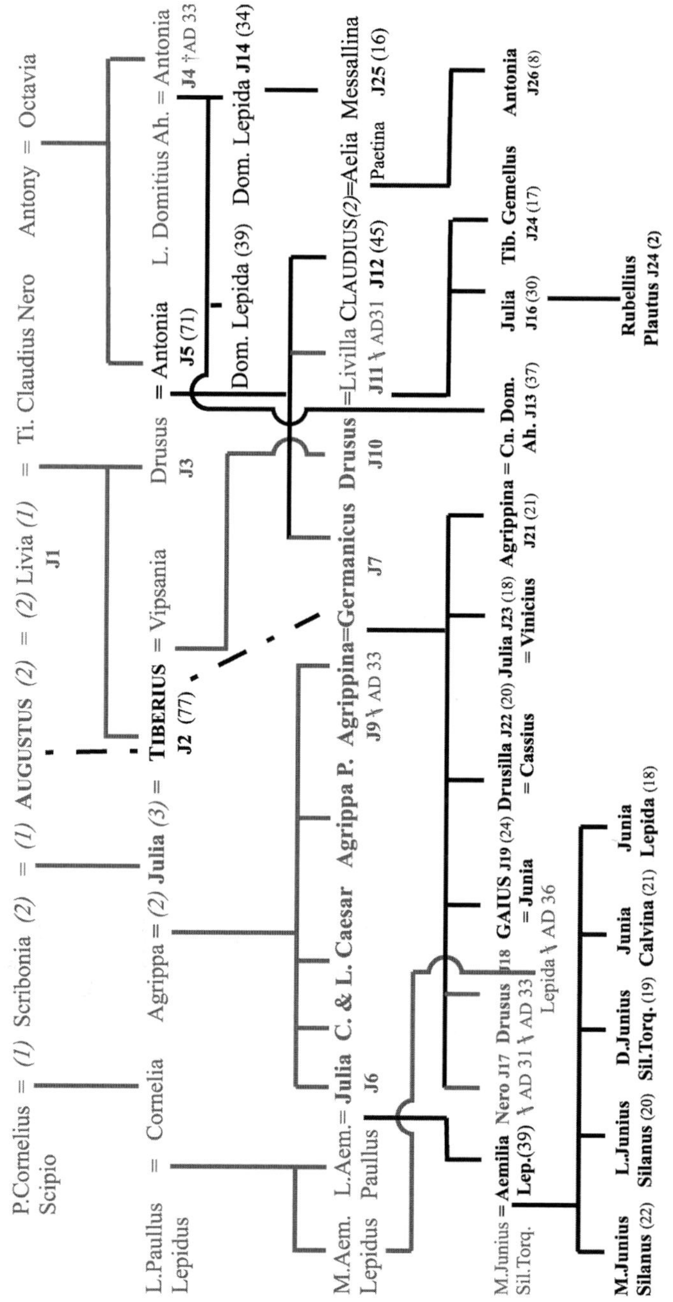

Family Tree in last year of Gaius' reign (Jan 1, AD 41)

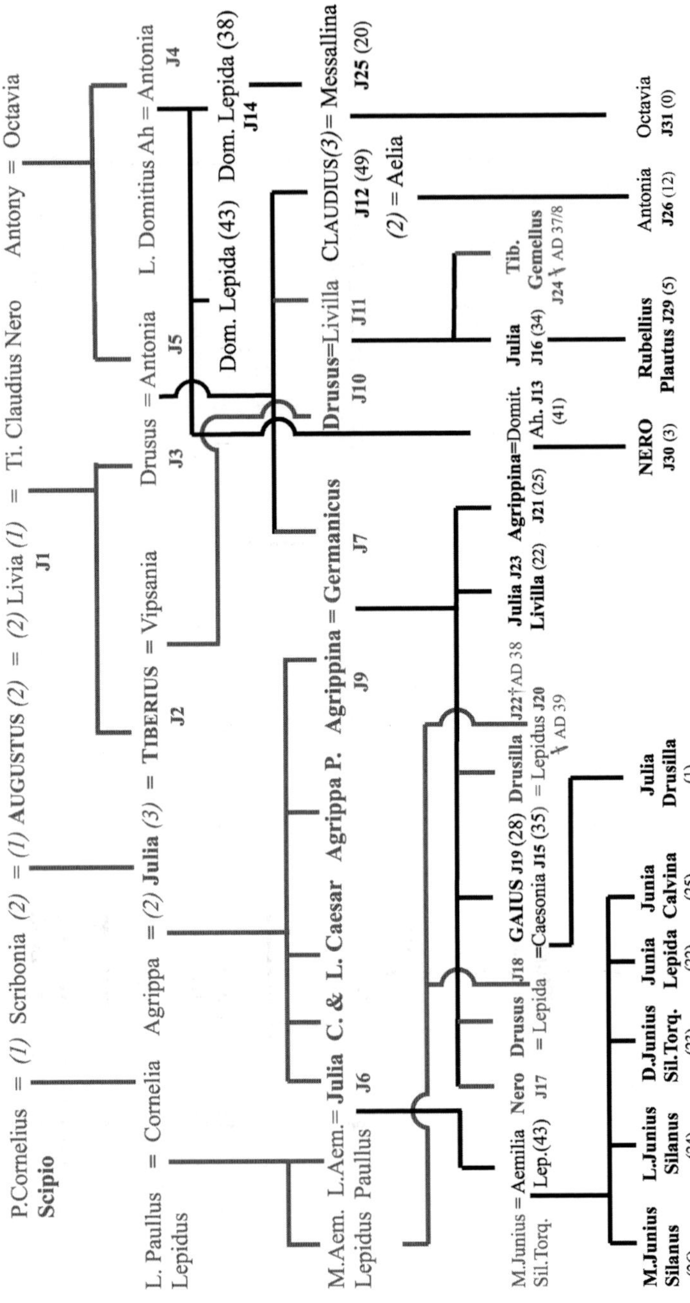

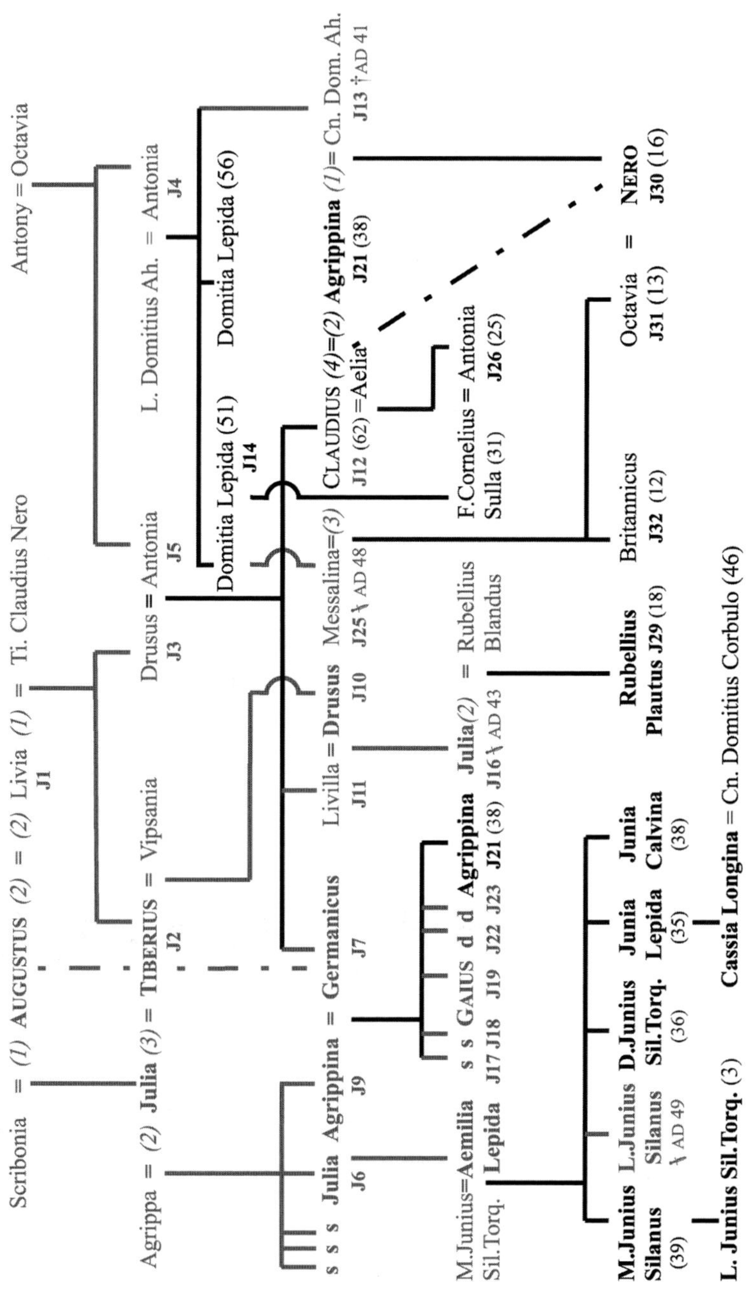

Family Tree in last year of Claudius' reign (Jan 1, AD 54)

Family Tree near end of Nero's reign (Jan 1, AD 68)

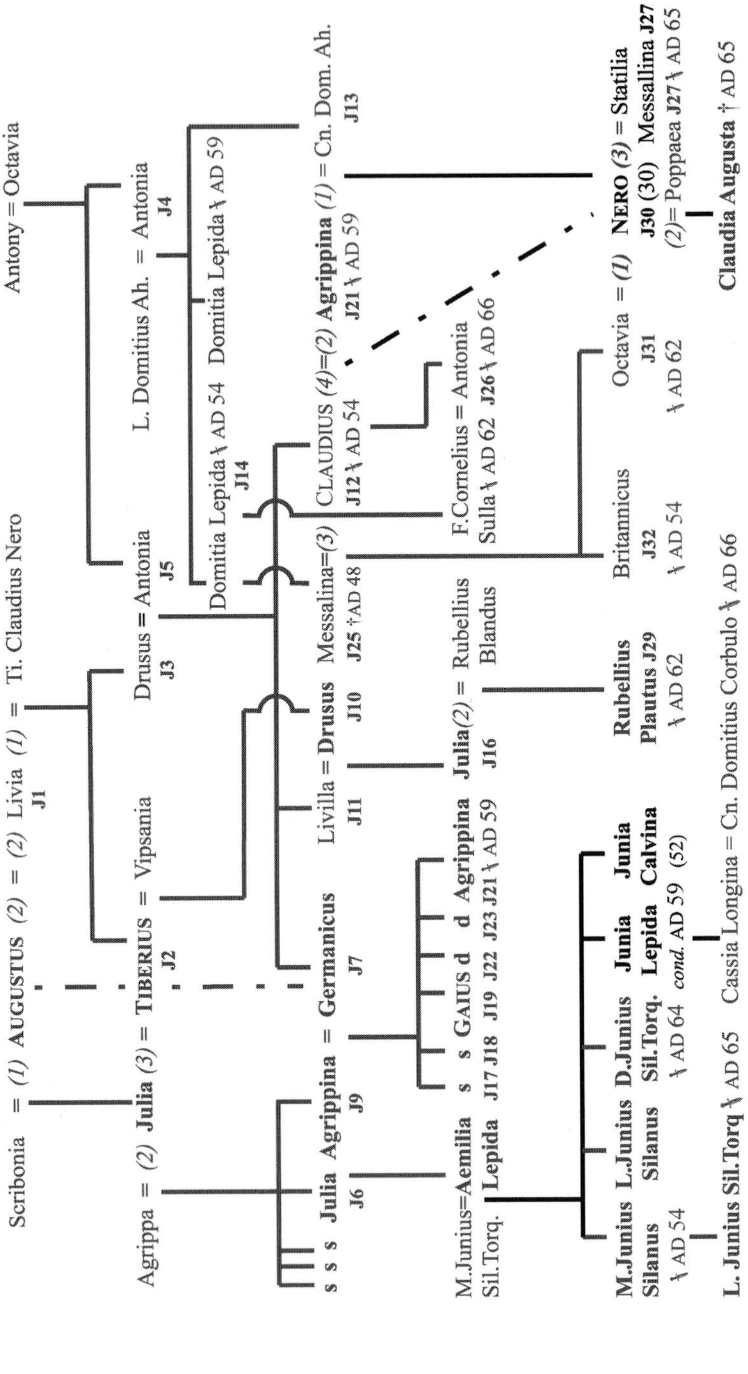